THE ENGLISH AS COLLECTORS

'The record of a single day's turnover at Sotheby's or Christie's, taken at random in any season of any year, bears more than ample testimony to the British genius for discerning acquisition.' F. H. Taylor

By the same author

*

Who Was Solly?

Sotheby's: Portrait of an Auction House

The Norton Simon Museum

*

All about the Giant Alexander
(*children's book*)

THE ENGLISH AS COLLECTORS

A Documentary Sourcebook

selected, introduced and annotated by

FRANK HERRMANN

OAK KNOLL PRESS
NEW CASTLE, DELAWARE

JOHN MURRAY
Albemarle Street, London
1999

This is a second, revised and expanded edition
The English as Collectors: A Documentary Source Book by Frank Herrmann
was originally published as *The English as Collectors: A Documentary Chrestomathy*
by Chatto & Windus, Ltd., London, and
by W.W. Norton & Company, Inc., New York, 1972

Author: Frank Herrmann
New typography: Andrew Burrell
Publishing Director: J. Lewis von Hoelle

This edition published in the United States of America by Oak Knoll Press
Published in 1999 by: Oak Knoll Press
310 Delaware Street, New Castle DE 19720

ISBN: 1–884718–83–3

Library of Congress Cataloging-in-Publication Data

Herrmann, Frank.
The English as collectors: a documentary sourcebook/selected, introduced, and annotated by Frank Herrmann.
p. cm.
Originally published: New York: W. W. Norton, 1972. With new introd.
Includes bibliographical references and index.
ISBN 1–884718–83–3
I. Title.
[N5245.H52 1999]
708.2—dc21 89–31924
CIP

This edition first published in Great Britain in 1999
by John Murray (Publishers) Ltd.,
50 Albemarle Street, London W1X 4BD

ISBN 0-7195-6144-2

A catalogue record for this book is available from the British Library

Printed in the United States of America on acid-free, archival paper

CONTENTS

INTRODUCTION

PART 1 • FROM THE BEGINNINGS TO 1824

CONTENTS

PART 2 • 1824 AND AFTER

CONTENTS

ILLUSTRATIONS

ACKNOWLEDGEMENTS

PERSONAL

I would like to express my particular indebtedness to a number of people without whom this book would never have seen the light of day. Firstly to my brother, Luke Herrmann, who gave most generously of his knowledge and time, and who corrected my errors of ignorance with patience and tact; to my wife, Patricia, who made me persevere as only she knows how when things went wrong, and for invaluable editorial advice; to Frank Simpson, for general encouragement and delightful hours spent in obtaining information from little-known sources, and in particular for providing the first clue in the solution of the great Solly mystery; to Mr E. Seligmann of Cecil Court, without whose immense knowledge of the literature I could never really have made any progress in the early days, for advising about and finding books, and for his generosity in loaning them to me when they were more expensive than I could afford; to Sir Philip Hendy, for giving me self-confidence when it was sadly lacking; to Gwynne Ramsey of *The Connoisseur* for unchanging encouragement and support; to Ellis Waterhouse for assuming that I knew as much as he did in long conversations at the Barber Institute, and for most useful information on source material; to Francis Haskell for a great deal of encouragement; to Dr Rüdiger Klessmann and Dr Helmut Börsch-Supan for invaluable assistance over the German Solly material; to Professor David Robertson, particularly over Eastlake material; to John Harris for allowing me to study his library of catalogues and guides; to my great-uncle, Jean Fürstenberg, a great collector in his own right, for many wise comments in years of correspondence; to John Steegman, who shortly before his death took a considerable interest in what I was doing, and allowed me to quote generously from his own book; to Francis Watson, who helped with the Hertford/Mawson correspondence when I thought I had got stuck; to A. J. B. Kiddell of Sotheby's for delightful reminiscences, for checking my facts on the collectors of oriental ceramics and for information on glass collectors; for useful pointers when I was still looking for source material to Professor Edgar Wind, John Gere, Professor J. D. Ettlinger, Dr Otto Kurz, James Byam Shaw, Colin Agnew, Michael Archer and Frank Davis.

After living with the idea of completing the work on this book for rather more than ten years, its gradual compilation has become almost a way of life. The delay in its completion will be appreciated by anyone who has experienced the conflicting claims of professional commitments, family responsibilities and private study for research. Fortunately, perhaps, I did not appreciate at the outset the extent of the work needed to produce even an *outline* history of collecting: it has involved the detailed scrutiny of nearly 5000 books, catalogues and papers; an enormously extensive correspondence; travel all over the UK, on the Continent (particularly in Holland and Germany) and round the USA – and has given me some of the happiest hours of my life. I have met a host of fascinating people I would never have come across otherwise – art historians, museum officials, art and antique dealers and auctioneers, antiquarian booksellers, specialist librarians, and collectors: all people with expert knowledge, to whom I can never express sufficient thanks.

Much of the work on the book was done before the general advent of the photostatting machine (bless it!) and my own execrable hand has been the greatest single obstacle towards accurate transcription. It is here that I have to thank a succession of secretarial helpers who have done their best to overcome this: Annette Pineles, Ann Langley, Jacquie Meredith, Sandy Duke and Frances Gosling. In particular my gratitude goes to Camilla Dinkel for general assistance at the early stages and, most of all, to Candida Geddes without whose all-round help the book would not have been completed for at least another two years! I am more than grateful to John Burke for the trouble he took over the compilation of the index.

TEXT SOURCES

I should like to thank many publishers and copyright owners for permission to reprint extracts from the following works, which are listed in the order that they appear in this book. *Earls of Creation* by James Lees-Milne (Hamish Hamilton Ltd): *Horace Walpole* by R. W. Ketton-Cremer (Methuen & Co Ltd and the Estate of the late R. W. Ketton Cremer); 'Journals of Visits to Country Seats' by Horace Walpole in *The Walpole Society*, Volume XVI (by permission of The Walpole Society); *The Letters of Sir Joshua Reynolds* edited by F. W. Hilles (Cambridge University Press, 1929: Archon Books, New York); 'A Case of Family Collecting' in the *Catalogue of the Earl of Radnor's Collection of Pictures 1910* (by permission of the Earl of Radnor); *Art in England*, Volumes I and II, by William T. Whitley (Cambridge University Press); *Artists and Their Friends in England*, 1700–1799, Volume I, by William T. Whitley (The Medici Society Ltd); 'Introduction to the Walker Art Gallery Foreign Schools Catalogue, 1963' by Hugh Macandrew and Michael Compton (by permission of the authors and the Walker Art Gallery); 'William Young Ottley as a Collector of Drawings' by J. A. Gere *in British Museum Quarterly*, Volume XVIII, No. 2. June 1 953 (by courtesy of the Trustees of the British Museum); *Let me Tell You* by A. C. R. Carter (Hutchinson & Co (Publishers) Ltd); *Victorian Patrons of the Arts* by Frank Davis (Country Life Books; by permission of the Hamlyn Publishing Group Ltd); *The Bernard Berenson Treasury* (Methuen & Co Ltd, London; Simon & Schuster Inc, New York; by permission of Laurence Pollinger Ltd and Baron Cecil Anrep); *Merchants of Art* by Germain Seligman (Meredith Press, New York); *The Sport of Collecting* by Sir Martin Conway (Ernest Benn Ltd); 'Introduction to the Courtauld Collection Catalogue, 1954' by Anthony Blunt (The Athlone Press); *The Nation and Its Art Treasures* by Robert C. Witt (William Heinemann Ltd); *Looking over my Shoulder* by C. Willett Cunnington (Faber & Faber Ltd and Winant Towers Ltd); 'Sir Karl Parker and the Ashmolean' by J. Byam Shaw and Ian Robertson in the *Burlington Magazine*, October 1962 (by permission of The Burlington Magazine); *On Art and Connosseurship* by Max J. Friedländer (by permission of Dr G . Hill of Bruno Cassirer); *Brave Day, Hideous Night* by John Rothenstein (Hamish Hamilton Ltd, London; Holt, Rinehart & Winston Inc, New York); 'Sir William Burrell's Purchase Books' by William Wells in *Scottish Art Review*, Volume 9, No. 2, 1963 (by permission of the author, Keeper of the Burrell Collection, Camphill Museum, Glasgow); the letters in the sections 'Lord Hertford and his Agent' and 'A Sidelight on Stowe' (by permission of the Trustees of the Wallace Collection). Other acknowledgements are made in the footnotes.

I would like to offer my apologies for any inadvertent omissions in acknowledgement and also to those literary heirs whom my publishers and I have been unable to trace. I hope they will accept this general acknowledgement for material I have quoted.

PICTURES

I am most grateful to the following for permission to reproduce illustrations: Thomas Agnew for plates 56 and 58; the Trustees of the British Museum, plates 25, 36, 40, 41, 42, 43; Christie's, plates 53, 57, 94; Colnaghi, plates 6, 7, 55; Fitzwilliam Museum, plate 11; Gemäldegalerie, Berlin-Dahlem, plates 61, 62, 63, 64; Illustrated London News, plate 52; Oscar & Peter Johnson Ltd, plate 39; Kunsthalle, Hamburg, plate 3; the Lord Chamberlain for plates 12, 59, reproduced by gracious permission of Her Majesty the Queen; Mr J. McBath, plate 95; Mr Denis Mahon, plate 67; Metropolitan Museum of Art, New York, plate 19; the National Gallery, plates 1, 26, 27, 60, 65, 66, 69, 70, 72, 73, 74, 75; National Gallery of Scotland, plate 14; National Monuments Record, plates 50, 51; National Portrait Gallery, plates 15, 24, 28, 29, 30, 31, 33, 34, 37, 76, 77, 78; the National Trust, plate 23; the Duke of Norfolk, plates, 8, 9; Rijksmuseum, Amsterdam, plates 4, 5; Sotheby's and Clark, Nelson Ltd, plates 2, 54, 89, 93; the Lord Spencer, plate 10; the Duke of Sutherland, plate 71; Thomson Newspapers Ltd, plates 48, 90, 91; Times Newspapers Ltd, plate 92; Towneley Hall Art Gallery, Burnley, plate 13; Trustees of Sir John Soane's Museum, plates 32, 46, 47 and the line drawing of a Section through the Museum 1827 on page 242; Victoria and Albert Museum, plates 38, 79, 80, 81, 82; Walker Art Gallery, plate 16; the Wallace Collection, plate 49; the Marquess of Zetland (who took particular trouble over the photograph), plate 17.

FOR THE 1999 EDITION

I need to make renewed, most grateful acknowledgements to my brother, Professor Luke Herrmann, as well as to Caroline Elam (editor of the *Burlington Magazine*) and to my wife, Patricia, for critical assistance with the updating introduction; also to Patricia for hours of patient labours on her computer; to my secretary of the past twenty years, Sheila Phillips, for her help on the initial drafts. Finally, I want to thank Peter Kraus for encouraging me to prepare a new edition of the book, and Bob Fleck for bringing it out.

AN INTRODUCTORY UPDATING
TO THE SECOND EDITION

It is a fortunate author who is given the opportunity to offer his work to a new generation of readers twenty-five years after his book first saw the light of day. He is even more fortunate if he can say with his hand on his heart that the solid core of information that makes up the body of his book can stand as it was. But the changes in the general framework that surrounds the subject of collecting have been dramatic and certainly deserve discussion, albeit of necessity mostly in summary form. In any canvas so large one can only pinpoint the salient highlights.

1. THE KEY CHANGES

Five factors in particular seem to me of major significance. Firstly, there is much greater interest in collecting history, not only at an academic level. Provenance is now regarded as of ever-increasing importance. If an object or a picture is known to have been part of a well-known and documented collection, its financial value increases dramatically.

Secondly, great changes have taken place in the world of the major British museums. The methods of displaying their contents have been the subject of much thought and have often improved immeasurably. This has gone hand in hand with diminished financial support from government sources which has, in turn, meant an increasing search for and dependence on outside, private help in the form of sponsorship.

Thirdly, museums and libraries have begun to shed selected items, so that books or pictures which twenty-five years ago were thought to have passed out of the collector's reach for ever, may become accessible once more. At present, de-accession, or de-acquisition as it is usually referred to in the press, is a much more common practice in America than in Europe or Great Britain, but one can envisage that with the enormous growth of museum holdings and a smaller contribution from public funds, it is likely to spread. Understandably, there is strong opposition to this (see pages xxxv and xlii), but in many ways what is much more regrettable is that the great remaining family-owned country house collections, such as Chatsworth, Houghton Hall, Althorp, Bute and Kedlestone (and many lesser ones) are being forced to part with some of their treasures, which constitute integral parts of historic entities, for reason of financial need.

Fourthly, of course, where major works of art or major examples of the decorative arts are concerned, the whole concept of value and money has changed fundamentally since 1972, reaching an unprecedented peak in the second half of the 1980s. The art market has become a global business. Catalogues are distributed worldwide. Many major art dealers have representatives, if not actual branches, on both sides of the Atlantic and elsewhere. Certainly the big auction houses now have tentacles reaching into every corner of the civilised world. The entry of the Japanese and, on a smaller scale, the Koreans some years later, produced an almost unreal element into the combination of artistic value and financial worth.

Fifthly, the English continue to collect vigorously. As will become evident, there are many new forms of what have come to be termed 'Collectables', as the traditional fields of the fine and decorative arts have become rarer and more costly. The interest in Victorian paintings, as one example, increased enormously in the 1980s but enthusiasm ebbed and prices fell when the major recession of the 1990s began to bite.

*   *   *

Since 1972, I personally have learned a great deal more at first hand about how the art market and the collecting world work. Soon after completing *The English as Collectors* I was asked to write a history of Sotheby's. It took me seven years. After the completion of that volume, Sotheby's asked me to join their management. I became responsible for the firm's offices and outstations in Europe and farther afield: there were twenty-five in Europe alone. The world certainly did not realise at that stage that more than half of what passed through the London saleroom came from outside the country.

It was particularly while I was at work on the Sotheby history, and in long discussions and arguments over the matter of diminishing availability with its then chairman, Peter Wilson, that I began to realise that the art world had reached a stage when it could no longer provide an unlimited supply of what collectors wanted. Perhaps this is most vividly illustrated by one of my favourite subjects, pottery and porcelain. Whereas in the 1970s Sotheby's and Christie's each held virtually a sale a week in this area, by the mid-1990s three or four sales a year is about all they can manage. The supply is a mere trickle of what has gone before. This alone will explain the enormous concomitant rise in prices. But life is not just as simple as that. Neither of the big auction houses has the overwhelming weight of expertise in ceramics they had formerly. The smaller auction house, Phillips, on the other hand, has built up theirs. So the drift of ceramic property to those auction rooms is very noticeable.

Another predictable factor has come into play since 1972. Nineteenth-century material, and to a considerable extent twentieth-century material too, are now regarded as eminently collectable. As the supply of earlier wares dried up, the auction houses made a determined effort to put this later material before the collector with a much more elaborate standard of cataloguing, and interest in it grew accordingly. The principal credit for pioneering this must go to Sotheby's in London who started a separate establishment which, because of its location, they called 'Sotheby's Belgravia'. Writers such as John Betjeman, Nikolaus Pevsner and John Steegman had been nudging taste toward a much greater appreciation of things Victorian. A little later the terms 'art nouveau' and 'art deco' became as familiar as baroque or rococo. The result was that people were prepared to accept the products of these periods back into their houses (and into their collections) which the previous two generations had been shedding and replacing with what they thought modern or more suitable. It also has to be said that with the spread of interest in collecting, or perhaps in this context one should use the word aggregation, buyers outside England, especially in the Middle East, had a particular love for objects with a degree of ornamentation that did not find a ready market in the UK or the US.

The hobby of collecting has been increasingly encouraged by the media, television in particular. 'The Antiques Road Show', put out by the BBC on Sundays, for example, has an enormous viewing public and has stimulated interest not only in the antiques or paintings themselves, but also in their value.

As daily newspapers have split themselves up into supplements dealing with specific areas of readership, varieties of collecting figure prominently in their leisure sections. All this has led to changes in supply. General antique shops as such have virtually become outlets where other members of the trade find their wares. If one takes two rural centres in England as far apart as Long Melford in Suffolk and Ludlow in Shropshire, one can find any number of antique shops in each place. Many actually have notices on the locked doors saying 'Please ring for business'. The business, as the owners will readily admit, is 90 per cent with other members of the dealing fraternity, and the prices marked are heavily discounted when objects actually change hands with them. The unfortunate collector is not always so lucky.

The cost of running galleries and antique shops has risen greatly, and as items such as staffing, rent and rates have climbed, the formerly ubiquitous antique shop has been largely replaced by antiques fairs held all over the country at weekends. They have become more and more numerous and are probably now the source of supply most used by collectors. Perhaps in the future even they will fade as the Internet and e-mail become more widely used and popular. It is already noticeable that subscribers to auctioneers' catalogues are on the wane as those firms whose business it is to scan saleroom catalogues on behalf of their customers, *fax* specific desiderata to specialist collectors on a daily basis.

2. REFERENCE MATERIAL AND NEW RESEARCH

But what has probably been most help to collectors of every kind is the growth of scholarship related to the art market. This again comes in many forms. In the case of English furniture, for example, it is undoubtedly the growth of the Furniture History Society that has been the catalyst for research. That body has taken our knowledge of English furniture makers a great deal further than in the days of Cescinsky, Macquoid and Edwards[1]. Or in the case of silver, the authorities we now look to are Arthur Grimwade and John Culme, instead of Jackson and Oman[2].

In the world of porcelain and pottery, the typical all-inclusive volume covering British wares has been replaced by a large number of books devoted to individual factories, or even periods of factory production. Diligent researchers like Geoffrey Godden have blazed the trail with volumes on specific nineteenth-century potteries, identifying their wares: knowledge which simply did not exist twenty-five years ago. Collecting societies of Spode, Derby and Wedgwood have come into being and flourish. Or take those venerable pioneers, Messrs Koysh and Haywood, who identified the individual makers of what was formerly simply lumped together as 'blue and white': they have spawned one of the most formidable bodies of pottery collectors.

There have been great changes, too, in the antiques-related periodical literature. *The Burlington Magazine* remains the most respected of the well-established periodicals: required reading for the professional art historian, although its coverage has been much widened to include the decorative arts and the contemporary scene. It has also published twice-yearly supplements (in February and August) called 'Documents in the History of Collecting' and has sponsored a number of conferences at the National Gallery on different historical aspects of collecting and the art market.[3] The venerable *Connoisseur* (founded in 1900) has disappeared. The editorship was transferred by its owners (the National Magazine Company) to New York to the former director of the Metropolitan Museum, Thomas Hoving. For a few years its circulation soared as it acquired an ever-more socialite character. Then it died. The ownership of *Apollo* has changed frequently: it became the plaything of European millionaires. The character of its contents has now veered more towards the *Burlington*. For a time *The Antique Collector* acquired more of the status of its

[1] Herbert Cescinsky, *English Furniture of the Eighteenth Century*, 3 vols, London 1909; Percy Macquoid and Ralph Edwards, *The Dictionary of English Furniture*, 3 vols, London 1924-7.

[2] Sir Charles James Jackson, *English Goldsmiths and their Marks*, 2nd edn. London 1921; Charles Oman, *English Domestic Silver*, London 1930 (and many other more specialist titles). Arthur G. Grimwade, *London Goldsmiths 1695-1837: Their Marks and Lives*, London 1976. John Culme, *Directory of Gold and Silver Smiths, Jewellers and Allied Traders, 1838-1914*, London 1987.

[3] See note 3, page xx.

former stable-mate, the *Connoisseur*, under the benign, long-lasting editorship of David Coombs. Then it changed hands and became distinctly more 'pop' until it, too, died in 1996.

Many collectors have turned to other publications. The most informative by far is a monthly which had existed for some years in Italy before bursting upon the astonished Anglo-Saxon world in English as *The Art Newspaper*. Its immense and immensely detailed coverage of events in art affairs all over the world has provided fascinating and original information to a growing readership since 1990, and the paper today is neatly divided between newsy items and the art market. Then there is the *Antiques Trade Gazette* with a circulation of nearly twenty thousand, which provides a detailed calendar of forthcoming auction sales, and tells its readers what happened at a great number of them afterwards. If it is price you are interested in as a collector, there is no better way of keeping in touch: it is truly a focused mirror on the art market and the glory of it is that it devotes almost more space to smaller auction houses dotted around the country than the giants in central London and overseas.

This is probably the place also to mention that there has been a regrettable decline in the coverage of auction sales in the better broadsheet newspapers. Regular reporting of sales has virtually ceased, except in the *Daily Telegraph*, which publishes a racy summary on Mondays. It is only the items with newsworthy stories attached to them that such papers as *The Times* and the *Independent* find room for. This is a sad retrogression after generations of excellent auction reporting. But before they are forgotten, two outstanding and intrepid reporters in this field continue to work. They are Geraldine Norman in the UK and Souren Melikien in Paris, who writes in English in the *International Herald Tribune*. Both have an immense knowledge of the art market and the collecting world and both are assiduously read by a body of devoted followers.

On the other hand, the history of collecting has acquired its own journal that appears three times a year, but keeps a very low profile. It is *The Journal of the History of Collections* (OUP). It came into being in 1989 as the result of a seminal conference on the origins of museums, held at Balliol College, Oxford, in 1983. The principal discussions there were on the subject of the sixteenth and seventeenth-century cabinets of curiosities. The collected papers eventually came out in book form as *The Origins of Museums* and set in train much further research.

The *Journal*'s appetite is omnivorous. It covers the collecting of every sort of artefact: from natural history items to medical apparatus, from American Indian objects to plaster casts of Greek sculpture. But it has one supreme merit: its articles re-scan collections that have been ignored in the past, very often, one feels, out of sheer snobbery. The best example of this in my eyes was an entire issue in 1992 devoted to the Lady Lever Art Gallery in Port Sunlight, Liverpool. Its dynamic begetter was the first Lord Leverhulme, the son of a prosperous wholesale grocer. He devoted his immense riches to collecting the furniture, the archaeological discoveries from expeditions he sponsored, the needlework, the majolica, oriental porcelain and Wedgwood, and the paintings *which he liked.* Fakes may have crept into his collections – which is not surprising when one knows the speed with which he bought and the scale on which he bought – but, overall, the visitor to the Gallery is almost overwhelmed by what he finds. And yet Lord Leverhulme did not exactly hide his light under a bushel. He sponsored the compilation and publication of a magnificently illustrated three-volume catalogue[1] which, although only 200 copies were printed for sale in Britain and 150 in the USA, was still available at the museum sixty-five years after its publication.

Last, and probably most important of all, has been the work done on the vast assemblage of documented information about works of art bought, sold and collected, in the *Provenance Index* of the Getty Art History Information Program under the aegis of Burton Fredericksen. Inspired initially by Sir Ellis Waterhouse, my own mentor of twenty-five years ago, it is available for reference on a huge computerised database and is also gradually being published in book form. Needless to say, sale and collection catalogues have been among the richest sources of information.

* * *

The literature on collecting has also grown extensively along traditional lines. Let me mention a very few books that are particularly relevant to the contents of what follows. Dealers and other sources of supply (see page 30) have, in particular, been the subject of much research. Louise Lippincott's *Selling Art in Georgian London: the Rise of Arthur Pond* (1984) revealed a whole new scenario about dealing in the Augustan art world. The author based her book on a close study of Pond's *Journal of Receipts and Expenses* (1734–1750) and his papers, both in the British Library, and her pioneering work was widely praised.

We are indebted to Hugh Brigstocke for a good deal of additional information on William Buchanan (see pages 127 *et seq.*).[2] Mr Brigstocke tracked down a hundred previously unknown letters from Buchanan addressed mostly to two of his agents, David Stewart, of whom we did not know at all, and James Irvine, of whom we did. The letters, which often consist of instructions, are wonderfully informative on Buchanan's wily methods of marketing his wares.

Mrs Jameson (see pages 65–71) has figured in many recent articles and books and has now achieved the recognition she deserves. My particular favourite,

[1] Vol.I, *English Painting of the XVIIIth-XXth Centuries*, by R R Tatlock (with an introduction by Richard Flight); Vol.II, *Chinese Porcelain and Wedgwood Pottery with other Works of Ceramic Art*, by R L Hobson; Vol. III, *English Furniture, Tapestry and Needlework of the XVIth-XIXth Centuries*, by Percy Macquoid. London 1928

[2] *William Buchanan and the 19th Century Art Trade, 100 Letters to his Agents in London and Italy*, London 1982.

Edward Solly (page 202–208), has to my knowledge been the subject of at least five PhD theses and much research, mostly in Germany. Christof Martin Vogtherr, using Solly as a starting point, has created a whole corpus of knowledge about the early days of the major German museums which were based on royal collections before Solly came along. That also, of course, involved a close and revealing study of that memorable man, Gustav Waagen (see page 3), to whom we are so deeply indebted.[1]

Jeremy Maas, himself a picture dealer, unearthed a great deal of new information about art dealing in the second half of the nineteenth century seen through the persona of Ernest Gambart, son of a Belgian print dealer who moved to England in the 1840s.[2] Gambart rapidly built up a sizeable business trading in contemporary reproductive prints and gradually moved more and more to dealing in the original work of contemporary painters, as did Agnew's and Colnaghi's (see page 31). Among his protégés were Alma-Tadema, Rossetti, Ford Madox Brown and the young Edward Poynter, later to become President of the Royal Academy. Gambart was an outstanding salesman and extremely popular with contemporary artists because he succeeded in obtaining unusually high prices for their work, mainly among the newly-rich industrialists, who were some of his best customers. His peak period of sales was in the 1860s.

The greater awareness of interest in the history of collecting and the art market continues to bring relevant archival material to the fore in auction rooms and with booksellers. Thus Charles Sebag-Montefiore found an album of over two hundred letters addressed to the art dealer, John Smith (1781–1835; see page 30). By dint of studying additionally the eighteen volumes of ledgers and day books surviving from Smith's business covering the era 1812 to 1908, which are in the National Art Library at the V&A, he was able to construct a very detailed picture of Smith's dealing activities.[3]

Smith appears to have started as a frame-maker and slowly progressed to supplying paintings quite regularly to such distinguished collectors as Sir Robert Peel (page 248), Lord Grosvenor, the Duke of Sutherland at Stafford House (page 140), Lord Northwick at Thirlestane House and even William Wells of Redleaf in Kent (page 228). What is particularly interesting is how much Smith travelled on the Continent, engaged both in finding pictures for his English collectors and selling stock items to continental clients. The firm was continued after John Smith's death by three further generations of his family.

The whole area of taste and fashion in collecting of that same era is brilliantly summarised by Francis Haskell in the five Wrightsman lectures

[1] 'Die Auswahl der Gemälde aus den Schlössern für das Königliche Museum in Berlin' in an as-yet unpublished thesis, 1991.

[2] *Gambart: Prince of the Victorian Art World*, London 1975. Maas died in 1996.

[3] In an (as yet unpublished) paper read to a conference organised by *The Burlington Magazine* with the *Provenance Index* of the Getty Art History Information Program, held at the London National Gallery in December 1994 on 'The History of the Art Market 1400-1900'. See also page xvii.

he gave in New York, which were later published in much enlarged form as *Rediscovering Art: Some Aspects of Taste, Fashion and Collecting in England and France* (1976). The book continues to be widely quoted, but also demonstrates just how difficult it is, generations later, to analyse what prompts selectivity unless we are left with written evidence to that effect.

3. MUSEUMS: THEIR GROWTH AND THEIR PROBLEMS

Much space in *The English as Collectors* is given over to the emergence of what I called 'the Official Collector' and the establishment and growth of museums. Since 1972, great changes have taken place in that world. The architecture, arrangement and display of objects, and the internal organisation of most such institutions had not changed substantially for two if not three generations. It was becoming clear that the public no longer accepted the old methods of presentation. In the competing world of communication, visitors wanted to know 'what they were looking at, why and how it was collected, how it was made, what it had to do with other objects nearby, and to be given enough information to "make sense of it"'.[1] All the great London museums, the National Gallery, the British Museum and the Tate Gallery had been greatly affected by these changes, but nowhere did this transmogrification become more publicly visible than in the case of the Victoria and Albert Museum in 1989.

THE VICTORIA & ALBERT MUSEUM

Sir Roy Strong, former Director of the National Portrait Gallery and a figure well-known to the British public through TV appearances and his writings, followed Sir John Pope-Hennessy as Director in 1974. But his period of office was bedevilled by the increasingly apparent inadequacy of funds provided by the government and internal dissension between him and his staff.[2] The post again became vacant in 1988. To general surprise, it was filled by the museum's own diminutive librarian, Elizabeth Estève-Coll. She had obviously had time to consider what changes she wanted to undertake and early in 1989 she began to put them into practice by suggesting a restructuring of the responsibilities previously held by the Keepers of each Department. But her plans were not put forward with the finesse such heady ideas required and the reaction was

[1] Quoted from Margaret Hall's *On Display: a Design Grammar for Museum Exhibitions*, London, 1987

[2] Detailed with riveting candour in his *Roy Strong Diaries, 1967 to 1987*, 1997.

fireworks, and the eventual departure of eight out of nine well-known and well-loved senior museum specialists.

Whatever the rights and wrongs of the case may have been – and there were a lot of wrongs initially as Mrs Estève-Coll herself eventually admitted – the enormous press debate focused the public mind on what was happening, and what was thought to be necessary, in the museum world. The V&A employs a thousand people. It has some one hundred and fifty-four galleries, which occupy twelve acres. Responsibilities were re-aligned. Modern management techniques were introduced. Research and management were separated, but not as originally planned. The watchword became accountability, for finance was all-important. Sponsorship was harnessed. Seven galleries were totally refurbished by this means. Mrs Estève-Coll, whose principal interest was in education as laid down by the founders of the South Kensington Museum, as it was first called in 1852, learned to smile again, after the most scathing personal attacks launched on a museum director in modern times. In 1995, she left the Museum for pastures new as Vice-Chancellor of the University of East Anglia, which houses the celebrated Sainsbury Collection. Her place has been taken by Alan Borg, for many years Director of the Imperial War Museum, who had earned nothing but praise from museum professionals and public alike. The V&A Trustees are said to have given him the job, which was hotly competed for, because of his brilliant plans for the future of the V&A. Soon after his arrival, he undid the much-resented management structure. Departments reverted to being called Departments. Morale amongst the curatorial staff soared, but the Treasury, as has so often been its wont, made his life more difficult by reducing the Museum's annual grant. He soon startled the art world by announcing plans for a new spiral Humpty-Dumpty sort of building for the Boilerhouse, designed by Daniel Libeskind, who had already designed – and carried through – a forked-lightning shaped addition to the Berlin Museum. The resulting controversy certainly focused attention once more on the V&A. So has the fact that a compulsory admission charge of £5 has been levied as a contribution to the running costs of the Museum.

THE NATIONAL GALLERY

The National Gallery had different problems, mostly ones centred on space, or lack of it. And yet right beside its own building was a site allocated by government towards expanding the Gallery's premises. In 1981 a competition was launched for a combination of galleries and commercial offices on the site. The Trustees saw this as the only solution for funding new galleries. The winning design did not win approbation, either from the planning authorities or Prince Charles, who referred to it as 'a monstrous carbuncle on the face of a much loved and elegant friend'. The situation was saved by a generous gift from the three brothers, John, Simon and Timothy Sainsbury for a new building. This was to be wholly devoted to the display of 250 late medieval and early renaissance works, as well as a lecture theatre, a gallery bookshop, a restaurant, research facilities and offices for the staff. After much searching and a second, limited competition, the American architect, Robert Venturi, was chosen to produce a new design.

Only six years later, the completed extension, now known as the Sainsbury Wing, was opened to the public. While, inevitably, there was some carping about the external appearance of the building Venturi had designed, under what must have been extraordinarily difficult circumstances, there was nothing but praise for the actual galleries and the way in which the paintings – really all well-known icons of their time – had been hung and displayed inside them. It was a veritable triumph of curatorial skills. It had taken place under the aegis of Neil MacGregor – the second former editor of *The Burlington Magazine* to have become Director of the National Gallery[1] – who in 1987 had replaced the distinguished Sir Michael Levey. MacGregor worked in close partnership with Lord Jacob Rothschild, who was the then Chairman of the Trustees. *Their* overall financial problems were considerably ameliorated after J. Paul Getty junior had endowed the Gallery with £50 million. This has enabled them to make extraordinarily fine acquisitions, which would certainly not have been possible out of the measly £3 million the government allowed them for the purpose at the time.

As a postcript it should be added that the whole process of conservation, picture cleaning and restoration has made huge strides since 1972. Then I mentioned Ruhemann's book on *The Cleaning of Paintings*, published in 1968. What were once a leading conservator's highly contentious, personal views have now been more widely accepted and nowhere can this be seen more clearly than on the walls of the National Gallery. Incidentally many of these galleries have themselves been wonderfully enhanced and rehung, often through the generosity of individual sponsors.

THE BRITISH MUSEUM

If it is a fresh design approach which has played a crucial role in the transformation of our major museums, this is probably most evident in the British Museum. Under the benign and very successful régime of its then-Director, Sir David Wilson[2], who followed Sir John Pope-Hennessy in 1977, almost every part of the Museum has been subjected to facelifts of environment and display.

[1] Sir Charles Holmes was the first in 1916; see also page 19, note 1.

[2] From 1977 to 1991. Before that, he was an archaeologist on its staff and then became Professor of Mediaeval Archaeology at the University of London.

A design officer, Margaret Hall, had been appointed as far back as 1964, initially to concern herself with the many special exhibitions the Museum stages each year. Among the most celebrated, for which she and her staff (currently 25 of them), provided the settings were the 'Treasures of Tutankhamun' in 1972 which attracted some three and a half million visitors and the Viking exhibition in 1980, seen by nearly half a million people. Incidentally, both were sponsored and widely publicised by newspapers.

It did not take the Museum authorities long to realise that some of these design and display techniques could be adapted for the longer-term presentation of its permanent collections. The consistency and ingenuity of Margaret Hall's approach to the phased re-design of Sir Robert Smirke's mid-nineteenth century building, with excellent new methods of display, lighting and labelling, are a model of what can be achieved on a limited budget in an elderly building. This applied particularly, of course, to the many entirely re-furbished galleries.

The Museum, which now has nearly seven million visitors a year, has continued to expand its existing collections, particularly those of the twentieth century, and here and there to fill gaps. For example, within the space of very few years, it has built up an outstanding collection of German Expressionist prints, an area earlier much neglected and further impoverished by A E Popham's refusal in the 1950s of an almost complete collection of the prints of Karl Schmidt-Rotluff as a gift. Its collection of modern American prints has become the best outside America. Its assembly of continental *art nouveau* material is impressive. The beginnings of a national collection of bank notes were made in 1978. The gift of jewellery of between 1700 and 1930 from that most eccentric of collectors, Mrs Anne Hall Grundy (as a permanent invalid she did all her collecting from bed on the telephone) filled 'one of the most conspicuous lacunae in the Museum's jewellery collection.'[1]

A worry which beset the Trustees and the Director from the late 1970s onwards was the increasing insistence by certain countries that items displayed in the Museum, which had originated in the countries concerned, should be returned to them. The most highly orchestrated of such pleas came from Melina Mercouri after she became a minister in the Greek government (having achieved fame as a film star in an earlier incarnation). She wanted nothing less than the return of the Elgin marbles (see page 154). She was not without supporters in this country and it took all of Sir David Wilson's diplomatic and forensic skills to persuade them that, on moral grounds as well as purely legal ones, such a return was not feasible from what was to all intents and purposes one of the greatest storehouses of the world's treasures, where the comparative study of cultures is paramount.

Ever since the British Museum's foundation in 1753, the Library had been an integral part of it. For reasons of space or lack of it – as one of the six

[1] Marjorie Cargill, *The Story of the British Museum*, London 1981

copyright libraries in the UK the British Library is presented with a copy of every new book published in Britain – new premises became essential. The first idea of providing these in Bloomsbury itself was firmly and publicly rejected because it meant pulling down some of the delightful streets around the Museum. So in 1976 the government paid six million pounds for an unwanted goods yard outside St Pancras station to provide an alternative site. Only a year later plans for a magnificent 200,000 square metre library to be built in three phases was approved in principle by the then Labour government, but no precise financial commitment was made. The go-ahead for Phase One of 76,000 square metres was given in March 1978, with the building work to start in 1979 and occupation projected for the late 1980s. The building was opened to the public in 1998 after a long concatenation of mishaps. The whole disastrous affair is a classic case of constant ministerial and Treasury interference which, far from the intended saving of money, had pushed up costs to an astronomical level. What is most incomprehensible of all is that, although it is already known that the Library will run out of space soon after completion, the present official intention is to sell off the currently unutilised parts of the site!

In the meantime the British Museum itself has plans for a vast new cultural complex (shades of Paris?) for the Millennium celebrations. A multi-level elliptical building designed by Sir Norman Foster is to be constructed around the celebrated Reading Room. The departure of the Library to St Pancras, when it has eventually taken place completely, will liberate no less than forty per cent of the Bloomsbury site. This will make possible the return of the ethnographic collections from distant Burlington Gardens where they have been housed as the 'Museum of Mankind' for many years. There are also plans for a display illustrating the history of the Museum itself in the magnificent King's Library, and eventually it may also enable large sections of the Museum collections now in storage to go on display.

THE TATE GALLERY

The Tate Gallery has also grown. After twenty-five years of negotiation, planning, building and tribulation, its new extension opened in May 1979. It increased the area for the display of works of art by fifty per cent and enabled the staff to display important works that had been in storage for years. Soon afterwards Sir Norman Reid, Director since 1964, retired; he had begun work at the Tate straight after coming out of the army in 1946. His friendship with many living artists on both sides of the Atlantic had led to a great enrichment of the Gallery. He was succeeded by Alan Bowness. It was also in 1980 that the Clore Foundation made an offer to the Trustees to provide a building for the re-united Turner Bequest (see page 327 *et seq.*). This consists of some two hundred and ninety oil paintings and over 19,000 water colours and drawings. All these were originally in the National Gallery, but the paintings had already long been transferred to the Tate Gallery and the drawings were deposited at the British Museum. The Clore Gallery opened seven years later. It was designed by Sir James Stirling. Again, it was much criticised, but there is no doubt that the spatial arrangement of the galleries is excellent.

1980 was something of an *annus mirabilis* for the Tate. It was in that year that Henry Moore finally presented the Gallery with thirty-six of his sculptures, a matter discussed for many years previously, and Paul Mellon gave the Tate collection of sporting pictures thirty such paintings from his own collection. They included two by Stubbs and two by the (now well-known, but not then) Swiss-born artist who came to England in 1800 and worked here for fifty years, Jacques-Laurent Agasse.

In 1988 Nicholas Serota took over as Director of the Tate. He had spent eleven years running the unquenchable Whitechapel Art Gallery and as a student his thesis at the Courtauld Institute had been on Turner's Alpine tours in Switzerland. He totally reversed the policies of his predecessors. He stripped out all the false walls and partitions that had gradually distorted the original gallery rooms and re-hung the entire Gallery. It stunned the art historical world. But the public and the press loved it.

The basis of the re-hanging was to show the evolution of English art through the centuries with occasional emphasis on major figures, such as Hogarth and Constable, by setting them against sympathetic pastel backgrounds with good explanatory labelling. The lack of clutter and the opening up of new vistas allowed the paintings to speak for themselves and English art came out triumphant: it sparkled. Serota re-arranged the foreign galleries on a similar basis; particularly to show parallel developments outside the UK. The policy was to be rotational: as only a selection of paintings could be shown at any one time, that selection was to change annually. Clearly this was an expensive undertaking. The backing of a major sponsor, BP, both initially and in later years, has made it possible.

The Tate, too, has ambitious plans for the future. It has already opened ancillary galleries in Liverpool and St Ives in Cornwall. Now it has well advanced plans to utilise an enormous, redundant power station facing St Paul's Cathedral on the South side of the Thames, for a museum devoted purely to modern art: London's answer to the Pompidou Centre in Paris[1]. Collecting contemporary art – though it may take strange forms – has become popular

[1] It was given a grant of £50 million towards this from the 'Millennium Fund' in November 1995. This fund and money from the recently established National Lottery (Heritage Lottery Fund) is to be used extensively to assist developments in the art world and will be of particular and heaven-sent help to museums: the only problem is that the money given is for capital projects only. A danger is that government may use it as an excuse to cut regular annual grants to museums.

both in the UK and in America (probably even more so there) and certainly such a venture would be a response to public interest.

Reading the Trustees' biennial reports, there is a familiar concern with insufficient funding. Then suddenly in 1992 one comes across a discreet mention of an anonymous benefactor, an Englishman long resident in the United States, who has given the Gallery its most generous single donation since its foundation by Henry Tate in 1897. He turned out subsequently to be Sir Edward Manton, a collector of Constables, who had been advised for many years by Leslie Parris, Deputy Keeper of the Tate's British Collection. But the museum has also made giant strides in attracting sponsorship, which all English museums will have to do in the future.

DULWICH

If the Tate showed the way in which museums today should hang their paintings, Giles Waterfield, until recently Director of the Dulwich Museum (see page 173), gave us plenty of food for thought on how our ancestors did it. Together with the dynamic Timothy Clifford, currently Director of the National Galleries of Scotland[1], he staged an exhibition in 1991 entitled 'Palaces of Art: Art Galleries in Britain from 1790 to 1990'. The aim was to put the debate of how collections should be displayed into an historical setting. He brought together some two hundred oil paintings, water colours, prints, drawings, photographs, architectural drawings and even gallery chairs for the purpose. 'As the oldest surviving art gallery in England, open to the public since its foundation, Dulwich seemed a particularly appropriate place to house such an exhibition devoted to the architecture of art galleries, to the lighting and hanging of picture collections, and to the decorations of the rooms in which they are displayed.'[2] It was a remarkable résumé, accompanied by a particularly good catalogue, which achieved exactly what it set out to do by starting a press and public debate on such matters. In an architectural sense, Dulwich itself has been an influential source for new galleries such as the Turner Clore Gallery and the Sainsbury Wing.

However, Dulwich nearly went out of business shortly thereafter. Dulwich College – or Alleyn's College of God's Gift, Dulwich, as it is properly called – was no longer prepared, or able, to support the museum. Giles Waterfield had to act with great speed to work out a new long-term financial support

[1] Clifford had himself initiated the total reorganisation of the display of paintings in the National Gallery of Scotland. Unlike the Tate, he had opted for the fiercely colourful backgrounds typical of galleries in the nineteenth century, and in general the result was deemed a great success. A considerable collector in his own right, he has also made a name for himself by challenging under the export licence regulations the export of major works of art, and raising the large funds needed to keep them within the UK.

[2] Quoted from the Introduction to the exhibition catalogue: a highly informative document of permanent value.

structure to assure its future. Once again, the by now familiar names came to the rescue. Lord Sainsbury, he of the new National Gallery Wing, became chairman of the Trustees in 1994. Of the £10 million needed for the endowment of the Museum, three quarters had been promised a year later. As a recent press report stated, the chairman's 'old association with Lord Rothschild, now chairman of the government's National Heritage Memorial Fund, cannot have been unhelpful in getting Dulwich its £3 million from the Fund'. But it was a great achievement to establish a new lease of life for Britain's oldest museum at a time when recession was still much in evidence.

SIR JOHN SOANE'S MUSEUM

Dulwich is one of the few remaining buildings designed by that brilliant, eccentric architect, Sir John Soane. His very own museum in London's Lincoln's Inn Fields (see page 241), has also undergone great changes. Sir John Summerson, one of Britain's leading architectural historians, was followed as Director there by Peter Thornton, who had been in charge of the Furniture Department at the V&A for many years. After considerable fund-raising efforts, he was able, phase by phase, to restore Soane's structure in Lincoln's Inn Fields to the same state in which Soane had willed it to the nation, for change within had been inevitable since Soane's death in 1837.

An interesting fact has recently come to light which is particularly relevant in these days of strict planning laws. Soane's external feature, the three-storey stone screen, embellished with idiosyncratic and abstracted classical motifs, set in front of Number 13 Lincoln's Inn Fields, departed from the normal austere flat fronts which had been more or less enforced on London houses by various Building Acts, particularly that of 1774, since the Great Fire in 1666. After the construction of Number 13 was completed, Soane was summonsed before the local magistrate and accused of breaching sections of the 1774 Act, and others. But his lawyers argued that, far from being a 'nuisance', the façade was an ornament to the surroundings and could not be termed a public nuisance as it stood within Soane's freehold land. The magistrate found in Soane's favour and thus the great collector was vindicated. It was a judgement much welcomed by other architects of the time.

THE COURTAULD GALLERY

The most fundamental change of all among London's great picture collections concerned the Courtauld Gallery (see page 382). Originally housed in a quiet backwater near London University in Bloomsbury, it moved – after eleven years of protracted negotiations – into the splendour of Somerset House in the

Strand. The fine rooms in the North Block of Sir William Chambers' grand design (originally to house government departments) had once been the home of three learned societies: the Society of Antiquaries, the Royal Academy and the Royal Society. The first two had moved to Burlington House and the third to Carlton House Terrace in the mid-1850s.

To the original collection, principally of French Impressionist paintings and drawings *and* Viscount Lee of Fareham's varied collection of mainly medieval art (see page 394), there had in recent times been added by bequest or gift various other wholly outstanding private collections. Among the most important was that of Thomas Gambier-Perry (1816-1888) of early Italian paintings (see page 383), which had remained virtually unknown, and that of Count Antoine Seilern, always referred to earlier as the 'Princes Gate Collection' (see page 431) in which the work of Rubens predominated. Thus there was an accumulation of some 500 paintings, 6,000 drawings and upwards of 26,000 prints, as well as the finest imaginable examples of early decorative art, that had to be moved across London in 1989. Somerset House opened to the public in 1990. The first much-criticised display arrangement has been considerably altered when Dennis Farr was succeeded as Director in 1993 by John Murdoch, formerly of the V&A.

In the following year, there was staged under his aegis an exhibition which is of seminal interest to anyone concerned with the history of collecting, and to which the catalogue is a lasting monument. Its subject was 'Samuel Courtauld as Patron and Collector'. The greater part of the works of art Courtauld had ever bought for himself, or for other people, were included and in most cases the prices he had paid for them and information on when and where he had bought them had been established. There can be little doubt that Impressionism and Post-Impressionism are the artistic eras which most ardently engage the public interest. This exhibition demonstrated brilliantly a number of different factors: the activities of a private person as a collector with a very special vision of his own; the way in which he passed his love of the arts and his possessions into the public domain; and his forethought in providing funds for various national institutions to continue the path he had first trodden. It also showed the gradual assimilation of what in its early days was regarded in general as rather an aberrant form of art[1] into lovable masterpieces; and, finally, it made clear what the deepening passion for French painting of that era has risen to in financial terms over seventy years.

[1] When reviewing an exhibition of Sir Hugh Lane's (see page 391) collection of Impressionists in London in *The Burlington Magazine*, C J Holmes had put it rather charmingly: 'Hitherto as a nation we have been curiously insular in our attention to modern continental art.' Though, of course, the official French attitude towards their own compatriot artists had not been much less hostile. Courtauld visited this exhibition of Lane's pictures and described it as 'My second real eye-opener'.

AN INTRODUCTORY UPDATING

The extract on page 383 from *The Courtauld Collection: a Catalogue* (1954) is the work of Anthony Blunt, one-time Professor of History of Art in the University of London, Director of the Courtauld Institute and Surveyor of the Queen's Pictures. He was amazingly active and authoritative on a large variety of art historical subjects, outstanding among which were his *Art and Architecture in France 1500-1700*, an early volume in the Pelican History of Art series (1953), and his catalogue raisonné of Poussin's works, the result of years of study. He retired from the Courtauld in 1974 after being showered with academic honours and honorary doctorates. He became one of the leading, if not the leading figure in the post-war academic world of art history. The general view now appears to be that his subsequent disgrace when he was uncovered as a Soviet spy and stripped of his honours should not be allowed to detract from his standing as an art historian.

THE ROYAL ACADEMY

My catalogue of major examples of change is almost complete, but three more institutions need mention. First, there is the Royal Academy (see page 14). Great breaths of new life have been breathed into it. The place hums. Many collectors of British art still take their first tentative steps towards becoming collectors at the Summer Exhibitions. The standard may vary from year to year, but the red dots proliferate. All the most advanced marketing techniques have been used, and used very successfully, to get the great British public to take an interest. Von Bode's pioneering efforts to enrol 'Friends' for the Kaiser Friedrich Museum at the beginning of the century have here been polished and brought to a fine art of persuasion – and temptation.

There are constant, seminal exhibitions, now almost invariably staged with sponsorship collaboration. When given the funds to do so, the Royal Academy took the brave step of asking Sir Norman Foster to create more attractive temporary exhibitn space for them and he did so, brilliantly, on the top floor, where once the old Diploma Galleries were located in Burlington House. With the money provided by Jill and Arthur M Sackler, he created three simple galleries that since 1991 have housed superb exhibitions of paintings with a multitude of themes and often, of course, culled from private collections. The addition is highly attractive because of Foster's ingenious use of light and space.

KETTLE'S YARD

Kettle's Yard in Cambridge is a unique little showpiece in the centre of the city that should have figured – just – in the 1972 edition of this book. It is the one-time home of Jim Ede and his wife, Helen. Ede had been Assistant Keeper at the Tate in the 1920s. There he became friendly with Christopher Wood, David Jones and, in particular, with Ben Nicholson. Although as poor as a church mouse, he bought – or was often given – work by all three. In 1926 he first heard of Henri Gaudier-Brzeska, the French sculptor, who had been killed in action in 1916. To quote Ede 'a great quantity of his work was dumped in my office at the Tate: it happened to be the board room and the only place with a large table. All this work ... had become the property of the Treasury and the enlightened Solicitor-General thought the nation should acquire it, but no, [it was] not even [to be accepted] as a gift. In the end I got a friend to buy three works for the Tate and three for the Contemporary Art Society, and the rest, for a song, I bought. Since then [this was written in 1970] it has seemed my task to get Gaudier established in the rightful position he would have achieved had he lived into this present time.'[1]

In 1936, Ede moved overseas for twenty years, living first in Morocco and France and then lecturing on art all over the United States. It became his dream to create a *living place* [his italics!] where young people could enjoy art in an informal setting. Kettle's Yard was the result. In 1966 he gave it to Cambridge University. After the addition of a large extension, designed by Sir Leslie Martin, it was opened to the public in 1970. It has been added to twice since then, but still retains the delightful informality of a home rather than a museum and shows to great effect the charm and strength of a very personal collection in which fine twentieth century art mingles well with earlier antiques and natural objects.

THE BURRELL COLLECTION: OPEN AT LAST

The last entry in the earlier edition of *The English as Collectors* concerned Sir William Burrell's 'Purchase Books', which were the records of what he bought for his vast collection between 1911 and 1957. He had given his collection in its entirety to the City of Glasgow in 1944 (see page 414) as well as a large sum towards a special building to house it. By 1972 little progress had been made towards that end. In fact it was only a stinging rebuke in 1963 to the Glasgow Corporation and the Burrell Trustees by that august body, the Standing Commission on Museums and Art Galleries, that finally catalysed the location of an acceptable site in the Pollok estate, at that time still in private ownership. It consists of three hundred and sixty acres only three miles from the centre of Glasgow and its fine gardens and park-like nature accorded well with Burrell's ardent wish for a rural setting.

[1] Quoted from his introduction to *Kettle's Yard, an illustrated guide*, Cambridge 1980.

Preparing the complex brief for an architectural competition proved a lengthy business and it was not published until 1970. 242 architects submitted plans. The eventual winners, announced in 1972, were a team of unknown architects, all tutors in the Cambridge University School of Architecture. The group was led by Barry Gasson and their design won universal acceptance, particularly because it fully exploited the natural setting of the site, especially the adjacent woodlands. Inflating costs, however, delayed the start of building further. It was the astonished reaction at the riches of the virtually unknown Burrell collection shown in a selective exhibition of treasures from it in the Hayward Gallery in London in 1975 that finally triggered the Secretary of State for Scotland's agreement to meet half the costs of the building, because Burrell's initial bequest for the purpose was now nowhere near enough to fund the project.

Even when the Museum finally opened in 1983, it was only possible to show a proportion of the 8,000 objects that Burrell had assembled, but its reception was rapturous and enormous crowds flocked to Pollok Park.

No single owner-collection of such size and scope had come into being in Britain in recent times, though they have of course done so in America. One has only to think of Pierpont Morgan or Henry Clay Frick, or more recently, Norton Simon. Burrell did not have the singularity of vision, which Frick brought to the Old Master paintings he assembled. Further more, Burrell's funding was on an altogether smaller scale: the most he ever spent in a single year was £20,000[1]. Though before the Second World War Burrell had purchased much of the material dispersed by William Randolph Hearst, the newspaper tycoon, in a series of London sales.

Burrell's greatest love was for Gothic art: the tapestries, the stained glass, the early room settings and in the new museum they mingled wonderfully well with his wide range of other interests: the silver, the European ceramics, the arms and armour, the Near Eastern carpets and ceramics, and his wide spectrum of paintings which includes a Hans Memlinc, a Giovanni Bellini, a Lucas Cranach as well as a Rembrandt self-portrait, a Frans Hals (at £14,500 the most expensive purchase Burrell ever made) as well as works by Boudin, Manet, Sisley, Cézanne and no fewer than twenty-two by Dégas.

For a decade, the flow of visitors was enormous. Now, it is said, sadly, that Glasgow corporation is concerned by a great reduction in numbers. They have already made severe staff cuts. More recently through the person of Julian Spalding, director of Glasgow Museums, they have sought to overturn an explicit codicil to Sir William's will under which he proscribed the loan of artifacts from the collection to overseas exhibitions. The Burrell Trustees have vigorously opposed such a step (which, in fact, requires an Act of Parliament). They have said with some vigour that it would fly directly in the face of Sir

[1] But few collectors have had the opportunity of eighty years of collecting. Burrell bought his first pieces as a 16-year old boy. He died aged 96, having continued to buy almost to the end of his life.

William's express desires and might well affect the generosity of future donors of collections, which is obviously a major issue. A commission was appointed to adjudicate, and while allowing loans to go overseas, hedged such permissions around with complex restrictions.

CARDIFF TRANSFORMED

And if I have ventured to Scotland to discuss what has happened to the Burrell Collection, I must in fairness go to Wales and to Cardiff, in particular, where the National Museum of Wales has been transformed in recent years. It has become one of Britain's great museums. With a purchase grant raised at last in the 1970s and 1980s, its new acquisitions in almost every field were brilliantly chosen[1]. I mentioned all too briefly (pages 392 and 428) that wonderful collection of some 260 Impressionists, Old Masters (including two charming 'Botticellis' - now thought to be of workshop origin) and British paintings left to the Museum by the Misses Davies, which they assembled at Gregynog over forty years from 1908 onwards. These works are now superbly displayed in discreet, well-lit, entirely new galleries in a building constructed over six years and opened in 1993.

The paintings are interspersed with very fine selections of Oriental porcelain and other examples of the decorative arts, and the architect has created some delightful vistas. In fact, it is another instance of effective collaboration between an architect, John Phillips, and the curatorial staff. And though it may be a strange thing to mention, the gallery seating by David Colwell, provided for the weary visitor, displays a combination of modernist ingenuity and sculptural quality rarely seen in a museum – and it is comfortable as well.

Perhaps because of its tiny acquisition budget in the past, Cardiff has benefitted enormously from the generosity of local collectors. Its first benefaction was of 36 paintings given by William Menelaus as far back as 1882. This included the magnificent Tissot, *Bad News* (or 'The Parting'). Later, James Pyke Thompson gave a sizeable collection of watercolours, including three by Turner. It was Pyke Thompson who devised the dual policy that the Museum should acquire the best work of Welsh artists on the one hand and of the finest available international artists on the other.

Often, frustrating obstacles barred the way. When Sickert's *Église Saint Jacques, Dieppe* was advocated as a purchase for £90 in 1918, the then Keeper of Art, Isaac Williams, wrote: "It is an example of the extreme impressionist school which [our adviser] seems to admire so much. In my opinion this particular class of work is quite unsuitable for a public collection as it only seems

[1] There was, of course, the odd hiccough: there is some argument, for example, whether the Rubens' tapestry cartoons, still on view, are the work of the Master.

to excite the eccentric imagination of a very small number of people who mistake their unhappy affliction for genuine artistic perception."

During the First World War also, Wilfred de Winton enriched the Museum with his vast collection of Welsh, English and Continental porcelain. His assembly of fine Swansea and Nantgarw porcelains gave the Museum supremacy in that field, which grew even further when Ernest Morton Nance left his similar collection of rare and provenanced pieces to the Museum. It was the recent munificence of Sir Leslie Joseph that allowed the Museum to display this to magnificent advantage.

4. MUSEUM PHILOSOPHY

For a very detailed account of what it feels like to be at the centre of the need for change in the museum world and its actual execution, readers should turn to a wonderfully cogent report on his stint of office by Sir David Wilson. He called it *The British Museum: Purpose and Politics* (1989). He pulls no punches. He covers every aspect of the modern 'official collector's' duties, chores and difficulties in a way few others with his level of responsibility have had the courage to do.

Wilson's chapter on 'Collecting' is of particular interest to us in two respects. Firstly, his views on the training and necessary abilities of museum curators today would be music to the ears of his predecessors. He writes, 'A good museum curator is, above all things, curious about all objects, whether they be in his own subject or in some entirely different area. The museum curator proves his worth in the field, in the saleroom or in the dealer's showroom [see also page 53]. He or she is trained to spot the important pieces. The curator who found [a] £20 Gainsborough is a specialist in Italian art of the Renaissance to the 18th century, but he is also a good museum man – a man with an eye.'

Secondly, Sir David stresses that the 'importance of gifts of objects or collections to the museum cannot be under-estimated ... a recent exhibition of the major donors to the Louvre was accompanied by a catalogue which listed all the benefactors of that great museum – nearly 2,700 in all. The British Museum probably has had a hundred times that number.' He mentions that in two calendar years chosen at random, 1985 and 1986, the British Museum received a total of 107 major donations and 832 minor ones, many of which in both classes were multiple gifts. The English as collectors live, and continue to be as generous as ever!

I mentioned that de-accession by museums could become an appreciable factor. Sir David states quite categorically that 'disposal is nearly always a mistake'. He quotes an example of a painting by Fantin-Latour sold by the Lady

Lever Art Gallery in 1958 for £9,045. When it re-appeared on the art market some years later, its selling price was £950,000. The British Museum is governed by an Act of Parliament which disallows the disposal of any part of its collections, though there are carefully defined exceptions. Much the same rules against de-accession apply to most major British museums at present, though in a less rigid form (see the footnote on page 50). However, when de-accession has taken place in the UK, it is usually from lesser or quasi-public museums which have fallen on hard times. Certainly some major British libraries have disposed of those sections of their book stock which are tangential to their core interest. In that way they have gained both space and funds for further purchases.

In America, where an even higher proportion of museum holdings consist of donations or bequests from collectors (there have, of course, been tax advantages in making such gifts which still do not exist in England[1]) great care is normally taken to consult the relevant benefactors or their offspring before disposals are put in hand. Often, indeed, the next generation is allowed to have a say in how the money raised through de-accession is to be used by the museum after the sale has taken place. Certainly Sotheby's in New York has had major sales which have been widely publicised as being museum de-acquisition material. An interesting factor from our point of view is that on many occasions such material has been bought by English collectors and incorporated into English collections. The ultimate question, however, is, will the possibility of later de-acquisition put off the donors of the future?

* * *

In contrast to Sir David's commanding stance and comments on the museum director's calling at the present time are those of Richard Oldenburg, who retired from New York's Museum of Modern Art in 1994 to become the new head of Sotheby's in America. On being asked about this switch from one side of the art world to the opposite pole, Mr Oldenburg said, 'It is so complicated right now to be a [museum] director ... A directorship has become such a demanding job that it almost precludes serious scholarship or work with exhibitions as a whole.' He stressed that, in consequence, such posts had become less and less attractive to art historians. 'The challenge', he said, 'is to make the directorship the job that shows that art is the primary function of the museum.'[2]

Even the *Economist*, a journal that does not normally concern itself with such matters, carried an article in May 1994 about the fact that no fewer than

[1] In the UK, there exists only a complex arrangement by which the Treasury is prepared to remit death duties and/or capital gains tax, when an owner of an exceptional work of art gives or sells it to a museum at a price agreed by the Treasury. This is known as the 'in lieu' arrangement.

[2] Quoted in *The Art Newspaper*, May 1995

nineteen American art museums were director-less at that time. Museum trustees had become too demanding, particularly over fund-raising. The future would show, the writer said, whether art historians or administrators would rule the roost. Curiously, it was a precisely parallel problem that had beset the major auction houses ten or fifteen years earlier and there, as we shall see, the administrators (cum-accountants) won.

* * *

Sir David Wilson mentioned the importance of museum donors. No less a body than the Museums and Galleries Commission in their report on *The National Museums* (1988), wrote that the national museum collections 'represent to a great extent the patronage, discernment and generosity of generations of benefactors'. On page 45 of this book, you will find me writing 'The wealth of museums in Britain stems largely from the generosity of private collectors over the last 150 years'. But not everyone thinks so today. In a volume entitled *Art Apart: Art Institutions and Ideology across England and North America*, edited by Marcia Pointon (1994), she states quite categorically in her introduction: 'The authors of this book reject the history of the selfless generosity of a series of great men'. In the recently published *Codes of Ethics* of the Museums Association, one reads the following guidelines: '... museum professionals are advised to eschew personal collections, mindful that the best opportunity for an object to be preserved for the public is in a museum'. An unexpected attitude when one considers some of the great English museum curators of the past, such as Augustus Wollaston Franks or Sir Hercules Read (see pages 49 and 291).[1]

But the situation becomes even more quirky. I stated in the original introduction to this book that I had made little attempt to concern myself with the psychology of collecting (page 5). However, many other people now have. A recent, extreme example is a volume by Susan M Pearce entitled *On Collecting: an Investigation into Collecting in the European Tradition* (1995). It draws heavily on the influence of other writers who have applied a new psychological and esoteric vocabulary to the collecting process, and breaks down collecting into three phases: practice, poetics and politics. I think most collectors would have difficulty in recognising themselves or, indeed, their collecting activities. There are overtones of imbalance, of abnormal behaviour. The approach seems to devalue the fun of collecting, the pleasures it can give and, indeed, the scholarly

[1] For an interesting account of just what Franks bequeathed to the British Museum, see Sir David Wilson's *The Forgotten Collector* (1984), one of the delightful little publications in the series of Walter Neurath lectures, published by Thames and Hudson in memory of their founder, and the more recently published collection of Essays to mark the centenary of Frank's death, *A W Franks, Nineteenth-Century Collecting and the British Museum*, 1997, edited by Marjorie Caygill and John Cherry, which contains wonderfully useful research into the precise nature of Frank's work.

bent that often prompts it. The pity is that such books are obviously intended for students: the author is a Professor of Museum Studies. One cannot help feeling that there is a link here with the philosophy expressed in that edict by the Museums Association. Such attitudes certainly exist at the present time[1]. One can only ask whether this 'other route', this deviant path, this Marxist angle, is here to stay or if it is an aberration which the effluxion of time will nullify.

5. A NEW SET OF VALUES

Earlier on, I mentioned the enormous changes during the last quarter of the century in the economics of collecting.

The art world, like most others, moves in cycles. There have been major recessions since 1972 on a scale that had not been experienced since the 1920s. 1974, 1982 and 1992 (and beyond) have left their scars on every dealer's heart. But for the shrewd collector, those moments produced unparalleled opportunities. Perhaps the most interesting experiment which blatantly combined collecting and investment was carried out by a corporate body, the British Rail Pension Fund, who embarked on a deliberate policy of investing a small proportion (4 per cent) of their annual income in Old Master paintings, engravings, oriental porcelain, books, etc. Although they were ably advised, this activity caused the most fantastic furore in the media. But the Fund was generous: it did not tuck away its holdings in bank vaults, but lent much of what it had bought to museums all over Britain. By now the sale of its early purchases has already gone a long way. The results for a body that does not have to pay tax seemed to this observer to be startlingly successful. Though it has to be said that investment professionals mock this opinion. They say that the Fund could have done better by investing in gilts. But what investment fund has ever attained the theoretical maximal optimum? British Rail's bold experiment only proved the old parameters. Luck, skill and a seeing eye were essential: luck in its timing; skill in its selection, and a seeing eye in buying mostly what were outstanding items in each field.

Perhaps this can best be demonstrated by singling out one watershed example to show the surge of prices which I mentioned at the outset of this introduction,

[1] An editorial in an issue of *The Art Newspaper* of November 1995 seems particularly relevant here: 'On a visit last month to a leading Northern contemporary art museum, the editor of this newspaper rashly expressed the opinion that the curator of the recent Whitechapel exhibition on drawing, none other than Goldsmith head Michael Craig-Martin, had wonderful taste. "Taste!", spat out the young curator to whom the remark was addressed, "I hate that word. I have no idea what it means." Resisting the impulse to point out that that was obvious from the works hanging on the walls, your editor retired to lick her wounds and reflect on the irony of it all.'

which goes *way beyond mere inflation* and really demonstrates the new assessment of value in the art market. In December 1986 Christie's in London sold what they described as 'The varied and very English collection formed with great taste and discernment by Mr & Mrs Philip Goldberg, mainly in the early 1960s. They bought at the major London modern picture galleries as well as in the auction room and they kept meticulously detailed records of the prices they paid for each picture. The Goldbergs originally paid a total of £220,000 for their collection. On 2nd December 1986 it fetched £4,159,329, an increase of 2,000%.'

A Ben Nicholson *Bottle* which they bought for £267 in 1958 made £66,000; a Chagall bought for £2,300 in 1963 made £198,000; a Giacometti which cost £1,850 in 1960 fetched £165,000; a Seurat costing £4,000 in 1962 made £170,000, and Henri Matisse's *Jeune Fille en robe Blanche* increased by a staggering £416,000 between 1962 and 1986 after being bought for £12,700. But the real point at issue is what sort of collectors acquired these items at their new prices? History, of course, does not relate, and taking the issue even further, who would buy them today at even more startling figures? What is interesting is how many other owners of collections of works of art and (in particular) now valuable paintings assembled since the Second World War, have *not* been tempted by the unceasing blandishments of the auction houses to turn what they own into mountains of cash. But resistance becomes ever more difficult as the threat of death duties approaches.

* * *

Nevertheless, many of the collections which I mentioned in my summary of the twentieth century (see pages 387-405) have been dispersed, after the deaths of their owners, often with great saleroom *éclat.* In the case of some of the most distinguished family collections, going back to the eighteenth century, a number of part-dispersals have taken place, each of which also caused much criticism. Thus a limited number of drawings were sold from the Duke of Devonshire's vast collection at Chatsworth, firstly in 1984 and again in 1987. In the second instance, some seventy were initially offered to the British Museum by a proposed private treaty sale, but the authorities considered the asking price too high. The drawings were then sold at auction by Christie's for a sum three times greater (£24,000,000) than had at first been mooted.

In 1995 one or two major Old Master paintings, and particularly fine pieces of furniture, were sold by the Marquess of Cholmondeley from Houghton Hall in Norfolk, also by Christie's. Again the prices were greatly in excess of even the high estimates and the sum realised was over £21,000,000. In the previous year, the famous Holbein of *An Unknown Woman with a Squirrel* from Houghton had been sold directly to the National Gallery for a huge sum.

The sale of items from Althorp, the home of the Spencer family, was carried out rather more secretively, in general direct to dealers, and the press afterwards was full of tittle-tattle that the prices realised had been less than adequate. The then Earl Spencer, with whom I had a long discussion when compiling the original edition of this book, particularly over the iniquities of levelling death duties on historic family properties, would have been less than pleased. His grandson, now in charge of Althorp – and famed for his funeral oration on his sister, Princess Diana – has indicated that there will be no further sales.

More recently, a number of works was sold by order of the executors of the Sixth Marquess of Bute. Among them was an unrecorded portfolio of thirteen gouaches and watercolours by Paul Sandby, showing the Bute estate in Bedfordshire as it was in 1763. The prices exceeded the high estimates by a factor of five. A North Indian enamelled gold dish and covered bowl of about 1700, one of the most important Mughal objects that had come up for sale for many years, raised £194,000 against an estimate of £7,000-£10,000.

6. JOSEPH MAYER: AN OMISSION

So much for the dispersals: but where are the new collectors that come to mind who follow in the footsteps of the great tradition? One name from the nineteenth century I should certainly have included had I known more about him. This is Joseph Mayer of Liverpool (1803-1886)[1] and I must make good this omission. At the age of 14 he discovered an urn in a field turned up by a plough, and then earned a reward from his grandfather for deciphering the inscriptions on it. Thus was born a love of antiquities which dominated his life.[2] He became a jeweller, and a very successful one at that. This enabled him, particularly as he never married, to indulge in the purchase of a vast range of items of archaeological and artistic interest. These included Egyptian, Assyrian, Babylonian, Etruscan, Greek, Roman and Anglo-Saxon antiquities; ancient engraved gems, and an extraordinarily rich collection of mediaeval ivories and Limoges enamels. He also put together a wonderful collection of illuminated manuscripts, 126 in all, about half being mediaeval and later Western, and the other half Burmese, Persian, Arabic and Turkish. But there was more to come: Mayer assembled over five hundred pieces of arms and armour; ceramics – including Italian majolica – and a truly outstanding collection of Wedgwood wares, as well as Chinese and Japanese porcelain, Chinese glassware, metalwork, jade and ivories. At one stage he owned a large collection of Napoleonic memorabilia, but this he sold *en bloc*.

Mayer was on very friendly terms with Augustus Wollaston Franks of the British Museum and a frequent visitor there. It is thought that Franks (see

[1] Though see page 389.

[2] *DNB*, though this conflicts in detail with other sources.

page 332) helped, if only to encourage Mayer's establishment of an extensive private museum of Egyptology in 1852, which he opened to the public.[1] In fact, though this housed the various categories of items enumerated above, the artefacts from ancient Egypt provided the dominant theme. Mayer often acquired entire collections of such material which he integrated into his own. This seems less astonishing when one considers that in the 1830s alone Sotheby's sold no fewer than five major collections of Egyptological material, and this does not include the initial *private* sale of the first two of the three famous Consul Henry Salt collections (see page 224) or that of Joseph Sams, an eccentric bookseller (much of which went to the British Museum).

Mayer's munificence to his native city knew no bounds. He established a lending library of 20,000 volumes, public gardens, a bowling green; he paid for the publication of many learned works which would never otherwise have been printed, and towards the end of his life he set up a second Art Museum, this at Pennant House in the village of Bebington outside Liverpool. On his death the contents of Pennant House were sold in their entirety (on Mayer's surprising, but specific instructions) to provide funds for the upkeep of his other benefactions. Thus were lost beyond recall the 20,000 prints and drawings with autograph letters and 'mementos of famous persons' which he had gathered for his (never completed) *magnum opus* on the history of the arts in Britain. Sadly the detailed record of all his purchases throughout his collecting career disappeared at the same time, but he left the entire contents of the 'Egyptian Museum' to the City of Liverpool, where most of it can still be found in the Merseyside Museums (with the exception of what was lost through bomb damage during the Second World War).[2]

7. FORD AND MAHON

If Joseph Mayer represents a major omission from the nineteenth century, what names should we add to those collectors I mention between pages 387 and 405? Two in particular come to mind. Both are now of an advanced age; both started collecting in the 1920s. Both are connoisseurs in the true and traditional sense of the word.

Sir Brinsley Ford started collecting while still at Oxford. Among his earliest purchases were two small bronzes by Henry Moore. As a young man he inherited part of the collection of his great-grandfather, Benjamin Booth (1732-1837) which included a fine group of paintings and drawings by Richard Wilson. Later

[1] Initially called the 'Egyptian Museum', the name was changed in 1862 to the 'Museum of Antiquities' and again in 1867 to the rather grander 'Museum of National and Foreign Antiquities'.

[2] For a detailed description of the collection, see *Joseph Mayer of Liverpool, 1803-1886*, edited by Margaret Gibson and Susan M Wright, London, 1988.

he inherited many paintings, drawings and some sculpture and maiolica from his grandfather, Richard Ford (1796-1858), the famous author of the *Handbook for Travellers in Spain.* To this foundation Sir Brinsley has added hugely: the highlight among his acquisitions being a wonderful Michelangelo *Torso of a Man,* from the sale of the Oppenheimer Collection (see pages 400 and 434). Another major acquisition was a group of fourteen late *Punchinello* scenes by Domenico Tiepolo. His interest in modern British art was as great as that in Italian, and his collection includes a splendid array of works by Sickert, Augustus John, Harold Gilman, Christopher Wood and John Piper. Sir Brinsley has always been a doughty fighter for the arts and was chairman of the National Art Collections Fund (the private charity which helps museums to fund new acquisitions), Trustee of the National Gallery and a host of other galleries.[1]

Sir Denis Mahon, two years younger than Sir Brinsley, was similarly educated at Eton and Oxford. His extensive collection concerns itself primarily with the work of Italian Seicento artists, particularly of the Bolognese school. His researches and writings on the subject are extensive and were soon recognised as being particularly authoritative in a relatively unexplored area. A reading of Sir Michael Levey's catalogue of the seventeenth-century paintings in the National Gallery shows the references to the background knowledge on many paintings to be studded with quotations from Sir Denis's published work. But as long ago as 1934, when he offered Sir Kenneth Clark, as a purchase for the National Gallery, his painting by Guercino of *Elijah fed by the Ravens* (from the Barberini Collection: there are many references to that collection as a source for others within the body of this book), Clark responded that, much as he himself admired it, he knew he could never persuade the Trustees to buy such a picture.[2] Because the era from which they stemmed was then so little appreciated, Sir Denis was able to acquire many of his finest paintings for very modest sums (see plate 67). Thus he owns outstanding works not only by Guercino (no fewer than ten paintings), but also by Guido Reni, Annibale Carracci, Domenichino, Luca Giordano, Salvator Rosa and eighteenth-century masters such as Creti and Crespi. It is known that many of his key pictures are intended after his death not only for the National Gallery in London but also the National Gallery of Scotland, the Birmingham Museum and Art Gallery, the Fitzwilliam and the Ashmolean Museums. The last already has a collection of his finest Guercino drawings on deposit, where they joined those collected for the Museum by Sir Karl Parker (see page 407) mostly in the 1940s.

[1] In 1998 the Walpole Society published an extensive, two volume catalogue of his collection to celebrate his 90th birthday. (Vol. 60).

[2] Quoted from James Byam Shaw's introduction in the catalogue for the Exhibition of Guercino Drawings from Denis Mahon's Collection shown at the Ashmolean Museum in 1986, which was published by the *Burlington Magazine.* In the same piece, Byam Shaw wrote about Sir Denis's scholarship, 'He is tenacious of his ideas to the point of pugnacity, but so careful in assembling his documentation that he is unlikely to be caught out in an error of fact'.

Sir Denis has also organised a great many exhibitions of Italian art and has recently battled hard to persuade the government to be more generous in allowing people to leave works of art to the State in lieu of inheritance tax. He has always figured prominently in such public debates about artistic heritage. In fact, he has recently stated that he will bequeath his collection – some 61 paintings now said to be worth £25 million – to the National Art Collections Fund who will retain legal ownership of them with the right to withdraw them from the intended museums, should those museums at any time dispose of any paintings or drawings from their permanent collections. This move is designed by him to protect public collections from being put under pressure by governments to sell works of art to raise funds. Interestingly enough, Sir Denis bought his last painting in 1972, when this work was first published. Since then, prices have been beyond his reach.

In summary, therefore, the Ford and Mahon collections are probably among the finest that still remain in the setting of private houses in central London today.

8. NEWCOMERS

The contrast of the works of art assembled by Charles Saatchi of advertising fame could not be greater. His interest is entirely in contemporary art at two levels: he has often bought the work of talented students who have only just launched out on their careers, as well as that of the foremost names of our time.

The collection is so vast that it is housed in two former factory buildings in St John's Wood in London. Mr Saatchi's is what in America is called a warehouse collection. It has become so widely representative of the best-known names among living artists from both sides of the Atlantic that it has virtually achieved public status. It has come into being at a time when a particularly talented generation of British artists is almost more admired and appreciated in the rest of the world than in Britain. In 1985 an extensive catalogue in four well-illustrated volumes appeared under the title of *Art of our Time.*

Many enthusiasts began to feel that the Saatchi Gallery had superseded the Tate Gallery as the most successful and adventurous purchaser of modern art in this country. It includes not only the works of Lucian Freud, Frank Auerbach, Howard Hodgkin and Leon Kossoff, but also extensive holdings of Julian Schnabel, George Baselitz, Anselm Kiefer, Francesco Clemente and many, many more. Mr Saatchi's taste has been called 'bizarrely catholic'. It has certainly stimulated a great deal of controversy on what form contemporary art should take. It has also aroused great ire among commentators that Mr Saatchi has at times bought so many examples of a young painter's work that it has created a reputation before it was deserved, and that the fame thus achieved has fallen flat when some of that work was sold out of the collection not much later.

It is surely open to a collector to make what changes he likes? It will be interesting to see what has become of the Saatchi collection in another thirty years.

Contemporary art is often scoffed at. It has certainly taken some unexpected turns in recent years. But just to show how much it can mean to a collector was demonstrated in an article on his own collection by the film critic, Alexander Walker[1]. 'Buying art', he muses, 'is an act of self-analysis, done standing up and not supine, achieved (if at all) in silent communion, not at full confessional spate to the analyst.' He explains that he has 'a penchant for pictures that catch the artist's moment when self-research found a new form, [Victor] Pasmore's epiphany, for example, turning from figuration to abstraction'; what Mr Walker elsewhere calls 'a premonitory moment'.

He also remarks that 'Watching the light of day change the pictures one owns is part of the joy of domestic possession.' One is reminded of Sir Robert Peel speaking to Mrs Jameson (see page 246). Mr Walker's final comment is 'Minimalism appeals to me because it forces me to slow down and really look hard and long. Sometimes, I confess, I wonder if what I see is really there.' Such an unusual revelation of a collector's inner world is surely the most rewarding comment an artist can ask for.

* * *

As we approach the end of the twentieth century there are not many people who can still collect the finest products of the Old Masters, the Impressionists or even the English School. Inevitably the prices are in millions. But millionaires do exist and continue to come into being, and some still devote their wealth to art collecting. Sir Andrew Lloyd Webber, composer of miraculously successful musicals, comes to mind. Published information of what he collects has only recently begun to emerge. His principal area of interest is in the paintings of the Pre-Raphaelite Movement, but he startled the ceramic world when, by apparently bidding through *three* agents, he swept up virtually every item in a sale at Sotheby's of a collection of pots by William de Morgan.

In 1993 he bought a fine Canaletto[2] at a Christie's sale in London for £10.2 million. The picture, *London: the Old Horse Guards from St James's Park*, is now on loan to the Tate Gallery. A Picasso portrait of *Angel Fernandez de Soto* which he bought in New York for over £18 million is on loan to the National Gallery in London.

[1] National Art Collections Fund journal, *The Art Quarterly*, Autumn 1993: a journal that has in recent years become an important source of information on collecting.

[2] Perhaps mention should be made at this point that the popularity of the Italian vedutists–Guardi, Canaletto, Bellotto and others–has soared since 1972, and so have their prices. In that year, Sotheby's sold two: one of *The Piazza San Marco* in Venice and another of *The Old Walton Bridge* outside London for £54,000 and £52,000 respectively. Today's (1997) prices at auction would be fifteen to twenty times that.

Even less is known about Sir Graham Kirkham, a Yorkshire miner's son who has built up a large and successful business retailing upholstered furniture. He pulled the chestnuts out of the fire when the Royal Holloway College, a nineteenth-century educational foundation, chose to sell major paintings it had been given many years earlier by its founder. Although the College considered the sale necessary to ensure its survival, there was a major controversy about it. Sir Graham is said to have bought their Gainsborough of *Peasants Going to Market* privately in 1993 for £3.5 million. It is currently on loan to the Tate Gallery. He also bought the Constable *View of the Stour* from Holloway in 1995 for £6.7 million[1] and – at Sotheby's in the same year – Monet's *Poplars on the Banks of the Epte*, a painting that has changed hands several times in the last few years, for £4,840,000. A 1995 private gallery catalogue implies that he owns other works of the same quality.

9. THE ROLE OF THE AUCTION HOUSES

In the article by Alexander Walker from which I quoted earlier, he was very emphatic about where he bought his paintings and prints. 'I hardly ever buy at auctions. A bargain is satisfying – so is the thrill of a tussle for possession. But I value far more the relationship with an art dealer which is the result of gallery buying over the years. The "premium" I pay is for my education.' There is still great support by individual collectors for working with a sympathetic dealer (see also page 400).

Nevertheless it is the auction houses that have played the dominant and most visible rôle in generating public awareness of the art market in all its myriad aspects – and they it was who lured ever more participants into the sport of collecting by propagating an infinitely subtle blend of the joy of art ownership with the prospect of sound investment.

The competition between them has not diminished. Sotheby's and Christie's are still locked in combat: Sotheby's the richer by 250 years of history, never previously chronicled, written by me; Christie's has had its innards exposed by John Herbert, its long-time and not uncritical publicist.[2] Both firms are as strongly established in New York as in London, if not more so, particularly in the case of Sotheby's. Both now function in infinitely more sophisticated premises than formerly. Both are public companies with a raft of shareholders. Both are driven by highly profit-conscious slave masters. The worthy Peter Chance at Christie's has been replaced by Christopher Davidge, son of a former Christie administrator, who learned the nitty-gritty of management when

[1] A case came to court in 1997, about this Holloway painting where one dealer claimed successfully that another had usurped his commission.

[2] Frank Herrmann, *Sotheby's: Portrait of an Auction House*, London 1982; John Herbert, *Inside Christie's*, London 1990.

running the subsidiary firm that prints all Christie's catalogues. Sotheby's lost its way in management terms after Peter Wilson's startlingly sudden withdrawal. The absence of his guile and his brilliance had left too large a hiatus. The firm was the subject of two takeover bids from America in the 1980s. The first was fended off by dint of a referral to the Mergers and Monopolies Commission; the second, by Alfred Taubman, an American property developer, won the day. It was a brilliant purchase and a rewarding investment. Since he took over, there has been a succession of chief executives in the UK, including Lord Gowrie, a former Tory Minister of the Arts. But the reins are now firmly in the hands of an American Thatcher-like figure, Dede Brooks, a one-time financial controller at Sotheby's in New York. Possessor of a dynamic personality, a great deal of determination and an intimate knowledge of the importance of the bottom line, but also with a sympathetic understanding of the problems of her experts, she is beginning to grow into the footsteps of Peter Wilson, though the firm she heads is a very different animal.

It was interesting that a group of very wealthy private investors considered the purchase of Christie's as a whole early in 1998 for £540 million but finally decided that the auction world provided insufficient certainty of a satisfactory financial return. The principal shareholder involved then sold out to François Pinault, a French billionaire businessman who had started life in the timber business, who offered a much higher price, so both our major auction houses – great duopoly that they are – have now gone truly global.

Both Sotheby's and Christie's have sizeable intelligence departments that keep records of every 'collectable' they hear of in private ownership. Both firms find it necessary to produce increasingly elaborate catalogues for major items. Both have perfected a standard of colour photography and colour printing in their catalogues that is virtually unmatched in any other industry. Both firms were badly burned in the recession after an unprecedented period of booming sales.[1] Both had to cut back on staff and offices, but both are now making a solid recovery, though the number of sales held has been reduced. To some extent, both have introduced a class system into their client base. The lesser items are sold at Christie's South Kensington or Christie's East in New York, or in Sotheby's Colonnade sales in London and New York. Only the best items

[1] The boom, which many people believe to have been initiated by the massive entry of Japanese buyers into the art market, reached its well-nigh unbelievable peak when, in May 1990, Christie's in New York sold Van Gogh's *Portrait of Dr Gachet* for £49,000,000; and Sotheby's, two evenings later, sold Renoir's *Moulin de la Gallette* for £46,000,000. These extreme prices had first come into being in March 1989 when Van Gogh's *Sunflowers* sold at Christie's in London for £24,700,000 and, in November 1989, Van Gogh's *Irises* had reached £30,200,000 (though the buyer could not eventually pay for it), while Picasso's *Les Noces de Pierette* had reached £32,900,000 and his celebrated self-portrait *Yo Picasso* sold for £29,000,000, many times what it had fetched a decade earlier. Needless to say, dealers had similarly exceptional seasons. 'No one can tell how long this phenomenon will last', a leader in the *Independent* stated at the time. We now know.

feature in the principal catalogues. Therefore, unless a collector subscribes to both, he is not fully aware of what is coming onto that part of the art market in which he is interested.

Both firms thought that the Far East held great promise for future expansion until the great Asiatic recession in 1998. Oriental objects of all kinds had increasingly returned to the areas where they originated long ago. Both firms have turnovers exceeding one billion pounds. Both find that it is still Impressionist paintings, really important Old Masters and jewellery that ultimately pay the bills; while often small, specialist departments are no more than tolerated, though the fickle business of contemporary art sales has become a major factor. And the bills are heavy: the overheads of running such worldwide businesses are staggering. Both firms have a much more rapid turnover of staff. In each firm it is still the experts that seem least happy. In the past it was virtually unknown that executives should move from one to the other: now it is a not-infrequent occurrence.

But both together, Sotheby's and Christie's, still dominate the art market and, of course, the collecting world. Their disappearance is unthinkable. Though one wonders how much longer they can keep going in their present form.

The style of selling in the saleroom has changed. Waving numbered paddles and anonymity have taken the place of having known names called. People attend sales less in person. Instead there are banks of manned telephones and no one except the staff ever knows who is at the other end.

Both firms have indirectly spawned a number of niche auction houses and galleries started by former employees. Recently contracts of employment have been tightened in order to preclude such moves, or at least to delay them. While both Sotheby's (who started long ago) and Christie's are heavily involved in the real estate property market, both continue to explore innovative sales of material not traditionally collected, often with some success. This is an essential investment in the future, whatever the ultimate financial results may indicate. Finally, both firms have called a truce over commissions charged to clients by standardising their terms and adhering firmly to the published figures.

Both have borne the brunt of public exposure for malfeasances: Christie's in New York and Sotheby's more recently in Milan. If one can make such a judgement, Christie's is currently half a length ahead in the race for getting hold of the best property.

But, of course, the two major auction houses do not have it all their own way. For one thing, they will not now accept goods below a certain, often four-figure value. This offers opportunities to other salerooms. Phillips continues to be a successful Number 3[1] and, after management changes some years ago, Bonhams

[1] It, too, has spread its wings. The firm now has a network of 25 salerooms in addition to 34 offices and representatives in Britain and elsewhere. In 1995 Phillips staged 875 sales. In 1997, Christopher Weston, who had built Phillips up to its present size, sold out and retired.

is getting a larger slice of the cake. A great number of independent provincial auction houses continue in business and seem to survive very comfortably. Indeed, they seem to be getting better goods that would formerly have been sold in London.

* * *

I have not attempted to enlarge the annotated bibliography which begins on page 418.[1] Certainly I have unearthed a great number of additional catalogues of collections, both in the private and sale categories. But those already listed are the ones most useful, taken in conjunction with the text.

On the other hand, one of the early readers of the first edition of this book, Charles Sebag-Montefiore (see page xx), was so intrigued by the bibliography as it stood that he set about collecting the works listed in it. After years of assiduous searching, he has extended the aggregate to four or five times the original number of volumes. He has endeavoured, as far as possible, to acquire copies with contemporary annotations. These, of course, add to their interest. He began compiling a new bibliography and for many years I have been encouraging him to get this published. It now looks as if his work may soon see the light of day. It will be most useful.

But mention must also be made of a most comprehensive and detailed guide to *The Fine and Decorative Art Galleries of Britain and Ireland*, the work of Jeanie Chapel and Charlotte Gere, which appeared in 1985 under the sponsorship of the National Art Collections Fund. It combined useful information on the founding, the donors, the architecture and the contents of virtually every UK museum of consequence: an essential work of reference for all those interested in the history of collecting, and it included a mass of practical details (telephone numbers, opening hours and precise location) for prospective visitors. Alas, the volume was remaindered after a relatively short existence in print and is now hard to find.

* * *

And finally ...

During the course of the years since *The English as Collectors* was first published, two questions have often been asked.

Why the use of the unusual word *Chrestomathy* in the sub-title of the earlier edition? At its simplest (see page 5), the dictionary defines it as 'a book of

[1] In fact, almost all the volumes concerned (some 300) were included in an exhibition held in 1972 at the National Book League, then at 7 Albemarle Street in London, together with 160 publications on collecting, newly issued by publishers. The exhibition and its catalogue aroused considerable interest, as no such bibliography had been put together previously.

selections'; in the nineteenth century it was often used in connection with books that taught foreign languages. It seemed to me preferable to the word *Anthology* because my commentaries took up so much of the book. Also, and perhaps slightly mischievously, I was hoping that the word would intrigue and catch on. It didn't: it merely caused puzzlement. So now the sub-title has become *A Documentary Sourcebook*, which is exactly what is intended.

The other question was why had I paid only scant attention to the whole subject of book collecting? It was certainly not through lack of interest: my whole working life has been involved with books but my years at Sotheby's convinced me that, while I loved the auction world, I loved it on a smaller scale. So I founded my own auction house, Bloomsbury Book Auctions, in 1983, which concentrated on books and manuscripts. It has established a strong toehold in that field.

I had no doubt, however, that the whole subject of book collecting really interested a different audience from the one I had in mind when compiling *The English as Collectors*. The literature on the collecting of books is vast, perhaps because the purchasers are particularly literate; and it would have meant reducing the number of extracts on the collecting of the fine and decorative arts for which I felt – and still feel – there is a particular need. However, for anyone interested in the bookish genre, there is one supreme example that I would recommend. It is Willmarth Lewis's *Collector's Progress*. Mr Lewis became interested in Horace Walpole and all that he stood for[1] in the early 1920s. With a pertinacity and perspicacity that is rare even among outstandingly manic bibliophiles, he hunted down everything he could find of Walpole's library and the contents of Strawberry Hill. For a particularly interesting part of the hunt, the reader is recommended to his chapters IX and X. They demonstrate with singular clarity that, where specialist collecting is concerned, timing and opportunity are everything. Mr Lewis had the means to pay for that which he sought. He also succeeded in what must be the collector's ultimate dream: he published the Walpole correspondence he had so assiduously searched for in 48 volumes, and eventually gave his entire collection to Yale, where interested students can examine at leisure the results of a lifetime's search.

Adieu.

[1] See pages 82, 90 and 116.

Introduction

TO THE
Amateurs
OF ENGLAND

1. PREFATORY

IN May of the year 1835 a small, bespectacled, highly articulate scholar arrived in England from Berlin. He came armed with a mass of introductions to many of the most eminent men of their time, and for six solid months he travelled round the country looking studiously and critically at the contents of their houses. The result of his extensive scrutiny and diligent note-taking was a three-volume work entitled *Works of Art and Artists in England.*[1] Its author was Dr Gustav Waagen, first Director of the Royal Picture Gallery in Berlin.

The book was a landmark. It made clear for the first time that the English were unrivalled collectors of works of art. It pointed out too that the number of outstanding pictures, antiquities and *objets d'art* in England was probably exceeded in only one other European country, Italy. It established, surprisingly, that the English were almost unique in their love of surrounding themselves with objects of beauty from many previous ages in the rooms in which they and their families passed their lives. Elsewhere in Europe up to that time such pieces were more usually confined to special cabinets and galleries.

Today the collecting of works of art has absorbed a considerable proportion of our national affluence for rather more than two centuries and has become firmly established as a delightful aspect of our intellectual life. Yet there have been few historical accounts of it since Dr Waagen's detailed conspectus. Perhaps this is not surprising. The subject is a vast one and yet the literary sources are limited and widely scattered.

Books about every aspect of art are legion, but the restless energy, persistence and expertise that are the hallmarks of the devoted collector have not often been rated of sufficient general interest to merit a volume to themselves. Most great collectors were poor authors or did not consider a detailed account of their own activities worth passing on. Those that tried were often cloyingly anecdotal. The extreme circumstance was overemphasised; the norm went unrecorded. The number of original accounts of collecting which show detachment and objectivity is so small that their authors have been subjected to a long concatenation of literary theft by generations of more or less skilful paraphrasers.

Rather than joining their ranks, it seemed to me possible that a useful chronological survey of the English as collectors could be compiled by choosing passages from earlier sources that were both well informed and readable. The extracts in this book therefore tell *most* of the story as they stand. Combined with brief introductions, explanatory annotations, some detail about the author of each piece, and reference to other useful literature—so that the interested reader can pursue

[1] For full bibliographical details, see pages 146 and 425.

the subject in much greater depth if he wants to – they form a fairly systematic account of the collecting of works of art in England. In fact, I have tried to produce the sort of book which I had hoped to find when I first became fascinated by the whole subject of collecting some years ago: not a fully-fledged history, but a documentary source-book for those who want to know more.

In general I have confined the subject matter of the excerpts throughout the book to the collecting of the works of painters and sculptors on the one hand, and to the products of the best craftsmen of all ages on the other. Overall, it must be confessed, my primary concern has been with pictures. I have concentrated furthermore on what Herbert Read has called 'purposive' collecting,[1] where a strong element of aesthetic discrimination is involved. Of its very nature collecting is a highly individualistic pastime and generalisations about it are always riddled with exceptions and contradictions. I have nevertheless attempted to single out the threads of what by common consent at any given time constituted a *trend* among the pursuits of the many. Sometimes, perhaps, this merely reflected the views of a particularly vocal minority.

I have deliberately retained a certain duplication of comment by different authors at different times because the very repetition highlights rather effectively the importance in the history of English collecting of such events as the dispersal of the Orleans Collection, the purchase by Beckford of the Altieri Claudes, the Stowe, Bernal and Hamilton Palace Sales, and the constant demand for and eventual establishment of a National Gallery in 1824. In fact, this last was probably the most important single event in the whole history. It was the realisation of an ambition that had possessed innumerable collectors before it occurred and its growth and development influenced a host of others afterwards. It is for this reason that I have used it as a dividing point between the two parts of this book.

In selecting material I have deliberately chosen authors like Horace Walpole, Dr Waagen and Mrs Jameson, who would have been well known to many active and successful collectors in their own day, and whose advice the collectors would have taken to heart and followed. I ought to stress that most of the extracts and ancillary information are culled from *books* rather than from the periodical literature. There are two reasons for this. It would be beyond the capacity of one person to read and know all the contributions relevant to collecting; and, secondly, information in journals is often of a more tentative nature. It seemed to me that once it was consolidated in the less ephemeral form of a book it could usually be regarded as more reliable. However, despite this, reference is made to many useful articles in journals, but these are not included in the select bibliography. The present work may be the more useful because many of the books quoted, although well known, were scarce ten years ago and have now become almost unobtainable.

I must admit also that I have avoided extracts from sources that appeared earlier

[1] In his introduction to Niels von Holst's *Creators, Collectors and Connoisseurs*, London, 1967.

than the middle of the eighteenth century, as these are often difficult to read. It should, however, be stressed that a great number of such sources have been consulted in my search for information.

There is little attempt at any explanation of the psychology of collecting.[1] (Though one might point out how often the greatest collectors have been men in high office who probably had little leisure to spare for such a pastime.) The aim instead has been to chronicle what was collected, by whom, the sources of supply, the transitory nature of private collections, the astonishing survival of family accretions, the growth of expert knowledge, the emergence of permanent public galleries very often due to the generosity of the enlightened private collector, and –quite incidentally–the gradual transformation of what were once merely articles of domestic decoration into what are now items of considerable financial significance. There is no emphasis on art as investment, which is a mere by-product of true collecting; though clearly it cannot be ignored, particularly at the present time. Paintings, antiquities, *objets d'art* are regarded as things that give pleasure to their owners by virtue of their excellence or beauty. But economic value must play an important part in availability and in determining what the interested collector can or could buy.

The whole subject is obviously immense, whether one considers what was collected or by whom. For every collection named or described two or three have had to be omitted. Inevitably the extracts must be regarded as representative and not exhaustive. This will explain my choice of the word *chrestomathy* in the subtitle of this book. It can be defined simply as a collection of favourite passages from a particular literature to show a trend. It seemed to me a more appropriate variant of the word anthology.

We have today reached a stage in the history of collecting where one factor has become increasingly important. This is provenance. The thought that an enlightened enthusiast can pick up a great work for a few shillings is what spurs on many. It does happen, but increasingly rarely. The wider diffusion of knowledge has made it almost impossible to discover significant objects that are either underrated or overlooked. It is much more important to have paid the right price at the right time! In a 'market' where the demand steadily increases and the supply must of its very nature dwindle, prices are always on the increase, particularly for the pieces which are genuinely what they are claimed to be. A fully documented sales or collecting history, a pedigree, or provenance, is probably as reliable a guide to authenticity as any other. In the past the study of provenance has been confined to pictures and antiquities. As values go up it will be used

[1] It is a subject which seems to fascinate writers in France and Germany. As early as 1911 Adolph Donath wrote a book called *Psychologie des Kunstsammelns*, and since the last war a number of French psychoanalysts have made a study of art collectors. Their startling conclusions are quoted by Pierre Cabanne in *The Great Collectors*, London, 1963. According to this writer and also to Maurice Rheims, French collectors seem to be infinitely more psychologically complex than their staid and simple English counterparts.

increasingly for other categories of works of art. This alone makes the study of the history of collecting particularly relevant today. Additionally the amalgam of taste, flair, fashion, patronage, connoisseurship, financial acumen, affluence and occasional flamboyance, makes it a fascinating subject which will gradually establish itself as an important aspect of our social history.

Probably the heyday of collecting was the period between 1770 and 1830. For this was the era when the general affluence of the English gentleman coincided with the decline of the famous aristocratic and royal families of Europe, and veritable treasures could be had for very little by those who had a discriminating eye, an urge to travel and a well-lined purse. However he may have affected the history of England otherwise, Napoleon must be regarded as the patron saint of English collectors at the beginning of the nineteenth century, because he dislodged from the European continent art treasures that no one had regarded as anything but absolute and permanent fixtures. A vast proportion of them found their way to England. The landed gentry[1] had that curiously English combination of taste for the stable *and* the drawing-room, and what was virtually unknown anywhere else in Europe–as mentioned earlier–they liked to *live* surrounded by their pictures and antiquities. No doubt the almost obligatory Grand Tour accounted for some of their enlightenment: certainly their predominantly classical education did not.

In any case, well before the middle of the nineteenth century England had become such a treasure house of art as to arouse considerable envy on the Continent. Dr Waagen was simply the most celebrated among a number of other European experts who came over here and wrote long and detailed accounts of the many collections they had visited. Once the model had been established, there was no lack of English authors who occupied themselves with this genre of literature. Without these invaluable conspectuses, which in many instances are our primary sources of information, we would know a good deal less about the subject.

It is an astonishing fact that in some parts of the country–Northamptonshire, for example–one can still follow in the footsteps of Dr Waagen and see the same houses with substantially the same contents as he did, *despite* depletions by the changing taste of six or seven intervening generations, despite financial depressions and the curse of death duty.

One must also remember that the most important phase of collecting in this country had occurred before the advent of museums, photography and easy travel made it a simple matter to study anything like the complete works of any one artist or even one school of painting, and certainly the 'Kunsthistoriker' had not yet come into his own. The only places where comparisons were possible were on the walls of the salerooms, and this increases our gratitude and respect for the catalogues of Christie's, Foster's, Sotheby's and the other famous auctioneers. However, the English in general have a little-recognised propensity for record-

[1] One must remember that as a middle class of well-educated and affluent non-aristocrats they were almost unique in the Europe of their time.

ing purely factual information and preserving documentation, and many collectors produced in their lifetime printed catalogues of their own collections. Again these prove to be wonderfully useful sources of information, though as we learn – in particular from Mrs Jameson – the attributions given were generally more optimistic than authoritative.

Collecting is a part of our history during the last two hundred years of which England (and Scotland, for that matter) can be justifiably proud. Very often our taste was ahead of the rest of the world. Italian Primitive painting, for example, was something we recognised as important years ahead of the Italians themselves or any other country in Europe. And we benefited because prices were correspondingly low. By and large we were generous in what we paid for what we brought back home. On the European continent our reputation for immense wealth can, I think, be attributed largely to what were regarded as the crazy prices we were prepared to pay for pictures and antiquities. Unlike most European countries we rarely pillaged or robbed. I hope that the relatively brief account of the acquisition of the Elgin marbles on page 154 may show that this too was a case not of robbery, but of rescue.

Of course there are aspects of English collecting about which, with hindsight, one can be critical: the slow re-awakening of interest after the terrible holocaust of Oliver Cromwell and the Commonwealth; our prolonged preference for seventeenth century Italian painters and our lack of interest in Renaissance art, particularly sculpture; our hesitancy in shaking off a maudlin preference for Victorian art when first faced with the products of the French Impressionists, and the occasionally slavish following of the dictates of fashion. Yet despite this our record is surely second to none in the appreciation of beautiful things, in making them our own for a time, and in our generosity in presenting them to the public ultimately.

The extraordinary fact is that the public today is still positively eager to flock to museums to see paintings by Old Masters, when so often the iconography of the subject matter – based as it is on remote classical mythology or little-known hagiographical or biblical events – must be totally lost on them, so that composition and style are admired for their own sake. Perhaps it is the very complexity of allusion of many great works of art that have come on the market in recent times that has deterred the private collector and appealed particularly to the official collector. Where paintings are concerned, in fact, it would not be unfair to say that the private collector has preferred the comparative simplicity of landscapes, of portraits and of still lives. All the more reason then that museums should hesitate less to help the visitor with more information about what a painting represents and how it came into being.

Many of the matters touched upon briefly in this section are discussed at greater length in the later sections of the introduction. These have been included to sketch in the background to collecting activities. Each one of them, if tackled in a comprehensive manner, could easily have been expanded to fill an entire book.

Finally a word about the recent past and the present. Treatment of the contemporary scene has had to be confined largely to brief references in the introduction. The status of collections lately or at present being formed is far too fluid for any but passing comment. Even the survey of the outstanding collections of the earlier part of the twentieth century shows how rapidly dispersal follows a decline in a collector's enthusiasm, and the frequency with which a lifetime's collecting activities have forcibly to be turned into cash as soon as the approaching hazard of death duties is realised. Applying the yardstick of historical perspective to those collections that survive is also difficult because of changing standards and sheer availability. All one can say with certainty is that the distinguished collectors of today, who are not men of enormous wealth, make their contribution by increasing specialisation. The most successful, in general, are several jumps ahead of fashion and the concomitant rise in prices.

But the most important single attribute of a great collector, as always in the past, is an eye for quality. It surmounts the boundaries of specialisation: it inevitably picks out the best in any field of art collecting.

2. HISTORICAL

When considering *what* people collected, the three principal factors are taste, fashion and availability. If serious purposive collecting from our point of view started in the eighteenth century it is important to remember that the Augustan philosophy was dominated by a rigid adherence to accepted principles. There was endless discussion of, and, apparently, general agreement upon, what constituted correct Taste. To us the word taste implies both standards and enthusiasm. John Steegman, one of the most discerning writers of recent times to study the subject, wrote:[1] 'It can include both those who not only know what they like, but know why they like it, and those who only know what the majority of other people like.'

Given that there will always be individuals endowed with powers of discernment out of the ordinary, in eighteenth-century England this led first to the establishment of the rules of taste; then to the establishment of rulers, and finally to the establishment of a tradition of obedience to those rules. And yet by general consent the eighteenth century can well claim to be considered as the golden age of English taste. The simplicity of form and ornamentation under Queen Anne was succeeded by a medley of styles, including the Baroque, Rococo, and Neo-Classical with much overlapping and intermingling. These met the capricious demands of a cultured cosmopolitan society, rich and enlightened enough to demand the latest mode from architects, designers, artists and craftsmen of immensely diverse talents and powers of invention. Though each style was basically

[1] His *Rule of Taste, from George I to George IV*, 1936, covers this ground with remarkable clarity and I have quoted him on it at some length.

imitative of an earlier era, the period was notable for an admirable resourcefulness in the adaptation of ancient forms to new purposes.

But the seventeenth-century background is important too in this context. The Reformation had led to 'a re-distribution of wealth and the rise to power of new men and to the building of new houses on a new scale of splendour. But the English still felt apart from Europe, and had a curiosity about that Europe which inspired them from early in the seventeenth century to travel either on the Grand Tour or to universities like Padua and Paris. This curiosity that engendered the habit of foreign travel engendered also the habit of collecting. For once it had become necessary for a young man to have travelled, it became necessary for him to show some tangible results of his journey; at first this was limited to the French or Italian cut of his clothes and to his partiality for French or Italian poetry. Soon, and especially under the very highly cultivated Charles I, it became important for him to possess works of art and to spend large sums of money in acquiring a collection of antiquities, curiosities, medals, gems, statuary or painting;[1] the habit of collecting spread, encouraged by the example of the Earl of Arundel, the Duke of Buckingham, the Earl of Pembroke, Sir Anthony van Dyck and the King himself; it gained impetus whenever a great collection, such as those of Rubens or the Duke of Mantua, was dispersed, but it was violently checked by the Civil War and the death or temporary eclipse of those who had most encouraged it; and after 1660 their successors, or those restored in fortune, were in a very different frame of mind.'[2] And so though the seeds of collecting were sown,[3] as Buchanan[4] and many writers in the time of George IV contended, a century of darkness followed upon the Civil War. Yet, Steegman continues, it was clear 'that during the reign of George II an interest in the Fine Arts spread again among the wealthy and educated. Not only was the mere acquisition of pictures and statuary becoming more valuable as a source of social prestige but it was considered desirable to possess,

[1] The educated English traveller on the Continent with an interest in such matters is likely to have seen one or more of the 'Cabinets' of art and unusual natural objects which many princely and aristocratic families maintained – and added to – in their ancestral homes. In Germany these were known variously as 'Wunderkammern' or 'Kunstkammern', or if their contents included regalia, jewellery and particularly valuable pieces of armour, as 'Schatzkammern'. For fuller accounts see Niels von Holst's *Creators, Collectors and Connoisseurs*, London, 1967; the same author's 'Kunstkammern des 18. Jahrhunderts', *Repertorium für Kunstwissenschaft*, 1931; and J. von Schlosser's *Kunst- und Wunder-Kammern der Spätrenaissance*, Leipzig, 1908; but in particular Caspar F. Neickel's *Museographie*, Leipzig, 1727, which laid down the principles upon which such repositories were to be set up. One of the most celebrated English collections of this kind, which combined works of art with examples of natural history specimens, was the Duchess of Portland's 'Portland Museum' which came up for sale in 1786. It included the 'Portland Vase' which Gavin Hamilton had obtained from the Barberini Palace in Rome only a few years earlier.

[2] Steegman, *op. cit.*

[3] And indeed ripened in a few memorable cases, where at least part of the pre-Civil War collections still remain, as at Burghley, Althorp and Chatsworth among others.

[4] 'The interval which succeeded the dispersion of that magnificent collection [of Charles I] down to the reign of our late worthy and beloved sovereign, George III, may in so far as regard the arts of painting and sculpture, be compared to a return of the dark ages.' William Buchanan, *Memoirs of Painting*, London, 1824, vol. I, p. 213.

if not expert knowledge of, at any rate an articulate enthusiasm for, the objects acquired; most persons of quality learned at least the jargon assiduously if not always very intelligently, and some, impelled by a curiosity originally no more than modish, discovered new pleasures of "sensibility";[1] indeed, it was not long before the Fine Arts came to be regarded as the one intellectual activity for which enthusiasm was not only admissible but desirable.'[2]

Guides to the orthodoxy of taste were not slow in coming forward. Among the first was the painter, Jonathan Richardson. In 1719 he published two discourses: an *Essay on the whole Art of Criticism as it relates to Painting* and, in the same volume, an *Argument in behalf of the Science of the Connoisseur*. In 1722, jointly with his son, who had done most of the work, he published an account of the art treasures to be seen in Italy.[3] Hogarth's *Analysis of Beauty*, 'written with a view to fixing the fluctuating ideas of Taste', appeared in 1753; Burke's *Essay on the Sublime and Beautiful* came out in 1756; James Barry's thunderous *Inquiry into the Real and Imaginary Obstructions to the Acquisition of the Arts in England* in 1775; Sir Uvedale Price's *Essay on the Picturesque* in 1794; the Rev. William Gilpin's *Essay on Picturesque Beauty* in 1792; Sir Joshua Reynolds' famous *Fifteen Discourses*, delivered to the students at the Royal Academy between 1769 and 1790 and first published collectively in 1797, had an enormous and lasting influence;[4] and so, among a more limited audience, had Richard Payne Knight's *Analytical Enquiry into the Principles of Taste*, which covered every facet of the whole subject and appeared in 1808.

The works listed represent only the landmarks in a substantial literature. The books on architecture alone that would have been essential reading for any gentleman contemplating the construction of his own 'seat' in an acceptable manner would fill a sizeable library shelf (particularly as many of the volumes were quartos and folios).[5] The frequent use of the word 'picturesque' is of more than a little significance. Again Steegman is enlightening: 'Nature was only admired when she resembled art, when, in fact, she became picturesque. . . . When [the word] was first applied to any scene, it meant, not that an artist ought to paint it, but that it looked as if it had already been painted, that it resembled a picture; the

[1] 'To the eighteenth century sensibility was a significant, and almost sacred word, for it enshrined the idea of the progress of the human race. Sensibility was a modern quality; it was not found among the ancients, but was the product of modern conditions. . . .' J. H. S. Tompkins in *The Popular Novel in England, 1770–1800*, London, 1932.

[2] Steegman, *op. cit.*

[3] *An account of Some of the Statues, Bas-Reliefs, Drawings and Pictures in Italy etc, with Remarks* by Mr Richardson Senior and Junior. One cannot help wondering to what extent this book was used later in the century as a source of information by English connoisseurs (and dealers) about what they could try to buy in Rome from the financially embarrassed aristocrats.

[4] An interesting comment on the influence of the works of Burke, Barry and Reynolds was made by William Buchanan, who actually started his career as an art dealer about 1802 because he felt that the climate for picture buying had been so vastly improved by the efforts of such writers.

[5] For a brief but informative summary of them see John Harris, *Georgian Country Houses*, London, 1968.

more a scene resembled a picture the more beautiful it was . . . For three-quarters of the eighteenth century Nature did not seem tender or gentle; she was neither intimate or sympathetic, she was not romantic and she was not tragic; in short she was hardly ever considered except in her relation to man; she was uncouth, ignorant, unpolished and unreliable, and if she was to be allowed into gentlemen's houses she must first be taken in hand and civilised; and the man whose business it was to do that was the artist.'

Landscape painting for its own sake was not therefore much appreciated, but painters like Canaletto and Samuel Scott and, to a lesser extent, Richard Wilson, provided an excellent contemporary compromise. Italian and French masters like the Carracci, Guercino, Salvator Rosa and Guido Reni on the one hand, and Claude and the Poussins on the other, with their subtle blendings of the lore of antiquity, allegory, myth and legend with artificially contrived landscapes, exactly met the bill; and this explains their continued popularity in England, to which reference will be found over and over again.[1] In general, paintings by Italian masters were regarded as more desirable than any others. They afforded *cachet* to any collection. (See, for example, Thomas Martyn on the subject on page 101.) As far as drawings were concerned, the English collectors of the eighteenth century most admired Raphael and his school, and after him examples of Flemish and Italian Baroque. Again, of course, Poussin and Claude were associated with this predilection.

Flair among English painters was for portrait painting, and evidence that our ancestors supported them substantially can be seen in most ancestral houses preserved since the eighteenth century. A less obvious talent was for 'conversation pieces', often of family groups, which were done with simplicity and charm. They provide interesting evidence of the interiors of middle-class English houses during the eighteenth century[2] and show how startlingly simple the furnishing of the average gentleman's living-quarters appears to have been. The almost universal inclusion of pictures on the walls as a means of interior decoration[3] is a

[1] By the turn of the century the continuing affection for such artists came under fire. Thus Irvine writing to Buchanan about 1802 says: 'As to Sir Richard Worsley's observations, they give a just account of the present low state of taste in England, and his preference of a Magdalen by Guido to the Raphaels does not surprise me, as that country has always been taken by *sleight of hand*. Guido may astonish for a while, but does not go deep; but Raphael is like a philosopher, who will not mislead the judgement in order to gain general applause, but contents himself with addressing the hearts of the few who have feeling to relish him. Sir Richard is a voluptuary, and judges accordingly.' And again, 'I am sorry to hear that the Raphaels are so little understood, for I am pretty certain that there is no *oil picture* by him in England that can be compared with them, considering their merit, preservation, and subject. But where *such persons* rule the taste of the collectors, nothing can surprise me.' Buchanan, *Memoirs of Painting*, Vol. II.

[2] In his *Painting in Britain 1530–1790* Ellis Waterhouse explains that this *genre* was the antithesis of aristocratic portraiture. In fact, its obvious appeal lay in recording the likenesses of several members of one family at a reduced cost.

[3] Whitley, *Artists and their Friends in England 1700–1799*, quotes a Frenchman visiting London in 1765 on the subject of the private collections of Old Masters among the wealthier English as follows: 'A taste for pictures makes an article of

useful pointer to the size of the picture 'market',[1] though of course as a proportion of the population the overall number of such potential purchasers would be limited. Pottery and porcelain ornaments and small bronze figures on mantelpieces were also common.

Statuary, so beloved, in particular by the Society of the Dilettanti, was reserved for special galleries (sometimes referred to as 'skylight rooms'), capacious entrance halls, corridors, grand staircases and occasionally for libraries.[2] Curiosities, gems, coins, medals, the lesser pictures, antiquities and the like would be kept in smaller, more intimate rooms known as cabinets. Lavishness in the grand style stemmed often from the very strong Palladian influence.

Architectural features gradually became important in themselves both externally and internally. There would also be opportunities for endless frescoes and painted ceilings. Perhaps of recent years we have become overconcerned with the initially rather limited interest in this vogue. For one thing, not many Englishmen had the money to carry Palladianism through in style and when they did, and succeeded in producing really remarkable houses, they were–like the third Earl of Burlington–men of unusual talent and ability. Horace Walpole on his visits to Country Seats was scathing of merely lavish expenditure in houses of consequence. Writing about Moor Park in 1760, which had been refurbished by Sir Lawrence Dundas (see Plate 16) at enormous expense, he said 'Few places have had so much laid out on them and yet there is little real beauty in it'. But when he saw Chatsworth, truly styled in the grand manner, he wrote 'the West Front is extremely beautiful, the masonry and ornaments executed in the most delicate perfection'. The external ornaments he thought 'in good taste'. 'The Ascent to the Apartments is grand and in a singular style.'

Yet it would also be fair to say that in those family houses where succeeding generations had been collectors of discernment the furnishings would be elaborate and rich. Thus at Melbury (see page 93), Walpole reports 'It is a sumptuous old Seat in a fine Situation, the House ancient but modernised by Lady Ilchester's Grandfather . . . the apartments are most richly and abundantly furnished with pictures, tapestry, fine tables, and the finest old China and Japan collected by Mrs Horner, and many family pictures.'

But for most of us it is probably the simple elegance of the unpretentious town and country houses, terraces and crescents which come to mind when the eighteenth century is mentioned, and the point should be made that many a collector of more modest means lived in such houses.

If one can generalise at all–and with such an immense subject to consider there were *always* exceptions–then by the third quarter of the eighteenth century

their luxury; they sacrifice to this taste in proportion to their fortune.'

[1] See also under 'Sources of Supply', page 25.

[2] Though mention should be made here of Robert Adam's astonishing ability to integrate collectors' moveables into their environment, a process which William Kent had begun.

England, fortified in spirit by military victory, stable government and economic calm, had set about and succeeded in a process of civilisation and appreciation of the visual arts, and private collecting had been a major factor in this. Orthodoxy of fashion, as we have seen, tended to restrict the English vision. Thus painters of the gothic era, and of the early Renaissance, were generally described as 'hard' or 'dry'. They were thought uncouth and were largely ignored. Admittedly most of Europe shared these sentiments. But by the turn of the century discerning individuals were widening their field of interest. One of the most outstanding–because his collecting career embraced considerable parts of both the eighteenth and the nineteenth centuries, and because he spent money with great restraint and caution –was Samuel Rogers. He patronised contemporary artists as he recognised their very real ability and yet he was also fascinated by the Italian and Flemish[1] Primitives and took a deep interest in the remains of classical antiquity.

The catholicity of his taste was clearly illustrated by the diversity of his collection when it was sold by Christie's in 1856. It included Egyptian antiquities, antique gold objects, antique glass, antique *cinquecento* bronzes, antique terracottas and marbles, archaic Greek vases in immense quantities, and pictures: pictures of the contemporary English school (many were painted by his intimate friends), Dutch, Italian from the thirteenth to the eighteenth centuries, and French; objects of art and virtue; silver; modern sculpture and plaster casts; drawings of virtually every school, but predominantly Italian; miniatures; illuminated manuscripts and fragments from them; missals; engravings; early photographs; an immense library; Greek and Roman coins; and a limited amount of fine porcelain (for use!), and fine furniture (ditto).

Although seventeenth-century Dutch paintings had been described contemptuously by Horace Walpole as 'those drudging mimics of Nature's most uncomely coarseness', they had been collected to some extent before 1750 and became extremely popular afterwards.[2] They were available in enormous quantities at reasonable prices. They were therefore the more likely to be genuine, and there began to be a growing sympathy for their documentary appeal and cheerful earthiness. It is reasonably certain too that for collectors like Sir Robert Peel, who specialised in the Dutch school, they contained a highly acceptable alternative to the more artificially 'picturesque' element of the seventeenth-century Italian school.[3]

[1] In this respect he was highly exceptional, for regrettably Flemish Primitives were rarely popular with English collectors until towards the end of the nineteenth century, and even at that time some of the best examples were sold to the Continent for relatively low prices.

[2] For further details see page 239.

[3] By 1835 the spread of Dutch pictures in England was so wide that Dr Waagen remarked on it more than once. He also mentioned the popularity of Dutch seascapes, particularly by the van de Veldes. But as always there were painters who were outstandingly popular (Paulus Potter, the two Teniers, Adrian van der Werff, Dou) and the competition for their work created artificially high prices. Of course they were assiduously sought after on the Continent too, particularly in France and Germany.

I have already stressed the impetus given to the collecting of really outstanding works of art during the Napoleonic era. This engendered a new tendency to combine the urge for artistic acquisition with speculation and this, in turn, led to a considerably increased number of people who took to dealing in works of art as a regular trade.[1] Although discernment by collectors was not invariably to the fore, a high proportion of the new influx of pictures went to a hard core of experienced connoisseurs, probably less than fifty in number. The primary collections started or enlarged at this time contained the great corpus of European works of art which came to rest in this country, and though obviously depleted by the erosion of taxation, death duties and economic decline, some of them are still among the greatest collections in private hands.

It was at the turn of the century that another influential factor began to increase the popularity of collecting and this was the growing participation by the royal family. Among the Hanoverians it was probably George II's consort, Caroline of Brandenburg-Ansbach (who rediscovered in the drawer of an old table a set of Holbein drawings now at Windsor) who first evinced real enthusiasm for the possession of works of art. Her son, Frederick Prince of Wales, though usually much abused, actively encouraged individual artists, and Vertue gives him credit for taste, connoisseurship and enthusiasm. It was Frederick who urged that the Royal collections at Windsor and Hampton Court should be well catalogued, and we learn from Vertue (who, one must admit, was one of his protégés) that the Prince of Wales was capable of compiling *from memory* an almost complete catalogue of all the art objects in the royal family's possession.

To Frederick's son, George III, must go the credit for actively supporting the foundation of the Royal Academy in 1768 but it was *his* son, the Prince Regent, later George IV, who exercised the greatest influence on the arts during the first thirty years of the nineteenth century. Under him the court virtually directed and helped to formulate taste for the first time since Charles I. If evidence were wanted to prove this, one has only to look at the vast number of books on the arts published at that time that were dedicated to him. Even discounting the flowery language of such pieces, there was genuine admiration, gratitude and respect for what the Prince Regent had achieved. 'He was not only a collector of very great distinction but a patron such as had never perhaps been seen on the throne before.'[2] In most of his endeavours in the field of the arts–and particularly in connection with purchases for the royal collection–he was ably advised and assisted by Charles Long, later Lord Farnborough (1761–1838), which explains why the latter's name occurs so frequently in the collecting records of that era.

By and large the arrival of the young Queen Victoria on the throne coincided with

[1] 'Carraccis, Claudes, Poussins, arrived by ship-loads. One stands amazed at the number of pictures introduced by the enterprise of private dealers into England between 1795 and 1815, during the hottest time of the war . . .' etc., etc. Anna Jameson, *Companion to the Most Celebrated Private Galleries of Art*, London, 1844, page xxxi.

[2] Buchanan, *op. cit.*

the end of the classical collecting era which had started under Charles I, had continued after a long hiatus under the 'rule of taste' for the first six or seven decades in the eighteenth century, had been spurred on by the release of treasure on an unsurpassed scale in the time of Napoleon and concluded with a truly sensational flourish throughout the first three decades of the nineteenth century.

The social and industrial revolution that was beginning to affect every walk of life, the quest for reform, the breaking down of privilege, the striving after improved education and a more democratic society for all, naturally made their impact on collecting. For one thing it became more specialised, which made it easier to acquire the relevant knowledge and less expensive to indulge in as a pastime. Almost imperceptibly at first, it moved into two new and quite distinct areas though, of course, the well-established facets of collecting continued unabated. The new areas were the much increased patronage of living artists on the one hand and the pursuit of *objets d'art*, that is the work of craftsmen rather than of artists, on the other. Both are dealt with at some length in the body of this book.

Patronage increasingly became the province of the men newly wealthy, who had not the patience to acquire connoisseurship in the old sense, and who were sensitive about being made to look ridiculous by the purchase of meretricious or simply bogus works of art. Psychologically too the outlay of money for the direct production of works of art appealed to them. Painters responded by producing what was most readily acceptable, and those who could satisfy this patronage best flourished exceedingly. It is probably true to say that the prices paid towards the end of the nineteenth century for new paintings, often before they were even finished, have never been exceeded. It was the revolt against the academism of the establishment that brought the Pre-Raphaelites into being, though they too were not unsuccessful in arousing the collector's interest. However, their rise to eminence induced many collectors to turn back to the Old Masters and eighteenth-century English artists, both of which came strongly back into favour towards the turn of the century.

Thereafter English artists were bad at publicising themselves and their work, and nothing makes more astonishing reading today than Lord Duveen's endeavours – and very successful they were – to do it on their behalf.[1] Though still with some degree of hesitation, one might well wonder today whether his eulogies of painting in Britain in the post-1920 world (which did *not* for a long time attract collectors) had not more than a morsel of justification in them!

Today after surveying the experience of two centuries it may be said to be almost axiomatic that in every generation there emerge a few collectors of particular discernment and exceptional flair who diverge from what have become the accepted realms of collecting. One such, for example, was Dr Mead, who in the 1750s bought the works of contemporary painters such as Watteau and Canaletto.

[1] See *Thirty Years of British Art*, Sir Joseph Duveen, Bt, London, 1930.

Half a century later Samuel Rogers, Edward Solly, William Young Ottley and William Roscoe took particular delight–probably unknown to each other in the first place–in what most of their contemporaries disdained, namely the 'primitives' among Italian and Flemish painters; and in the middle of the nineteenth century the 4th Marquess of Hertford was almost alone for many years[1] in his appreciation of eighteenth-century French painters and in seeking out the finest pieces of furniture produced by French craftsmen a hundred years earlier.

As soon as the active pursuits of the enlightened few are reviewed and discussed in printed form–first in periodicals and after more consideration in book form–the many follow. A fashion becomes established. A market is created. Prices soar. As the speed of communication increases, a wider interest is aroused more quickly. But thorough understanding and methodical study, the prerequisites of expertise, are essential before new knowledge can be consolidated and committed to paper. In the field of the arts, research and scholarship seem to grow in direct proportion to rises in value.[2] Not surprisingly, as prices increase, and the commitment to each purchase of a single object involves the outlay by a collector of a higher proportion of his available funds, he wants to be assured that he *really* is buying what he thinks he is buying. He is less prepared to take a risk. He consults the literature or the dealer does it for him. But when there is no literature, judgement–and value–is much less certain. This was the position with regard to ceramics, tapestry, glass and furniture, in fact to most of the decorative arts of those highly productive (and distinguished) centuries–the seventeenth and the eighteenth–in the thirties of the nineteenth.

One of the collections with a new outlook, though it was not formed by an Englishman, or in England, is of particular interest in this context because its *subsequent* influence on English collectors was considerable. This was the collection formed between 1830 and 1840 by Jules Soulages, a French advocate, which eventually found its way to the Victoria and Albert Museum. The Soulages Catalogue of 1856 compiled by J. C. Robinson, then Curator of the Museum of Ornamental Art (as the Victoria and Albert Museum was known) contains the following note about the formation of the collection.[3] 'It was the result of repeated tours through Italy, made with the express purpose of acquiring specimens of Art: M. Soulages, in the outset of his pursuit, devised for himself a definite scheme or idea of a collection, and all his acquisitions were made strictly with reference to it. . . . His aim appears to have been to get together a complete series of decorative objects of utility, and of those minor productions of great artists, which are not usually thought to deserve the designation of "high art". . . . The idea of such a

[1] He was, of course, later followed by various members of the Rothschild family–though in their case the interest was more understandable–by John Bowes of Barnard Castle and by the 10th Duke of Hamilton.

[2] For a further discussion of this point see page 34 *et seq.*

[3] It was probably written by Henry Cole (see page 290), one of three signatories of the introduction. For full details of the collection, see page 290.

1 Paintings showing the interior of art galleries – more often imaginary than real – were a popular subject frequently commissioned from Flemish painters in the seventeenth century, when Antwerp was the centre of the art world. This one in the National Gallery, London, was formerly attributed to Hans Jordaens: the authorship is now regarded as uncertain. Frans Francken the Younger and David Teniers the Younger were also exponents of this genre.

2 Here in contrast is the picture gallery of the Antwerp merchant, Cornelis van der Geest, painted by Willem van Haecht in 1628 showing many actual pictures by Pieter Breughel, Rubens, Snyders, Elsheimer and others that have been identified. Portrayed in the foreground are the Spanish Regents visiting the gallery accompanied by their courtiers and a number of artists whose work is represented, including Rubens, Snyders and van Dyck. This picture, which had been in New York for many years, was sold by Sotheby's in 1969 for £24,000.

3 One of the earliest European forms of collecting was to set up 'cabinets of curiosities', containing jewellery, outstanding examples of craftsmanship, unusual natural objects and, later, paintings. English visitors to the Continent must have seen these in princely and aristocratic houses, particularly in Germany. This painting by Joseph Heintz II of such a cabinet dates from about 1650.

4, 5 After the turbulence of the sixteenth century, painting in Holland flourished to a remarkable extent during the early part of the seventeenth century. In the absence of a clearly defined patrician class, patronage of painters was almost universal. English travellers were amazed to see good pictures in the simplest houses. Later on art collecting became a form of investment, and in the eighteenth century the simplicity and realism of the Dutch School became popular all over Europe as well. After 1750 English collectors took a particular interest in Dutch interiors, landscapes and marine painting.

These two pictures by Adriaan de Lelie (1755–1820) show the Gallery of Jan Gildemeester (above) and that of a collector named Brentano (below).

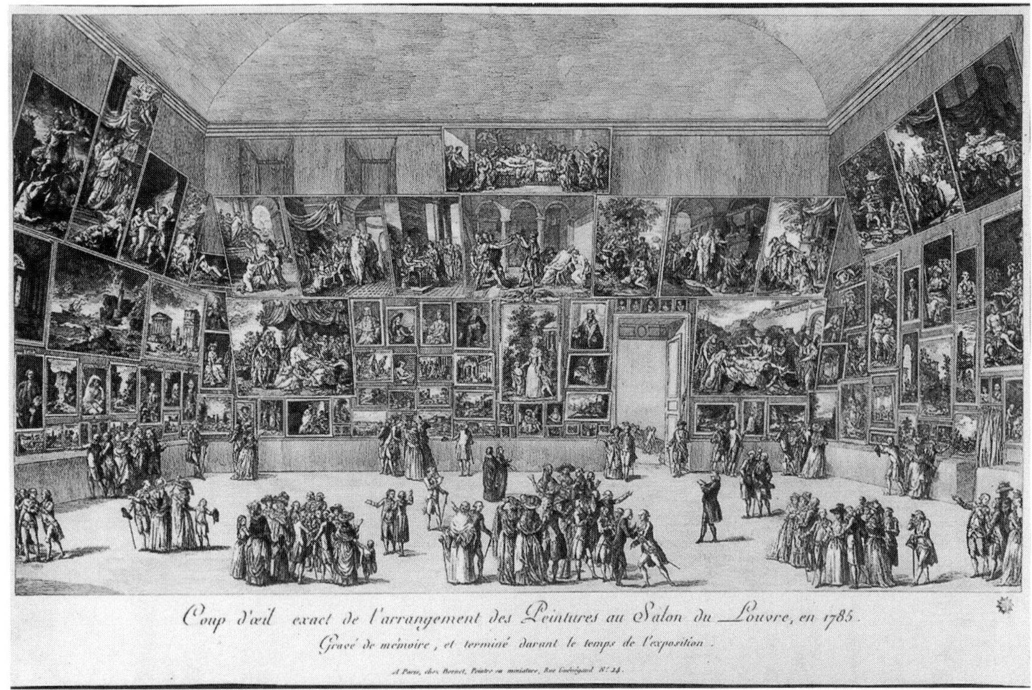

6, Although there had been continuous demand from as early as 1747 that the art treasures of the French royal
7 family in the Louvre should be permanently on view to the public, the palace was not officially opened as a museum until 1793. The exhibitions of 1785 and 1787 shown here contained the work of French Academicians held in the Salon of the Louvre. Many such exhibitions were visited by English travellers. These engravings are the work of Pietro Antonio Martini (1738–1797) who made similar engravings of two Royal Academy exhibitions held in Somerset House in 1787 and 1788.

8, 9 These portraits of Thomas Howard, Earl of Arundel and Surrey, and of his wife Anathea Talbot, are by Daniel Mytens (c. 1590–1647) who came to England from the Netherlands after 1612 and succeeded van Somer as Court Painter in 1621. Arundel was almost the first and certainly one of the greatest of all English collectors. He and his wife spent some time in Italy while they were young, and it is largely due to their inspiration and enthusiasm that we owe the strong bent towards Italian art, both of the Court of Charles I and among later English collectors. A very similar pair of portraits (attributed, as these once were, to van Somer) was sold at the Northwick Sale in 1859 for 200 guineas.

11 Charles Compton, 7th Earl of Northampton (1737–63), painted in Rome by Pompeo Girolamo Batoni in 1758. Batoni (1708–87), who was originally trained to be a goldsmith, was much patronised as a portrait painter by foreign visitors to Rome, and usually took pains to pose his clients of differing nationalities against suitable backgrounds. His portraits of aristocratic Englishmen often included a dog.

10 Robert, 2nd Earl of Sunderland (1641–170[illegible] painted in Rome in classical costume by [illegible] Peter Lely. He was one of the earliest memb[illegible] of the Spencer family to start the great coll[illegible] tion that can still be seen at Althorp in W[illegible] wickshire. As ambassador to Paris and Mad[illegible] he bought a considerable number of Italian [illegible] Dutch pictures.

12 In 1772 Joseph Banks asked the painter Johann Zoffany to accompany him and Captain Cook on a journey to the Pacific in order to paint the flora and fauna. But Zoffany withdrew at the last moment. Instead he was commissioned by George III and Queen Charlotte to paint the Grand Duke of Tuscany's celebrated collection in Florence. The task eventually took him six years and resulted in the painting called *Tribuna of the Uffizi*. Zoffany endlessly re-positioned the objects on it to suit his composition, and included many English connoisseurs and travellers who happened to be in Florence. Though the painting was a sort of apotheosis of the Grand Tour it did not eventually please Zoffany's royal patrons, who would have preferred it without the multiplicity of portraits, which are of particular interest to us today. The beautiful picture in the foreground is Titian's *Venus*. Standing to the right of it (holding a dress sword) is Sir Horace Mann, British representative in Florence for many years, friend and correspondent of Horace Walpole and inveterate collector in his own right and on behalf of his friends and acquaintances. The painting on the extreme left is Raphael's *Madonna della Sedia*. The group below it to the right includes the Earl Cowper on the extreme left, who eventually bought the Raphael 'Niccolini-Cowper' *Madonna* being admired. For many years it remained at Panshanger. It is now in the Washington National Gallery.

13 Zoffany's painting of Sir Charles Towneley surrounded by his favourite antiquities in the Sculpture Gallery of his house at 7 Park Street, Westminster (now Queen Anne's Gate) was first shown at the Royal Academy in 1790. Again Zoffany had taken artistic licence by uniting in one room the most important marbles selected from all over the house. Towneley was descended on his mother's side from the Earl of Arundel. He lived in Rome from 1765 to 1772, was an intimate friend of Sir William Hamilton and was closely associated with Gavin Hamilton and Jenkins in their highly successful archaeological excavations, from which many of his best pieces stem. After his death the British Museum acquired his collection for £20,000.

collection, even at this comparatively recent period, was a novelty – an abundance of materials was available, and consequently there is no doubt but that, in proportion to the means and endeavours employed, it was far more effectively carried out than would be practicable at the present time, even with greatly increased expenditure of funds, time and personal exertion. . . . An infinity of interesting objects was therefore to be obtained, all over the Continent, and more especially in Italy, at prices very much below their present value.' Cole then goes on to make this vital point: 'Collectors are rapidly acquiring increased knowledge and judgement, and the establishment of public Museums and other causes, are rendering the taste for collecting almost universal amongst educated persons', and certainly, during the second half of the nineteenth century, a steadily increasing stream of books to guide the interested amateur through most fields of collecting began to be published.

At about the same time, but unfortunately without relevant documentation until much later, Ralph Bernal (see page 293) and Felix Slade (see note on page 288) were forming outstanding collections of *objets d'art* in England.[1]

Lady Charlotte Schreiber's enormous industry in the collecting of pottery and porcelain, and her efforts to seek out more information about the manufacture of different English wares, was still highly unusual in the third quarter of the nineteenth century. Her nephew Montague Guest's fascinating account of what was *not* being collected in the 1860s is again highly illuminating (see page 331).

By the beginning of the twentieth century collecting was so well established as a pastime of the educated English that Antiquity Shops[2] – as they were called – had become much more common (they had replaced the Victorian curio and bric-à-brac shops[3]). 1901 saw the first issue of *The Connoisseur* followed shortly by the *Burlington Magazine* (*Apollo* first appeared in 1925). These specialist journals catered for collectors at varying levels of expertise. They supplemented *The Art Journal* (1849–1912) which had itself taken over from *Art-Union* (1839–1848). *The Art Journal* had faithfully reported upon every aspect of the arts during its long period of publication and, incidentally, it had fought hard to protect the Victorian collector from a multitude of frauds that were continually being devised and perpetrated on a large scale. The frank nature of these disclosures makes fascinating reading today.

Many general weeklies also had a regular feature for collectors. Occasionally these were gathered together in book form. *The Queen* magazine issued two such volumes, called *The Collector*, in 1905; these were followed by a third volume in

[1] During the earlier part of the nineteenth century, the acquisition of such collections as those of Soulages and Bernal was considered particularly useful, as the objects contained in them could serve as models for those concerned with industrial design. This goes some way towards explaining why in Victorian times extraneous and frequently unexpected ornament was added to the design of purely functional objects.

[2] See *Quinneys'* by H. A. Vachell. The book came out in 1914. By 1950 it was in its 23rd impression.

[3] See Major H. Byng Hall's *The Bric-à-Brac Hunter*, London, 1875.

1907. They were 'intended primarily for an interchange of ideas amongst those with small collections'. Collecting, stated the preface, 'in whatever form, should be undertaken because it pleases, because it cultivates and enlarges the mind; not because it is a fashion.' The subjects covered (which in general might be classified – and often were – as bygones) are a useful guide to their popularity at the time[1] and are given in some detail for this reason.

There were general sections on porcelain, pottery, lustre, enamels (in detail these included articles on Chelsea, Worcester, Spode, Lowestoft, Dresden, Sèvres, St Cloud, Rouen, Wedgwood, Leeds, Staffordshire, Caughley, Rockingham, Dutch Delft, silver lustre, copper lustre, purple lustre, Bilston and Battersea enamels, and European peasant pottery); engravings; old needlework; Egyptian and Grecian antiquities; books, autographs, play bills; old silver, pewter, pinchbeck and brass; coins and medals; miniatures. And included under the heading 'miscellaneous' were clocks, watches, glass, netsukes, patch and snuff boxes, ormolu, memorial jewellery, ancient gloves, Turkish curiosities and posy or poesy rings.

In the second volume the main pattern was repeated but the section on ceramics was much longer and included articles on Worcester, Chelsea, Coalport (past and present), dated wares, Derby, the decorator William Billingsley, Lowestoft, kiln finds, Bow, Rockingham, heraldic china, Italian majolica, Imari porcelain, Capo di Monte, Lille faience, the Portland Vase, antique figures, puzzle jugs, bellarmines, English stoneware bottles, the Willow Pattern, pot lids, Delft tiles, Limoges enamels, and general hints for collectors. There was a useful article on lace. Under 'miscellaneous' there were articles on tea caddies, silhouettes, fans, old English scratchbacks, puzzle portraits, playing-cards, printed ephemera, old violins and antique jewellery.

The third volume of 1907 only had four main sections: pottery and porcelain, prints and coloured books, glass and a miscellaneous one. Under ceramics there were covered Crich ware, slipware, salt glaze, Astbury, Whieldon, ceramic decoration in Staffordshire including transfer printing, the Woods, John Turner, Adams ware including jasper, Humphrey Palmer, John Voyez, Staffordshire figures, eighteenth-century fine stoneware, eighteenth-century battles on pottery, marked pieces by minor potters, pottery jugs, early English teapots, Toby jugs, silver lustre, resist silver lustre, the Liverpool pottery and John Sadler, Leeds, Plymouth and Bristol porcelain, Swansea Etruscan ware, Swansea faience, Nantgarw porcelain, medallions by the Tassiers, Pharmacy jars, Dutch Delft drug jars, Jesuit china, Palissy, Continental porcelain factories and Zürich porcelain. The miscellaneous section included articles on English pictorial embroidery, Dutch needlework pictures, Valenciennes and Mecklin lace, Alençon lace, pinchbeck,

[1] One still occasionally finds very fully illustrated volumes dating from the turn of the century on relatively humble items which were collected with great fervour then, but which have virtually disappeared today. Lead tobacco jars and leather buckets are instances that come to mind.

silhouettes, ancient ivories, knife boxes and vases, impressed horn boxes, apostle spoons (sixteenth–eighteenth century), English silver tankards and engraved gems. A curious omission is the lack of any mention of furniture, but a great deal was being written about it elsewhere at that time.

As the popularity of collecting increased the literature grew and grew, but one must admit that much of it was at a pretty degenerate level. Apart from the 'Chats-on' type of volume and ghastly anecdotal reminiscences (the stories had some resemblance to the angling memoirs of the same period), quite competent authorities deliberately wrote down to the catchpenny market. One of the maddest volumes of that era was C. J. Holmes'[1] *Pictures and Picture Collecting* (1903), the first volume in Trehearne's 'Collectors' Library'. Although the prefatory note explains that the book is aimed particularly at those of moderate means its first chapter is on collecting for the millionaire; the second is for the merely rich! Advice in the first chapter suggests starting off with a Leonardo, a Titian to give the collection distinction, and examples by Mantegna, Botticelli, Filippo Lippi and Bellini, because they 'are things of such obvious beauty as to be always among the most desirable of possessions.'

The first world war brought about an immense decline in collecting activities, both major and minor. Yet the years between the wars saw an enormous growth in knowledge on almost every subject. This meant that those few who were fortunate enough to have not only flair and connoisseurship but also funds available could and did acquire things of superb quality at prices that seem the more painful today for having been paid so comparatively recently. Sad from the private collector's point of view too was the passing of an increasing proportion of every sort of collector's *desirabilia* into the museums. This subject is dealt with at some length on page 406. However, the overall lack of funds did lead to the increased collecting of objects which could give enormous pleasure for relatively little outlay, such as drawings[2] and ceramics (both European and oriental).

From 1948–50 onwards collecting burgeoned, and we were soon in an era where the investment aspect became of increasing importance, because prices had soared, but so, obviously, had available funds[3]–or was it the other way round?

One cannot really tell what the future holds, although we have learned from the past that what one age discards, another discovers, and that the interval between

[1] Later editor of the *Burlington Magazine*; Director, first of the National Portrait Gallery, and subsequently of the National Gallery. His autobiography, *Self and Partners*, London, 1936, is of considerable interest.

[2] In the preface to his book *Old Master Drawings: A Handbook for Amateurs and Collectors*, London, 1922, for example, H. S. Reitlinger expresses astonishment at the enormously increased interest in the collecting of drawings that had occurred in the previous few years.

[3] Once upon a time–it seems almost laughable to mention it–prices remained stable for decades at a time and longer–and often even *plunged!* Reflections of these factors is evidenced by such phenomena as the *Times*-Sotheby indexes of changing values of different objects and books on art as investment, but it should be stated that these have not by any means met with universal approval.

these two stages is usually more than a single generation. The astonishing increase of interest in industrial archaeology is a recent example of this. What can be had for the asking today will probably achieve a 'market' tomorrow. The crazes of one age become of interest to the collector when examples have largely disappeared some years later.[1]

However, good design and craftsmanship have certainly not disappeared. It is delightful that in a machine age increasingly concerned with automated production, the design and graphic content of many consumer goods is improving. For all we know collectors of the twenty-first century may be looking for those gay tea-towels and highly decorated carrier bags of the 1960s!

3. THE ACQUISITIVE IMPULSE

What I have always hoped to find, in reading through the literature on collecting, is the dispassionate description of the moment in time when a collector found something he wanted to own; his detailed inspection of the piece; the moment he realised that he could afford to buy it; his hesitation whether to plunge or not; his doubts as to whether his wife would ridicule the purchase–or welcome it; the actual instant when his hesitation hardened into a positive decision; and, finally, the moment when he pulled out his cheque book and pen.[2] It is this concatenation of events that makes a man a collector; they, as much as the subsequent delight of ownership, are what gives collecting an edge.

The process involves knowledge in the recognition of the piece; connoisseurship in the appraisal of its origin, its date, its authenticity, its value. Implicit in all this are taste, which sparked off the collecting of the object in question in the first place; and flair, if only in knowing where to look for it at a given moment and in picking it out from a multitude of other alternatives.

There is a curious antithesis of objectivity between the professional art historian or museum curator on the one hand and the private collector on the other in the purchase of what may be virtually the same pieces. The professional regards taste as a vague, ambivalent characteristic; he tends nowadays to profess scientific detachment, he must shun prejudice. 'He must', as Herbert Read says, 'arrange and categorise with Linnaean assiduity' to fill his gaps, to be representative, ultimately to educate. The collector's considerations are far more personal.

[1] Built-in obsolescence and shortage of storage space are new factors here, for they have largely destroyed the careful habit of our ancestors in storing away things for another generation, and they will almost certainly affect what one might call the random survival rate of the antiques of the future.

[2] In fact, Lord Eccles' book, *On Collecting*, London, 1968, covers this ground admirably. Even more enlightening on the process of becoming a collector is an article by Ella Winter called 'I bought a Klee' in *Studio International*, Vol. 172, July 1966.

Does the object appeal to him; does he think it beautiful; is it sufficiently different from what he already owns; will it 'go' with the rest of his belongings?

In the realm of pictorial art, collectors often seem to have a better eye for paintings than professional art historians, because they see in the round, they can register an immediate sense of enjoyment, an 'I-must-have-it' feeling. To the extent that many outstanding art dealers have been collectors at heart, they too can share this immediacy of response.[1] Connoisseurship, involving the critical examination of the object in question, can only follow the first joyful reaction. It is these rare moments of personal selection from among a mass of seemingly similar objects in an auction room, a gallery, or a shop which precede acquisition, that are the real highlights of a collector's career and – sadly – accounts of them hardly ever find their way into books or catalogues.

At this stage we might well consider when an accretion becomes a collection. We have already excluded the mere accumulation of family possessions of a decorative kind, by confining the subject matter of this book to purposive collecting. Not, it should be added hastily, from any sense of disdain, for above all it is the embellishments and utilitarian objects, which conform to our taste and with which we surround ourselves, that transform a house into a home.

The footnotes in the articles of the professional art historians are studded with references to this or that 'collection', indeed the term is now almost synonymous with ownership. More realistically a collection is styled as such when the owner has acquired sufficient objects of a kind *and* enough connoisseurship to impress the professionals active in the same field. In the past it was simply when documentation of a collection was extant. Many collectors, of course, produced their own printed catalogues, which were given away to friends and acquaintances, or sold direct to touring visitors, or through local bookshops. Occasionally the appellation came into use on the strength of a hand-written inventory that had been preserved, often accidentally; but most commonly of all it was after an owner had died and an auction catalogue had shown for the first time that there was a mass of objects of a similar kind in sufficient quantity to attract to the sale other collectors of the same thing. Thus many a man has only achieved posthumously the documented status of collector.

One of the most delightful sources of information of collections in the eighteenth, nineteenth and even the early part of the twentieth centuries was the sale catalogue preceded by an informative introduction about how the collection came to be formed. This even contained the occasional, purely human detail about the collector. One cannot help lamenting that Sotheby's and Christie's have virtually given up this admirable custom. One can entirely appreciate the difficulties of the authorship of such pieces[2] in providing the correct amalgam of authoritative

[1] Except, of course, that they classify things into highly saleable, saleable, and unsaleable!

[2] An interesting instance when authorship of the catalogue was allowed to go to an unfortunate extreme was the Doetsch sale held at Christie's in 1895. The owner, a merchant of German descent

information and human interest; but while the scholarship of contemporary cataloguing is usually of a high standard, it leans heavily on this very source material from the past, which it fails to supply for future generations.[1] One might also plead here for the more frequent inclusion in sales catalogues of photographs of well known collections *in their own setting* before they are split up. Detailed visual evidence of this kind is a fascinating record in the history of taste.

Collecting is a form of self indulgence, but by and large it is a beneficial one. Probably the simplest differentiation between the dabbler and the genuine collector is that the latter has stilled once and for all any inhibition against spending money on the inanimate objects of his choice. Once this resolute state of mind has been reached and some money is available, progress is assured. The preservation of many of the world's greatest works of art in the face of deliberate destruction, contempt or neglect has been due to the collector's acquisitive urge, the quest for beauty, the indulgence of taste and the desire for association and continuity with the past. Works of art are permanent (or nearly so!): collectors come and go. Horace Walpole commented sagely: 'How insecure is the permanency of heirlooms'; and so one must be grateful that the desire for collecting goes on and that one generation of collectors succeeds another. One could see this particularly clearly in the nineteenth century, when a single painting might pass through Christie's hands three, four or even five times in less than a century–and those were times when collections were *not* formed or dispersed as lightly as today for mere profit.

No chronicler of the English as collectors could dare to ignore the sporting appeal of the subject. 'Collecting', said Denys Sutton, 'is a pursuit which suits our taste, combining a love of the arts with an element of chance and sport.'[2] Sir Robert Witt had stated 'It is the chase, not the quarry, that counts; the pursuit of the unattainable, the discovery of the unexpected, with all its vicissitudes of success and failure.' Sir Martin Conway obviously shared this view, which seems to have come to the fore at the beginning of the present century, because he called the story of his (very considerable) collecting career *The Sport of Collecting* (1914). And Robert Benson, who formed a great collection of his own about

and some substance, had collected in an unusually methodical way nearly 500 pictures of different schools, which included some of considerable merit. The trustees decided to ask J. P. Richter to undertake the cataloguing for the sale and to give him a free hand over what he considered to be more authoritative re-attributions. Damaging rumours about this circulated before the sale. In consequence the auctioneers dissociated themselves from ultimate responsibility and the pictures fetched some £11,000 instead of over £100,000 as expected.

[1] For a particularly interesting catalogue that *does* supply such information see Christie's catalogue of the Lansdowne Marbles sold on 5 March 1930. Perhaps the habit is coming back to us from across the Atlantic. The catalogue of the Roudinesco collection of paintings of the School of Paris sold by Parke-Bernet in New York, 10 October 1968, contains a highly informative preface by Dr Roudinesco himself on how he came to buy the paintings concerned.

[2] In his introduction to the catalogue of *Some British Drawings From the Collection of Sir Robert Witt*, an exhibition staged by the Arts Council in 1948.

1900,[1] wrote in the introduction to the Holford Collection Catalogue[2] 'pictures are the big game of collecting', which emphasises in an illuminating way the varying degrees of social prestige of different types of collecting. Indeed no one could deny that there are good aesthetic reasons for this. Clearly certain arts express a wider range and a greater depth of feeling, while others involve a higher degree of skill.

A collector must be an enthusiast; he can and should take risks. Learning the hard way that one's judgement has been at fault widens one's knowledge by much more than the mere recognition that a piece is not what one thought it to be. Sir Alan Barlow[3] said that if a collector 'boasts that he has never acquired an object, the authenticity of which was subsequently disproved, we should surely admire his judgement or his caution less than we deplore his poorness of spirit'. For taking a risk can work conversely too: many collectors have bought for very little an anonymous painting because its quality appealed to them and have subsequently established its authorship, which has enormously enhanced its value. The late Captain George Spencer-Churchill labelled a whole section of his collection 'The Northwick Rescues' because he had acquired them in this way (see page 323).

4. SOURCES OF SUPPLY

Early instances of picture buying and selling appear to be closely linked with the Englishman's love of travel. Until near the end of the eighteenth century those who made their living by dealing in works of art had usually started life as painters or professional antiquaries. We have a surprising amount of information about dealing in the time of Charles I, Arundel and Buckingham because the correspondence between them and the agents whom they personally employed to discover works of art in Europe and Asia Minor has survived and has been studied in some detail. Arundel had connections with most of the King's ministers and ambassadors overseas, and used them, as well as a host of other agents, particularly painters, to advise him of any interesting collections or single objects that came onto the market. One of his greatest coups was the purchase of the entire 'cabinet' of drawings in Venice which belonged to Daniel Nys, into which other collections had already been incorporated.[4] When Sir Thomas Roe sought out antiquarian treasures from Turkey for the Duke of Buckingham, Arundel retaliated by sending the Rev. William Petty to do the same for him. Charles, during his youthful

[1] See the *Catalogue of Italian Pictures at 16 South Street, Park Lane, London and Buckhurst in Sussex, collected by Robert and Evelyn Benson*, London, 1914.

[2] *The Holford Collection at Dorchester House*, two vols., Oxford, 1927, edited (anonymously) by Robert Benson; research by Tancred Borenius.

[3] In a paper first read to the Oriental Ceramic Society in April 1937 and reprinted in 1961, called 'The Collector and the Expert'.

[4] For full details see 'Thomas Howard, Earl of Arundel as a Collector of Drawings' in the *Burlington Magazine*, Vol. 139, (January to March 1947), by Denys Sutton.

travels to Spain, obtained superb treasures merely for the asking! In 1623 he asked for and was given by the Spanish King Titian's *Pardo Venus* (now in the Louvre) and Titian's *Woman in a Fur* (now in the Vienna Gallery) and yet again Titian's portrait of Charles V (now back in Spain in the Prado). He was on friendly terms with Rubens and van Dyck, and not only commissioned and bought paintings direct from them, but also engaged them to find other works of art for him. This was not difficult, as both men were shrewd and experienced collectors in their own right. However, Charles obtained his greatest treasures direct from Venice. From there he brought back to England the outstanding della Nave collection which included paintings by Antonello, Giorgione, Titian, Veronese, Palma Vecchio and Lorenzo Lotto. It would be delightful but idle to speculate how interest in the arts might have progressed in England after the wonderful start that had been made in the seventeenth century, if what Buchanan had termed 'the dark ages' had not intervened. There was the example of Arundel's passion for Holbein, for classical sculpture, for masterpieces of the High Renaissance as well as from the Quattrocento, and for drawings from Germany as well as Italy; and George Villiers' love for Titian (he is said to have owned nineteen paintings by him) and for his own contemporary, Rubens, whose collection of sculpture he had purchased when the painter was temporarily in financial difficulties. Most important, however, was the superb display of art with which the king, Charles I, had surrounded himself. Yet the dazzling and unaccustomed burst of culture at court[1] was probably one of the principal factors which brought about the demand for a return to puritanism.

By the end of the seventeenth century the undisputed centre of the art world was Antwerp,[2] but during the early eighteenth century Paris, Venice and Hamburg[3] became of increasing importance. By the middle of the eighteenth century an astonishing number of English and Scottish painters and antiquaries had settled in Rome. Their principal purpose may have been to study the arts there but, in fact, they spent most of their time as guides and mentors to young English and Scottish visitors. 'A regular Course with an Antiquarian generally takes up about six weeks; employing three hours a day, you may, in that time visit all the churches, palaces, villas and ruins worth seeing', wrote Dr John Moore, tutor to the 8th Duke of Hamilton.[4] The antiquary introduced his client to the gay, social scene of

[1] By 1642 the much-quoted complaint was being made that the King was being deceived by 'gifts of paintings, antique idols and such like trumperies brought from Rome'. (See G. H. J. Albion, *Charles I and the Court of Rome*, Louvain, 1935.)

[2] See in particular J. Denucé's *Kunstausfuhr Antwerpens im 17. Jahrhunderts: die Firma Forchoudt*, Antwerp, 1931.

[3] The concourse of Englishmen travelling through Hamburg was such that a Dresden dealer sent paintings there in 1770 for the sole purpose of displaying them so that 'rich Englishmen passing through might acquire them', and in 1786 'an English collection of pictures which had been intended for Russia was auctioned in Hamburg'. (See Niels von Holst, *Creators, Collectors and Connoisseurs*.)

[4] Quoted from the invaluable *Scots in Italy in the Eighteenth Century*, by Basil Skinner, Edinburgh, 1966.

Rome and procured introductions to all the best collections in the great palaces. He acted as banker, as artistic and financial adviser and he was often responsible for organising 'the safe dispatch home of whole consignments of paintings bought on an extensive tour of Italy'. Though as Skinner says, each young traveller 'took home with him from Italy much more than his cargo of paintings, sculptures and antique marbles, the tangible souvenirs of his excursion to the south. He took home as well a sophistication of taste and an appreciation of the virtues of classicism which only contact with the Mediterranean inheritance could impart'. Furthermore, these antiquaries introduced the young gentry to other English painters in Rome so that works could be commissioned, and they probably also arranged for portraits of their clients by such native painters as Carlo Maratti and Pompeo Batoni, who both posed so many travelling English milords against quasi-classical settings (see Plates 9 and 10).

Most celebrated among these resident mentors was Gavin Hamilton (1723–1798), a painter and distinguished archaeologist in his own right, who had excavated Hadrian's Villa in Tivoli and had acquired from the Palazzo Barberini the piece that was to become famous later as 'the Portland Vase'. In fact, his patrons were often to become the purchasers of the antiquities he had excavated. Most of these young men became the leaders of the taste of their time: they included the Duke of Dorset, Lord Egremont, Viscount Palmerston, Lord Shelburne, Lord Spencer, Lord Hope and Sir James Grant.

Among Hamilton's fellow archaeologists were James Byres (1734–1817) and Thomas Jenkins (died 1798); and other antiquaries who turned for profitability to dealing in classical finds were Colin Morison (1732–1810, who became particularly friendly with J. J. Winckelmann, the great German theorist of neo-classicism) and James Clarke (died 1799) who practised as a leading *cicerone* in Naples.

To the artists from England and Scotland visiting Rome for any length of time 'the lucrative speculation in older pictures was probably more profitable than selling their own works', and such men as James Irving, James Campbell, George Augustus Wallis and Jacob More spent many years combing Italy for paintings, sometimes for collector clients and sometimes for dealers.[1] Others again came to Italy on special journeys commissioned to find particular works of art, though just as frequently such journeys were undertaken on the artists' own initiative without specific commissions. Andrew Hay is said to have made at least six journeys to Italy and at least as many to France, and was instrumental in forming the collections both of Sir Robert Walpole and the Duke of Devonshire, while both John Thomas Seton and William Mosman bought collections of drawings which they carried back with them and sold in Scotland.

In addition, three other sorts of British resident in Italy – diplomats, bankers and political exiles – turned their hands to dealing in works of art. The last group, of course, were accounted for by the Jacobite court in exile, who were under papal

[1] See 'Irving reports to Buchanan', page 167.

protection.[1] Most prominent among the banker-collectors was a Mr Sloane, with whom Buchanan treated unsuccessfully. He was known to ask unusually steep prices for the paintings in his possession and in 1802 Irving, on Buchanan's behalf, failed yet again to make a deal with Sloane's son after the old man's death.

Most celebrated among the dealing diplomats in Italy–'the acquisitive English Consuls'[2] as they became known–was, of course, Joseph Smith (1675–1770), the friend and patron of Canaletto. Smith, in fact, only became English Consul in Venice in 1744 after long residence there. He was originally a merchant in meat and fish; then he became deeply involved in publishing books of an antiquarian nature with the firm of G. B. Pasquali. This led to his increased interest in the arts and he began to buy books, gems and pictures for himself and his clients. In 1763 he resigned his consulship and sold the bulk of his library and most of his pictures, including 53 by Canaletto, to George III.[3]

Smith was well known and in close contact with most of the leading painters of his day and was frequently visited by English connoisseurs who had come to Venice. Horace Walpole, Richard Wilson, Sir Joshua Reynolds and Robert Adams were all made welcome by him; but though respected he was not, apparently, much liked.

The artists whom Smith patronised before 1744 were Tiepolo, Sebastiano Ricci, Marco Ricci, Rosalba Carriera and Carlo Cignani. Canaletto probably started working for him about 1728. Although Smith directed Canaletto's output almost entirely into English hands, the exact nature of the relationship between artist and patron remains uncertain, though Smith clearly enjoyed the combination of vicarious patronage in Venice on the one hand with the apparent granting of favours to the aristocracy in England on the other. His brother, John Smith, seems to have acted as link-man with prospective clients in London. Certainly Canaletto also obtained many commissions direct: we know, for example, of the execution of twenty views for the Duke of Bedford; another series of twenty for Sir Robert Harvey and of seventeen for the Earl of Carlisle. The relationship was interrupted for some years by some unknown cause and during this time Smith occupied himself with the purchase of Old Master paintings and drawings, particularly of the Dutch School, for his own collection and for those of others. But he and Canaletto again collaborated successfully later.[4]

[1] See in particular Lesley Lewis' *Connoisseurs and Secret Agents in Eighteenth Century Rome*, London, 1961.

[2] For an interesting example of the manner in which such posts changed hands, see Thomas Moore Slade's account (on page 132) of how he came to acquire the Vitturi Collection.

[3] They were finally bought through the agency of Richard Dalton, the King's librarian, whose knowledge of paintings was considerable. But most of the negotiations with Smith had been carried out by James Stuart Mackenzie, who held a diplomatic post at Turin. His brother, the Earl of Bute, was a close friend and financial adviser of George III.

[4] Much of this information comes from Francis Haskell's fascinating *Patrons and Painters, a Study in the Relations between Italian Art and Society in the Age of the Baroque*, London, 1963. But the literature on Consul Smith and Canaletto is extensive. See in particular Sir Karl Parker's *Canaletto's Drawings at Windsor Castle*, Oxford

Smith's career in Italy was probably one of the longest in time of Englishmen abroad. But while most careers were briefer they were also rewarding, in terms of works of art collected, not only on the diplomats' own behalf, but for their friends and acquaintances. There was, for example, Horace Mann, Horace Walpole's friend and correspondent and British Envoy to Florence; Sir William Hamilton at Naples, celebrated collector of Greek vases and antiquities, and, of course, Emma's husband; the brothers Udney: Robert had been Consul at Leghorn; Sir John Dick, who had been Consul at Leghorn from 1754 to 1766; and Robert Fagan, who had been British Consul-General in Sicily and particularly active as a dealer (see page 162). The diplomats in their turn needed local agents to find works of art for them and there were many Italian dealers in most major cities who specialised in supplying pictures to foreigners. Probably the best known was Giuseppe Maria Sasso, who formed a close relationship with yet another highly acquisitive diplomat, John Strange, the British Resident in Venice after Smith. When Strange returned to England, he introduced Sasso to his successor, Sir Richard Worsley, who was yet another inveterate connoisseur.

The extent to which highly prized works of art, paintings, busts, marble statues and urns had been moved from Italy to English town and country houses during the eighteenth century had not remained unnoticed by continental connoisseurs, who looked upon the exodus with a mixture of admiration and resentment. The position was summarised neatly by Winckelmann, who is reported to have commented: 'Before we know where we are, the British will take the whole of Trajan's Column to London!'

We have scant records of London picture dealers in the first half of the eighteenth century. They appear to have travelled extensively on the Continent, assembled a sizeable collection there and then returned to London to dispose of it at leisure from their own homes or through the auction rooms. Through sales records we know of men such as Peter Anthony Mottaux, Samuel Paris and Robert Bragge, all of whom worked in this way.[1] After 1770 there was an increase in the number of picture dealers resident in London, whose business it was to find clients for the growing number of foreign canvases which were being sent to England from the Continent by agents there. Whitley[2] mentions a London dealer 'named Goodall, of Marsham Street, Westminster, who was exhibiting more than a thousand pictures lately consigned from abroad, including many attributed by him to eminent masters. All these, together with bronzes, carvings, miniatures, drawings

and London, 1948; Michael Levey's *The Later Italian Pictures in the Collection of Her Majesty the Queen*, London, 1964, and Sir Anthony Blunt's *Venetian Drawings at Windsor Castle*, London, 1957.

[1] See the invaluable 'Dutch Paintings in England before 1760' by Frank Simpson in the *Burlington Magazine*, Vol. XCV, February 1953.

[2] *Artists and Their Friends in England, 1700–1799*, London, 1928, Vol. I, page 261.

and objects of art generally, were displayed at his house in some twenty rooms, and half-a-crown was charged for admission.' Whitley goes on to mention an exchange of letters between an American artist, resident in London, called John Greenwood, and Copley, the American painter in Boston. Greenwood had 'turned to picture dealing[1] and finally became an auctioneer, a profession in which he gained well-deserved success and a reputation for probity'. In one letter, Greenwood wrote: 'Since I've left the Indies I've been visiting most of the Courts of Europe and admiring the thousands of fine paintings that one finds distributed among them, though at present England bids fair to become the seat of the Arts and Artists. Almost everything that is not immoveable is brought here from every country, as none pays so generously for real good pictures as the English; though I must confess I think it begins to fall off somewhat. You will be surprised when I tell you that I have brought into London above fifteen hundred pictures and have had the pleasure of adorning some of the first cabinets in England. . . .'

But, in fact, from about 1730 onwards it was the auction houses through whom the highest proportion of every form of work of art passed. One of the first London auctioneers known to us was Edward Millington,[2] who had established a saleroom known as 'The Vendu' in the fashionable locality of Covent Garden as early as 1690. When the London season[3] was over, Millington moved with his stock to Tunbridge Wells, then becoming a fashionable health resort, 'for the diversion of ladies and gentlemen'. By 1720 Cock's auction room was doing well and by 1741 he was so well established that he was asked to undertake the sale of the celebrated collection of Edward Harley, Earl of Oxford. When Langford took over the business, the taste for collecting pictures by Old Masters was well and truly established. It was Langford who sold the famous collection of Dr Mead in 1754 and 1755. Both Redford and Roberts[4] assert that the great majority of paintings sold through the auction houses before the middle of the eighteenth century were 'doubtless good old copies', because the prices paid rarely exceeded £20. But this contention now seems unlikely.

Clearly by 1733 the attendance at picture sales was already regarded as a popular

[1] One of Greenwood's most substantial customers was Sir Lawrence Dundas, who bought a considerable number of Dutch and Flemish paintings from him in 1762. See 'The Dundas Pictures' by Denys Sutton, *Apollo*, September 1967.

[2] See George Redford's *Art Sales*, 1880, Vol. II.

[3] The 'season' continued to be of importance in a commercial sense throughout the whole of the eighteenth and nineteenth centuries. Thus Lord de Tabley's (formerly Sir John Leicester) famous collection of pictures was sold very soon after his death in July 1837. When the resulting prices were called in question William Tijon in a letter published by the *Morning Chronicle* said: 'The pictures . . . were sold in the month of July, when the Session of Parliament had terminated and when many of the most eminent patrons and collectors had left town for the season.' Quoted from Whitley's *Art in England, 1821–1837*, page 137.

[4] George Redford, *Art Sales*, London, 1888; W. Roberts, *Memorial of Christie's*, London, 1897.

form of entertainment, for in that year an anonymous rhymster published *The Man of Taste, occasioned by an Epistle of Mr Pope's on that Subject* which included the following lines:

In curious paintings I'm exceeding nice
And know their several beauties by their Price.
Auctions and Sales I constantly attend,
But chuse my pictures by a skilful friend.
Originals and Copies much the same,
The picture's value is the painter's name.
My taste in sculpture from my choice is seen,
I buy no statues that are not obscene.

It was in 1762 that that redoubtable Scot, James Christie, started his auctioneering business. It was some years before he got into his stride as an auctioneer of works of art, but once he had done so, he and his successors in the firm dominated the London saleroom business for the best part of 150 years; and fortunately their records are remarkably complete. Sotheby's, founded by one Samuel Baker, had, in fact, started earlier (about 1744) but tended to specialise in the disposal of 'literary property' and libraries, and only came to the fore in a wider context of art sales in the later half of the nineteenth century.

Other firms who conducted outstanding sales towards the end of the eighteenth century and in the first half of the nineteenth were Skinner and Dyke (who sold the Calonne Collection after it had been brought to England) and Greenwood (who sold the Dundas Collection in 1794). H. Phillips of 73 New Bond Street, noted for the flamboyance of the introductions to his catalogues (see the Fonthill and Northwick Collections), started in 1796. His name is still perpetuated in the firm of Phillips, Son and Neale. Important too, particularly in the picture world, were Foster's, who started under Peter Coxe in 1794, and whose catalogues as 'Coxe, Burrell and Foster' were widely distributed. Puttick and Simpson (more recently merged with Phillips, Son and Neale, and a haunt of most pre-war ceramic collectors) also started in 1794. Their saleroom was in the former studio of Sir Joshua Reynolds, though again for many years they specialised in the sale of libraries. George Stanley achieved some prominence early in the nineteenth century both as an art dealer and auctioneer. Mrs Cosway, widow of the miniaturist, Richard Cosway, wrote of Stanley in 1822 'I have always found him polite, attentive and *ready in payment*. His price is $7\frac{1}{2}\%$. I went round and visited all the auctioneers, and really must say, I liked him better than any!' By tradition many auctioneers were very slow to pass on the proceeds of a sale. Stanley was exceptionally business-like and prompt in his payments.

Among a host of other names that of George Robins deserves mention, for he brought twentieth-century methods of publicity to the promotion of his sales early in the nineteenth century. All those mentioned so far were London firms. In

Liverpool, Thomas Winstanley, now best known for his association with the collector, William Roscoe (see page 179), rose to some eminence as an auctioneer of works of art. He was the author of *Observations on the Arts* (1828), which appears to have been quite widely read by collectors, and he was responsible for the famous Eldin Sale in Edinburgh in 1823.[1]

In fact, picture dealers, in the sense in which we know them today, only came into their own to any significant extent early in the nineteenth century. Among the doyen of their trade was William Buchanan, author of *Memoirs of Painting*, who had a dynamic and distinguished career to which frequent references will be found. His business in Oxendon Street, London, was taken over eventually by George Yates, who was also exceedingly successful. His later Bond Street Gallery was destroyed by fire in 1836 with devastating loss, said to be largely uninsured. The Woodburn brothers were the principal dealers in drawings early in the nineteenth century and are particularly associated, initially with the formation, and subsequently with the dispersal, of the monumental collection of drawings of Sir Thomas Lawrence. John Smith specialised for many years in the sale of Dutch and Flemish pictures. He was the author of that astonishing undertaking, the nine volume *Catalogue Raisonné of the Works of ... Dutch, Flemish and French Painters.* The first volume appeared in 1829; the eighth in 1837. A 900-page Supplement appeared in 1842. Like Winstanley, Smith was anxious to warn collectors of the crooked dealings of many of his fellow dealers. In the introductions to several of the volumes he prevails upon collectors to pay attention to the conservation of the works of art in their possession; and he also bemoans the difficulties of authorship and publication involved in the immense task he had set himself in the compilation of his catalogue.[2] Of considerable importance too was the Flemish dealer, C. J. Nieuwenhuys, who settled in this country (he was succeeded in his business by his son). Like so many of his contemporary fellow dealers, he took to authorship. In 1834 he published his *Review of the Lives and Works of Some of the Most Eminent Painters*, which contained one of the first accounts in English of the inventory of Rembrandt's personal collection of paintings. Nieuwenhuys' book is of particular interest because of his comments on the acquisitions of Buchanan and Smith. His own collection was sold at Christie's in 1833.

Buchanan, Yates, Smith, the Woodburns and Nieuwenhuys never pretended to be anything but dealers in works of art. But already in the eighteenth and right through the nineteenth century there was a host of gentlemen collector-dealers, who actively benefited in their dealings from their social positions. Many of them

[1] This sale achieved some notoriety, not only because of the quality of the pictures, which was high, but because the floor of the upstairs room in which it was held gave way during the sale, with considerable injury to all those attending it!

[2] It is still useful in the study of collecting today in its own right, but much more so is Dr C. Hofstede de Groot's *Beschreibendes und Kritisches Verzeichnis der Werke der hervorragendsten Holländischen Maler des XVII. Jahrhunderts*, in ten volumes, Esslingen/Paris/London, 1907–1928, which was based on the nucleus of Smith's compilation, but which is a vastly improved and more scholarly work.

were indeed knowledgeable connoisseurs[1] but many others were sharks and charlatans. Among the more distinguished was Michael Bryan, whose importation into England of collections from the Continent (particularly the Orleans Collection) was of extreme importance. He was the author of the *Dictionary of Painters and Engravers*. The activities of N. J. Desenfans are discussed at some length on page 172; Alexis Delahante, who came to England from France because he was exiled by Napoleon as a Royalist, was also prominent in the London art dealing scene. Edward Solly (see page 202) took to dealing in works of art after his long sojourn in Germany in 1821 and again achieved a considerable reputation, as had William Young Ottley to a much greater extent (see page 186) some years earlier.

Much more numerous than dealers in paintings were those who traded in prints and engravings. Often, of course, this was combined with bookselling, which in its turn was linked to publishing, so that books, prints and pictures could often be bought on the same premises. But early in the nineteenth century this combination became rarer, though prints and pictures still remained natural commercial companions. Ancillary businesses, like those of colourmen and framemakers, sometimes developed into picture galleries. Those twin bastions of the art trade, Agnew's and Colnaghi's, have grown from such beginnings. The first Agnew, Thomas, became a partner in Manchester in 1817 of one Vittore Zanetti, who described his firm in contemporary advertisements as 'Carvers and Gilders, Looking Glass and Picture frame Manufacturers, Opticians, Ancient and Modern English and Foreign Print sellers, Publishers and Dealers in Old Coins, Medals and all kinds of Curiosities'. The firm also dealt extensively in scientific instruments and styled themselves as Barometer, Thermometer, Hydrometer and Saccharometer Makers! The 'Repository of Arts' from which the two partners traded flourished and had several times to be enlarged, and by 1835 Thomas Agnew was left as sole partner. He had gradually developed the picture dealing side. He travelled to Italy on buying expeditions; he bought Dutch pictures from John Smith in London; he made regular purchases from Christie's; he patronised contemporary artists: in short he laboured with shrewdness and skill to satisfy the growing appetite for art collecting of the increasingly wealthy merchants and manufacturers in the north of England in the middle of the nineteenth century. When he retired in 1861, the business was continued by his two sons, William and Thomas, and though Thomas Junior opened a branch in London in 1860, it was William who dominated the business and laid the foundations of the really great business that survives to this day.

[1] In this connection, Buchanan's definition of a connoisseur is of interest: 'The title *connoisseur*, which implies a knowledge of being able to judge correctly of works of art, is more frequently bestowed than deserved. No-one can be a connoisseur who does not at the same time possess taste, as on taste depends the capability of forming a just discrimination, and a delicacy of choice–a power of separating the good from the indifferent.'

Colnaghi's too had started with print selling and scientific instruments. In fact, in 1785, Paul Colnaghi joined the London business started by Giovanni Battista Torre, who combined a flair for pyrotechnics with print selling and scientific instrument making. Colnaghi came of a distinguished Milanese family, but had to seek his fortune abroad after his father died heavily in debt. He was 'a man of high intelligence, with a lively charm that captivated men and women, young and old, alike. Added to this he was an untiring worker and of unassailable integrity and it will be understood how he was able to build up a position of high prestige in the art world.'[1] Unfortunately Paul's sons, Dominic and Martin, quarrelled, so the original business was eventually continued by Dominic alone (though Martin prospered in his own right). Colnaghi's reputation in the world of engravings and drawings became world wide and in the collecting literature allusions to the firm are legion. As at Agnew's, the generations of partners genuinely befriended many collectors among their clientele, and so it came about that both firms dealt with several successive generations of families of collectors, though Colnaghi's entered the realms of Old Master dealings somewhat later.

Up to the third quarter of the nineteenth century English art and antique dealers largely dealt with private collectors. Thereafter their horizons were widened by the gradual acceleration of purchases by museums all over the world and by the awakening of interest in the arts in America. Dealers in London, Paris and Berlin were quick to see their opportunities, and as far as England was concerned the number of pictures of high quality that began to leave the country probably exceeded the number coming in. It was really at this time that the international art market, as we know it today, began. It would also be fair to say that the corresponding increase in the value of fine paintings tempted still more people to interest themselves in less expensive *objets d'art* such as those listed by *The Collector* and mentioned in the previous section. But there was always a limit to the number of any variety of object that had survived from previous ages, and dealers began to become very expert at foreseeing the swings of fashion.[2] Of course to some extent they promoted them. Thus in the 1920s the antique shops still contained a good many examples of genuine seventeenth-century furniture and silver. Despite the economic depression most of these had passed into private or public possession here and in America by the early thirties, when dealers concentrated more on eighteenth-century things, which in turn rapidly disappeared. After the second world war the craze for the Regency period soon emptied the shops of the cheaper worthwhile pieces, and today the vastly increased number of antique shops are filled with Victoriana and even with *art nouveau* and later pieces. In my own local antique shop the owner and I greet each other periodically with the caustic remark that 'the stock is getting younger and younger'!

[1] *Colnaghi's, 1760–1960*, London, 1960.

[2] 'A dealer can seldom afford to initiate taste, but a dealer with a flair can anticipate his circumstances in which taste changes and by doing so accelerate that change.' Geoffrey Agnew, *Agnew's*, 1967, page 10.

In the last five years the unceasing exportation on a gigantic scale of antique English furniture to Italy, Germany and the United States has brought about a scarcity of such goods that few people even in the 'trade' could have envisaged at the beginning of the 1960s. In contrast, one suddenly senses a greatly increased interest in smaller Roman antiquities (which have been almost totally ignored for decades) and in fine, if simple, seventeenth-century furniture from Italy, Flanders, France and Spain.

By and large in this country the men who control intermediately the sources of supply for collectors – the dealers – have long had a deservedly high reputation for honour, integrity and expertise. But in the field of works of art, where age is one of the principal criteria and where the number of non-genuine objects probably far outweighs the genuine, there is always room for dishonesty, or at least for turning a blind eye in order to make a quick profit. And the nefarious tradition of the dealers' ring seems hard to stamp out. Generally the most successful collectors have been those who could appreciate quality themselves, who had a much more than superficial knowledge of what they collected, and who had a sure instinct about whom they should trust and whom they shouldn't.

In general the English – and this applies particularly to collectors – shy away from anything resembling aggressive salesmanship. The prospective purchaser only needs encouragement to bolster his self-confidence when he has already made up his mind to buy. No one knows this better than dealers in pictures and antiques. Quinney's advice to his wife, Susan, was exactly right: 'Find out what they want, and don't be too keen to sell 'em. Most men, my pretty, and nearly all the women go dotty over the things hardest to get. Our best stuff will sell itself, if we go slow.'[1]

5. THE GROWTH OF EXPERTISE

After the beginning of the nineteenth century the continued study of works of art gradually led to a great deal of theorising about their production, particularly in the case of paintings. Interest was divided between attention to content, style, technique and to a lesser extent provenance. All were vitally important when it came to identifying authorship, for on attribution depended the value of a picture. Artistic expertise and art criticism have always been something of a tug-of-war between aesthetic and commercial considerations. A literary or music critic will not normally make an immediate impact on the recognised merit of a work by an author or composer long dead because intangibles are involved, but critical comment by an expert on a painting can prove highly damaging (or, indeed, highly beneficial) because, unlike a literary or musical composition, a picture or a

[1] H. A. Vachell, *Quinneys'*.

work of art is a piece of negotiable property.[1] Inevitably this gives the art historian or expert who is the recognised authority on a specialised period or a particular painter a good deal of power, and makes it essential that scholarship in this field should be combined with complete integrity.

The cultivation of connoisseurship already flourished, as we have seen, in the eighteenth century. Its development was of vital interest to the enthusiastic collector. But the methodical study of works of art that was less dependent on subjective criteria, really coincided with the emergence and growth of public galleries both in England and on the Continent. One single aspect of the matter was that the custodians of such institutions were hesitant to make mistakes in the expenditure of public funds where examples by well-known masters at high prices were involved. But the appointment of intelligent and highly educated men to these posts afforded opportunities and incentives for the systematic study of painting and the other arts. Almost inevitably in the first half of the nineteenth century the senior administrative posts in museums in England went to painters who had not really made their mark, though many of them had outstanding ability and judgement, which was no doubt helped by their practical appreciation of artistic techniques. Probably no less a factor was the methodical compilation of documentary evidence by the building up of excellent libraries of books and magazines on the arts, and of engravings and photographic reproductions, which were there for immediate and permanent reference.

Technical expertise in the sense that we know it today was given a vigorous push forward in this country by the visits of Passavant and Dr Waagen, particularly by the latter, who established a technique of critical examination of pictures which had previously not been much exercised.[2] Dr Waagen seemed to set the pattern too for a scientific comparison of the work of one artist with the rest of his *œuvre*–as far as this was possible before the invention of photography. Our own Sir Charles Eastlake carried all this several stages further at the National Gallery, and Sir George Scharf and Sir J. C. Robinson did it on a lesser scale at the National Portrait Gallery and the Victoria and Albert Museum.

If progress so far had been achieved by professionals, we now come to an achievement by two amateurs that was to make a lasting impression, and that was the literary partnership between Joseph Archer Crowe and J. A. Cavalcaselle. Crowe was a journalist and later became a diplomat. Cavalcaselle was Italian, a painter and a political revolutionary. Both men shared an innate love of the arts. They became firm friends, travelled and haunted private collections and museums together and then pooled their knowledge, reactions and judgements. As Cavalcaselle knew little English and Crowe was a professional author, it was the latter

[1] This aspect of art criticism was discussed at some length by Professor Ellis Waterhouse in a formal lecture delivered at Essex University on 21 February 1969 entitled 'The Role of the Art Expert in the World Today'. But see also Max Friedländer in the extract on 'Problems of Connoisseurship', page 377.

[2] Though, in fact, the doctor himself did not practise it over-assiduously on his visit to England!

who was responsible for most of the writing. Cavalcaselle's system of pictorial analysis consisted of redrawing each painting himself and then noting down and pinpointing stylistic characteristics. In order of publication the collaboration produced *The History of Flemish Painting* (in 1857), *The History of Italian Painting from its Origins to the Sixteenth Century* between 1864 and 1871, and two monographs on Titian (in 1877) and on Raphael (in 1882). The results of their researches attacked and frequently demolished vested interests in a big way and set new and lasting standards in recognition and attribution, particularly of Italian painting.

Another Italian who made a considerable contribution to the analytical study of painting was Giovanni Morelli (1816–1891). He had been trained as a doctor, with a particular interest in comparative anatomy[1] but he again was a fervent patriot who devoted much of his life towards the liberation and unification of Italy, and it was only late in life that he was able to start publishing his perceptive but revolutionary ideas in the arts. His particular method of study was the analysis of repeated physical characteristics of subjects portrayed by a particular painter and his stylistic idiosyncracies. In fact, Morelli's submission was that one should look for detail in a picture rather than to respond to a general impression.[2] There is some dispute whether the mantle of Morelli's expertise subsequently fell on J. P. Richter's or Bernard Berenson's shoulders, but both men again contributed greatly to our knowledge of Italian painting. To some extent the reputation of both has been vitiated by their involvement with art dealing. Indeed the role of the art expert after the 1880s became exceedingly difficult. The rewards of pure scholarship were small and those of co-operation with the art trade at a time of great expansion could be enormous.[3] What the dealers, and ultimately the collectors, demanded as an accompaniment to the pictures they bought for ever-increasing prices were certificates of authentification from the known experts in the field. This custom was particularly strong in Germany[4] where in the early part of the present century the outstanding figures in the expertise of attribution were Wilhelm Bode (see page 385) and Max Friedländer (see page 377).

As we approach the present day it becomes increasingly difficult to select the

[1] For a much more recent example of the effectiveness of medicine as an analytical training in the arts, see 'Collecting Costume' by Dr C. Willett Cunnington, page 384. Dr Cunnington's systematic analysis of British costume throughout the centuries was in its way almost as revolutionary as Morelli's in the world of painting.

[2] For an illuminating appraisal of Morelli's place in the development of art appreciation, see Professor Edgar Wind's 1960 Reith Lectures, published as *Art and Anarchy* in 1963.

[3] Duveen is said to have paid Berenson an annual retainer of £25,000!

[4] Though the demand for such certificates late in the nineteenth century was also considerable from America where they helped to give reassurance to the rising tide of new and inexperienced collectors. 'The name of a leading authority on a piece of paper or on the back of a photograph seemed a protection against a buyer's mistrust of his own judgement, or the ignorance or unscrupulousness of a dealer.' W. G. Constable, *Art Collecting in the United States of America*, London, 1964.

really outstanding critics. But there can be little doubt that Roger Fry had an enormous influence in his own day, dragooning into the British public's mind an understanding of the Post-Impressionists, and to Herbert Read must go the highest tribute as an interpreter of modern art. He provided the intellectual backing for the remarkably creative generation of English and European artists of the second quarter of the twentieth century, whose work was usually far in advance of the comprehension of the general public. So effective was Read's championship of contemporary painting, with its almost total abandonment of art as illustration, that much of the success of the multitude of galleries who sell such works to collectors in London, New York and Paris may be said to be due to his espousal of the cause. The assessment of his complex character will need time, but curiously enough Read seems to have descended in a direct line from those eighteenth-century gentlemen who combined a love for the land with a love for the arts. Thus Read wrote of himself: 'in spite of my intellectual pretensions, I am by birth and tradition a peasant. I remain essentially a peasant. I despise the whole industrial epoch . . . the only class in this community for which I feel any real sympathy is the agricultural class including the genuine remnants of a landed aristocracy.'[1]

We have seen how increased professional curiosity in the arts during the last century built up a growing corpus of speculative opinion and sometimes of fact. Naturally such accretion of knowledge led to constant changes of mind (and sometimes, of heart!). As far as the history of collecting is concerned it led to a highly confusing pattern of changes in attribution. Exceptions were those pictures whose history of ownership since they had been painted was continuously documented, or the pictures that had remained the property of succeeding generations of a single family. But naturally such cases of watertight provenance, which precluded speculation about authorship, were comparatively rare.

One of the reasons why the painter's name attached to a picture changed so frequently in England was, of course, the particularly devastating era of ignorance that prevailed in the eighteenth century after the wholesale and largely anonymous importations from the Continent. Mrs Jameson in 1844 was one of the first writers to condemn vehemently, but delightfully, our 'quackery and ignorance' where genuineness, or more simply, attribution, was concerned. 'We must take it for granted', she wrote, 'that in many cases, a Titian, a Paul Veronese, etc. means simply a Venetian picture, of the style and time of Titian or Veronese.' It was the diligent work of William Young Ottley, of Eastlake, of Crowe and Cavalcaselle and their followers that brought about at least increasing accuracy of speculation.

An interesting example of the sort of thing which could happen[2] during the course of establishing an attribution was Michelangelo's unfinished *Entombment*, now in the National Gallery (No. 790). According to Redford[3] it belonged at the

[1] *Poetry and Anarchism*, 1938.

[2] See also the story of the Solly 'Raphael' on page 322.

[3] *op. cit.*, Vol. I, page xix *et seq.*

beginning of the nineteenth century to Cardinal Fesch in Rome, who was a diligent, if not particularly discriminating, collector. The *Entombment* came to be stored in the basement vaults of the Falconieri Palace during Fesch's lifetime. After his death it was sold, among a host of other pictures, by the Principe di Musignano to a Roman picture dealer called Vito Enei. In 1846 some of these pictures were bought in one lot by R. Macpherson, an English photographer resident in Rome (who happened to be Mrs Jameson's brother-in-law). Macpherson singled out the *Entombment* as of particular merit and, after cleaning it, showed it to the German painter, Peter von Cornelius, who declared it to be by Michelangelo. In consequence of the *éclat* following upon this attribution, Macpherson nearly lost the painting in a lawsuit, but eventually brought it from Rome to London. In 1868 Sir William Boxall, the then director, bought it for the National Gallery for £2000. In 1881, Sir J. C. Robinson challenged this attribution (in a letter to *The Times*) and suggested that it was the work of Baccio Bandinelli 'as far as the design was concerned', but thought it was probably painted by Agnolo Bigio. Robinson's principal argument was based on a seemingly relevant passage in Vasari. Since that time the authorship of the picture has been a veritable battlefield for the cognoscenti, the full details of which can be found in the National Gallery Catalogue[1] where the attribution to Michelangelo is upheld. The basis of the present assessment is an excellent example of the use of a combined analysis of content, style, technique and provenance (the picture had been in the Farnese Collection at the beginning of the seventeenth century) that has gradually developed since Waagen's day. However, it should be made clear that as far as this book is concerned, the attributions given are those thought to be correct at the time when the excerpt quoted was written, unless an alternative ascription is specifically stated.

More so in recent years perhaps than ever before, English collectors have become noted for the determined pursuit of knowledge in the field of their particular interest, and many of them have themselves made useful contributions to the almost explosive growth of specialist literature on every aspect of artistic endeavour. But there can be no substitute for *looking at* pictures and for *handling objets d'art*.[2] This intimate contact is not only the basis of all knowledge, it also engenders enthusiasm, that most essential quality in all real collectors. One frequently comes across the term 'gloating' applied to a collector after he has acquired a possession. It seems to me a total misnomer for a form of deep-seated

[1] Cecil Gould, *The Sixteenth Century Italian Schools* (excluding the Venetian), 1962.

[2] This is not to decry the great improvements in the processes of graphic reproduction that have taken place in the last few years, particularly where the use of colour is concerned. But in the case of paintings, the difference in scale between the actual object and a reproduction in a book or magazine alone is enough to negate total effectiveness, and with three-dimensional objects this is even more strongly the case. It is to be hoped that more attention will be paid in future to technical developments leading to improved accuracy of colour reproduction without prohibitive cost. At present most exhibition catalogues containing colour reproductions unblushingly tell their own sorry tale.

satisfaction that follows upon the combined use of expertise and personal enthusiasm when the piece acquired is removed from gallery or auction room to the setting of a collector's own home.

But quite clearly today the men and women with the greatest expertise after long professional training and a lifetime's experience are to be found in the major museums and the most important auction houses, and it is of inestimable advantage to the collector that he may call upon their knowledge at will.

6. THE ECONOMIC FACTOR

Until recent times the most surprising characteristic of the English as collectors has been their complete candour about the prices they paid for the things they bought. The same state of affairs was certainly not true either on the Continent or in America, where there has always been great secrecy about the monetary side of collecting. It may well be that this comparative outspokenness in England stems from our much longer tradition of buying works of art through the auction houses where knowledge of the prices paid is public property.

The fluctuations of prices have depended only on the extent to which works of art were available and the degree to which people wanted to own them. But the economic side of the whole history of art collecting is made intensely interesting because the outstanding objects are virtually unique, or at any rate never available in any quantity, and because there have usually been a few (sometimes only two) people who have very badly wanted to own one and the same thing.

In any historical consideration of collecting price is of interest, but what really matters is value on the one hand and the relative purchasing power of money on the other. The essence of value is quality. The phrases 'first class', 'fine quality' and 'important' abound in any description of a collection. As far as the art of painting is concerned they are justifiably applied in the case of a work that marks an achievement rarely reached even by a master who has made a unique and distinctive contribution in the history of his craft. That achievement should represent a combination of imaginative accomplishment with stylistic verve and technical mastery. But works of genius are rare; and even flair occurs only a few times in each generation, so one must take it that 'important' and 'first class' have become tired commercial horses which auctioneers' cataloguers hardly ever allow back into their stables. After more than a century of continuous purchases by the world's museums, one must also accept that what is left in the 'private sector' of the art world cannot often compete qualitatively with what has already gone permanently into the 'public sector'.[1] That above all is the reason why when something of really

[1] 'The stock of masterpieces still in private hands is continually diminishing; it is no exaggeration to say that in the next two or three decades it is likely to be almost totally exhausted.' *The National Gallery Report for January 1965 to December 1966*.

exceptional quality is up for sale, the price reached is such that it hits the headlines the day after the auction. To this extent ours is a completely different era from any that has gone before. Today *everything* has its price tag and its label. The old bargain appeal only applies most exceptionally (and then usually because a dealer is handling something outside the normal range of his expertise). The determined collector today has come to terms with the fact that he must buy not only when he thinks the price is right but when opportunity offers, or cease collecting. Clearly under such conditions the purchasing power of money has reached a nadir, and it becomes almost tedious to talk of new auction records. They are merely the reflections of an age in which art and finance have come so close to each other that to the sufficiently affluent they have become virtually synonymous. It is sad but presumably inevitable that in an era of constant political and financial crises and uncertainties, the stock and money markets of the world have become so disturbed that the art and craftsmanship of past generations have become a form of gilt-edged commodity. In this climate the London auction houses have undoubtedly benefited from their long tradition and have played not *a*, but *the* leading role. They have achieved enormous success because they have quietly, but none the less assiduously, bred a fantastic level of confidence among both sellers and buyers.[1] If, in the past, they could be regarded as the wholesalers of the art and antique trade, today the prices reached during sales quite often exceed those of the 'stock' already on display to the public in the shops. The natural consequence, of course, is that these are marked up.

It is a fascinating coincidence that the development of economics as a science has progressed more or less on a parallel with the growth of collecting, both starting from small beginnings after 1800. It is interesting to remember too that that outstanding collector, Edward Solly, wrote and published a paper at the beginning of the nineteenth century[2] in which he stressed the importance of production and consumption in an economic sense and demonstrated the uselessness of idle money, and that these views were regarded as highly controversial, if not downright dangerous at the time. Collecting, like patronage, has of necessity to be the pastime of those with money surplus to their daily needs. The purchase of works of art for ready cash might well have been regarded as money stagnating until relatively recent times, and yet a long book could be written on 'Bankers as

[1] In this connection it is of interest that when Peter Wilson, at present Chairman of Sotheby's, became a partner in the firm in 1938 (after two years' service in the furniture department), the company's annual turnover was about £350,000. The combined turnover for Sotheby's and Parke-Bernet (which it has owned since 1964) for the 1967/68 season was just over £30,000,000. Wilson became chairman of Sotheby's in 1951, the year in which the company's turnover really shot ahead. More than any other man he seems to have been the architect of the boom in the world art market during the last decade.

[2] *Considerations on Political Oeconomy*, Berlin, 1814. The first part had originally been written and privately published while Solly was living in Sweden in 1812. The principal edition appeared in English with a simultaneous German translation.

Collectors throughout the Ages'. Clearly the pleasure of the possession of works of art more than compensated for interest forfeited. The interplay of social history, the rise and fall of capital and its relation to collecting could again be discussed at great length. What is of interest to us in the history of collecting is that the substantial English landowners who were the great collectors of the eighteenth century in this country had relatively little ready cash, and that the purchase of paintings and antiquities meant the outlay of much more than the mere price paid might indicate today. In fact, for the landowner, collecting became progressively more difficult as the nineteenth century advanced and as the supply of negotiable capital grew more restricted. After 1840 it was the new generation of industrialists and merchants who had the money available for the immediate purchase of works of art. Later still it was the growth of a middle class that led to the spread of higher education and the increased popularity of the sort of collecting evidenced by *The Collector* of 1905. 'Collections', said F. H. Taylor,[1] 'are merely the tangible illustrations to the ordinary processes of economic history and show the trends of historic taste. These form the records of the life story of successful men in successful times.' From the late 1870s onwards the increasingly depressed state of agriculture and the competition from abroad to many of our major industries steadily took its toll of established collections. The unusually large number of quite magnificent sales that took place in the 1880s and 1890s bear witness to this. The prices obtained were often disappointing but the increasing interest from Germany and the U.S. in the picture market helped to keep prices relatively buoyant.

The reader who wishes to know more of the Economics of Taste should turn to Gerald Reitlinger's monumental work of that title. The first volume is subtitled 'The Rise and Fall of Picture Prices from 1760 to 1960', and the second volume concerns itself with *objets d'art* prices since 1750.[2] This very detailed survey is of particular interest because while concentrating on prices and fashions in this country it also takes account of what was happening simultaneously on the Continent and subsequently in America. The author has worked out a scale of monetary values throughout the period he covers and the surprising result of applying this is that recent peak prices are often found to be only on a par with what past generations have paid; though probably the most fascinating feature of both volumes is the very low prices which many pictures and *objets d'art* fetched until comparatively recently. Here one must remember what Tancred Borenius said about the first Lord Northwick's collecting activities around 1800: 'the value of works of art was one of taste and appreciation rather than of mere commerce'.

The collectors who have most concerned themselves with the relationship of present-day equivalents of particular currencies with their purchasing power at various times in the past are the coin collectors. Gold and silver content only go a little way towards providing an answer; nor are wages and values of a standard

[1] *The Taste of Angels*, 1948.

[2] The third volume is concerned with the art market in the 1960s.

measure like a bushel of wheat true absolutes because of varying social and industrial circumstances. So that while the real value of a unit of currency–say, the pound sterling–lies in the quantity of goods or services it can command, some outside factor usually distorts true equivalence. The American economic historian, Preserved Smith, put it at its most graphic when he said: 'A fat ox now weighs two or three times what a good ox weighed four centuries ago!'[1] But while an ox is an ox is an ox, in the case of collecting such features as scarcity, artistic content, condition, demand and the timing of a sale obviously affect individual prices enormously.[2]

The scale of equivalent values for picture prices which Reitlinger devised in 1960 meant that in order to get a 1960 equivalent of a 1760–1795 price one would have to multiply by twelve; for a 1850–1914 price the multiple was six; for a 1921–1939 price it was 3·7. But during the ten years that have elapsed since 1960 there has occurred what is probably the most dramatic inflation of art prices since they have been recorded, so that today's scale would already be very different.[3] A scale of present-day equivalents of one pound sterling worked out by Spinks as of 1 January 1966[4] was slightly more sophisticated in giving alternatives for purchasing power and apparent value. For the first period quoted from Reitlinger (1760–1795) the two equivalents were multiples of five and thirty, and for 1854–1876 they were four-and-a-half and twelve. This only goes to show how rapidly fluctuations occur, and how very approximate such calculations are. For this reason I have not tried to give modern equivalents of the prices quoted in the text of the extracts that follow.

Obviously one cannot discuss the economic factors affecting collecting at the present time without some reference to the taxation system current in the United States. There the Federal Government encourages gifts and bequests to galleries and museums by including these among charities and by allowing substantial exemptions from tax to benefactors because, in fact, the number of museums in the United States established and maintained to any extent by public authorities is extraordinarily small. This subsidising of artistic purchases is the greatest single factor to have catalysed the uplift of prices in recent times. Conversely, of course, it is also this factor that has drained away already, and is continuing to do so, a high proportion of the finest works of art that come onto the European market. Other European countries have followed the American taxation model,

[1] Preserved Smith, *The Age of Reformation*, New York, 1920.

[2] One collector of my acquaintance proudly displays a superb piece he bought at a sale on 3 September 1939 for £1, which one might reasonably expect to fetch five figures today, but it would only be a very determined collector indeed who would have attended a sale on the first day of the second world war!

[3] In fact, in Reitlinger's third volume, published late in 1970, the scale has already changed enormously: the equivalents of 1750–1795 prices have to be multiplied by between 20 and 16 times; those of 1850–1895 by 10 to 8 times; and 1921–1939 prices by 5 times.

[4] Spink and Sons, *Numismatic Circular*.

and perhaps one day our own traditionally shortsighted government will do the same. All that they have done in recent years is to make it more difficult than ever for works of art to be retained within the same family by closing every loophole to legitimate tax avoidance as far as death duties are concerned.

7. THE LITERATURE

There is by tradition a strong link in England between art and literature. Clearly there must have been a sizeable readership for the pamphlets, journals, discourses, books and biographical dictionaries about the arts which began to appear in growing numbers in the second half of the eighteenth century. Often the authors were themselves artists who had strong feelings about this or that point relevant to their calling which they expressed with vigour and wit. Obviously too as the interest in collecting works of art gained impetus there was an increased demand for books which concerned themselves and could be used as guides to every aspect of the subject. Publishers soon realised that collectors liked to read about other collectors, and so fortunately a series of volumes began to appear after the beginning of the nineteenth century without which it would be very difficult today to construct a historical survey of collecting. Extracts from most of these are given in this book, but it may help the reader to survey them briefly beforehand.

Far and away the most important work of its kind, because its coverage was so very comprehensive, was Dr Waagen's *Treasures of Art in Great Britain* of 1854.[1] This was, in fact, the second and greatly enlarged edition of *Works of Art and Artists in England* which had been published in three much shorter volumes in 1838 and had been written during 1835. A description of how Dr Waagen tackled the work and an account of his life is given on page 146. He had himself used and heavily relied upon William Buchanan's invaluable *Memoirs of Painting* which had appeared in 1824 (see pages 127 and 167). Dr Waagen had probably been encouraged to tackle the whole project because of the obvious inadequacies in the work of his fellow countryman, J. D. Passavant's *Tour of a German Artist in England, with Notices of Private Galleries etc.* which had appeared in English in 1836 but had been written in 1831 (see page 219). It is still of considerable interest to us today nevertheless.

Passavant himself makes generous acknowledgement to the two most informative eighteenth-century sources on collecting. These were, first, the works of Jonathan Richardson and his son, the earliest of which appeared in 1715 (*Theory of Painting*, *Science of a Connoisseur* and *The Art of Criticism*) and which were republished in various forms (finally in a collected edition in 1773); and, secondly, Thomas Martyn's–originally anonymous–compilation, *The English Connoisseur*,

[1] A fourth supplementary volume, called *Galleries and Cabinets of Art in Great Britain*, appeared in 1857.

of 1766 (see page 99). This contained accounts of some thirty prominent collections.

All these volumes were carefully scrutinised, assimilated and to some extent utilised before the middle of the nineteenth century by Mrs Anna Jameson in the compilation of her *Handbook to the Public Galleries of Art in and near London*[1] of 1842 and her particularly interesting *Companion to the most Celebrated Private Galleries of Art in London* of 1844. Frequent references to Mrs Jameson's work will be found in this book. All the authors writing after 1829 had also drawn heavily on John Smith's *Catalogue Raisonné of the Works of the most Eminent Dutch, Flemish and French Painters*, mentioned on page 30, and to a lesser extent on C. J. Nieuwenhuys' *Review of the Lives and Works of some of the most Eminent Painters* of 1834. But far and away the most important source of information about English art had been James Dallaway's five-volume revision of 1826 of Horace Walpole's *Anecdotes of Painting in England* of 1762–1780, which in turn had been based on Vertue's *Notebooks* (see page 57).[2] This itself had been supplemented by Edward Edwards' *Anecdotes of Painters*, posthumously published in 1808. Allan Cunningham's *Lives of the most Eminent British Painters, Sculptors and Architects* of 1829 covered the same ground. John Pye's *Patronage of British Art*, 1845, did so from a particularly idiosyncratic point of view.[3]

The opening of the National Gallery in 1824 clearly gave a strong fillip to the interest in other collections already extant. This resulted in the publication of C. M. Westmacott's *British Galleries of Painting and Sculpture*, 1824, and the long, rambling *British Galleries of Art* by P. G. Patmore also in 1824. The book was published anonymously. Of particular interest to collectors was Thomas Winstanley's *Observation on the Arts* of 1828. A slightly earlier volume which reviewed the collections of drawings in this country was Henry Reveley's relatively rare *Notices Illustrative of the Drawings and Sketches of some of the most distinguished Masters* of 1820.

Clearly the number of collection and auction catalogues is so great that it would be quite impossible to list them. But there are a few of both kinds which contained such invaluable source material that they deserve mention. In the first

[1] This was published by the firm of John Murray, who had also published both editions of Dr Waagen's book. Roberts in *Memorials of Christie's* was the first to point out that John Murray I and the first James Christie both hailed from Scotland and left the navy within a few months of each other to start work in London. Both were part owners of the *Morning Chronicle*. The house of Murray's major contributions to the nineteenth-century literature on the arts included the works of Mrs Jameson, Sir Charles and Lady Eastlake, Layard, Crowe and Cavalcaselle and their own famous guides, as well as Waagen. Much of the correspondence relating to the publication of these books is still extant in the firm's archives.

[2] Another edition with even more extensive notes compiled by Ralph Wornum, later Keeper of the National Gallery, appeared in 1849. It was reprinted in 1862 and reissued by a different publisher in 1888.

[3] Pye's must have been one of the first volumes of art historical studies in English in which the footnotes and supplementary material heavily outweighed the author's text!

category Horace Walpole's *Aedes Walpolianae*, 1747 and 1752, the catalogue of his father's collection at Houghton Hall in Norfolk, is outstanding. Of great interest too was the catalogue published as *Authentic Memoirs of the Life of Dr Richard Mead, M.D.*, 1755, and James Kennedy's *Description of the Antiques and Curiosities in Wilton House*, 1769. Later examples of interest are John Britton's *Catalogue Raisonné of the Pictures belonging to the Marquis of Stafford in the Gallery of Cleveland House*, 1808, William Young Ottley's immense four-volume *Catalogue of the Marquis of Stafford's Collection in London*, 1818, and T. F. Dibdin's magnificent *Aedes Althorpianae: an account of the Mansion, Books and Pictures at Althorp, the Residence of George John Earl Spencer, K.G.*, 1822.

Among the more memorable auction catalogues were those for the sales at Fonthill Abbey (Christie's, revised by Phillips), 1823 (see page 214); Stowe (Christie's), 1848–the priced and annotated catalogue was subsequently edited by Henry Rumsey Forster; Strawberry Hill (George Robins), 1842; Ralph Bernal's sale (Christie's), 1855; Samuel Rogers' collection (Christie's), 1856; Lord Northwick's collection at Thirlestane House, (Phillips), 1859; and the Hamilton Palace Sale (Christie's), 1882; again a priced and annotated catalogue appeared later.

In the second half of the nineteenth century there were three works in particular which threw much light on the history of collecting. The first was by another German visitor to England, Adolf Michaelis. His book, *Ancient Marbles in Great Britain* was written between 1861 and 1878 and was published in 1882. It was the most complete survey of Greek and Roman antiquities in private and in public collections in this country. The next work was even more monumental and is an absolute mine of information. Extracts from it and references to it occur frequently in this work. It was compiled over many years by *The Times* Sales Correspondent, George Redford, and was published in two folio volumes in a limited edition to subscribers in 1888. Its full title was *Art Sales: A History of Sales from 1628 to 1887 of Pictures and other Works of Art with Notices of the Collections sold, Names of Owners, Titles of Pictures, Prices and Purchasers*. Redford's list of sales was revised in more accurate form and enlarged by Algernon Graves and appeared as *Art Sales* in three volumes between 1918 and 1921. The third important work consisted of extracts from a diary kept between 1869 and 1885 largely relating to purchases of ceramics and antiques–the unique, two-volume *Journals* of Lady Charlotte Schreiber. The book in fact appeared in 1911; for a full description and long extract, see page 329.

The present century has seen an immense number of books which touch upon the history of collecting in this country.[1] Surprisingly only five works are major reviews of the main aspects of the subject. William T. Whitley is the author of two of them, each in two volumes. The first, *Artists and their Friends in England*,

[1] Many are written in the style so aptly described as 'the manner of the relaxed raconteur of the pre-1939 period'.

1700–1799 was published by the Medici Society in 1928. *Art in England, 1800–1820* and *1821–1837*, was published by the Cambridge University Press in 1928 and 1930. Whitley spent years combing through contemporary newspapers, journals, catalogues, letters and documents. Invaluable though *Art in England* is, it unfortunately lacks any references to sources, though his entire material and notes are available in the British Museum with a most useful index compiled by Ruth Simon.

The newly discovered *Farington Diary*, the journals of Joseph Farington, R.A. (1747–1821), was edited by James Greig and selections published in eight volumes between 1922 and 1928. Mixed in with a mass of other detail, it contains much useful information on collecting. A new and scholarly edition is in preparation.[1] The first attempt at the wider canvas of an international and historical survey of collecting 'from Rameses to Napoleon' came to us in 1948 from the director of the Metropolitan Museum in New York, F. H. Taylor, entitled *The Taste of Angels*. Unfortunately he did not live to complete the second volume, from 1815 to the present day, which had been planned. In 1961 appeared Gerald Reitlinger's *The Economics of Taste*, as already mentioned in Section 6. The first volume reviewed picture prices and the second (1963) prices of *objets d'art*.

Among the earlier books mentioned, the works by Martyn, Buchanan, Passavant, Waagen, Mrs Jameson, Redford and Michaelis must be regarded as the classics in the field. Apart from a mass of source material in individual articles in the *Burlington Magazine*, *The Connoisseur* and *Apollo*, the corpus of publications by the Walpole Society since its foundation in 1912, probably contains the most outstanding contributions towards shaping the history of collecting in England.

8. THE EMERGENCE OF THE OFFICIAL COLLECTOR

The wealth of museums in Britain stems largely from the generosity of private collectors over the last 150 years. On the continent of Europe the emergence of the great national galleries and museums was based much more on the gradual transference of dynastic heirlooms to public ownership. In the first place celebrated princely collections were shown only to distinguished visitors. But then the increasing number of interested connoisseurs led to the opening of such galleries at fixed times and, in due course–particularly where the tourist trade was important–the general public came to be admitted regularly. The process began in Italy in the eighteenth century when, for example, the superb collection of the Medici passed to the Tuscan State in 1737. In 1768 the extensive collection of the Saxon royal family in Dresden was opened to the public, and as early as 1747 there

[1] The complete diary is in the Royal Library at Windsor. A typed copy of the whole MS is in the Department of Prints and Drawings of the British Museum.

had been vociferous clamour in Paris that the contents of the Louvre should not remain invisible forever. The 'Belvedere Gallery', as the Vienna Art Gallery was known, became a public museum in 1781.

An account of the way in which public demand in this country, stimulated by increasing travel to the Continent, eventually led to the establishment of our own National Gallery in 1824 is given on page 263. London shared with Amsterdam the privilege of having for its principal picture gallery an entirely new creation, though to some extent even the Rijksmuseum was based on the former collection of the House of Orange. Again it would be interesting to conjecture what would have happened if Charles I's magnificent collection had not been dispersed. The long delay in the re-establishment of a royal picture collection of any importance inevitably meant that it compared poorly with other European royal collections until late in the eighteenth century. Yet in a way the strength of our monarchy has been demonstrated by its deliberate retention of its own art treasures, though the public is, and always has been, given many and generous opportunities of seeing them, of which the recently opened Queen's Gallery at Buckingham Palace is only one example. One might well speculate on the extent to which English taste in the arts has been moulded through the years by the accessibility of the royal van Dycks and the Raphael cartoons[1] at times when few other great works of art were to be seen in England.

The spread of interest in the arts and the demand for better education in the nineteenth century culminated in the establishment of other museums in London and in the provinces. Private benefactions played a very important part in this. In London the Dulwich Gallery, the Sir John Soane's Museum, the Wallace Collection and the Tate Gallery originated entirely through the generosity of great collectors; so in the present century did the National Maritime Museum, Kenwood House, the Courtauld Institute and the Percival David Collection. In the provinces, municipal consciences coupled with gifts and acquisitions from local residents led to the establishment of municipal art galleries in Liverpool, Manchester, Birmingham, Norwich, Leicester and Leeds. Both Oxford and Cambridge benefited from private munificence; so did Glasgow and, rather later, Edinburgh. In London the South Kensington Museum originated through what was basically the Prince Consort's initiative. More recently museums at Brighton, Port Sunlight and Lincoln were again established by outstanding collectors, while the Barber Institute in Birmingham was founded by an enlightened benefactor. Barnard Castle was endowed by John Bowes before it was taken over by Durham County Council. The National Trust owns a great multitude of houses, many with superb collections, most of which were gifts from private owners to the nation.

Against all this one has to set a deeply engrained tradition of governmental

[1] '27 April 1812, Monday. Rode to Hampton [Court] on Wilkie's horse. Spent a delicious four hours with the Cartoons. What an exquisite, Heavenly, delightful mind Raphael had.' *The Diary of Benjamin Robert Haydon*, edited by W. B. Pope, Cambridge, Mass., 1960.

reluctance to spend money on the arts. With a few outstanding exceptions, usually as the result of public pressure, the record of successive British governments until the era of the redoubtable Miss Jennie Lee has been 'too little and too late'. Over and over again the extracts quoted later in this book bear this out.

One of the museums which was constantly bedevilled by the twin problems of having to provide an educational lead while hampered by a shortage of funds was the Victoria and Albert Museum. Matters had apparently reached something of an impasse by 1913, when a number of departmental sub-committees were established to investigate and to report upon their principal deficiencies. At that time the Director could only personally sanction purchases of up to £20. For objects exceeding that sum permission had to be obtained from the Board of Education in Whitehall. Apart from inconvenience at home, this also meant that officers on the Museum staff could hardly ever make purchases when they were travelling abroad and when they saw things which they wanted to snap up. The Ceramics Department stated: 'the Director and Keeper are compelled to let the best things go past them, or to fall back upon what is cheap – the fatal snare of the second-rate collector. The collector who buys only cheap things, in spite of occasional coups, soon finds his collection *déclassé*. . . . Further, it ought not to be the principal function – as it is rapidly becoming their function – of the Director of the Museum and the Keeper of the Ceramics Department to beg and borrow off private individuals in order to supplement the inadequate allowance of roughly a thousand pounds per annum made by the state. The Authorities cannot seriously wish it to be considered that the best beggar is the best Keeper, but if they do, they must no longer expect to command the services of the best men – gifted by nature to feel the difference between a masterpiece and an average work – and entitled after years of training to become heads of departments. There is no scope, as matters stand, for their gifts or their industry. The money question *must* be faced. . . .'[1]

The same author had quoted earlier in his report one of the six canons laid down in the foundation of Chinese aesthetics by Hsieh Ho, a Chinese critic of the sixth century A.D. Ho's edict stated simply: 'Collect masterpieces!' That edict should be 'the first principle of any good collector', the report continued, 'and should be the special object of a Museum designed to help, directly or indirectly, the tens of thousands of workmen and workwomen – potters, cabinet makers, masons, metal workers, jewellers, weavers, embroiderers and others who spend their lives in hard labour to satisfy the demands of taste. For only masterpieces are the source of inspiration – and by the number of its masterpieces a collection is finally judged.'

This attitude reflected in unalloyed form the strictly educational mandate laid down at the time of the Victoria and Albert Museum's foundation. Later a more liberal purpose was added to the original aim: 'To select and to preserve, *for their*

[1] *Victoria and Albert Museum Advisory Council, Reports of the Sub-Committees upon the Principal Deficiencies in the Collections,* 1913.

own sake, the finest products of artistic craftsmanship.' 'This idealistic project', wrote Sir Trenchard Cox,[1] 'won the sympathy of the art-loving public and, instead of the Museum becoming a utilitarian teaching establishment, a series of incomparably rich gifts and bequests from private donors made it, within a generation, one of the greatest treasure houses in the world. These benefactions also gave to the Museum that character of connoisseurship, which is still evident in the markedly personal nature of its now vast collections.' But in contrast he added: 'The public is still not fully alive to the fact that the high quality of the collections in any great national museum depends, not so much upon the persuasive ability of the administrators to conjure up the necessary amount of money from public or private sources, as on the scholars who know exactly at what point the collection under their care should be strengthened and enriched.'

Clearly the foresight of the 1913 committees had borne fruit. Many of the deficiencies pointed out in each field of craftsmanship[2] were slowly and painfully made good, often at vastly greater cost than would have been necessary if earlier opportunities had been seized. Nevertheless, the museum authorities continued to cultivate and advise collectors who enjoyed the aesthetic discrimination of collecting if it was known that their complete collections would ultimately go to the Museum, but help was given just as frequently when this was not certain.

Already in 1913 it was foreign museums who were the principal competitors in the fields where fashion had not as yet shown the way to the private collector. At that time too the purchasing policies of the great London museums were still not clearly defined and the arrangement of a conference of the Directors concerned was called for to avoid undue overlapping of interests. In one area in particular the American museums had overtaken the British because they were able to obtain the necessary finance more readily: this was in archaeological excavations all over the world. Thus between 1901 and 1904 Dr Berthold Laufer had unearthed ceramic treasures in China of a degree of antiquity hardly known before (such as mortuary pottery from the Chow Dynasty, 1122 B.C.) and in 1906 Pierpont Morgan began to finance archaeological expeditions to Egypt under the aegis of the Metropolitan Museum and was so successful that by 1908 one hundred and eighty-five cases of finds were ready to be shipped back to New York.

The primary museums in London were staffed by the Civil Service and there

[1] 'The Museum in a Changing World', *Victoria and Albert Museum Bulletin*, Vol. I, No. 1, January 1965. This delightful periodical publication was aimed at the specialist *and* the interested public. Unfortunately it appears to have failed in its sales to the latter and it ceased publication in 1969 in view of the current economic stringency.

[2] The overall list from all eight departments was immense. It included Romanesque, Gothic and English medieval sculpture; Byzantine, early Persian and Central Asian ceramic works, early Chinese, Korean and Japanese pottery; Italian stained glass; sixteenth- and seventeenth-century English silver, English ironwork of the seventeenth and eighteenth centuries; Southern German tapestries, early Persian carpets; surprisingly perhaps, seventeenth- and eighteenth-century English furniture showing excellence of design and workmanship rather than elaboration of ornament, and examples of Chippendale.

can be no doubt that the entrants to professional keepership were of the highest standard.[1] Although there was no professional training except experience, by the end of the nineteenth century a remarkably high level of expertise and scholarship had been established. Indeed it is scholarship, rather than any outstanding ability at display or arrangement, which has been the hallmark of the best English 'official' collectors. Until the time of the first world war they were frequently men with private means. This enabled them to form collections of their own which they often left to the very museums that they had served. This independence gave keepers an ability to mix with private collectors on equal terms and led to the formation of friendships which in turn resulted in substantial bequests. In the British Museum, Sir Augustus Wollaston Franks and Sir Hercules Read were two such men who have probably never received the gratitude they deserved.

Yet until fairly recently, before the expansion of museums in the rest of the country, this concentration of talent in London meant that there were too many good men who could not and did not get the promotion they deserved. They turned sour or sought refuge in excessively obscure areas of specialisation. This tended to give the senior staff in museums a stuffy and unpopular image in the public eye, which in most cases was quite undeserved.

During the second world war most museums in this country had evacuated their finest possessions to places of safety. After 1945 renewed display on fusty, traditional principles seemed not to accord with the spirit of the times and there was a gradual movement to make visits to museums more enjoyable and enlightening for the public. The undoubted leader in the movement towards better visual presentation was Sir Leigh Ashton at the Victoria and Albert Museum. He devised the revolutionary change of dividing the Museum's collection into two categories: 'the primary galleries which present a synthesis of the entire collection irrespective of material; and the Study Collections in which the objects are still arranged by material for the convenience of the specialist student'.[2] This arrangement has proved a huge success.

Under Sir Philip Hendy the National Gallery too evolved vastly better methods of display and, most interesting of all, decided to open its reserve collections to the public. The arrangement of the pictures cheek by jowl is probably the nearest we can get in this country to the bad old times when the National Gallery was still in Pall Mall.[3] However, the opening of the reserve collections makes it possible to

[1] One of the most remarkable examples of this was the British Museum's Department of Prints and Drawings soon after the first world war, when it contained what James Byam Shaw has described as 'one of the most distinguished group of scholars ever to grace one department'. The team consisted of Campbell Dodgson, A. M. Hind, Laurence Binyon, Arthur Waley, A. E. Popham and K. T. (now Sir Karl) Parker. (The separate Oriental division had not then been established.)

[2] Trenchard Cox, *op. cit.*

[3] Exquisitely described by W. G. Constable as showing 'the tendency of the day to favour large and gloomy canvases of sombre brown tone and grandiose intention' (in an article on 'The Foundation of the National Gallery' in the *Burlington Magazine*, April 1924).

keep only the best on view in the principal galleries. Furthermore, they demonstrate better than anything else can the changes of taste and unavoidable mistakes in purchases that must occur in the history of any considerable picture gallery. They make clear too the astonishing advances in conservation and restoration that have taken place. Anyone fortunate enough to have seen at work the carefully considered and scientific approach to the cleaning of paintings in the National Gallery Laboratory must surely have grave misgivings about the continuously vocal and traditionally uninformed public outcry on the subject.

In recent times the security hazard has become another important factor in museum life. The National Gallery, the Dulwich Museum and the Sir John Soane's Museum have all suffered in this respect. The work and money involved in conservation and security alone give the 'official' collector an enormous advantage over the private collector. This is particularly evident in the ancestral collections open to the public in family residences where such factors as air-conditioning and conservation on a gallery scale are clearly not possible and the average condition of the pictures is consequently much less good.

Against this disadvantage one must set an enormous plus. American museums are particularly rich in their ownership of rooms complete with panelling, door furniture, decorated ceilings, fenestration, pictures, furniture, carpets and decorative objects. These project period atmosphere and taste extraordinarily effectively and are very popular with visitors. We in England, on the other hand, have a lot of complete houses containing many such rooms *which are still lived in* and can be visited by the public at particular times. These exude atmosphere to an even more pleasurable extent and will always seem more attractive than the simulated scenario of a museum. In such settings the condition of the pictures seems of much less importance!

One aspect of 'official' collecting, which has already become acute and will become more so, is the shortage of space, particularly for the display of secondary material. If museum curators have a common problem ahead of them in the future, it is to make the latter more readily available to students and to the public. For it has always been a mistake for a museum to *sell* parts of its collections because of changes in taste and qualitative appreciation, to say nothing of financial losses incurred.[1]

* * *

[1] I have recently seen in a private house in Sussex an unusual but attractive landscape by Cézanne. It had been bought by the owner from the Tate Gallery for £80 after a Cézanne exhibition in the thirties because the museum authorities considered the picture untypical of the artist's style. Also alarming are the unconfirmed stories that circulate about the deliberate destruction of material by museum authorities: porcelain forgeries and unidentified canvases in bad condition are the objects most frequently mentioned. The Victoria and Albert Museum's policy on disposal is interesting: all pieces are scrutinised by a Board of Survey. They are then either given or sold to another institution, or sold anonymously at auction. Fakes never leave the museum and are destroyed.

In the cataloguing of pictures and drawings British museums are supreme, and fortunately the National Collections have never indulged in the irritating continental habit of cataloguing the paintings in reserve collections separately. The National Gallery and the Wallace Collection provide both scholars and the public with particularly useful catalogues. But where the decorative arts are concerned the problems of cataloguing become much more difficult simply because of the number of objects involved. Both the British Museum and the Victoria and Albert Museum disappoint in this respect: catalogues have become very expensive or are simply not obtainable. The little picture books which *are* available make pleasant reminders of visits to museums but are of limited value to the serious student. Another irritation to the specialist collector is the policy held by some museum authorities of printing collection catalogues in small editions initially and allowing them to remain out of print indefinitely as soon as stocks are exhausted. Instances of this are known to every collector. If examples are wanted, one might list at random[1] the catalogues of the Glaisher Collection of ceramics in the Fitzwilliam Museum,[2] the Schreiber Collection at the Victoria and Albert Museum,[3] and Volume I of the Catalogue of the Collection of Drawings in the Ashmolean Museum (Netherlandish, German, French and Spanish schools) by Sir Karl Parker, 1938.

Although the hiatus is now filled, exactly forty years elapsed between the fifteenth edition (1928) and the sixteenth (1968) of the Wallace Collection catalogue of pictures and drawings! It might well help if more pressure by the public was brought to bear on the governing bodies of museums to rectify this situation.[4] It is always difficult for the curatorial staff to find the time that has to be devoted to the compilation and revision of catalogues when the almost universal shortage of staff forces them to undertake so many other tasks. It may well be that in future this work should be given to independent art historians trained in the task and prepared to move from place to place. Certainly continuous and uninterrupted concentration on such work under local supervision might achieve more rapid results and would probably cost less in the long run.

Cost, of course, is always the bugbear, though a few authorities seem to find that a vigorous publications policy is profitable! The possibility of making entrance charges to museums has been discussed at length just recently and now decided upon. My feeling is that a reasonable entrance charge (not for children or students, but for adults only) will deter relatively few people and could provide a useful source of income so long as it was clearly earmarked for new acquisitions,[5]

[1] At the time of writing in 1970.

[2] In two volumes by Bernard Rackham, 1935.

[3] In three volumes, also by Bernard Rackham, 1924–30.

[4] Provincial museums are still the principal offenders in not having catalogues of any sort available, even where full-time curators are employed. One can only regret, for example, that the delightful Christchurch Mansion in Ipswich, Suffolk, which contains a number of good paintings by Constable, Gainsborough and others, as well as furniture, ceramics and antiquities, has not had a catalogue for many years.

[5] The Rijksmuseum in Amsterdam, for example, uses the profits from the sales of its publications to buy new works of art. This policy is actually

for subsidising catalogues, or for modernising museum facilities, which are often desperately antiquated, and not simply for administrative purposes. Entrance charges are made all over the Continent and in America, and museums there are probably better rather than worse attended than our own.

Many of the other improvements in museum presentation that one would like to see eventually simply depend on having more money available. One aspect of museum display of particular concern to collectors is the labelling of works of art. Obviously one reason why many gifts to museums are made is to preserve the object in association with the donor's name. Yet labels are often difficult to read, their positioning is inconvenient and it is only rarely that one sees consistency in the presentation of the information upon them. Full acknowledgement of donors is a small return for their generosity and is often of interest to visitors, particularly when a piece comes from a well-known collection.

But enough of carping: most museums in Britain achieve miracles on inadequate budgets. The official collector is an honourable and deserving rival to the private collector. Particularly in those immense twilight areas where works of art and archaeological remains become indistinguishable from mere artefacts, the preservation of which is of the greatest interest to scholars and historians while relatively unattractive to the private collector. In fact, the acquisition of what our ancestors loosely termed antiquities has become almost entirely the preserve of museums, if for no other reason than that there are few private collectors who can accommodate them today in flats or houses, and even fewer who possess the scholarship essential to their accurate identification. Where the tailends of ancestral collections of this kind *do* remain in private possession they usually have a fusty, neglected look about them, as if the present owners found them something of an embarrassing encumbrance.

The constantly increasing value of works of art in public possession causes increased hazards where security is concerned, but it is nothing new. Thus already in 1913, the Department of Metal Work in the Victoria and Albert Museum, in the report mentioned earlier, stated that 'The great enamelled Ettemberg Reliquary purchased in 1861 for £2142, is now valued at £100,000; the Byzantine enamelled Pectoral Cross, purchased in 1886 for £315, would now probably realise £10,000; and the gold enamelled Missal Cover attributed to Cellini, purchased in 1864 for £700, is now worth over £20,000!'

In many ways the great museums of today have become the national treasuries. While Hans Tietze wrote:[1] 'National art treasures have become as much an inalienable symbol as a consecrated crown once was', he says later in the same piece that 'the least part of their value lies in the millions they would fetch in the market; their real worth lies in the intellectual labour and in the spiritual pleasure stored

stated in their catalogues. The London National Gallery uses similar profits to subsidise its more specialist catalogues.

[1] *Treasures of the Great National Galleries*, London, 1955, page 8.

up in them'. It is this dual aspect that makes the work of the custodians of such treasures fascinating. There can be little doubt that it is the power to acquire further objects either by shrewd purchase in the open market or by the cultivation of potential benefactors that is one of the intangible rewards of a curatorial career. An almost unique recognition of this fact occurs in the *Report of the Committee of the Ashmolean Museum*[1] which states: 'It was urged [upon us] that to deprive the keepers of their right to buy objects was to take from them one of their most prized functions and one in which they had often showed special skill–Sir Karl Parker's purchases were often cited to us, with justice, as proof of this–and to diminish the attractiveness of their posts and, therefore, the prospect of a university of obtaining the services of distinguished scholars.'

Yet the sums available for purchases are usually so limited that it is becoming more and more difficult to equate them with objects of the sort of quality already in museums. A comparatively recent and startling development is that prices have increased so enormously that the great bulk of works of art changing hands in the auction house and elsewhere is no longer going into museums *but is staying in private hands*. Often, whether one likes it or not, this is at least partially for investment reasons. Museums, even in the United States, can only afford to go after the really exceptional piece. Fifteen years ago that doyen of official collectors, Sir Karl Parker, could write: 'The time will shortly come when in retrospect even the 1930s and 1940s will appear to a future generation of collectors almost as a time of plenty.'[2] Indeed it has, particularly where buying for official collections is concerned! New acquisitions are the life blood of a museum: without them it stagnates. One of the likely consequences is that museums will concern themselves increasingly with the purchase of contemporary works of art and industrial products because their money will go much further on such objects and because today so much gets lost or forgotten so quickly. But, as Douglas Cooper said:[3] 'We should be sure that the art which is being sponsored and put into museums is good art. And that will always depend on people with imagination, flair and insight.'[4] Contemporary art is art untried, without the benefit of historical perspective, and one suspects that the survival rate beyond the taste and fashion of our time may not be high.

The last word about what *really* matters to those who administer our museums

[1] Published as Supplement Number I to the [Oxford] University Gazette, Vol. XCVIII, November 1967, page 25.

[2] *Catalogue of the Collection of Drawings in the Ashmolean Museum*, Vol. II, Italian Schools, 1956, page xx.

[3] *Great Private Collections*, London, 1963, page 12.

[4] It is only fair to say that he continued the passage as follows: 'However these are just the attributes which will never be developed by the hordes of art-administrators into whose hands the power to shape taste has been placed in the last twenty years. For that reason it is my conviction that any society which genuinely believes in upholding cultural values should show respect for the initiative, powers of aesthetic judgement and devotion to scholarship of men like the great collectors to whom this book [*Great Private Collections*] is dedicated with the admiration which is their due.'

[5] 'Art and Society', *The Cornhill Magazine*, Centenary No. (No. 1025), London, 1960.

should go to Lord [Kenneth] Clark. 'I believe', he wrote,[5] 'that the majority of people really long to experience that moment of pure, disinterested, non-material satisfaction which causes them to ejaculate the word "beautiful"; and since this experience can be obtained more reliably through works of art than through any other means, I believe that those of us who try to make works of art more accessible are not wasting our time.'

PART ONE

From the Beginnings to 1824

NOTE

Footnotes which are part of the original quoted texts are set in *italics* and are referred to by typographical symbols, thus *†. Explanatory footnotes included by the present editor are set in roman type and they are referred to by superior figures, thus [1].

In general, the original material in the extracts has been reprinted as it first appeared. This accounts for the apparent inconsistencies in punctuation, capitalisation and spelling, particularly of artists' names.

THE GREAT TRIO · CHARLES I, ARUNDEL AND BUCKINGHAM

THE literature on Charles I as a collector is extensive, but Dr Waagen's account of the great royal collection was one of the first that was both comprehensive and analytical. This was only to be expected from the penetrating mind of the first director of the Berlin Royal Gallery.

The principal documents from which Waagen drew his information were Horace Walpole's *Anecdotes of Painting in England* of 1762, which was itself based on the painstaking researches of the engraver, George Vertue. Walpole says: 'Mr Vertue had for several years been collecting materials for this work. He conversed and corresponded with most of the virtuosi in England; he was personally acquainted with the oldest performers in the science; he minuted down everything he heard from them. He visited every collection, made catalogues of them, attended sales, copied every paper he could find relative to the art, searched offices, registers of parishes, and registers of wills for births and deaths, turned over all our own authors, and translated those of other countries which related to his subject. He wrote down everything he heard, saw or read. His collections amounted to near forty volumes large and small.' It was the greatest source book on early art in England of all time. Vertue assembled his material between 1713 and 1757, but it needed the diligence and literary skill of a Walpole to turn it into printed form.

The other two catalogues of the royal pictures were published by William Bathoe in 1758. The following advertisement for them was again written by Horace Walpole:

1. A Catalogue and Description of King Charles the First's capital Collection of Pictures, Limnings, Statues, Bronzes, Medals and other Curiosities, with the Measure of the Pictures, and an Account of whom or by whom purchased. To which is added, an exact Alphabetical Index of the Painters, and the names of the Pictures, now first published from an original Manuscript in the Ashmolean Museum at Oxford: the whole transcribed and prepared for the Press and a great part of it printed, by the late ingenious Mr Vertue, and now finished from his Papers. The Second Edition. With the Addition of the Valuation of the Pictures of the several Palaces, the Value of the whole Collection, and the Prices that the capital Pictures, &c. were valued at and sold for. Price 10s 6d.[1]

[1] When the Rev. James Dallaway republished Walpole's *Anecdotes of Painting in England* in 1826 ('with considerable additions') he wrote that the Bathoe Catalogue 'is now extremely

2. A Catalogue of the Collection of Pictures, &c. belonging to King James the Second. To which is added, a Catalogue of the Pictures and Drawings in the Closet of the late Queen Caroline, with their exact Measures; taken, at the Queen's Command, by the late Mr Vertue. And also, of the principal Pictures in the Palace of Kensington; with compleat Indexes of the Painters, and the Names of the pictures. Price 10s 6d.

Our debt to Abraham van der Doort, a Dutch engraver who came to this country in 1609 and stayed until his death by suicide in 1640, is very considerable. For it was he who compiled the principal inventories of the royal collection. For a very full account of his career and a definitive version of the *Catalogues of the Collections of Charles I* edited by Oliver Millar, see the 37th volume of the Walpole Society 1958–1960.

But what about Charles himself? One of the pithiest judgements of the royal career occurs in the Rev. W. Gilpin's *Observations on the Western Parts of England* (written in 1775, though not published till 1798). 'If Charles had acted with as much judgement as he read, and had shown as much discernment in life, as he had taste in the arts, he might have figured among the greatest princes. Every lover of picturesque beauty, however, must respect this amiable prince notwithstanding his political weaknesses. We never had a prince in England whose genius and taste were more elevated and exact. He saw the arts in a very enlarged point of view. The amusements of his court were a model of elegance to all Europe and his cabinets were the receptacles only of what was exquisite in sculpture and painting. None but men of the first merit in their profession found encouragement from him: and these abundantly. Jones was his architect, and Vandyck his painter. Charles was a scholar, a man of taste, a gentleman and a Christian; he was everything but a king. The art of reigning was the only art of which he was ignorant.'

And this eventually was his undoing and led to the dispersal, as we learn from Dr Waagen, of what was probably the finest collection ever assembled in England. But though this tragedy was great it was not finite or everlasting: Charles II recovered some elements of the collection, and many others that had gone to Europe were incorporated into the French royal collections. And a substantial portion of these, as we shall see later,[1] came back to these shores in 1798 with the Orleans Collection.

EXTRACTED FROM Dr Gustav Waagen's *Treasures of Art in Great Britain*, Vol. I, 1854.

THE taste for collecting works of art in England originated with the court. King Henry VIII, a friend of the fine arts, and a great patron of Holbein, was the first who formed

scarce'. It is not only scarce, but also very expensive today.

[1] See page 134.

a collection of pictures. It was, however, of moderate extent, since, including miniatures, it contained no more than 150 works.[1] The glory of first forming a gallery of paintings on a large scale belongs to King Charles I, who lived a century later. As this prince united an extraordinary love for works of art with the most refined taste, and spared neither pains nor expense, he succeeded in forming a collection of paintings, which was not only the richest of that age in masterpieces of the time of Raphael, but is perhaps scarcely to be equalled even in our days.

The king began to collect before he ascended the throne. After the death of his elder brother, Prince Henry, who was likewise a lover of the arts, the gallery was increased by the addition of his cabinet. But the chief portion consisted of the collection of the Dukes of Mantua, purchased through the Duke of Buckingham, most probably of Duke Charles I, in the year 1629.* He is said to have paid £80,000 for it–a very large sum in those days. That collection was, however, one of the first in Italy; the family of Gonzaga at Mantua, who reigned till 1627, having been 150 years in forming it; and this family was second only in patronage of the arts to that of the Medici. In the fifteenth century they attracted the great Andrea Mantegna to their court, and in the sixteenth Raphael's greatest scholar, Giulio Romano. In this collection there were then, besides several other pictures by the first-named master, his celebrated Triumphal Procession of Julius Caesar, and by Giulio Romano a number of capital easel-pictures. Raphael probably painted for the Gonzagas the famous Holy Family, now known in the Escurial by the name of the Pearl; Correggio painted his Education of Cupid, now in the English National Gallery, and two allegorical pictures; Titian, among many others, the celebrated Entombment, now in the Louvre, and the twelve first Caesars. All these and admirable works by other masters were purchased for England.

The king obtained also, through the intervention of Rubens, the seven celebrated cartoons by Raphael. Three-and-twenty fine pictures of the Italian school were purchased of one Frosley. Lastly, foreign sovereigns and his own subjects vied with each other in adding to the collection by most valuable presents. On his visit to Madrid when Prince of Wales, King Philip IV of Spain gave him the famous picture by Titian, called after the palace where it had so long been kept, the Venus del Pardo. The subject is properly Jupiter and Antiope, in one of the grandest and finest landscapes by Titian with which we are acquainted. It is now in the Louvre. Louis XIII King of France presented him by his ambassador, M. de Lyancourt, with a St John the Baptist, a highly-finished picture, by Leonardo da Vinci, now likewise an ornament of the Louvre. Among the many Englishmen

[1] See *Anecdotes of Painting in England* collected by George Vertue, digested and published from his original MSS by Horace Walpole, edited with considerable additions by the Rev. James Dallaway, 1826, Vol. I, p. 337 for a partial inventory of Henry VIII's 157 paintings. Much fuller details are given in *Three Inventories of Pictures in the Collection of Henry VIII and Edward VI* edited by W. A. Shaw, London, 1937. An excellent account of collecting under the Tudors is given in Francis Henry Taylor's *The Taste of Angels*, London, 1948.

* *This date appears to be determined beyond question by a picture by Domenico Feti in the Belvedere Gallery at Vienna, on the back of which, besides the usual C.R. and the crown, which distinguished the pictures of the collection of Charles I, there is a ticket with the words* 'From Mantua, 1629, No. 159'.

who presented the king with pictures, those who above all distinguished themselves were Thomas Howard, Earl of Arundel, the Lord Marshal; the Earl of Pembroke, Lord High Chamberlain; the Earl of Suffolk; Lord Hamilton and Lord Abbot Montague.

Though the king preferred the great Italian masters, he duly appreciated the principal painters of the German and Flemish schools. Of the earlier masters of the fifteenth and sixteenth centuries he possessed works by Gerhard van Harlem, Holbein, Albert Dürer, George Pens, Lucas Cranach, Lucas Van Leyden, and Antonio More. He endeavoured to induce Rubens, the greatest painter of his time, to settle in England; and failing in this, he loaded him with marks of favour, and not only engaged him to paint the ceiling of the banqueting-room in the palace of Whitehall, built by Inigo Jones, but also purchased some of his best easel-pictures. On the other hand, he was so fortunate as to attach entirely to his service the most distinguished of the scholars of Rubens, [namely] Vandyck; and the number of masterly pictures which this painter executed for him, from the year 1632 to his death in 1642, was very considerable.

The above particulars will alone give you[1] a very favourable idea of the collection of King Charles I. A comparison of three existing catalogues, however, will bring the treasures of this collection more fully and also more particularly before you. One of them is an extract from a catalogue of all the pictures and works of sculpture which the king possessed, with a statement of their estimated value, and the price for which they were sold by auction after the lamentable execution of the king.

It appears that the number of pictures in all the royal palaces was 1387, and that of the works of sculpture, 399. Of all these, only 88 pictures are particularly mentioned as capital works, and the estimated value and sale-price added. The second document is a catalogue drawn up about the year 1679, by Vanderdoort, keeper of the royal collections, which comprehends 77 smaller pictures in St James's Palace, and all the works of art in the palace of Whitehall, which was the principal gallery. The number of pictures there, including the miniatures, was 497, and of works of sculpture, 79. But of the 574 pictures inserted in this catalogue, there are only 38 of the 88 specially enumerated in the above mentioned extract. Now, as besides these 38 pictures, there are among the 574 enumerated by Vanderdoort 216 by eminent masters, among which are works of the highest class, such as the Education of Cupid by Correggio, Christ with the Disciples at Emmaus by Titian, we may infer with great probability that, besides the other 50 pictures out of the 88, which came from the king's other palaces, Somerset House, Hampton Court, and the greater part from St James's, there was in them, as well as in Whitehall, a considerable number of other valuable pictures. This inference is partly confirmed by the third document, a catalogue of the collection of King James II. We find in it, in the first place, two paintings marked as by Raphael, two by Giorgione, two by Parmegiano, and one by Titian, of which it is expressly stated that they were part of the collection of Charles I, but which are not included in the selection of 88 pictures, nor in Vanderdoort's catalogue.

With the addition of those seven, we still have only 629 out of the 1387 which Charles I

[1] The 'you' referred to is Dr Waagen's wife. The passage quoted was originally in the form of a letter to her about art in England generally.

possessed. But there is in the catalogue of King James II's collection a considerable number of other pictures under the names of Leonardo da Vinci, Raphael, Giulio Romano, Giorgione, Titian, the two Palmas, Paul Veronese, Tintoretto, Bassano, Parmegianino, Dosso Dossi, Holbein, Rubens, and Vandyck, which are not named either among those 88, or in Vanderdoort's catalogue, most of which I am convinced, were part of the 758 pictures in King Charles I's collection, respecting which we have no information.

But if we look only to what, according to these three catalogues, certainly belonged to the collection, we are astonished at the number of works by the greatest masters which it contained. Of the Florentine school there were, by Leonardo da Vinci, one; by Andrea del Sarto, three: of the Roman school, by Raphael, thirteen; by Giulio Romano, twenty-seven; by Perino del Vaga, one; by Garofalo, one: of the Lombard school, by Luini one; by Correggio, nine; by Parmegianino, eleven: of the Venetian school, by Giorgione, five; by Titian, forty-five; by Pordenone, four; by Sebastian del Piombo, one; by Palma Vecchio, five; by Paul Veronese, four: of the Bolognese school, by Annibale Carracci, two; by Guido Reni, four: of the German school, by Albert Dürer, three; by Hans Holbein, eleven; by George Pens, two; by Aldegrever, one: of the Flemish school, by Lucas Van Leyden, seven; by Mabuse, two; by Rubens, six; by Vandyck, eighteen. Now, though it may be assumed that the genuineness of many of these pictures was doubtful, or that many were not remarkable; yet by far the greater number were of the highest class. . . .

Among so many works, the king had selected the finest of all to be placed where he could daily enjoy the pleasure of contemplating them; for the forty-six pictures which adorned the three rooms in which he lived at Whitehall, were, with the exception of one by Michael Cocxie, only by Raphael, Correggio, Titian, Giulio Romano, Polidoro da Caravaggio, Andrea del Sarto, Giorgione, Luini and Parmegianino. In his private gallery adjoining he had a collection of portraits of different princely houses of Europe, particularly of the kings of England, and of his own family.

In Vanderdoort's catalogue, seventy-nine works of sculpture are noted, among which are but few of any importance. Most of them are busts, or small copies of modern works—for instance, by Fiamingo, Bernini, &c. The chief collections of sculpture were in the royal palaces of Greenwich and Somerset House. In the former there were 230 specimens, in the latter 120. Little information respecting them has come down to us; but as the king caused Sir Kenelm Digby, then Admiral in the Levant, to make purchases for him there, and as the sculptures were valued at £17,989, and some articles were sold for £200 and £300, we may conclude that there must have been works of value among them. The King was particularly fond of medals. Vanderdoort enumerates 443, which, however, with the exception of some Greek, and the Imperial Roman medals, are of the sixteenth and seventeenth centuries. Lastly, he had a collection of drawings by great masters, some of which Vanderdoort has likewise specified, for instance, a drawing-book of Michael Angelo Buonaroti.

In this general and refined love of the arts the king had a worthy counterpart in the Earl of Arundel, already mentioned; nay, it was he who first inspired the king with the taste. He, too, collected, with the most universal and discriminating feeling, and with princely magnificence, paintings, drawings, engraved gems, but, above all, antique sculpture and inscriptions. During his long travels on the Continent, he himself made many purchases; and afterwards employed persons, well versed in such matters, in different parts of Europe. Thus Edward Norgate, a painter, and John Elwyn, a man of learning, were very fortunate in the purchases they made in Italy. William Petty collected a number of sculptures for him in Paros and Delos, all of which were unhappily lost by shipwreck: the Earl, however, obtained, especially from Asia Minor, a number of highly important inscriptions, and numerous pieces of sculpture. This endeavour to draw from the original source, which occurred to no-one else, proves the high cultivation of mind in this great connoisseur. The collection in his house and garden in London, and in his garden at Lambeth, contained thirty-seven statues, one hundred and twenty-eight busts, two hundred and fifty marbles with inscriptions, besides sarcophagi, altars, fragments, and valuable engraved gems. The earl had a special predilection for the works of Holbein, and had succeeded in collecting an astonishing number of paintings and drawings by that master. He had also succeeded in obtaining admirable drawings by Albert Dürer, by the purchase of a part of the celebrated Imhoff collection at Nuremberg.

The Duke of Buckingham, the unworthy favourite of Kings James I and Charles I, holds the third place as a collector of works of art in England at that time. Sir Thomas Roe, ambassador to the Porte, collected works of sculpture for him. He bought of Rubens his fine collection of paintings, and other works of art for £10,000. Sir Henry Wotton, the English ambassador at Venice, made important purchases for him in that city in his various travels, while the duke himself added to his gallery. All these treasures were placed in York House in the Strand. The following details will enable you to form some general notion of the value of this collection.

After the assassination of the Duke in 1628, his property was sequestrated; and on that occasion a great part of the works of art were dispersed. Some pictures, and certainly not the worst, were purchased by the king, the Duke of Northumberland, and Lord Montague. Yet, among the remainder, according to a catalogue that still exists, there were three pictures by Leonardo da Vinci, one by Andrea del Sarto, three by Raphael, one by Giulio Romano, two by Correggio, two by Giorgione, nineteen by Titian, two by Pordenone, two by Palma Vecchio, thirteen by Paul Veronese, seventeen by Tintoretto, twenty-one by the Bassanos, six by Palma Giovane, two by Annibale Carracci, three by Guido Reni, nine by Dominico Fetti, eight by Holbein, six by Antonio More, thirteen by Rubens; besides several by other masters. Many of these pictures undoubtedly were not genuine, others of little worth; but there were many capital pictures among them, for instance, the celebrated Ecce Homo, by Titian, with nineteen figures as large as life, for which the Earl of Arundel in vain offered the duke £7000 either in money or land, a very large sum for those days: there were also the finest hunting pieces and landscapes by Rubens. We have no particulars respecting the collection of sculpture; that of engraved gems seems to have been of considerable value.

The example set by the king and the first men in the kingdom, amongst the nobility and other wealthy individuals, could not fail to find imitators; so that the English were then in a fair way of acquiring an elevated and pure taste in the fine arts, by the more general diffusion of works of the finest periods. The political events, however, which led to the death of Charles I and the Protectorship of Cromwell, put an end for a considerable time to this fair prospect. For in July 1650, it was resolved by the Parliament to sell by public auction all the pictures and statues, valued at £49,903 2s 6d, with the rest of the king's private property. The sale took place in that year and in the year 1653, and attracted vast numbers of agents from foreign princes, and amateurs from all parts of Europe.

The principal purchasers were, 1. The Spanish ambassador, Don Alonzo de Cardenas. He purchased so many paintings and other valuable articles, that eighteen mules were required to convey them from Corunna to Madrid. Among the pictures was the large Holy Family, by Raphael, from the Mantua collection. Philip IV is said to have exclaimed on seeing it, 'That is my pearl!' hence the name by which this picture has since been known to lovers of the arts.

2. M. Jabach, the banker, a native of Cologne settled at Paris, who afterwards sold his valuable collection to Louis XIV, purchased many of the most capital pictures, among which were, by Correggio, Jupiter and Antiope, and two allegorical designs; by Titian, the Entombment, and Christ with the Disciples at Emmaus, all of which are now among the chief ornaments of the Louvre. Those allegorical designs are also in the rich and excellent collection of cartoons and drawings in the Louvre, which has been unhappily withdrawn from the eye of the public for several years past.

3. The Archduke Leopold William, at that time Governor of the Austrian Netherlands. He expended a large sum in the purchase of some excellent pictures, particularly of the Venetian school. On his accession to the Imperial throne in 1658, these, with his whole rich collection, were transferred to Vienna, and are now in the Imperial gallery in the Belvedere palace.

4. Mr Reynst, an eminent Dutch connoisseur of those days. He purchased several fine pictures, which he had engraved in the work on his collection.

5. Christina, Queen of Sweden. She purchased chiefly the most valuable jewels and medals, and likewise some pictures at high prices.

6. Cardinal Mazarin. He bought especially works of sculpture, and rich embroidery, tapestry, and carpets, to adorn his palace at Paris.

Lastly, Sir Balthasar Gerbier, and the painters De Critz, Wright, Baptist, Leemput, were eager purchasers. The sum paid for the whole was £118,080 10s 2d. Thus the greater part of the noble works of art which King Charles I had collected were scattered over all Europe. The celebrated seven Cartoons by Raphael were purchased by Cromwell's order for the nation, for £300. Many other purchases were made by Englishmen, and thus at least retained in the country. . . .

The collections of the Earl of Arundel and the Duke of Buckingham also experienced a similar lamentable fate. That of the last-mentioned nobleman was removed by his son to Antwerp during his banishment, and there sold by auction, to obtain means of subsistence. There, too, the Archduke Leopold William was a liberal purchaser, and obtained the fine picture by Titian, the Ecce Homo, which is now in the Belvedere gallery.

When the Earl of Arundel left England, in 1642, it is said that he took his collection with him; but this is probably to be understood only of his cabinet pictures and engraved gems. Most of his pictures by Holbein, of which the engravings by Hollar give us an idea, were lost. The greater portion of Albert Dürer's drawings were destroyed by the populace in the civil wars, or perished in the great fire of London. Only a series of eighty-seven portraits by Holbein, which the Lord Chamberlain the Earl of Pembroke had exchanged with King Charles I for a picture by Raphael, representing St George, which he afterwards gave to the Earl of Arundel, are at present in the Royal collection of drawings. They are known to the public by Bartolozzi's engravings in Chamberlaine's work. His eldest son, the Duke of Norfolk, presented the marbles with inscriptions to the University of Oxford, where they have become celebrated throughout the learned world, under the name of 'Marmora Oxoniensia'. Of the statues in Arundel House, which were confiscated during Cromwell's usurpation, several were purchased by the Spanish Ambassador, Don Alonzo de Cardenas. What remained were sold in 1678, when streets were built on the site of Arundel House and gardens; and the most important articles in the house were purchased by the Earl of Pembroke for his collection in his country seat at Wilton, where they still are. Those in the garden were bought by Lord Lemster, father of the first Earl of Pomfret, for his country seat, Easton-Neston. But in 1755 these also were presented to the University of Oxford by the Countess of Pomfret.

The joyless spirit of the Puritans, hostile to all art and poetry, which prevailed in England, was not favourable to the collecting of works of art, and if the succeeding kings, Charles II and James II, took some pleasure in such works they did not possess their father's refined taste. The endeavours of the first, however, to recover the dispersed pictures of the collection of Charles I merits the most honourable commendation. Nor were those endeavours by any means fruitless. After the death of the above-mentioned Mr Reynst, the States-General purchased all the pictures which he had bought from the collection of Charles I, and presented them to Charles II. This monarch also gathered together so many others, that of those mentioned in the select eighty-eight, and in Vanderdoort's catalogue, seventy may be certainly pointed out, among which the nine pictures of the Triumph of Caesar, by Mantegna, are the most important. . . .

Charles II again increased the Royal collection to above 1100 pictures, and above 100 works of sculpture. Among the latter were many articles of the Cinquecento style. What James II added was not considerable either in number or value. Among the pictures, which amounted to little more than 100, the most important are two by Vandyck, two by Wouvermans, five sea pieces by William Van de Velde, and seven pictures by Schiavone.

These treasures were distributed among the palaces of St James, Hampton Court, Windsor, and Whitehall. The latter was still the principal gallery, and contained no less than 738 pictures, many of which were by the most eminent masters. The Royal collection, therefore, suffered a new and irreparable loss by the destruction of the palace of Whitehall by fire in 1697. Of the three by Leonardo da Vinci, three by Raphael, twelve by Giulio Romano, eighteen by Giorgione, eighteen by Titian, six by Palma Vecchio, six by

Correggio, seven by Parmegianino, twenty-seven by Holbein, four by Rubens, thirteen by Vandyck, fourteen by William Van de Velde, which were in that palace, and of which a very considerable part were evidently genuine, the greater portion were destroyed on that occasion.

Among the private collections in the time of King Charles II the most important was probably that of Sir Peter Lely, who at that time filled the same place as portrait painter which Vandyck had occupied under Charles I. Among the 167 pictures which it contained there were two by Titian, eight by Paul Veronese, five by Rubens, and three by Claude. The principal pictures in the collection, however, were those of Vandyck. Of the twenty-six by him, twenty-three were portraits, chiefly of great excellence. There was also a series of thirty-seven portraits of eminent persons, painted on a small scale in brown chiaroscuro, for the use of the engravers. Twelve of them are in the Munich gallery; most of the others in the possession of the Duke of Buccleuch, at Montague House, in London. Lely's collection was also rich in drawings by the great masters, especially by Raphael, Polidoro, and Michael Angelo, and also in engravings. After his death the whole were sold by auction in 1680.

THE FIRST COLLECTORS

Dr Waagen's rather statistical account of Charles I, Arundel and Buckingham as collectors was first published in England in a slightly briefer and less accurate form in 1838 (it is quoted here from the revised edition of 1854). It had certainly been read by Mrs Anna Jameson, who began to get into her stride as a popular author on the arts–with a particular interest in collecting–in 1842 when her *Handbook to the Public Galleries of Art in and near London* was published. It was followed by her *Companion to the Most Celebrated Private Galleries of Art in London* in 1844. We know that her respect for Dr Waagen was high, but quite clearly she felt that the first stirrings of interest in the collecting of pictures and sculpture in England could be recounted in a warmer and more romantic manner. As her influence on the educated readers of her time was substantial, her account of Arundel, Buckingham, Charles I and Lely is quoted here.

THE FIRST COLLECTORS

EXTRACTED FROM Mrs Anna Jameson's *Companion to the Most Celebrated Private Galleries of Art in London*, 1844.

FOREIGNERS and critics love to flout at English taste; it is therefore a curious fact, and one we have reason to be proud of, that the earliest instance on record of any private individual indulging a taste for art, was our own Lord Arundel. I believe he was the first collector, of private rank, in civilised Europe. It was not till the end of the fifteenth century that painting, from being wholly ecclesiastical, began to be devoted to civil and social purposes–that portraiture came into fashion, and that compositions from the classical poets, and small decorative and devotional pictures, began to be painted. Even these, up to the end of the sixteenth century, were very rare; and most of the panel paintings of this time which remain to us have been cut from the doors of cabinets and presses, the friezes of bedsteads, the tops of harpsichords, and other pieces of furniture. Pictures must have multiplied, and become articles of trade, as well as common for mere decorative purposes, before the idea of collecting those most remarkable could have suggested itself. The Venetians and the Flemings first made pictures articles of commerce. As early as the fifteenth century a few Flemish pictures were imported into Italy, and bought as curiosities; and in the middle of the succeeding century we find the Bassano family carrying on a sort of manufactory of small pictures, recommended by their splendid colours, and various, though low and common-place treatment. These were dispersed through Italy, and sold at fairs as articles of commerce, much like the Dutch and Flemish pictures of the same and succeeding periods. More than a century later, we hear of the Feria–the *markets* for pictures, at Cadiz and Seville, where the young Murillo sold his wares.

I find no mention of collectors of pictures, and founders of picture galleries, before the middle of the sixteenth century, and then they were all princes of the sovereign houses of Italy–the Medici, the Gonzaga, the Este, and the Farnese families. It is true that there had previously existed collections of works of art, if not of pictures: witness Isabella D'Este, and her cabinet of gems and antiques at Mantua, open to the learned and to artists, before the time of the Medici, and before Lorenzo's famous Accademia; but *she* was a sovereign princess. I can find no example of any *private* individual indulging this costly, magnificent taste, previous to that of the Earl of Arundel. He appears to have been, not only the first Englishman, but the first subject in Europe, who, out of his own private fortune, and inspired by a genuine feeling of their beauty and value, collected round him ancient and modern works of art, as statues, busts, ancient inscribed marbles, gems, drawings, pictures, chased work in gold and silver, everything, in short, which the Italians class under the general name of *virtu*. Lord Arundel was, in fact, the first *virtuoso* not only of his own country but his own time. I never look at his portrait by Van Dyck, in the Sutherland Gallery, with its thoughtful, melancholy, refined expression of countenance, without a deep interest; and those works of art which he obtained have, through association with his name and fate, a value, to my fancy, beyond their own.

The Laughing Boy, by Leonardo da Vinci, now, I believe, in the possession of Mr Beckford; Raphael's Little St George, now at Petersburg; the Pomfret marbles, at Oxford;

the antique statues and busts, at Wilton; the Marlborough gems, famed throughout the world–formed only a part of the Arundel collection. The Duke of Buckingham followed Lord Arundel–but it is almost an injustice to name them together! What was taste and enthusiasm in Arundel, was sheer vanity and ostentation in Buckingham. What a proof we have of the spirit which actuated Buckingham, in one anecdote of him! Arundel had employed William Petty, uncle to that Sir William Petty, who was the ancestor of the present Marquess of Lansdowne, to collect antiques for him in Greece and Syria. Buckingham, then all-powerful, gave a similar commission to Sir Thomas Roe, English ambassador at Constantinople, and instructed him, at the same time, to throw every possible obstacle in the way of Petty! Dallaway relates the anecdote.* He does not quote his authority, but one can believe anything of Buckingham – at once so haughty and so servile – so magnificent and so mean! At Paris and at the court of Madrid he had made the acquaintance of Rubens, and persuaded the painter to cede to him the collection of pictures, gems, antiques, &c., formed by himself when in Italy, and since his return. Rubens sold the whole to him for £10,000, reluctantly, as it appears, for he did not want the money;[1] and as for Buckingham, he scarcely lived to call himself possessor of the treasures he had coveted.[2] Assassinated a few months after (in 1628), many of his pictures were dispersed. King Charles, Lord Arundel, and Lord Montague, purchased several from the family; others descended to his young son, the Duke of Buckingham. The old catalogue of this collection, published by Bathoe, is now lying before me; it contained 220 pictures; among them, three by Raphael, three by L. da Vinci, nineteen by Titian, seventeen by Tintoretto, and thirteen by Rubens himself.

It is clear that, previous to 1643, the works of art accumulated in England were of the highest value and importance. The gallery of Charles I was unequalled by that of any crowned head.† No subject in Europe possessed such treasures as had been collected by Arundel and Buckingham. But then came the deadly struggle between Charles and his Parliament: all these precious objects were lost, dispersed, and went to enrich and adorn foreign capitals. Charles' collection was confiscated, and sold. Of Lord Arundel's, a portion was sold in Holland, for his subsistence; the rest scattered among different members of his family: and as for the rich collection of the Duke of Buckingham, part was sold in the Netherlands, for the maintenance of the young duke, some pictures were pawned to Sir Peter Lely, the rest were confiscated by Parliament.

The next private collection of which we hear anything, was that of Sir Peter Lely. He had purchased a number of pictures, drawings, &c., from the widow of Van Dyck. On the sale of King Charles' collection, and the dispersion of the Duke of Buckingham's, he obtained others. His collection might be termed magnificent, for a private individual; it

* *Anecdotes of the Arts in England.*

[1] In fact, it is now thought that he did.

[2] An interesting account of Buckingham, 'Portraits of a Great Connoisseur' by Charles Richard Cammell, appeared in *The Connoisseur* in September 1936, page 127 (Vol. 98, No. 421). Clarendon wrote about Buckingham: 'His ascent was so quick, that it seemed rather a flight than a growth; and he was such a darling of fortune that he was at the top before he was seen at the bottom.'

† *For a particular account of the Royal collections in England from Charles I to the present time, see the 'Companion to the Public Galleries'.*

contained 167 pictures, 26 by Van Dyck, and many by Titian and Rubens. The original drawings possessed by Lely were also particularly valuable. Many of those I have seen in Lawrence's collection bore Lely's mark on them, and must have been part of the plunder of the cabinets of Charles I and Arundel. There is a passage in Roger North's Life of Lord Guildford, which, for its quaint and forcible expression, dwells in the memory. He was an intimate friend of Lely; and after telling us that he had a whole magazine of original sketches of the best masters, he adds, 'and drawings, likewise, of divers finishings, *which had been the heart of great designs and models*'. If Roger North had been a dilettante of the first water, he could not have expressed better the peculiar value and sentiment and significance of a genuine drawing.

COLLECTING AS A FASHION · MRS JAMESON SURVEYS THE EIGHTEENTH CENTURY

Mrs Jameson was one of the first writers to be openly critical of the English preference for the later Italian schools of painting. One of the painters she couldn't stomach, for example, was Albano.

In her biographical note on this artist she writes: 'A painter who without one element of strength or greatness, one touch of true or earnest feeling, painted agreeable pictures, in which the slender graceful figures, have all a pretty pastoral air: the landscapes are pleasing, airy, and arcadian; the colouring tender and brilliant. His faults are a total want of mind and variety in conception, and the most wearying insipidity and uniformity in form and expression. . . . I know not any painter of celebrity with whom one becomes so quickly and so easily satiated as with Albano.'

She also resented the slapdash nature of most of the catalogues that came her way. Self-taught, she was a natural scholar; unusually scholarly, in fact, for a popular writer on the arts. She did not achieve this lightly and describes her difficulties with some feeling.

'I have at least endeavoured to be accurate. I say, *endeavoured*, for as to achieving complete accuracy, those alone can tell who have tried how difficult is the mere attempt; those alone can tell who have tried what it is to hunt a fact, mis-stated, through a dozen volumes – to trace a name mis-spelt – to ascertain a date – to decide between opposing authorities – to compare disputed points – or, hardest task of all! to knock down a charming theory or a pretty story with a dry row of figures – to take from some favourite picture its pretension to authenticity, and stick a doubt or a lie on the face of it . . . we must take it for granted that in many cases, a Titian, a Paul Veronese, etc. means simply a Venetian picture of the style and time of Titian or Veronese. I firmly believe, for instance, that half the pictures which bear Titian's name, were painted by Bonifazio, or Girolamo de Tiziano, or Paris Bordone, or some other of the *Capi* of the Venetian school, which produced such a swarm of painters in the sixteenth century.'

EXTRACTED FROM Mrs Anna Jameson's *Companion to the Most Celebrated Private Galleries of Art in London*, 1844.

WHAT had been taste in Arundel, magnificence in Buckingham, science in Lely, became in the next century a *fashion*, subject to the freaks of vanity, the errors and absurdities of ignorance, the impositions of pretension and coxcombry. The great Duke of Marlborough filled Blenheim with pictures – the fruit of his campaigns – the gifts of cities and princes – and the Blenheim collection remains to this day one of the finest in England. Sir Robert Walpole, the minister, formed a large collection at Houghton; after his death, purchased by the Empress Catherine for £30,000, and now at St Petersburg. Luckily, some of the finest Van Dycks – those of the Wharton family – had been sold previously to the Duke of Devonshire; they used, within my memory, to adorn Devonshire House; but are now among the glories of that glorious palace, Chatsworth, where they are empanelled in the dining-room. Richardson, the painter, whose admirable book on his own art met in his time with more scoffers than readers, left a collection of drawings and pictures, sold in 1747.*

In 1758, was sold by auction, a collection formed by Sir Luke Schaub, a merchant and banker, the Angerstein of his time. It produced £8000. Among his pictures was the Sigismunda of the Duke of Newcastle. The price given for it (400 gs., a large sum in those days) provoked Hogarth to wrath and envy, and a vain competition which covered him with ridicule. Others of Sir Luke Schaub's pictures were, the Christ healing the Lame Man, now in the Queen's Gallery[1]; 'The Tent of Darius', in the Grosvenor Gallery[2]; and Van Dyck's small study for the portrait of Venetia Digby.† Another great collector in the beginning of the last century was Sir Andrew Fountaine, of Narford, whose descendant, the present Mr Fountaine, has inherited the elegant tastes of his ancestor.[3]

Dr Mead, the physician, had at this time a very good collection, dispersed on his death

* *The drawings,* 4749 *in number, sold for* £1966. *The pictures for about* £700.

[1] By van Dyck. [2] By Le Brun.

† *It was lately in the possession of Sir Eliab Hervey. The large picture is at Windsor, No.* 6.

[3] Sold after his death in 1873 by Christie's.

in 1754. General Guise bequeathed his pictures 220 in number, to Christ Church College, Oxford, in 1765. A Mr John Barnard, of Berkeley Square, possessed at this time sixty-six pictures. A certain Mr Jennens, then of Ormond Street, could boast of the possession of 358 pictures. Mr Bouchier Cleeve, of Foot's Cray, in Kent, possessed seventy-seven pictures: among them the two large pictures of Salvator Rosa, now in the Grosvenor Gallery; the Pordenone, in the Sutherland Gallery; the Jan Steen and the Van Dyck, in the Queen's Gallery; and eight sea pieces of Van der Velde. In the collection of Sir Gregory Page were two fine pictures by Rubens, now in the Grosvenor Gallery, and twelve pictures of the History of Cupid and Psyche, now at Hampton Court, also, I believe, the two great Landscapes by Francesco Mille, now in the Bridgewater Gallery. This Sir Gregory Page was a personal friend and great admirer of Adrian Van der Werff, and had twelve of his best pictures:[1] eight were purchased for the Louvre, at the price of 33,000 fs; one is now in her Majesty's Gallery.*

All these collections were formed previous to 1765, about which time the first Earl Grosvenor laid the foundation of the magnificent Grosvenor Gallery. The collections of the Duke of Devonshire, at Devonshire House, of Lord Methuen,† of Agar Ellis,‡ the first Marquess of Lansdowne,§ and Lady Holderness,‖ were formed between 1760 and 1790. Mr Hope, of Amsterdam, brought over his fine gallery of Dutch pictures from Amsterdam to England about 1790.

This enumeration goes to prove that the purchase of pictures had by this time become a *fashion*. But was it anything more? In looking over the catalogues it is impossible not to feel, that with no want of money or zeal, there was a want of elevated taste, as well as a want of knowledge. 'A Landscape', Claude; 'a Holy Family', Raphael; a 'sea-piece,' Van der Velde; 'an Old Man's Head', Rembrandt; 'a Riposo', Ludovico Carracci *or* Carlo Cignani!! 'Hector and Achilles', Nicholas Poussin *or* Peter Festa!! 'A Landscape, with a Magdalen in it', Albani *or* Breemberg!! 'Conversation, with dancing', Annibal Carracci; and so on, page after page. What reliance can be placed on such an absurd nomenclature? In those days, when a great or rich man built a house, 'some demon whispered Visto!, have a taste!' and forthwith he gave an order to the connoisseur of the day, some Mr Dalton, or Mr Smith, to buy him pictures and antiques, in the same spirit, we may presume, as Prince Korkasoff's order to his bookseller: 'Buy me a library: large books at bottom–small books at top!'

In the midst of all this quackery and ignorance, there was still something *truly* respectable in the wish to possess books and pictures as an appendage to rank, instead of horses, diamonds, ribbons, and uniforms. The wish to possess is followed by delight in the possession. What we delight in, we love; and love becomes in time a discriminating and refined appreciation. *In time*–but it must be allowed that the progress to such refinement

[1] Mrs Jameson had extracted many of these details from Thomas Martyn's *The English Connoisseur*, see page 99.

* *No.* 162. *The pictures of Sir Gregory Page Turner were sold at Blackheath in* 1816.

† *Now at Corsham.*

‡ *Merged in the Grosvenor collection.*

§ *Sold and dispersed.*

‖ *Sold in* 1802. *She was by birth a Dutchwoman, and possessed, by purchase or inheritance, many exquisite pictures of the Dutch School.*

was, and *is*, in this cold, working-day country of ours, wondrous slow. Let us turn again to the old catalogues. It is clear, that in the middle of the last century the elder Italian masters were considered gothic and barbarous. Every Venetian portrait was 'a Titian', and every hard-looking German head 'a Holbein'. The Bassani were popular; but the Carracci and their school–Domenichino, Guido, Guercino, Albano–seem to have been most sought after, and their names almost as ridiculously misapplied as those of Raphael and Correggio. The feeble and superficial masters of the later degenerate schools of Italy abound–Carlo Dolce, Carlo Maratti, Pietro da Cortona, Giordano, Lucatelli, and such *gentaccia*.

Yet such, it should seem, was the fashion everywhere. Not in France, nor even in Italy, where the productions of a better age, of the highest style of art, were at hand for comparison and reference, did a better feeling exist. And we must needs allow, that for Claude, for Nicolo and Gaspar Poussin, for Salvator Rosa, there has existed in England a real taste,[1] for it was not merely a fashion. The predilection for Claude–dating from early in the last century, when Frederic Prince of Wales bought them wherever they were to be met with–has been such, that, I believe, all the best pictures and drawings of that prince of landscape painters are, with few exceptions, now in this country. Of the Flemish school, Rubens, and above all, Van Dyck, from his long residence in England, were most frequently met with; yet Sir Joshua Reynolds tells us, that in the early part of the last century, the man who should have placed Van Dyck above Kneller would have been scoffed at; and we all know the story of the gentleman who employed a painter to wig his Van Dycks.

[1] The strong predilection for Claude and Poussin among English collectors is a recurrent theme among writers on collecting. Mrs Jameson herself said of a Claude in the National Gallery: 'the predilection of the English for this charming painter, perhaps because the sunny, classical, and ideal beauty of his scenery presents so strong a contrast to that of their own land, and the high prices given in England for his pictures, are the cause that most of his works have found their way to this country. Very few of his more valuable productions are now to be met with on the Continent. The National Gallery contains nine landscapes by his hand.' Ruskin, too, had much to say on the subject. For a fascinating and scholarly appraisal of the English interest in landscape painting, see John Hayes' three articles on the subject in *Apollo* for June 1965, March and June 1966.

DR WAAGEN AGAIN

EXTRACTED FROM Dr Gustav Waagen's *Treasures of Art in Great Britain*, Vol. I, 1854.

WHEN the taste for collecting pictures revived after the commencement of the eighteenth century, it was not encouraged either by the Crown or by Parliament, but solely by private individuals, who, at the same time introduced the custom of placing their collections for the most part at their country seats. The following families have been more or less distinguished by their love of art: The Dukes of Marlborough, Bedford, Devonshire, and Hamilton; the Marquises of Lansdowne and Bute; the Earls of Pembroke, Exeter, Leicester, Warwick, Spencer, Burlington, Radnor, Egremont; Sir Robert Walpole, Mr Paul Methuen, and Mr Welbore Agar Ellis; the three latter more particularly deserve mention.

These collections which were formed by the end of the eighteenth century, are, however, of a very different character from those of the time of Charles I. They betray a far less pure and elevated taste, and in many parts show a less profound knowledge of art. We, indeed, often find the names of Raphael, Correggio, and Andrea del Sarto, but very seldom their works. The Venetian school is better represented, so that there are often fine pictures by Titian, Paul Veronese, Tintoretto, and the Bassanos. Still more frequent are the pictures of the Carracci and their school, of Domenichino, Guido, Guercino, Albano;[1] but there are among them but few works of the first rank.

Unhappily the masters of the period of the decline of art in Italy are particularly numerous; for instance, Castiglione, Pietro Francesco Mola, Filippo Lauri, Carlo Cignani, Andrea Sacchi, Pietro da Cortona, Carlo Maratti, Luca Giordano. At this time also a particular predilection for the works of certain masters appear. Among these are, of the Italian school, Carlo Dolce, Sasso Ferrato, Salvator Rosa, Claude Lorraine, and Gaspar Poussin, pictures by the two latter being frequently the brightest gems of these galleries. Of the French school, Nicholas Poussin and Bourguignon are esteemed beyond all others. Of the Flemish school, Rubens and Vandyck, and, though not in an equal degree, Rembrandt. Of all these favourite masters we see the most admirable specimens. Here and there are found fine sea-pieces by William Van de Velde, choice landscapes by Ruysdael and Hobbema, and pretty pictures by Teniers. On the other hand, we seldom meet with a genuine Holbein, still more rarely with a Jan Van Eyck, or with any other masters of the

[1] Clearly Mrs Jameson had read Dr Waagen very carefully! *She* lists these four painters in exactly the same sequence. This does not mean that she went in for the literary larceny so common in the domain of the chronicling of collecting. In fact, Mrs Jameson says in a letter after she had completed her *Companion to the Most Celebrated Private Galleries of Art in London*: 'It is the sort of thing which should have fallen into the hands of Dr Waagen, or some such bigwig, instead of poor little me!'

old Flemish and German schools. As the only collection which forms an honourable exception, and was made in the elevated taste of Charles I, I must here mention that of the Earl of Cowper at his country seat, Panshanger, in Hertfordshire. This collection, which was formed towards the close of the century, contains chiefly pictures by Raphael, Andrea del Sarto, and Fra Bartolommeo.

The amateurs of the eighteenth century were likewise very ardent in collecting drawings. Among the numerous cabinets thus obtained the most distinguished were those of the Dukes of Devonshire, the Earls of Pembroke, and of George III, which still exist; and those of the two Richardsons and Sir Joshua Reynolds, which have been broken up.

Private collections of ancient sculpture, some of them very numerous, arose at this period. But here the first glance is sufficient to show that the refined critical knowledge of art possessed in our times did not preside in the formation of them. We accordingly find works of superior merit more or less mixed with the restorations of Roman workers in marble. The most considerable collections of this kind are those of the Marquis of Lansdowne and Mr Hope in London, of Lord Leicester at Holkham, of the Duke of Bedford at Woburn Abbey, of the Earl of Carlisle at Castle Howard, of the Earl of Egremont at Petworth, of Mr Blundell at Ince, of Mr Smith Barry at Marbury Hall, and of Sir Richard Worsley at Apuldurcombe House, in the Isle of Wight. The most important of all, that of Mr Charles Townley, now forms a portion of the British Museum. Lastly, other articles of ancient art, such as small bronzes, painted vases, terra cottas, household furniture, ornaments–in a word, all that is comprehended in the name of antiquities;– also medals and engraved gems were eagerly sought for. The most eminent collectors, for instance, of terra cottas were Mr Charles Townley; of vases, Sir William Hamilton; of engraved gems, the Duke of Devonshire, the Earl of Carlisle, Mr Joseph Small, and Sir R. Worsley; of small bronzes Mr Kemp (whose collection was sold in 1720); and for objects of antiquity of all kinds, Dr Mead.

But England was destined to sustain another grievous loss of works of art. In the year 1780 the gallery of paintings belonging to Sir Robert Walpole at Houghton Hall, of which I have already spoken, and which was very considerable both in extent and value, was sold for £30,000 to the Empress Catherine of Russia, and is now one of the most important parts of the imperial gallery in the Hermitage. A number of capital works by Rubens and Vandyck were thus lost to England. A collection, too, of eighty antique works of sculpture belonging to Mr Lyde Brown, mostly collected at Rome by the well-known English banker Jenkins from the Barberini Palace and from recent excavations, went in the same manner to St Petersburg.

The time, however, soon came when the consequences of the French Revolution brought a full indemnification to this country for all its preceding losses in works of art.

AN EXEMPLARY GRAND TOUR

ONE of the most delightful features of the upbringing of youthful members of the landed gentry in the eighteenth century was a tour of the Continent in the company of a tutor. This was an amalgam of seeing the sights, meetings with outstanding personalities, discussions with scholars, and a period of residence in some seat of learning. The ultimate goal was always Italy and a prolonged stay in Rome. Though a particular study of the arts was not inevitably a primary objective, funds were usually available for the purchase of books, paintings and antiquities. If the resulting taste in painting was often for the later Italian schools, this was probably due to two simple reasons: there was a preference among educated Italians themselves for the sophisticated output of the Mannerists; and therefore the dealers stocked these readily saleable items rather than the products of the Renaissance and pre-Renaissance era, which in any case at that time were firmly in the hands of ecclesiastical establishments or the Italian aristocracy.[1]

Both Thomas Coke's parents died in 1707 when he was only ten. The young heir went to live with his grandfather in Gloucestershire and then with a cousin in Derbyshire. It was the latter who prevailed upon the grandfather to send the delicate but remarkably precocious boy abroad. Tom Coke's father had left his affairs in a parlous tangle of mortgages and debts, but 'because of the extraordinary diligence and expert management of the family estates by the faithful agent, Humphrey Smith, matters had by 1712 enormously improved, and Coke had a spendable income in the region of £10,000 a year'. Dr Thomas Hobart, a learned and cultivated fellow of Christ's, Cambridge, was employed as a tutor and the preparations for their extensive travels – they were absent for six years[2] – were undertaken with great thoroughness. Practically every step of the journey can be traced by means of the meticulous record kept by a 'superior servant', Edward Jarrett.

Mr Lees-Milne's account of this memorable tour is a charming condensation of what are often rather dull examples of contemporary documentation.

EXTRACTED FROM James Lees-Milne's *Earls of Creation*, 1962.

THE party left London with a coach and four horses, two grooms, of whom one was shortly to be replaced by a Frenchman, and a valet, Abraham. The faithful agent,

[1] This was not the case, of course, after the advent of Napoleon (see page 16).

[2] 21 August 1712 to 18 May 1718.

Humphrey Smith, and his son Edward accompanied the young master, Dr Hobart and Edward Jarrett as far as Dunkirk, whence having sped them on their way they returned to England and to Holkham. The travellers reached Paris on 24 September where they stayed six weeks. The Invalides, the Luxembourg Palace and Notre-Dame were visited. There were excursions to the gardens at Marly and Versailles. Dr Hobart, grimly determined to avoid all social distractions and dissipations, moved his charge early in November to Angers. There they remained for five months, which in spite of lessons in riding at the Academy, in fencing, dancing and music, did not appeal to Tom. He complained ruefully to his grandfather of the fogs of Angers, the execrable French spoken by the inhabitants and the indifferent teachers. Dr Hobart had occasion to mention the number of other young English bloods in the town and his fear of bad influences.

In April 1713 the party leave Angers. Throughout the summer they are almost perpetually on the move. Nantes, La Rochelle, Toulouse (where some rare little books are bought), Narbonne, Montpellier, Nîmes, Arles, Avignon and then Lyons do not delay them for more than a day or two each. Along the route Tom Coke pays his respects to governors, marshals and presidents of parliaments who presumably return their compliments to this bright adolescent. The cursory items in the account books remind us closely of Lord Burlington's expenditures. 'For a flute', 'for a flagiolet', 'for a trumpet' speak of Tom's indefatigable music exercises, interspersed with visits to the opera in the towns they pass through. Tips or 'vails' and gifts of charity to the poor, or the galley-slaves in Marseilles are regular and unavoidable exactions. 'For painting the shaze', 'for broken windows and new springs', and 'for a dog fowling a silk carpet' are no less familiar entries. Only the entry, 'given to too prety women, by my master's order', has no counterpart in the record of Burlington's unimpeachable conduct. On 4 November 1713, they cross the Mont Cenis pass by mule and on the 7th arrive in Turin. The next fourteen months are spent in Italy.

From the very start of the journey Turin Academy has been looked upon as a fitting seat of learning to claim the young traveller's studies. But it was not yet to mean a halt of more than a few weeks. Even so an excursion was undertaken by chaise to the Palazzo Stupinigi where the King of Piedmont sometimes resided. The party soon continued to Genoa, thence by sea to Lerici, and so to Pisa and Florence, where courtesies and presents were exchanged with the Grand Duke of Tuscany. In January 1714 they were in Venice where operas and masquerades were the rule. There was a little loitering in the lagoons, however, and the beginning of February saw them at Ravenna and Rimini. By the 7th they were in Rome, and put up for their first two nights at the Golden Mountain Inn.

There is every indication that in Rome Tom Coke did much serious sightseeing between attending brilliant receptions, like that of the Queen of Poland. He visited the Villa Borghese, the Villa Ludovisi, the Palazzo Farnese, the Vatican and Quirinal palaces and gardens, the Palazzo Odeschalchi, the Palazzo Rospigliosi, the Palazzo Aldobrandini, the Palazzo Chigi and the Palazzo Spada, as well as countless churches by renaissance and contemporary architects. But, curiously enough, there is no mention of his studying the antiquities of the Forum or the remains of ancient temples. He had Italian lessons and bought pictures. He also engaged one Signor Giacomo, an 'architecture master for a month', and acquired 'instruments to learn architecture'. Then after a rushed visit of a fortnight to Naples he seems for the first time to have met, probably at the studio of the painter Benedetto Luti, and struck up a friendship with the thirty-year-old William Kent. Under 1st June in Jarrett's account book there appears the first of many entries relating to the man who was to wield such tremendous influence upon Coke's taste in the arts–'Paid to Mr Kent 60 pauls.' Almost immediately the cavalcade again left Rome for the north, this time taking Kent in its train. The very first entry in a scrappy journal which Kent began at this date records: 'Rome: I had ye honour to waite of Mr Coke & Dr Hubert from thence June ye 6–on ye 8 whe came to Siena.' Since Kent's journal is concerned almost exclusively with pictures (he had learnt painting under Luti's tuition), it is just possible that Tom Coke's enthusiasm first turned the older man's interests in the direction of architecture. We learn that together they looked at Siena Cathedral and visited Giuliano da Sangallo the elder's villa at Poggio a Caiano, which had been taken from Inigo Jones as a model for the river front of his Queen's House at Greenwich. After Bologna they entered the Republic of San Marino. 'Whe returned', Kent recorded in his halting but picturesque style, 'from ye Bright Republick with ye sounding of Trumpets & came to our calash & set out for Ravenna.' There they were much impressed by 'ye famous church of St Vitale ye plan being an ottangle & they say ye form of St Sabbcna at Constantinople'. The neighbouring sepulchre of Galla Placidia was likewise inspected.

On 22nd July they reached Venice. The next day they visited St Mark's (the Cathedral 'very much Gotic but ye great arches are round & all of mosaic upon ye frount without are four noble horses of a green gusto'); and in the afternoon crossed the water to 'ye cieling divided into several divisions' (Kent noted down). Santa San Giorgio Maggiore, 'the architecture of Palladio, ye library in Maria della Salute' was seen, the canvases of Tintoretto and Titian receiving special praise. Kent made a rough plan of the octagon and on the opposite page a half-elevation sketch of Palladio's San Francesco della Vigna. Before leaving Venice Coke, like Burlington seven months later, had his portrait done in pastel by Rosalba.

On 18th August they took what Kent calls a 'bootcello* very convenient to come by water' to Padua, stopping on the way 'to see the villa of ye famous beauty, Motzenigo Procuratess', and admire the frescoes, 'some of Veronese's first manner things relating to ye family'. At Padua the paintings of Giotto were–surprisingly–commended. Next came Vicenza, with it Palladian palaces and the Teatro Olimpico, 'ornamented with statues and basso relievos with fifty marble pillars' which Kent sketched. Then Verona with its Roman amphitheatre, and on 4th September Mantua, with the Palazzo del Té 'without ye gate very fine, but most ruined by ye Germans'. Kent approved the very fine grotto at the end of the garden–'ma per disgratia e per la vertu va tutte in ruina', the Signor breaks into Italian, ending the brief entry with, 'write this at ye Peacock in Parma upon my bed for not having more Room'.

* *By* bootcello *Kent meant* burchiello, *a large covered water omnibus with oars which plied between Venice and Padua at regular times.*

At Padua Coke had parted from Kent who returned on 3rd October by slow stages to Rome, his expenses as far as Parma at least having been paid by his young friend. Coke and Dr Hobart proceeded to Turin where at last the youth–he was now seventeen–settled down for the winter at the Academy. From the account he gave to his grandfather he hated every moment of it. 'I did intend', he wrote, 'to have desired you to defend me from being whip'd in this Academy, for I heard a very ill character of it, but, I having Governour, am obliged to no rules. . . . I am sure you would not desire that I should be treated like a child, as the Piedmontese are in this Academy. . . . I think of all the Academies that I have seen, except at Rome and Naples, this is the worst'–which last sentence suggests that very few, if any, from his limited acquaintance with them, would have met with Tom's unqualified approval.

In the spring of 1715 they move, much to Tom's relief, from Turin into Savoy. At Aix-les-Bains the doctor takes the waters and his pupil lessons in geography, mathematics and again architecture. In July they are in Geneva and in August at Basle, where a chestful of books including *The Habits of Basel* and *The Death Dance of Holbein* is purchased. Also the young master's head is shaved preparatory to him wearing a new wig. The party then proceeds by water to Frankfurt in the company of two new friends, a Mr Warner and a Mr Richard Mongoe, upon whom the cautious governor looks askance. Here a whole consignment of volumes is bought through a Greek agent. By now the youthful pupil is so well indoctrinated by his learned governor that a passion for book collecting has taken firm hold of him. At Mainz three boxes of books are packed. At Langres a missal is found; and at Lyons for 30,000 livres some forty manuscripts are acquired from the discalced Augustinians' convent of the Croix-Rousse. This haul, which was Coke's first and most spectacular purchase of a whole collection, comprised the famous library of Raphael de Marcatellis, the natural son of Philip the Good. In December the party are at Marseilles. On Christmas Day they leave the 'Bons Enfans' hotel and pack themselves, the chaises and plenty of provisions, including candles and two chests of Côte-rôtie, on board a ship bound for Sicily.

January 1716 saw Mr Coke in Palermo, which he thought a beautiful city; but the inns of Sicily were so atrocious that it was out of the question to settle comfortably in any of the island towns for long. He saw Messina, Syracuse and Catania, and even crossed to Malta for 'while things continue so troubled in England, one can't keep too far from it', a sentiment inspired by the recent change of dynasty and the menace of a Jacobite restoration. In May he went to Naples where he met Kent again, who introduced him to Solimena from whom he commissioned two pictures. More important still was his acquisition of the cream of the Giuseppe Valletta collection of manuscripts. There are payments to Kent for his journey to Naples, his lodgings, and other necessaries as well as 'for pictures and drawings that he bought for my master at several times'. Together they went in June to Rome where they put up at the Black Eagle. Numerous paintings by Procaccini, Garzi, Conca, Luti as well as anonymous views of the city and its palaces were bought. These adorn the walls of Holkham to this day. The month of August and the first half of September were particularly devoted to the study of architecture. Signor Giacomo, 'the Architect master', is again paid for his tuition and supply of drawing paper; and is given a present 'for goeing about the town with my master and larning of him architecture'. It is apparent that Mr Coke's intensive study, not only of the history but also of the technicalities of the science, was done for an ulterior motive. At the back of his mind in these early years of his life he cherished a determination to rebuild, on the palatial lines which suited his ever accumulating fortune, the home of his ancestors. There in a suitable neo-classical setting he would display the magnificent books, pictures and sculpture amassed during his travels.

He now began in all seriousness to buy marbles. A colossal bust of the Emperor Lucius Verus, found when the port of Nettuno was cleared, and a bas-relief were his first acquisitions in this department of the arts. On 12th September he left Rome for Florence and the northern cities, chiefly in pursuit of books of which a rare edition of Livy was the prize. Kent accompanied the party and was taken ill at Modena where he was attended by doctors at Coke's expense. In January 1717 they were back in Rome for a stay of three busy months of sightseeing and collecting both pictures and statues. Signor Giacomo was paid for preparing plans of the Palazzo Farnese just as he had been paid the previous autumn for drawing Andrea Pozzo's rich altar of St Ignatius Loyola in the Gesu. A 'Great Statue' of Jupiter was transported to Civitavecchia to be shipped to England, but the wagon carrying the colossal burden stuck fast in the snow. A headless statue of Diana, still in the gallery at Holkham–at the time highly prized but actually very stiff and dull–was dispatched to Leghorn. For its extradition out of the Papal States without a licence Coke was, according to Matthew Brettingham and Kent, very properly arrested and nearly imprisoned.

Before leaving Rome for the last time the *Cavaliere* Coke, as by now he was known all over Italy, had his portrait painted by Angelo Trevisani. He was then twenty years old, and by no means good-looking. He is represented sitting in a richly carved chair, his left hand resting on the head of a mastiff. Busts to indicate the young virtuoso's tastes are set in the background. The angular face is enveloped in a close-fitting wig. The nose is long and very prominent; the eyes are deep and earnest, the lips sensual; the chin is slightly receding. It is the portrait of a wilful but intelligent youth of a serious and brooding cast of mind.

Having said good-bye to Kent who was to remain in Italy for another two years Coke and Dr Hobart departed for the north. Once more they passed through Florence where Coke commissioned Signor Biscioni, Prefect of the Laurentian Library, to collate the current printed text of the three decades of Livy with twenty-six manuscripts in the Library. The formidable task was not completed until 1728. Biscioni gave the young man an introduction to the scholar Apostolo Zeno in Venice, who reluctantly parted with several valuable manuscripts in return for a mere £60. Zeno and other Italian scholars of the early eighteenth century gravely resented their need to part with rare manuscripts to young milords from the north, most of whom, unlike Thomas Coke, had more riches than education. A brief excursion to Padua resulted in the purchase of a large section of the library of the Canons Regular of San Giovanni in Verdara which had been given them in the fifteenth century.

After being shown over a number of Venetian palaces by a specially hired guide Coke and his attendants left for Vienna, by way of Innsbruck and Salzburg, completing the journey down the Danube. In Vienna the *Cavaliere* made elaborate preparations to take part in a campaign then being waged against the city of Belgrade. Horses, tents, baggage and equipment of all sorts were mustered at heavy expense in a special room hired for the purpose, in spite of the remonstrances of Dr Hobart. Alas, the glorious prospect of winning golden spurs was rudely scotched through the cunning instance of his governor, who had already warned the young man's guardians. Appalled, they ordered the governor to prevent this folly at whatever cost. Accordingly the wise Dr Hobart, in order to diminish his pupil's recriminations against himself urged the Austrian police forcibly to intervene. Abashed and disappointed the would-be warrior sought consolation in flute practice and gambling, after inditing a rather touching apology for his intemperate behaviour to his grandfather. The letter addressed from Prague began: 'I beg ten thousand pardons for what you may by this time be informed of, of my intention to see the Army in Hungary, not withstanding Sir Edward Coke, in the name of my guardians had refused.' His excuse for having wanted to see active service at least showed spirit and his lack of resentment against the tutor a good-humoured and philosophic temper. 'Mr Hobart (who in deference to my Guardians I forgive, they having recommended him) got the Governor of Austria to put me in arrest,' the letter continues. And then, 'Vienna is a very dull place' is followed by an equivocal description of the Emperor Charles VI's ladies of the court, whom His Imperial Majesty commands to shoot every afternoon at a target in the palace grounds. 'I can't call these Ladys Amazons, one must find a new name, for they, instead of one breast being cut off, have two as big as four other women can have. The sexes are so changed at Vienna, that as the Ladys shoot, the men are obliged to make curtsies.'

Perhaps after this disappointment it was just as well that the doctor and his pupil separated for a few weeks. After Dresden and Berlin, where valuable manuscripts and two illuminated Byzantine Gospels were bought from the library of Andreas Erasmus Seidel, Coke went alone to Hanover, Amsterdam and The Hague. There he joined forces with Lord Leslie and his brother. The three young men visited Brussels together where they joined Lord Bruce. Finally, February 1718 saw *Cavaliere* Coke and Dr Hobart in Paris. Thomas was nearly twenty-one years old and practically his own master. Dr Hobart's responsibilities were accordingly nearing an end. Now the life the pupil chose to lead in Paris was his own affair. The situation was radically different from that five and a half years ago when the doctor had been at pains to keep him away from the dissipations that beset a boy from every quarter. He lived in luxurious apartments and was waited upon by four servants in livery. Lord Stair and Lord Essex were his constant companions; his young brother Neddy had joined him from London. He patronised expensive tailors, had his shirts ruffled and bought periwigs of the latest fashion. He went to balls and was sent a present of flowers by the King of France's gardener. He purchased more pictures, including the large equestrian portrait by Vandyke of the Comte d'Aremberg which hangs in the saloon at Holkham. In May there were great preparations for a return to England. Crates of books, pictures and statuary, not already dispatched from Civitavecchia or

Leghorn by sea, had first to pass through the customs, then be coded and sealed. Two smart new berlins were bought to take the great quantities of luggage. The crates, boxes, trunks and packages, the servants, Dr Hobart and lastly, Mr Coke himself all embarked at Calais. On 18th May they landed at Dover, where the faithful Humphrey Smith, come specially from Holkham, greeted his young master on the pier.

AEDES WALPOLIANAE

It is easy to forget today, after the unremitting labours of Mr Wilmarth Lewis and Mr Ketton-Cremer, that Horace Walpole has only recently emerged from an aura of derision and ridicule.[1] The facets of Walpole's interests and activities were so many and varied that we must claim him here firmly as one of the patron saints of English collecting; not only as a remarkable collector in his own right,[2] but also, as we have already seen, as a chronicler of what had gone before.

'*Aedes Walpolianae*, or a Description of the Collection of Pictures at Houghton-Hall in Norfolk, the Seat of the Right Honourable Sir Robert Walpole, Earl of Orford,' was one of the earliest *catalogues raisonées* of a private picture gallery to be printed in England. It saw the light of day when Sir Robert's youngest son was only twenty-six. His style was diffuse and his judgements opinionated. Even modern views about it vary enormously. 'It is a remarkable work, the outstanding piece of English criticism of the eighteenth century before Sir Joshua, and except for the prejudices of youth, no less penetrating than the *Discourses*,' says F. H. Taylor.[3] 'The art-criticism of any period almost inevitably causes pain and bewilderment to future generations; and Horace Walpole's introduction to *Aedes Walpolianae* is no exception. . . . There was some good criticism and sound appreciation scattered about the introduction, and almost too much of Walpole's habitual vivacity; but the general standard of performance can best be judged by the paragraph of resounding nonsense with which it closes,'[4] says R. W. Ketton-Cremer.[5] While there is obvious truth in the latter judgement, *Aedes Walpolianae* is an outstanding and interesting document in the field of collecting literature. The scathing passage on art jargon is enough to justify its existence.

[1] Engendered as much by Macaulay (in the *Edinburgh Review* of October 1813) as by the nastier barbs of Lady Mary Wortley Montague.

[2] See page 116.

[3] *The Taste of Angels*, page 431.

[4] See page 88.

[5] *Horace Walpole, a Biography*; see also page 116.

14 A pleasant conversation piece of three collectors of engravings. The picture is attributed to Allan Ramsay and the sitters may be connected with the Hope family of Hopetoun House, Edinburgh.

15 The artist Francis Hayman (1708–76) with a sitter until recently thought to be Sir Robert Walpole. Hayman lived a most convivial life. He started as a scene painter at Drury Lane and was well known for his decorative work in Vauxhall Gardens. He illustrated many books with engravings and was the Royal Academy's first librarian.

16 Henry Blundell (1723-1810), like his great friend Charles Towneley, was a passionate collector of ancient marbles. At his death his collection consisted of 500 or more, chiefly Roman copies of Greek originals. They were arranged in two specially built galleries at Ince: a large rotunda attached to the house, called the 'Pantheon' and the other a 'Garden Temple' in the grounds. This is an interior view of the 'Pantheon'.

17 Zoffany's portrait of Sir Lawrence Dundas with his little grandson, Lawrence Dundas, afterwards 1st Earl of Zetland, in the library or Pillar Room at 19 Arlington Street, London, was painted in 1769. Dundas amassed an enormous fortune and became known as the 'Nabob of the North'. He had further residences at Aske in Yorkshire, Dundas House in St Andrew Square, Edinburgh and Moor Park, Hertfordshire. He furnished them all lavishly, both with objects newly commissioned and with antiquities. He bought many pictures from abroad which the dealer Greenwood (see page 28) found for him in France and Holland. Behind him, over the mantelpiece, is a seascape by van de Capelle; the table is probably by Chippendale. The bronzes on the mantelpiece are still in the possession of the present Marquess of Zetland at Aske.

18,The Hope family left Scotland in the seventeenth century and settled in Holland. There they
19 achieved great opulence as bankers and merchants. Thomas Hope (1769-1831) returned to London and used his wealth and taste to impress on Regency society the principles of Neo-Classicism. While he collected Old Masters, antique statuary and vases, he also patronised such contemporary artists as Flaxman, Thorvaldsen, Benjamin West and Haydon. He designed his own furniture and dabbled in architecture. His original picture gallery is shown above, and the new one which he designed in conjunction with William Atkinson in 1819 for the reception of his collection of Flemish pictures is shown below. Hope was unusual as a collector in allowing the public to view his collection.

20 View of the New Gallery at Cleveland House in 1824. Its owner, the Marquess of Stafford, was one of the most enlightened collectors of his day and the first regularly to admit the public into his Gallery (from May 1806 onwards). The large picture in the centre of the left hand wall is Annibale Carracci's *Danae on a Couch with Cupid.*

21 Thirlestane House, Cheltenham, was the home of John Rushout, 2nd Lord Northwick (1769–1859). His enthusiasm for collecting was such that it was bought originally only to house the overflow of pictures that could not be accommodated at Northwick Park! It was generally believed that both house and collection were to be left to the City Fathers of Cheltenham, but as Lord Northwick died intestate both had to be sold up. The house was later occupied by Sir Thomas Phillips, doyen of book collectors.

22 Fonthill Abbey, the home of William Beckford (1760–1844), certainly one of the most colourful and exotic personalities among English collectors. Fonthill was designed by Wyatt and the building of this piece of Gothic extravaganza began in 1796. There was endless trouble with the tower, which was 280 feet high and which eventually collapsed. Beckford, who liked to live in seclusion, spent many years at Fonthill making improvements to the house, the garden, the grounds and adding to his splendid collection of pictures and other works of art, and his immense library.

23 The Altieri Claudes were among the most discussed collectors' items in the nineteenth century. They were bought in Rome from the Altieri family by the dealers Fagan and Grignion. Nelson made himself responsible for their transport to London. William Beckford bought them for the incredible price of £6825 in 1795. In 1808 R. Hart Davis, an early National Gallery benefactor, bought them for 12,000 guineas. They are shown here in their final resting place, Anglesey Abbey, now the property of the National Trust.

24 Horace Walpole (1717–1797), one of the most important arbiters of taste in England during the eighteenth century, painted by J. C. Eccardt in 1754.

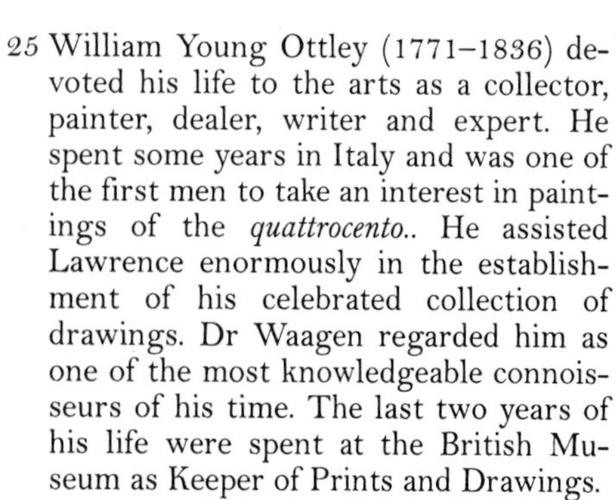

25 William Young Ottley (1771–1836) devoted his life to the arts as a collector, painter, dealer, writer and expert. He spent some years in Italy and was one of the first men to take an interest in paintings of the *quattrocento*.. He assisted Lawrence enormously in the establishment of his celebrated collection of drawings. Dr Waagen regarded him as one of the most knowledgeable connoisseurs of his time. The last two years of his life were spent at the British Museum as Keeper of Prints and Drawings.

26 To Sir George Beaumont (1753–1827), here portrayed by Hoppner, must go the lion's share of the credit for the eventual establishment of the National Gallery in 1824, to which he gave his own collection during his lifetime. Sir George was a generous patron in many fields, an influential figure in the arts, a friend beloved by many and an enthusiastic landscape painter.

27 John Julius Angerstein (1735–1823) portrayed by Sir Thomas Lawrence. His collection of paintings was bought by Lord Liverpool for £57,000 in 1824 as a nucleus for a National Gallery.

28 This, the most elaborate in a series entitled 'Patrons and Lovers of Art, studies from the life for an imaginary picture gallery', was painted in 1826 for General Sir John Murray, G.C.B., by P. A. Wonder of Utrecht. Shown here are G. Watson Taylor, M.P. (kneeling), an enthusiastic collector; the Rev. William Holwell Carr, one of the first great benefactors of the National Gallery; General Murray; and the artist.

Walpole's account of the paintings must be read in conjunction with Mr Ketton-Cremer's description of Houghton. 'Houghton is a magnificent house; but it is quite unjust to condemn it for ostentation. Beside the stupendous palaces of Vanbrugh, or the vast Palladian structures raised later in the century, its scale might almost be described as modest. There is nothing in the design to mark it as the fulfilled ambition of a wealthy parvenu; it is simple, massive, dignified, and every foot of its surface is remarkable for its sober perfection of detail and finish. In its spacious magnificence, it was the perfect expression of Sir Robert; and it is hard to believe that he could have ever wished it smaller by a single foot. The house matched the man. There was something of his personality in all its pictures and in all its furnishings – in the solemn massive east front; in the more ornate west front which faced the gardens; in the astonishing hall and its famous lantern, which was so often ridiculed in *The Craftsman*; in the Marble Parlour, with its cool alcoves and granite cistern, refinements to aid deep drinking and heavy dining on a hot day; in the bedchambers with their superb tapestries and marvellous embroidered bed hangings; in the velvet, the gilding, the friezes and doors and chimney pieces; and above all in room after room filled with pictures from floor to ceiling, the Gallery, the Salon, the Carlo Maratti Room and all the other rooms with their profusion of pleasant family portraits, indifferent hunting scenes, and unrivalled masterpieces by every painter whose work was admired by the *cognoscenti* in the reign of George II.'

Sir Robert began the building of Houghton in 1722 in the midst of his great political career and it was not completed in every detail until 1738. He acquired his collection by relying heavily on the advice of others – but then he was always a sound judge of advisors – and it became the greatest collection of art in England since the time of Charles I. 'He had agents all over Europe buying pictures for him; diplomats and friends, too, sent them either as thank-offerings or to curry favour with so influential a politician. His own direct purchases in the art market bear striking witness to his enthusiasm. The prices he paid were often record ones for the period: £500 for Salvator Rosa's *Prodigal Son*, £700 for Guido Reni's *Consultation of Fathers of the Church*, £320 for Poussin's *Holy Family* (a letter to Lord Waldegrave shows him to have been willing to go up to £400). When complete the collection totalled over four hundred paintings, and included twenty van Dycks, nineteen Rubens, eight Titians, a large number of Carlo Marattas, five Murillos, three each by Veronese and Reni, two Velasquez, and a Frans Hals (both singularly discerning purchases in that age), a Raphael, an outstanding Poussin and the works of dozens of other highly esteemed old masters.'[1]

It is said that Walpole spent some £35,000 on his collection and he certainly died in debt in 1745. Thereby hangs another tale, for Houghton eventually became

[1] From F. J. B. Watson's article on the present-day Houghton Hall and its collection (now the property of the Marquess of Cholmondeley) in *Great Family Collections*, edited by Douglas Cooper, 1965.

the property of Horace Walpole's nephew, George, 3rd Earl of Orford. This Orford lived a profligate life and was given to fits of insanity. Horace frequently had to look after his nephew's affairs. Even so the indebtedness grew larger and in 1779 the third Earl 'requited the generosity of his uncles by dispoiling Houghton of its supreme glory, Sir Robert's collection of pictures. He sold them for a sum variously stated to be £40,000 and £45,000, to the Empress Catherine of Russia.'[1]

Negotiations for the sale lasted some time and there was a general outcry against it. John Wilkes advocated the establishment of a National Gallery to be contained in the British Museum. 'I understand that an application is to be made at Parliament that one of the first collections in Europe, that in Houghton, made by Sir Robert Walpole, of acknowledged superiority to most collections in Italy and scarcely inferior even to that of the Duc of Orleans in the Palais Royal at Paris may be sold. I hope it may not be dispersed but purchased by Parliament and added to the British Museum. I wish Sir, the eye of painting as fully gratified as the ear of music is in this island, which at last bids fair to become a favourite abode of the polite arts. A noble gallery ought to be built in the garden of the British Museum for the reception of this invaluable collection.'

But it was to no avail. The Houghton pictures went to Russia.[2]

The excerpts from *Aedes Walpolianae* that follow consist of a memorable passage from Horace's dedication; the main substance of his introduction (a number of Latin quotations and some digressions are omitted); and finally, almost a third of the room-by-room description of the contents. I have inserted within square brackets after each painting sold to Catherine the Great the figure at which it was valued for the sale.[3] Paintings without these figures were not included in the sale.

---

[1] Ketton-Cremer, *ibid.*, page 294.

[2] For an unusually detailed account of their Russian setting, see J. Beavington Atkinson's *An Art Tour of Northern Capitals in Europe*, 1873, particularly pages 175–181, where he describes the newly completed Hermitage at St Petersburg.

[3] This information has been collated from a copy of *Aedes Walpolianae* in the Westminster City Reference Library (though there are a number of copies with such additions extant). The volume contains a handwritten note on the flyleaf which states 'in the margin of the following catalogue is specified the price of each particular picture as they were valued for the Empress of Russia, Catherine II, who purchased the whole Collection, the Family Portraits excepted'. The grand total for the 232 paintings valued was £40,220. Though Mrs Jameson states emphatically in her *Handbook to the Public Galleries of Art in and near London* that the Empress never paid more than £36,000 for the pictures and was so indignant at the cost that she even refused to look at them!

The last item in Redford's *Art Sales*, Vol. II, contains a similar valued inventory of the Houghton Collection. The valuation had been prepared by Messrs West, R.A., and Cipriani, R.A. (There is a letter extant from Horace Walpole to the Rev. W. Cole in which he thought the pictures were overvalued.) The number of paintings listed here is different; so is the total sum, by some £305. Redford explains this difference in a footnote of his own in *Art Sales*, Vol. I, page 135. Catherine wanted to buy a portrait of Sir Robert Walpole, as the Collector, included with

HORACE WALPOLE

Extracted from Horace Walpole's *Aedes Walpolianae*, Second Edition, 1752.

DEDICATION

Your power and your wealth speak themselves in the grandeur of the whole Building. . . . And give me leave to say, Sir, your enjoying the latter after losing the former, is the brightest proof how honest were the foundations of both.

INTRODUCTION

The following account of Lord Orford's Collection of Pictures, is rather intended as a Catalogue than a Description of them. The mention of Cabinets in which they have formerly been, with the addition of the measures,* will contribute to ascertain their originality, and be a kind of pedigree to them.

In Italy, the native soil of almost all Vertù, descriptions of great Collections are much more common and much more ample. The Princes and Noblemen there, who lov'd and countenanc'd the Arts, were fond of letting the world know the Curiosities in their possession. There is scarce a large Collection of Medals but is in print. Their Gems, their Statues, and Antiquities are all published. But the most pompous works of this sort are the AEDES BARBARIAE and GIUSTINANAE, the latter of which are now extremely scarce and dear.

Commerce, which carries along with it the Curiosities and Arts of Countries, as well as the Riches, daily brings us something from Italy. How many valuable Collections of Pictures are there established in England on the frequent ruins and dispersions of the finest Galleries in Rome and other Cities! Most of the pictures in the famous Pallavicini Collection have been brought over; many of them are actually at Houghton. When I was in Italy there were to be sold the Sagredo Collection at Venice, those of the Zambeccari and San Pieri palaces at Bologna; and at Rome, those of the Sacchetti† and Cardinal Ottoboni; and of that capital one I mention'd, the Barbarini: but the extravagant prices affix'd had hindered the latter from being broke. Statues are not so numerous, and consequently come seldomer, besides that the chief are prohibited from being sold out of Rome: a silent proof, that the sums sent thither for purchases are not thrown away, since the prohibition arose from the profits flowing into the City by the concourse of Strangers who travel to visit them. For however common and more reasonable the pretext, I believe,

the other paintings. The Earl demurred. The picture was retained. It finished up in the refectory at Strawberry Hill.

This information is given in some detail in order to set aside the uncertainty so often expressed about the sum paid by Catherine for the Walpole Collection.

It has now emerged that the first James Christie had also played a major role in the valuation.

* *They have been newly measured, end are more correct than in the first edition.*

† *The Sacchetti Collection has been since purchased by Pope Benedict XIVth and placed in the Capitol.*

Ten travel to see the Curiosities of a Country, for one who makes a journey to acquaint himself with the Manners, Customs, and Policy of the Inhabitants.

There are not a great many Collections left in Italy more worth seeing than this at Houghton: in the preservation of the pictures, it certainly excells most of them. That noble one in the Borghese palace at Rome, is almost destroyed by the damps of the apartment where it is kept.

The Italian Collections are far more numerous and more general. Lord Orford has not been able to meet with a few very principal Hands: but there are enough here for any man who studies Painting, to form very true ideas of most of the chief schools, and to acquaint himself with most of the chief Hands. Knowledge of this sort is only to be learnt from Pictures themselves. The numerous volumes wrote on this Art have only serv'd to perplex it. No Science has had so much jargon introduced into it as Painting; the bombast expression of the Italians, and the prejudices of the French, join'd to the vanity of the Professors, and the interested mysteriousness of Picture-merchants, have altogether compiled a new language. 'Tis almost easier to distinguish the Hands of the Masters, than to decypher the Cant of the Virtuosi. Nor is there any Science whose productions are so capricious and uncertain a value. As great as are the prices of fine Pictures, there is no judging from them of the several merits of the Painters; there does not seem to be any standard of estimation. You hear a Virtuoso talk in raptures of Raphael, of Correggio's Grace, and Titian's Colouring; and yet the same man in the same breath will talk as enthusiastically of any of the first Masters, who wanted all the excellencies of all the three. You will perhaps see more paid for a picture of Andrea del Sarto, whose colouring was a mixture of mist and tawdry, whose drawing hard and forced, than for the most graceful air of a Madonna that ever flowed from the pencil of Guido. And as for the Dutch painters, those drudging Mimicks of Nature's most uncomely coarseness, don't their earthen pots and brass kettles carry away prices only due to the sweet neatness of Albano, and to the attractive delicacy of Carlo Maratti! . . . Nicolo Poussin had the greatest aversion for Michael Angelo Caravaggio, for debasing the Art by imitations of vulgar and unrefined Nature. His lights and shades are as distinct and strongly opposed, as on objects seen by candle-light. It was not so much want of Genius in the Flemish Masters, as for want of having searched for something better. Their only idleness seems to have been in the choice of their subjects. Rottenhamer and Paul Brill, who travelled into Italy, contracted as pleasing a Stile as any of the Italian Masters. Lord Orford's Landscapes of the latter are very near as free, as pure, and as genteel as Claude's and Titian's.

There was something in the Venetian School, especially in Paul Veronese, which touches extremely upon the servile imitation of the Dutch: I mean their ornaments of dress and gawdy embroider'd garments. It puts me in mind of a story of Apelles, who looking on a Picture just finished by one of his Scholars, which was mightily decked out with gold and jewels; 'At least, my lad,' said he, 'If you could not make her handsome, you have made her rich.'

If ever Collections cou'd be perfect, the present age seems to be the period for making them so. Another century may see half the works of the great Masters destroy'd or decaying: and I am sorry to say, that there seems to be a stop to any farther improvements, or continuation of the perfection, of the Art. . . .

The first and acknowledged Principal School was the Roman: it was particularly admired for Drawing, Taste and great Ideas; all flowing from those models of improv'd Nature, which they had before their eyes in the Antique Statues and Bas-reliefs. Their faults were, minute and perplex'd Draperies, and a hardness of Colouring: faults arising from the same source as their perfections, they copied too exactly the wet Draperies which the ancient Statuaries used to cling round their Figures very judiciously, to show the formation of the limbs, and to give a lightness to the Marble, which would not endure to be encumber'd with large folds and flowing garments, but which are the great beauties of Painting. Raphael towards the end of his life grew sensible of this, and struck out a greater Stile in his Draperies. Their hard Colouring too was owing to their close Application to the study of the Antique, and neglecting Nature. Raphael's superior Genius made him alone comprehend both. The many volumes wrote on this Subject make it needless to say more of Raphael. Michael Angelo Buonarotti alone of all the Roman School fell into the contrary extreme: he follow'd nature too closely, so enamour'd with that ancient piece of anatomical skill, the Torso, that he neglected all the purer and more delicate-proportion'd Bodies. He was as much too fond of muscles, as Rubens afterwards was of flesh; each overloaded all their compositions with their favourite study. This great School, after the death of the Disciples of Raphael and Michael Angelo, languished for several years, but reviv'd in almost all its glory in the person of Andrea Sacchi,* who carry'd one part of the Art to greater perfection than any before him or since, the Harmony of Colours. His countryman and competitor Pietro Cortona was a great ornament to Rome. He had rather a great richness than a fruitfulness of fancy. There is too remarkable a sameness in his ideas, particularly in the heads of his women; and too great a composure in his expression of the passions. No collection can be compleat without one picture of his hand, and none wants more than one, except of his greater and less sort, for his small pieces are his best. Lord Orford has one in his Cabinet, which is very capital. He had an extreme good scholar, Ciro Ferri. Andrea Sacchi bred up a most admir'd scholar, the famous Carlo Maratti. This latter and his scholars form'd a new Roman School, and added Grace, Beauty and Lightness, to the Majesty, Dignity, and Solemnity of their predecessors. Indeed Carlo Maratti has unluckily been one of the Destroyers of Painting, by introducing that very light stile of colouring which in less skillful hands has degenerated into glare and tawdry. The Drawing-Room in this Collection, call'd the Carlo-Marat Room, is a perfect School of the Works of Him, Nicolo Beretoni, and Gioseppe Chiari, his Disciples.

Contemporary with the Elder Roman School was the Venetian, as renown'd for their Colouring, as the other for their Drawing. Titian, Giorgione, Pordenone, Paul Veronese, Tintoret, the Bassans, Paris Bourdon, Andrea Schiavoni, and the Palma's, were the chief

* *He first study'd under* Albano.

Masters of it: Titian and Paul Veronese by far the best. The Landscapes of the former, and the Architecture of the latter, were equal to their Carnations. Giorgione had great ideas. Pordenone and Tintoret were dark and ungraceful. The Palma's were stiff, and the Bassans particular. The elder Palma is remarkable for ill-drawn Hands and Arms, of which he was so sensible, that he seldom has shown above one of each figure. The Bassans have always stooping Figures, and delighted in drawing the Backs of them. Their Landscapes are dark, and their greatest Lights consist in the Red Draperies, which they promiscuously distributed to almost every Figure.

The same Century produc'd that universal Genius, Lionardo da Vinci, whose Colouring of Flesh does not yield in roundness to Titian's; nor his skill in Anatomy to his Cotemporary Michael Angelo's; his Judgement in it was greater. Tho' he was not born at Milan, yet his residence there establisht a kind of Milanese School. It was the fate of that City not to have its greatest Ornaments born its Natives. The Procacini, who were of Bologna, retir'd thither on some disputes with the Caracci. Camillo, who was most known of the Three, was very particular in his Colouring. The variety of Tints in his Flesh, the odd disposition of his Lights on the verges of the Limbs, and his delighting in clustering Groupes, made his Pictures extremely easy to be known.

There is little to be said of the Florentine School, as there was little variety in the Masters; and except Andrea del Sarto, and the two Zucchero's, their names are scarce known out of Tuscany. Their Drawing was hard, and their Colouring gawdy and gothic.

The Lombard School was as little universal, but far more known by producing those two great Men Correggio and Parmegiano: the first, for Grace and Sweetness confest the first of Painters; and the latter as celebrated for the Majesty of his Airs. His Works are easily known by long Necks and Fingers and by a certain greenness in his Colouring. . . . Frederico Barroccio was a great imitator of Correggio, but seems rather to have study'd what Correggio did, than what he did well; his beautiful Colouring and bad Drawing are both like Correggio's.

The Neapolitan School has produc'd little good; if Lanfranc was a good painter, which in mind I do not think, he was bred up in the school of the Caracci. His manner was wild, glaring and extravagant. What Luca Jordano did well, he ow'd to his Master Pietro Cortona. His careless and hasty manner prevented his Pictures from almost ever being excellent. His hand is often difficult to be known, as it was the most various and uncertain. There cannot be three manners more unlike, than in the Cyclops, the Judgement of Paris, and the two small ones in the Carlo-Marat Room, all by him. Generally indeed his Pictures are to be distinguished by deep blue skies, blue and white draperies, and vast confusion of unaccountable lights, particularly on the extremities of his figures. His genius was like Ovid's, flowing, abundant, various, and incorrect.

The greatest Genius Naples ever produced resided generally at Rome; a genius equal to any that city itself ever bore. This was the great Salvator Rosa. His thoughts, his expression, his landscapes , his knowledge of the force of shade, and his masterly management of Horror and Distress, have plac'd him in the first class of painters. In Lord Townsend's Belisarius, one sees a Majesty of Thought equal to Raphael, an Expression great as Poussin's. In Lord Orford's Prodigal is represented the extremity of misery and low nature; not foul and burlesque like Michael Angelo Caravaggio; not minute, circumstantial and laborious like the Dutch painters. One of them would have painted his eating broth with a wooden spoon, and have employed three days in finishing up the bowl that held it. In the story of the old man and his sons, one sees Drawing and a taste of Draperies equal to the best collected from the antique. Salvator was a Poet and an excellent Satirist. Here again was a union of those Arts. His pictures contain the true genius and end of Satire. Tho' heighten'd and expressive as his figures are, they still mean more than they speak. . . .

The French School has flourished with several extreme good Masters. One character runs thro' all their Works, a close imitation of the Antique, unassisted by Colouring. Almost all of them made the voyage of Rome. Nicolo Poussin was a perfect Master of Expression and Drawing, though the proportion of his Figures is rather too long. Le Soeur, his disciple, to the style of his Master, and the study of the Antique, join'd an imitation of Raphael which, had his life been longer, would have raised him high above Poussin. The man kneeling on the fore-ground in Lord Orford's Saint Stephen might be taken for the hand of Raphael. And in the Moses in the Bullrushes, the distant woman is quite in the great Master's Taste. The Cloyster painted by him at the Chartreuse at Paris, is, in my opinion, equal to any composition extant, for the Passions and fine thoughts. His fault was in his Draperies; the folds are mean and unnatural. Sebastian Bourdon was liker Poussin, only that as Poussin's figures are apt to be too long, his are generally too short, and consequently want the grace which often consists in over-lengthen'd Proportions. Le Brun's Colouring was better than any of the French, but his Compositions are generally confused and crouded. Lord Orford's Icarus is much beyond and very unlike his usual manner. It is liker to Guercino, without having the fault of his too black shadows. France and Lorrain have produc'd two more painters, who in their way were the greatest ornaments to their profession; Gaspar Poussin and Claude Lorrain: the latter especially was the Raphael of Landscape-painting.

I shall not enter into any detail of the Flemish Painters, who are better known by their different Varnishes, and the different kind of utensils they painted, than by any style of Colouring and Drawing. One great Man they had, who struck out of the littleness of his Countrymen, tho' he never fell into a character of graceful beauty: but Rubens is too well known in England to want any account of him. His Scholar Vandyke contracted a much genteeler Taste in his Portraits. But what serv'd other Painters for models of beauty, was to him a standard of miscarrying: All his Portraits of Women are graceful; but his Madonnas, which he probably drew from some Mistress, are most remarkable for want of beauty.

It will easily be observed that I have yet omitted one of the principal schools, the Bolognese; but as I began with the Roman, I reserv'd this to conclude with. This, which was as little inferior to the Roman, as it was superior to all the rest: This was the School, that to the dignity of the Antique, join'd all the beauty of living nature. There was no perfection in the others, which was not assembled here. In Annibal Caracci one sees the ancient Strength of Drawing. In his Farnese Gallery, the naked figures supporting the ceiling are equal to the exerted skill of Michael Angelo, superiorly colour'd. They talk of his Faults in Drawing, but those Figures and Lord Orford's little Venus are standards of proportion for men and women. In Guido was the grace and delicacy of Correggio, and colouring as natural as Titian's. I can not imagine what they mean, who say he wanted knowledge in the Chiaro Oscuro: It was never more happily apply'd and diffus'd than in Lord Orford's Adoration of the Shepherds. In Albano was finishing as high as in the exactest Flemish masters. His Scholar Mola form'd compositions as rich as the fam'd Barbarini ceiling by Pietro da Cortona; Lord Orford's Curtius is an instance. There are numbers of figures less crouded, more necessary, and with far more variety of expression. If nature and life can please, the sweet Dominichini must be admir'd. These two never met in one picture in a higher degree than in Lord Orford's Madonna and Child, by him. One can't conceive more expression in two figures so compos'd, and which give so little room for showing any passion or emotion. Ludovico Caracci, the Founder of this great School, was more famous for his Disciples than his Works; tho' in Bologna they prefer him to Annibal: but his Drawing was incorrect, and his Hands and Feet almost always too long. In one point I think the Bolognese painters excell'd every other Master; their draperies are in a greater taste than even Raphael's. The largeness and simplicity of the folds in Guido's Dispute of the Doctors, is a pattern and standard for that sort of painting.

I shall conclude with these few Recapitulations. I can admire Correggio's grace and exquisite finishing; but I cannot overlook his wretched Drawing and Distortions. I admire Parmegiano's more majestic Grace, and wish the length of limbs and necks, which forms those graceful airs, were natural. Titian wanted to have seen the Antique; Poussin to have seen Titian. Le Soeur, whom I think in drawing and expression equal to Poussin, and in the great ideas of his heads and attitudes, second to Raphael, like the first wanted colouring, and had not the fine draperies of the latter. Albano never painted a picture, but some of the figures were stiff, and wanted grace; and then his scarce ever succeeding in large subjects, will throw him out of the list of perfect painters. Dominichini, whose Communion of Saint Jerome is allow'd to be the second picture in the world, was generally raw in his colouring, hard in his contours, and wanted clearness in his carnations, and a knowledge of the Chiaro Oscuro. In short, in my opinion, all the qualities of a perfect painter, never met but in Raphael, Guido, and Annibal Caracci.

DESCRIPTION

On the right-hand you enter a small Breakfast Room.

Over the chimney is a very good picture of Hounds, by *Wootton.*

A Concert of Birds, by *Mario di Fiori*; a very uncommon picture, for he seldom painted anything but flowers; it belonged to *Gibbins* the carver, and is four feet seven inches high, by seven feet nine and a quarter wide.

The Prodigal Son returning to his father; a very dark picture, by *Pordenone,* the architecture and landscape very good. It is five feet five inches high, by eight feet eleven and half wide. This picture belong'd to *George Villiers,* the great Duke of *Buckingham.*

A Horse's Head, a fine sketch, by *Vandyke*. [50]

A Grey-Hound's Head, by old *Wyck*, who was *Wootton's* master.

Sir Edward Walpole, grand-father to Sir *Robert Walpole*. . . .

Robert Walpole, Son to Sir Edward, and father to Sir *Robert Walpole*: he was Member for *Castle-Riseing*, from the first of *William* and *Mary* till his death in 1700. His wife was *Mary* only daughter to Sir *Jeffery Burwell*, by whom he had nineteen children.

Horatio, Lord *Townsend*, father to *Charles* Lord Viscount *Townsend*.

Mr *Harold*, Gardener to Sir *Robert Walpole*, a head by *Ellis*. . . .

[The Supping Parlour, the Hunting Hall, the Coffee-Room omitted.]

THE COMMON PARLOUR

This room is thirty feet long by twenty-one broad. Over the chimney is some fine Pear-tree carving, by *Gibbins*, and in the middle of it hangs a portrait of him by Sir *Godfrey Kneller*. It is a master-piece and equal to any of *Vandyke's*. Three-quarters.

King *William*, an exceeding fine sketch by Sir *Godfrey*, for the large Equestrian Picture which he afterwards executed very ill at *Hampton-Court*, and with several alterations. Four feet three inches high, by three feet wide.*

King *George* the first, a companion to the former, but finished. The figure is by Sir *Godfrey*, which he took from the King at *Guilford* Horse-Race. The horse is new painted by *Wootton*.

A Stud of Horses by *Wovermans*; two feet one inch and three-quarters high, by two feet nine wide. [250]

Venus Bathing, and *Cupids* with a Carr, in a landscape, by *Andrea Sacchi*; one foot ten inches and half high, by two feet six inches wide. It was Lord *Halifax's*. [180]

A Holy Family by *Raphael da Reggio*, a scholar of *Zucchero*; two feet two inches and three quarters high, by one foot and a quarter wide. [70]

A fine picture of Architecture in Perspective, by *Steenwyck*, one foot nine inches high, by two feet eight wide. [80]

A Cook's Shop, by *Teniers*. It is in his very best manner. There are several figures; in particular his own in a hawking habit, with Spaniels; and in the middle an old blind fisher-man, finely painted. Five feet six inches and three-quarters high, by seven feet seven and three-quarters wide. [800]

Another Cook's Shop, by *Martin de Vos*, who was *Snyder's* master, and in this picture has excell'd any thing done by his scholar. It is as large as nature. There is a greyhound snarling at a cat, in a most masterly manner. Five feet eight inches high, by seven feet ten and half wide. [200]

A *Bacchanalian*, by *Rubens*. It is not a very pleasant picture, but the flesh of the *Silenus*

* *Mrs Barry and another actress sat for the two emblematic figures on the foreground, in the great picture.*

and the Female Satyrs are highly colour'd. There is a small design for this picture revers'd, in the Great Duke's Tribune at *Florence*. Two feet eleven inches and three-quarters high, by three feet six wide. [250]

The Nativity, by *Carlo Cignani*. The thought of this picture is borrow'd (as it has often been by other painters) from the famous *Notte* of *Correggio* at Modena, where all the light of the picture flows from the child. Three feet seven inches and half high, by two feet ten and half wide. [250]

Sir *Thomas Chaloner*, an admirable portrait, three-quarters, by *Vandyke*. Sir *Thomas* was Governor to *Henry* Prince of *Wales* (vide *Strafford* Papers, Vol. 1, page 490) and in 1610 appointed his Lord Chamberlain. (Vide *Sandford's* Genealogical Tables, page 529.) He died in 1615, and was buried at *Chiswick*. [200]

Sir *Thomas Gresham*, the Founder of *Gresham*-College, by *Antonio More*. Two feet six inches and a quarter high, by two feet and half wide. [40]

Erasmus, by *Holbein*, a half length, smaller than the life. [40]

A Friar's Head, by *Rubens*. [40]

Francis Halls, Sir *Godfrey Kneller's* master, a Head by himself. [40]

The School of *Athens*, a copy (by *Le Brun*) of *Raphael's* fine picture in the *Vatican*. Three feet two inches high, by four feet two and three-quarters wide. [250]

Joseph Carreras, a *Spanish* Poet, writing: He was Chaplain to *Catherine* of *Braganza*, Queen of *Charles* II. Half length, by Sir *Godfrey Kneller*.

Rembrandt's wife, half length, by *Rembrandt*. [300]

Rubens' wife, a head, by *Rubens*. [60]

A Man's Head, by *Salvator Rosa*. [40]

Mr *Locke*, a Head, by Sir *Godfrey Kneller*.

Inigo Jones, a Head, by *Vandyke*. [50]

Over the door, a Daughter of Sir *Henry Lee*, three-quarters. By Sir *Peter Lely*. She was married to Mr *Wharton*, afterwards created a Marquis; and was herself a celebrated poetess. *Waller* had address'd a Copy of Verses to her on the death of Lord *Rochester*, whose great friend and relation she was.

Over another door, Mrs *Jenny Deering*, mistress to the Marquis of *Wharton*. These two came out of the *Wharton* Collection.

Over the two other doors, two pieces of ruins, by *Viviano*. [40]

[The Library, the little Bed-Chamber, the little Dressing-Room, the blue Damask Bed-Chamber, the Drawing-Room omitted.]

THE SALON

Is forty feet long, forty high, and thirty wide; the hanging is crimson flower'd velvet; the ceiling painted by *Kent*, who design'd all the ornaments throughout the house. The chimney-piece is of black and gold marble, of which too are the tables.

In the broken pediment of the chimney stands a small antique bust of *Venus*; and over the garden-door is a larger antique bust.

On the great table is an exceeding fine bronze of a man and woman, by *John* of *Boulogne*. When he had made the fine Marble Groupe of the Rape of the *Sabines* in the *Loggia* of the *Piazza del Gran Duca* at *Florence*, he was found fault with, for not having expressed enough of the softness of the woman's flesh, on which he modell'd this, which differs in it's attitudes from the other, and has but two figures; but these two are Master-pieces for Drawing, for the strength of the man, and the tender delicacy of the woman. This bronze was a present to Lord *Orford* from *Horace Mann*, Esq; the King's Resident at *Florence*.

On the other tables are two vases of Oriental Alabaster.

Over the chimney, *Christ* baptised by St *John*, a most capital picture of *Albano*. His large pieces are seldom good, but this is equal both for colouring and drawing to any of his master Caracci, or his fellow-scholar *Guido*. It is eight feet eight inches high, by six feet four and a half wide. There is one of the same design in the church of *San Giorgio* at *Bologna*, with an oval top, and God the Father in the Clouds, with different Angels; two are kneeling, and supporting *Christ's* Garments. This picture belong'd to Mr *Laws*, first minister to the Regent of *France*. [700]

The Stoning of *St Stephen*; a capital picture of *Le Soeur*. It contains nineteen figures, and is remarkable for expressing a most masterly variety of grief. The Saint, by a considerable Anachronism, but a very common one among the *Roman* Catholics, is drest in the rich habit of a modern priest at high mass. Nine feet eight inches and a half high, by eleven feet three and three-quarters wide. [500]

The Holy Family, a most celebrated picture of *Vandyke*. The chief part of it is a Dance of Boy-Angels, which are painted in the highest manner. The *Virgin* seems to have been a portrait, and is not handsome; it is too much crowded with Fruits and Flowers and Birds. In the air are two partridges finely painted. This picture was twice sold for fourteen hundred pounds: Since that, it belonged to the House of *Orange*. The Princess of *Friesland*, mother to the present Prince of *Orange*, sold it during his minority, when Sir *Robert* bought it. 'Tis seven feet and half an inch high, by nine feet one and three-quarters wide. [1600]

Mary Magdalen washing *Christ's* Feet; a capital Picture of *Rubens*, finished in the highest manner, and finely preserved. There are fourteen figures large as life. The *Magdalen* is particularly well coloured. Six feet and three-quarters of an inch high, by eight feet two wide. It was Monsieur de *Morville's*. [1600]

The Holy Family in a round, by *Cantarini*. The Child is learning to read. Three feet six inches every way. [300]

The Holy Family, by *Titian*. It belonged to Monsieur de *Morville*, Secretary of State in *France*. Four feet seven inches and a half high, by three feet four and a half wide. [100]

Simeon and the Child; a very fine picture of *Guido*. The design is taken from a statue of Silenus with a young *Bacchus*, in the *Villa Borghese* at *Rome*. This was in Monsieur de *Morville's* Collection. Three feet two inches and a half high, by two feet seven and a half wide. There is another of these, but much less finished, in the Palace of the Marquis *Gerini* at *Florence*. [150]

The *Virgin* with the Child asleep in her arms, by *Augustine Caracci*. Three feet six inches high, by two feet nine and three-quarters wide. [200]

An old Woman giving a Boy Cherries, by *Titian*. It is his own Son and Nurse, four feet ten inches high, by three feet six and three-quarters wide. [100]

The Holy Family, by *Andrea del Sarto*. This and the last were from the collection of the Marquis *Mari* at *Genoa*. Three feet one inch and a quarter high, by two feet seven and a quarter wide. [250]

The Assumption of the *Virgin*; a beautiful figure supported by Boy-Angels, in a very bright Manner, by *Morellio*. Six feet four inches and three-quarters high, by four feet nine and a half wide.* [700]

The Adoration of the Shepherds its companion: All the light comes from the *Child*. [600]

The *Cyclops* at their forge, by *Luca Jordano*. There is a copy of this at St *James's*, by *Walton*. This belong'd to *Gibbins*. Six feet four inches high, by four feet eleven wide. [200]

Daedalus and *Icarus*, by *Le Brun*. In a different manner from what he generally painted. Six feet four inches high, by four feet three wide. For the story, see it twice told in *Ovid's Metamorphosis*, Lib. 8 and Lib. 2. *de Arte Amandi*. . . . [150]

HORACE WALPOLE'S JOURNALS OF VISITS TO COUNTRY SEATS

In the midst of his many other activities between 1751 and 1784, Horace Walpole undertook almost every year a lengthy excursion to see country houses whose contents or architecture were of interest to him. Descriptions of these survive in the form of two notebooks that were transcribed by Paget Toynbee and published by the Walpole Society in 1928.[1] Forty-five such peregrinations were described, of which extracts from two are included here.

Melbury, which Walpole visited in July 1762, was the seat of the Fox-Strangways (the Earls of Ilchester), a family well to the fore in the history of English collectors.[2]

* *The Duke of* Bedford *has a large picture like this, except that it wants the Virgin, by the same hand, brought out of* Spain *by Mr* Bagnols, *from whose Collection the Prince of* Wales *bought some fine pictures.*

[1] Toynbee tells us that they were sold at Sotheby's among a mass of other Walpoliana by Sir Francis Ernest Waller in December 1921 and fetched £50 and £35 respectively! This shows, as much as anything else, how Walpole's reputation has changed in the last forty years.

[2] See also 'A Generous Donation' on page 299. Giles Stephen Fox Strangways, the Sixth Earl of Ilchester, was one of the most distinguished presidents of the Walpole Society (1943–59).

A catalogue of pictures belonging to the Earls

Walpole visited Burghley in July 1763. It is interesting that he knew the English copyists of many of the quasi-Italian paintings which he saw. When Dr Waagen came to Burghley in 1835 he remarked that 'the great masters of the time of Raphael are here rather in name than in reality'. Gustav Waagen arrived just as the Marquess of Exeter was going hunting and he was at first shown round by a housekeeper. He went on to say: 'I have seen no other seat which affords so completely, and on so grand a scale, a view of the taste in the arts which prevailed among the English nobility from the middle of the seventeenth till about the end of the eighteenth century.'

Burghley is one of the few houses rich in printed documentation; among the several early guidebooks were ones published in 1797, 1815 and 1847.

The reader must remember that the pieces which follow are transcribed direct from Walpole's jottings in his notebooks. The style is thus a good deal more abrupt and less polished than in Walpole's other published writings.

EXTRACTED FROM the Sixteenth Volume of the
Walpole Society, 1928.

M*elbury* in Dorsetshire, Seat of Stephen Fox Strangways Earl of Ilchester who married the daughter and sole heiress of Mr Horner, whose wife was the last of the Strangways, who possessed Melbury above 500 years & were allied to most of the ancient nobility. It is a sumptuous old seat in a fine situation, the house ancient, but modernised by Lady Ilchester's grandfather, under the direction of Thomas Sutton, styling himself Architect to Thomas Strangways Esq. There is a very ancient octagon tower, remaining, rising above the house, and adorned with arms and matches of the family in painted glass; as there are others about the house. The apartments are most richly and abundantly furnished with pictures, tapestry, fine tables & the finest old China and Japan, collected by Mrs Horner, & many family pictures; as, a whole length of Sir John Strangways temp. Elisabeth. His wife & little daughter, by Vansomer. Gyles Strangways, his son, who was confined in the Tower by Oliver Cromwell, & of whom there is a medal. It is a very good half length; I believe by Walker. Heads of *Nicholas and Dorothy Wadham.* The present Henry Lord Digby, nephew of Lord Ilchester, in a pink domino, & Mrs Colebrook, daughter of Lord Harry Poulett, afterwards Duke of Bolton, both by Eckardt. Three or four Knights of the Garter, heads 1509. Duke Hamilton & his second Dutchess, sister of Mrs Horner, whole lengths. Two copies by Jervase of the two best Carlo Marattis at Houghton, good whole length of Judge Vaughan, I believe by Riley. Eight heads in stone-coloured frames, of a Master & fellows of a college in Oxford by Mrs Beales; among them, are Tillotson & Stillinfleet. Mrs Mary Digby, the friend of Pope, a small

of Ilchester (at Melbury, Redlynch, Abbotsbury and 42 Belgrave Square) was published privately in 1883. A second volume of those at Holland House appeared in 1904.

Watteau. Lady Sundon, whole length by Amiconi. Lady Susan Fox Strangways, by Ramsay, half length, very good, 1761: she is eldest daughter of Lord Ilchester; in white and green ribbands. Sir Rob. Long, by Rosalba, in crayons. There is a great deal of carving by Gibbons over the Chimnies. The staircase is painted by Thomas Hill, & represents the father and mother of Mrs Horner & all their children. Fine glasses in frames of blue glass & cut.

Near the house stands the parish church, which serves for the chapel. It is built in the shape of a Greek Cross, & is a sweet little building, & tho exceedingly old, looks as if designed for ornament by modern taste. It is quite compleat, with shields and quarterings of painted glass in the windows, & full of tombs of the family of Strangways, from great antiquity to the present times. On each side are two altar tombs, with flying canopies of the best gothic, and Knights lying on them, entire; one, a Strangways the other a Browning; each with a collar about his neck, like the order of the Toison d'or. A table monument for Thomas, brother of Mrs Horner, the epitaph by Dr Friend. Another for Mrs Horner, the inscription composed by Mr Henry Fox, Paymaster, & Mr Philip Francis. A brass on the floor for Sir John Strangways, who died at the siege of Boulogne, temp. Henry 8, & who sold land to fit himself for the interview in the vale of cloth of gold. The font is Saxon & extremely ancient. The altar piece is the only thing unworthy of this valuable little temple, being a square piece of red velvet, bordered with a carving of wood gilt, & adorned with grapes and ears of corn to represent the bread and wine; a design of Mrs Prowse & put up by Mrs Horner, who has also given very magnificent plate to the altar, as she did to three other churches, the two Melburys & Abbotsbury; two churches she built.

The great apartment of the house is unpainted oak.

Close by the house stands a garden seat, ancient & newly adorned with shields and matches of the family.

A lake is near the house, & noble grove of large trees, as there are in the Park; & without it, a charming wood of 200 acres, cut into wild walks with a natural water, & two beautiful cascades. It rises to a very large circular field, round which is an Etoile of six walks, commanding rich views.

Sir John Strangways, of whom I have mentioned the whole length portrait, left an account of his Estate in verse, still preserved in the family.

The Kitchen and Servants' Hall are vey spacious; near them is a cell, built by Mrs Horner to receive beggars. She gave away £3000 a year in charity.

There is a pretty aviary; & in one of the orange trees in the court, I saw a goldfinch sitting on its nest close to the house.

Burghley. A noble pile! the inner court is beautiful scenery. The lesser stair case is very pretty, the roof adorned in fret work and ascending vaulted with the flights of steps. The present earl has made great repairs & newly furnished several chambers gorgeously.

There are prodigious numbers of pictures by Carlo Maratti, Gioseppe Chiari, Carlo Dolce, Luca Jordano & Philippo Laura. The Seneca by Jordano is very capital, some of the Dolces and Lauras very good; the Coriolanus by Chiari one of his best; but the rest are not above middling. In an old unrepaired chamber is a French masqued ball in tapestry. The chapel is too low, & not yet restored: Some of the ornaments & in other parts of the house have been in good taste of grotesque. The eating room is hung with portraits of the family: the great Salon painted by Laguerre; He and Verrio have done a vast deal here; in the Salon the former has in one corner painted two young gentlemen of the family. There is much too of Gibbon's carving, *particularly the last Supper in alto Relievo.* Vast quantities of exceeding fine China & Japan; particularly three small pieces in very good taste, *said to be China made by the second Villiers Duke of Buckingham.* There is tapestry after Albano; several other suits not put up; silver sconces, very fine gilt plate, an old enamel casket; and *a most valuable cabinet, front & sides all painted by Rubens.* Two Chimney-boards painted with birds by Barlow, very good, but quaere. Two fine small Gaspars. Charles Cavendish, a boy, painted after his death by Carlo Maratti. Heads of *Sir Godfrey Kneller and Verrio,* by themselves; the latter strong and good. Fine gold bed & tapestry. Dead game and flowers in glass, by *Vandermin,* who lived long with the last earl. Two flower pieces in work by Miss Gray. Charles I & another of his children, by old Stone, poor. Mr W. Cecil, young, by Wissing, good. Two large & fine flat vessels of the Raphael Fayence, bought by this lord at Mr Hampden's sale, who had them from Jarvis's widow. They cost my Lord £38. Two Gaspars richly coloured, with figures by Philippo Laura. In the best closet are many curiosities: the Adoration of the Magi by Hoskins after Rubens. Qu. Venus & Adonis after Titian by Peter Oliver. Fine enamel after Raphael. Profile of a boy in Brown with snappers* in one hand—*a most capital work of Hoskins,* & of exceeding nature. *Sir Edward Cecil afterwards Lord Wimbledon* by Do. Countess of Devon. Do. *Acteon and Diana by Alex Cooper.* Lord Roos, 1677 P.C. Small holy family, by Carlo Maratti, fine, & other small pieces in oil & waters; particularly St Peter on the waves over the chimney by Lanfranc. In the same closet is a glass case full of rich vases, caskets, trinkets & in pretious stones, crystal, enamel, gold, Philigree &c. Particularly a crystal vase adorned, in the front a cameo of Queen Elizabeth. A fine casket with cameo of Henry 8th & his three children. Enameld ring, & triangular saltseller, that were Queen Elizabeth's. In another chamber a large piece of the Cecils and Cavendishes, by Wissing, bad. Three of the Cecils by Verrio. Head of Queen Elizabeth probably by Mark Garrard, like my coin† & the description in Hentzner.‡ The tribute money, small black & white, Rubens. Head of St John like that at Houghton, by Carlo Dolce. Death of the Virgin, Raphael in his second manner. Lady Herbert by *Ashfield* very highly finished & well. Two Vandermeulens. *Armida enchanting the Sword of Rinaldo, Gennaro.* Stucco

* *Castanets.*

† *Walpole's coin of Queen Elizabeth was engraved by Grignion for his* Royal and Noble Authors (*see* Journal of the Printing-Office at Strawberry Hill, pp. 7, 30).

‡ *That is,* A Journey into England, by Paul Hentzner, in 1598, *printed at Strawberry Hill,* 1757.

cielings in the good loose taste of Charles II. *Susanna & Elders, Lely,* very large Castiliogne–*Second Lord Exeter.* Claud, with figures by Nicolo Poussin. Andrea del Sarto like that at Houghton. Still life of jewels &c in the family. *Earl of Exeter by Carlo Maratti.* An old Knight of the Garter, qu. who, & if not by Dobson. Vast hall & staircase, not yet restored. In the kitchen which is vast, an ox cut open by Snyders. Brown is ornamenting the park & has built a Gothic greenhouse & tables, which are not bad, except that they do not accord with the house which is not Gothic.

PRINCIPLES OF SCULPTURE COLLECTING

KENNEDY'S *Description of the Antiquities and Curiosities in Wilton House* is one of the few accounts which gives the *principles* upon which a collector formed his collection. Thomas Herbert, 8th Earl of Pembroke (1664–1732), was an avid collector of classical antiquities. In 1720 he added more than 1300 busts and other sculptures from the Roman Palace of the Giustiani, a large quantity of objects from the sale of Cardinal Mazarin's collection[1] and many more from the impoverished Neopolitan family of the Valetta. One presumes that he did not adhere too rigidly to the rules he had laid down for his own guidance among these massive purchases. Certainly he was teased by his contemporaries–Winckelmann and Horace Walpole[2] were among them–for being over-zealous in the detail of his attributions. However, Pembroke endeavoured to take the best advice available. From an early guide book to Wilton[3] we learn that 'the first sketch of an account of this collection was drawn up by Earl Thomas with the assistance of one or two friends. On this groundwork, Nicola Haym, an Italian antiquary, was employed to labour;

[1] For fuller details see Michaelis' *Ancient Marbles in Great Britain*, 1882, page 42 onwards. Michaelis tells of the unfortunate fate that befell the original collection and how so many later imitations and repaired pieces came to be part of it.

[2] 'An ancient virtuoso indeed would be a little surprized to find so many of his acquaintances new baptised.' Walpole, *Anecdotes.*

[3] *Aedes Pembrochianae,* a new Account and Description of the Statues, Bustos, Relievos, Paintings, Medals, and other curiosities in Wilton-House. By 1784 the tenth edition of this book was in print: the first had come out in 1774. The first guide, *A Description of the Earl of Pembroke's Pictures*, 1732, was compiled by Count Carlo Gambarini. Kennedy had also written a *New Description of the Pictures . . . at Wilton.* First published in 1758, it had gone into a ninth edition by 1779.

and after him Sir Andrew Fountaine, Martin Folke Esq., president of the Royal Society, and Dr Pocock, communicated their remarks.'

EXTRACTED FROM James Kennedy's *Description of the Antiquities and Curiosities in Wilton-House*, 1769.

THE Earls of Pembroke had from the reign of Henry VIII been encouragers of the fine arts, and very early shewed their taste in employing Holbein and Jones in improving and adorning their noble seat at Wilton; however it was reserved for Earl Thomas, to raise it to a degree of magnificence and splendour, beyond any this nation afforded, and which justly made it vie with the most celebrated abroad.

This Nobleman possessed every qualification, necessary to constitute a real connoisseur and virtuoso, in a very eminent degree. He had an exquisite natural taste, improved by extensive learning, and a fondness for the study of antiques. His conversation with the best Italian Antiquaries of his age, cherished his own propensities, and he resolved to form a collection on a plan, which would render it valuable, and be always a monument of his superiority in this way.

Before he began to purchase, he confined himself by the following limitations:

I. He resolved not to run into all sorts of curiosities but to buy such as were illustrative of antient history and antient literature. It would have been an endless matter to have endeavoured to acquire Gems, Statues, Medals, Relievos, Bustos, domestic utensils and a thousand other antiques, which however Cardinal Albani, many of the Popes, and the present King of Naples have done. Being on the spot when any of these were found, they had opportunities of completing sets, which no foreigner can possibly have. It was therefore certainly more prudent, to decline what he had no hopes of perfecting, than to fill his house with fragments, which would neither satisfy the ignorant nor please the connoisseur.

For this reason he rejected Cameos, Intaglias, and the smaller Lares and Penates. Bustos he was particularly fond of, as they expressed with more strength and exactness, the lineaments of the face. Besides the viewing of these brought to the spectator's mind the history and glorious exploits of antient kings and heroes.

Though his Lordship had a superior esteem for the Antique, yet he greatly praised the grand Duke of Tuscany's collection, consisting of above eight hundred modern Statues. Lewis XIV in his estimation, deserved not less applause, for his encouragement of French artists, who made many Statues in marble and lead after originals, and ornamented his gardens with them. These made excellent models for young statuaries and engravers to copy.

Lord Pembroke was sensible, that in a few years sculpture would receive but little encouragement, that Antiques would be monopolised in a few hands, and therefore was willing, before this event took place, as many copies might be taken, as would disseminate a correct taste, and give a relish for antient beauties. This accordingly is come to pass, at present a sculptor of the best genius can scarce find employment, while every paultry painter, who can sketch a likeness, is caressed.

II. No duplicates were admitted. This rule is so necessary for every collector to observe that it seems strange any should violate it. What purpose can statues with similar heads, trunks and draperies serve? Undoubtedly none useful; they can only occupy spaces, which may easily be filled up with other things more valuable.

The case is widely different in respect of Divinities. As the symbols of many of these could not with propriety be represented together, so more figures than one of them became necessary. To exemplify this: *Venus rising from the sea* cannot be exhibited but in that one action. Suppose her chariot drawn by Doves, with Cupid, Mars, Adonis, and a variety of other Actions and Deities belonging to here were introduced into one piece, what would be the consequence, but that it must disgust every observer, as all things so crouded universally do? *Venus picking a thorn out of her foot*, and *Venus holding a shell*, are as different in attitude, as if they no way related to the same person.

The same reasoning will hold good of Apollo, Hercules, Bacchus and others, so that his Lordship most judiciously multiplied such Statues as were explanatory of different Attributes; for thereby, as it were a history was made of these Divinities.

Altars, Urns and such like came under the denomination of Duplicates, for the most part; however some of them preserved in Relievo many curious things, relative to the sepulture, marriages and other rites and ceremonies of the Greeks and Romans; when this was the case, they were valued and retained. Accordingly here are eleven sorts of interment and five different Altars.

III. Lord Pembroke rejected whole Nations, as the productions of Egypt, Hetruria and Magna Graecia; though he admitted a few to diversify his collection. The numerous and whimsical Egyptian Deities, which captivate the eyes of some connoisseurs, were looked on by his Lordship with indifference. The Hieroglyphics wherewith they are loaded, at present are unintelligible, or if they were known, could communicate nothing worthy attention. He therefore was satisfied with an Isis, Osiris and Orus, nor was he solicitous about more; though he greatly admired the Jaspers and marbles of that Country.

HETRUSCAN figures are not less *outré* and inexplicable than the foregoing, yet great regard has been paid to the works of that country and much pains taken to elucidate them. Some of their Vases, particularly are beautifully relieved and painted; but not easily to be met with, unless in the Cabinets of the Curious. Even were they to have been procured they would have answered none of his Lordship's views.

For the same reason, the Basso Relievos of Valetta who lived in Magna Graecia (the kingdom of Naples) were not purchased, though antient, because Sculpture did not flourish in that country till after its decline in Greece. There were but little hopes of finding valuable pieces there, especially as we know the Romans pillaged all the neighbouring Kingdoms to adorn their capital.

IV. Even works of the best ages were bought with limitations. As images were objects of adoration with the heathens from the earliest times, they consequently were multiplied, each family having many, and the temples great numbers. To this religious opinion concerning statues, that they represented the Deity under a human appearance, is owing the improvement and perfection of sculpture. Statues at the beginning, were as gross as Mens conceptions, being little better than rude stones and blocks without shape. As politeness and improvement advanced, they entertained more becoming ideas of the divine nature, and the only means they had of expressing them suitably, were to exhibit them under those appearances most esteemed among men.

Thus beauty, or a just conformation of features, with a complexion suited to the climate, has always and ever will claim the love and admiration of the beholder. Hence the most beauteous persons were the models for their Gods and Goddesses, and the closer they followed the original, the nearer they approached to perfection. His Lordship observed, that this perfection was not to be expected in the antient productions of the Grecian artists, it was a work of time, advanced but slowly, and was confined, in some measure, to a particular Epoch.

Nothing does more honour to Lord Pembroke's taste than confining his choice to the best Ages. . . .[1]

COLLECTORS FIRST COLLECTED

THE full title of the two little volumes from which the following extracts are taken is *The English Connoisseur: containing an account of whatever is curious in painting, sculpture, &c., in the palaces and seats of the nobility and principal gentry of England, both in town and country.* The work was published anonymously in 1766 but the editor and author of the preface has been identified as Thomas Martyn (1735–1825), a botanist. Full details of the sources of the material, which was almost entirely taken from earlier publications, are contained in a fascinating article by Frank Simpson, 'The English Connoisseur and its Sources', *Burlington Magazine*, Vol. XLIII, 1950.

The two volumes include descriptions[2] of the contents of the house of Mr John

[1] Kennedy mentions two other tenets which the Earl of Pembroke observed when forming his collection. He avoided inscriptions ('which some value so highly') unless they were of some particular historical significance. He did not purchase 'unknown Heads' or fragments, 'His Lordship's design being, as is apparent from what has been said, to make a Collection of Antiques not mutilated, he could not, consistently, include any in it which were so. They did very well for Statuaries to copy, but otherwise were mere lumber.'

[2] The spellings given are Martyn's.

Barnard, Belvedere (Sir Samson Gideon, afterwards Lord Eardsly); Blenheim (Duke of Marlborough); Chatsworth (Duke of Devonshire); Chiswick (built by the Earl of Burlington, then owned by the Duke of Devonshire); Devonshire House, Piccadilly (Duke of Devonshire); Ditchley (Earl of Litchfield); Foot's Cray Place, Kent (Mr Bouchier Cleeve); Hagley Park (Lord Lyttelton); Hampton Court; Houghton Hall (Sir Robert Walpole); the house of Mr Charles Jennens in Ormond Street, Holborn; Kensington Palace; the Leasowes, Shropshire (Mr William Shenstone).

In London Martyn covered the Antiquarian Society; Banquetting House, Whitehall; Barber's Hall; Bartholomew's and Bethlehem Hospitals; Bridewell; Charing Cross; Foundling Hospital, in Lamb's Conduit Fields; the Royal Palace of St James's; the House of Lords: St Mary le Bow; the Monument; Northumberland House; the Painter Stainer's Hall, College of Physicians; Queen's Palace (then containing the Raphael cartoons); St Paul's Cathedral; Shaftesbury House; Somerset House; the house of Colonel Sothby in Bloomsbury Square; St Stephen's, Walbrook; the house of James West. Outside London he described the collection of Mr Paul Methuen, at some length; then Okeover, in Derbyshire.

In Oxford he described All Souls College; the Ashmolean Museum; the pictures in the Bodleian Library; Christ-Church including the collection of books left to the college by General Guise; St John's College; Magdalene [sic] College; the Music School; New College; the Picture Gallery; the Pomfret Statues; the Theatre (Sheldonean); University College and Wadham College; the house of Sir Gregory Page in Blackheath; Kedleston, near Derby (Lord Scarsdale); Stowe (Earl Temple); Wilton (Earl of Pembroke) and Windsor Castle.

Martyn's normal treatment tends to be rather monotonous, but one of the most interesting descriptions is that of the collection of Mr Paul Methuen. This was in fact based on a catalogue compiled by Horace Walpole. The collection passed by descent to Lord Methuen of Corsham House near Bath, where the great majority of the paintings still are; some were disposed of in sales at Christie's in 1840, 1899 and 1920.

EXTRACTED FROM *The English Connoisseur*, Vols. I and II, 1766.

PREFACE

THE great progress which the polite arts have lately made in England, and the attention which is now paid them by almost all ranks of men; seem to render an apology for a work of this nature wholly unnecessary. The only way, by which we can ever hope to arrive at any skill in distinguishing the stile of the different masters in Painting, is the study of their works: any assistance therefore in this point cannot but be grateful to the rising Connoisseur. It is well known at how few of those houses into which, by the indulgence of their illustrious owners, the curious are admitted, any catalogues of the paintings and other curiosities, which adorn them can be obtained; and without such catalogues it must be confessed little use can be made, by the yet uninformed observer of these valuable collections, besides that general one of pleasing the eye and the imagination, by viewing a variety of delightful objects. The editor of the following trifle, aware of the necessity of such assistance, when he first designed to travel about his native country, in order among other views to become acquainted with the manner of such principal masters in painting, looked out for books giving an account of the curiosities which the seats of the nobility and gentry, in various parts of the kingdom, contain. From the few that fell into his hands, he abstracted what he thought was to his purpose; and in his progresses, corrected in them whatever he thought amiss, and made addition when he found them deficient. Where no catalogue had been before printed he endeavoured to obtain one, or to make out such an one as he was able to do, from a survey of the house and information. If this work, which the editor here offers the young student in the polite arts, should at all contribute to promote or facilitate the study of them among his countrymen, he will have gained all the end which he aims at.

The curious observer will find ample and instructive lessons on the Italian schools in the houses of our nobility and gentry. Mr Walpole* scruples not to assert that 'there are not a great many collections left in Italy more worth seeing than that at Houghton. In the preservation of the pictures it certainly excells most of them.'

It should be observed in commendation of the taste which our illustrious countrymen in general have showed, that they have preferred the greatness of design and composition in which the Italian masters are so well known to excell, before the gaudy Flemish colouring, 'or the drudging mimickry of nature's most uncomely coarseness,'† upon which the Dutch so much value themselves. To deny these their proper share of merit, or to refuse them a place in a collection, would be ridiculous; but surely to set them in competition with Italian sublimity is much more so.

When the editor was in Holland, the great predilection of the Dutch for their own painters could not escape his observation; scarce anything being seen in their cabinets but the laboured productions of their own masters. In France, where he had the pleasure of surveying abundance of Italian pictures, and where the Orleans Collection alone would compensate the pains of any traveller; he could not but often smile to see the tawdry productions of their own artists set upon a level, nay sometimes, with true French vanity even jostling or thrusting aside the divine productions of the Italian Pencils. At this time he could scarcely help felicitating his own countrymen, upon their not having produced artists of sufficient eminence, to give them a pretence of burying a taste for real merit and greatness under national prejudice.

When this, however, is said in commendation of the predominant taste of the English, it is not to be understood, as if there were wanting among us sufficient specimens of either

* *Aedes Walpolianae, Introduction.* † *Ibid.*

Dutch or Flemish schools; we only have them not in so great number or perfection as in Holland and Flanders. . . .

The editor cannot help concluding with a wish that the nobility and gentry would condescend to make their cabinets and collections accessible to the curious as is consistent with their safety. The polite arts are rising in Britain, and call for the fostering hand of the rich and powerful: one certain way of advancing them, is to give all possible opportunities to those who make them their study, to contemplate the works of the best masters, that they may not form a bad taste and a poor manner upon such productions as chance throws in their way. It ought to be acknowledged with gratitude, that many of the collections of the great, are ever open to the inspection of the curious; who have been permitted by some in the most liberal manner to take copies of their paintings, and to make drawings from them; but at the same time it must be lamented that some cabinets are not accessible without difficulty and interest. It should be mentioned to the honour of the French nation, that their collections are come at, even by foreigners, with great facility: in particular the royal pictures are not locked up in private apartments from the eye of the people, but are the pictures of the public.

To anyone who is desirous of becoming acquainted with the principles of Painting without much labour, the editor would recommend *Count Algarotti's* elegant little treatise or *Essay on Painting*, written in the Italian language and lately translated into English.

PAUL METHUEN ESQ.

In Grosvenor-Street

ON THE FIRST FLOOR [The second floor has been omitted.]

IN THE HALL AND STAIR-CASE

Over the Chimney

A Naked Boy blowing bubbles, and treading on a Death's Head, representing Vanity by *Elizabeth Sirani.*

Near the Street Door

A large picture of Dogs and Foxes, by *Peter Snyders.*

Over the Door that goes into the first Parlour

A Man's Head, by *Gioseppe de Ribera,* commonly called *Il Spagnoletto.*

On the Landing Place

A large picture of David and Abigail, by *Sir Peter Paul Rubens.*

Over the Door

The Adventure of Don Quixote and the Barber, by a Spanish Painter.

Fronting the Landing-Place at the Top

The Portrait of the Duchess of Mantua, Grand-daughter to the Emperor Charles the Fifth, with her Son in her lap, who was the last Duke of Mantua, with some allegorical figures, armour, &c. by *Giovanni Benedetto Castiglione.*

Under it

A Landscape, and a musical conversation, painted by *Sir Peter Lely*; being the portraits of himself and his whole Family, drawn by the life.

Fronting the Windows

The Judgement of Paris, by *Gerard Lairess.*

Under it

The Judgement of Midas, by the same hand.

Over the Looking-Glass

A young Lad blowing bubbles, said to be painted by *Annibal Caracci.*

IN THE FIRST PARLOUR

Over the Chimney

A Dutch Kermis, or Country Fair, painted by old *Peter Brughel.*

On each side of the Chimney–Next the Window

The Portrait of a Turk, by *Rembrandt Van Ryhn.*
David with the Head of Goliath and his sling, by *Leonello Spada.*

Between the Windows

A Man's Head, said to be that of Massaniello the Fisherman, who caused the great revolution of Naples, by *Salvator Rosa.*

The Portrait of Francisco de Taxis, the first inventor of the Posts in Europe, for which reason the direction of them has always remained in one of his Family in all the dominions that belong to the House of Austria, by a hand not certainly known.

Over the Doors out of the Hall

The Folly of spending our Lives in the Pursuit of Love, Wine, Music and play, an emblematical picture by *Johannes Schorel.*

The Virgin, Our Saviour, Mary Magdalen, St Peter, John the Baptist and St Jerome; by *Jacobo Palma.*

Over the Marble Table

The Birth of Our Saviour, and the Adoration of the Shepherds, by *Giac. Bassan.*

Under it in the Middle

St John the Baptist asleep in the desart, by *Andrea del Sarto.*

On both Sides of it

Two small Sea Pieces, a port in the Mediterranean, and a fight with the Turks, by *William Vandevelde,* Junior.

Under them, in the Middle

An emblematical picture, representing a guardian Angel pointing out the way to Heaven to a soul, under the figure of a young girl, by *Carlo Dolce.*

On both Sides of it

Two very highly finished Landscapes on Copper, by *Salvator Rosa.*

Between the two Doors

The Portrait of the Duke of Richmond and Lenox, of the Stuart Family, at whole length, with a Dog, by *Vandyke.*

Over the Door to the Back Parlour

Vulcan at his forge, with the Cyclops, by *Jacob Jordans,* of Antwerp.

Over against the Windows–in the Middle

The Head of our Saviour crowned with Thorns, by *Ludovico Caracci.*

On both Sides of that

Two Fruit Pieces, by *Michael Angelo Pase,* called *Michael Angelo del Campidoglio.*

Under them, in the Middle

A Bacchanal in two colours, by *Rubens.*

On both Sides of it

Landscape, with a Robbery, and a Battle, both painted by *Giacomo Cortese,* commonly called *Il Bourgognone.*

Under them, in the Middle

A pretty large landscape, and figures of Dutch Boors, by *Adrian Van Ostade.*

On both Sides of it

A Stag-hunting, and another of Hern Hawking, by *Philip Woverman.*

Under them

Two Conversations of Boors within doors, by *Ostade.*

IN THE SECOND PARLOUR

Over the Chimney

Lot and his two Daughters, with the city of Sodom on Fire, by *Lorenzo Lotti,* a great imitator of *Giorgione* and *Titian.*

Over the Closet Doors–Next the Window

The great amphitheatre at Rome, and other buildings, by *Viviano Cadaborra.*

A Sea Port, with Buildings and Ruins, by *Salviouch,* and the Figures by *John Miele.*

Over the Door to the First Parlour

Omphale the Mistress of Hercules, with the Lion's Skin and his Club by her, by *Augustin Caracci.*

Over the two Doors

Two Battles in the style of *Bourgognone,* but the hands not certainly known.

IN THE PASSAGE ROOM

Over the Doors

A Philosopher with a Book in his hand, by *Pier Francesco Mola.*

Mary Magdalen, by *Giacinto Brandi.*

Our Saviour meditating on the Sins of the world, by *Giovanni Antonio Regillio,* a competitor of Titian, and commonly called *Il Pordenone.*

IN THE GREAT ROOM

Over the Door at which you go in

The Portrait of a young Man on wood, by *Andrea del Sarto.*

Between that Door and the Windows

The Head of St James the Apostle.

The Head of St John the Evangelist.

N.B. These two last pictures are by a hand not certainly known.

Under them

A Bacchanal painted on copper, by *Cornelius Polemburgh.*

Between the Door and the Wall–in the Middle

A pretty large picture of Our Saviour and the Samaritan Woman, by *Giovanni Francesco Barbiori da Cento,* commonly called *Il Guercino.*

On the Side towards the Door

The Virgin and Child, by *Il Cavalier Giovanni Langfranchi.*

On the Side towards the Wall

Venus dressing, and Cupid holding her Looking Glass, *by Paolo Veronese.*

Under them, in the Middle

The Virgin and Child, by *Raphael de Urbino.*

On the Side towards the Door

The Virgin and Child in the Clouds, and several Angels, by *Bartholomeo Murillo.*

On the Side towards the Wall

The Virgin and our Saviour, by *Carlo Cignani.*

Next to the Door

The Annunciation of the Virgin Mary, by *Paolo Veronese.*

Next to the Wall

The Birth of our Saviour, &c. by *Jacopo Robusti,* commonly called, *Tintoretto.*

Over the Chimney

Tobit and the Angel, by *Michael Angelo Caravaggio.*

Between the Wall and the Chimney–in the Middle

The Portrait of a Man, by *Antonio Allegri,* commonly called *Il Corregio.*

Towards the Wall

The Head of some Spanish General, by *Giovanni Giachinette,* commonly called *Il Bourgognone delle Teste.*

Towards the Chimney

The Portrait of the Famous Fernando Cortes, conqueror of Mexico, by Titiano Vecelli, called *Il Titiano.*

Under them

A large Battle in an oval, painted by *Luca Jordano.*

Between the Chimney and the farthest Wall–in the middle

St Sebastian, by *Guido Reni.*

Next to the Chimney

The Portrait of St [sic] Anthony Vandyke, painted by *Himself.*

Next to the Wall

The Portrait of a young Girl, with a little dog asleep in her hands, by *Rembrandt.*

Under them

A large oval Battle, painted by *Luca Jordano.*

Over the Closet Door

The Portrait of a Man with a book in his hand, said to be the famous satyrist Berni, by *Giorgio Barbarelli,* called *Il Giorgione.*

Between the Door and the Wall

A She Saint, with Angels, by *Pietro Beretini,* called *Pietro Cortona.*

Under it in the Middle

A small Battle, by *Bourgognone.*

On both sides of it

Two small pictures, done from the Gallery of Arch-Duke Leopald, the one from Paris Bourdon, and the other from young Palma, by *David Teniers.*

Between the Door and the Window

A large picture, representing our Saviour at the Pharisee's house, and Mary Magdalen anointing his feet, with the portrait of the person for whom it was painted, as a servant waiting at table, by *Carlo Dolce.*

N.B. This Picture is out of the stile of *Carlo Dolce's* paintings, who never before attempted so great a subject and composition; and was done by him after the drawing of *Ludovico Cigoli.*

Under it in the Middle

The Portraits of three of Henry the 7th's Children, viz. Prince Arthur, Henry the 8th, and Princess Mary, who was afterwards Queen of France, and Dutchess of Brandon, by a hand not certainly known.

On both sides of it

Two pieces of the history of Judith, the one where she is presented to Holofernes, and the other where she is entertained by him at a feast, by *Paolo Veronese.*

THE RESTA DRAWINGS FOR SALE

English collectors have always been enthusiastic collectors of drawings and any number of quotations could be cited why this was the case. There were three principal reasons: drawings were often more informative about the artist's style, technique and work than the finished paintings for which they were preliminary sketches, and many collectors thought them more beautiful; a large number of drawings could be kept in a small space—latterly in Solander cases; and, finally, they could be acquired for a tiny outlay in comparison with framed oil paintings.

Talman's offer to the Dean of Christ Church of the celebrated collection of drawings assembled by Padre Sebastiano Resta, a Milanese *dilettante*, is included here as one of the earliest and most mouth-watering morsels in its class ever to come on to the English market—2111 drawings by some of the greatest painters of Western civilisation for the sum of £750, which, according to Talman, might well be reduced to £600 after bargaining! That this letter was something of a classic is borne out by its inclusion by Bathoe in the Catalogue of the Duke of

Buckingham's Collection in 1758. The editor of this volume[1] was Vertue once again, and he no doubt was encouraged by Horace Walpole.

John Talman, who died in 1726, was the son of William Talman, the architect of the Palace of Chatsworth built by William, 2nd Duke of Devonshire (1665–1729), who was himself the owner of an important collection of drawings. Talman spent much of his life in Italy and became the first director of the Society of Antiquaries in 1718. He was a considerable collector of drawings in his own right and there are three albums of prints and drawings which he assembled in the Ashmolean Museum.

He succeeded in selling at least part of the Resta Collection in England to Christ Church on the one hand, and John Lord Somers (1651–1716) on the other.[2] Many of the latter's drawings, bearing the so-called Resta-Somers mark, are now in the collection of the Duke of Devonshire at Chatsworth. One complete volume has survived and is in the Ambrosiana Library at Milan.[3]

Copy of a letter from Mr J. TALMAN to Dr ALDRICH, Dean of Christ-church recommending the fine collection of drawings of the Bishop of AREZZO, collected by Father RESTA

FLORENCE, March 2 N.S. 17 09/10

SIR,

I have lately seen a collection of drawings, without doubt the finest in Europe, for the method and number of rare designs; nor is the price, considering the true value, at all too much. Mr Envoy I have waited on to see them, who is of the same opinion; and has desired me to let an abstract of my catalogue, which I am making with all exactness, to be copied out to send to my lord president: I send an abstract with this post, as I have done to Mr Topham, to shew to several lords. This collection belonged to Monsignor Marchetti, bishop of Arezzo, now in the possession of chevalier Marchetti of Pistoia, nephew to the said bishop: which collection is to be sold. It consisteth of sixteen volumes in folio, gilt on the back and sides, and most of them bound in red turky leather. These books were at first collected by the famous father Resta, a Milanese, of the oratory of St Philippo Neri at Rome, a person so well known in Rome and all over Italy for his skill in drawings, that it would be needless to say any more of him, than that these collections were made by him

[1] It also included a catalogue of Sir Peter Lely's collection; a description of Easton-Neston in Northamptonshire and its contents, and a description of the Cartoons at Hampton Court.

[2] They were dispersed again by auction after his death.

[3] For fuller details of the Resta Collection, see the article by A. E. Popham in *Old Master Drawings*, Vol. XI, No. 41, June 1936. The author mentions a manuscript catalogue in the British Museum which is a copy by the Richardsons of the 'remarks' written by Resta in some of the volumes of one of his collections of drawings.

and that through the whole work he has added abundance of observations (gathered by the application and experience of fifty years) no where else to be seen, every book being filled with notes on each drawing; with several corrections of those that have wrote the lives of the painters. The design of this work is to shew the rise and fall of painting in divers periods of time.

In the first volume, (which is bound as above mentioned, and is fourteen inches broad and twenty high) painting is divided into Pittura nascente, crescente et adulta. In the first page are the heads of those popes who reigned during the said periods; the first beginning in the time of Gregory IX, 1227, containing twenty-one popes; the second, in the time of Innocent VI, 1352, containing fourteen popes; the third period, in the time of Paul II, 1464, containing five popes. In the index are all the names of the painters whose works are contained in this volume, which contains sixty-nine pages, and one hundred and thirty-seven drawings. Numbers of drawings of the most considerable masters in this book are, Albert Durer two, Leonardo da Vinci four, M. Angelo four, Andrea Mantegna twenty-three, P. Perugino six, Raff. Urbin seven; under every drawing in this and all other books is set down the master's name, from whence it came, by whom given, and when.

The second volume, red as the former, containeth the golden age, or painting compleat, with a copious index. There are nine pages in all relating to the works of Buonaroti, Titian and Corregio, the heads of the golden age. Leonardo da Vinci, as being the most antient, and first who gave light to this age, is placed by himself, and forms a class alone: but by way of introduction to shew the drawings of this bright period, here are exhibited some specimens of the masters, of the masters of the foresaid four heads of grand families of this compleat age, viz. of Girlandaio to Raphael, of Andrea Mantegna master to Corregio. The first drawing in this book is the ritratto of Bramantini, a Milanese painter, who tho' properly belonging to the former period, yet to do honour to the country of father Resta, a Milanese, where he did so much in the art of painting, as to be esteemed the introducer of the golden age into that city; is therefore placed in the front. Before the annotations, is set the ritratto of father Resta, looking in this volume, and as it were shewing of it, with great joy, to Carlo Maratti. This drawing was made by the said Carlo, 1689, as his own hand-writing underneath shews. This book contains one hundred and sixty-nine pages, and three hundred drawings. That age began in the pontificate of Julius II and comprizes that of Paul III &c. this tome ends in the reign of Julius III and the last design but one is a beautiful cartel containing the arms of the pope, supported by the figures of justice and victory, to intimate that this age terminated triumphantly. Number of drawings of the principal masters are And. del Sarto six, Bandinelli six, Corregio five, D. de Volterra six, Giorgioni seven, Giul. Romano fifteen, Leonardo da Vinci [*missing*], M. Angelo fourteen, Pordenone nine, Polidoro twenty-eight, Parmegiano sixteen, Penno nineteen, Raphael seven, Titian six, and Vasari four.

The third volume contains the Bracheal, or age of experience, beginning in the time of Pius IV, anno 1560, comprehending ten popes, to 1591. The division is into three grand schools, Zuccari, Mutiano, and the Caracci, under three heads; all the other masters are ranged. This book has two hundred and twenty-two pages, three hundred and thirty drawings.

The fourth volume is called the age of painting, restored by Caracci, is bound as the former, and is as it were a second part of the last school in the third volume, pages one hundred and forty-four; to an appendix seven pages, drawings in all two hundred and twenty-one.

Fifth volume (this volume bound more richly than the other four) is against Vasari, or Florentine Vasari, against Bolognese Vasari; the title of the book is Felsina Vindicata, or, Felsina in aureo sæculo argentea in argentea aurea; the last drawing in the book is a victory of Corregio, to shew that Lombardy justly triumphs over Tuscany, page 87; drawings, all bordered with gold, one hundred and nine.

Sixth volume. This contains the antient Greek painting in the mosaick at Rome and elsewhere, all by one hand, numb. 24. bound in parchment, gilt back and side.

Seventh volume. Curious landscapes and views of towns, with borders of gold about. them, pages sixty, drawings sixty-nine; bound in plain parchment, no index; these drawings are of all the great masters.

Eighth volume. Saggio di Secola (curiously bound in blue turkey leather, all gilt sides and back) or specimens of painting for five centuries, viz. 1300 inclusive to 1700 inclusive, beginning with the story of Coriolanus, done by Caracci from the baths of Titus Romæ, and a most curious miniature of Cimabue; no index; the drawings bordered with gold, one hundred and ten; pages seventy-nine: the two last drawings are of Caracci. Finis habet rationem optimi. See at the end.

Ninth volume. This is called the senators in the antient cabinet, or, The cabinet council of the grand judges of art, to whose works exhibited in this book all causes of appeal are to be carried. These senators are, Leonardo da Vinci, M. Angelo, Andrea del Sarto, Georgione, Titian, Raphael, and Corregio, the grand tribunal for the golden age. Beginning of the silver age, the judges are: Zuccari, Barrocci, and Procacino; at the end of that age. The judges are the Caracci: thus none are admitted, but such as are truly worthy and experienced persons. Lanfranco, with his Corregiescan and Carracuscan genius, is the last of those in this book and of the cabinet council; his school opens the grand senate: but Annibal Caracci by a special privilege, can vote in all causes. The drawings are forty-three, and are bordered with gold, and are of the prime masters only. In twenty-four pages.

Tenth volume. Saggio del Secoli shewing specimens of painting in the early ages, beginning with the drawing of a Greek, in the time of Cimabue and Giotto. Drawings one hundred and fifty, all bordered with gold.

Eleven and twelve. Two books (red turkey leather) eleven inches broad, sixteen inches high, full of curious drawings of all sorts of masters, for two hundred years, merely designed for entertainment, without any regard had to the history of painting, though every drawing has notes to it; in the first book one hundred and eleven pages, and drawings one hundred and forty-four. In the second book, seventy pages, and one hundred and seventy-two drawings; amongst which a great many of Raphael and other great masters.

Thirteenth volume. A small but very excellent series of drawings (bound in parchment, gilt) beginning with P. Perrugino, 1446, and brought down to the present time. Here, amongst the drawings of Raphael, is one which the father calls the oriental pearl; pages forty, and drawings seventy-two, adorned with gold.

Fourteenth volume. This book contains Schemata prima, Scholi magni monumenta laboris, or several designs for the cupola at Parma, viz. three different designs for the assumption, and two for the apostles; all in red chalk, by Corregio. Pages seven, drawings five with abundance of notes.

Fifteenth volume. This has more designs for the said cupola of the hand of Corregio, and with abundance of notes. This volume, with the last, are of a size bigger than all the rest, broad eighteen inches, high twenty-eight inches.

Volume sixteen. It contains abundance of designs of all the great masters, as of Corregio, his disciples and imitators, &c. In the title page is an emblem with this motto, Nostri quondam libamen amoris, pages sixty-five, drawings two hundred and nineteen, that is of principal masters. Del Sarto four, Procacino three, Barrocio four, Remini two, Corregio thirty-five, Lud. Carraci twelve, Annibal Carraci twelve, Polidor four, Parmegiano nineteen, Cortona three, Raph. Urbin ten, And. Sacchi two, and Titian four; Tad. Zuccari is the last drawing but one, is a lofty and noble portico called the academical, in which are represented father Resta and several figures bringing this collection to the bishop, who is sitting in a chair, with the cavalier Porchetti his nephew standing by him, to whom the bishop, by laying his hand on his breast, shews the great satisfaction he has in being possessor of so noble a collection; which consists of two thousand one hundred and eleven drawings. This great drawing is of the design of Passeri, and finely coloured. Total number of drawings in this whole collection of principal masters, except those books where there are no indexes: Leonardo da Vinci twelve, M. Angelo twenty-seven, Andr. Mantegna twenty-three, Perugino six, Ralph Urbin twenty-five, And. del Sarto ten, B. Bandinelli six, Corregio sixty-three, Dan. di Volterra sixty-one, Georgione seven, Julio Bonasoni fifteen, Pordenone nine, Polidor thirty-two, Parmensi thirty-five, Perino twenty-one, Titian twelve, Berninis fourteen, Sacchio eight, and Carraci seventy-four, Domenichino forty-five, Guido six, Della Bella twelve, Callot many, in all, with the rest mentioned in that catalogue, five hundred and twenty-seven, and with two thousand one hundred and eleven drawings; they demand three thousand crowns, or seven hundred and fifty pounds sterling. I hope they will fall one thousand, which will bring it to six hundred pound. If they are worth any money, they are worth six hundred pound sterling.

Sir,

Your most humble servant,

JOHN TALMAN

[Bathoe or Vertue added the following comment:]

This collection was purchased, I think, by lord Somers; and Mr Richardson, painter, collated, purchased and exchanged many, which were sold and dispersed in his sale.

N.B. Mr Talman was a gentleman of fortune, and was many years in Italy; he copied very accurately, in water colours, the inside of churches, marbles, &c. He was afterwards admitted a member of the society of Antiquaries in London, for whom he made several very fine drawings, many of which he presented to the society.

[*For a very full account of John Talman's work and life, and an annotated re-printing of his letter book , 1707–1712, as well as details of his collections, see the 59th volume of the Walpole Society, 1997.*]

REYNOLDS REPORTS TO THE DUKE OF RUTLAND

WHEN Sir Joshua Reynolds set out for Brussels in 1785 he was sixty-two and had been President of the Royal Academy for seventeen years. So the Duke of Rutland could hardly have chosen anyone better to act as his agent at what promised to be a most important sale of paintings. In the event, it proved to be a disappointment, though Reynolds did ultimately spend nearly £1000 during the course of the sale's six weeks duration.[1]

Reynolds was a penetrating critic with a taste ahead of his time, and a collector on a grand scale in his own right. After his death in 1792 Christie's sold his own collection of 411 paintings. Reynolds' executors said in their preface to the catalogue: 'In this collection was vested a *large*, if not the *largest* Part of his Fortune and he was not likely from *Ignorance*, *Inattention* or want of practical or speculative judgement to make great expenses for things of small or uncertain value.'[2] However, one cannot help wondering about this statement when one reads that there were 70 paintings by van Dyck, 54 by Correggio, 32 by Tintoretto, 12 by Leonardo, 44 by Michaelangelo, 32 by Rubens, 24 by Raphael, 19 by Rembrandt and 13 by Titian! But there can be no doubt that Reynolds formed one of the major collections of his time, which was made particularly interesting by his fascination for portraits of other artists including, for example, Raphael by Rembrandt, and Rubens with two fellow artists by van Dyck.[3]

---

[1] *Life and Times of Sir Joshua Reynolds*, Leslie and Taylor, London, 1865.

[2] The total for the sale of the Reynolds pictures was £10,319.

[3] A detailed study of Reynolds' Collection appeared as editorials in three consecutive issues of the *Burlington Magazine* for June, July and August 1945.

SIR JOSHUA REYNOLDS

FROM *Letters of Sir Joshua Reynolds*, edited by F. W. Hilles, 1929.

To the DUKE OF RUTLAND

London, 19 July 1785

. . . I set out tomorrow morning for Brussels, and consequently take the liberty of writing to your Grace in the midst of hurry and confusion. I have but just received a catalogue of the pictures which are now on view at Brussels. The Emperor has suppressed sixty-six religious houses, the pictures of which are to be sold by auction. Le Comte de Kageneck* informs me the Emperor has selected for himself some of the principal pictures; however, there is one altar-piece which belonged to the Convent of the *Dames Blanches* at Lovain, which is to be sold. The subject is the Adoration of the Magi, ten feet by seven feet eight inches, which I take to be about the size of your picture of Rubens.† I do not recollect this picture accurately, and, what is *valde diflendus*, I have no notes to refer to – they are, alas in your Grace's possession‡. This picture, I suspect is the only one worth purchasing if your Grace has any such intention, or will honour me with discretionary orders in regard to other pictures. I shall leave orders for your letter to be forwarded to me at Brussels. The sale does not begin till the twelvth of September; during the whole month of August the pictures are shut up, but for what reason I cannot imagine. The principal object of my journey is to re-examine and leave a commission for a picture of Rubens of a St Justus – a figure with his head in his hands after it had been cut off – as I wish to have it for the excellency of its painting §; the oddness of the subject will, I hope, make it cheap. Whether it will be a bargain or not I am resolved to have it at any rate. I have taken the liberty to take Mr Crab's verses|| with me, having but just now received your Grace's letter in which they were contained. I shall have time to examine them critically on the road. I shall have the honour of writing to your Grace again from Brussels. . . .

London, 22 August 1785

. . . I set out for Brussels the day after I wrote to your Grace, but left word that if any answer arrived it was to be sent after me, but my stay abroad was so short that I missed it; however, I have since received it in London. I was much disappointed in the pictures of the suppresed religious houses; they are the saddest trash that ever were collected

* *Envoy extraordinary and minister plenipotentiary from Austria and Germany* (1782–1786).

† *In* 1779 *Rutland had bought at the Verhulst Sale at Brussels Rubens' famous picture of the Virgin and Christ, St Catherine, and other female saints.*

‡ *About 'The Adoration of the Magi' Reynolds had written: 'a slight performance. The Virgin holds the Infant, but awkwardly, appearing to pinch the thigh'.* (The Literary Works of Sir Joshua Reynolds, *ii*, 412.)

§ *'Every part of this picture is touched in such a style that it may be considered as a pattern for imitation.'* (Works, *ii*, 328 et seq.)

|| *Possibly the Lines on* Belvoir Castle. *V. Huchon's* Crabbe, *Paris* 1906, 226 *n. The poet was Rutland's chaplain.*

together. The Adoration of the Magi, and St Justus, by Rubens, and a Crucifixion by Vandyck, were the only tolerable pictures, but these are not the best of those masters. I did not like the Justus as well as I did before, but I think of sending a small commission for it; the two others I dare say will not go to above £200 each. The Vandyck was in the church of the Dominicaines at Antwerp. I was shewn some of the pictures which were reserved by the Emperor, which were not a jota better than the common run of the rest of the collection.

Though I was disappointed in the object of my journey, I have made some considerable purchases from private collections. I have bought a very capital picture of Rubens of Hercules and Omphale,* a composition of seven or eight figures, perfectly preserved, and as bright as colouring can be carried. The figures are rather less than life; the height of the picture, I believe is not above seven feet. I have likewise a Holy Family, a Silenus and Baccanalians, and two portraits, all by Rubens. I have a Virgin and Infant Christ and two portraits by Vandyck, and two of the best huntings of wild beasts, by Snyders and De Vos, that I ever saw. I begin now to be impatient for their arrival, which I expect every day. The banker, Mr Danoot, was very ill when we were at Brussels, supposed to be dying; if that should happen his pictures will be sold.†

There are no pictures of Mieris‡ either at Antwerp or Brussels. All the pictures in those two places which were worth bringing home I have bought—I mean of those which were upon sale—except indeed one, the Rape of Sabines, for which they asked £3500; excepting this. I have swept the country, and for this I would not exchange my Hercules and Omphale.

10 September 1785

. . . Though I have not been so punctual in answering your Grace's letters as I ought, yet I took care that nothing should prevent me from writing to my correspondent in Flanders, to desire he would go so far as four hundred guineas for the Vandyck, and three hundred for the Rubens. I could not in conscience give him a higher commission. I must beg leave to mention to your Grace the person I have employed in this business; his name is De Gray,§ a very excellent painter in *chiaro oscuro*, in imitation of *basrelievos*. He paints likewise portraits in oil and in crayons extremely well. He was very civil and attentive to me when I was at Antwerp, and was the means of my purchasing some very fine pictures. He then told me he intended going to Ireland, having been invited by Mr Cunningham; and I promised to recommend him likewise to your Grace's protection, which I can with a very safe conscience, not only as a very ingenious artist, but a young man of very pleasing manners. I have no doubt but he is very happy in this opportunity of doing anything to oblige your Grace, and will be very zealous in the performance.

* *'Hercules with a distaff, Omphale chastising him by pinching his ear.' (Catalogue of Ralph's Exhibition, reprinted by Graves and Cronin,* 1904, *where the other pictures here mentioned are also listed.*)

† *For Danoot's collection v.* Works, *ii*, 264, et seq.

‡ *Frans van Mieris* (1635–1681).

§ *De Gree* (*d.* 1788), *a native of Antwerp, Sir Joshua had met on his first trip to Flanders in* 1781. *He eventually made his home in Ireland.*

I don't know how to account for the pictures at Antwerp not appearing so striking to me this last journey as they did the first. I was disappointed in many other pictures besides those on sale.* It ought at least to teach me this lesson—not to be very impatient when anyone differs with me about the degree of excellence of any pictures, since I find I differ so much from myself at different times.

I have enclosed the title and that part of the catalogue which has the Rubens and the Vandyck which I apprehend is all that your Grace wished to see.

The picture will be sent away on Monday by way of Liverpool.† In the hurry of pictures I have neglected thanking your Grace for your kind sollicitations in my favour with Mr Pitt. I am, as I certainly ought to be, as grateful as if it had been crowned with success. . . .

London, 22 September 1785

. . . I am sorry to acquaint your Grace that there is nothing bought at the sale. I have enclosed Mr De Gree's letter, by which it appears they went much above even the commission that you wished me to send. I cannot think that either the Rubens or Vandyck were worth half the money they sold for. The Vandyck was an immense picture and very scantily filled, it had more defects than beauties,‡ and as to the Rubens, I think your Grace's is worth a hundred of them. They are so large, too, that it would cost near two hundred pounds bringing them to England. I have sent the catalogue to Lord Sydney's§ office to be forwarded to your Grace. . . .

London, 26 September 1785

. . . Immediately on the receipt of your Grace's letter I wrote to Mr De Gree to make enquiry to whom the pictures were sold, and whether they would part with them again at a certain profit; at the same time, I am confident if your Grace saw them you would not be very anxious about possessing them. The Poussin's are a real national object and I rejoice to hear that the scheme of their coming to England is in such forwardness.

* *'On viewing the pictures of Rubens a second time, they appeared much less brilliant than they had done on the former inspection. He could not for some time account for this circumstance; but when he recollected that when he first saw them, he had his note-book in his hand, for the purpose of writing down short remarks, he perceived what had occasioned their now making a less impression in this respect than they had done formerly. By the eye passing immediately from the white paper to the picture, the colours derived uncommon richness and warmth. For want of this foil they afterwards appeared comparatively cold.'* (*Note by Malone in* Works, *i*, *lxxii* et seq.)

† *The portrait of Lords Charles, Robert and William Manners. In his account-book Sir Joshua wrote: 'Duke of Rutland for his three sons sent to Ireland, September* 1785, *£*300'. (*Graves and Cronin*, 614 et seq.)

‡ *'For its defects ample amends is made in the Christ, which is admirably drawn and coloured.'* (Works, *ii*, 298.)

§ *Thomas Townshend, first Viscount Sydney* (1753–1800), *the 'Tommy Townshend' of Goldsmith's* Retaliation, *at this time Pitt's Secretary of State for the Home Department.*

Mr Boswell has just sent me his 'Johnsoniana', which is one of the most entertaining books I ever read. If your Grace pleases I will send it by the same conveyance as the catalogue. I think you will be agreeably amused for a few hours; there are Johnson's opinions upon a great variety of subjects, and Boswell has drawn his character in a very masterly manner. The Bishop of Killaloo, who knew Johnson very well, I think will subscribe to the justness and truth of the drawing. . . .

STRAWBERRY HILL

WHEN there is talk of English collectors, the names of Horace Walpole and Strawberry Hill are some of the first to spring to mind. The documentation on Strawberry Hill, both the house and its contents (and certainly of the life of its owner), is enormously extensive: one might almost say, complete.[1]

The description quoted here comes from that minor classic among recent biographies, R. W. Ketton-Cremer's *Horace Walpole*,[2] and ideally it should be read in the context of this whole life. As Ketton-Cremer says: 'It is interesting to note how his own [Walpole's] artistic standards have altered since he had compiled the *Aedes Walpolianae*. His tastes had shifted from the lavish and spectacular to the small, detailed and exquisite; Houghton had given place to Strawberry Hill; and the critic who was enraptured by Rubens and Salvator Rosa now regarded with equal enthusiasm the miniatures of Oliver and the enamels of Petitot.'

The contents of Strawberry Hill were put up for sale forty-five years after Horace Walpole's death (in 1842). The auctioneer responsible was 'that famous master of his craft', George Robins. The catalogue is an example of his fulsome style. In the introduction he wrote:

'The individual who has received instructions from the Right Honourable the Earl of Waldegrave, to distribute to the world the unrivalled and wondrous Collection at Strawberry Hill, formed by his Lordship's great ancestor, Horace Walpole, Earl of Orford, and has thus had placed within his power the ability to

[1] *Description of the Villa at Strawberry Hill, in an inventory of the Furniture, Pictures, Curiosities, etc.* Strawberry Hill: Printed by Thomas Kirgate, 1774. The same with additions, 1784, and again with corrections, in the second volume of the edition of Lord Orford's *Collected Works*, 1798.

[2] It must be one of the few recent biographies that has been almost continuously in print after initial publication at an injudicious moment at the beginning of the second world war: thus, Duckworth's, 1940; revised edition, Faber & Faber, 1946; revised again, Methuen and University Paperbacks, 1964.

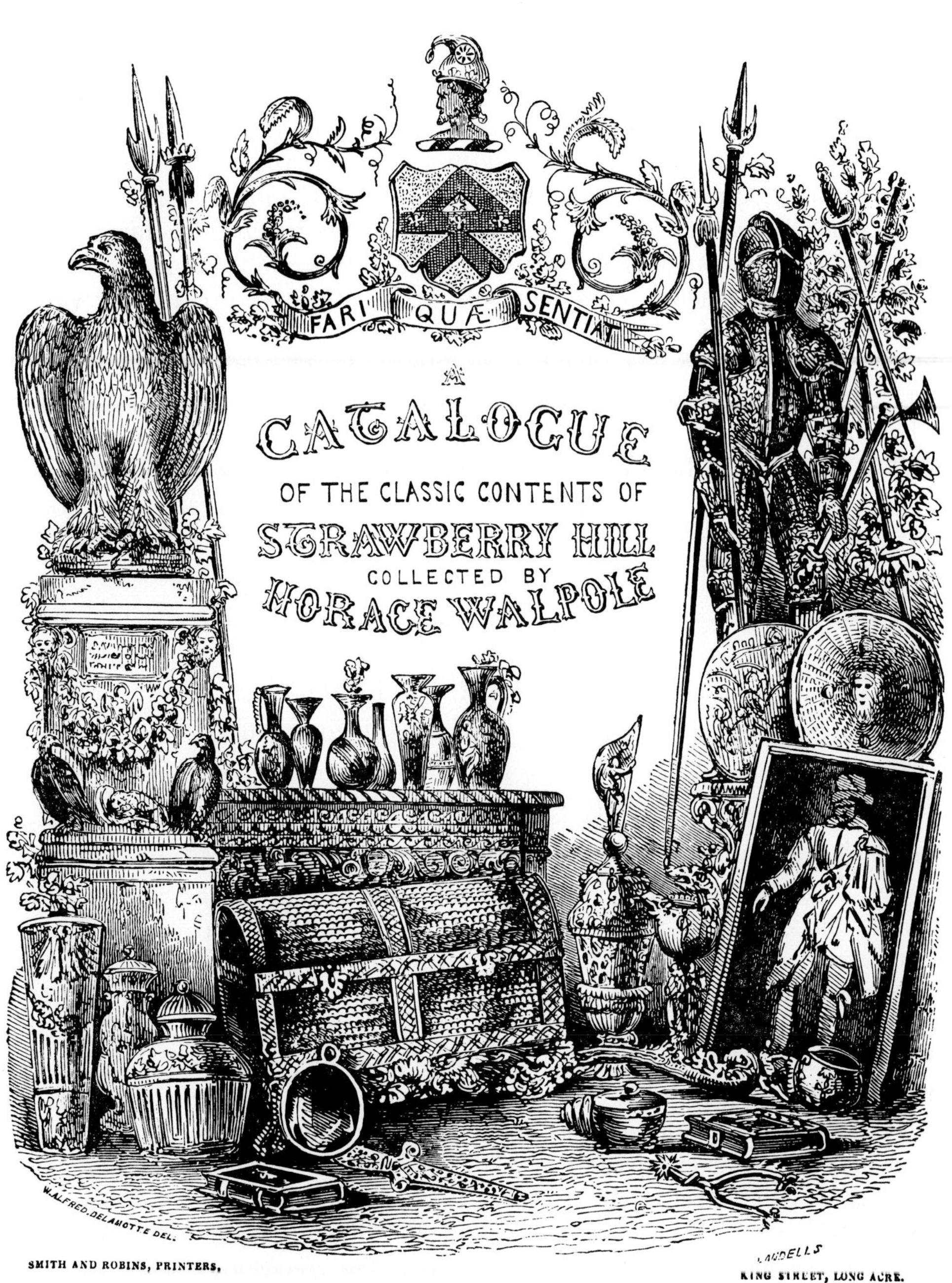
FARI QUÆ SENTIAT
A
CATALOGUE
OF THE CLASSIC CONTENTS OF
STRAWBERRY HILL
COLLECTED BY
HORACE WALPOLE
W. ALFRED. DELAMOTTE DEL.
LANDELLS
SMITH AND ROBINS, PRINTERS,
KING STREET, LONG ACRE.

enrich the royal and national collections of every civilised country, the galleries of the cognoscenti, and the cabinets of amateurs in every class of the highest walks of Art, has had the singular good fortune, during a long professional career, to be the favoured agent in introducing to the public, in endless variety, unique collections of all that is rare in taste and *vertu*, and although, through his instrumentality, he has exchanged properties extending over several millions of pounds sterling, yet he approaches his present herculean undertaking with feelings such as he never experienced on any former occasion, fully sensible that the distribution of this precious museum, crowded with the tangible records of past ages–treasures consecrated by the hand of time and of genius–far exceeding in interest and importance all that has preceded it in the chronicles of auctions, and that no future sale can by possibility enter into rivalry with it.'

The sale, which *The Times* described in the derisory manner to be expected of Walpole's repute at the time, lasted twenty-four days *in situ* and resulted in a total of £33, 450 11s 9d.[1] Many pieces were bought by the great collectors of that time, Lord Northwick, the Duke of Bedford and the Duke of Sutherland among them.

EXTRACTED FROM R. W. Ketton-Cremer's
Horace Walpole, Third Edition, 1964.

THE Gallery must have presented a noble spectacle when it was filled with all its treasures. Though not a remarkably large room (it was fifty-six feet by thirteen) it was the largest room at Strawberry Hill; and in it Walpole assembled many of his finest pictures, his most spectacular pieces of porcelain, his most precious marbles and bronzes. Light streamed through the five large windows in which Peckitt had depicted all the quarterings of the Walpoles in painted glass. On the other side of the room were five deep canopied recesses, the middle recess containing a chimney-piece designed by Chute and Pitt. The furniture was covered with the same crimson damask as the walls; its woodwork was painted in black and gold. The walls were loaded with pictures, the recesses were filled with them–portraits of relations and friends, portraits of the celebrities of the sixteenth and seventeenth centuries, the painting by Mabuse of the marriage of Henry VII, landscapes and subject-pieces by an endless variety of artists. There was work by Cornelius Hansen, Rubens, Lely, Rosalba, Liotard, Reynolds–an extraordinary medley of periods and styles. On an ancient sepulchral altar stood the famous Boccapadugli eagle, which had been dug up in the Baths of Caracalla in 1742, and which Walpole liked to think had inspired Gray with the line about the 'ruffled plumes and flagging wing'.* And

[1] This did not include prints and engravings which were deferred to be sold in London. See Redford, *Art Sales*, Vol. I, for a great deal of information on the sale.

* Progress of Poesy, *I. 2. Gray however noted that this passage was 'a weak imitation of some incomparable lines' of Pindar.*

between two of the windows hung Van Somer's portrait of Henry Carey, Lord Falkland, all in white', a picture which haunted its owner strangely. It became a part of the fantasy which found expression in *The Castle of Otranto*, and was transformed in that story into the portrait of Duke Manfred's grandfather,* which sighed so deeply and descended from its frame, and 'marched sedately but dejectedly' along the gallery of the visionary castle.

The Round Tower was built at the end of the wing formed by the Cloister and Gallery, and was the western termination of the house. It was a sturdy tower of three stories, battlemented and machicolated, with a great bow-window (considerably later in style) overlooking the road to Hampton. Each floor contained one big circular room. The ground floor became the new kitchen; the first floor was called the Round Drawing Room, and was approached from the Gallery through a small lobby. Its main features were the bow-window, and chimney piece 'taken from the tomb of Edward the Confessor, improved by Mr Adam, and beautifully executed in white marble inlaid with scagliuola, by Richter'.† Adam's 'improvement' amounted to a much-needed simplification of the Confessor's gaudy mosaic sarcophagus, and he also designed a pleasant frieze for the walls. The Round Drawing-Room was hung, like the Gallery, with crimson Norwich damask; the chairs were of aubusson tapestry, of flowers on a white background, with green and gold frames.

* Works, *ii.* 466; *Lewis i.* 88 (*Walpole to Cole, 9 March* 1765).

† Works, *ii.* 468.

It contained a few good pictures, and many of Walpole's larger books and volumes of prints.

The Chapel, which later came to be called the Tribune, opened off the Gallery. It was a small room, square with a semi-circular recess in the middle of each wall; the roof, vaulted in imitation of that of the chapter-house of York Minster, rose to an apex formed of a large star of yellow glass. The windows were entirely filled with ecclesiastical stained glass, and the dominant light of the room was the 'golden gloom' which filtered down

through the great star. In one of the recesses stood an altar of black and gold, copied from a tomb in Westminster Abbey. 'The sable mass of the altar', Walpole wrote, 'gives it a very sober air, for notwithstanding the solemnity of the painted windows, it had a gaudiness that was a little profane.'* The ecclesiastical atmosphere was, however, so successfully conveyed that the Duc de Nivernais, the French ambassador, pulled off his hat when he entered the room; after which 'perceiving his error, he said, "Ce n'est pas une chapelle pourtant" and seemed a little displeased.'† Walpole, of course, had never intended to distress the faithful by making a frivolous imitation of a chapel; he was growing ever more serious about his buildings, and in the construction of a Gothic castle the chapel held a very special place. Great hall, south tower, armoury, cloister, gallery, round tower,

* Lewis, *x.* 64 (*Walpole to Montagu,* 14 *April* 1763).

† Toynbee, *v.*314–315 (*Walpole to Mann,* 30 *April* 1763).

chapel – one after another they were coming into being. His fantasies found concrete form; the little house called Strawberry Hill was fast assuming the splendours of the Castle of Otranto.

It is possible that when Monsieur de Nivernais was shown the Chapel, quite soon after its completion, it still retained a degree of austerity which the ever-increasing pressure of Walpole's collections was soon to dispel. If he had inspected it in 1774, the date of Walpole's printed *Description of Strawberry Hill*, he would have found that its walls and niches were adorned with very secular objects indeed. Walpole never allowed any Gothic prejudices about uncrowded rooms or undecorated surfaces to interfere with his remorseless and incessant accumulation of objects of art. He selected the Chapel as the repository of his smaller and more exquisite treasures; and, with cabinet-pictures and miniatures crowding the walls, and shelves and brackets loaded with trinkets extending in all directions, it must indeed have reverted to the gaudiness which he had originally felt to be 'a little profane'. In the niches were placed casts or bronzes of the Venus de Medicis, an Antinous, the Apollo Belvedere, the Farnese Flora, and his own mother. Above the altar was a cabinet which contained his marvellous collection of miniatures – the Olivers, the Coopers, the Hoskins – and his superb enamels by Petitot and Zincke. The antiques belonging to Conyers Middleton, which he had bought after the Doctor's death, were placed about the room. In two glass-cases were some of his supreme treasures – the bust of Caligula in bronze, with silver eyes; the missal 'with miniatures by Raphael and his scholars'; and the silver bell carved with miraculous ornament by Benvenuto Cellini. Jostling them were such curiosities as Henry VIII's dagger, a mourning-ring of Charles I, the great seal of Theodore, King of Corsica, and the cravat carved in wood by Grinling Gibbons. The entire room was an indescribable display of pictures, bronzes, carvings, ivories, enamels, faience, pot-pourri jars, snuff-boxes, kettles, tea-pots, cups and saucers, seals and rings.

A CASE OF FAMILY COLLECTING · THE EARLS OF RADNOR

One of the great joys of England even today–and certainly one of its principal tourist attractions–is the great multitude and wealth of historic houses which the public is free to view in exchange for a mere 25 pence. Many of these houses produce their own guide books and catalogues of contents. One such is Longford Castle belonging to the Earls of Radnor. This collection, like some of the finest still extant in England today, is not the outcome of one man's collecting activities but the result of purchases by several, not necessarily successive, generations of collectors.[1] Occasional depletions are brought about by financial stringencies or the need to meet death duties. Thus three fine paintings (Holbein's *The Ambassadors*, *Portrait of an Italian Nobleman* by Moroni, and a portrait then thought to be by Velazquez but now catalogued as by Mazo) were sold to the National Gallery for £55,000 in 1890. Messrs N. M. Rothschild, Lord Iveagh and Charles Cotes each contributed £10,000 towards their purchase: the Treasury made a special grant towards the rest.

Very often some member of the family with enthusiasm for the task has compiled the original catalogue and a professional antiquarian or historian has been charged with its subsequent revision. This is the case in the extract that follows:[2]

'The fifth Earl succeeded to the Longford estates on the death of his father in 1889, and it has been the privilege of his wife (the present writer) to arrange and classify the family Collection of Pictures. It has always been believed by the last generation that there was no authentic record as to when, where or by whom these pictures had been collected: indeed it has been stated in print that they were bought *en masse* from Mr Seguier, a picture-cleaner employed by the National Gallery in the first half of the nineteenth century. The writer had, however, the good fortune to find in the Muniment Room at Longford several private account-books embracing a period of over a hundred years which had been very carefully kept by the first Viscount Folkestone and the first and second Earls of Radnor, and a searching perusal of these resulted in the very satisfactory discovery not only of the dates of the different sales where the purchases were effected, but also of the prices given for nearly all the more important pictures between the years 1720 and 1823.'

The picture collection includes examples of the work of Hobbema, Cuyp,

[1] For two particularly interesting and well-illustrated examples of such collections see Michael Jaffé on Chatsworth and Kenneth Garlick on Althorp in *Great Private Collections*, edited by Douglas Cooper, 1963.

[2] In 1909 a complete and very fine catalogue of the collection, prepared with the assistance of Mr W. Barclay Squire, and containing illustrations of over a hundred of the principal pictures, was privately printed by Jacob, Earl of Radnor.

Rubens, van Dyck, Frans Hals, Holbein, Claude, Poussin, Murillo, Correggio and Mabuse, as well as a host of family portraits. The Radnor Collection made history once again when, in November 1970, the magnificent Velazquez portrait of Juan de Pareja[1] was put up for sale at Christie's and fetched a world auction record of £2,310,000. The sum was so high that the British Government did not feel that it could match it, and the exportation of the picture to the United States was allowed. The public outcry which followed drew attention once again to restricting the exodus of really great works of art from our shores, but the enormous price of the picture introduced an air of unreality into the art world. However, this has happened on almost every previous occasion when a work of art was sold for a really phenomenal record sum, and no doubt the price of Juan de Pareja will eventually become a mere notch in the yardstick of the economics of art.

A consequence of the sale, which was probably not foreseen, was that a number of pictures of like quality was sent to the saleroom by their owners in the expectation of realising similar prices, such as the Harewood Trust's *Death of Actaeon* by Titian and Lord Derby's *Study of Negro Heads* by van Dyck. This may yet force the government to bring the present death duty laws into line with the more favourable ones in the United States and on the Continent.

TAKEN FROM *The Catalogue of the Earl of Radnor's Collection of Pictures*, 1910.

ON the return (*circa* 1650) of Lord Colerane to his home he found the house in terrible state.[2] The beautiful vines on the walls had been cut down, and 'his Lordship was saluted with nothing but filthiness and desolation, except itt were an Infinite Swarm of fleas, that pitched upon his white boote hose, there was noe other Liveing Creature left for him'.* However, he took heart and did the work of restoration so well that he left the place in much better condition than when he first bought it, and this work was carried on by his son Henry, second Lord Colerane, who succeeded his father (who was 'choak'd endeavouring to swallow the rump of a Turky') in 1667. This Henry was a great antiquary and brought many stone carvings, marble-topped tables etc., from Italy to embellish the Castle. He was succeeded (in 1708) by his grandson, Henry, who apparently preferred the other family place (at Totteridge, near Tottenham, Herts) as a residence and obtained an Act of Parliament to allow him to break the entail and sell Longford, to provide the money for the dower of his Aunt Cecilia, his grandfather's favourite child.

[1] It was probably acquired by the 2nd Earl of Radnor in 1811 for £151 14s 5d. It was previously in the collection of Sir William Hamilton sold at Christie's on 27 March 1801 and, according to Buchanan (see *Memoirs of Painting*, ii, p. 76) it came from the Baranello Collection at Naples.

[2] Cromwell besieged the house after the Battle of Naseby. It surrendered to him on 18 October 1643.

* *Pelate MS*, ut supra.

Thus in 1717 Longford, and the lands belonging to it at that time, passed into the hands of Sir Edward Des Bouveries, Bart., from whom they have descended to the present owner.

Sir Edward made great alterations in the house, turning the Chapel on the ground floor into a Long Parlour and making a large Entrance Hall, two stories high, quite out of keeping with the style of the building. Sir Edward died in 1736, and, leaving no children, was succeeded by his brother Jacob, who in 1747 was made first Viscount Folkstone. This Jacob, who was a man of great artistic taste and judgement, was the first President of the Society for the Encouragement of Arts and Sciences. He greatly beautified the place; bought Chippendale furniture for the Gallery, Green Drawing-Room, etc.; imported velvet and damask from Lyons for the walls and tapestry from M. Neptune at Brussels; employed Peter Scheemakers to carve marble mantelpieces, John Michael Rysbrack to execute busts and Thomas Hudson to paint portraits of himself and his family. He bought over a hundred of the principal pictures (including 'Erasmus', 'Aegidius', the two Claudes, the two Poussins, etc.) – and thought nothing of giving £25 for an embroidered waistcoat for himself! He was altogether a princely gentleman in his ideas as to spending money, but his descendants may indeed thank him for the very judicious way in which he laid out so much in the lasting embellishment of his house and on the art treasures he placed in it. He was succeeded in 1761 by his son William who was created 1st Earl of Radnor in 1765. He also was a very judicious buyer, and there are notes in his account books of his having bought about seventy-five pictures. He did not acquire other works of art, but he employed Reynolds and Gainsborough to paint portraits of many members of his family, he himself being depicted by Gainsborough and his three wives respectively by Hudson, Reynolds and Cotes. His successor, Jacob, 2nd Earl of Radnor, reigned as lord of Longford for over fifty years, from 1776 to 1828. He added over eighty pictures to the collection and it was he, alas! who conceived the idea of rebuilding the Castle with six round towers instead of three. All the plans were made and the work was begun towards the close of the eighteenth century. He got as far as pulling down the North-West tower (the 'Filius' of the three Elizabethan towers) and had actually built three of the six contemplated new towers, when fortunately money failed, and the greater part of the work was left a shell, until completed by his grandson, the 4th Earl of Radnor, in 1874. The 2nd Earl added one great treasure to the collection, viz., the Imperial Steel Chair. He bought it at the close of the eighteenth century from Gustavus Brander, F.R.S., a descendant of a Swedish family to whom it had belonged since the days when it was looted by the Swedes from the Imperial Museum at Prague, where it has been placed by the Emperor Rudolph II, to whom it had been presented (about the year 1577) by the town of Augsburg. The 2nd Earl also bought the inlaid ivory chairs in the Gallery, to which a certain amount of interest attaches owing to their having formed part of a set brought from India by Warren Hastings for Queen Charlotte.

THE DIFFICULTIES OF VIEWING COLLECTIONS

'I KNOW not for my own part, more than one or two isolated instances in which admission has been refused to an artist or stranger who came *properly introduced*,[1] or whose name was known,' said Mrs Jameson, and as an inveterate student of other people's collections she ought to have known. But it was not everyone who could get introductions. Even with them it required a great deal of patience and organisation if one wanted to see, in quick succession, a *number* of private houses containing collections, as Dr Waagen found over and over again. And even when he had achieved entry into such houses, he was endlessly haunted by the spectre of starchy housekeepers rattling their keys, hurrying him from room to room, as he tried to inspect the pictures (often in bad light) and attempted to make notes on them.

However, it was by no means impossible to arrive unheralded at some fine residence in order to examine its contents and to gain admittance without difficulty even in the absence of the owner.[2] This was the case particularly in the first half of the nineteenth century. Nor were all servants as demanding as those in the piece that follows.

In London there were fixed days and times for viewing the more celebrated private galleries. Cleveland House was open from '12 to 5 o'clock during Wednesday in May, June and July'. There were set regulations for entry. 'No person can be permitted to view the Gallery without a ticket. To obtain which it is necessary that the applicant be known to the Marquis, or to some one of the family; otherwise he or she must have a recommendation from a person who is. Applications for such tickets are inserted in a book by the Porter, at the door of Cleveland-House, any day except Tuesday; when the tickets are issued for admission on the following day. Artists desirous of tickets for the season must be recommended by some member of the Royal Academy. It is expected, that if the weather be wet, or dirty, that all visitors will go in carriages.'[3]

However, Mrs Jameson tells us that some people took advantage of the liberality of those owners who opened their galleries freely to the public. One can clearly detect the voice of the ex-governess.[4] 'We can all remember the public days

[1] My italics; from her *Companion to the Most Celebrated Private Galleries of Art in London*, 1844, page xxxv.

[2] See for example Jane Austen's *Pride and Prejudice*, Chapter 43. What a pity it was though that Elizabeth Bennet was so little interested in the paintings around her as she was being shown the picture gallery of Pemberley by the housekeeper!

[3] Taken from the *Catalogue Raisonné of the Pictures Belonging to . . . the Marquis of Stafford in the Gallery of Cleveland House*, John Britton, 1808.

[4] In her youth Mrs Jameson had been governess to the families of the Marquess of Winchester and

at the Grosvenor Gallery and Bridgewater House, we can all remember the loiterers and loungers, the vulgar starers, the gaping idlers, we used to meet there –people, who, instead of moving among the wonders and beauties . . . with reverence and gratitude, strutted about as if they had a right to be there; talking, flirting; touching the ornaments–and even the pictures!'[1]

EXTRACTED FROM William T. Whitley's *Art in England, 1800–1820*, 1928.

NOTHING had been done to encourage the artistic taste of the people at large, and England had as yet no public picture gallery.[2] A few portraits and some sculpture were at the British Museum, but admission to that institution was still hedged about with many of the restrictions against which William Hutton had protested in 1784, and it is safe to say that at the dawn of the nineteenth century the great majority of the people in England had never had an opportunity of seeing a good picture. It is true that exhibitions had been held in London since 1760, but only a small fraction of the population had visited them; and to the royal collections of works of art and those in the great private houses, there was no access for a poor man unless he entered the rooms that contained them in the capacity of a workman or a servant.

Even for people of the middle class admission to the important private collections was difficult because of the consequent expense. In the *Monthly Magazine* of February of this year a letter was published from a correspondent who had recently visited the collection at Wilton House. After describing some of the things he had seen there he goes on to say:

'Our walk over the house and gardens had already cost us six shillings, and we flattered ourselves that we had no more exactions to encounter. But as we were going past the porter's lodge, a servant stopped us with a fresh demand, informing us in plain language that "they were all stationed here for their fees, and nobody could come in or out without payment". We accordingly submitted to be fleeced once more. I am told that this kind of tax is peculiar to England.'

The writer had good reasons to resent such demands, for what he paid to see Wilton and its gardens corresponded to more than a guinea today. But in making his complaint he was only repeating what had been said a hundred times in the eighteenth-century periodicals. The exactions of the servants who showed great houses had been a scandal for years, and when Carlo Vanloo, the French King's painter, came to England in 1764 to see some of our collections, the London newspapers warned him of the rapacity of those who had charge of them. Some years later Governor Thicknesse, Gainsborough's friend, complained bitterly of the insolence and attempted exactions of the servants at Blenheim. He

later to Lord Haverton. See the editor's third article in the series 'Collecting Classics' in *The Connoisseur*, May 1966.

[1] *op. cit.*, page xxxiv.

[2] This was in the year 1800.

compared their behaviour with the treatment he experienced at Versailles, where he was shown over the palace by one of the King's personal attendants, who, after paying him every courtesy, declined a fee. To take it, he said, would be repugnant to his royal master's dignity. However, at Blenheim the servants obtained nothing from Thicknesse, who was the last person in the world to suffer imposition meekly. 'We saw Versailles and Blenheim gratis,' he says, 'the first because the servants would not take and the latter because we were determined not to give.'

THE VITTURI COLLECTION IN ENGLISH HANDS

THIS piece is extracted from William Buchanan's *Memoirs of Painting, with a chronological History of the Importations of Pictures by the Great Masters into England since the French Revolution.* It was published in two volumes by Ackermann in 1824, and together with Waagen's *Works of Art and Artists in England* of 1838 (which was written in 1835) and Passavant's *Tour of a German Artist in England* of 1836 (which was written in 1833), it forms a trio of the most important printed sources on collecting in England of that period.

Buchanan was a law student in Edinburgh when he became passionately interested in the arts, and upon completion of his studies in 1802 he decided to come to London to set up as an art dealer, having obtained financial support from various sources. He realised that the great turmoil in Europe caused by Napoleon's ambitions had brought about remarkable opportunities for buying works of art that had become dislodged, for the first time in centuries, from the iron grasp of the church on the one hand and many princely and aristocratic families on the other, and that such opportunities would never recur. Accordingly he sent his own skilful agents to Italy and Spain. Their instructions were to buy only the best. Buchanan always preferred a few really high-priced items to a great number of relatively cheap ones. He was exceedingly knowledgeable about pictures; he was shrewd, he was immensely enterprising and he could be infinitely patient. It was a rare combination of talents and it paid remarkable dividends in that it brought an unbelievable wealth of pictures to England that would never otherwise have crossed the English Channel. But in many respects Buchanan's enlightenment and taste were far ahead of those of his contemporaries and, like many art dealers since his day, he had to engage himself in the education of his customers on a grand scale! For many years–and they were the years of his greatest successes–he received little in the way of recognition or financial reward. Three times in his long career he gave up in disgust and disappointment. But after each lapse he could not resist the offers of great collections, and started dealing again. Eventually he made a great deal of money.

He had three ambitions beyond mere financial gain. He campaigned unceasingly for the founding of a national gallery.[1] As much as anything else this motivated the quality of his acquisitions and the way he disposed of them to his favourite customers. He wished to obtain some honour, some mark of distinction from the government of his day, for the efforts he had made, ultimately as he thought for the good of the nation. In this he failed. Finally, he wanted to record, in as much detail as he could muster, the major transactions in the art world that had occurred during his own initial, turbulent twenty-two years' career as a dealer, and in the five or six years immediately preceding it; and this he did. And in many instances we have precious little detail of such events except those contained in his book.

He listed the major collections that came up for sale, how they had been formed and how they were disposed of. They included the Orleans[2] and Calonne Collections and those of John Trumbull, Michael Bryan, the Greffier's Fagel, Countess Holdernesse, John Udney, William Young Ottley,[3] Citizen Robit, Sir William Hamilton and a host of others.

He also listed in detail his own importations (see page 167) and transactions and a number of items –such as the letter from Thomas Moore Slade which follows –which he thought would be of interest to posterity.

Buchanan's book appeared in 1824, the year of the opening of the National Gallery (when he was 47), so he knew that he had succeeded in his primary objective. He lived another forty years and, although he continued to import paintings on a less magnificent scale, one has only to look at the catalogue of the Holford Collection for which he had supplied so many pictures (it was sold at Christie's in 1927 and 1928) to see how high his standards remained. We know[4] that he intended to write a second work taking the story up to the end of his life, but as the *Art Journal* noted at the time of his death in 1864, 'the unfortunate failure of his eyesight interrupted the progress of his labours and the volume remains in an unfinished state'. Regrettably, it has never been found.

Buchanan's wife (the daughter of Lord Elibank) died seven years before him and it seems[5] that his daughter 'had a pension from the government on account of

[1] See page 168 (Irvine reports to Buchanan: introduction).

[2] See page 133.

[3] See page 186.

[4] *Memoirs of Painting*, Vol. I, page 220. Buchanan's own collection was sold at Christie's in 1825.

[5] From a handwritten note in a copy of *Memoirs of Painting* presented by the author to Studley Martin.

MEMOIRS

OF

PAINTING,

WITH

A CHRONOLOGICAL HISTORY

OF

The Importation

OF

Pictures by the Great Masters

INTO

ENGLAND

SINCE THE FRENCH REVOLUTION.

BY W. BUCHANAN, ESQ.

" La chûte du trône de Constantin porta dans l'Italie les debris de l'ancienne Grèce ; la France s'enrichit à son tour de ces precieuses dépouilles."

J. J. ROUSSEAU.

VOL. I.

LONDON:
PRINTED FOR R. ACKERMANN, STRAND.
1824.

her father's services in importing so many fine paintings'. He declined this pension for himself and commuted it to her.

Buchanan would have died a happier man if he could have seen a brief, hastily-pencilled note I found among the Whitley papers in the British Museum quoting an authority writing about Buchanan in 1896, who said that by that year '. . . upward of a third of the pictures in the National Gallery has passed through Buchanan's hands . . .'.[1]

EXTRACTED FROM William Buchanan's
Memoirs of Painting, 1824.

An account of the formation of this collection, with the history of some other pictures of a high class which belonged for many years to Thomas Moore Slade, Esq., will be best rendered by giving here a copy of the letter on that subject, which the author of these compilations received from Mr Slade himself.*

'In answer to your inquiries regarding the Vitturi collection of pictures which I purchased at Venice, and also the pictures of the St Ursula by Claude, the Pythagoras of Salvator Rosa, the celebrated Cuyps, &c. now in possession of the Ranelagh family–all of which were for a long time my property–I send you the following information, part of which may be deemed interesting as in reference to your work, and of which you may make whatever use you think proper.

'The celebrated picture of the St Ursula by Claude, lately purchased by the British government, was brought from Italy with a few other fine pictures by Mr Locke about sixty years ago. It was purchased out of the Barberini Palace by that gentleman, and was considered at that time a most important acquisition to the stock of fine pictures in England, the number of which was not then very great, there being many copies among the originals in the collections of this country.

'Mr Locke, on leaving his house in Portmansquare, sold the St Ursula along with some other fine pictures to Mr Van Heythusen for £3000, among which was a fine picture of a Holy Family with Angels, by Nicholas Poussin, afterwards in the Lansdowne, now in the Grosvenor collection; and a fine Bacchanalian by Sebastian Bourdon, very little inferior to Poussin.

'Mr Van Heythusen had about the same period purchased the collection of Sir Gregory Page at Blackheath, and conceiving that he had invested too much capital in pictures, he

[1] For further details of Buchanan, see the editor's article on him in *The Connoisseur* for April 1966.

* *An account of the formation of this collection, as well as other purchases made abroad at that time, becomes the more interesting, as the arts had for a very long period been much neglected in England; and it was the importation of works of a high class which first roused the attention of the public to their importance. Mr Slade, who has ever been a most enthusiastic admirer of works of art, was among the first of those gentlemen who set an example of giving liberal prices, which alone could draw those treasures from foreign countries.*

became alarmed, and disposed of the pictures which he had purchased from Mr Locke to Mr Des Enfans,[1] who again sold the Poussin to the Marquis of Lansdowne, and the St Ursula Claude to myself for £1200. I purchased from Des Enfans at the same time the Pythagoras of Salvator Rosa, and its companion, which had been brought from Italy by Gavin Hamilton, as also a fine picture by Schidone, and some others of consequence; and I paid him for the lot £2800, *argent comptant.*

'This purchase, as well as that of the Flemish part of the Orleans, was long before your time, and before the period when you undertook your spirited enterprise of bringing from Italy so many capital works of art, for which this country must ever be your debtor. The conquest of Italy by the French opened a door for the acquisition of works of that high class, which it was needless to think of obtaining before that event; and the Vitturi collection, which I purchased in Italy before either of the above purchases, was deemed one of the most consequential which had been brought from thence at that early period.

'I must here state to you, that in those days I was a man of very independent fortune, left to me by my father, Sir Thomas Slade. After having dedicated two years in making a tour through England, Scotland, and Ireland, I set out in June 1774, for Italy. My friends, who knew my strong predilection for pictures, and that I had plenty of money to purchase them, earnestly guarded me against imposition. I travelled through France, Switzerland, Italy, visited Malta, and Sicily, and reached Venice without purchasing a single picture. On my arrival there, I saw all the famous collections; amongst the rest, that of the Count Vitturi, a noble Venetian, who had for the last twenty or thirty years been purchasing pictures out of the other great collections, when he knew that their possessors wanted money. I made my notes upon the principal pictures of this collection, as I did on others, never, however, imagining that they should afterwards become my own. It so happened, however, that instead of spending two or three weeks at Venice according to my original intention, I became *incatenato*, and *cavaliere servente* to a certain *Contessa* of the first consideration, and I remained in that fascinating city for nearly two years.

'During this period the Count Vitturi died, and his collection was to be sold. The Empress of Russia and Mr Hope of Amsterdam had agents for them at Venice, and also Mr Jenkins of Rome desired to purchase it, but Mr Udney, who was then consul at Venice, by his clever management and address, got the promise of them, but could not raise the money for the acquisition. There were no English at Venice except the Duke of Gloucester and myself, and, having the greatest command of money, Mr Udney applied to me to purchase them jointly with him, proposing that I should have the choice of a few of those that I liked at a fair value, and that he should dispose of the rest. With this idea I consented, thinking to have a few pictures for myself at a moderate price. I advanced the whole money for the purchase by bills on my banker in London, and Mr Udney gave me his for half the money on his brother, Robert Udney, Esq., a man of large property.

'The pictures being thus secured, were all brought to Udney's apartments and hung up, but on my selecting four or five pictures which I particularly wished for my own private

[1] See page 172.

collection, instead of putting a moderate price upon them, according to agreement, he put a most exorbitant one. This, I expostulated with him, was contrary to the spirit of the agreement, for when I advanced the whole money, the acquiring some of the best pictures for my own private collection was my sole inducement. At the very moment that we were discussing this point, the post arrived from England with advice that all the bills which I had given on my bankers had been regularly paid, but that all the counter-bills, which Mr Udney had given me for his half, had been protested.

'This being the actual state of matters, I told Mr Udney that by right the whole purchase should belong to me; but as I did not choose to avail myself of that advantage, it was agreed that I should pay a certain sum of money to induce Sir John Dick to resign in his favour the consulship of Leghorn, which I accordingly did, and he was appointed to that situation, where he afterwards made a good fortune.

'Upon this arrangement being made I became sole proprietor of the Vitturi collection,[1] and had the satisfaction of enjoying them for a whole year at Venice, where I still remained fascinated with that fine city and its *agrémens*, and should probably have been there much longer, but the American war breaking out, I was called to England by my friends. My pictures, and other objects of virtù, of which I had formed a most valuable assemblage, were sent by sea; and as war with France was expected, I had them all cased up under the name of Illustrissimo Signor Cavalli, who happened to be then going on his embassy to England; I took the precaution likewise of writing all the lists and memoranda in Italian, and well I did so, for the vessel was captured in the Mediterranean by a French privateer, and carried into a Spanish port. Cavalli, however, claimed them as his property, and after much difficulty they were delivered up, and shortly afterwards to my great joy arrived safe in England.

'Having returned from Venice *via* Germany, I had a public situation under government assigned to me at Chatham; and when the Vitturi collection arrived I built a gallery to receive it at my house at Rochester, where, with the famous St Ursula Claude, the Salvators above mentioned, the Ranelagh Cuyps, and many other fine pictures, I had the gratification of possessing them for fifteen years, where I was visited by all the principal connoisseurs of this country, who came to enjoy a view of these fine works.

'It was not decreed that these happy days should last for ever. I became engaged in a grand speculation of making broad cloth without spinning or weaving, and I was induced, in conjunction with Mr P. Moore, to accept of being agent to this great concern, and to resign my place at Chatham. My pictures were then removed to London, but unfortunately this great scheme did not succeed, although you may imagine that there was much plausibility in it, when such cautious, long-headed men as the late Lord Kinnaird and Messrs Moreland and Hammersley, were concerned in it, while several established clothiers left the usual mode of weaving to work under our patent.

[1] As listed by Buchanan this collection consisted of 56 paintings. Among them were seven by Titian, two by Veronese and one each by Giorgione, Raphael, Antonello da Messina, Andrea del Sarto, Tintoretto, Rubens, Rembrandt, Gerard Dou, van Dyke, Guardi (composed and painted for Slade!) and Caravaggio.

'By the failure of this speculation, instead of becoming, as Lord Kinnaird had presaged, one of the richest men in the kingdom, I lost a fine fortune, and was compelled to break up my collection. Most of the principal pictures I let my good friends the Earl of Darnley and Sir Philip Stephens have, and some of less note passed into the collection of Commissioner Brett. Most of those to Lord Darnley are still in his lordship's grand gallery at Cobham Hall, particularly the Titians, and the fine Pythagoras of Salvator Rosa; the famous long landscape of Cuyp was amongst those belonging to Sir Philip Stephens; my charming St Ursula of Claude I likewise offered to Lord Darnley and Sir Philip Stephens, as also to the late Lord Kinnaird, for the same price I gave Des Enfans for it, which was £1200, although I was certain I could get much more, but they all declined it. I then got £1700 conditionally, and it was soon after sold to Mr Angerstein for £2500. Amongst the Marine Claudes it certainly stands pre-eminent; so fascinating is this picture, that it has always been the admiration of every connoisseur of art.'

. . . Besides the above collection of pictures, Mr Slade imported the famous collection of prints and drawings which he had from the Count Durazzo, the Imperial Ambassador at Venice, and a capital collection of gems, intaglios, and cameos, which he purchased from Vitturi, along with a complete series of gold and Greek medals of the greatest perfection. The late Duke of Marlborough offered 1200 guineas for three of the cameos only, which was refused. The gems were sold for £2500, and the Greek medals to Dr Hunter and Sir Roger Gascoigne.

BUCHANAN ON THE ORLEANS COLLECTION

BUCHANAN's account of this historic collection is remarkably complete. In full it takes up the lion's share of the first volume of his *Memoirs of Painting*–well over 200 pages. Most of his introduction is included here. Obviously it is not possible to list all the paintings, but a partial, numerical summary[1] of the Italian, Spanish and French paintings[2] may be of interest: Leonardo da Vinci (3), Michelangelo (2), Bronzino (1), Andrea del Sarto (2), Raphael (12), Giulio Romano (3), Sebastiano del Piombo (3) Caravaggio (1), Baroccio (4), Andrea Sacchi (2),

[1] This list is based on the one reproduced by Redford in *Art Sales*, Vol. 1, page 73, which included some pictures that do not appear to have come to England. I have used Buchanan's spellings in the list above.

[2] For the Flemish part of the collection see page 142.

Correggio (9), Parmegiano (6), A. Carracci (24), Ludovico Carracci (7), Agostino Carracci (2), F. Albano (9), Schidone (2), Guido (16), Domenichino (8), Guercino (4), Mola (4), Titian (27), Giorgione (9), Pordenone (3), Bassano (1), Tintoretto (12), Schiavone (3), P. Veronese (19), Palma Vecchio (7), Francesco Bassano (5), P. Veronese (2), Spagnoletto (5), Luca Giordano (2), Velazquez (2), N. Poussin (6), Claude (1). A large number of minor pictures were sold separately by auction at Bryan's Gallery, Pall Mall on 14 February 1800 by Cox, Burrell and Foster.

Extracted from William Buchanan's *Memoirs of Painting*, 1824.

During the conflicting storms which ravaged the continent of Europe, Great Britain alone presented a bulwark to which foreign nations looked with awe and with respect; and although at war with her politically, they still confided in her honour and in her strength: they transmitted their moneyed wealth to her public funds, and their collections of art to private individuals, either for protection, or to be disposed of for their use. The collections of Monsieur de Calonne, and of the Duke of Orleans, with many selections of the highest importance from the palaces of Rome, Florence, Bologna, and Genoa, which had escaped the plunder of an invading army, were imported into this country, and roused an emulation and a taste for the acquisition of works of Art, which had been almost dormant in England since the days of its illustrious patron and protector, Charles the First.

From this period may be dated a new and a distinct era in the art, with reference to modern times: the collections of Great Britain, heretofore possessing but few genuine works of the Italian schools, were now enabled to enrich themselves from their precious stores, and were soon placed on a par with those of Rome herself. . . .

The late Mr President West[1] used to remark, that next to the merit of having painted a picture which should do honour to the art, and become an ornament to the state wherein it was produced, was the credit of having brought from foreign countries works of the great masters. The importation of such works tends to enrich the nation which receives them, it holds out a bright example for imitation, and rouses and calls into action the native talents of those who feel the sacred flame of emulation.

The irreparable loss which this country sustained in the dispersion of the magnificent collection which had belonged to King Charles the First, a collection formed upon the soundest principles of good judgement, aided by the elegant and refined taste of the

[1] Benjamin West was President of the Royal Academy from 1806 to 1820. He was born in America but settled in London in 1763, and is principally remembered as a painter of historical pictures (many of which are in the royal collections).

monarch himself; the subsequent diminution of its riches in the transfer of the Houghton collection to a northern Potentate,[1] the meagre state of the collections which remained to us, in works of the Italian school, made us strongly feel in our own case the truth of the worthy president's remark, and the public was prepared to avail itself of the first opportunity which should occur, to remedy in part these heavy losses.

The period was not far distant which offered such an occasion. . . . In 1792, the Duke d'Orleans gave orders for disposing of his magnificent collection of pictures; and the casualties of the times afterwards forced the purchasers to send it for protection to our more happy shores. The storm of Revolution at last burst forth with all its terrors, and with it sprung up those causes, which in a measure forced upon us a species of remuneration in the Arts, for our former heavy losses.

As the introduction of a collection of so much importance as that of the Orleans into this country formed of itself an era, it cannot but be interesting to trace it to its origin, to observe the new turn which it gave to the prevailing taste of the date; to know the objects of which it was composed, with the value attached to each; and to learn the names of those men who first gave its reception into this country, a marked patronage and encouragement: matters almost as interesting to those who appreciate a correct knowledge of chronological events, as to the lover of art himself.

The gallery of the Palais Royal was always regarded as one of the finest in Europe.

In 1639, the Cardinal Richelieu either from vanity, or gratitude for the favours which he had received from the king, ceded to him by a deed *inter vivos* his palace, with the furniture and other valuables which it contained; and he confirmed this gift by his testament executed at Narbonne in May 1642.

In the year 1643, Anne of Austria, Queen of France and Regent of the Kingdom, accompanied by her two young sons, Louis XIV and the Duke D'Anjou, quitted the palace of the Louvre to take possession of that of the Cardinal, and to establish her residence there. The Marquis of Toûville, who was then great maréchal of the king's household, conceiving that it was not fit that her majesty should inhabit a palace which bore the name of a subject, prevailed upon her to change its title and substitute that of the *Palais Royal*–at the intercession however of the Duchess D'Arguillers, this name was afterwards for a time suppressed, and the original inscription of *Palais Cardinal* replaced.

Louis XIV ceded this palace to Philip his only brother, afterwards Regent of France, and by him this collection was rendered the finest and the most important private collection at that time existing in Europe–from that period this palace again bore the name of Palais Royal.

Philip Regent Duke of Orleans was a man of a high and proud spirit, of a refined and cultivated taste–he considered that no man could perpetuate his name so effectually with posterity, as by a just and liberal patronage of the fine arts–he fully appreciated the high value which had been attached to the name of De Medicis–a family, which, having sprung from the commercial classes of society, had, by a liberal and refined encouragement of literature, and of the arts and sciences, founded for themselves a reputation which may be

[1] See page 82.

deemed immortal; neither did he lose sight of the splendid example which François Premier, one of his illustrious predecessors, had left in his own country.

Philip with the power which he possessed in the state, joined to his own wealth, had ample means afforded him of gratifying his taste, as well as his ambition. He employed some of the most celebrated artists of the day to select for him by purchase, the finest works of the great masters which could be procured in the various countries of Europe, while many of the minor states desiring to pay their court to him, made presents to the Regent of such works as were likely to yield him satisfaction, or to secure his favour and protection, and in general, the whole collection was formed upon the broad and liberal view of rendering it one of the most splendid and consequential in Europe; Philip employed twenty years of his life in forming this magnificent gallery.

Queen Christina of Sweden was possessed of forty-seven pictures of the highest importance, which her father had possessed himself of on the reduction of Prague. Among these were ten by Correggio. When she abdicated the crown she retired to Rome, and carried with her this precious collection of chefs-d'oeuvres. Out of this collection she presented to Louis XIV the famous picture of the Leda of Correggio, and on her death these pictures were sold in Rome and purchased by Livio Odeschalchi, Duke of Bracciano, nephew of Pope Innocent XI, from whose heirs again, the Regent Philip made the purchase of this rich collection.

The other cabinets from which the Regent made acquisitions in the formation of his gallery, were those of the Cardinals de Richelieu, Mazarin, and Dubois; of Lord Melford, of the Duke de Grammont, the Abbé de Maisainville, Deval, Forest de Nancré, de Nosse, de Seignelay, Tambonceau, Paillet, de Lannay, de la Ravois, of the Duke de Noailles, de Menars, de Hautefeuille, of the Duke de Vendôme, Corberon, de Bretonvilliers, du Cher, de Lorraine, l'Abbé de Camps, Dorigny, etc. etc.

The above list of amateurs proves the high and general regard in which the art of painting was held in France, at the period at which this collection was forming; and it is worthy of remark, that it was principally composed of the works of the ancient masters.

Among the different pictures which were purchased for the Regent, the prices which he paid for some of these have come down to us. For the celebrated picture of the raising of Lazarus, now in the Angerstein collection, he paid to the chapter of monks at Narbonne the sum of 24,000 francs; a sum certainly much under its value even in those days, when it is considered that for the Seven Sacraments of Poussin now in the Stafford gallery, he paid 120,000 francs; and it was well known that *price* never was the bar to the acquisition of whatever was truly excellent; the good fathers no doubt had their reasons for ceding this celebrated picture for so small a sum.

For the Saint Roch and Angel by An. Caracci, which was formerly in the Church de St Eustache of Paris, he paid 20,000 francs; and for the Saint John in the Desert by Raphael, he paid likewise 20,000 francs; but it has been asserted, that had this last picture been indubitable, it must even at that period have cost four times that sum, as the works of Correggio, which cannot be placed above those of Raphael, were paid for in that proportion.

By the means of these various acquisitions, the gallery of the duke regent contained during his lifetime 485 pictures, of the best choice, and in the finest state of preservation.

At the death of Philip, his son Louis took the name of Duke of Orleans. He was a man of weak understanding, and was guided in all his actions by priests, and monks. To please the fancy of these worthies, and prove how much he was devoted to them, he caused all pictures which represented 'nature unadorned' to be destroyed, or sold. The fine picture of Leda, by Correggio, which had been made a present of by the Queen of Sweden, was among the first objects to fall a sacrifice to his blind zeal: it was ordered to be cut into quarters, which was literally obeyed; but not having been committed to the flames, as was the case with many others, the director of the gallery, Coypel, contrived means to secrete the fragments, and had them put together. At the death of Coypel it was sold to Pasquier, and, at his sale of pictures, in 1755, it was purchased for the King of Prussia at the sum of 21,060 frs. and afterwards placed in the gallery of Sans Souci.[1]

After these various dilapidations and outrages committed on the works of these great men, whom the world has always been taught to regard with veneration, this collection passed down quietly until the epoch of the meeting of the National Convention. In 1792, the Duke d'Orleans, for the purpose of procuring money to agitate the national spirit, of which he always hoped ultimately to profit, sold all the pictures of the Palais Royal. A banker of Brusselles, named Walkuers, bought those of the Italian and French schools at the price of 750,000 livres, who again sold them to Monsieur Laborde de Mereville, a gentleman of fortune, for 900,000 frs. This gentleman, either as an amateur, or guided by feelings of national pride and philanthropy, made this purchase with the sole view of preserving the collection for France. For this purpose he gave orders to build a superb gallery, connected with his own hotel, in the Rue d'Artois. The works were already far advanced, when the storm of the revolution burst out in all its force, and obliged Mons. Laborde, with thousands of other refugees, to seek safety in England, whither he had the good fortune to transport his collection, which proved to him a resource during this period of his misfortunes. They did not, however, stop here; for, anxious to revisit his native country, for motives at present unknown, he was recognised by the reigning faction of the day, and fell a sacrifice to the revolutionary cause.

The pictures of the Flemish, Dutch, and German schools were likewise sold in 1792, by the Duke of Orleans to Thomas Moore Slade, Esq.[2] who paid for them 350,000 francs, and who by great management succeeded in having them sent to this country at the moment that matters begun in France to wear the most serious aspect. This purchase was made for the late Lord Kinnaird, Mr Morland, and Mr Hammersley, in conjunction with Mr Slade.

The principal part of this magnificent collection, consisting of the Italian schools, was consigned, on the part of Mons. Laborde de Mereville, to a house of eminence in the city of London, and it is believed that they were in the hands of that house when a treaty was entered into by the late Mr Bryan, as authorised by and on the part of the late Duke of

[1] Today it can be seen in the Gemäldegalerie, Berlin-Dahlem (No. 218).

[2] See next article.

Bridgewater, the present Earl of Carlisle, and the Earl Gower, now Marquis of Stafford, for the purchase of that part of the collection, including also the French school, which was agreed on at the price of £43,000 sterling.

When this important purchase was concluded, which secured for England one of the richest collections, and at the same time one of the most valuable acquisitions which had presented itself in modern times, it was determined on by these three noblemen to select a certain proportion of the pictures for their own private collections, and to allow the remainder to be sold by private contract, under an exhibition to be made of the entire collection.

This exhibition commenced on the 26th of December, 1798, in the rooms belonging to Mr Bryan, in Pall-Mall, and at the Lyceum, in the Strand, neither of these places being individually sufficiently extensive to contain the collection. It continued for six months; at the end of which time all pictures sold were delivered to the purchasers.

The pictures reserved for the original purchasers are indicated in the following catalogue,[1] at their estimated valuation, and amounted to 39,000 guineas. Those sold during the sale by private contract amounted to 31,000 guineas, while the residue sold afterwards by Mr Coxe, joined to the receipts of exhibition, which were considerable, amounted to about £10,000 more, thus leaving a valuable collection of pictures to the purchasers, as a bonus and just reward, for securing for this country so splendid a collection, and enriching it with works of the first class.

. . . The interest which this famous collection had excited was great beyond anything which had preceded it. The amateur was anxious to secure the genuine works of those masters which had long been sought for in England; and the present was among the first opportunities which had occurred where the same could be obtained to any extent. The whole pictures of the Bolognese school were engaged in an incalculably short time, although it formed the most numerous branch of this collection; and the amateurs seem to have vied with each other in gaining possession of the works of particular masters.

On the first morning of opening for the private view to the principal amateurs, the late Mr Angerstein became a purchaser of some of the most important pictures in the collection; in particular, of the Resurrection of Lazarus, by Sebastian del Piombo, which he immediately, and without hesitation, secured at the price demanded of 3500 guineas.[2] The late Sir Francis Baring was likewise an early visitor, and named a certain number of those pictures which were marked for sale, as objects which would suit his taste. The price demanded was 10,000 guineas; the offer made was £10,000. Mr Bryan had no power to diminish. The worthy Baronet would not advance, and the treaty was not concluded. This anecdote, which the author of these sketches had from Bryan himself, not only proves the off-handed decision, and liberality, which always mark the character of a British merchant, but the intrinsic value which was attached to the collection itself, the proprietors not admitting of the principle of naming a price, greater, than would actually be taken.

Lord Berwick, the Viscount Fitzwilliam, the Earl Temple, Mr Maitland, Mr Hope,

[1] Not included here; see pages 25–216 of *Memoirs of Painting*, Vol. 1.

[2] Since 1824 it has been No. 1. in the catalogue of the London National Gallery.

and Mr Hibbert, were all early, and considerable purchasers from this collection, as were likewise the late Mr Willett, the Earl of Darnley, the Earl of Suffolk, Mr T. Hope, Mr Troward, Mr W. Smith, the Baroness Lady Lucas, now Countess De Grey, Mr Udney, Mr Long, Sir A. Hume, Mr Fitzhugh, etc. etc. etc. This list sufficiently proves the great and general interest which this collection had raised in England; and at the same time disproves the assertion which foreigners had till then made,* that we were a nation possessing no love for the Fine Arts, nor any knowledge of them.

Until the arrival of the Orleans Collection in England, the prevailing taste and fashion has been for the acquisition of pictures of the Flemish and Dutch schools;[1] this likewise had for a long period been the rage in France. These were much more easily to be acquired, and came more frequently before the eye of the public than works of the Italian masters; it might, therefore, be deemed somewhat singular to see with what avidity the present collection was seized on by the amateurs of painting in general; and it will not be deemed surprising, that, from that time, a new turn was given to the taste for collecting in this country. Subsequent importations of the works of the Italian masters, gave an opportunity of improving that taste, and brought the English collections, generally, to a standard of consequence, which they could not boast of before that period.

THE ORLEANS DISPERSAL · AN EXPLANATORY POSTSCRIPT

AFTER the Duke of Bridgewater had bought the nucleus of the Orleans Collection in 1798, and allowed his nephew, the Earl Gower, a share of it, the separate parts of the collection descended down the family. The names Bridgewater, Stafford, Sutherland, Egerton, Ellesmere, and Gower are ones that constantly recur in the subsequent chronicles of English collecting, and as their relationship (and the nomenclature of their separate galleries) is extremely confusing, this is a good point at which to attempt an explanation of it.

Let us draw on Mrs Jameson (who was writing in 1844) for assistance. She says:

* *Montesquieu, Winkelmann, etc. etc.*

[1] Buchanan's assertion may have been true in the few years immediately preceding the importation of the Orleans Collection but, though it is repeated by Waagen and others, it is open to dispute as far as the second half of the eighteenth century is concerned.

'The Duke of Bridgewater already possessed some fine pictures, and after the acquisition of his share of the Orleans Gallery, continued to add largely to his collection, till his death in 1803, when he left his pictures, valued at £150,000, to his nephew, George, 1st Marquess of Stafford (afterward 1st Duke of Sutherland). During the life of this nobleman, the collection, added to one formed by himself

Cleveland House about 1824, home of the Marquess of Stafford.

when Earl Gower, was placed in the house in Cleveland Row, and the whole known then–and for thirty years afterwards–as the Stafford Gallery, became celebrated all over Europe. On the death of the Marquess of Stafford, in 1833, his second son, Lord Francis Leveson Gower, taking the surname of Egerton, inherited under the will of his grand-uncle, the Bridgewater property, including the collection of pictures formed by the Duke. The Stafford Gallery was thus divided; that part of the collection which had been acquired by the Marquess of Stafford fell to his eldest son, the present Duke of Sutherland; while the Bridgewater Collection, properly so called, devolved to Lord Francis Egerton, and has resumed its original appellation, being now known as the Bridgewater Gallery.'

To make confusion worse confounded the Bridgewater House of Mrs Jameson's day was being demolished at the time she was writing. The paintings were housed in temporary premises where they were ill displayed while a new Bridgewater House was being constructed to the plans of Sir Charles Barry.

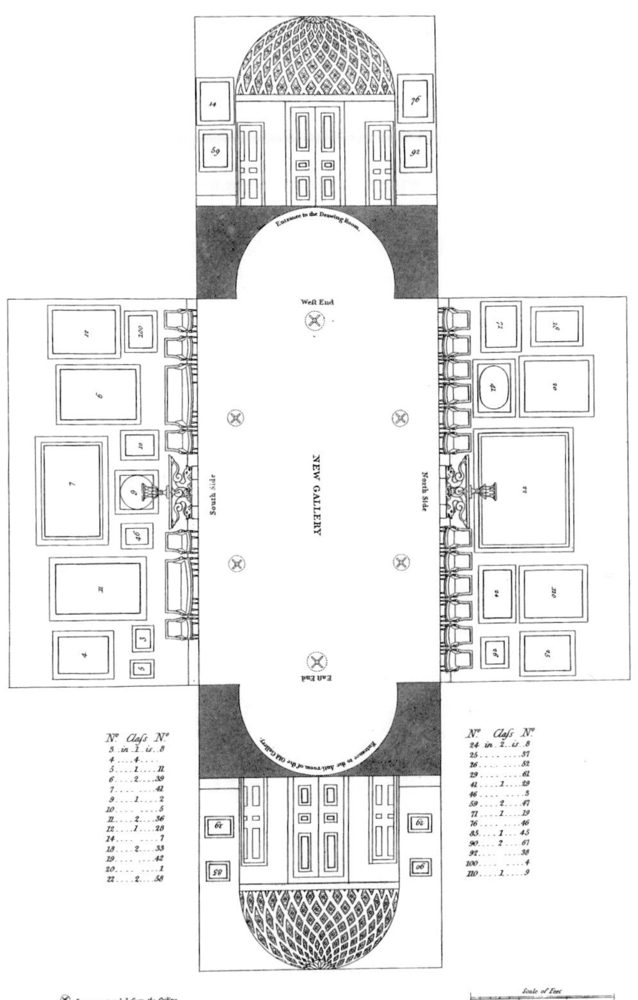

Plan of the New Gallery in Cleveland House (see also Plate 20).

A brief history of this house will explain why it is referred to by such a multiplicity of names. It was built as *Cleveland House* in 1626, and was bought by John Egerton, 4th Earl of Bridgewater in 1700. It was considerably altered by Francis Egerton, 3rd and last Duke of Bridgewater, who also added the picture gallery in

1797. He left the house and collection to his nephew, George Granville Leveson-Gower, who became Marquess of Stafford in 1803 and added the *Stafford Gallery* from designs by C. H. Tatham in 1805–6. It was known by this name until his death, although he had become Duke of Sutherland in 1823.

The second son, referred to by Mrs Jameson as Lord Francis Egerton, became Earl of Ellesmere in 1846. He re-styled that part of the collection which he inherited the *Bridgewater Gallery*, but demolished the original house and had the new *Bridgewater House* designed by Charles Barry.

The Stafford Gallery is most fully and sumptuously documented in a four-volume catalogue, complete with plans of the house and the pictures in each room (see above), engravings of every painting and detailed notes on them by William Young Ottley. This appeared in 1818. There was an earlier *Catalogue Raisonné* of *The Pictures in the Gallery of Cleveland House* compiled by John Britton in 1808. The same engraved frontispiece for this (see Plate 20) is also used in C. M. Westmacott's *British Galleries of Painting and Sculpture*, 1824, which contains a less detailed description of Cleveland House.

The *Sutherland Gallery* belonged to Lord Ellesmere's elder brother, the 2nd Duke of Sutherland. It was contained in *Stafford House*.[1] Both Smirke and Barry had had a hand in completing this 'magnificent mansion, or rather palace'.

FRANK HERRMANN

THE FLEMISH PART OF THE ORLEANS COLLECTION

THE account of the purchase of the Vitturi Collection which Buchanan received from Thomas Moore Slade has already been quoted. Slade, who must have been an unusually dynamic collector, also gave Buchanan details of how he eventually purchased the Flemish and Dutch part of the Orleans Collection. It was subsequently broken up and sold to the foremost collectors of his day. It consisted of twelve paintings by Rubens, ten by van Dyck (the famous portrait of Lord Arundel was not included in Slade's purchase though it also came to England), nine by

[1] Cleveland House was on the north side of Cleveland Row. Stafford House was south of Cleveland Row. In 1916 it was bought by Viscount Leverhulme who renamed it Lancaster House.

Teniers, six by Rembrandt, three by Gerard Dou, four by Wouvermans, three by Francis Mieris, seven by Vetscher and three by Adriaen van der Werff.[1]

Extracted from William Buchanan's *Memoirs of Painting*, 1824.

Long before the introduction of the Italian part of the Orleans Collection into England, and even before the Duke of Orleans had disposed of any part of his gallery of paintings, proposals were made to him on the part of T. M. Slade, Esq. to purchase the entire collection so far back as the year 1792. The author of this work will here give the information which he received from Mr Slade himself, in reference to that negotiation and which is exceedingly interesting.

Mr Slade in his letter to him, dated 2 February, proceeds:

'In the month of May 1792, the late Lord Kinnaird and Messrs Morland and Hammersley asked me, if I would join them in the speculation of purchasing the whole of the Orleans Collection; for which they were to provide money, and I to find judgement as to their value. This proposal suiting me, I readily acquiesced in it; and on the 8th of June I set off from my house at Rochester for Paris, carrying with me a letter of credit on the house of Peregaux and Co. for fifty thousand pounds sterling. I arrived at Paris the very day the king had fled: the city was in the greatest confusion and under martial law; however, the keepers of the gallery had orders to let me have free access at all hours, and to take down any pictures which I wished to inspect.

'A negotiation on the part of Lord Kinnaird had been begun through the means of a Mr Forth, a gentleman who was intimate in the family of the Duke of Orleans. After two or three days that I had been in Paris, I was requested on the part of the Duke of Orleans to make a valuation of all the pictures in the collection, and to make an offer. This I represented was contrary to all usage, as it was for His Royal Highness to fix the price, and to make a demand–all expostulation, however, on this point was in vain: for unless I acceded to these conditions the negotiation could not be entered into. I was therefore compelled to make a valuation, which I presented to the Duke; but when he saw it, he got into a rage, and said he was betrayed, and that I was in league with Monsieur le Brun, the director of His Royal Highness's gallery, as there was only 20,000 livres difference between his valuation and mine. I most positively assured the duke that such could not be the case as I was not acquainted with Monsieur le Brun; had never spoken to him in my life; and only knew him by reputation. This casualty, however, gave a check to the affair. The Orleans party at this time became every day stronger at Paris, and the duke so

[1] The beautifully finished works of van der Werff (1659–1722) were particularly prized by collectors in the eighteenth century. During his lifetime van der Werff obtained prices far higher than Rembrandt had ever received. His paintings were bought with especial avidity in Germany: his principal patron there was the Elector Palatine of Bavaria.

popular, that he flattered himself he should speedily be elected regent–he suddenly, therefore, resolved not to sell that collection, on the credit of which he had already borrowed considerable sums of money for the purpose of influencing the public mind: thus was this first, and most important negotiation broken off, to my great mortification, and I returned to England, having accomplished nothing.

'I had not long left France, when Lord Kinnaird informed me that the Italian part of the Orleans Collection had been disposed of; that the duke had lost a large sum of money at billiards to Monsieur la Borde, the elder; and that the bankers were so pressing upon him that he was compelled to let them have the Italian pictures to pay his debt; that the Flemish and Dutch pictures still remained, but there was not a moment to be lost in endeavouring to secure them for his country. I accordingly set off a second time for Paris, and on my arrival was again required to make a valuation, which I did; and, strange to say, it again came within 10,000 livres of Monsieur le Brun's valuation.

'On this occasion my offer was accepted, a memorandum of agreement was signed, and I conceived all to be settled; but the duke having learnt that he could obtain a larger sum from the Empress of Russia objected to ratifying the sale, unless he was allowed the difference of exchange, which was at that time exceedingly favourable for England: this I acceded to, being anxious to terminate the affair, and I flattered myself that all obstacles had been removed; but no! the duke had nearly outwitted himself by this delay. The numerous creditors, to whom he had pledged different parts of the palace, rose up and claimed the pictures as part of the furniture, and refused to let them be removed. I consulted an able advocate, who advised me, as I spoke the French language fluently, to plead my own cause. I accordingly attended the first meeting of the creditors, in the great hall of the Palais Royal–from thirty to forty claimants were present–I urged the justice of my claim, which they did not seem to allow; and I boldly declared, that, if they would not suffer me to remove the pictures, I had the power, and would enforce it, of lodging a protest against their being sold to any other person; in which case, the duke could not satisfy their demands to any extent. This threat had the desired effect, and next day I was informed that I might remove them at my own risk. I lost no time in availing myself of this permission, and had them carried to a large warehouse adjoining the Palais Royal.

'Here again I had fresh difficulties to encounter; and considering the state of the times, very considerable risk; for while I was having them cased up, I was surrounded by a parcel of people, many of them artists, who declared that it was a shame so capital a collection should be permitted to go out of the kingdom, and seemed from their language determined to prevent it. Some of them asked privately by what route they were to go; I had told the people employed in the *emballage* that they would be sent off by land for Calais: so soon however as the packing was completed, I had them all privately in the night put on board a barge which was in readiness, and sent by the Seine to Havre de Grace; from whence they were immediately forwarded to England, and were safely landed at the Victualling Office at Chatham.

'I was at that time a man of good fortune, and held a place under government. My house was at Chatham, where I had a very excellent gallery of pictures for my own gratification.

So soon as these pictures were landed, I had them arranged in my gallery, and for some months had an opportunity of gratifying visitors with a view of my acquisition; of which, considering the risks I had encountered, I was very proud.

The following season the collection was carried to London, where it was exhibited for sale by private contract, at the Old Academy Rooms in Pall Mall, under the direction of Mr Wilson of the European Museum; and you may judge of the general interest which this collection created, when I inform you, that above one hundred pounds per day was received during the last week of the exhibition, at one shilling admittance only. I had the entire control over this valuable property, and fixed those prices which I considered as fair, but which have since proved to be much under the real value of the pictures. Many of the finest were sold in the course of a few days, and I can give you the names of the purchasers with the prices of the principal pictures; but not having retained one of the marked catalogues, I must refer you to Mr Wilson for the prices of those which were not of so great value, although it may be said that the whole collection was good.'

The above letter is here given as containing a short and interesting history of the introduction of this branch of so important a collection into England.

The names of purchasers of this part of the collection, which the author of these compilations received from Mr Wilson, are as follows: The Duke of Richmond, the Marquis of Lansdowne, the Earl of Carlisle, the Earl of Ossory, the Earl of Darnley, the Baron Nagel, Lord Eardley, Viscount Dudley and Ward, —Danby Esq. of Yorkshire, Walter Fawkes Esq. of Portland Place, Lady A. Polwarth, Joseph Smith Esq., Mr Vandergucht, the Count de Bruhl, the Earl of Buckinghamshire, General Craig, Sir Francis Basset, Lord Gower, Miss Ottway, the Earl of Gainsborough, Viscount Clermont, William Smith Esq., M.P., Monsieur Mickel Basil, Payne Knight Esq. M.P., the Countess of Hardwicke, Sir John Nelthorpe, W. Beckford Esq., J. Davenport Esq., George Hardinge Esq., —Taylor, Esq., and Sir Philip Stephens.

DR WAAGEN SURVEYS THE POST-ORLEANS ERA

THE piece that follows is probably the most detailed, and yet compact, conspectus we have of the major European collections that were dispersed around the turn of the eighteenth century, and of their subsequent re-distribution in England and elsewhere. Only the master mind of a Gustav Waagen was capable of such a feat of compression of detailed knowledge, based on occurrences that were barely documented at all in his own time.

Waagen was born in Hamburg in 1794, the son of a little-known painter. He studied at Breslau and Heidelberg: his subject, the history of art, was then still a most unusual course of study. He had a remarkable visual memory and soon showed extraordinary gifts of discernment. He spent some years in Rome and then his mentor, Carl Friedrich von Rumohr, a distinguished figure in the German world of art and learning at the time, selected him for the post of first Director of the Royal Picture Gallery at Berlin. Waagen started work on the project around 1821 though the museum was not completed till 1830.

During his life he achieved much for the museum. His revolutionary catalogues alone would have merited a niche for him in the history of art. They were model compilations–clear, concise, highly informative and ingeniously organised–and their typographic presentation was a joy. But Waagen suffered under the frequent official squabbles and the poor pay that went with the job, so he was constantly applying to the Prussian authorities for leave to go abroad on tours of study. His meticulous notes, diaries, letters home, official reports and sketches were the raw material for a whole series of books that were guides to the works of art that could be seen in England, France, Italy, the Netherlands, Spain, Russia and Germany itself. He also wrote a number of general books on art: his principal work being a monograph on 'Hubert' and Jan van Eyck (1822). He died on yet another journey to Copenhagen in 1868.

His first journey to England took place in 1835. An account of this was originally published in German and the work was brought out in an English translation by John Murray in 1838 as *Works of Art and Artists in England* in three volumes. It is supposedly based on thirty long letters to his wife, and she is the 'you' that so frequently figures in the text. As will be seen from the ensuing article, Waagen–like some latter-day Baedeker or Pevsner–had done an immense amount of homework before his journey and had a very shrewd idea of what he was going to see. The only feature missing in his book which one would dearly love to see is a detailed list of printed sources he had consulted both before the journey and afterwards.[1] He travelled in England for five months on this occasion, but 'despite unremitting exertions was compelled to leave various collections of great masters unvisited'.

He made good these omissions on his return to England at the invitation of Sir Charles Eastlake fifteen years later, in the spring of 1850. The result was additional accounts of twenty-eight collections in London, nineteen outside and seven in Scotland that he had not previously seen. It proved too difficult merely to add them to *Works of Art and Artists in England* and to re-issue this in an enlarged

[1] He does mention four *major* works in his introduction, but not the innumerable local catalogues he must have consulted. The four were Buchanan's *Memoirs of Paintings* (on which he drew heavily), John Smith's *Catalogue Raisonné of the Works of the Most Eminent Dutch, Flemish, and French Painters*, C. J. Nieuwenhuys' *Review of the Lives and Works of the Most Eminent Painters* and Allan Cunningham's *Lives of the Most Eminent British Painters, Sculptors and Architects*. It was Edward Solly (see page 202) who gave him most information otherwise.

edition, so a completely re-written and expanded edition was prepared for publication only in England. Lady Eastlake undertook this mammoth task of revision and translation and the result appeared as *Treasures of Art in Great Britain* in three much enlarged volumes in 1854. But one must confess that though much more detailed, and probably more reliable, it is an infinitely less readable work than the 1838 edition. Lady Eastlake had ironed out all Waagen's freshness of vision and stylistic fervour in her translation. Furthermore, the English taste in collecting had changed considerably in the interval between the two editions: there had been a decided shift towards patronage of living artists.

However, the book was a great success, and Waagen's further visits to Britain in 1851, 1854, 1856 and 1857 led to a fourth supplementary volume, *Galleries and Cabinets of Art*, published in 1857. By this time his influence on English life and thought was considerable. He gave evidence before a Parliamentary Commission; he came over for three months as a juror to the Great Exhibition of 1851 and he organised the momentous Fine Arts Exhibition at Manchester in 1857.[1] It seems likely that the Prince Consort had suggested him for the task, because Waagen was the only man who knew where the best exhibits were to be found.

But the bibliographical story of Waagen was still not complete. The two principal editions were so widely read and quoted (see, for example, Christie's catalogues after 1840) that in 1912 Algernon Graves published a *Summary of and Index to Waagen*. This included over 9200 pictures referred to by the assiduous doctor and a second part of the volume listed those pictures mentioned in the tour of 1835, but not repeated in the later work. There is also a special index of 1130 portraits, followed by an index of owners.

It is quite clear from the extract that now follows that Dr Waagen had not long previously been reading Buchanan's *Memoirs of Painting*. Many of the celebrated English collections he mentions are discussed in separate excerpts in the present work.

EXTRACTED FROM Dr Gustav Waagen's *Works of Art and Artists in England*, Vol. I, 1838.

BY the dispersion of the pictures of these two collections in England,[2] a taste for fine pictures was increased in an astonishing manner; and succeeding years afforded the most various and rare opportunities to gratify it in a worthy manner. For, when the storm of the French Revolution burst over the different countries of Europe, and shook the foundations of the property of states, as well as of individuals, the general distress, and the

[1] For a detailed description, see page 312.

[2] The Orleans and Calonne Collections.

insecurity of property, brought an immense number of works of art onto the market, which had for centuries adorned the altars of the churches as inviolably sacred, or ornamented the palaces of the great, as memorials of ancient wealth and splendour. Of these works of art, England has found means to obtain the most and the best. For scarcely was a country overrun by the French, when Englishmen skilled in the arts were at hand with their guineas. In Italy, Mr Day, a painter, had in particular made very important acquisitions in the years 1797 and 1798. Next to him, Mr Young Ottley, afterwards Mr Buchanan, a picture-dealer, and Messrs Champernowne and Wilson successfully exerted themselves. Instant, pressing necessity induced many families to dispose of celebrated pictures to English bankers. In this manner Mr Sloane especially obtained many valuable pictures in Rome. Thus it happened, that most of the great families of Italy lost more or less all of their treasures of art. This fate fell with peculiar severity on Rome, and especially on the families Aldobrandini, Barberini, Borghese, Colonna, Corsini, Falconieri, Giustiniani,[1] Ghigi, Lanzelloti, and Spada; then on Genoa, where the families of Balbi, Cambiasi, Cataneo, Doria, Durazzo, Gentile, Lecari, Marano, Mari, and Spinola, sold the whole or part of their collections of art. In Florence, the palace of Riccardi; in Naples, the royal palace, Capo di Monte, lost many admirable pictures. Lastly, a great number of churches in all Italy parted with their altarpieces.

In the same manner, and with the best success, the English have exerted themselves from the year 1798 to the present time in Belgium and Holland. At the beginning, Mr Bryan, who had taken so great a part in the purchase of the Orleans collection, was especially active; and afterwards Buchanan, and John Smith, dealer in works of art. Of the astonishingly great number of valuable pictures spread over the two countries, from their national schools, the greater portion of the finest have been brought to England. It is there we must now look for so many pictures which in former times have adorned the collections of Van Zwieten, Van Hasselaer, Lubbeling, Van Leyden, Schlingelandt, Lormier, Braamcamp, and numerous others, and which even in this century belonged to Smeth Van Alpen, Muilman, Brentano, and Van Goll. Two collections, moderate in size, but very choice, that of the Countess Holderness, formerly belonging to the old Greffier Fagel,[2] and that of the banker, Crawford, were sold by auction in London in 1802 and 1806.

It was not till the French invasion, in the year 1807, that an opportunity offered of procuring a number of works of art in Spain. This opportunity was the more important, because till that time very few pictures by Spanish masters were to be met with out of Spain, the exportation of them being prohibited, under very severe penalties. Besides, it was the more difficult to make any acquisition of importance, because the most valuable

[1] The bulk of the Italian paintings from this celebrated collection went to Paris and were bought by the King of Prussia in 1815 with the intention of forming a nucleus for a national gallery. The English Solly Collection (see page 206) was added to it in 1821, but the Berlin Royal Gallery as such did not open its doors to the public till 1830.

[2] A very fine collection of drawings belonging to the Greffier Fagel was also sold in London by Thomas Philipe in a six-day sale of 644 lots in May 1799.

pictures belonged either to the Crown, or to rich convents, or were heir-looms in great families. Mr Buchanan, whom I have already mentioned, took the resolution of profiting by the events after 1807, to obtain works of art, and had the good fortune to find in the celebrated English landscape painter, Wallis, a commissioner who succeeded in triumphing over all the difficulties and dangers which the dreadful state of the country threw in the way of his undertaking. Thus, chiefly by his own exertions, but in some instances by those of others, pictures of the first class were brought from Spain to England. In Madrid, the principal were the celebrated Murillos from the palace of Santiago, and many capital pictures from the collections of Alba, Altamira, and the Prince of Peace; nay, some pictures were even obtained from the Escurial: besides this, the convent of Loeches near Madrid, gave the celebrated colossal pictures of Rubens, and Seville many fine Murillos.

While the English, with so much judgement, profited, by the circumstances of the times, to collect works of art in Italy, Belgium, Holland, and Spain, they by no means lost sight of France, where they had made such a splendid commencement of all their operations, by the acquisition of the Orleans gallery. Accordingly, when the collection of Citizen Robit, which was very rich in master-pieces of the Flemish, Dutch, and French schools, was sold by auction at Paris, in 1801, Mr Bryan, with two connoisseurs, Sir S. Clarke and Mr Hibbert, purchased forty-seven of the best pictures in that collection, and brought them in the following winter to London, to be sold by auction, Sir S. Clarke and Mr Hibbert retaining a certain number at a stipulated price. In the sequel Mr Buchanan also went to France for the same object. Besides several valuable acquisitions from different quarters, he brought to England some admirable specimens of the Dutch school, from the rich collection of Mr Laperrière, the receiver-general, which was sold by auction in 1817. His most important operation, however, was the purchase, in the same year, of the collection of Prince Talleyrand. It consisted of forty-six pictures, the greater part of them being the most celebrated works of the Dutch school, from the principal collections in Europe. Many of these pictures have certain names: thus there were, from the collection of the Duke of Dalberg, 'Les Fagots', by Berghem; from the collection of the Duke of Choiseul, 'La Leçon de Musique,' by Gabriel Metzu; from that of the Duke of Alba, 'Les Oeuvres de Miséricorde', by Teniers; from that of Van Leyden, in Holland, 'La Paix de Munster', by Terburg. In the latter are original portraits of the sixty-nine ambassadors of the several European powers, who signed the treaty of Westphalia. There was likewise in this collection an admirable Claude Lorraine from the Electoral gallery at Cassel. This choice cabinet, for which 320,000 francs were paid, was divided, with the exception of a few pictures, between two English gentlemen, Mr John Webbs and Mr Allnut. The English have also purchased most of the good pictures from the collections of Erard and Lafitte, which were recently sold by auction in Paris.

In proportion as the number of capital pictures which gradually came to England increased, the more did a taste for them spread, so that the demand being greater, the prices continued to rise. The natural consequence was, that whoever in Europe wished to sell pictures of great value sought to dispose of them in England. Accordingly, the number of pictures consigned to England is astonishingly great. From the Netherlands, a Mr

Panné, and more especially the families of Nieuwenhuys, brought many, among which were some of the highest class, from old family collections. As even in the smallest towns in Holland, there were often pictures by the best masters, that country was formerly explored like a hunting-ground by the picture dealers; and in such little towns notice was given by a public crier, that those who had old pictures might come forward. By this means the most charming works of Hobbema, Ruysdael, and other masters, were brought to light. In the year 1815, Lucien Bonaparte's collection of 196 pictures, containing many good specimens of the Italian, Dutch and Spanish schools, was brought from Italy to be sold by auction in London.* About the same time the collections of Spanish masters were brought to London, which General Sebastiani, and the Chevalier de Crochart, Paymaster general of the French army, had found means to obtain while they were in Spain: among them were some pictures of great value. Lastly, those pictures are of great importance, which Messrs Delahante, Erard, Le Brun, and Lafontaine, brought from Paris to England. They were chosen from the celebrated French collections of Randon de Boisset, of the Duke de Praslin, the Duke de Choiseul, the Prince de Conti, Poulin, Sereville, Sabatier, Tolazan, Robit, Solirene, &c., and from the great mass of excellent pictures which the Revolution had brought to France from Italy, Spain, Belgium, Holland and Germany. Those gentlemen, especially Delahante and Le Brun, were such profound judges of paintings, that it is no wonder that among these pictures was a series of master-pieces of all schools.

I have been obliged to write so many pages to give you a concise view of the most valuable paintings which have been imported into England since 1792. Add to these the great number of excellent pictures which Englishmen have obtained, or purchased singly, during their travels, or dealers of less weight have brought to England, and you will be able to form a tolerable idea of the extraordinary treasures which this country possesses.

The eagerness to possess some of these works was very great in England; yet here too, the decided direction of the national taste manifested itself, which in general preferred those of the Flemish and Dutch schools of the seventeenth century, and, among the Italian, had a great predilection for the school of the Carracci. Thus the immense number of pictures of that school, which were in the Orleans gallery, were the first purchased, and with great avidity. A chief ground of this preference is, that the English generally employ pictures to ornament their apartments, for which purpose the pictures of that school are peculiarly suitable, by their agreeable and finished execution. Above all, there was a rage for certain masters of the Dutch school, particularly Hobbema, Cuyp, Potter, Pieter de Hooge, Teniers, Adrian and Isaac Ostade, and the marine painter William Van de Velde. But at the same time the ancient affection for the works of Rubens, Vandyck, Rembrandt, Claude, Nicolas and Gaspar Poussin, and Carlo Dolce, remained in full force.

In conclusion, I give you here a list of the most distinguished collectors in England since 1792, who, by diffusing the most admirable works of art in their century, have conferred upon it a lasting benefit: the Duke of Bridgewater, the Marquis of Stafford, the Earl of

* *About twenty of the best pictures were left at Rome.*

Carlisle, the Duke of Buckingham,[1] Earl Darnley, the Marquis of Lansdowne, the Duke of Richmond, Lord Berwick, Viscount Fitzwilliam, Lord Kinnaird, the Earl of Suffolk, Lord Northwick, Sir Abraham Hume, Sir Francis Basset, Lord Farnborough, Lady Lucas (since Countess de Grey) likewise Messrs Henry and Thomas Hope, Angerstein, Samuel Rogers, Hibbert, Maitland, Willet, William Smith, Penrice, Elwyn, Hart Davis, Lord Radstock, Messrs Aufrere, George Byng, Watson Taylor, Walsh Porter, W. Wells, Jeremiah Harman, Champernowne, Sir Thomas Baring, Coesvelt, Sir Simon Clark, Lord Grosvenor (now Marquis of Westminster), Lord Dudley, the Rev. Holwell Carr, W. Beckford, the Duke of Wellington, the Marquis of Londonderry, Mr Miles, Lord Ashburton, and Sir Robert Peel. I have made this enumeration nearly in the order in which these collections became of some importance. Finally, I must mention as one of the most distinguished, the private collection of King George IV, the formation of which coincides, in point of time, with the two last. About a third of these collections are now partly dispersed, partly transferred to public institutions, and partly become of less importance, by the sale of some of the pictures; of the others, which still exist, several are, however, continually increasing.

The ancient fondness of the English for drawings by the old masters,[2] likewise found the amplest gratification after the breaking out of the French Revolution. In Italy, Mr Young Ottley embraced the opportunity of acquiring an admirable collection of designs by the greatest Italian masters, especially Raphael and Michael Angelo. Subsequently, Mr Samuel Woodburn, the most eminent dealer in works of art in England, was extremely successful. In Pesaro, he purchased of the Marchese Antaldo Antaldi the remainder* of the collection of drawings which he possessed, and which had belonged to Timoteo della Vite, a scholar of Raphael's, among which, there were especially choice drawings by his great master. The harvest that he gathered in Rome was far more important. Mr Vicar, a painter residing in that city, a man of refined taste in the arts, had, in his character of one of the commissioners of the French Republic for selecting works of art in Italy, to be sent to his own country, had an opportunity of forming for himself a collection of drawings, which contained a selection of the most excellent, and especially a rare treasure in drawings by Raphael. Mr Woodburn purchased this collection for 11,000 scudi. At Paris, he bought for 140,000 francs, the celebrated collection of drawings of Paignon Dyonval; a selection from that of the well-known Baron Denon, which, as French commissioner-general for all works of art (which France appropriated to itself in the countries occupied by its armies) he had obtained in different parts of Europe; and lastly, the collection of Mr Brunet, the architect. In Holland too, every opportunity was seized to obtain drawings by the ancient masters of that country, from the collections of old families. In the same manner, many articles from the celebrated collection of Count Fries in Vienna, were transferred to England. The greater part of all these treasures flowed into the collection of Sir Thomas Lawrence, late President of the Royal Academy, who, with an enthusiastic passion for works of art of this description, spared no expense, and is said to

[1] See 'The Stowe Sale', page 274.

[2] See page 107.

* *The others were bought in 1714 by the famous French dealer Crozat.*

have laid out £40,000 upon them.[1] Other important collections were formed, the best known of which were those of Messrs Esdaile, Richard Ford, Hibbert, Payne Knight, Mordant Cratcherode, and General Sir Charles Greville.

Another branch of the fine arts of which the English were very fond, were MSS illustrated with miniatures, which are of so much importance in the history of painting; for, as greater monuments of the early centuries of the middle ages are entirely wanting in most countries in Europe, and are very rare in others, it is only by means of those miniatures that we can obtain a knowledge of the state of painting from the fourth to the fifteenth century. They teach us how Christian art, long faithful to its mother the antique, in the conception and mechanical part, gradually assumed in both a new and peculiar manner; and how, subsequently, the ideas of the different nations were impressed upon it. In them alone is contained the complete, extremely large circle of representations and inventions which the paintings of the middle ages have embraced. Nay, from them proceeded even the whole of the great advance of the art of painting, both in Italy and the Netherlands in the fifteenth century. For the celebrated Fiesole, who was the first in Italy who in his paintings made the happiest use of the variety of intellectual expression in the human countenance, and thereby led to a new era in the arts, was the pupil of a miniature painter, and first cultivated that property in this branch of the art. In like manner, the celebrated brothers, Hubert and John Van Eyck, the founders of the great Flemish school, were essentially disciples of that school of miniature painters which in the second half of the fourteenth century was flourishing, and had attained so high a degree of perfection in the Netherlands. Of the great number of such important monuments, which were brought to light, especially by the dissolution of so many monasteries in all parts of Europe, an astonishing proportion has come to England, and is preserved there, partly in public institutions, partly in private collections. The interesting collections of Messrs Edward Astle, Dent and Mark Sykes, are already dispersed. Of those that still exist, those of the Duke of Devonshire at Chatsworth, of Mr Coke at Holkham,[2] the Duke of Sussex at Kensington, Sir John Tobin at Liverpool, Mr Young Ottley in London,[3] contain very valuable specimens. One of the most considerable of all, that of Mr Francis Douce, has been very lately bequeathed by him, to the Bodleian Library at Oxford.

[1] See page 189.
[2] See page 219.
[3] See page 186.

DR WAAGEN ON THE ELGIN MARBLES

HERE, to introduce one of the outstanding events in the history of English collecting, is Dr Waagen.[1]

EXTRACTED FROM *Art and Artists in England*, Vol. I, 1838

COMPARED with the great extension of taste for works of design in all the various branches, that for works of sculpture appears in England, since the French revolution, only in individual instances. The taste for modern sculpture is the most prevalent, and the works of Canova, Thorwaldsen, and the English sculptors, are, therefore very numerous in England. On the other hand, hardly more than a single English private person is known to have acquired works of ancient sculpture, of very great importance.[2] But then, this has been done on so grand a scale, that this one may be counted for many; nay, his acquisitions may be very well laid in the balance, against all those splendid treasures of pictures which we have just reviewed. This one man is Lord Elgin, and these acquisitions consist in nothing less than in the principal works, which have come down to us from the brightest era of Greek sculpture, and are known to every person of education in Europe, by the name of the Elgin Marbles.

. . . By the exhibition of these sculptures in London, and by the distribution of plaster casts of them all over Europe, all friends of the arts had, for the first time, the opportunity of making themselves acquainted, by actual inspection, with works which may be indisputably assumed to have been executed partly by the greatest of the Greek sculptors, Phidias himself, and partly according to his designs, and under his directions. The most celebrated antiquaries and artists in Europe, Visconti, Canova, vied with each other in their enthusiastic admiration of the perfection of these sculptures, which very few of the antiques previously known approach in excellence. In my opinion these works are as far superior to all the antique sculptures before discovered, with very few exceptions, as the works of Homer to the later Greek and Roman poems. The acquisition of them by civilised Europe is, therefore, of as much importance, with respect to the fine arts of antiquity, as it would be with respect to ancient poetry, if the works of Homer had been lost, and considerable fragments of them been found of late days in the library of some Greek monastery. Many Englishmen have collected articles of virtu of all kinds in Greece, as well as in Italy, so that a great portion of the finest of such monuments is also in England.

[1] For fuller details, see the next article.

[2] Waagen here seems confused. There were many fine private collections of classical sculpture. See Michaelis' *Ancient Marbles in Great Britain* (Bibliography, page 422). But certainly it was true that Renaissance sculpture was totally ignored by English collectors until comparatively recently.

LORD ELGIN'S RESCUE OF THE SCULPTURES FROM THE PARTHENON

THE literature on the wonderful sculptures in Pentilic marble carved by the hand of Phidias which Thomas Bruce, 7th Earl of Elgin, imported into England between 1802 and 1812 is sufficient to form a not inconsiderable library. The subject can be looked at from so many points of view. The architectural and aesthetic; the archaeological; the sociological; the diplomatic and political. For this important landmark in the history of English collecting, I have deliberately chosen a rather dry, impassive, and reasonably impartial account written by a scholar noted for his conservatism, not too long after the dust of the Elgin affair had settled. Sir Henry Ellis, a genial, fat and friendly man, was principal librarian at the British Museum. He had been an assistant at the Bodleian, had gone to the British Museum in 1806 and became Secretary to the Society of Antiquaries in 1814. While he remained universally popular he was not much respected towards the end of his career because of his unchanging ways in the midst of progress round about him.[1] This account of the importation of the Elgin marbles is the first chapter in his little two-volume work on the *Elgin and Phigaleian Marbles of the Classical Ages in the British Museum*, published in 1846.

One of the most interesting contemporary descriptions of the affair–but not all of it is relevant here – is the *Memorandum on the Subject of the Earl of Elgin's Pursuits in Greece*, second edition, corrected 1815, which was written by Elgin's former secretary, W. R. Hamilton.[2] Much of this Ellis paraphrased but he omitted to tell us some of the depressing twists of fortune which Elgin suffered.

One must remember that during Elgin's spell as ambassador there, Greece was an outlying province of the Turkish Empire and that the Turks had been there for centuries. Hamilton tells us how Elgin bought the house of a Turkish 'janizary' built immediately under and against the columns of the portico of the Parthenon. After demolishing this and excavating beneath it he found 'the greatest part of the statue of Victory in a drapery which discovers the fine form of the figure, with exquisite delicacy and taste. He also found there the torso of Jupiter, Neptune and Vulcan, the breast and part of the head of Minerva together with other fragments. Here was also procured that most inimitable statue in a reclining position, supposed to represent a river god. . . . Then Lord Elgin obtained leave, after much difficulty, to pull down a (second) house also and continue his researches. But no

[1] He was succeeded by that most dynamic of the British Museum's principal librarians, Antonio Panizzi, in 1856. For a detailed account of the relationship between the two men, see *Prince of Librarians*, the Life and Times of Antonio Panizzi, by Edward Miller, London, 1967.

[2] The first, very rare, edition of the book came out in 1811.

fragments were here discovered, and the Turk who had been induced, though most reluctantly, to give up his home to be demolished then exultingly pointed out the places in the modern fortifications, and in his own buildings, where the cement employed had been formed from the very statues which Lord Elgin had hoped to find. It was, in fact, afterwards ascertained on incontrovertible evidence that these statues had been reduced to powder and so used. *Then and only then did Lord Elgin employ means to rescue what still remained exposed to a similar fate.*'[1]

As much as any of the many other harrowing tales of wanton destruction that have come down to us, this incident demonstrates what would have happened to the Parthenon sculptures if Lord Elgin had not come to their rescue. It is easy to overlook the sheer magnitude of the rescue operation involved. After Elgin obtained the celebrated firmaun in 1801, permitting him to undertake this work, he employed between 300 and 400 workmen for a year in lowering the sculptures from the Parthenon and the other edifices in the Acropolis. Among the material shipped to England–after innumerable adventures–were 'the principal pediment figures, fifteen metopes, and fifty-six slabs of the frieze from the Parthenon (as well as numerous fragments), one of the sculptured "Korai" from the Erechthenon, four slabs from the frieze of the temple of Athene Nike, besides a number of architectural remains and more than a hundred inscribed stones'.[2]

Later Elgin consulted Canova, the celebrated Roman sculptor, about restoring the statues and bas-reliefs. To his eternal credit Canova refused point blank to consider such an undertaking. 'His expression was', Lord Elgin wrote, 'it would be sacrilege in him, or any man to presume to touch them with a chisel.' In addition to his other troubles Elgin lost an entire boat-load of bas-reliefs in his own vessel, *Mentor*, in a storm off the island of Cerigo, but thanks to Hamilton's endeavours over two years all the cases were eventually extricated by divers from the hold of the ship.

Feelings about the Elgin marbles still run high and discussion of their (wholly unwarranted) return to Greece occurs in the press several times a year. Despite the noble inheritance he had left the nation, Lord Elgin's personal life after his return from overseas was beset with misfortune. In fact, of all our many acquisitive diplomats at the tailend of the eighteenth and the beginning of the nineteenth centuries, he must have been one of the most unlucky. He left England as ambassador to Constantinople in 1799 with everything a young man could desire: personal success in the army and politics; a pretty wife; a considerable fortune; the prospect of a great diplomatic career, and good looks into the bargain.

When he came home six years later his wife had left him for another man; his career was in ruins; he had run up enormous debts; disease had ravaged his countenance–but he was owner of the finest collection of classical antiquities that any man in the British Isles had ever got together.

[1] My italics.

[2] Adolf Michaelis, *Ancient Marbles in Great Britain*, 1882, page 135.

There can be no doubt that his motives in amassing this collection were of the highest. Personal gain was the last thing he considered: it was his enthusiastic interest in antiquities that drove him to assemble in Italy a team of draughtsmen and artists who, together with scholars from England, could study, mould and make drawings of the great classical remains in Athens. It was in recognition of his very considerable successes in diplomacy that the occupying power in Greece at the time, the Turks, granted one of his associates permission to remove what sculptural remains he wanted. Had Elgin not removed them it is certain that the French would have done so, and had the French failed to do so, the Turks would have destroyed them–as they had already destroyed in ignorance masses of other sculptural treasures–or sold them piecemeal to visiting travellers.

For those who would like to pursue further details about the Elgin marbles there are three excellent source books: Adolf Michaelis' *Ancient Marbles in Great Britain*, 1882; A. H. Smith's very detailed *Lord Elgin and his Collection*, reprinted from the *Journal of Hellenic Studies* in 1916, and most exhaustive of all, William St Clair's recent *Lord Elgin and the Marbles*, which is a wonderfully lively account of the great rescue operation and its devastating effect on the personal life of Thomas Bruce, 7th Earl of Elgin, one-time Ambassador Extraordinary and Minister Plenipotentiary of His Britannic Majesty to the Sublime Porte of Selim III Sultan of Turkey.

Extracted from Sir Henry Ellis' *The Elgin and Phigaleian Marbles*, Vol. I, 1846.

In the summer of 1799, at the period of the Earl of Elgin's appointment to the Embassy to Turkey, Mr Harrison, an experienced architect, who was then working for him in Scotland, suggested to his Lordship, that though the public were in possession of everything to give them a general knowledge of the remains of ancient art at Athens, yet they had nothing to convey to artists, particularly to students, that which the actual representation by cast would more effectually give them. Upon this suggestion, Lord Elgin made a communication to his Majesty's government; but the probability of incurring an expense of an indefinite nature, and doubt as to the successful issue of the undertaking, deterred the minister from adopting the proposal as a national object. Nothing therefore was done to promote Lord Elgin's views, in England.

In his voyage to Constantinople, Lord Elgin touched at Palermo, where he consulted with Sir William Hamilton, who not only encouraged his idea of procuring drawings and casts from the sculptures and architecture of Greece, and more especially from the specimens existing at Athens, but applied to the King of Naples for permission to engage his Majesty's painter, Giovanni Battista Lusieri, then at Taormina, who went with Mr

Hamilton* to Rome and, upon a plan arranged by Sir William Hamilton, engaged five other artists, the best assistants Rome could afford, who accompanied him to Turkey. These five persons were, two architects, Signor Balestra, and a young man of the name of Ittar; two modellers; and a draughtsman, Theodore, a Calmuc, of great talent in drawing antique figures. They reached Constantinople about the middle of May 1800, when the French were in full possession of Egypt. They were sent, however, as soon as opportunity offered, to Athens, where Lusieri afterwards joined them, and where, from August 1800 to the, month of April 1801, they were principally employed in making drawings, at a very considerable expense on the part of Lord Elgin.

In proportion to the change of affairs in the English relations towards Turkey, the facilities of access were increased, and about the middle of the summer of 1801 all difficulties were overcome. Lord Elgin then received very strongly expressed firmauns from the Porte, which were carried by the Rev. Dr Hunt, the chaplain of the Embassy, to the Vaivode of Athens and the Disdar of the Acropolis, and which allowed his Lordship's agents not only to 'fix scaffolding round the ancient Temple of the Idols', as the Parthenon was called, 'and to mould the ornamental sculpture and visible figures thereon in plaster and gypsum', but 'to take away any pieces of stone with old inscriptions or figures thereon'; a specific permission being added, to excavate in a particular place. Lord Elgin subsequently visited Athens himself with additional firmauns, and having received while at Constantinople very urgent representations from Lusieri on the almost daily injury which the originals were suffering from the violent hands of the Turks, who were engaged in dilapidating the building piecemeal, in order to dispose of the fragments to travellers, he was at length induced to consent to the removal of whole pieces of sculpture, and thus after some years spent in the operation, succeeded in acquiring all those exquisite statues, and *alti* and *bassi rilievi* which are now called the Elgin Marbles.

At his Lordship's departure from Turkey in 1803, he withdrew five out of the six artists, sent home what he had collected, and left Lusieri to continue such further operations as might tend to make his collection more complete.

In 1811, Mr Perceval was disposed to recommend the sum of £30,000 to be given for the collection as it then existed, but the offer was declined on the part of Lord Elgin, who still continued to add to his treasures. As late as 1812, eighty cases additional to the collection arrived in England.†

In 1815 the negotiation was renewed, Lord Elgin offering, in a petition to the House of Commons, to transfer the property of his Collection to the public, upon such conditions as the House might deem advisable, after an enquiry upon evidence into its merits and value.

In the House of Commons this proposal met with a partial opposition. On one side, it

* *William Richard Hamilton, Esq., afterwards British Minister at Naples.*

† *Among the articles added at this time, were the neck and shoulders of the colossal central figure of the western pediment, called Visconti Neptune; the forehead of Minerva; and the two heads of the horses of Hyperion; three metopes, the most perfect in the collection, marked* 6, 9 *and* 13, *in Visconti's list; twenty slabs of the procession on the frieze; an antique lyre, and two ancient flutes of cedar wood; a bronze urn, with a marble urn which enclosed it; and a cabinet of medals.*

was regretted that these sculptures should have been taken from the spot where they had remained for so many ages; that the most celebrated temple of Greece should have been stripped of its noblest ornaments. The method of obtaining these antiquities was termed dishonest and flagitious. The House was reminded, that when the firmaun was presented to the Vaivode of Athens, presents of value were acknowledged to have been delivered to him. In short, that it was in his official character alone that the permission to carry away these marbles was obtained by the ambassador; and that, as a representative of his Majesty, Lord Elgin had laid himself under obligations to a foreign court, to which he was sent in order to watch the interests and maintain the honour of his country.

In answer to this, it was contended that these objects were lying in their own country in a course of destruction; that the Turks viewed them with apathy, and were even in the habit of shooting at them;* that Lord Elgin went into Greece with no intention to commit ravages on her works of art; that his first design was to take drawings of her celebrated architectural monuments, and models of her works of sculpture, both of which had been executed into his design till he saw that many of the pieces of which his predecessors in this pursuit had taken drawings, had entirely disappeared; that some of them were buried in ruins, some burnt into lime, and others either converted entire, or even pounded into materials for building; in short, that the malice of man had done more injury to these remains than either time or accident, and that they were subjected to daily dilapidations and constant ruin; that in Turkey upon all introductions, whether with or without a firmaun, the local authorities must be propitiated with presents; that so far from having brought away these marbles in his character of ambassador, not a piece had been removed from Athens till Lord Elgin had returned, and, of course, till his official influence ceased. Lusieri continued to be employed in 1816 under his Lordship's orders.

The committee of the House of Commons, to whom enquiry concerning the collection was referred, came to an unanimous opinion in favour of Lord Elgin's conduct and claims, an opinion distinctly expressed in the Report which was the result of their examination.

They stated that, before Lord Elgin's departure for Constantinople, he communicated his intentions of bringing home casts and drawings from Athens, for the benefit and advancement of the fine arts in this country, to Mr Pitt, Lord Grenville, and Mr Dundas, suggesting to them the propriety of considering it as a national object, fit to be undertaken and carried into effect at the public expense; but that this recommendation was in no degree encouraged, either at that time or afterwards.

It is evident, their Report says, from a letter of Lord Elgin to the Secretary of State, 13 January 1803, that he considered himself as having no sort of claim for disbursements in the prosecution of these pursuits; though he stated, in the same dispatch, the heavy

* *That the Turks were in the habit of mutilating the Parthenon figures before the Christians took an interest in the ruins of Athens, is evident from what the Sieur de la Guilletiere says in his 'Athens Ancienne et Nouvelle', 12mo Par. 1675, p. 192. 'Tout cela a couru grand risque d'estre ruiné par le scrupule de la religion Mahometane, qui ne souffre aucune figure de choses animées. Il y en a mesme quelques-unes qui sont mutilées. Mais enfin les plus honnestes gens d'entr'eux ont expliqué leur loy plus favorablement, et arresté la suitte de ces debris; et mesme la puissance du ciel s'en est meslée,' &c. The interior at this time was used for a Mosque.*

expenses in which they had involved him, so as to make it extremely inconvenient for him to forgo any of the usual allowances to which ambassadors at other courts were entitled. It could not, therefore, be doubted that he looked upon himself in this respect as acting in a character entirely distinct from his official situation. But whether the government from whom he obtained permission did, or could, so consider him, was a question which could be solved only by conjecture and reasoning, in the absence and deficiency of all positive testimony.

The committee further observed that the only other piece of sculpture which according to evidence, had been removed from its place on the Parthenon for the purpose of export, was taken by M. Choiseul Gouffier, when he was ambassador from France to the Porte; but whether that nobleman did it by express permission, or in some less ostensible way, no means of ascertaining were within the committee's reach.

It was undoubtedly at various times an object with the French government to obtain possession of some of these valuable remains; and it seemed probable, according to the testimony of Lord Aberdeen and others, that at no great distance of time they might have been removed by that government from their original site, if they had not been taken away and secured for this country by Lord Elgin.*

Chandler says that Morosini, after the siege, was ambitious to enrich Venice with the spoils of Athens; and, by an attempt to take down the principal group of the western pediment, hastened its ruin.

The charges attending the formation, removal, and placing of Lord Elgin's collection in London, including conveyance, salaries, board and accommodation to artists at Athens and literally all their supplies, scaffoldings, packing-cases, payment to Turkish labourers, transit of some of the property in hired vessels to England and loss occasioned by the wrecking of one; the weighing up of the marbles, which formed the sole cargo of one of these, by means of divers procured from the distant islands of Calymna, Cos, &c;† the unfavourable exchange of money, the cost of erecting convenient and sufficient buildings for the marbles when they arrived in London; arranging the casts, and attendance on the collection; formed a large and heavy amount from 1799 to 1803, of £62,440, including £23,240 for the interest of money; and, according to a supplemental accompt continued from 1803 to 1816, to no less a sum than £74,000, including the same sum for interest.

Two valuations, and only two in detail, of the collection were laid before the Committee of the House of Commons, differing most widely in the particulars, as well as in the total.

* *See also the Memorandum of the Earl of Elgin's Pursuits in Greece, 4to* 1810, *p.* 5. *Some of the persons employed in collecting for M. de Choiseul Gouffier's Museum were remaining at Athens when Sir John Hobhouse was there in* 1810, *having, as he expressed it, 'the same views, which nothing but inability prevented them from accomplishing'.* Journey through Albania &c., *p.* 246, *note.*

† *Lord Elgin, in the Appendix to the Committee's Report, p.* 65, *says 'There was, besides the loss of my vessel (the Mentor), an English copper-bottomed yacht which was cast away off Cerigo, with no other cargo on board than some of the sculptures. The prices and charges on this vessel (which from the nature of her voyage, could not be insured in Turkey), and the operations, which continued three years, in recovering the marbles cannot be stated under* £5,000.'

One from Mr Richard Payne Knight[1] amounted to £25,000, and the other from Mr William Richard Hamilton amounted to £60,800.

The following are the details of these valuations:

MR PAYNE KNIGHT'S

	£
'Recumbent statue of Hercules, as on the coins of Croton, with little of the surface remaining	1500
Trunk of a male statue recumbent	1500
Back and shoulders of a trunk, on which the head of Hadrian appears to have been	200
Fragment of the head of a horse, very fine	250
Fragments of about ten draped trunks, from the pediments of the Parthenon, most of which appear to be of the time of Hadrian	2000
Fourteen Metopes, of various degrees of merit all corrosed, and mostly much mutilated	7000
Twelve pieces of the frieze of the Cell with parts entire	3600
About thirty-five more, completely ruined	1400
Three capitals, and part of a column, from the same temple	500
Plaster casts from ditto, and other temples	2500
A granite Scarabaeus	300
A white marble Soros, complete and entire, but coarse	500
Various shafts and blocks of marble	350
Ditto of porphyry	350
Various fragments of statuary and relief	500
Various ditto of architecture	300
Caryatis from the Propylaea, much injured	200
Nine broken marble urns	450
One wrought brass ditto	150
One inscribed earthen ditto	150
Inscriptions &c.	300
Medals	1000
	£25,000

[1] Ellis makes little mention of the extreme venom of the campaign against Elgin which was led by Payne Knight. The latter's most vocal supporters included Lord Byron and the Society of Dilettanti. Among those who spoke up in favour of the unique quality of the marbles were many of the artists who had seen and studied them soon after their arrival in London. They included Benjamin West, who was President of the Royal Academy, Benjamin Robert Haydon, Sir Thomas Lawrence, Farington and the sculptor, Nollekens.

MR WILLIAM RICHARD HAMILTON'S VALUATION

Theseus	£4000	
Ilissus	4000	
Female group	4000	
Ditto	4000	
Iris	2000	
Three Horse's heads	2000	
Torso of Neptune	500	
Remainder of the pediment	2000	
Pediment		22,500
Metopes (19)		10,000
Fifty-three pieces of the frieze at £400		20,300
Bacchus		1,000
Caryatis		700
Casts from the Parthenon		1,000
Doric Columns and architecture		400
Ionic ditto and ditto		800
Inscriptions		2,000
Etruscan bas-reliefs		200
Vases from Athens		200
Bronze vase		400
Medals		800
Drawings		500
		£60,800

'Articles on which no value whatever is set in the foregoing list:

Casts from the Temple of Theseus
Ditto from the Choragic Monument
Sun-dial
Various heads from Athens
A unique lyre in cedar wood
Two flutes in ditto
Sarcophagus, Fragments of architecture, and sepulchral Monuments.'

The only other sum mentioned as a money price, was in the evidence of the Earl of Aberdeen, who names £35,000 as a conjectural estimate of the whole, without entering into particulars.

The committee having ascertained the prices paid for other celebrated collections of marbles, more especially for the Townleyan Marbles, and those from Aegina, and from

Phigaleia in Arcadia, came to the resolution, that they should not be justified, in behalf of the public, if they were to recommend to the House any extension of Mr Perceval's offer to a greater amount than £5000. Under all the circumstances of the case they judged £35,000 to be a reasonable and sufficient price for this collection. The act of legislature by which it was procured for the public was dated 1 July 1816. The policy of acquiring it is becoming every day more evident. It is a fact worthy of record, that, with a view to wait the event of the English parliament purchasing or refusing these marbles, the present King of Bavaria had lodged £30,000 in an English banking-house. The possession of this collection has established a national school of sculpture in our country, founded on the noblest models which human art has ever produced.

FAGAN, AN EARLY IMPORTER

THE British consuls in various parts of Italy during the latter half of the eighteenth century were among the most enterprising seekers after antiquities and pictures on behalf of clients in England. The list is long and includes Consuls Smith, Robert Udney, John Udney, Sir Horace Mann and Robert Fagan.[1] The definitive book on their activities in this field has still to be written.

EXTRACTED FROM William T. Whitley's
Art in England, 1800–1820, 1928.

IN 1800, except for portraits, English artists were receiving few commissions, and the war was hurting them, too, in another way. As the French occupation of Italy became more complete, the owners of historic collections showed increasing readiness to dispose of their pictures, for there was always a possibility of their appropriation by the invaders. Among the English they found their principal buyers, and there were in Italy plenty of enterprising dealers from this country, both amateur and professional, prepared to buy pictures and to take the risk of getting them away by sea. Numbers of Old Masters were therefore imported in 1800 and their sale in London was naturally detrimental to the interests of the home artists.

One of the most diligent and successful importers of Old Masters at this time was

[1] See 'Sources of Supply', page 27.

Robert Fagan, the British Consul-General for Sicily. Fagan, who had been trained as a painter in the Royal Academy schools, was the principal agent in the importation of the Altieri Claudes in 1799, and he had since been indefatigable in his search for good pictures, as he shows in the following extract from a letter addressed to a friend in England and dated Rome, 23 May 1800:

I enclose a list of fifty-five pictures of the first class which you can send to Mr Penn, Mr Beckford and others. I am sorry the beautiful Venus by Titian from the Villa Borghese [see Plate 12] has met with a little injury on the thigh on the way to Leghorn by land, as likewise two other pictures. I have requested Mr Grignion to have them adjusted by some able person, but as he is not of the profession will you, if possible, have the goodness to look over this and only let be done what is absolutely necessary.

If this collection I have made is published in the different papers it may be exceedingly advantageous to the sale; mentioning that 'Mr Fagan, artist at Rome, who sent to London the famous Altieri Claudes, has selected from the first galleries sixty of the most choice pictures which are daily expected in England', mentioning in such a manner as you think proper to word it, the Venus from Villa Borghese. Besides these I have five capital pictures here; the Rembrandt of Palazzo Corsini; the schoolmaster and Calvin of Villa Borghese; the portrait of Ludovico Carracci by himself from Palazzo Bolognetti; and the Virgin, Child and St Catherine by Titian, which Artois copied in the finest style. The price set upon the five is 2500 guineas, and if I cannot obtain that sum I shall keep them for myself as examples of fine art.'

One of the two pictures mentioned as coming from the Villa Borghese is that wonderful Moroni known as *Titian's Schoolmaster*. It was sold by Fagan, with other pictures, to William Buchanan, who in turn sold it for 600 guineas to the second Marquis of Stafford. It is now in the collection of Lord Stafford's descendant, the Duke of Sutherland. This is the picture that astonished Hazlitt and which Waagen preferred to anything in the Duke of Sutherland's gallery.

THE ALTIERI CLAUDES

THESE two paintings were regarded as the ultimate prize by English collectors in the early nineteenth century and one comes across references to them over and over again. Their history in brief was that William Beckford bought them for the incredible price of £6825 (as a pair) in 1799; they were sold to a dealer named Harris for 10,000 guineas in June 1808; R. Hart-Davis, M.P. (an early National Gallery benefactor) bought them for 12,000 guineas three months later; they passed into the possession of Sir Philip Miles[1] of Leigh Court, near Bristol and were sold in the Miles Sale in 1884[2] passing to a Captain R. B. Brassey. They then became the property of the late Duke of Kent in 1940 and were sold in 1947 to Lord Fairhaven. He left them to the National Trust in 1966 (see Plate 23).

EXTRACTED FROM William T. Whitley's *Artists and their Friends in England, 1700–1799*, Vol. II, 1928.

DURING the last years of the eighteenth century large numbers of works of art found their way to England from Italy, whose princes and nobles were forced by the French invasion to dispose of pictures that had been in the possession of their families for generations. Many of these were purchased by English artists settled in Rome, such as Robert Fagan, Charles Grignion and James Irvine, who combined the buying and selling of pictures with the practice of painting, and took the risk of smuggling the canvases out of Italy by ships whose commanders had to face the possibility of capture by French privateers or Algerian corsairs.

In 1799, Fagan and Grignion managed to acquire[3] and send to London the famous landscapes known as the Altieri Claudes. At great risk, and at a time when the roads were crowded with country people flying before the advance of the invaders, they carried the Claudes in a waggon from Rome to Naples. Here they transferred themselves and their precious packages to a polacca, in which, shut up in a small cabin with thirty or forty other fugitives, they endured the discomfort and danger of a passage to Palermo in such stormy weather that the Italian crew at one crisis gave up all hope of saving the ship.

Nelson, with part of his fleet, was at at this time at Palermo, where Grignion obtained an introduction to him and painted his portrait. The artist when dining with Nelson at the table of Sir William Hamilton mentioned his anxiety concerning the Claudes, and their great value and artistic interest. 'This', said Nelson, 'is a national concern', and calling for pen and paper he wrote a letter on the spot to the Governor of Gibraltar requesting him to give a convoy to the *Tigre*, a small armed vessel in which the owners of the pictures had arranged to send them to England. The *Tigre*, though chased by several enemy ships of superior force, reached Falmouth in safety; but as Fagan and Grignion had omitted to state to whom the Claudes were consigned they were unclaimed, and were actually put up to auction, and only saved at the last moment from being sold for a small sum.

In the early spring of 1799 the two pictures were taken to London, where the romantic story of their conveyance from Italy and the intervention of Nelson was already public property. Shown privately at Lincoln's Inn Fields, they were seen by most of the London connoisseurs, and in a short time were bought by Henry Tresham, R.A., for William

[1] See Annotated Bibliography.

[2] See Redford's *Art Sales*, Vol. I, pages 361–366.

[3] The price they paid according to C. F. Bell's *Annals of Thomas Banks*, 1938, was only about £500.

Beckford of Fonthill. The sum paid for the two Claudes and four smaller Old Masters that had been sent with them from Italy was seven thousand guineas–an enormous price for the period.

Soon after the sale of the Claudes, Tresham received a long and interesting letter concerning them from Charles Heathcote Tatham, the architect, who was well acquainted with Prince Altieri, the original owner of the pictures. Tatham (who was the grandfather of Sir William Richmond, R.A., and the father of William Blake's friend Frederick Tatham) said that two years earlier when he was at the Altieri Palace, the Prince's son conducted him to where the Claudes were hanging and asked him if he would like to buy them, as his father was convinced that if they remained in Rome they would fall into the hands of the French. Tatham, to his deep and lasting regret, was compelled to decline the proposal.

'I found', he said, 'that I could not accept the offer without making the most imprudent risk of losing them and perhaps exposing them to absolute destruction. The Mediterranean was so infested with corsairs and privateers that scarce a barchetta could pass in safety from one port to another; and the insurance on property was then at the rate of thirty per cent and upwards. I therefore found myself obliged to forgo the pleasure and advantage of a purchase, to have completed which must have been a matter of the highest gratification to any lover of the arts.

'About six months since the Prince honoured me with a letter in which he mentions with the deepest regret that the pictures are gone, and that he had sold them to Mr Fagan for nine thousand scudi. The extraordinary escapes they have had in their conveyance here you are well acquainted with; and I am sure are as happy as I am, that since, to the regret of every amateur they have been removed from the place of their actual nativity–the great and natural university of art–they have at last arrived safely in a country that knows how to appreciate their value.'

Tatham in the concluding paragaph of his letter throws some light on the origin of the Claudes, and tells the tragic story of the two Princes who, living in a great house filled with treasures of art, were denied the blessing of sight: 'The Princes Altieri, both father and son, have the misfortune to be blind; the elder, I was informed, lost his sight when he was about forty years of age, the younger when he was near twenty. The pictures alluded to were, I believe, painted by Claude for the grandfather of the present Prince, and were first placed in the same magnificent room in which they ever afterwards remained till they were sold to Mr Fagan. There were also many other valuable pictures in the Palace and a large collection of antique statues and busts, the latter of which were collected chiefly by the present Prince, prior to his loss of sight. Since that heavy affliction he used to take strangers round his gallery, and pointed out the various pieces as they stood when he was able to see them. It as an affecting sight to see two such illustrious characters led about their own gallery by attendants, and capable of enjoying the remembrance only of the beauties which adorned it.'

AND A POSTSCRIPT · THE ALTIERI CLAUDES

EXTRACTED FROM William T. Whitley's *Artists and their Friends in England, 1700–1799,* Vol. II, 1928.

ACCORDING to the writer of Fagan's life in the *Dictionary of National Biography,* Beckford gave only £1500 for the Claudes and 'a few small Italian pictures' that were imported with them, but this price is very wide of the mark. I have seen letters from Thomas Grignion, who was intimately connected with all the business affairs of his brother Charles the painter, in which, after mentioning Beckford's sale of the Claudes to Hart Davis for ten thousand guineas, he says: 'Mr Beckford gave us only £6825 and £525 for the small cabinet pictures by renowned masters that came over with them. So he made a good bargain.' He states further that he discovered afterwards that Beckford was so anxious to acquire the Claudes that his agent Tresham was authorized to go as far as ten thousand guineas for them alone if the sellers stood out. Beckford, says the same authority, had always longed to possess the two pictures since he saw them in Italy when he was young, and made lavish offers to Prince Altieri which were refused.

The house in Lincoln's Inn Fields in which they were shown soon after they had been brought to England was that of Mr Charles Long, afterwards Lord Farnborough. Thomas Grignion states that he was present when, 'by the kindness of my dear friend, Mr Long, they were shown in his drawing-room, and all the most enlightened dilettanti attended and were lavish in their praise, especially of what is termed the *best* picture'. Nathaniel Dance, who at this time (1799) was devoting himself to landscape painting, was among the connoisseurs who met at Mr Long's and Grignion says that he was 'in raptures with the *best* picture', and having perused it for a long time he went to the other and considered it with the utmost attention; and then exclaimed, 'They may say what they will of this picture, but there are *many* fine passages in it', which he pointed out to the company.

When the two Claudes arrived in London they were hailed by some critics as the finest works of the master. Modern authorities do not agree with this estimate, but there is reason to believe that the pictures are not in the condition in which they were in 1799. Forty years later a well-informed reviewer of Waagen's *Works of Art and Artists in England* said, when speaking of the harm done by ignorant or careless picture cleaners:

'Among the most atrocious destructions of late years was the flaying and dissection of the two celebrated Claudes now in the possession of Mr Miles of Bristol, who had them from Mr Hart Davis, who purchased them from Mr Beckford of Fonthill. West and Sir Thomas Lawrence called at the house of the distinguished "flayer" to whom they had been entrusted to clean; the servant inadvertently showed them into a room where these exquisite pictures were–actually excoriated–the ground apparent in several places, the foliage in many parts totally obliterated, and all the surfaces for ever destroyed. The *cleaner* entered the room. The mild, courtier-like Lawrence was for once enraged and exclaimed: "I see, Sir, we have been where we were not wanted, and I am sorry–for this destruction (pointing to the Claudes) will deprive me of my rest." West, who was a man of great command of temper, stood as he was wont when angry, working his closed lips; then looking at the destroyer, he said: "Sir, you deserve to have been flayed as you have flayed those pictures." The conceited varlet replied: "Oh gentlemen, it is nothing–all very easily put to rights." "Yes", said West, "when you can get Claude to come from his grave to do it, not before." The two artists immediately left the house.'

IRVINE REPORTS TO BUCHANAN FROM ITALY

JAMES Irvine was a painter and dealer who spent a large part of his life in Italy. He and Buchanan got to know each other in 1799 when Buchanan was still a law student in Edinburgh. Irvine had been living in Rome for almost twenty years, and was intimately acquainted with the colony of English connoisseurs resident there. He and Buchanan quickly became friends and the younger man introduced Irvine to an Edinburgh collector, James Gordon, for whom Irvine bought a considerable number of paintings on his subsequent return to Italy. The two friends continued to correspond and the friendship kindled in Buchanan an extraordinary enthusiasm for the arts. So much so that he decided to devote his life to a career connected with them and to forsake the law.[1]

In April 1802 Buchanan decided to set up as a dealer in London and asked Irvine to become his Italian agent. Irvine was delighted by the idea and the project was financed in part by James Gordon and in part by another dealer, James Champernowne. The role of agent suited Irvine particularly well because he was consistently unlucky when transacting business on his own behalf, so much so that he believed himself born to misfortune. 'Such is the luck', he declared, 'that attends all my concerns, that were I to turn baker I believe people would give over eating bread.'[2]

But his lack of assurance and self-confidence militated, if anything, in his favour

[1] Buchanan, *Memoirs of Painting*, Vol. II, page 80.

[2] Quoted by Whitley, *Art in England, 1800–1820*, page 60.

during the often protracted negotiations with the Italian aristocracy and their intermediaries, who usually thought they had bested him in any deal. This uncertainty emerges very clearly in the many letters from Irvine that Buchanan quotes, but coupled with Buchanan's own determination and knowledge of what his clients would pay, they made a formidable and exceedingly successful team. Many of their joint purchases are now among the masterpieces of British museums.

Buchanan was well aware of Irvine's exceptional knowledge of art in Italy. At the very outset of their partnership he writes of his decision 'of availing himself of the services of Mr Irvine for the purpose of obtaining a few of the most capital works which could then be procured in Italy. He [Buchanan] considered well the consequence that such would be to the country, and the *éclat* which had been derived by the French nation from the formation of their gallery of art which had been recently opened; and he entertained an idea that if a sufficient number of works of importance could be still brought together so as to form an important nucleus of art of a high class, it was not too late to make the attempt of inducing His Majesty's ministers to form, through the means of such objects, the commencement of a national gallery.'[1]

EXTRACTED FROM William Buchanan's *Memoirs of Painting*, Vol. II, 1824.

Genoa, 25 Sept. 1802

'I wrote to you this day se'nnight of my arrival here, and that there were hopes of being able to procure something of consequence, in which I have not been disappointed. I have now concluded the purchase of three capital pictures by Rubens, in one of the Balbi palaces. In my last, I think I mentioned the subjects of these pictures, one of which is taken from Andrea Mantegna's triumphs of Julius Caesar, and should be worth, I think, about £1000 in England. It is painted on a fine canvas, pasted on wood, and injudiciously enlarged to fill a particular place. The other two are capital landscapes, which you know are very rare and highly prized; so that I am at a loss what opinion to give of their value, as it depends on circumstances that here I cannot judge of with certainty; but I imagine about £3000 the two. They are on board, and rather large, but being thin they are not heavy. They have also been a little enlarged; but the additional pieces must be taken off. The frames being of no value, I have left them, not to enlarge the case, which is ordered, and shall be sent by the first opportunity. Unfortunately, I am a few days too late for a vessel that sails today; but another goes in about a month. I have been in pursuit of a very capital Rubens, of figures the size of life; but the proprietor declares he will take nothing less than 1000 sovrani (nearly £1500): however, a priest is retained in the cause, which is always a

[1] Buchanan, *Memoirs of Painting*, Vol. II, page 96.

good thing; and should success for the present fail, another occasion may offer. I had also another in view; but being a subject rather unfavourable (the brazen serpent, of which there is a print), and the execution slight, I do not think it an object until better fail. In another palace there are four or five fine pictures, for which I have made proposals, but they object to separating them. As the collection is not numerous, and so large a proportion fine, it might answer well enough to take the whole. The fine pictures are

1. Bacchanalian Boys–Vandyck.

2. Finished sketch of St Ignatius bringing to life a Boy, &c. The large picture in the Jesuits' church here. A charming thing.

3. Dejanira, a whole-length, naked, and her maid with the poisoned shirt–Rubens.

4. Judith with her Maid receiving the Head of Holophernes–Guido. Quite different from Mr Gordon's and more in his second manner. Seems very capital, Half-length.

'Till now I had no idea of the number of collections, great and small, to be seen in Genoa. I have done nothing but run through them, and yet some of the best are still concealed. Others have been sold during the late revolution. I have formed a connection with a person here, conversant with them all, and acquainted with many of the proprietors, who has engaged to keep a sharp look-out and acquaint me when the moment for purchasing arrives; for most of them are still obstinate in refusing to sell. He gives me hopes that the finest collection in Genoa, at present concealed, and the proprietor out of the country, may by-and-by come to sale, if an offer were made for the whole. He means to go to Milan on purpose, as the owner is expected there some time hence. I have agreed to allow this person 5 per cent on the purchase of any thing he may find for me, which I hope you will think well bestowed; and I have reason to think him honourable, as he has assisted me hitherto effectually, and without any endeavours to enhance prices for his own benefit. Indeed, on such occasions, I take care to declare at a proper time that I will not lay out more than a certain sum, including all expenses. On the present occasion, I limited it to 25,000 livres, and he undertook to get them for less. The truth is, that I would have given the price asked rather than leave them, as it was by no means extravagant for a first demand; viz. for the two landscapes £1000 sterling, and £600 for the other, which was the highest valued. When I first saw them, I determined to go as far as £1500, or more, for the three. My first offer was 20,000 livres, and I was told that nothing less than £1000 sterling could be taken: but I was advised not to advance too quickly, as there was always time for that; but it was necessary to add something, and the bargain was concluded as above.

'With regard to the other two objects in view I am at a loss. On reading your instructions, I am strongly inclined to risk a few hundred to procure the fine Rubens, as your object at present seems to be as much to produce capital works as to secure a great profit. This picture ought to be worth £3000 when compared with the prices of other pictures lately sold in London; yet there is a risk attending these matters, and the sum is great. My best way will be to wait further instructions, and still I should like to receive and pack it up myself. In this dilemma you must send me immediate instructions, and in the mean time I shall see whatever else can be procured in other places between this and Rome. Could I find a picture equally valuable by some other master, I should, perhaps, give it the preference for the sake of variety: but for this there would still be a handsome sum left. From what I have learnt since writing the first part of this letter, the pretensions for the other collection are fully as high, and it might be better to have one Capital Piece at present, and leave the others for a future occasion. My chief inducement to attempt the purchase of the other collection is the Guido, which, as far as I could judge, is very capital, and would give more variety. Tomorrow, or next day, I shall again visit both, and fix more precisely my ideas, as well as attempt coming to something more decisive with the proprietors.'

Another capital purchase was concluded by Mr Irvine at Genoa, a few days after the date of the above letter, as the following one will show.

Genoa, 1 Oct. 1802

'In my letter of the 25th ult. I mentioned the different pictures I had in view, and gave you a list of some that I thought might be objects to offer a fair price for. On again returning, I did not find them of so great consequence as to be put in competition with the other mentioned also in that letter, and which grew upon me every time I saw and examined it more attentively. I found, also, on reading over again your instructions, that you particularly recommend choosing works of the *first class*; and rather to give £800, £1000, or *even more*, for *one capital picture*, than take two or three for the same price, but of inferior merit, even though they might bring more money at a sale. Reflecting attentively on these directions, I determined to risk something for so capital a piece, and went to the country to find the priest and try what could be done. After some conversation and promises of recompense, I offered 25,000 livres of Genoa (the price asked was above 43,000); but he told me it was needless to propose such a sum, as he was sure it would not be accepted. After a great deal of talk, and my advancing to 28,000, he declared he could not propose to the proprietor the selling it for less than 30,000 livres, as that sum had repeatedly been offered and refused. In a word, finding him obstinate, I was obliged either to give it up or agree to make this offer, which I at last did; and this morning he informed me of its being taken, and of course claimed much merit for having induced the proprietor to agree to it, as he insisted (he said) on 4000 Genoese crowns, which make 32,000 livres. In addition to this, I have to give 5 per cent. on the above to be divided between the priest and the person who acted as mediator; so that the picture will cost you altogether above £1100 sterling, which I am afraid you will think too much, and which I would not have given on any other occasion than the present, when your object seems to be to carry a point by producing something truly of consequence. The picture has much need of being new lined, and put into proper order, when I am confident it must forcibly strike every person of taste and knowledge in the art. It is an allegory that Rubens has repeated in another picture, but composed differently, and of which there is a modern print engraved by one Henriquez; but I greatly prefer this. It contains almost every thing in which Rubens excelled – women, children, a man in armour, a satyr, a tiger, fruit and furies; making altogether a composition wonderfully rich and pleasing. It is known in Genoa by the name of Rubens' family, and has always been a well-known and celebrated picture, esteemed the best or second best by him in this city. It is in the collection of George Doria, a branch of the celebrated family of that time. I have ordered a roller for it, as it is rather large, and has been increased as usual here to fill up the side of a room. With regard to putting it in order, I shall write to you on a future occasion; but you must not imagine from this that it is not in good preservation. In the course of tomorrow I hope to have it packed and put on board, and at night shall set off with the courier on my return to Florence, whence you will probably hear from me again.'

The picture described in this letter turned out afterwards to be the famous picture which was presented by Rubens to Charles I.[1] On its arrival in England, the picture was relined as advised by Mr Irvine, and on taking away a former canvas on which it had been lined, the Royal Crown of England, with the letters C.R. in large characters, were found on the back of the original canvas. This discovery led Mr Buchanan to make a search in the catalogue of the pictures of Charles I published by Vertue, when he found it particularly mentioned in two different parts of the catalogue, and the exact size as there given, corresponding with the picture itself. It is mentioned as one of the pictures which was in the Bear Gallery at Whitehall, and is there called a picture of 'Peace and Plenty, with many figures as big as the life, by Rubens'. It is also described in another part of the same catalogue, as an emblem of Peace and War, 'which Sir Peter Paul Rubens, when he was here in England, did paint, and presented it himself to the king, containing some nine figures'.

This picture, with the two Rubens' landscapes above mentioned, and the Triumphal Procession, along with some other capital pictures which are mentioned hereafter, were, on their arrival in England, offered by Mr Buchanan to the British Government, he having previously purchased up Mr Champernowne's interest in them, and having flattered himself that works of that high consequence would meet with a favourable reception on the part of His Majesty's Ministers. They were not, however, accepted, on the ground, as then alleged, that the Government was not in a state at that time (during Mr Pitt's administration) to lay out money on objects of that description. They were therefore offered to Mr Angerstein as a select Collection of objects of a leading class. He also declined them for the reason that, having purchased several of the Orleans pictures, and likewise part of the collection imported by Mr Day, he had not room in his house in Pall Mall for them. Mr Buchanan then determined on separating them, when the great Rubens was purchased by Earl Gower, now Marquis of Stafford, for £3000. One of the landscapes by Rubens was purchased by Lady Beaumont for £1500, and made a present of to Sir George; the Rainbow Landscape* was also valued at £1500, and was exchanged with Mr Champernowne for his picture from the Falconieri Palace, now in the

[1] Charles I was already a great admirer of Rubens' work when, in 1628, the latter came to England on a diplomatic mission from Philip IV of Spain. He was at once commissioned to paint several pictures for the royal collection. He took particular care over 'Peace and Plenty', as it was originally called, and Charles was so delighted when it was presented to him, that Rubens' request for a treaty with Spain was soon granted. After the sale of Charles' collection, it passed into the Doria Collection, Genoa, and after Irvine had found it for Buchanan it was sold to the Duke of Sutherland who presented it to the National Gallery in 1828 (No. 46). It is shown in Plate 60.

* *This picture was lately sold by Mr Christie at the public sale of Mr Watson Taylor's pictures, for £2730, and was purchased by the Earl of Orford.*

possession of Mr Penrice of Yarmouth; and the Triumphal Procession was purchased by Mr Champernowne for £800. The celebrated picture of King Charles the First in three views [see Plate 59], which formed one of this small collection, was retained by Mr Buchanan for several years. It is now in the possession of His Majesty. The fine Claude, representing a View of the Bay of Naples, and surrounding scenery, was sold to the late Earl of Wemyss for £1500. The Plague of Poussin, from the Colonna Gallery of Rome, was sold to Mr Harris for £800. A beautiful small Ludovico Caracci was sold to Lady Lucas, now Countess de Grey. The fine picture of the Marriage of St Catherine by Francesco Parmigiano, from the Colonna Palace, for which Mr Buchanan paid £1000 in Rome, was afterwards sent back to Italy, in consequence of not fetching the price set upon it in England, and as it had been sought after for Lucien Buonaparte; and the pictures by Raphael purchased by Mr Irvine for Mr Buchanan at Florence, were for the same reason also sent back to that country.

This formed the commencement of the numerous purchases made for Mr Buchanan at subsequent periods, as well in Italy by Mr Irvine, as in Spain by Mr Wallis, and in France, Flanders, and Holland, by himself; and which he is proud to have it in his power to say comprise many of the most capital pictures of all the schools of painting which came to this country during the late war.

DESENFANS · THE AMATEUR PROFESSIONAL

NOEL Desenfans was born in Douai in 1745 and was educated there and in Paris. He came to London as a teacher of languages and '. . . being possessed of considerable taste and much love of the fine arts, he spent much of his time in attending picture sales. At one of these he bought a small picture by Claude which he sold to George III for £1000. The profitable nature of this transaction induced him to turn his whole attention to picture-dealing.'[1]

A provident marriage with a former pupil, Margaret Morris, sister of Sir John Morris of Clasemont, Glamorganshire, probably helped to finance his career as a dealer, in which he ultimately achieved considerable success.

Desenfans was friendly with the younger brother of the King of Poland and

[1] Preface to the fourth edition of *A Descriptive and Historical Catalogue of The Pictures in the Dulwich College Gallery*, 1905. See also Redford's *Art Sales*, Vol. I., page 42 *et seq.*

through him was commissioned to buy paintings for King Stanislaus, who had come to the throne in 1764[1] and wanted to establish a national gallery in Warsaw. However, Poland was partitioned in 1795; Stanislaus was forced to abdicate and Desenfans eventually had to dispose of the collection he had formed on the King's behalf.

He was an early protagonist of a National Gallery and published a plan for the advancement of the Fine Arts in England in 1799. He died in 1807 and left his extensive collection of pictures to his friend Sir Peter Francis Bourgeois, whom he had encouraged to be a painter and who was, in fact, appointed landscape painter to George III in 1794.

When Bourgeois died in 1811, after a fall from a horse, he left his pictures and a sum of £12,000 to the Master, Wardens and Fellows of Dulwich College. And there they are to this day, housed in a special gallery designed by Sir John Soane.[2]

[1] Carlyle had a poor opinion of him: 'Not a sublime specimen of human nature, this poor Stanislaus! Ornamental wholly, the body of him, and the mind of him, got up for representation, and terribly plucked to pieces on the stage of the world. You may try to drop a tear over him, but will find mostly that you cannot.' Thomas Carlyle, *History of Friedrich II of Prussia.*

[2] See page 241. The gallery was in fact destroyed by bombing in the second world war and rebuilt subsequently. Fortunately, the pictures had been evacuated.

The pictures are of variable quality. Thus Waagen wrote in 1854: 'I had heard this collection so highly extolled in many quarters, that my expectations were very highly raised; but on the whole they were not fulfilled. In none of the galleries which I have hitherto seen in England do the pictures agree so little with the names given to them, nor is so much that is excellent mixed with so much that is indifferent and quite worthless. . . .'[1]

Nevertheless, though today we would consider that there are a large number of outstanding paintings among them, the museum was probably the most ill-visited public gallery in the London area until January 1967, when eight paintings, including three by Rembrandt and three by Rubens, were stolen in a spectacular nocturnal raid. They were all subsequently recovered in circumstances that were never fully explained.

The gallery was again much in the public eye when, contrary to the terms of Bourgeois' will under which he bequeathed his pictures 'to the Master, Warden, and Fellows of Dulwich College *for ever*', the Trustees decided to sell Domenichino's *The Adoration of the Shepherds* at Christie's in March 1971. The picture fetched £100,000 and was bought for the National Gallery of Scotland.

EXTRACTED FROM William T. Whitley's
Art in England, 1800–1820, 1928.

AT the time of deciding between the two Turners the Academy was considering a larger offer of pictures – the collection formed by Robert Udny [sic], brother of John Udny, Consul-General at Leghorn. Robert Udny, who died in January 1802, was a wealthy man who had inherited estates and had also made money in commerce. 'He was', says one of his biographers, 'much distinguished for his taste in the fine arts, and ranked with our best judges of painting, for which he had a sound taste, and possessed a very fine collection of pictures.' John Udny appears to have been anxious to promote the study of the arts in England, and to have realised how much English students were handicapped by the lack of public collections. According to his will he had made his collection partly with the idea of 'forming a complete school of painting, in aid of the Royal Academy', and he directed that the Academy was to be given an opportunity of acquiring the collection before any attempt was made to place it on the market. Udny's executors therefore invited the Academy to make an offer for the pictures, but the Council declined to negotiate and they were afterwards sold by Christie in 1804.

Robert Udny no doubt desired that this collection should form the nucleus of some kind of national gallery, plans for which had been proposed more than once; notably by Desenfans, who, when Udny's executors were approaching the Academy, was endeavouring to dispose of the large number of pictures he had acquired as agent for the King of Poland. He

[1] Waagen, *Art Treasures Of Great Britain*, Vol. 2, 1854, page 341.

little thought that many of those he failed to sell in the spring of 1802 were destined to figure, twelve or fifteen years later, in the first public collection shown in England at the Dulwich Gallery.

Noël Joseph Desenfans, to whom that gallery owes so much, was a Frenchman who came to England in the latter half of the eighteenth century and for some years practised as a teacher of languages before drifting into picture-dealing. He was well acquainted with Sir Joshua Reynolds (who had but a small opinion of him as a judge of art), and from Sir Joshua he bought the picture with which he commenced to form the collection of which he was now trying to dispose. This was *The Basket of Grapes* by Jordaens. Desenfans also knew Gainsborough and other eminent artists; and had been the schoolfellow of de Calonne, that distinguished exile from France and collector of English pictures, who took up his abode in London some years before the revolution of 1793. He bought for de Calonne, and had friends among other collectors abroad through whom he acquired works by Old Masters that were sold at a profit in England. In particular he was intimate with the French dealer, Lebrun, husband of the well-known artist Madame Vigée Lebrun, who was now in 1802 practising in England with great success.

Although Desenfans dealt on a large scale, he always posed as an amateur, and there was no love lost between him and the admittedly professional dealers, who resented his indefinite position and suffered from his skilful self-advertisement, particularly in the newspapers. For no one could write better than he the paragraphs, paid for as advertisements, and inserted as news, that were accepted without question in the London journals of the time, in whose columns his ingenious puffs are frequently found. And in those columns too appeared sometimes paragraphs of a less complimentary nature, paid for by his rivals. This is one of them:

'A certain foreign gentleman who is said to be a great encourager of the arts, has discovered that of dealing in pictures without posing *as a dealer*, of exhibiting them without being an *exhibitor*, and of heaping money without passing as a monied man. When he buys pictures it is *out of love for the art*; when he sells them he *only parts with them to oblige his friends*; and when he exhibits them in Pall Mall he puts them on view at one shilling entrance, to be sure, but this is *only to keep out the mob.*'

Desenfans had friends in high positions in Poland, who obtained for him the appointment of Polish Consul-General in England: and from Stanislaus, King of Poland, he received what appears to have been a general commission to buy pictures with a view to the foundation of a National Gallery at Warsaw. Of the particulars of this commission nothing is known except that Desenfans received considerable sums from King Stanislaus for the purchase of pictures, which were left on the hands of the amateur dealer when the partition of Poland cost the King his throne. In 1802 Desenfans determined to dispose of these pictures and for this purpose hired a gallery in Berners Street, two or three doors from Oxford Street; and compiled a catalogue of nearly four hundred pages in which he described and commented on the 187 canvases 'purchased for his Majesty the late King of Poland'.

His idea was to exhibit the pictures and sell them in the gallery by private contract, and the conditions of sale are set forth in the preface to the catalogue. He pledges himself that each picture shall be offered at the price paid for it, 'no lucre whatever being aimed at by the sale of the collection', and that purchasers shall be allowed to see his receipts.

This was the original plan of Desenfans and it has always been believed that such pictures as he disposed of on this occasion were sold by private contract. But I have discovered that for some reason or other he abandoned this idea, and placed the collection in the hands of Skinner and Dyke, a well-known firm of auctioneers, who sold them under the hammer in the gallery in which they were exhibited. The sale lasted several days and concluded on 19 March, and it is said that the Marquis of Hertford, Lord Gower, Lord Yarmouth, and M. de Calonne were considerable purchasers. The following are the titles and prices, published at the time, of the principal works sold, all of which are described in Desenfans' catalogue:

Andrea del Sarto	*The Madonna*	800 gns
Vanderwerff	*Judgment of Paris*	385
Salvator Rosa	*Dice Players*	200
Vernet	*Landscape with Fishermen*	100
Guido	*St Sebastian*	215
Wouwerman	*Landscape with figures*	210
do.	*Halt of Horsemen*	100
do.	*A Farrier's Shop*	200
do.	*A Landscape*	130
Teniers	*Figures Merry Making*	160
do.	*Landscape and Fortune Teller*	195
A. Ostade	*A Conversation*	105
Gerard Dou	*Lady at Harpsichord*	170
Hobbema	*A Landscape*	180
Titian	*Departure of Adonis*	245
Claude	*Seaport*	200
do.	*A Landscape*	110
do.	*A Landscape with Cattle*	180
N. Poussin	*Flight into Egypt*	160
do.	*Landscape with Orion*	150
Rubens	*Mary de Medici*	100
do.	*Landscape*	105
Cuyp	*Cattle and Figures*	130
do.	*A Landscape*	105
do.	*Landscape and Figures*	180
Carlo Dolci	*St Veronica*	125
Jan Both	*A Landscape*	110

Altogether the pictures realised about £10,000. This was £2000 less than they had cost, according to Desenfans, who complained bitterly of the opposition of the dealers, and of the artifices practised to degrade the collection in the estimation of the public. On his

29 From the same series as plate 28, this picture shows (left) 1st Baron Farnborough (Sir Charles Long), art adviser to George IV and the royal family; his father-in-law, Sir Abraham Hume (seated), who had a large collection of Dutch and Italian pictures and wrote a book on Titian; and the Earl of Aberdeen, President of the Society of Antiquaries and founder of the Athenian Society.

30 Sir Robert Peel (left), who owned a superb collection of Dutch paintings; the painter, David Wilkie; and (seated) the 3rd Earl of Egremont, patron and collector (at Petworth, where he built the North Gallery to house his acquisitions).

31 Three of the greatest collectors of their era: on the left, Mr Agar-Ellis (later 1st Baron Dover); Earl Grosvenor, 1st Marquess of Westminster; and in the frame, George Granville Leveson-Gower, 2nd Marquess of Stafford and first Duke of Sutherland, owner of Cleveland House. Earl Grosvenor swallowed Agar-Ellis's collection whole in 1806 (for 30,000 guineas, before it came up for sale at Christie's). His father had been one of the first active English collectors as far back as 1755.

32 Sir John Soane (1753–1837) painted by Lawrence in 1828.

33 Robert Vernon (1774–1849) was one of the new generation of collectors, who favoured the patronage of living artists. His collection was left to the nation in 1847. This portrait is the joint work of H. Collen and G. Jones. The latter painted the background. He had advised Vernon on the formation of his collection.

34 Samuel Rogers (1763–1855) poet, banker and connoisseur, portrayed at the age of 85. His house by Green Park in London contained the harvest of nearly fifty years of assiduous, shrewd and enlightened connoisseurship. The sale of its contents at Christie's in 1856 took twenty days.

35 Lady Charlotte Schreiber (1812–1895), a woman of immense vigour and intellectual ability, was one of the greatest collectors of pottery and porcelain before the end of the nineteenth century. She also made definitive collections of lace and playing-cards which she left to the British Museum. An immense ceramic collection went to the Victoria and Albert Museum. Even so there was enough left for a generous distribution to her ten children after her death.

36 Dr Gustav Waagen (1794–1868), first director of the Royal Picture Gallery in Berlin. He was an inveterate traveller in search of knowledge on the arts and a frequent visitor to England, where he played an increasingly influential role in the arts. His monumental book, *Treasures of Art in Great Britain,* is the most important work in the history of English collecting.

37 Mrs Anna Brownell Jameson (1794–1860) from a photograph by David Octavious Hill taken about 1845. Her life was complicated by an unhappy marriage, a permanent shortage of money and two invalid sisters. Yet she toiled on cheerfully and indomitably and became a popular author on the arts. Her style had freshness and vigour, and her work was an important link between the murky sentimentality of the old school of art history and the scientific criticism of the new.

38 A painting by F. Mackenzie of the principal room in the original National Gallery at No. 100 Pall Mall, where the Angerstein Collection was first shown to the public. It had previously been Angerstein's own house. The large picture on the right is *The Raising of Lazarus* by Sebastiano del Piombo, which is No. 1 in the National Gallery catalogue.

39 The British Institution held an annual exhibition where collector-members could show their latest acquisitions. This view by Alfred James Woolmer is dated 1833. The picture beside the easel is Rembrandt's *Lucretia*.

40 The Elgin Marbles in the temporary Elgin Room at the British Museum in 1819, with distinguished visitors and chief members of the Museum Staff: Sir Henry Ellis (wearing glasses) is standing in the centre of the group on the left. The painting is by A. Archer, who is shown sketching in the foreground (right).

41 Another view of the temporary Elgin Room, by W. H. Prior. This room was used between 1817 and 1832, when it was succeeded by a New Elgin Room.

42 Front Quadrangle of the Old British Museum, Montague House, 1842. A water-colour by J. W. Archer.

43 Entrance Hall of the Old British Museum. A water-colour by George Scharf, dated 1845.

44 A nineteenth-century view of the Lycian Room at the British Museum. The museum authorities had themselves organised several successful archaeological expeditions to the semi-Greek mountain country of Lycia which had revealed an extraordinary wealth of remarkable monuments.

45 Bank Holiday in the 1880s at the popular Bethnal Green Museum.

part, he said, the sale was conducted with absolute fairness, for the auctioneers declined to undertake it until he had signed an agreement that he would not buy in a single lot, directly or indirectly. And the following announcement is printed on the cover of the sale catalogue: 'N.B. Messrs Skinner and Dyke pledge their word of honour to the public that the pictures will be sold without reserve.'

This means that every work mentioned in the bulky descriptive catalogue compiled by Desenfans was sold for what it would fetch; and assuming that the list I have quoted includes all those that realised the best prices, the famous Watteau, *Le Bal Champêtre* (No. 173 in Messrs Skinner and Dyke's sale catalogue), must have been knocked down for less than £100. It seems incredible that it could have gone for so little, but Desenfans, who by some means recovered possession of the picture, valued it at only £200 when he insured his collection in 1804.

Le Bal Champêtre, which is the finer of the two pictures by Watteau at Dulwich, has been admired by generations of artists and connoisseurs. It is the Watteau of which Constable speaks in a letter addressed to C. R. Leslie in 1831. The picture was then at the Royal Academy, lent to the school as an object of study, and Leslie made a copy of it, which Constable saw and thus criticises:

'Your Watteau looks as it should look, colder than the original, which looks as if painted in honey–so tender–so soft and so delicious–so I trust yours will be–but be satisfied if you touch the hem of his garment, for this inscrutable and exquisite thing would vulgarise even Rubens and Paul Veronese.'

Wilkie, according to his friend Mrs Thomson, worshipped *Le Bal Champêtre* and its fellow-picture *Fête Champêtre*. She says:

'I remember with delight a long day at Dulwich–the Watteaus there attracted Wilkie's close attention, he saw nothing but these–his cynosures. I found him, as I walked about, always in the same spot. "There is so much air," he said, as if speaking to himself, and he mused for half an hour as we quitted the gallery and retraced our steps along the quiet village to find our horses.'

Although *Le Bal Champêtre* is the subject of a long note in the catalogue of 1802, Desenfans does not say how he acquired it, but on this point some information was given in a valuable note published in *The Times Literary Supplement* on 10 January 1924. The writer of the note had recently seen a catalogue of the collection of that well-known connoisseur, Sir Abraham Hume with annotations from his hand. In one of these Sir Abraham states that *Le Bal Champêtre* once belonged to him and that he obtained it from Desenfans in 1792, in exchange for another picture, the title of which he does not mention. In another note he explains how he parted with the Watteau: 'This picture', he says, 'I exchanged, April 1797, with Mr Desenfans, for one by Mola of *Hagar and the Angel*–a Landscape.' According to the writer of the note in *The Times Literary Supplement* the Mola when sold in 1923 fetched only 25 guineas, and the present value of the Watteau is £20,000.

DESENFANS TRICKED BY SIR JOSHUA REYNOLDS

EXTRACTED FROM William T. Whitley's
Art in England, 1821–1837, 1930.

DURING Sir Joshua's later years William Cribb was his picture-framer and occasional business agent. He was the proud possessor of a portrait of Sir Joshua, presented to him by the artist in 1790; and of one of his palettes, the gift later of Lady Thomond, Sir Joshua's niece. The portrait with the palette set in the lower part of its frame, realised two hundred guineas when sold at Christie's in 1871.

This portrait was sold as part of the estate of William Cribb, the younger, who had carried on for more than thirty years the business founded by his father, of whose connection with the artists of the past he told many tales. One of these –*Gentlemen Connoisseurs in Painting*–appeared in print in *Willis's Current Notes* in 1857. It concerns Noël Desenfans to whom we owe the existence of the Dulwich Gallery. Desenfans believed himself to be a fine judge of pictures, but he was deceived, not only in the instance described by Cribb, but also by copies of Old Masters, bought by him as originals, although actually the work of Ibbetson. He was well acquainted with Sir Joshua, who thought little of his opinions and became so weary of his eulogies of the dead artists and his depreciation of the living, that he determined to give him a lesson.

Sir Joshua, therefore, instructed his assistant, Marchi, to make an exact copy of a Claude which hung above the mantelpiece of the dining-room at Leicester Fields–a picture which was the object of general admiration and the theme in particular of constant praise by Desenfans. The copy was then dried and smoked to give it an appearance of age, and placed in the frame of the original picture. At this point the assistance of Cribb was called in. He was informed by Sir Joshua of the trick that was to be played upon Desenfans, and given a letter which might be shown to the 'gentleman-connoisseur', in spite of an injunction to secrecy which figured in the postscript. This letter, which the younger Cribb did not quote in his article in *Willis's Current Notes*, still exists. It runs as follows:

'Dear Sir

Go to my house and tell George to deliver to you a picture which hangs over the chimney in the blue chamber, and get it lined and varnished, which it much needs as it has not been moved for thirty years. It is a copy after Claude; if it were original it would be worth a thousand pounds, and as a copy, I should think it worth half. At any rate, I will not sell it under two hundred guineas; if you cannot sell it at that price, let the handsome frame it has be new gilt, and let it be hung up in the parlour by the time I come to town.

Yours sincerely
J. Reynolds

P.S. Don't let anybody know to whom the picture belongs.'

It was relined and placed, in the original frame, in a prominent position in the back part of Cribb's shop, then No. 288 High Holborn. Two or three days afterwards, Desenfans, who also dealt with Cribb, came into the shop, and seeing the picture, exclaimed at once, 'Why, you have got Sir Joshua's Claude!' Cribb said he did not think so, and allowed him to see Sir Joshua's letter about the relining. Meanwhile Desenfans eyed the supposed Claude with admiration, never doubting that it was the picture above the mantelpiece, and certain from his own judgement that it was an original, despite Sir Joshua's denial. He expressed a strong desire to become its possessor, and asked Cribb to approach Sir Joshua in the matter, but on no account to mention his name.

To sharpen the appetite of the would-be purchaser, Sir Joshua remained silent for a week, every day of which Desenfans called to know if an answer had been received, and to look again at the picture, which, he said would require careful cleaning. Sir Joshua wrote at length to say that, although he was in no way desirous of selling, he would let the gentleman have it for two hundred pounds. Desenfans at once gave a cheque for the amount, which was forwarded to Sir Joshua, who pretended to have learnt for the first time the name of the purchaser. He returned the cheque with a polite letter in which he stated that the picture was only a copy made by his assistant for practice, and expressed his surprise that so consummate a judge of Old Masters as Mr Desenfans should have been so easily deceived. Sir Joshua made no secret of the success of his stratagem, which caused an estrangement between him and Desenfans, who never knew that Cribb was implicated.

WILLIAM ROSCOE[1]

FROM the Introduction by Hugh Macandrew and Michael Compton to the *Walker Art Gallery Foreign Schools Catalogue*, 1963.

. . . He was the son of an innkeeper and market gardener but made himself a successful attorney in Liverpool. From an early age he wrote poetry, studied languages and developed a taste for the Arts. He participated in the foundation of two societies for the encouragement of the arts in 1773 and 1783. Both were short-lived.

He probably began by collecting books but his interest extended to prints by 1782 and by 1785 he was lecturing on *The History of Art* and *The Knowledge and Use of Prints* and *The History and Progress of the Art of Engraving*. By the same year he had conceived the idea of a chronological collection of prints and wrote an essay on the subject (which must have been an improved version of Heineken's *Idée Générale d'une collection complète*

[1] 1753–1831; one of the first English collectors (Edward Solly, see page 202, was another) to concern himself with the early Italian schools. The principal source of information about him is the two-volume *Life of William Roscoe*, 1876, by his son Henry. The otherwise excellent article on him in the *Dictionary of National Biography* gives little detail of his activities as a collector.

d'Estampes). This, together with *Remarks on Etching*, was intended for the third volume of Joseph Strutt's *Biographical Dictionary of Engravers*, which was never published. In the preparation of the preceding volumes, however, Strutt had received a great deal of help and advice from Roscoe, whose essay, *The Excellency of the Art of Engraving* had been published anonymously in volume one (pp. 1–3).

At about the same time he began to collect modern British paintings. There is no evidence that he was buying foreign pictures for his own collection but he may have bought some for friends and was already at least thinking of doing so for himself by 1792.

In 1796 Roscoe published his *History of Lorenzo de' Medici*, containing a chapter on the Arts, which was a very great success and made him not only a national but an international figure. He began to correspond with learned men in Italy but there is little or nothing about the arts in what remains of this correspondence.

Roscoe himself never at any time left England but in 1790 William Clarke, who was travelling in Italy and searching the archives for material for Lorenzo, wrote to him that he had met the Chevallier d'Agincourt who 'had been for many years preparing a Raggualio of the state of the Arts from their decline in the time of Constantine to their resurrection in the West after Constantinople fell a prey to the Turks. . . . His design was to take a summary of the state of the arts from century to century during this dark period. . . .' This scheme must have appealed to the author of the abortive *An Idea of a Chronological Collection of Engravings* and by 1804 he had certainly begun to form a collection of pictures, as well as of prints and drawings, to illustrate the rise of the arts. Among his first purchases were some of the most important. These include the Simone Martini and the predella panel attributed to the young Perugino, both from the sale of Colonel Matthew Smith, Governor of the Tower of London.

The collection grew rapidly, mainly through the energy of Thomas Winstanley, the Liverpool auctioneer and dealer, and by 1814, Roscoe was evidently preparing a catalogue.

In the meantime he had written another history, *Leo X*, as well as numerous political works; had been a Member in the short-lived Parliament of 1806–7; had helped to found the botanical gardens in Liverpool; had taken on a large scheme of reclamation of marsh land at Chat Moss and had become a partner in a bank.

It was not out of choice that Roscoe entered banking; he had been called in as an attorney to examine the affairs of his old friend's bank, Clarkes, and he was obliged to stay on as an active partner after the problems had been resolved. But the bank suffered from a run on capital by Liverpool merchants engaged in the American trade, and had to suspend payments in January 1816. Roscoe, together with his partners, was declared bankrupt in 1820 although in an effort to save the situation in 1816, he sold almost everything he had including all, or virtually all, those parts of his collection that were not personal gifts. Of these, 156 paintings are listed in the catalogue of his sale, some twenty-five were sold as extra lots or privately and there were about seventy pictures listed as presents, including the thirty-nine small Italian portraits.

The catalogue was certainly intended by Roscoe to be a memorial and even to give some kind of permanence to his collection. His 'Advertisement' to the sale of his drawings and paintings defines concisely his aims in forming the collection: 'The following works . . . have been collected during a series of years, chiefly for the purpose of illustrating by a reference to original and authentic sources the rise and progress of the arts in modern times, as well in Germany and Flanders as in Italy. They are therefore not wholly to be judged by their positive merits, but by a reference to the age in which they were produced. Their value chiefly depends on their authenticity and the light they throw on the history of the arts; yet as they extend beyond the splendid era of 1500, there will be found several productions of a higher class which may be ranked amongst the *chef d'oeuvres* of modern skill. . . . Hopes had been indulged by the present possessor that the works of Literature and Art included in this, and the two preceding Catalogues [i.e. of books and prints] might have formed the basis of a more extensive collection, and have been rendered subservient to some object of public utility. . . . The Catalogues may serve, however, to give an idea of the entire collection, when the works that compose it are again dispersed.'

Among the pictures that were to illustrate the rise and progress of the Arts were some forty-three (also about two not in the catalogue) that Roscoe believed to have been painted before 1500. To us they form the most interesting and valuable part of the collection for Roscoe was one of the first in England to collect such works on such a scale and they included the two outstanding masterpieces of the Walker Art Gallery's present collection, the Simone Martini and the Ercole Roberti.

Roscoe's hopes for the permanence of his collection were not wholly disappointed for T. W. Coke (later Lord Leicester) offered to buy the pictures that Roscoe valued most while some of the other lots were not bid for or passed, some were not claimed by the buyers and some were apparently bought in by the agency of local dealers and booksellers. A group of these pictures chosen by Roscoe and Dr Traill and valued at 1553 gns. were deposited at the Liverpool Royal Institution and in 1818–19 a subscription was raised and a group of thirty-five were purchased for about 1200 gns. at Roscoe's offer and presented to the Liverpool Royal Institution [Letter to Traill 16.8.1818, Roscoe Papers 4861A]. A similar subscription had secured a number of the books for the Athenaeum.

It is not clear whether by Roscoe's design or whether by the uninterest of the buyers at the sale a large proportion of these pictures (twenty-four out of the thirty-five) were supposed to be of the period before 1500, that is Primitives; just half of what Roscoe had owned in this class. The others were of the sixteenth century. All thirty-five are now in the Walker Art Gallery. Judging from these it cannot be said that Roscoe's aim of providing authentic specimens was very perfectly realised: only the two signed works and one that was virtually documented were correctly attributed but others were not too badly misnamed and most were at least of about the right period and school according to the standards of the time. Roscoe was several times deceived by Flemish imitators both of Italian masters and of their own predecessors and he made one or two howlers which is not surprising, considering that there were very few authentic specimens in England. He was forced to rely for comparisons almost entirely on engravings and even these were rare for the early periods. For the most part it is clear he depended on the attributions of a few collectors and dealers, among them Smith, Woodburn, Greville and Ottley.

ROSCOE LATE IN LIFE

EXTRACTED FROM J. D. Passavant's *Tour of a German Artist in England*, Vol. II, 1836.

MY journey to this large and interesting commercial city [Liverpool] was chiefly undertaken for the purpose of becoming personally acquainted with the celebrated Mr Roscoe, hoping through his means to obtain various important particulars regarding my purposed life of Raphael. On arriving, therefore, I repaired immediately to Lodge Lane, the residence of this venerable antiquarian, and was gratified by finding that the object of my visit was sufficient passport to the kindest of receptions. My hopes of assistance from Mr Roscoe had been founded upon the authority of M. Bossi, the Italian translator of Mr R.'s 'Life of Leo X', from whom it appeared that Mr R. was acquainted with several hitherto unpublished letters by Raphael. To these, therefore, my first enquiries related; but I was disappointed in finding that M. Bossi had been misled in this respect, and that his statement of having made the personal acquaintance of the biographer of Leo X was no less incorrect. Not only had Mr Roscoe never seen M. Bossi, but, what in the present age is rather extraordinary, had never visited the French capital. This error perhaps originated in a mistake of persons, M. Bossi having become acquainted with a son of the author, in Paris, Mr Thomas Roscoe, the editor of the Landscape Annual, a gentleman who also takes great interest in all matters relating to art.

I spent nearly two days with this excellent person, who, although physically declining (being in his seventy-eighth year), still retained every mental faculty unimpaired. Having passed a long and active life in the unceasing cultivation of art, science and literature, it will readily be believed that my plans respecting the life and works of Raphael were met by him with the liveliest interest. He eagerly communicated to me all the information in his power, and shewed me several rare English works which he conceived would further my undertaking.

Among the original drawings in his possession, a small one by Raphael particularly interested me. It was the fragment of a Holy Family, most spiritedly drawn with the pen – the figure of the infant St John, standing on the lap of the Virgin; still preserved. This drawing, with many other rare and interesting objects, was bound into a quarto edition of Leo X; a method of illustrating historical works very generally adopted in England, and which not only greatly enhances the real value of the work, but imparts an individual interest, and contributes to press its contents more forcibly on the memory of the possessor.

Another interesting drawing was the design for the cenotaph erected to the memory of Michael Angelo, and minutely described by Vasari in his life of the artist.

Before quitting this delightful abode, the daughter of Mr Roscoe, at his request, fetched down for my inspection a large work, which he had compiled upon the different species of flowering plants in and around Liverpool, embellished with plates, which, in point of truth of imitation and beauty of colouring, left nothing to desire.

On taking leave, the excellent old man, in the true, hearty English style, shook me warmly by the hand, and reminding me that he was not long for this world, gave me his parting blessing. His words were prophetic: before I reached London, he had peacefully passed to that world for which his spirit had here so ardently longed. His memory will always be sacred to me, and I am only thankful that the opportunity was granted me of knowing one who inspired affection and respect alike to all who, whether intimately or remotely, enjoyed that privilege.

WAAGEN MEETS WILLIAM YOUNG OTTLEY

ONE of the most professional of all English collectors was William Young Ottley (1771–1836). The son of a guards officer, he studied in the Royal Academy School and then lived in Italy for ten years. His knowledge was not only extensive, but acquired with a well-nigh scientific rigour of purpose. It was not surprising that of all the innumerable acquaintances Waagen made in England he should have regarded Ottley as closest to himself in outlook and interests. Like Waagen, Ottley concerned himself with most forms of art: he collected paintings, drawings and illuminated manuscripts. There is no doubt that he financed his collecting with very active dealing. At the very end of his life he became Keeper of the Department of Prints and Drawings in the British Museum.

From contemporary accounts he was clearly a sympathetic and warm-hearted person. He wrote a good deal and published a series of finely illustrated books of his own engravings. A graphic account of Ottley's pictures is given by J. S. Sartain, who assisted him with the engravings of the plates for the *Early Florentine School* from 1823 to 1825. Sartain wrote:

'My engraving table stood in the corner of a picture gallery, the walls covered with admirable paintings by great masters. If I raised my eyes from my work to the south wall opposite, there was a first-class Rembrandt, a nude woman seated, an old woman wiping her feet after a bath. . . . To the left was a Domenichino of

Cephalus and Aurora, figures larger than life. To the right of the Rembrandt a large picture of *The Battle of the Angels*, a noble composition by Mr Ottley himself, painted in black and white, evidenced consummate mastery in drawing the nude figure. It was his intention to paint over it in solid colour, but whether he ever did so I do not know. A line of works of lesser dimensions occupied the space beneath, among them a Guido, a Schedone, a Correggio study in oils, a Giorgione, and in the middle an antique torso of a cupid, not unlike the marble known as the *Genius of the Vatican*.

'On the west wall, opposite the fireplace, and over the Print Cabinets, was among other large pictures, a very large Titian, a *Madonna and Child* with landscape background. Just back of where I sat, was another Titian, the *Rape of Europa*, a beautiful picture of captivating colour, and lighter in tone than any other work of his I have seen. Below the Titian, and level with the eye, was the *Nativity* of Sandro Botticelli. . . . On the west side of the door of entrance was a large Salvator Rosa, St George pouring upon the Dragon some liquid from a bottle. Over these hung two Bassanos that extended across the whole width of the gallery, the subjects of course treated after his accustomed manner, but the colouring very rich and fine, though dark. Both recesses on each side of the fireplace were filled with books. [There was] a large table in the middle . . . on which was an accumulation of all kinds of things, books, drawings, prints, and what not–piled on one another in a confused way as if valueless. To reach this gallery from the dwelling the way was through another smaller gallery, also lighted from above, the walls of which were covered from floor to ceiling with pictures by the old Pre-Raphaelite artists, which Mr Ottley had collected in Italy during the latter part of the last century. Most of them were taken from churches during the occupation by the French soldiery, and but for Mr Ottley's intervention might have been destroyed.'[1]

Extracted from Dr Gustav Waagen's *Works of Art and Artists in England*, Vol. II, 1838.

The day before yesterday I was invited to dinner by Mr Ottley, whose extensive knowledge of the history of art and his enthusiasm for art itself, in its manifold epochs and forms, have led to a great intimacy between us. I went as early as two o'clock in order to examine more at leisure his collection of paintings of the Tuscan school, from the thirteenth to the fifteenth century.[2] It is very advantageously distinguished by two cir-

[1] J. S. Sartain, *The Reminiscences of a Very Old Man*, New York, 1899, pages 96 ff.

[2] These are discussed in considerable detail by Professor Ellis Waterhouse in 'Some Notes on William Young Ottley's Collection of Italian Primitives' in *Italian Studies Presented to E. R. Vincent*, 1962.

cumstances. It contains, with few exceptions, excellent works by masters, the most eminent of their time, whereas in the greatest galleries we find only the rudest performances of those ages. But Mr Ottley is also a great enemy to picture-cleaning, so that most of the pictures are still in a pure state, a circumstance peculiarly important in pictures in distemper, because, with the original varnish, their glaze-colours, and with them the harmonious mellowness, is lost.

Some genuine Byzantine pictures of great age and skilful execution are at the head. But the paintings of the old school of Siena are peculiarly important. To my great joy I found here the larger portion of the panels of the picture by UGOLINO DA SIENA, which, according to Vasari, he painted for the high altar in the church of St Croce at Florence. . . .[1]

. . . When Mr Ottley, who had meantime returned home, came into the room to call me to dinner, he was surprised to find me still busy with the old pictures; and when I expressed my approbation, and assured him that it would now be difficult, nay, impossible, to form in Italy a collection of this quality, he said it was a real consolation to him at length to see justice done to his old masters; for, so long as he had been in England, nobody had paid so much attention to them as myself. Mr Ottley is one of the few persons who recognised the noble and rich intellectual treasures in these ancient works of art at a time when they were, in general, despised or forgotten. Unfortunately, this is still the case in England. . . .

After dinner a new pleasure was prepared for me. Mr Ottley fetched his portfolios with ancient miniatures, of which he certainly has 1000, from the eleventh to the seventeenth century, of all the schools, among which, however, the Italian is by far the richest. With the exception of a few, they are cut out of old MSS in parchment. By being thus detached from the documents to which they originally belonged, they are unfortunately deprived of the principal means of ascertaining the place and time of their origin. The number of those that are interesting and beautiful is considerable.

[1] Waagen then went on to describe in some detail, as was his wont, a *Crucifixion* by Giunta Pisano; another by Duccio; a third by Ambrogio Lorenzetti; two miniature-like subjects by Simone Martini; 'a little gem' by Taddeo di Bartolo; an *Annunciation* by Cimabue; lesser pictures attributed to Orcagna and Spinello Aretino; major pictures by Fiesole, Masaccio, Andrea del Castagno, Pesello Peselli, Sandro Botticelli, Cosimo Roselli, Domenico Ghirlandaio and Gentile da Fabriano.

OTTLEY'S LIFE AS A COLLECTOR

THE best account by far of Ottley as a collector of drawings, and his relationship with Sir Thomas Lawrence in this field, is an article by John Gere in *The British Museum Quarterly*.[1] Only part of it is quoted here.

THE years 1791 to 1798 Ottley spent in Italy. It was then that he acquired, not only the knowledge and connoisseurship which so impressed his contemporaries, but the greater part of his no less astonishing collections. He was fortunate in being there during the French invasion of 1796, for such inconveniences as, even in that comparatively enlightened period, he would have to put up with in an enemy-occupied country must have seemed trifling in comparison with the bargains in works of art which were everywhere to be found, in an Italy thrown into confusion by the impact of the French Revolution. 'I purchased at Florence, from a broker', records Pryse Gordon, 'several portfolios of drawings of old masters, the weedings of the gallery; there were 1500, and cost me only 20 dollars . . . in this collection were masterly sketches. I put them into the hands of the celebrated connoisseur Mr O—y, whom I knew in Rome, he selected about 150, for which he gave me a liberal price.'* This can have been only one of many such opportunities, for the drawing of the Resurrection, attributed to Tintoretto, 'purchased by the proprietor near thirty years ago . . . the first ancient design of which he made the acquisition',† was the nucleus of a collection which has only failed to become as famous as any in the succession of 'classic' English collections of drawings because of the difficulty of identifying its contents. Part of Ottley's livelihood came from dealing in drawings, which is no doubt why he rarely used his collector's mark (of which Lugt gives five variants) and why, even when it has been put on a drawing, it is often scratched out. Many drawings known to have been his have, however, a particular style of mount, as characteristic in its own way as the 'Mariette' or 'Lawrence', but not setting off the drawing so well, and so more often discarded. The 'Ottley' mount is of yellowish unglazed cartridge paper, on which the drawing is surrounded by thin ruled lines, usually one black and two red. The artist's name, and sometimes a short description of him, is inscribed below in italics. Ottley described and engraved about eighty of his drawings in *The Italian School of Design*, but an idea of the extent of his collection can only be obtained from the catalogues of his sales of drawings, of which at least three are known, in 1804, 1807, and 1814. . . .

These various sources throw some light on his collecting activities in Italy. He bought

[1] 'William Young Ottley As A Collector Of Drawings', *The British Museum Quarterly*, Vol. XVIII, No. 2, June 1953.

* *Pryse Gordon*, Personal Memoirs, *London*, 1830, *Vol. ii*, *p*. 39.

† 1814 *Sale, lot* 1117.

drawings from the Martelli collection, and that of Lamberto Gori, in Florence; of Antonio Cavaceppi in Rome; of the Neapolitan Royal Family; and of the Zanetti family in Venice from whom, like Vivant Denon in 1791, he bought an important group of Parmigianinos. Only one drawing is described as being 'from the old Medici collection', so that the purchase of 120 drawings from the Uffizi was evidently too commonplace an affair to be worth remembering. It was probably for other reasons that Ottley was silent on the subject of what seems likely to have been the most important single source of his collection; the one formed by the rival collector J. B. J. Wicar, a French painter who was in the advantageous position, for a collector of drawings, of being in charge of the official looting of pictures in Italy. The Woodburns' discreet reference to this: '[Wicar] had, however, entrusted a large and very valuable portion of them to a friend in Florence; which were afterwards purchased by W. Y. Ottley, Esq.' is true so far as it goes; but it omits to mention that the drawings were stolen. An enemy of Wicar's, Antonio Fedi, took advantage of his hurried departure from Florence in July 1799 to steal his collection, and managed somehow to dispose of part of it to Ottley, who had returned to England the previous March. . . .

In March 1799* Ottley returned home and settled in London, where he spent the rest of his life as an expert, writer on art, and amateur dealer. He constantly added to his collection, and was a buyer at most of the important sales in the early years of the century. 'His presence on such occasions, together with that of a few of his brother collectors, used to give a zest and stimulus to the business of the auction-room, which subsequently it has often lacked.'† He was never openly one of 'the trade', as Samuel Woodburn, for instance, was; but he put his knowledge to very profitable use, using the saleroom, as well, to dispose of his drawings. His 'entire Cabinet of original Drawings' was sold by T. Philipe, 6–8 June 1814, and before this there were at least two anonymous sales. The 'Gentleman of well-known taste going abroad', whose collection of prints was sold by T. Philipe on 19 March 1804, is identified, on a copy of the catalogue in a volume containing the bookplate and annotations of the contemporary collector Charles Lambert, as *Mr Otley*; a notice in the catalogue says that 'a capital collection of drawings . . . the property of the same Gentleman will be sold early in April'. There can be little doubt that this second sale was that held anonymously, by the same auctioneer, on 11 April 1804. . . .

Italian drawings, as one would expect, predominate in Ottley's collection. The great masters of the other schools–Claude, Rubens, Rembrandt, Dürer–are well represented, but there are drawings by every Italian artist of any importance from the fifteenth to the eighteenth century. It is as complete and impersonal as a museum, and tells us even less about its owner's personal taste than most large collections of drawings. Many of the drawings are the work of minor masters, but Ottley seems to have been as interested in their authenticity as examples of a particular artist as in their aesthetic value as objects.

* *He advertised a collection of* '26 *capital pictures, purchased at Rome in Dec.* 1798 . . . *brought to England in March* 1799' *for sale by private contract.*

† *Obituary in Literary Gazette,* 1836, *pp.* 363 ff.

His collection was neither a vast miscellaneous accumulation, nor a small, fastidiously chosen, cabinet of masterpieces. Formed rather like a museum collection, as much from the historical as from the aesthetic point of view, by a scholar gifted with equal taste and learning, to whom every stage in the development of Italian art was of interest, it is significant of the new and more scientific attitude to the study of drawings which Ottley's friend and fellow collector, William Roscoe, defined in the catalogue of his own collection: 'the following works have been collected . . . chiefly for the purpose of illustrating, by a reference to original and authentic sources, the rise and progress of the arts in modern times. . . . They are therefore not wholly to be judged of by their positive merits, but by a reference to the age in which they were produced. Their value chiefly depends on their authenticity, and the light they throw on the history of the arts.'

It was inevitable that Ottley should sooner or later have made the acquaintance of Sir Thomas Lawrence, the greatest collector of drawings of the period. They found each other so congenial, that it is only surprising that they were not on terms of intimate friendship long before 1823. Collecting drawings was the lasting solace and insatiable passion of Lawrence's life. He indulged it with magnificent extravagance and disregard of financial obstacles, and by the time of his death in 1830 he had absorbed the pick of every collection which had come on the market for the past thirty years. One of these was Ottley's 'entire cabinet', which he bought for £8000. A letter from Lawrence to Ottley (undated, but postmarked February 1823) almost certainly refers to this transaction:

'I must retain your pledge to keep the subject of your collection of drawings scrupulously secret, even for two or three months. In addition to this mark of friendship, think that your vigilence and knowledge are still to work for me and to be exerted with confidence and courage. My income is not small, and professional employments are still before me to ensure me a certain even continuance of such a portion of it as to leave me justified in expence for such an object. More pictures I certainly shall *not* buy, more drawings I may, but only by the first masters and of the first quality, and this limits my further acquisitions to very few.'

J. A. GERE

LAWRENCE'S COLLECTION SPURNED

THE whole history of *official* collecting in England is an indictment of successive governments since about 1770 (and a tribute to the generosity of private individuals of means and taste). One of the most lamentable incidents in the unchangingly parsimonious attitude of the Treasury towards the arts was their refusal to buy the superb collection of drawings which Sir Thomas Lawrence had got together after a lifetime's devoted pursuit of the finest drawings by the world's most outstanding masters.

Clearly drawings fascinated the artist in Lawrence, because they were usually the first, intimate and revealing attempts by earlier masters to represent graphically important detail before this was translated into the more formal composition of a painting in oils. Often they were only animated doodles. Yet they retain a quality of permanence as tools of instruction by artists of one generation for artists of another. They would nourish creativity and stimulate powers of invention. Additionally, we know that Lawrence found them a source of infinite pleasure.

Lawrence was always short of money and there can be little doubt that the principal reason for his constant personal financial embarrassment was his almost fanatical collecting activity. Thus George IV, who gave the painter innumerable commissions, could never understand what Lawrence did with his money. 'I have paid him £24,000', said the King, 'and have not yet got my pictures. The Duke of Wellington is £2800 in advance to him. All the world is ready to employ him at a thousand pounds a picture, and yet I am told he never has a farthing.'[1] Many instances are recorded of times when Lawrence needed urgent, if not desperate, financial assistance. Among those who helped him was Samuel Rogers, who as a fellow collector probably appreciated Lawrence's plight, but as a banker found it difficult to comprehend his lack of financial acumen. However, Lawrence was constantly helping others who were in difficulty and his own, almost profligate, generosity was widely known.

It is particularly ironic that the man who should have played such an active part in persuading the government of Lord Liverpool to buy the collection of John Julius Angerstein as a nucleus for the National Gallery in 1824, should have his own, no less important collection, rejected a few years later.

The present account of the disposal of the Lawrence Collection is taken from Redford's *Art Sales*. Redford acknowledges his debt for much of the information to J. C. Robinson's *Critical Account of the Drawings by Michel Angelo and Raffaello in the University Galleries, Oxford*, 1870. Robinson describes the fate of the drawings at length in his introduction. A great deal of additional light is thrown on

[1] Quoted by Whitley, *Art in England, 1820–1837*, page 179, *et seq.*

these events by Lady Eastlake in the *Memoir* of her husband. This occurs in *Contribution to the Literature of the Fine Arts* (second series) by Sir Charles Eastlake, 1870, which she edited for Murrays after Sir Charles' death.

More recently Sir Karl Parker has described the dispersal of the Lawrence Collection–which he calls 'perhaps the most deplorable incident in the whole history of art-collecting in England'–in his introduction to the *Catalogue of the Collection of Drawings in the Ashmolean Museum*, Vol. II, Italian Schools, 1956. He gives the story in some detail but is, of course, particularly concerned with the Italian section and how the Ashmolean came to acquire Lawrence's superb Raphael and Michaelangelo drawings, largely because of the perseverance of Dr Henry Wellesley 'who fought for them with the conviction of a real enthusiast'. Sir Karl gives particular credit to the dealer Samuel Woodburn. He quotes Wellesley, who had written 'It is in some respects unfortunate, that the only individual (now that Sir Thomas Lawrence and Mr Ottley are no more) who is as well qualified to decide on the value of the drawings should be the present proprietor; and if it be asked how it happens that so clear-sighted and experienced a judge should desire to sell entire what would produce more money if broken up, the only answer is that Mr Woodburn is as public-spirited as he is intelligent, and must view any profit from the transactions as far subordinate to the character and reputation he has to sustain.'

EXTRACTED FROM George Redford's *Art Sales*, Vol. I, 1888.

SIR Thomas Lawrence besides being the most eminent portrait painter of his time was distinguished for his fine taste in art, which was especially shown in his love for the drawings of the old masters. For many years he devoted himself to the formation of a collection of these invaluable works of the great masters, frequently outbidding the great dealers, who provided him with drawings, when any were to be sold privately, and paying such prices for fine things as would allow of no profit to a dealer. The well-known expert and most active collector of his day–Samuel Woodburn–was constantly engaged in finding drawings worthy of the collection which Sir T. Lawrence was forming, and no-one knew better than he did the great value of such a collection. After his death in 1830 the proposal was made to the Government to purchase the Lawrence Collection and a public subscription was started, headed by the Royal Academy with £1000 to acquire the drawings for the National Gallery; but it was neither taken up by the Government of the day nor by the governing bodies of the British Museum and the National Gallery, so that the promoters did not, unfortunately, succeed in carrying out a scheme which would have rendered a most important public service in the interests of art. Sir T. Lawrence had in his unbounded liberality, encouraged by the large income he derived from his position as the fashionable portrait painter of the day, expended a large sum–about £40,000–upon his collection, and being one of the handsomest and most courtly men in society it is not to be wondered at that his expenditure was spoken of as extravagance.[1] In fact he was led in his enthusiastic love and admiration for these old drawings to exceed the means at his command, so that his executors found his estate in debt to Messrs Woodburn to a considerable amount. There is something touching in the words of his will, dated 28 July 1828, as he contemplated the possible dispersion of these treasures of a life, with a hope evidently, but faintly expressed in the desire that 'My collection of genuine drawings by the old masters which in number and value I know to be unequalled in Europe' should be offered at the modest price of £20,000, about half what it had cost him, first to the King (George IV) and if not accepted, then to the British Museum, to Sir Robert Peel, or the Earl of Dudley.* 'And if none of such offers be accepted, the collection shall be forthwith advertised for sale and if within two years a purchaser shall not be found, the same may be sold by public auction or private contract in London, either altogether or in separate lots, at such price or prices and in such manner as the executors may think best.' In the end, an offer of £16,000 was made by Messrs Woodburn and this was accepted. They then arranged in 1836–7 several exhibitions of the drawings during two London seasons, with the prices they asked. These were for the Raphael drawings alone (160) £15,000. For the Michael Angelo drawings, about 150, no price was named. For the Rubens drawings (150) £3000. The other masters were also priced at considerable sums and many of them were sold to private collectors. In 1838, the remaining designs were exhibited again but without any great result, and the Woodburns declared their intention to sell them separately with the exception of the Raphael and Michael Angelo drawings. These they took to the Continent, and eventually they were offered to the Prince of Orange, afterwards King of Holland, William II, but at a price beyond the means at his disposal. He however proposed the purchase of some, and this being agreed to certain drawings were selected, but according to Sir J. C. Robinson, who wrote the valuable catalogue of the Oxford Collection, to which many of these drawings finally came, 'the greater number of the really important authentic works both of Raffaello and Michael Angelo, especially the invaluable preliminary studies and designs, were unwittingly disregarded and sent back to England'. In 1840 and 1842 fresh efforts were made to induce the Government to purchase but without success, and then a committee endeavoured by subscription to obtain the remaining part of the Lawrence Collection for the University Galleries then being built. Only about £3000 was subscribed, but the collection was valued by a competent judge at £14,000 and the price named by Messrs Woodburn was only 10,000 guineas, includ-

[1] R. & S. Redgrave in their celebrated *A Century of Painters of the English School*, 1890, recount the story as follows: 'Lawrence was during all his life in difficulties as to money, although, latterly at least, in the receipt of large sums from his profession. Lord Durham paid him for 'Master Lambton', 600 guineas; yet we find him writing for payment in some instances before his portraits were completed. This improvidence has been much commented upon, and a charge of gambling was entered against him, but we think without foundation. A portion, at least, of his family were for years dependent upon him, and his only extravagance seems to have been in works of art; it was too well known that a fine drawing by the old masters was a temptation too strong to be resisted, if money could be had, at whatever disadvantage.'

* *This was not the late Earl nor his father, but the great political Lord Dudley of that time.*

ing many fine drawings added from the Harman Collection which Sir T. Lawrence did not possess. It is very creditable to the public spirit of Messrs Woodburn that they reduced their price to meet the views of the Committee, and the necessary sum was made up by the liberality of Lord Eldon who gave £4000 to complete the purchase for the University of this most important series of drawings by these two great masters.

But we have still to follow out the dispersion of this splendid Lawrence Collection as regards those drawings which passed into the King of Holland's possession. 'The number of drawings by or ascribed to Raffaello selected by the Prince amounted to eighty; but of these not more than about thirty were authentic, and the number of drawings by Michel Angelo, are about sixty, and of these probably a somewhat larger proportion were genuine' (Robinson). The King died in 1850 and his collection was sold by auction at the Hague (August 1850). Samuel Woodburn then bought at the sale thirty-three drawings by Michel Angelo, and thirty-four by Raphael. The Duke of Saxe Weimar, for the Weimar Gallery, bought chiefly the Michel Angelo drawings; the Louvre and Frankfurt Museum represented by M. Passavant, others. These Institutions securing five or six by Michel Angelo and about eighteen by Raphael, the rest passed into the hands of English and Continental collectors. Woodburn sold a few of the drawings to the Rev. Dr Wellesley of Oxford, whose collection was a fine one[1] dispersed by auction at Messrs Sotheby's in 1866; retaining most of them which he restored to the residue of the Lawrence Collection still in his possession, till his death in 1853, after which they were offered at Christie's in 1854, but without effecting a complete sale, for the auction was stopped on the second day. Finally, however, in 1860 the Woodburn collection was sold at Christie's, and then some of the Lawrence drawings were purchased by the Government; but even then, although a special grant of money was made by the Treasury to the British Museum for the purpose of acquiring the finest works in the sale, a large proportion of drawings 'equal if not superior to those actually acquired' (Robinson), were bought by private collectors at little more than nominal prices, while a sum of several hundred pounds was actually returned to the Treasury which was intended to be spent in the purchase of these drawings.

[1] See page 300.

BUCHANAN HIMSELF AT WORK

AFTER Napoleon's downfall and the return of peace in Europe, Buchanan gave up the use of agents and did his own buying on the Continent. The passage quoted describes his activities just after he had brought off one of the major *coups* of his career: the purchase of Talleyrand's entire collection of Dutch and Flemish paintings in Paris.

EXTRACTED FROM William Buchanan's *Memoirs of Painting*, Vol. II, 1824.

A SHORT account of Mr Buchanan's[1] proceedings, in regard to the purchases which he then made, will be found in a letter written from Amsterdam, which having been preserved by the friend to whom he then wrote, he is now enabled to give here.

Amsterdam, 25 August 1817

'After writing to you from Paris, a piece of information came to my knowledge which has brought me here in all haste. I learnt that the fine Paul Potter, belonging to the Burgomaster Hoguer, would be sold in the course of a few days, and that several amateurs were on the look-out for it.

'A few days ago Monsieur le R. did me the honour of a call, evidently for the purpose of learning my movements for the rest of the season. The conversation turned on the beauty of the south at this season of the year; and fearing that my views might have been directed towards Flanders or Holland, he strongly recommended my seeing the banks of the Loire before leaving France, especially as the vintage was fast approaching. I told him that I had long intended to make an excursion to Orleans, Tours &c. and had some thoughts of going there before returning to England. This seemed to quiet his suspicions of finding me a competitor in the north; for having so recently purchased the Talleyrand collection, which excited some degree of jealousy among the Parisians, he imagined to find me his opponent also in Flanders and Holland. I enquired where he meant to spend the autumn; when he said he was going in the course of a short time, on account of his health, to drink the mineral waters of Mont-d'Or. After some farther conversation upon indifferent matters, he then took his leave of me, and we parted wishing each other *bonne santé et un bon voyage*.

'Having learned that much interest was likely to be excited among the amateurs in this

[1] Buchanan refers to himself in this manner throughout both volumes of *Memoirs of Painting*.

quarter, and hearing that it was the intention of Monsieur le R. and some of his friends to leave Paris in the course of a couple of days for Amsterdam, I had my passport *visé* by the minister of police for Brussels, and set off the following afternoon in a light travelling calesh, accompanied by Mrs B. and my servant Antoine, an old campaigner. We travelled all night, as is usual in France, and the following morning stopped for a couple of hours at Cambray, to see the British troops reviewed by the Duke of Wellington,* having just reached that place as his Grace had got upon the ground. The day was beautiful, and the troops made a most brilliant appearance.

'From Cambray we passed over much ground celebrated in the annals of war, and got by the afternoon to Valenciennes, the siege of which occupied so much attention at an early period of the Revolution. From thence, the next point which brought us up was the Hotel Royal of Brussels.

'After waiting on old Gaumare, the banker, I took the earliest opportunity of calling upon Monsieur Van Reyndaers, to see his two celebrated pictures by Hobbima, which I have the pleasure to inform you I purchased, along with a fine Philip Wouvermans, and a Backhuysen, for 40,000 francs, which, although it may appear a good price to give off hand, yet, next to Mr Gray's large Hobbima, at Hornsey, I consider these to be about the best pictures of the master which I have ever seen; and there was no time to lose, as I was only a few hours a-head of several connoisseurs, who had set off like myself on a voyage of discovery, and carried heavy metal. This, to begin with, I consider to be a pretty little acquisition.

'Being exceedingly anxious to get to Antwerp to see the picture of the Chapeau de Paille, and three other fine pictures, by Rubens, which are soon to be sold, we left Brussels after dinner, intending to remain at Antwerp during the night; but, on considering the risk I ran of losing the opportunity of seeing Hoguer's pictures a day previous to the sale, in order to enable me to form a judgement on their merits, I determined on passing through Antwerp without stopping. We arrived at that city in time to gain admittance, although the gates had been shut, and were re-opened to us per favour; but at the post-house we were informed that no one could get out without an order from the Governor of the place; being determined however to make the attempt, and having agreed to pay for the hire of fresh horses whether we should or should not succeed in passing the gates, we obtained them, and drove up to the post, when I handed out to the guard of the night my passport and a small piece of paper enclosing a Napoleon, saying rather loudly, "Voila Monsieur, mon passeport, et l'ordre du Gouverneur." The order was instantly recognised, and the massive gates moved on their hinges. The following morning we breakfasted at Breda, at an early hour, and by the route of Gorcum and Utrecht we arrived at Amsterdam the same evening.

'It now became a matter of some importance to see the collection of Van Hoguer privately, without encountering my Parisian friends. This I easily succeeded in doing through the means of the bankers on whom I had credits; while, to keep competitors in the dark as to my intentions, I adopted the following *projet*.

* *The army of occupation.*

'Antoine, as I have already said, is an old campaigner, and a fellow of much humour and drollery, with a countenance of most immovable muscle. He was well known as Antoine to all my Parisian friends; but when tolerably rouged, with a suit of black clothes, and a well-powdered wig, no one could imagine that he had ever before seen Monsieur Jolli. My own attendance at the sale, as *a bidder* would have been imprudent, and was likely to meet with opposition from more quarters than one; I therefore determined on relinquishing the contest to Monsieur Jolli, who, having received his instructions, acquitted himself *à merveille*, and had the honour of seeing his name entered in the sale-roll of the Burgomaster Hoguer as the purchaser of the famous young bull of Paul Potter, for 7925 guilders; and of being congratulated by many of the dilettanti present, as a gentleman of most undoubted taste and good judgement.*

'The aid which this auxiliary afforded, enabled me to enter the room as an indifferent observer. The first person who caught my eye was Monsieur le R. whom I had so lately left in Paris. We recognised each other with a laugh–'Eh bien, Monsieur, comment vous trouvez vous des eaux du Mont-d'Or?'–'Et vous, Monsieur, que dites vous de la belle Statue de Jeanne d'Arc sur la place d'Orléans?'

'This sale contained very few pictures of consequence. I have purchased at it two pictures by Backhuysen, a small Vandevelde and Jan Steen; and since the sale I have purchased a Philip Wouvermans, and a half interest in a very capital picture by Jan Steen, which escaped me at the sale through a mistake.†

'The little Paul Potter, which I have had the good fortune to acquire, is of much greater importance than some of those who have come after it seem to be aware of. It is painted at the best period of the master, viz. in 1647, the same year in which he painted his famous large picture of the young bull, which is in the gallery of the Hague. It is composed of three animals; one of which, a beautiful cow, is lying in the foreground, and appears chewing the cud; a second animal is foreshortened; and the third and principal of the group is a young bull, which has just started up, and is bellowing lustily. You absolutely hear him. His eye is fixed upon the observer, and is full of fire and animation, while you can discover the humidity of his breath resting on the tip of his cold nose. The whole form of this animal is compact and good; and being of an uncommon breed, and of great excellence, the Board of Agriculture will certainly vote me the medal of this year for so rare and valuable an importation.

'I shall send you in my next a full account of the principal collections of this place. That of Mademoiselle Von Winter is a most admirable collection of the best examples of the principal masters of the Dutch school. It possesses the finest Gerard Dow I have seen; besides some splendid pictures of Albert Cuyp, Both, Hobbima, Berchem, &c.

'The collection of Van Loon stands next to it in point of fine choice, and has the finest Philip Wouvermans which is probably extant. In the front of the picture there is a fine gray horse, which stands about 18 inches high. I have offered, by the means

* *This picture was sold by Mr Christie, at the sale of Mr Watson Taylor's pictures in* 1823, *for* 1210 *guineas, when there was a strong competition for it.*

† *This Jan Steen was afterwards sold to the Duke of Wellington in the sale of Monsieur le Rouge's pictures at Paris, in* 1819.

of an agent here, 1000 guineas for this picture, which has been refused. It is worth any money.

'Believe me to be
'Yours, &c. &c. &c.'

After the sale of the Burgomaster Hoguer's pictures, Mr Buchanan remained but a short time at Amsterdam. He purchased a very fine portrait by Rembrandt for Mr Gray; and he returned by the Hague, Rotterdam, Dort, and Breda to Antwerp, for the purpose of endeavouring to make a purchase of the Chapeau de Paille, and other pictures by Rubens, belonging to the Von Havre family, which were to be sold by private contract. The sum demanded at that time for the whole was only 100,000 francs; and he should certainly have given that money, but he was persuaded by a person (who afterwards proved to have had interested views), that by not pressing matters they could, after a short time, be obtained for 80,000 francs, and he therefore only purchased one of them, being the Helena Forman, taking a promise that he should have the refusal of the others if any diminution was to be made on the price demanded.

The estimation then set on these pictures by the family was

	Francs
Chapeau de Paille	50,000
Landscape, with the Chateau de Laaken	30,000
Elizabeth Brants	12,000
Helena Forman	8,000

making up the sum total which was demanded.

A singular mistake into which the family to whom these pictures belonged had fallen, may here be remarked, connected as they were by descent from the family of Rubens. They had misplaced the names of the two wives of Rubens, and called the Elizabeth Brants Helena Forman, and vice versa: while the character of Helena Forman, his second wife, is not only known to all amateurs, by the many old engravings which exist; but the most beautiful of all his portraits, the famous picture of Elizabeth Brants, which is in the gallery of Munich, is the same character as that which was in this collection, though differently habited.

Mr Buchanan, having left Antwerp soon afterwards for Paris, was informed that the landscape of the Chateau de Laaken had been sold without any communication being made to him; and he some time afterwards found it in the collection of Monsieur Aynard of Paris, who was at that time forming a collection of the finest objects which he could purchase of the Flemish and Dutch schools; the whole of which, about two years afterwards, he offered to dispose of to Mr Buchanan, as mentioned hereafter.[1]

[1] The Aynard Collection was offered to Sir Charles Long (later Lord Farnborough) who acted for the Prince Regent, but it was not accepted. Buchanan was then consulted, and advised about

While in Paris, Mr Buchanan made a few other acquisitions before returning to England; among which was a celebrated picture by Gerard Dow, known by the name of 'l'Epicière', and which had been in the Choiseul gallery. This picture afterwards passed into the collection of his present Majesty, where it now is.

In the following year, 1818, Mr Buchanan intending to make the tour of Germany, for the purpose of seeing the different collections in that country, and particularly one which had been much talked of as being at Soëder, near Hildesheim, he again passed by Ghent to Antwerp, where he found the Chapeau de Paille still in the possession of the same family, but the other two sold. This picture which, the year before, might have been purchased for 50,000 francs, or £2000, was no longer to be had at that price; and when Mr Buchanan did make an offer of that sum for a personage of high distinction, for whom he had been commissioned to purchase the same, his offer was not accepted. It is well known that subsequently the picture was purchased at public sale, and was brought to England. The author of this work is not informed in whose possession it now is, or whether it has again been sold.[1]

From Antwerp, Mr Buchanan passed by Dort, Rotterdam, the Hague, and Haarlem to Amsterdam; and while there, he made every effort to induce Mademoiselle Von Winter to part with a few of the pictures of her fine collection, in particular the small picture of a girl looking out of a window, and holding a basket of fruit, by Gerard Dow, and a large picture of a sea-piece, by Albert Cuyp. For these he offered 30,000 florins, viz. 18,000 for the first, and 12,000 for the second, being a sum nearly equal to £3000. Nothing, however, could tempt that lady to dispose of these beautiful works of art. She said she had inherited them from her father with a very ample fortune, and having no occasion whatever for money, she could not think of separating them from it.

At this time, nothing very fine could be procured at Amsterdam; and with several collections which he had in view in Germany, Mr Buchanan made but a very short stay there, and soon set off for Deventer, and by the back part of Holland he passed into Hanover, taking the route of the castle of Bentheim, so often celebrated by the pencil of Ruysdael,* who has given a faithful representation of that beautiful chateau and its vicinity. . . .

Much fault has been found with the badness of the roads in Germany; but this applies principally to the northern districts, which are sandy, and not to the centre of Germany, where the roads are much better than travellers have been led to expect. . . .

After traversing a wide expanse of country, which certainly well repays the traveller by

the saleability in England of some of the items. The Rubens Landscape of the Chateau de Laaken was bought for Carlton Palace at Buchanan's suggestion and is still in the Royal Collection.

[1] It was bought by the dealer Nieuwenhuys. He offered it in vain to George IV, and after being publicly exhibited for three months it was bought by Sir Robert Peel for 3500 guineas. The National Gallery acquired it with the bulk of the Peel Collection in 1871.

* *A capital large picture of the chateau de Bentheim was formerly in the collection of William Smith, Esq. M.P. It was consigned by him to the care of Mr Buchanan, and afterwards passed into the possession of a gentleman at Bristol. It was valued at 500l.*

its interesting and beautiful scenery, Mr Buchanan arrived at the place where one of those collections was to be seen, where, like many other of the German collections, he found the walls of a chateau covered with acres of canvas and old panels, but unfortunately most of these pictures ill suiting the characters of the masters to whom they were ascribed. In Germany the traveller finds the galleries of Dresden, of Munich, of Vienna, and of Hesse Cassel, well worthy of his attention, especially the two first of these, which will amply satisfy the expectations which he may have formed of these galleries of art; but he must not expect to find collections of the works of the great masters in the possession of individuals; such are only to be found in Italy and in Great Britain. France, at the present day, possesses but few of them, and in the Low Countries they are rarely to be met with; while it must be remembered that such works themselves do not multiply and increase upon us. They are already scarce, and are every year rapidly becoming scarcer.[1]

PICTURES WITH PEDIGREES...

THOMAS Winstanley is best known as the Liverpool auctioneer and art dealer from whom William Roscoe bought many paintings for his collection. Winstanley was also the anonymous author of the charming *Observations on the Arts*, with Tables of the Principal Painters, which first appeared in 1828. These tables of painters were evidently so useful that a second edition was called for. His style is somewhat verbose but there were interesting chapters on purchasing paintings, on copies, on damaged paintings and attempts at cleaning, on the value of pictures and on picture dealing. These were a healthy antidote to the many over-enthusiastic and less professionally knowledgeable publications of that time.

Winstanley's comments, in the extract which follows, are particularly interesting because they pinpoint very clearly a sharp fall in picture prices after the era of great enthusiasm which had been engendered by Buchanan and some of his fellow dealers at the end of the Napoleonic wars.

---

[1] No one had done more than Buchanan and his agents to establish in Europe the image of the wealthy English dealer/collector who could pay what were then almost unheard-of prices for anything really outstanding; and the European royal families of Prussia, Bavaria, the Netherlands and even Italy, and the Emperor Alexander of Russia, had followed where Buchanan had blazed a trail!

THOMAS WINSTANLEY

EXTRACTED FROM Thomas Winstanley's *Observations on the Arts*, 1828.

THE desire of possessing a fine picture is doubtless much increased by such picture having *a pedigree*–that is, that it is known to have been in the possession of some illustrious family, or celebrated individual. This is the case with many pictures which the political storms of Europe have cast upon our shores, where, however, they have not met with shipwreck or destruction, but protection and preservation.

The immense fortunes which have been made by individuals during the late war–the abundance of wealth accumulated by those who have been successful in money transactions of late years, and various other sources of riches from which Great Britain has drawn both collectively and individually the power of possessing whatever is precious–is another cause of the great price now to be obtained for articles of high taste and virtu. A portion of the superabundance of wealth is now devoted to decoration and ornament; and this taste pervades all ranks of society. Paintings are universally acknowledged to be objects worthy of possession, and the wealthy are anxious to obtain works of art of first rate excellence, and are willing as well as 'Rich enough to pay the price'.

Having thus, I presume in some measure accounted for the high prices which pictures of the first class bear in the commerce of the Arts at the present moment, I shall proceed to account also, as far as I am able, for the apparent reduction in the value of pictures of the old masters of inferior merit.

It is well known that since the termination of the late continental war, every corner of Europe has been searched–and, as it were, hunted for pictures, both by the collector and dealer. That amateurs in order to possess a few gems of value have purchased whole collections, the rejected of which, regulated by their taste, they have thrown unreservedly into the public market in this country. Eminent dealers have followed this example and those of less eminence and who have no other feeling for the works of art but as they produce profit, have sought for paintings in every city, town and almost every village in Holland, Flanders and Germany, to satisfy the cravings of their English customers. Even when the importation duty was considerable, the facilities of smuggling gave opportunities of importation to hundreds, I may say of thousands of inferior pictures, the only recommendation of which was –that '*they came from the Continent*'. Since the duty was reduced, I have been informed that small vessels have been wholly freighted with pictures, many of which have been already sold in London, and others have been kept back for future trials. Another powerful cause operating against pictures of inferior quality, is the rapid improvement of the public taste, which improvement I consider to have been effected in this country by the various exhibitions of the finest works of ancient and modern Art annually at the British Institution. Dull and insensible must be he who can have viewed the splendid specimens both of the British and Foreign Schools which have been of late years exhibited there, and more especially those which his present Majesty has graciously pleased to permit his subjects to enjoy the pleasure of contemplating and of studying for two successive seasons without finding their judgement corrected and improved, and their taste refined. This refinement of taste and power of judgement are also increased by the facility of travelling upon the Continent of Europe, where a knowledge of and examination of the Works of Art–which is at first a mere amusement–becomes progressively a delightful and almost necessary study. Thus before a more exalted taste and a more cultivated understanding of the works of the painters, sink those of a second class or inferior quality.

The artists of the present day have also lent a helping hand to the depreciation of the more humble labours of their predecessors, and I must take the liberty to say that I think their conduct in this respect unjust and impolitic. It appears to me, that before they thus condemn the productions of Foreign Art and of the by-gone painters, they should reflect–that in such conduct there is the imminent danger of bringing the arts, considered in the aggregate, into contempt and disuse. . . .

Notwithstanding all that has been said respecting the depressed state of the arts in England at the present moment, I cannot think that such a state is hopeless, or even to be lamented; on the contrary, I think that pictures are now arriving at their real and true value.

The avidity with which pictures have been purchased in Great Britain for the last twenty-five years, has opened the door to the excessive and almost fraudulent prices with eagerness on the one side, and rapacity on the other, having in many instances produced–prices at once ruinous to the purchaser, and hurtful to the progress of the arts among us. The artful have taken advantage of the unwary, and the few whose wealth has enabled them to purchase at high prices the works even of second-rate or inferior artists, must now be content to suffer a depreciation of value in their collections–consoling themselves that every species of property is at present reduced in value.

At the exorbitant prices formerly asked for pictures very few persons could afford to possess a collection even of a middling class, for the prices have been so enormous that in such a collection a man must have expended a moderate fortune. At present for a sum which then would scarcely purchase one picture, a respectable collection may be obtained. This state of things will not operate against the traffic of pictures–for the man of taste but moderate fortune will no longer be envious of his more wealthy neighbour–but may gratify his inclination in the possession of a tasteful collection of pictures for a sum of little comparative consequence.

[In an entire chapter devoted to copies, Winstanley quotes this illuminating excerpt from an Italian authority.]

. . . Lanzi also tells us that it is a custom not only with private individuals but with the noble and wealthy of the Continent, to replace an original picture which has been sold, perhaps in their necessity, with a copy made by an able modern copyist, in order that the catalogue of their collection may be complete in its description; and it is to this cause perhaps that we find so many copies purchased and brought to England, with the most authentic records, of their having been purchased with or having formed a part of a celebrated collection.

...AND PICTURES WITHOUT

As a rider to Winstanley's comments it is interesting to quote the views expressed by another distinguished auctioneer at the end of the nineteenth century. This was the celebrated Thomas H. Woods ('Old Woods'), a senior partner of Christie's, talking to George Redford, author of *Art Sales*.

TAKEN FROM A. C. R. Carter's *Let me Tell you*, 1940.

GREAT disappointment is often felt at the poor prices realised by the majority of the Italian pictures accumulated in country houses and recently sold off. Yet the reason is plain. Buyers know much more about art than they did fifty years ago, and the Italian pictures bought by noblemen and gentlemen on the Grand Tour, as they called it–the Virgins, Saints, and Martyrs (with great painter's names attached to them)–cannot find a purchaser.

'It is hard to make anyone believe that some twenty-five years ago a peer, just dead offered a now deceased Duke ten thousand pounds for a Carlo Dolci, and was refused. This seems impossible so greatly has the later Italian art depreciated. When this has happened to a picture of undoubted authenticity, is it to be wondered at that school pictures, copies and imitations hardly tempt many people to carry them away? And of this rubbish many country houses are full, with Sir Joshuas, Gainsboroughs, and Romneys of great value or admirable Dutch pictures to leaven the mass.'

EDWARD SOLLY

ISAAC Solly was the head of a highly successful family firm of merchants engaged in the Baltic timber trade in St Mary Axe in the City of London. There were four other brothers in the business and collectively they were widely known for their integrity, hard work, intelligent anticipation and sound commercial sense. All the brothers were zealous Non-Conformists, which meant that they suffered a great deal of social ostracism. During the wars with France the firm obtained immense contracts for supplying the government dockyards with Polish and Prussian oak-plank for shipbuilding. They also traded extensively in hemp, flax and cereals. By 1800 they owned a large fleet of merchantmen.

Isaac's third brother, Edward (1776–1844), moved to the Continent soon afterwards so that he could buy on the spot when it came to negotiating bulk purchases. For some years Edward lived in Stockholm. Then he moved to Berlin. There he settled and married. As the Sollys' trade grew, the business prospered and the brothers–but Edward in particular–became extremely wealthy. He appears to have been a man of outstanding intelligence and great charm. He moved in the highest social circles in Berlin. He was well liked and on very friendly terms with ministers of state, with the Prussian royal family and their Court officials, with artists and intellectuals and with the trading community. Although he spoke German fluently he was always regarded as particularly English, and, though he never had an official appointment, he appears to have enjoyed quasi-diplomatic status.

He began to take an active interest in the arts around 1810 as a form of relaxation from his dynamic and enterprising life. Naturally he travelled a great deal. After he had made a study of pictures and the history of painting in various European private and public galleries, he began to buy pictures himself. From the first he seems to have enjoyed cleaning and restoring them with his own hands.

His growing interest in collecting after 1811 coincided with an unprecedented influx of works of art, particularly Italian Old Masters, into Berlin. There were two main reasons for this: the so-called 'Secularisation of Religious Institutions', a decree that permitted the transfer of 'surplus' works of art out of Italy; and a change in Prussian law which made it possible for people to change their occupation at will (having previously been restricted from doing so by apprenticeships, guild memberships, etc.). One result was the gradual emergence of what was virtually a new trade in Germany–picture dealing. As news of Solly's readiness to buy paintings spread he was approached by dealers from all over the Continent. The Napoleonic wars and their consequences meant that there were more sellers than buyers, and Solly was able to use his professional skill in buying at exceedingly low prices.

A CATALOGUE

OF THE

COLLECTION

OF

DUTCH PICTURES

Of the First Class,

The Property of the well-known Amateur,

EDWARD SOLLY, ESQ.

INCLUDING

Many of the most Precious Quality, and fine and undoubted Specimens of

DE HOOGE	W. VANDEVELDE	BOTH
RUBENS	BACKHUYSEN	VAN DYKE
HOBBIMA	K. DU JARDIN	EGLON V. DER NEER
BERGHEM	METZU	CAMPHUYSEN
TENIERS	JAN STEIN	RUISDAEL
W. MIERIS	SNYDERS	MUSCHER
A. CUYP	VANDER NEER	DE LORME
POTTER	REMBRANDT	VAN OSS
VAN TOLL	DIETRICI	OSTADE

AND A FEW

CABINET ITALIAN PICTURES,

Collected at a vast expence from Private Sources, and the following known Collections:—

The Brentano, Malmaison, M. Wallscott, Baron Becker, Rezzonico Palace, Accajuoli Palace, M. Hoffmann of Dort, Ocke of Leyden, M. Blondel de Gagny, M. le Grand, l'Abbé Renou, M. Bickerstein, M. de Smeth, Prince de Gavre, M. Siebel.

WHICH WILL BE SOLD BY AUCTION,

BY

MESSRS. FOSTER & SONS,

At the Gallery, 54, Pall Mall,

On WEDNESDAY, the 31st of MAY, 1837,

AT ONE O'CLOCK.

May be Publicly Viewed Three Days prior, and Catalogues had, at 1s. each, of Messrs. FOSTER, 14, Greek Street, and 54, Pall Mall; of M. HERIS, Brussels; of M. DE LA HANTE, Paris; and of M. LAMME, Rotterdam.

He soon developed a marvellous eye and showed a particular liking for Italian pictures. He was most unusual, if not unique at the time, in his expressed preference for the earliest schools. Paintings of the *trecento* and the *quattrocento* had been preserved almost exclusively in churches and religious establishments. Now they became available in quantity. Solly bought and bought. But he did so cautiously, and with intelligence. He got together a committee of friends and connoisseurs, professional experts on various schools of painting, to a man. He found agents in Italy, especially in Milan, who would send him details, including documents showing where the paintings had come from, before he had to commit himself. If he liked the picture and his 'selection committee' approved, the deal went through. In this way authentification became almost a condition of purchase, and because many paintings had come from the churches and monasteries for whose walls they had been commissioned these came with unshakeable provenances. But Solly continued also to buy in Germany (he was among the first to buy the works of the fourteenth- and fifteenth-century German masters), in Switzerland (where he bought Holbein's *The Merchant, Georg Gisze* for 60 guineas after it had failed to find a buyer for three years) and in the Low Countries (the early Flemish masters were another of his favourite schools and in 1818 he bought six two-sided panels from van Eyck's altar piece, the *Adoration of the Lamb*). (See Plates 62, 63 and 64)

By 1820 he had acquired the astonishing total of 3000 paintings. They were housed in his immense residence at 67 Wilhelmstrasse in Berlin. The Italian part of his collection alone was hung in six or seven galleries. Almost every well-known master was represented. There were one or more examples of Giotto, Taddeo Gaddi, Lippo Memmi, Botticelli, Fra Filippo and Filippino Lippi, Pollaiuolo, Piero di Cosimo, Verrocchio, Vivarini, Giovanni and Gentile Bellini, Cima, Antonella da Messina, Mantegna, Signorelli, Raphael and Titian. Visitors from all over the world came to look. It was probably the largest collection in private rather than princely hands. But it was not to last.

No one had been more deeply impressed by this fantastic assemblage of works of art than the intellectual élite in Berlin. And with good reason. For Solly's highly personal choice of paintings represented a clear departure from what had been the accepted norm before. He was only mildly interested in the Baroque: he was passionately devoted to the development from the Byzantine to the Gothic, and then the flowering of the Renaissance. Apart from anything else his taste was a long way ahead of that of his English contemporaries, even of Roscoe and Young Ottley, of whom at that stage he had probably no knowledge at all.

Solly was truly grateful for his successful years in Berlin. He wanted that city to benefit from his own enthusiasm. In this he was encouraged by politicians and writers, by artists and connoisseurs. They included Hardenberg, the Chancellor; von Altenstein, the Minister of Culture; the politicians, Scharnhorst and Stein; Schinkel, the architect; Cornelius, the artist; Aloys Hirt, the art historian; von Rumohr, Waagen's sponsor; and even Goethe, who took up the cudgels on Solly's

CATALOGUE

OF THE

VERY INTERESTING AND VALUABLE COLLECTION

OF

ITALIAN

PICTURES,

OF THE RAFAELLE PERIOD,

FORMED BY

EDWARD SOLLY, Esq., Deceased,

Whose profound knowledge and discriminating taste, particularly in Italian Art, have established the reputation of this noble Collection throughout Europe:

WHICH

Will be Sold by Auction, by

Messrs. CHRISTIE & MANSON,

AT THEIR GREAT ROOM,

8, KING STREET, ST. JAMES'S SQUARE,

On SATURDAY, MAY the 8th, 1847,

AT ONE O'CLOCK PRECISELY.

May be publicly viewed Two days preceding, and Catalogues had, at Messrs. CHRISTIE and MANSON'S Offices, 8, *King Street, St. James's Square.*

behalf against the brothers Boisserée, celebrated collectors in their own right, who were jealous of Solly's achievements.

Solly's financial success probably reached its zenith in 1816. Afterwards the Baltic trade between England and Prussia declined. Already some years earlier the family business had suffered a severe blow when twenty of their vessels, while plying their contraband trade, were captured and confiscated by the Danes (who were under Napoleon's control) and taken to Copenhagen. Solly lost not only the ships but also their cargoes. Although both governments were deeply involved, neither the English nor the Prussian would at first accept even partial responsibility for the loss. Solly, though under pressure, continued trading *and collecting*. His reserves were enormous. Inevitably an idea that would restore his personal solvency and simultaneously benefit Prussia began to take shape in his mind. It was that his collection should be bought by the Prussian State. The Chancellor himself wrote to the King, Frederick William III, to suggest it. Some years earlier, in 1815, the King had already bought what was left of the Italian Giustiani Collection in the hope that it would form a nucleus for the sort of public gallery that had recently opened in almost every other capital in Europe. But Prussia was still recovering from the defeats inflicted on it by Napoleon. The great striving towards more liberal government was hampered by a shortage of cash.

At first the King refused even to consider the suggestion. But after three years of protracted negotiations, considerable opposition, some hard bargaining and the involvement of almost every major politician in the land, Solly was saved on the brink of bankruptcy by a payment for his collection of what was the then unheard-of sum of 500,000 gold Thaler. This included 200,000 Thaler in compensation for the loss of his fleet.

Solly had been near despair at times as one delay in settlement followed upon another, but his goodwill towards the purchasers never wavered. Though at one stage he had had to resort to the stratagem of sending certain of the best paintings to London and the threat to put them up for sale at Christie's. He calculated that, in all, his collection had cost him £750,000 of which he recovered only two-thirds. In November 1821 the pictures finally became the property of the Prussian king.

By this time Solly had already moved back to London. Upon the suggestion of von Rumohr, Dr Gustav Waagen was appointed first Director of the prospective Royal Berlin Gallery. A magnificent building was planned and designed by Schinkel. It opened nine years later and consisted in the main of the Solly pictures, the Giustiani Collection and a large selection of the cream of the paintings from the many Prussian royal residences. 676 Solly pictures were put on show immediately; 538 were distributed among the royal residences to replace those transferred to the museum; and 1783 were put into the reserve collection. Some of these were gradually moved to other museums but many of the geese thus left turned out to be swans after further research and restoration. It is a remarkable fact that the collection on which the greatest of the German museums was based had been formed for the personal delectation of an eccentric Englishman.

Because of the political complications of the time, the acquisition of the Solly Collection remained something of a mystery[1] for many years. The world at large only became aware of its true significance in 1904, when the old Royal Gallery moved to the vast new building complex, of which the picture gallery was styled the Kaiser Friedrich Museum, which had been the brainchild of Dr·Wilhelm Bode. Writers on the arts in England suddenly realised what the nation had missed. In 1905 *The Times* wrote in a leading article: 'Who was Solly? It is surprising that in these days when everything that bears upon the history of masterpieces and great collections is made the object of microscopic research, nobody seems to have written the life of a man who was evidently one of the most remarkable collectors that ever lived, and one of the most conspicuously in advance of his time.'

There is now little doubt that after his return to London Solly forsook the timber trade and settled down to pursue his interest in the arts. He soon began to form another collection, and he became something of a dealer. In England his taste – or perhaps it was merely his opportunities – seem to have changed somewhat, because his interest narrowed to a much greater liking for the Raphaelesque period. Indeed we have his own evidence on this point. In 1836 he was asked to appear before the Select Parliamentary Committee of Arts and Principles of Design which was carrying out an investigation into the purchasing policy – or lack of it – of the London National Gallery. Solly was asked: 'Have you made pictures almost the study of your life?' To which he replied: 'I may say I have.' He was asked: 'To what pictures in particular have you directed your mind?' He replied: 'Particularly the Italian School; to the different schools of the period of Raphael, which I consider the period of perfection.'

This was almost exactly a year after his old friend, Dr Waagen, had visited him in London. Solly appears to have been living at 7 Curzon Street, Mayfair, because *A Descriptive Catalogue of some Paintings of the Rafaelle Period in the Collection of E.S.* listing some 26 pictures has remained extant. Waagen thought Solly was living in splendour; but Solly himself considered his circumstances much reduced! Lugt records no fewer than eight sales at Stanley's, Foster's and Sotheby's between 1825 and 1837 in which Solly disposed of quantities of paintings, drawings and engravings. Yet Solly did not forget his early collection. Several times he effected exchanges for some of the original 3000 pictures. A German museum official

[1] Until it was unravelled for English readers with some delight by the present author in a series of five articles in *The Connoisseur* entitled 'Who Was Solly?'. Four articles appeared in April, May, July and September 1967. A fifth appeared in September 1968 and a sixth and final one, after the discovery of an authenticated portrait of Solly and his wife, in April 1971. Many of the original inventories and a great number of original documents (all of which had long been regarded as lost or destroyed) had by then been unearthed and scrutinised.

A condensed translation of *The Connoisseur* articles, with some newly-discovered material, appeared in the Jahrbuch Preussischer Kulturbesitz, 1969.

assessing the original Solly Collection in 1880 expressed astonishment that these exchanges were so highly unfavourable towards Solly. But quite clearly this was Solly's discreet method of adding what he considered important works to those already hanging among his former treasures in the Berlin Royal Gallery. Indeed later Waagen cast envious eyes on the pictures in Solly's house, but by this time Solly had too many other clients to consider. One of the last was John Bowes of Barnard Castle who considered him 'a first rate judge and collector'. Bowes bought nine pictures from Solly between 1840 and 1845. The cream of Solly's own pictures was sold at Christie's on 8 May 1847 some time after Edward's death. During the last twenty years of his life he established a formidable reputation in England as a connoisseur, but there can be no doubt that this very great English collector made his most lasting impression on the cradle of 'Kunstgeschichte' in Berlin. He is still a shadowy figure in the history of collecting, and he well deserves further study.

FRANK HERRMANN

THE REMARKABLE ACQUISITION OF CORREGGIO'S EDUCATION OF VENUS

MRS Jameson's exciting account of the acquisition of this famous painting and its companion, *Ecce Homo*, is not widely known. The picture, which was also called 'The School of Love' for many years, is now titled *Mercury Instructing Cupid Before Venus*.[1]

---

[1] There are many versions of the painting. The National Gallery catalogue lists five. It also blandly states: 'various other copies of No. 10, of uncertain date could be listed'. The writer may well have had in mind the claims of a Mr Jesse Landon to own *the* original which he bought in 1904 for 12s 6d. Mr Landon wrote and published a book on *The Education of Cupid . . . Rescued after three Centuries of Obscurity* in 1912. Mention is made of it here as being typical of a whole genre of such books in which the owners claim that they own the original of celebrated paintings of which they maintain that copies are in public galleries.

ANNA JAMESON

EXTRACTED FROM Mrs Anna Jameson's *Handbook to the Public Galleries of Art in and near London*, Vol. I, 1842.

THIS picture was painted for Frederigo Gonzaga, Duke of Mantua, the predecessor of him who, a hundred years later, admired and patronised Rubens. Its subsequent history is exceedingly interesting. When Charles I of England purchased the Mantuan collection, in 1630, for £20,000, this picture, and three others by Correggio, were included in the acquisition. It hung in Charles's own apartment at Whitehall, and is designated in his catalogue as 'A standing naked Venus, whereby Mercury sitting, teaching Cupid his lesson, entire figures almost as big as life.'* On the sale of the king's effects by order of the parliament, it was purchased by the Duke of Alva, and from his family it passed into the possession of the famous Godoy, Prince of Peace. When his collection was sold by auction at Madrid during the French invasion, Murat secured it for himself on the morning fixed for the sale, and took it with him to Naples, where it adorned the royal palace. On his fall from power, this picture was among the precious effects with which his wife, Caroline Buonaparte, escaped to Vienna. The rest of its strange eventful history I am enabled to give accurately, through the kindness and in the very words, of the Marquess of Londonderry, its next possessor.

'During the congress of the sovereigns at Verona, in November, 1822, General M'Donald, who was chamberlain to Madame Murat (then known as the Countess Lipona), arrived from her residence near Vienna to sell her collection of pictures, amongst which the two famous Correggios were the most conspicuous. The General communicated with the ministers of all the powers, and had various negotiations, on and off, with them. Many were desirous of obtaining possession of the two *chef-d'oeuvres*, but were indisposed to take the indifferent ones; while General M'Donald naturally wished the Correggios to assist in selling the others. I heard, by mere accident, of these circumstances, as it was not imagined I was an amateur, much less a connoisseur; and my informant acquainted me that the Emperor Alexander's ministers, Capo d'Istrias and Nesselrode, had obtained permission of the Emperor of Austria to export the pictures to Russia, if they could agree on the purchase. I waited immediately on Prince Metternich, and I asked him if, in the event of my closing a bargain with General M'Donald (as I understood the pictures were not yet actually sold), he would obtain for me, as British plenipotentiary, the same liberty of taking these gems to England that he had accorded to Russia? The prince smiled, and looked *en moqueur*, saying "Mais, oui, mon cher! certainement oui!" I then said I wished he would give me an official line under his hand to that effect; and I did not leave him until he gave me the paper, subject to the pleasure of the Emperor. The moment I obtained the order I went to General M'Donald, and enquired how his negotiation stood. He informed me the Russians stood out against taking the whole for the larger price,

* *A beautiful miniature copy (8 by 5½ inches) was executed by Peter Oliver, for Charles I, in 1636, when the original was in his possession; and now exists (or ought to exist) in the Royal collection. It used to hang in Queen Caroline's closet, at Kensington, and was then enclosed in an ebony frame with folding doors.* [It is now at Windsor: *Ed.*]

and wanted the Correggios alone. I asked him if he would close with me, and take my bills within a certain period for the whole? He immediately acquiesced; and within twelve hours after the bills were signed and my courier *en route* for Vienna, with the order for the pictures, which were conveyed by him to England almost before the Russians knew they were finally disposed of.'

An attempt was made to overtake and stop the courier, but the pictures had already reached the Hague; and the promptitude of Lord Londonderry on this occasion eventually secured to the nation two *chef-d'oeuvres* of art. This picture and the *Ecce Homo*, were purchased from his Lordship, in the year 1834, by parliament, for 10,000 guineas.

Sir Thomas Lawrence used to relate that when he was at Rome in 1819 the fate of these pictures was matter of great curiosity and speculation, as well as the dexterity of the ex-queen in secreting them; they were, even *then*, concealed at Rome; and Lawrence was allowed a furtive glimpse of them, in the hope that he would recommend them to a purchaser in England. He says in a letter, 'I had them brought down to me, and placed in all lights and I *know* them to be most rare and precious.' By his recommendation, Mr Angerstein offered £6500 for the two which was declined.*

THE BECKFORD COLLECTION SOLD

Eccentricity is not a particularly common trait among English collectors.[1] However, a few unusually colourful and exotic personalities, such as Horace Walpole, William Beckford and Sir John Soane, have succeeded in giving the English as collectors a slightly lurid patination.

William Beckford (1760–1844) was brought up in circumstances of great wealth. His father, twice Lord Mayor of London, owned extensive plantations in the West Indies. Beckford was able to vent his extraordinary gifts in whatever direction he pleased. By the time he was twenty-six his wife was dead, *Vathek* had been written and the beginnings of a tempestuous and probably orgiastic life were already behind him. So was his involvement with the boy, William Courtenay, at Powderam Castle. The resulting scandal meant almost permanent social ostracism. Although he travelled widely,[2] Beckford preferred or was forced into

* *Vide Life of Sir T. Lawrence, Vol. ii, p.* 169.

[1] It appears to be much more characteristic of the great, though not necessarily monied, French collectors of the same period.

[2] See his *Italy, with Sketches of Spain and Portugal*, 1834. This is based on letters written a good deal earlier. His descriptions of collections seen tend, sadly from our point of view, to be

a life of seclusion, and in 1796 Wyatt started to build for him Fonthill Abbey, probably the wildest piece of Gothic extravaganza of its time. Here Beckford lived the life of a recluse, but with a frantic zest for activity. He was constantly making improvements to the house, the gardens, the grounds and adding to his splendid collection of pictures and other works of art and to his immense and superbly selective library.[1]

By 1822, the income from his estates in Jamaica had dwindled and his own resources had been shrunk by constant expenditure if not extravagance. In fact, although he spent lavishly, after his middle life at any rate, he spent knowing full well where his money was going. This is borne out by many of his letters adjuring his agent at home to 'the strictest attention to unexpensiveness'.[2]

His straitened financial circumstances forced the sale of Fonthill and most of its contents. (Beckford retained the finest pictures and furniture and the cream of his library: they were transferred to his house in Lansdown Crescent in Bath.) Christie prepared the catalogue but John Farquhar, a Scottish millionaire gunpowder manufacturer, stepped in and bought the house and contents for a sum said to be in the region of £350,000. Only a short time later Farquhar entrusted the arrangement of a new sale to the auctioneer Phillips who, while using the Christie catalogue as a basis for his own, is said to have swollen both the number of pictures and books very considerably. Whitley[3] quotes a correspondent of the *Museum* who pointed out that the number of pictures had increased from 115 in the Christie catalogue to 415 in the revised Phillips' version. Christie had mentioned a single painting each by Teniers and Ostade, while Phillips catalogued twenty-one and ten respectively.[4]

As a collector Beckford is of interest in more than one respect. He was prepared to offer what were regarded as quite fantastic prices to other collectors or dealers for paintings he really wanted. Thus he had offered Angerstein £16,000 for

frivolous. Thus in Antwerp, on 23 June, 1780, he writes: 'First I went to Monsieur Van Lenkeren, who possesses a suite of apartments, lined, from the base to the cornice, with the rarest productions of the Flemish school. Heaven forbid I should enter into a detail of their niceties! I might as well count the dew-drops upon the most spangled of Van Huysum's flower-pieces, or the pimples on the possessor's countenance; a very good sort of man indeed; but from whom I was not at all sorry to be delivered.'

[1] See in particular *Life at Fonthill 1807–1822, with interludes in Paris and London,* from the correspondence of William Beckford, translated and edited by Boyd Alexander, London, 1957.

[2] An interesting example of this was a letter shown in an exhibition devoted to William Beckford (held in the Menstrie Museum at Bath in the summer of 1966)–No. 98.

[3] *Art in England, 1821–1837*, page 53.

[4] The pagination of the Phillips catalogue of 1823 is rather puzzling at first sight: it appears not to follow any logical sequence. But there is an explanation. The sale was to take 37 days in all and the days follow each other in the correct order in the printed lists. But the items were divided roughly into (i) Books, (ii) Effects and (iii) Pictures. For those owners of the catalogue who wanted their binders to bind up the parts in this grouping, the pagination works logically enough! The books were sold in 20 days (Day 1–Day 10; Day 19–Day 23; Day 33–Day 37). The effects were sold in 13 days (Day 11–Day 18; Day 28–Day 32). The pictures were sold in four days (Day 24–Day 27).

A · CATALOGUE · OF · THE · COSTLY · AND · INTERESTING · EFFECTS · OF · FONTHILL · ABBEY
1823
PRICE 12
Stedman Whitwell Arch. del.
Thomas Higham sculpsit.

THE UNIQUE AND SPLENDID EFFECTS
OF
FONTHILL ABBEY.

CATALOGUE
OF
THE EXTENSIVE ASSEMBLAGE
of Costly and Interesting
PROPERTY,
WHICH ADORNS THIS MAGNIFICENT STRUCTURE;
EMBRACING PART OF
THE FURNITURE;
THE BIJOUTERIE, COMPOSED OF PRECIOUS GEMS;
THE INIMITABLE
Carvings in Ivory by Fiamingo and Benvenuto Cellini;
THE BRONZES AND MARBLES;
The Matchless Collection of Raised Gold Japan,
And elegantly mounted AGATES;
THE
RARE ORIENTAL, JAPAN & SEVRES CHINA;
The sumptuously Gilt and Chased PLATE;
The Ancient Stained Glass;
THE EBONY, AMBER, FLORENTINE AND BUHL CABINETS,
THE MINIATURES, CAMEOS AND INTAGLIOS;
The Miscellaneous Elegancies, and Objects of Taste and Vertu;
And also part of the HOUSEHOLD LINEN, and CELLAR of WINES.

Which will be Sold by Auction,
BY

MR. PHILLIPS,

AT THE ABBEY,
On TUESDAY, the 23d of SEPTEMBER, 1823,
And Seven following Days,
And on THURSDAY, 16th of OCTOBER, and Four following Days
(Sundays and Mondays excepted)
At HALF-PAST TWELVE each Day precisely.

TICKETS for VIEWING, at *One Guinea* each, to admit Two Persons, or *Half a Guinea*, to admit One Person, on any two Days—Also, TICKETS to admit *Three* Persons every Day, during the View and Sale, at FIVE GUINEAS EACH, including the Four CATALOGUES, may be had at The ABBEY GATES; Beckford Arms, in *Fonthill Park;* the Lamb Inn, *Hindon;* at Messrs. Brodie and Dowding, and Mr. Earle's Libraries, *Salisbury;* Mr. Skelton's Library, *Southampton;* White Lion and York Hotels, *Bath;* Mr. Frost's Library, *Bristol;* Mr. Thomas's Library, *Weymouth;* Mr. Rutter's Library, *Shaftsbury;* Bath Arms, *Warminster;* Black Horse, Antelope, White Hart, and Lamb Inns, *Salisbury;* Gazette Office, *Devizes;* at Garraway's, *Cornhill*, and at Mr. PHILLIPS's, No. 73, *New Bond Street*, *London*, where, (and at the before mentioned places) the FOUR CATALOGUES, complete, may be had at 12*s*. or the Furniture, China, &c. at 5*s*.—the Books at 5*s*. and the Pictures at 2*s*. 6*d*.

Sebastiano del Piombo's *Raising of Lazarus*,[1] six Hogarths and an Annibale Carracci, and it was he who had bought the Altieri Claudes[2] for £6825. It is said that he had permitted his agent in the purchase, Henry Tresham, R.A., to go up to 10,000 guineas if necessary. In fact, Beckford sold the paintings for that sum nine years later.

He was prepared to buy any object he regarded as aesthetically interesting.[3] Thus Dr Waagen was astonished to see a mass 'of the earthenware called *majolica* . . . enamelled vessels . . . strikingly beautiful . . . vessels of agate and nephrite which attract attention by the beauty of their material . . . a gold vessel of the early part of the middle ages is very remarkable, as well as another of Chinese bronze, the colour of which is more delicate than I have ever seen before. The Chinese glass vessels and those of the middle ages are likewise remarkable for the beauty of their colour and the exquisite workmanship. . . . Choice pieces of Japan and Chinese porcelain were not wanting. The furniture corresponded in magnificence. . . . The tables are slabs of giallo and verde antico and other rare marbles. . . . What especially pleased me was that all these things bear a due proportion in size to the moderate apartments in which they are and are so arranged that they serve richly to adorn each, without producing as so often happens, by over-loading and confusion, the disagreeable effect of auction rooms.'[4]

Beckford died at the age of 83[5] after only a short illness. He was a man of such tremendous personality and intellect that one cannot help regretting that he failed to couple his collecting activities with some other constructive outlet that would have given lasting benefit to his time and to his country.

EXTRACTED FROM George Redford's *Art Sales*, Vol. I, 1888.

THE sale of the collection formed by the celebrated William Beckford, author of *Vathek* at Fonthill Abbey, in Wiltshire, a few miles from Salisbury, in September and October 1823, was the most noted dispersion of the time, and attracted all the world of rank and fashion to the place. The magnificence of this may be imagined from the view of it in its completed state, and before the vast structure fell to the ground through inadequate

[1] This painting, like the Altieri Claudes, represented one of the touchstones of early nineteenth century taste. It was not for nothing that it was Number 1 in the National Gallery catalogue! Angerstein himself had paid £4500 for it.

[2] See page 163.

[3] For a fiercely critical, contemporary account of Beckford's taste based on an inspection of Fonthill before the sale, the reader should turn to William Hazlitt's *Criticisms on Art and Sketches of the Picture Galleries in England*, 1843. Hazlitt is not quoted in the present work. In his writing there is too much carping, discursive introspection and not enough fact to be immediately useful to the student of collecting.

[4] Waagen, *Works of Art and Artists in England*, Vol. III, page 119, *et seq*.

[5] Not 84, as stated by Redford in the extract which follows.

provision in the foundations, a catastrophe that happened during the lifetime of the owner, who lived to the great age of eighty-four, when he died in the spring of 1844.*

The sale we are now about to speak of was necessitated in consequence of the loss of two large estates in a lawsuit, the value of which may be inferred from the fact that in these West India properties no less than 1500 slaves were included. After having expended a large sum in his taste for the fine arts, Mr Beckford decided to sell everything and quit Fonthill, notwithstanding that he had so provided for his seclusion as to build a wall 17 feet high, with iron spikes on the top, all round the domain, about seven miles in extent. It is recorded that he had consulted Mr Christie, and intended that he should sell the collection. The catalogue was made, and 1500 sold at a guinea; but, before it was available, an offer was made in 1822 by a Mr Farquhar, to purchase the whole Fonthill property, with the collection for £350,000; and this was accepted. The sale by auction of the works of art, the library, and furniture, &c., being placed in the hands of Mr Phillips, was conducted at the abbey during September and October. Accommodation was provided in a pavilion in the park, beds being charged 3d 6d single, and 5s double; and guinea tickets gave admission to the abbey for two persons, half-guinea for one, the catalogues being charged 12s, giving admission to the saleroom only. *The Times*, noticing the view before the sale said: 'He is fortunate who finds a vacant chair within twenty miles of Fonthill; the solitude of a private apartment is a luxury few can hope for. . . . Falstaff himself could not take his ease at this moment within a dozen leagues of Fonthill. The beds through the country are literally doing double duty: people who come in from a distance during the night must wait to go to bed until others get up in the morning. Not a farm-house, however humble, not a cottage near Fonthill but gives shelter to fashion, to beauty, and rank; ostrich plumes, which by their very waving, we can trace back to Piccadilly, are seen nodding at a casement window over a depopulated poultry yard.'

The books and prints occupied twenty days; the furniture and works of ornamental art, thirteen days; the pictures and miniatures, &c., four days: altogether there were forty-one days' sale producing £43,869 14s; the 424 pictures amounting to £13,249 15s. Some very fine things of historic interest were amongst the furniture, such as the set of chairs of

* *By a strange fatality the old Fonthill Abbey, which took its ancient name from the number of springs arising round the hill on which it stood, and was built on the estate that belonged to the Gifford family so far back as the time of William the Conqueror, was burnt down, and rebuilt, it is said, by the famous Inigo Jones. Then this abbey, being bought by Beckford the father, the wealthy Lord Mayor of London, and much enlarged, was destroyed all but one wing, by fire in* 1755. *Another abbey was built by the elder Beckford, which was so defective that it had to be demolished; and a new building, designed by Mr James Wyatt was begun in* 1795; *under the direction of Mr Beckford, the author, and erected at the cost of* £273,000. *The chief feature of this structure was the tower,* 280 *feet high, and the whole was an attempt to represent the favourite ideal of 'Vathek' in his 'Hall of Eblis'. Beckford was as impetuous in the building of his tower as in the writing of his romance (which was written when he was only twenty, and in French, in three days and two nights at a single sitting), and he had the work continued by torchlight night and day, with relays of workmen. Again the fates pursued him: his tower caught fire, and 'Vathek' is said to have looked on, enjoying the magnificent spectacle. Still the place was doomed: the restored tower fell to the ground and Fonthill Abbey was eventually left a ruin in the lifetime of its owner. One reason for hurrying on the works was that Beckford wished to have his mansion ready for the visit of Lord Nelson and Sir William Hamilton with his beautiful lady.*

ebony which belonged to Cardinal Wolsey, and came from his palace at Esher. A magnificent state bedstead, of ebony, with crimson damask hangings, and a rich purple silk quilt worked with gold, which belonged to Henry VII; a matchless state bed-quilt of Brussels point-lace over a damask ground and a toilette table-cover of similar work. Ebony tables with slabs of Verde antique; a table inlaid with precious marbles, jaspers, and oriental onyx, with arabesque border of costly marbles, from the Borghese Palace; cabinets of the time of Queen Elizabeth and James I; Japan cabinets, from the Collection of the Duc de Boillon, and the Duchess of Mazarin; and a superb coffer of raised Japan work, with animals in gold and silver, which belonged to Cardinal Mazarin. Services of Sèvres and Dresden porcelain; silver-gilt and silver plate, of various designs, as a plateaux, candelabra and many fine candlesticks, caskets, toilette-services &c., &c. Amongst the objects of Oriental art was a matchless Hookah, carved in jade and set with jewels, mounted in silver-gilt, and the stand elaborately chased, which belonged to Tippoo Sahib, and was taken as plunder from his palace of Seringapatam. The bronzes were many of the size of the antique: The LAOCOON,* cast and chased by Carbonneau, to which the gold medal of the Institute was awarded; the Medici Venus; a vase of the largest block of Hungarian topaz known, set with diamonds and gold mounts enamelled, made as a present to Catarina Cornaro, the work of Cellini; a commode and a secretaire, inlaid by Riesener, from the *Garde Meuble*, Paris, and bearing the cypher of Queen Marie Antoinette. These were, no doubt, those sold in the Hamilton Palace Sale, and were bought in at this sale, as were many other objects included in the catalogue. The pictures were sold on October 10, 11, 14, 15–385, lots, nearly all single pictures. The miniatures, only nineteen in number all French. The cameos and intaglios, twenty, with fifty-four cameos in oriental alabaster of large size, called antique, but no doubt of modern work from ancient sculptures at Rome. The noticeable pictures, as named in the catalogue were: COELLO, The Duke of Alva in a cuirass, with bâton. ORCAGNA, Crucifixion, on gold ground, from the Campo Santo. RUBENS, 'Le Jardin d'Amour', with portraits of Rubens, his Wife, Vandyck, Snyders, and the 'Chapeau de Paille' portrait. MANTEGNA, 'Christ in the Garden', with figures in a landscape, and angel with the cup in the sky. VAN EYCK, 'Entombment of a Cardinal', from Lord Bessborough's Collection. G. JAMIESON, 'The Regent Murray in Highland dress'. METZU, Woman cleaning fish, a kitten on a brass kettle, from Collection of Duke d'Alberg. ANT. MORO, Portrait, Jeanne d'Archel; portrait of Dona Juana of Austria. J. BELLINI, 'Marriage of St Catherine', from the Oratory of the Doge Loredano. P. DE HOOGE, Lady, with a spaniel, in white satin, a servant caressing a hound, in interior. Interior, woman weighing money. VAN HUYSUM, Vase of Flowers, from Duc de Praslin Cabinet. WOUWERMANN, Battle-piece, from the Collection of the P. of Orange. REMBRANDT, A Rabbi, from Vandergucht Collection; An Architect and his Wife. BONIFACCIO, Virgin and Child, St Catherine, St John, St Jerome, and Mary Madgalen, in a landscape—a gallery picture. TENIERS, A Village Fête, called 'Sign of the Teniers'. ALBERT DURER, Virgin with the Infant on a table, with the word '*Veni*' in gold before his extended hand, in a landscape;

* *This was the fine bronze sold in the Hamilton Palace Sale* 1882, *though that was said to be by Crozatier. It was afterwards sold to the Duke of Buckingham, and was again sold at Stowe in* 1848.

presented by Philip V to a convent at Saragossa. L. DA VINCI, 'The Laughing Boy with a Toy'. G. DOW, 'The Poulterer's Shop',[1] from the Choiseuil Collection. JAN STEIN, 'The Poultry Market', from the Aynard Collection. BERGHEM, A Sea Port, 'Embarquement des Vivres', Gulf of Genoa, from Duc de Praslin Collection. P. VERONESE 'St Jerome at Devotion', from the Monastery of St Benedict at Mantua, where it was the companion to the 'Communion of St Jerome' presented by the British Institution to the National Gallery. RUBENS, 'Holy Family, with SS John and Joseph', of gallery size. CUYP, Landscape with a camp, officer and other figures, soldiers playing cards. PALMA, 'Martyrdom of a Saint', large gallery picture. BONIFACCIO, 'Adoration of Magi', in a landscape, grand gallery picture. VAN EYCK, The Virgin, with the Infant on her lap, an angel presenting an apple, a saint kneeling, a landscape and fortified city in distance. K. DU JARDIN, 'Le Manège', upright landscape, with horses exercising, from the Aynard Collection. GAINSBOROUGH, A grand Landscape woody scene, with cattle in distance; a girl with milkpail, and man on horseback refreshing his horse with water; shepherd and flock coming to the brook.

When this sale took place, Mr Beckford was in his 63rd year; but he was not parting with his favourite pictures, for he reserved them at prices which were not nearly approached then; and in 1839 (as will be seen on referring to the catalogue of the National Gallery) he sold three pictures, one of which was the 'St Catherine' by Raphael, which was not in the Fonthill Sale, to the National Gallery for £7350; and in 1841, three years before his death, the Perugino 'Holy Family' (No. 181) for £800. 'The Laughing Boy', by Leonardo, and other pictures, were long afterwards to be seen on the walls of Hamilton Palace, where they passed with the choicer part of his fine library as dowry of his daughter, who became the wife of the Duke of Hamilton, and were sold finally in 1882. Had the collection at Fonthill been sold at the present time, the prices would have been far higher than any then bid as was seen at the Hamilton Palace Sale.[2]

[1] See page 248.

[2] See page 348.

ROGERS ON FONTHILL ABBEY

ONE of the most lively accounts of a visitation to Fonthill in its prime is a letter written by Lady Bessborough to Lord Granville Leveson Gower[1] in October 1817, on the day after Samuel Rogers had recounted his adventures to her.[2] Rogers and Beckford continued to correspond and to see each other for many years.

HE was received by a dwarf[3] who, like a crowd of servants thro' whom he passed, was covered with gold and embroidery. Mr Beckford received him very courteously, and led him thro' numberless apartments all fitted up most splendidly, one with Minerals, including precious stones; another the finest pictures; another Italian bronzes, china, etc. etc. till they came to a Gallery that surpass'd all the rest from the richness and variety of its ornaments. It seem d clos'd by a crimson drapery held by a bronze statue, but on Mr B's stamping and saying 'Open! the statue flew back, and the gallery was seen extending 350 feet long. At the end an open Arch with a massive balustrade opened on to a vast Octagon Hall, from which a window shew'd a fine view of the Park. On approaching this it proved to be the entrance of the famous tower–higher then Salisbury Cathedral: this is not finished but great part is done. The doors, of which there are many, are violet velvet covered over with purple and gold embroidery. They pass'd from hence to a chapel, where on the altar were heaped golden candlesticks, vases and chalices studded over with jewels; and from there into a great musick room, where Mr Beckford begg'd Mr Rogers to rest till refreshments were ready and began playing with such *unearthly* power that Mr Rogers says he never before had any idea how delighted one might be with him, that he thinks even Lady Douglas fails in the comparison. They went on to what is called the refectory, a large room built on the model of Henry 7 Chapel, only the ornaments gilt, where a Verdantique table was loaded with gilt plate fill'd with every luxury invention could collect. They next went into the Park with a numerous cortege,[4] and horses and servants etc., which he described as equally wonderful, from the beauty of the trees and shrubs, and manner of arranging them, thro' a ride of five miles. They were met at the setting out by a flock of tame hares, that Mr Beckford feeds; then pheasants, then partridges; and lastly came to a beautiful romantick lake, transparent *as liquid Chrysolite* (this is Mr

[1] See page 141.

[2] Quoted in *The Caliph of Fonthill*, H. A. N. Brockman, 1956, page 168.

[3] The dwarf Perro was still with him when Beckford moved to Bath in 1823. The move of the legendary figure caused a great stir in Bath at the time. But Perro appeared to be the only outward sign of flamboyance of an apparently respectable and only mildly eccentric elderly gentleman.

[4] It appears that Beckford always liked an entourage about him. Even when he travelled as a young man he was rarely accompanied by fewer than four or five retainers.

Rogers' not my expression), cover'd with wildfowl. Mr R. was hardly arrived at the Inn before a present of game follow'd him, and a note beginning the unfortunate Vathek was too sensible of the favour confer'd upon him by Mr Roger's visit not to keep something back to allure him to a repetition of it, and then pressing him so strongly to return next day that he did so, and was shewn thro' another suite of apartments fill'd with fine medals, gems, enamell'd miniatures, drawings old and modern, curios, prints and manuscripts, and lastly a fine and well furnish'd library, all the books richly bound and the best editions etc. etc. An Old Abbé, the Librarian and Mr Smith, the water-colour painter, who were there, told him there were 60 fires always kept burning, except in the hottest weather. Near every chimney in the sitting rooms there were large Gilt fillagree baskets fill'd with perfum'd coal that produced the brightest flame.

HOLKHAM HALL, 1833

THE two German art historians who dominated the first half of the nineteenth century were Gustav Waagen and Johann David Passavant. Both were 'Connoisseurs' in the new sense. They did not concern themselves much with theory or introspection but were fascinated by provenance and detail. Passavant, born in 1787 and seven years older than Waagen, tended more towards the eighteenth century; Waagen moved aggressively into the nineteenth. In features Passavant was gentle and doe-eyed; Waagen calm certainly, but incisive and calculating. Stylistically Passavant is the more bloodless of the two; though neither of them had great literary pretensions. Furthermore, Waagen quite frequently expresses a healthy contempt for Passavant's opinions.

From our point of view both Passavant and Waagen are of the greatest importance, because they were the first surveyors of the works of art that were to be found in the British Isles by the 1830s. Passavant came over to this country in 1833. The principal purpose of his journey was to see as many examples of work by Raphael as possible because he was at work on a major book on that Master.[1]

[1] Published eventually as *Raphael von Urbino und sein Vater Giovanni Santi*. For an amusing dissertation on its value to the present-day scholar, see Wilhelm Waetzold's *Deutsche Kunsthistoriker*, Vol. II, page 25 *et seq*. Waetzold deserves mention here as a most useful informant on the lives of Passavant and Waagen and their circle. First published in 1924, the work was reprinted without correction in 1966. Although revisions would certainly have been of advantage it appears that no one could be found to emulate Waetzold's breadth of reading (which verges on the improbable!) and certainly it would have been a brave man who would have tampered with Waetzold's very personal, literate and yet highly readable style.

He found, incidentally, as he explains in the preface to his *Tour of a German Artist in England*, that there was a complete dearth of books describing the art treasures of the British Isles, and this lack he set out to remedy. Hence the sub-title 'with Notices of Private Galleries, and Remarks on the State of Art'. The book was first published in German, and translated into English in 1836 by Elizabeth Rigby, later to become wife of Sir Charles Eastlake.[1]

Passavant was deeply impressed by the wealth of the English collections he saw, and it may very well have been the reading of Passavant's book that stimulated Waagen to come to this country to attempt an improved version of the same project.

Passavant was the son of a successful merchant who specialised in English goods. He embarked upon a life of commerce but forsook this to train as a painter. He studied in Paris under David, and in Rome where he was strongly influenced by the German Nazarene movement, but, as in the case of Waagen, it was von Rumohr who found for Passavant a suitable training ground in Florence. But Passavant did not thrive as a practising painter either and turned to art criticism instead. By 1840 he had written a good deal and was appointed curator of the Frankfurt City Gallery which had been founded by Städel. At his death he left behind thirty notebooks of accounts of his many journeys. It was one of these that became *Tour of a German Artist in England.*

We already know Holkham Hall–seen through Passavant's eyes in the extract which follows–from Thomas Coke's 'An Exemplary Grand Tour' on page 74. The Thomas William Coke mentioned here is the eldest son of the Thomas mentioned earlier.

EXTRACTED FROM J. D. Passavant's *Tour of a German Artist in England*, Vol. II, 1836.

THIS magnificent seat, situated in the county of Norfolk, belongs to Thos. William Coke, Esq., the rightful heir, though not bearing the title, of the Earldom of Leicester. Although merely a brick and mortar building, this is one of the finest edifices in England; the material having been burned expressly for the purpose, and even the cornice moulded in the most beautiful form. The coup d'oeil presented by the entrance-hall, supported on Corinthian pillars of the finest Derbyshire spar, is magnificent beyond description. Altogether, the arrangements of the interior are on the grandest scale, and well worthy of a royal residence. The building was planned by Kent, the architect, in the beginning of the foregoing century; and to that period must the slight incongruities observable in the

[1] For a further view of Passavant's place in the emerging pattern of English nineteenth-century taste, see 'The Changing Taste of Collectors' quoted from John Steegman, *Consort of Taste 1830–1870*, on page 235.

different portions of the architecture be ascribed. A particular description of Holkham, with ground-plan and sketches, published in 1711, by Brettingham, the architect, contains every necessary detail, excepting that of the name of the architect.

A chief object of splendour here, is a large circular saloon, adorned with antique statues. Among these, a draped figure of a Venus is particularly conspicuous, somewhat resembling the Venus of Arles. Also a male figure of most excellent workmanship.

The state rooms are, almost without exception, adorned with the most splendid pictures, of which the following are the most remarkable.

Michael Angelo. Small picture, in *clair-obscure*, from the Pisa Cartoon of the Soldiers Bathing. A composition which Michael Angelo painted, in connection with Leonardo da Vinci, for the great hall in the old palace at Florence, and than which no production is more celebrated in the world of art. . . .

Raphael. The original Cartoon to the Madonna with the Infant Saviour and St. John, called '*La belle Jardinière*', now in the Louvre. This cartoon is drawn in black chalk heightened with white. It is much injured, and soaked with oil, which greatly disfigures it. Three feet one inch wide, by two feet two inches high.

Also the portraits of Julius II and Leo X, with Julius di Medici, and Cardinal Rossi, after Raphael. The last-mentioned picture from the collection of Mr Roscoe.

Annibale Caracci. A small and very interesting fresco picture. Polypheme seated on a rock, playing on a pipe of reeds; Galatea, with her nymphs, sailing on the sea. This delicious little *morceau* is a most masterly sample of fresco painting; in excellent preservation, and about eighteen inches square.

In the collection of old drawings, many interesting pieces by Annibale Caracci also appear. A head, in particular, a study from nature; full of life and truth.

Ant. van Dyck. The Duke of Richmond; a whole-length standing figure. In point of gradation of tone, and harmony of colour, this is one of the master's finest pictures, at the same time uncommonly simple in composition.

A picture of more pretension is the large Portrait of Count Aremberg, on a horse in full gallop. This picture is much celebrated; but I must own, that the stiffness of the composition, and the coldness, almost approaching to hardness, of the colouring, did not permit of my admiring it.

Claude Lorrain. A large number of original pictures by this master appear in the Holkham Collection; principally rich landscapes; some of the greatest beauty. It is a thousand pities that the cleaning of these pictures should have been entrusted to so unskilful a hand, not a trace of the glazings being left. By this means they have been robbed of their greatest charm, and are striking examples of how little the form and local tints of a landscape avail, when deprived of that tone of colour which may be termed, as it were, the soul of the picture. In many of these Claudes, only the under-painting remains, which has little interest beyond that of exhibiting to the eye of the artist this master's mode of execution. By this it appears, that his colours were cold, and his forms, not excepting even his clouds, very decided, and even hard. Only by repeating paintings and glazings, was Claude able to produce that exquisite airiness of tone, which forms the chief charm of his pictures. A few of the number, however, are in excellent preservation; as also some original drawings in bistre.

Gaspard Poussin. Many specimens of this great landscape artist are also contained in Holkham, chief of which are well known by engravings. It is only to be lamented, that they should have so darkened with time. Those portions where the original colour has been preserved, exhibit a quality of tone admirably in unison with the arrangement and treatment of the subject, and display a freshness and decision of character which will stand their ground, even in competition with the fairy tones of Claude.

Over the fire-place, in the library, is placed an antique mosaic, of tolerable size, representing a Fight between a Lion and a Leopard; an excellently drawn group, and full of animation. This mosaic belongs to the beautiful remains of Roman art.

What principally determined me on visiting Holkham was the report of its containing a volume of architectural drawings by Raphael, the knowledge of which had reached me, even in Germany. This volume, as intimated in the envelop-sheet, had formerly belonged to Carlo Maratti. It contains thirty-five sheets, drawings principally from antique capitals, pedestals, mutules, cornices &c. Eighteen of them bear the impress of the same hand, being drawn with the pen, and touched with red chalk, quite in the manner peculiar to Raphael; often with accompanying notices, indicating whether taken from antique or modern models; sometimes the place where these existed; the latter, especially, in the second leaf, which contains capitals, pedestals, cornices, and urns, copied from various fragments in Padua. Another leaf, entirely from Raphael's hand, are sketches to grotesque work, in a semi-arch; also a landscape and a pen-drawing from Michael Angelo's fresco of the Brazen Serpent, in the Sistine Chapel.

I should have no hesitation in pronouncing these twenty-one drawings to be the work of Raphael's own hand, of which they bear the most indubitable proofs, did not the writing, which does not exactly tally with those letters of Raphael, written 1508, to his uncle Ciarla (which are known by repeated fac-similes), rather stagger me. The sonnets by Raphael, accompanying some of his sketches to the Disputa, which I had the opportunity of investigating both in the British Museum and in the collection of the late President, belong to the same period as these letters and bear precisely the same character of hand. A gap of ten years, at least, having, however, intervened between the date of those letters, and that of these architectural drawings, which Raphael is acknowledged to have executed towards the latter part of his life, it is quite possible that his handwriting may have materially altered, and assumed that irregularity of character which has given rise to these surmises. . . .

Besides this original MS,[1] Mr Coke possesses another old copy, written in the more conventional direction, and consequently easier to decipher. It were highly desirable, that this interesting work should be perpetuated in a printed form. With the exception of

[1] A treatise on the nature, gravity and current of water, with explanatory pen-drawings by Leonardo da Vinci, in his own hand, but reversed, so as to be readable only when reflected in a mirror.

these volumes, I remarked nothing else of interest, as far as regards the history of art, among the Holkham collection of manuscripts. Mr Roscoe, in his complete catalogue, of ten large folio volumes, has fully described this collection, which contains above a thousand volumes. His intention was to have published this work, and he was desirous, as a last preliminary, of going through it with some gentleman of equal erudition, for the purpose of making every final correction and addition. The death of the venerable compiler has delayed the publication. In the meantime, however, the learned public, next to the intelligent liberality of the possessor, are indebted to Mr Roscoe for rescuing this invaluable treasure from the really deplorable situation to which time and long neglect had reduced it. When Mr Coke, the last heir of the house of Leicester, took possession of the estate, now above fifty years ago, he troubled himself little about the literary treasures contained within the walls of Holkham, devoting all the energies of his mind, and the activity of his fine person, in the arrangement and improvement of his large estates; his leisure hours being fully occupied in the pleasures of the chase, and the convivial entertainment of his numerous guests. It was not till after the lamented death of his first wife, a circumstance which withdrew him more into the circle of his own family, and disposed him for pursuits of a graver kind, that he began to examine his hereditary stores of art and science, to which his friends had already been anxious to call his attention. To promote this, he immediately engaged the services of the gentleman who acted as superintendent of the royal collections, who commenced a regular investigation, and not only established the reputation of his numerous and splendid pictures, but discovered, in one of the turrets of the mansion, a quantity of manuscripts, thrown together in the greatest possible confusion, which appeared to him of inestimable value. In examining one volume after the other, he remarked a number of square holes, regularly cut in the broad margins of the parchments, a circumstance which remained inexplicable, till Mr Coke recollected in former times having always used similar pieces of parchment at the card-table, with which, on account of their great beauty, he had desired his servants always to supply him, and thus had been himself the unconscious abettor of these mutilations. Fortunately, only the white part of the parchment being serviceable, the text itself had remained untouched.

Highly gratified at finding himself the possessor of so unexpected a treasure, Mr Coke gladly availed himself of the assistance of Mr Roscoe's antiquarian knowledge, in throwing further light on their value. Without more delay, it was determined to spare no effort or expense for their arrangement and future preservation; in furtherance of which object, Mr Roscoe annually received in Liverpool a chest full of these manuscripts, which, after undergoing his scrutiny, were secured from further injury by the costliest bindings. By this means the catalogue originated, and the entire collection was gradually arranged with that order and discrimination it so richly deserved.

Just to give an idea of the copiousness and variety of this collection, I here annex the following hasty summary. Many copies of the Evangiles of the thirteenth and fourteenth centuries, with miniature illustrations, and their covers richly adorned with gold leaf and precious stones. Among the Italian poets, six copies of the *Divina Commedia*, two upon parchment of the fourteenth and four others of the fifteenth century; also, an old copy of the *Convitio*; of Petrarch's Sonnets, and *Canzoni*; the *Trionfi*, of the fifteenth century, upon paper; a collection of Italian sonnets and poetry, compiled by *Felice Feliciano*, 1462 . . . Many manuscripts contain most splendid miniature illustrations; for instance, *Les Chroniques des Comtes d'Hainault*, 2 vols. folio, on parchment; another of the Counts of Flanders, of the same period.

After spending five days beneath the hospitable roof of Holkham, I returned with my excellent friend, Mr Callcott the artist, to Cambridge.

VIEW BEFORE THE SALE

ENGLISH consuls were as interested in antiquities as in paintings. Here Dr Waagen views the celebrated collection of Egyptian antiquities got together by Henry Salt (1780–1827), British Consul-General in Egypt from 1815 to 1827, and discoverer of the Abu Simbel inscriptions. A considerable part of this collection was sold by Sotheby's in 1835. The British Museum bought many of the pieces. They had bought several items earlier from Salt, in 1818, and he gave them others from time to time.

EXTRACTED FROM Dr Gustav Waagen's *Works of Art and Artists in England*, Vol. II, 1838.

YESTERDAY I went to view the collection of Egyptian Antiquities left by Mr Salt, the English Consul in Egypt, who died in the year 1827, and which will shortly be sold by auction. Among the connoisseurs and friends of antiquity and art, whom the same interest brought together here, I became acquainted with Mr Wilkinson, the most eminent scholar that England now possesses in the language and antiquities of Egypt; and likewise Professor Reubens from Leyden, who enjoys great celebrity on the same account. Of the 1283 lots which the catalogue of this collection contains the majority are smaller articles, many of which are highly interesting, for the light which they throw upon the arts, the civilisation, and the history of the ancient Egyptians. How far these masters of the ancient world, in all the mechanical part of the art, had advanced in the treatment of sculpture in bronze, is proved by some admirably preserved little statues, most beautifully finished in the severe Egyptian style (Nos. 813 and 815 of the catalogue). Yet the art of gilding on metal appears not to have been known to them, for, in two gilded bronze statues, the gold is laid on a coating of chalk (No. 270 and 821). That they had peculiar, and, at the same time very pleasing forms, is evident from several vessels (Nos. 84 and 413). A vase of earthenware (No. 86) is distinguished above all the rest by the taste and elegance of the ornaments. But I have never yet seen such a treasure of the most beautiful Egyptian ornaments of gold and engraved stones as here. The most elegant was a necklace of amethysts, cornelians, and agates, which sometimes alternated with ducks, executed in the most beautiful manner, in which the layers of the agate were very ingeniously taken advantage of, to give the colours of certain parts, for instance, the wings. In another necklace I admired the peculiar and pretty invention of the golden clasp, which was still in perfect preservation. In the class of Ethnography, the greatest rarities were two models of ships, such as were used in funerals (Nos. 513 and 514); but they appeared small and insignificant in comparison with those which have been transferred with Passalacqua's collection to our Egyptian Museum at Berlin. Something quite new to me was the wooden model of an old Egyptian dwelling-house, of the simplest kind, which was found in a sepulchre with the two ships. Four boards enclose a square space, which forms a small court; only a narrow piece of this is covered, and divided into two stories. The lower one contains four provision chambers, with sliding doors–the upper one, the side of which is open towards the court-yard, and to which a very steep and narrow stair-case leads, is properly the dwelling, in which the owner is represented sitting, while his wife is busy in the court-yard, preparing corn; both, as the Egyptians are always represented on the ancient monuments, are of a red colour. None but the hot climate of Egypt, where there is no rain, would admit such an arrangement. A painter's palette of alabaster is also remarkable: it has seven hollows for colours, of which red and a very brilliant blue are still on it (No. 789), and a kind of drawing-board, on which a sitting figure is drawn in very black outlines (No. 243). Lastly, the mummies, with their sarcophagi, are one of the most important parts of the collection. You know that I once wrote an essay upon some such mummies in the Munich Collection, which was printed in the Transactions of the Bavarian Academy of Sciences, and since that time have examined a great number of such monuments. But I here found some, which in splendour and richness of ornament, surpass all that I had hitherto seen. The most costly of them, over a most careful envelope of linen of a reddish colour, has a mask of sized byssus, of which the face, the breast-cloth, and innumerable figures, are gilt. The face of the sycamore sarcophagus which closes upon it, as well as single figures and borders, is strongly gilt, and even the inside of the lid, richly adorned with figures and hieroglyphics. Lastly, the great sycamore sarcophagus, in which the first was placed is covered with hieroglyphics (No. 852). In another mask, the principal figures are laid on in a mass, so that they are rather raised: from the breast downwards, the mass is filigree. Lastly, a mask (No. 1126) is distinguished by the extraordinary fineness and beauty of the gilt countenance and eyes of the well-known Egyptian earthenware let in, in imitation of real eyes.*

* *Almost all the above, and many other interesting articles, were purchased at the sale for the British Museum.*

THE BRITISH INSTITUTION

It is certainly unusual in the history of learned and institutional bodies in this country to find one that was well endowed financially from its very inception. The British Institution, which was founded in 1805, must be almost unique among organizations devoted to the encouragement of the fine arts in having had sufficient wealthy patronage to ensure a really successful launching. Its principal object was to 'encourage and reward the talents of the artists of the United Kingdom, and to open an exhibition for the sale of their productions'. This broke the virtual monopoly of the British Academy, but the Academicians flocked to exhibit there.

Among the initial subscribers were such distinguished collectors as Lord Northwick, Sir George Beaumont, John Julius Angerstein, the Rev. W. Holwell Carr, Henry and Thomas Hope, Sir Abraham Hume and the Duke of Bedford. They and a host of others raised some £7000 and almost immediately bought the Shakespeare Gallery in Pall Mall for £4500, which had come onto the market because of the bankruptcy of Boydell, the engraver and publisher. The gallery, which consisted of three principal exhibition rooms, was fitted out with taste and skill for another £800, and the first exhibition was arranged by a committee of subscribers which included the Marquess of Stafford, Charles Long (later Lord Farnborough), Sir George Beaumont, Sir Francis Baring, Lord Lowther, Richard Payne Knight (Lord Elgin's great enemy) and the Earl of Dartmouth. The exhibition proved very popular and the total sales were substantial.

But the directors of the Institution did not rest on their laurels. As soon as the first exhibition of modern pictures had closed, the gallery was rehung with a small but choice collection of Old Masters which students and artists were permitted to copy. There were 23 paintings in all and they included works by Rembrandt, Rubens, van Dyck, Teniers, Wouwermans, Ostade, Murillo, Velazquez, Reynolds and Richard Wilson.[1] This school for copyists proved immensely popular.

In 1813[2] the directors of the British Institution broke new ground by holding an exhibition devoted entirely to the works of Sir Joshua Reynolds (21 years after his death). Two years later, the usual spring exhibition was followed by another innovation–the first public exhibition in England of Old Masters drawn entirely from private collections. The show was devoted to Flemish and Dutch pictures. 'In presenting this collection to the public', the Directors wrote in their introduction to the catalogue, 'it is to the works of *Rubens*, of *Vandyke*, and of *Rembrandt*,

[1] The full list is given by Whitley, *Art in England, 1800–1820*, p. 111.

[2] The original catalogues are not often found nowadays (particularly as they were printed by W. Bulmer and are therefore collected by students of printing history) but an anonymous author summarised their contents (for the years 1813–1823) in a single volume entitled *An Account of all the Pictures exhibited in the Rooms of the British Institution from* 1813–1823, *belonging to the Nobility and Gentry of England: with remarks, critical and explanatory;* this was published in 1824.

that the Directors desire particularly to call the general attention. Each of these Masters has his peculiar merit: and from each may be derived abundant sources both of study and delight.' There were 146 paintings in all: 25 attributed to Rubens; 19 to Rembrandt and 18 to van Dyck! Other painters represented in force were Wouwermans, Paulus Potter, Dou, Metsu, Adriaen van Ostade, Hobbema, Cuyp, Teniers and Frans van Mieris. Such exhibitions now followed almost every year until 1867 when the lease of the British Institution expired. (They are thus the direct precursor of the Royal Academy's present Winter Exhibitions.) Such exhibitions were invaluable from the educational point of view and did much to mould the taste of English collectors. They also afforded them an opportunity to show their most highly prized items to the general public.

But in this connection it is necessary to point out two factors which are easily overlooked today: first, the absence of public galleries until the opening of the National Gallery in Angerstein's house in Pall Mall in 1824;[1] and, in contrast, the anger which exhibitions of the works of the 'Dead Masters' stirred in the hearts of many of the practising artists of those days. They felt, with some justification, that they had few enough opportunities to bring their work before the eyes of potential patrons. This thought was very much to the fore in the minds of the British Institution's Directors. Again, in the introduction to the catalogue of the Reynolds Exhibition in 1813, they wrote '. . . let the Artist, while he contemplate the almost absolute perfection in the management of the tool and employment of the material, which distinguishes the best of [the pictures], seriously reflect that such perfection was the result of long and continued exertion . . . let the Lover and Patron of Art, and the Collector of Pictures, also reflect that it is employment only, which can produce such exertion . . .'

This was the British Institution then, nearly half way through its life, which so filled its distinguished visitor, Dr Waagen, with rapture. 'Nothing is so well calculated to give a foreigner an idea of the astonishing treasures which England possesses in good pictures, as this exhibition.' It could be held 'nowhere in the world besides England'. It was just praise at a time when private collecting in England had probably reached its zenith.

EXTRACTED FROM Dr Gustav Waagen's *Works of Art and Artists in England*, Vol. I, 1838

At about ten o'clock in the evening I drove with Mr Eastlake, in a cab (the usual name given here to a cabriolet), to the British Institution, to see a fine exhibition of

[1] One of the most active members of the British Institution, and for many years its Deputy President, the Marquess of Stafford, was one of the few connoisseurs who regularly allowed the public to see his magnificent collection.

pictures. This, you will say, is a singular hour for such a purpose; and yet it is the most fashionable time for seeing this gallery.

The British Institution was founded in the year 1805 and opened for the first time in 1806. Under the patronage of the king and the presidency of one of the highest of the nobility, a number of friends of the art united, in order to promote a taste for the art by annual exhibitions of pictures. A suitable house in Pall Mall, the best part of London, was purchased by the contributions of the members, in which the pictures of living artists are exhibited in the spring, and the works of ancient masters in the summer. To form the latter, the king and most of the owners of fine collections contribute; so that in a series of some years a person may here become acquainted with the most valuable portion of ancient pictures now in England.

Through the donations of some individuals and the profits of the exhibitions (the price of admission being 1s), the society has already accumulated so large a capital, that it has purchased several pictures at high prices up to £3000, and presented them to the National Gallery; and yet it possesses the sum of £8500 in the Funds. In the year 1834 the receipts amounted to £2434 17s. 11d., of which only £1719 9s. 8d. were expended. Of the remaining £715 8s. 3d., £455 were employed in the purchase of £500 Consols, and the remainder kept in hand.

Six evenings in each season these pictures are lighted up in the most brilliant manner, and a certain number of tickets of admission distributed among the members, who give them away as they like. I had mine from the Duke of Sutherland, the president, whose bust, by the celebrated sculptor Chantrey, a remarkable likeness, was placed in the middle room. A very numerous and elegant assemblage of gentlemen and ladies were viewing the pictures, which covered all the walls. The most eminent artists and connoisseurs meet here and communicate their observations to each other.

Nothing is so well calculated to give a foreigner an idea of the astonishing treasures which England possesses in good pictures, as this exhibition. Only forty persons out of the very considerable number of owners of pictures, besides the king, have on this occasion lent some from their collections, and yet there are 176, most of which are good, and many of the highest class. Now as a picture which has once been exhibited is not admitted a second time till after an interval of several years, the greater portion of pictures exhibited annually is always new. This can be done nowhere in the world besides England. Next to the king, from whose collection there is a celebrated picture by Rembrandt (the Master-Shipbuilder and his Wife), and a capital picture of Cuyp, the most valuable contributions were those of the Duke of Sutherland, Sir Robert Peel, and Mr William Wells[1]. In number, as well as in value, the pictures of the Flemish and Dutch schools of the seventeenth and

[1] A wealthy collector of pictures by old and modern masters, who was a Trustee of the National Gallery. He lived in Redleaf, near Penshurst in Kent. Whitley (*Art in England 1821-1837*) quotes a contemporary description: 'You can imagine nothing more beautiful than Redleaf. The house is the most tasteful place I ever saw, old-fashioned, full of beautiful pictures and furniture. The grounds are charming and it has the most famous flower gardens in England.' Wells was on friendly terms with many of the artists of his time, and died in 1847.

eighteenth centuries have on the whole a decided preponderance; for of the 176 pictures, 108 belong to them.

I content myself at present with noticing some of the principal pictures belonging to collections, respecting which it is uncertain whether I shall have an opportunity of seeing them, and I therefore always add the name of the owner. . . .

Of the old Italian school there is only one, but a very capital one; namely, the Triumph of Scipio by Andrea Mantegna, painted in black and white, executed with the greatest care, and in admirable preservation (George Vivyan). This is a work of his best time, when he better understood how to reconcile his imitation of ancient statues with the laws of painting. This picture shows that Mantegna had conceived, after his manner, a worthy idea of the old Romans, for the heads of the figures, which are in manifold and dignified attitudes, are full of vigour and animation. The free draperies, which are after antique models, are particularly masterly. Judging by the rather less marked fulness of the forms, this picture, which is treated quite in the manner of a bas-relief, on a ground which is in imitation of a variegated reddish marble, may have been painted a little earlier than the Triumph of Caesar at Hampton Court, and in some manner as a preliminary study for it. The wretched condition of the picture at Hampton Court renders this still more valuable. A Venus, with Cupid, by Paul Veronese, formerly in the Borghese palace, now in the possession of Lady Clarke, is distinguished by a rare transparency and brightness, with which the naked parts, in the full light, are very delicately rounded. The head, as is often the case with this master, is unmeaning, and by no means corresponding with the idea of a Venus.

In the nobly conceived and admirably coloured picture of St Cecilia (Wells), ascribed to Domenichino, neither the sentiment nor the painting appeared to me to be those of that master. I take it to be a very fine work of Christofano Allori, well worthy of being placed as a companion to his celebrated Judith in the Pitti palace. A marine view by Claude (Sir W. W. Wynne), is of the best time of that master. In the depth and transparency of the illuminated surface of the water, in the union of admirable harmony in the whole, with decisive indication in the parts, it strongly reminds us of the beautiful picture, with Acis and Galatea, in the Dresden Gallery. One of the rarest ornaments of the exhibition is San Thomas of Villa Nueva, distributing alms to the sick and the poor, by Murillo (Wells). This fine picture was formerly in the Church of the Franciscans at Genoa. It is of the second period of the master, in which, after his return from Madrid with a lively recollection of the pictures of Velasquez, he united great fidelity to nature in the design, and precision in the single forms. The subject was a peculiarly happy one for Murillo. In the head of the Saint in which priestly dignity and gravity are admirably expressed, he has proved how equal he was to such religious subjects from the legends of the monkish saints. The cripples and the sick afforded him, on the other hand, an ample field to show his skill in representations from common life, which we so highly admire in his beggar boys. The calm intellectual action of the Saint forms a striking contrast with the lively excitement of the distressed, whose whole consciousness is concentrated in their eagerness for the momentary satisfaction of their bodily necessities.

Rembrandt's portrait of his mother, in her eighty-third year, painted in 1634 (Wells), has a very powerful effect. The head, which is represented directly in front, is painted with great breadth and skill in the most brilliant gold tone – the colours thickly laid on; but the cap, the white collar, the black dress, very delicately treated. Rembrandt alone was capable of such energy of effect. There is here a remarkably rich picture by Paul Potter, the greatest animal painter of the Dutch school; for there are in front of a farmhouse, besides five cows, one of which is being milked, a calf, a goat, and five sheep, and a whole flock in the meadows at a distance. This picture, which came from the celebrated Dutch collection of M.V.L. van Slingelandt, is coloured with great solidity, and very diligently executed, and in this respect, a capital work of the master. The date 1646, with which it is marked, shows that he painted it in his twenty-first year. The touches of the pencil accordingly have still a little dryness, the forms a certain hardness, and the general tone is cold. To give you an idea of the high value in which the pictures of this master are held, I observe that this piece, which is not even of his best time, was purchased in the year 1825 at the sale of Lapeyrière, at Paris, for 28,200 francs. The picture now belongs to the Duke of Somerset. A special favourite of mine is a picture by Ruysdael, in the collection of Mr Wells. Few landscapes so thoroughly express the peculiar turn of mind of this master. A still, dark piece of water, on the surface of which the lotus, with its broad leaves and yellow flowers, flourishes in the refreshing coolness, is overshadowed by the gigantic trees of a forest; in particular an already decaying and dying beech leans its white stem far over it. On the right side of the picture are some hills in the distance; the bright daylight of the scarcely clouded sky cannot penetrate into the mysterious gloom of the water protected by its trees. The artist has felt, and represented with rare perfection the sense of solitude and quiet repose, which at times so refreshes the human mind in nature itself.

Though I would very gladly enumerate many other pictures, I must stop here. It was twelve o'clock when I returned home, highly gratified with what I had seen.

AN EXTREME VIEW

NOT everyone approved of collecting in its heyday. Sheldrake, the surgeon who treated Byron for his lameness, reports the poet's opinions at one of their meetings. Perhaps one should also bear in mind that Lady Byron, after her estrangement from her husband, became Mrs Anna Jameson's most intimate friend and shared the latter's great love of the arts.

WILLIAM T. WHITLEY

QUOTED BY William T. Whitley,
Art in England, 1821–1837, 1930.

HE talked much and freely upon literary subjects, but expressed a settled determination never to take any steps towards forming a collection of pictures or other works of art. He said that all dealers in pictures, etc., made a strong push to get every young man of rank and fortune, when he first entered public life, into their snares that they might make him their dupe and plunder him of his property. He declared his belief that all such dealers as well as gamblers of every kind, were complete scoundrels, whose object was fraud, and expressed his fixed determination never to have any dealings with them, a determination I believe he adhered to, during the whole of his life.

ADVERTISEMENT

The Author having during his whole life made the cultivation of the fine arts his peculiar study, and particularly directed his attention to the cleaning, restoring, and preserving from further decay, works of art, by the old and modern Masters, offers his services to those Noblemen and Gentlemen who may have ancestral portraits, or other pictures, in their possession, which require restoration.

With a due regard to the exigencies of the times, his charges will be extremely moderate, for having other resources, employment in a pursuit congenial with his taste, is more his object than emolument; and in all cases the strictest honour may be depended on.

To those who may favor him with a commission, testimonials as to his qualifications will be shewn, if required, from several distinguished Artists and Collectors.

Brook Lodge,
High Wycombe, Bucks.

Final page from *Advice to Proprietors of the Care of Valuable Pictures painted in Oil, with Instructions for Preserving, Cleaning, and Restoring them when Damaged or Decayed.* By an Artist, 1835. (The author appears to have been the son of a Marlow glass painter called Lovegrove.)

PART TWO

1824 and After

THE CHANGING TASTE OF COLLECTORS

THE extract which follows is taken from John Steegman's *Consort of Taste.* This assessment of Victorian taste was a pioneer work and remarkably perceptive. It is only now achieving the recognition it deserves, as interest in the period is growing.[1]

EXTRACTED FROM John Steegman's
Consort of Taste 1830–1870, 1950.

IT is hardly ever possible to assign definite dates to changes in taste. All that can be said here is that the standards that prevailed among collectors during the eighteenth century were still applicable in the 1820s; and that during the 1830s a very marked change took place. This change was the combining of patronage with collecting. It was no longer necessary to claim connoisseurship in the field of Old Masters in order to form a collection that should be highly esteemed even by quite exacting critics. Contemporary painters of genre, history, landscape or narrative suddenly found themselves enjoying a lavish patronage which had hitherto been bestowed on the portrait-painters alone, and saw their names in print along with those of Raphael, Claude or Teniers. Their golden age had begun.

It has been so often repeated as to have become a truism, that this new phenomenon of the patron-collector was a result of the rise to power of the middle-class. Lady Eastlake herself provides contemporary authority for this,* in saying that during the years between 1830 and 1840 the patronage which had till then been the privilege of an exclusive few was 'now shared, and subsequently almost engrossed, by a wealthy and intelligent class chiefly enriched by commerce and trade'. This is undoubtedly true. Yet such a class was a notable element long before 1830, and was indeed as old as the Industrial Revolution. In those days, however, the 'new' man hardly ever appeared as a patron of the arts except, like Alderman Boydell, for business or commercial reasons. If he wished to acquire a status in society which he had not inherited by birth, he was generally able to do so by securing a seat in the House of Commons. This cost a very great deal of money, but was usually held to be

[1] The book was re-issued in 1970 as *Victorian Taste: A Study of the Arts and Architecture from 1830 to 1870,* a title agreed with the author before his death in 1966. The reissue contains an appreciative foreword by Sir Nikolaus Pevsner, who terms the book a classic.

* *Lady Eastlake:* Memoir of Sir Charles Eastlake.

worth it.[1] Thus directing his aim, the 'new' man was content to leave the arts to those who had the education and the traditions to understand them. The Reform Bill of 1832, while not exactly the liberating affair that the majority of Englishmen hoped it would be, did facilitate entry into the House of Commons for many of those who lacked family, Court or territorial influence. It was therefore no longer so desirable for the socially ambitious, who as a result began to turn their attention to the other former preserve of the aristocracy, the arts.

Obviously England was not so precisely divided into art-loving aristocrats and philistine parvenus as this rather facile argument suggests. But it is demonstrable that after the Napoleonic wars many newly-enriched men did begin to form collections, while not ceasing to be business-men. And being business-men they soon realised that forming a collection has its pitfalls. Some of them bought so-called Italian masters and quickly regretted it; others contented themselves with expensive copies of well-known pictures, playing rather dully for safety; while others again, who began by buying copies, tired of these and developed a wish to own original works of art, and combined this desire with safety by buying modern pictures. There are exceptions to this generalisation who fit into none of these categories. John Julius Angerstein, who made a fortune in the city, formed a collection of Old Masters mainly on his own taste and partly with the help of Sir Thomas Lawrence, which was of a sufficiently high standard to be bought by the Government in 1824 as the nucleus of the National Gallery. On the other hand, Sir John Leicester, who was the heir of an old-established Cheshire family, an intimate friend of the Prince Regent and a widely travelled man, collected almost exclusively contemporary English pictures[2].

Of those collectors who became rich through the intensive phase of the Industrial Revolution or as a result of the Napoleonic Wars, John Sheepshanks and Robert Vernon were most characteristic. The former, a Yorkshire woollen manufacturer, bought pictures by Turner, Constable and Bonington, Stothard and Linnell, Landseer and Mulready, Wilkie, Crome and Nasmyth, and presented the entire collection to the nation in 1857, six years before his death. The latter, of very humble birth, became a horse-dealer, and made a large fortune out of army contracts during the Napoleonic Wars; he, like Sheepshanks, bought exclusively the work of his contemporaries and was therefore not only a collector but in the true sense a patron as well, for he aimed throughout his collecting life at founding and endowing a school of modern art. He bought entirely on his own initiative, without the intervention of any dealer,* deliberately to benefit the artist as much as

[1] See, for a late example of this practice, Lady Schreiber's *Journals*, Vol. II.

[2] 6th Baronet; he was created Lord de Tabley in 1826 and died in 1827. For details of his collection, see: *A Catalogue of Pictures by British Artists in the possession of Sir John Fleming Leicester, Bart* by John Young, 1825. In the same series, and also by John Young, appeared *A Catalogue of the Celebrated Collection of pictures of the late John Julius Angerstein*, July 1823; *A Catalogue of the Pictures at Grosvenor House, London*, April 1821; *A Catalogue of the Pictures at Leigh Court, near Bristol; the Seat of Philip John Miles Esq. M.P.*, 1822, and finally *A Catalogue of The Collection of Pictures of the Most Noble the Marquess of Stafford, at Cleveland House, London*, 1825. All these volumes contain descriptions of the pictures, every one of which is accompanied by an engraving. Young was Engraver in Mezzotint to the King and Keeper of the British Institution.

* *Vernon Heath:* Memoirs, 1892; *he was the nephew of Robert Vernon.*

possible, and continually weeded out his collection, each rejected picture being replaced by a better example of the same artist, until in 1847 he judged it complete enough to be presented to the National Gallery, where and at the Tate Gallery most of it still is.

This, then, was the attitude of the average collector of pictures in this country, a century ago; and by collector is meant a man beginning to form a collection, not an inheritor of an ancestral collection formed in the eighteenth century. The incentive to collecting was often, as it may be in any age, the desire for rivalry and emulation. The choice of object to be collected was dictated by common-sense, since antiquities and Old Masters are dangerous and often unsatisfactory things. Many even of the eighteenth-century collectors had made expensive mistakes, and those who now took their place were not inclined to run the same risk; having generally made their own money, they did not wish to spend it on things they did not thoroughly understand. Contemporary painting, however, as Lady Eastlake pointed out, they could understand, and it had the additional advantage of being unassailably genuine.

An ever-increasing number of collectors abandoned the Old Masters and followed the new fashion of patronising their own contemporaries; both the Queen and the Prince did their duty in this respect, by buying the work of Wilkie, Frith, Landseer, Callcott, Francis Grant and a good many other modern painters year after year. Even so, *The Times* saw fit, in 1843, to criticise the Queen for her failure to encourage the arts and sciences. 'There is too much room', said *The Times*, 'for those frequently-heard remarks on Her Majesty's remissness.' And *Punch*, which repeatedly attacked the Palace,* even went so outrageously far as to accuse the Queen and the Prince of taking advantage of their position in buying from artists at less than the normal price. Whether the Court led or followed the new fashion, there was pretty general agreement among the collector-patrons about whom to patronise; and about whom not to patronise, also. They nearly all refrained from buying either Turner or Constable, for example. Eminent those painters might be, but that did not prevent them from seeming unsound, wrong-headed and extravagant. It was with relief and almost with unanimity that the patrons turned away from these eccentricities to purchase the landscapes of Sir Augustus Callcott, which were felt to be so much more elevating and ennobling.

The new fashion, however, though so widely followed, never quite ousted the old. While many rich men, whether peers or army contractors, began forming collections of modern pictures, the collecting of Old Masters, and especially of Old Master drawings, was still a flourishing pursuit among the descendants of the eighteenth-century *cognoscenti*, as well as being found occasionally among exceptional members of the new industrial or commercial rich, like Angerstein or Sir Robert Peel. The German, J. D. Passavant, gives us a good deal of information about the public and private collections of England in 1832.† His observations, though unleavened by any hint of humour and not distinguished by accurate scholarship, are still valuable as evidence. The primary purpose of his visit was to examine such Raphaels as were still in this country, since he was projecting a work of

* *See esp.* Punch, *Vols. 4, 6, 8, 10; 1843–5.*

† *J. D. Passavant,* Kunstreise durch England, 1832. *Translated by Elizabeth Rigby* (*afterwards, Lady Eastlake*), 1836; see page 220.

that Master. He was, as he tells us, able to visit most of the first collections in the country–collections which then were of an almost incredible richness. Rich though they were, however, the visitor even at that date uttered the now familiar lamentation that within the last sixty years so many pictures had quitted the English shores.

At a time when the masses of the people were becoming the objects of more attention from educationists and reformers than they had ever been before, Passavant was very much alive to the importance of the great private collector and to his responsibility towards the public. He noticed that several exhibitions had been arranged in London to excite public interest in the work of living painters, which was no doubt meritorious enough. But, thought Passavant, it might also prove dangerous if public taste should ever come to determine the direction of art. So unformed was public taste that in his opinion these exhibitions tended to keep the state of art at a low ebb. He was not among those who believed that the voice of the public was the voice of true taste. On the contrary, he believed that that voice was confined to a few individuals guiding the public and even, rather vaguely, appealing to them for co-operation; meaning, presumably, patronage of those whom the voice of taste had indicated as being worthy of it. 'The fact is established', said Passavant with undeniable truth, 'that to the fostering influence of a few noble individuals the world is indebted for the finest production of genius.'

The collecting of Old Masters might very likely have died out, and the voice of the few individuals no longer have been heard, had not the Revolutionary and Napoleonic upsettings of Europe provided a fresh stimulus; such a stimulus, for example, as the sale of the Orleans Collection.* After 1815 a further impetus was given by a few great importing dealers in London like Colnaghi, Buchanan, Nieuwenhuys and, especially, Samuel Woodburn. Woodburn was the greatest dealer of the nineteenth century, and one of the most acute connoisseurs of his day. He had a leading hand in forming the collections of the Duke of Hamilton and Lord Fitzwilliam, and a large share in forming Sir Thomas Lawrence's unparalleled collection of Old Master drawings. The Antaldi collection of Raphael drawings at Urbino was bought by him, and he is said to have given £14,000 for the Dijonval collection of Old Master drawings at Paris; all the best things from both these collections were bought from him by Lawrence. Woodburn continued his great career till his death in 1853, with splendid establishments in London, first in Park Lane, and after 1846 at No. 134, Piccadilly. Success also enabled him to join the ranks of the country gentlemen, with the estate of Coedwgan Hall, in Radnorshire. The collectors for whom these and their confrères ransacked a devastated Europe represent the intermediate stage between the rather undiscriminating accumulations of the eighteenth-century Grand Tourists and the more austere *expertise* introduced by the Prince Consort and Sir Charles Eastlake. They shared certain steady and pronounced tastes, inherited from their fathers, for Guido Reni,

* *Sold by the Duke of Orleans in Paris,* 1792. *The French and Italian pictures were bought by M. Le Borde for* 70,000 *louis, and sold by him in London to Mr Jeremiah Harman for* £40,000; *he in turn disposed of them to a syndicate composed of the Dukes of Bridgewater and Sutherland and the Earl of Carlisle. These three divided the cream of the collection among themselves, and sold the residue in London during* 1799; *this residue alone made about* £80,000 *for the syndicate.* (See page 134.)

Domenichino, the Carracci and Nicolas Poussin; and, in addition, they developed a new taste, formed in the days of their own youth, for the masters of the Dutch School. George IV had collected these with scholarly discrimination and an unfailing eye for quality, and there is no doubt that Hobbema, the Ruysdaels, Cuyp and all the Dutch painters were more popular by far in England than anywhere else in Europe, and so indeed they remain.

PRINCE ALBERT AS COLLECTOR[1]

PRINCE Albert showed quite remarkable diversity of taste as a collector. One can only assume that some of what he bought was what he really liked; and the rest was what a sense of duty compelled him to think instructive, or improving, or simply right for its time.

EXTRACTED FROM John Steegman's *Consort of Taste 1830–1870*, 1950.

FEW were the Old Master collectors who turned their critical attention to the pre-Renaissance painters, the painters of the fifteenth and earlier centuries; what Lady Eastlake called 'not only the fruits of art but the gems'. No eighteenth-century connoisseur had ever bothered himself very much about them. Reynolds did bestow a word of qualified praise, in his Discourses, on Dürer. But down to the 1830s nobody[2] in England considered the Early Masters, as they were called before the foolish word Primitives came into use, as having any beauty or technical merit whatever. And in an age of militant Protestantism such pictures were not likely to be thought of as Improving.

The first person to show appreciation of these Early Masters was William Young Ottley,[3] certainly one of the most perceptive connoisseurs of his day. From about 1805, when he was thirty-five years old, till his death in 1836, Ottley was accepted as a leading authority on taste, especially with regard to Old Master drawings. In fact, his collection of drawings formed a very substantial part of Sir Thomas Lawrence's own collection, in due course and at the price of £8000. Ottley, who became Keeper of Prints and Drawings

[1] See also *Prince Albert and Victorian Taste* by Winslow Ames, 1968; particularly Chapter 11.

[2] This can now be regarded as an over-assertive contention. A few collectors *did* take an interest in the 'Early Masters' before 1830; see in particular the pieces on Solly and Roscoe.

[3] See page 186.

at the British Museum, wrote much which, though today superseded, had considerable influence in forming scholarly taste at the time. Hard on the heels of Ottley followed Prince Albert. His collection would be remarkable even today, when the Early Masters are more highly esteemed than those of the Renaissance. In the 1840s, when the reverse was the case, not only was it even more remarkable than it would be now, but the very fact of its being formed at all marks a definite point in the history of taste. Admittedly, in the history of English taste, Ottley, as an Englishman, is more to the point than Prince Albert; but in the history of taste in England the Prince played a part of the first importance.

This history of the Prince's collection is partly that of his relation's, Prince Ludwig-Kraft-Ernst of Oetingen-Wallerstein. When, in 1848, the latter found himself compelled to sell his collection, he sent the pictures to London on Prince Albert's advice, and they were put on view at Kensington Palace. A catalogue was compiled by Waagen; and the admirers of Carlo Dolci, Parmigianino and the Carracci, of Teniers, Cuyp and Brouwer, found themselves contemplating the Schools of Cologne, Van Eyck and Roger van der Weyden. There were no purchasers. The Prince thereupon bought the entire collection himself. He may in part have been impelled by the wish to help a poor relation whose hopes he had so vainly raised. But he certainly had a stronger motive than that; to educate the taste of his adopted country in a direction of which it was yet ignorant. After his death, the Queen carried out his wishes by presenting the best of his pictures to the National Gallery.*

The Prince's collection† consisted by no means only of the pictures from Schloss Wallerstein. He occasionally bought at Christie's, as for example the Cranach triptych, now in the National Gallery on loan from the King, which was then attributed to Grunewald. But the most important of his purchases were those of the early Italian Schools; the famous Duccio triptych, the Fra Angelico 'St Peter Martyr', and 'Madonna and Child', the central panel of the Gentile da Fabriano altarpiece and several other extremely important early pictures which hardly anyone else at that time would have dreamt of buying. The Italian purchases were made shortly before the Prince bought the Schloss Wallerstein collection. The years 1846 and 1847, saw the most important acquisitions, most of them bought by the Prince, but a few bought by the Queen and given to him by her in August 1847, as a birthday present of which he was probably not ignorant beforehand. The Prince's chief agents in Italy seem to have been Grüner, who afterwards acted as Eastlake's travelling agent for the National Gallery, and Warner Ottley, a relation of William Young Ottley.

* *See* National Gallery Annual Report, *1863. The pictures included in the Queen's gift are Nos.* 701–22.

† *See Sir Lionel Cust:* Pictures in the Royal Collection, *1911. Also catalogue of Exhibition of the King's Pictures, Royal Academy, 1946–7.*

46 A view of some of the classical antiquities in the 'Dome' of the Sir John Soane's Museum. A bust of Soane of 1828 by Chantrey can be seen in the centre.

47 Soane's ingenious solution of moveable planes for showing a multitude of pictures within a restricted space.

48 The Picture Gallery at Northwick Park photographed before the dispersal of the Spencer-Churchill Collection in 1965. In fact, this gallery was built in 1832 by the second Lord Northwick. It was when the 56 rooms in the house were filled to overflowing that he bought Thirlestane House (see plate 21).

49 A gallery at Hertford House in the 1880s at the time when Sir Richard and Lady Wallace were living there. It is now the Wallace Collection.

50 Barry's Picture Gallery at Bridgewater House photographed at the beginning of the century. It shows the arrangement that survived until 1939. Bridgewater and Dorchester Houses were the last of their kind: after them the purely classical approach to architecture involving mere vastness as an important feature was abandoned.

51 The Grand Salon at Dorchester House photographed in 1905. It was built for Sir George Holford about 1850. His immense collection, formed with much assistance from the dealer William Buchanan, was sold in three memorable sales at Christie's in 1927/8.

52 View of the Great Hall specially built for the Manchester Art-Treasures Exhibition of 1857. This epoch-making event was inspired by the Prince Consort. It was the first occasion when the general public was permitted to see the pictures, sculpture and ornamental art which private collectors had been amassing in the previous fifty years. Dr Waagen, with his unrivalled knowledge of what was available, assisted in the organisation. There were approximately 1100 Old

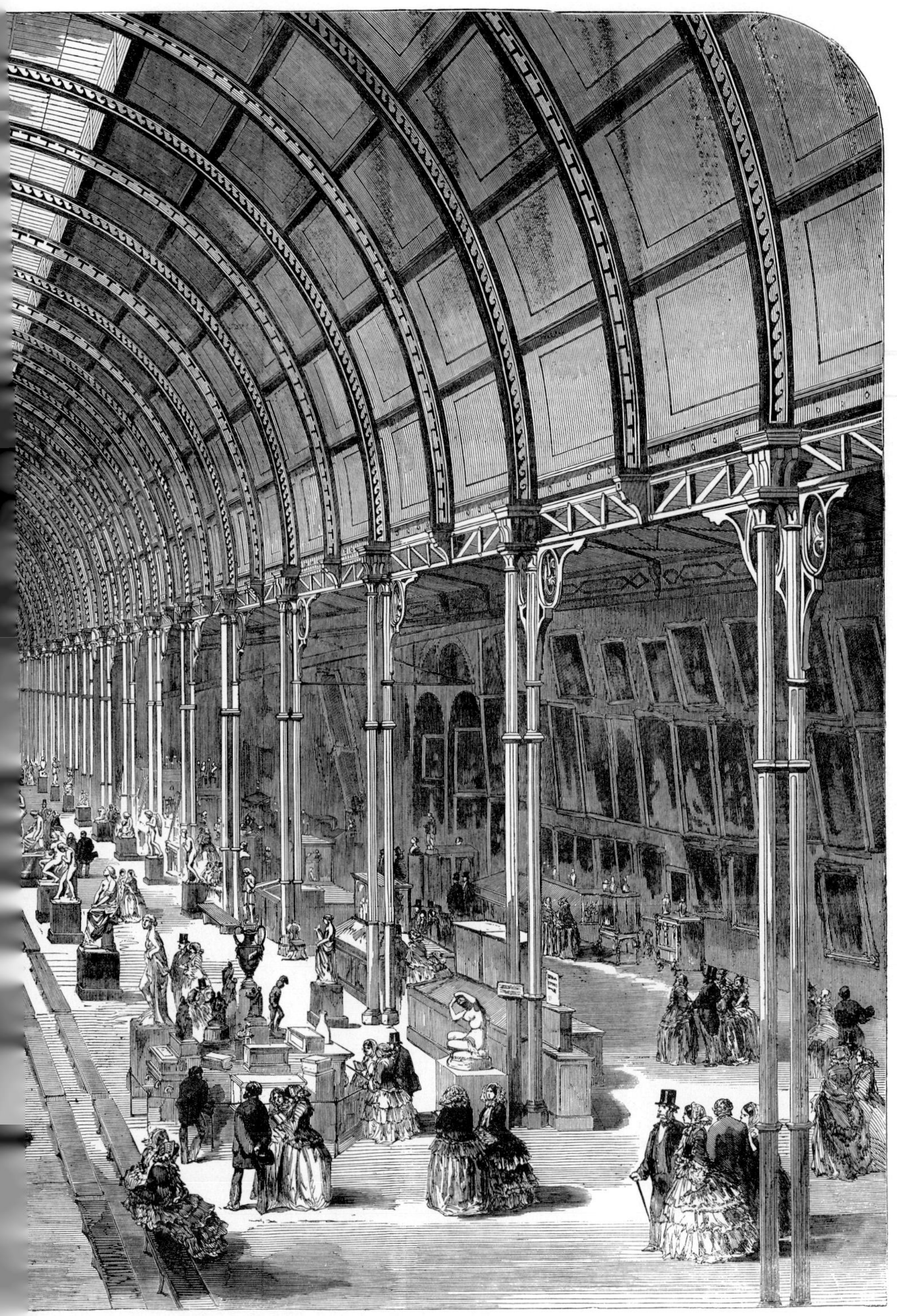

Master paintings, 700 works by contemporary artists, 386 British portraits, 1000 watercolours, the whole conglomeration of the Museum of Ornamental Art, as well as contributions from the British Museum and Marlborough House and the entire Soulages Collection. (See pages 312–320.)

53 Thomas Gainsborough's portrait of James Christie, who founded the auction house in 1766.

54 John Sotheby, who gave his name to the firm founde by his uncle, Samuel Baker, in 1744.

55 Paul Colnaghi (1751–1833).

56 Thomas Agnew (1794–1871).

57 A painting by J. Gebaud of the Carysfort Sale of pictures from Elton in Huntingdonshire at Christie's on 14 June 1828. Being sold is Sir Joshua Reynold's *Snake in the Grass*. It was bought by Sir Robert Peel for £1260. He is the first tall, upright figure in a top hat on the left. The room is the famous Octagon at King Street, and the auctioneer is the second James Christie.

58 Agnew's started in Manchester. Here is the interior of their Exchange Street Gallery about 1840.

59 One of the most enterprising and influential art dealers at the beginning of the nineteenth century was William Buchanan, author of *Memoirs of Painting*. His agent in Italy, James Irvine, secured this triple portrait of Charles I from the Palazzo Bernini in Rome in 1802 and Buchanan put it up for sale at Christie's in 1804. George IV eventually bought it in 1822 for 1000 guineas. It had been painted by van Dyck in 1635 and sent to Italy by Charles so that Bernini could execute a bust.

60 Another very important acquisition in Italy by Irvine on behalf of Buchanan was Rubens' *Peace and War*. Buchanan only discovered after the painting had reached England that it had formerly belonged to Charles I (see page 171). In fact, Rubens had painted it in 1627 in England especially for the great collector–king. The Duke of Sutherland bought it from Buchanan for £3000 and presented it to the National Gallery in 1828.

SIR JOHN SOANE

One of the most unusual collections made during the nineteenth century is that of Sir John Soane, R.A., architect to the Bank of England from 1788 to 1833. It is the more interesting in that the house – 13 Lincoln's Inn Fields – and its very diverse contents form a whole which has remained unchanged since Soane's death. The major influence in the formation of the collection was the architecture that was Soane's profession, but his interest also extended to pictures, sculpture, porcelain, bronzes and manuscripts.

In the Preface to his *Description of the House and Museum* (1836) Soane explains what he had tried to achieve:

One of the objects I had in view was to shew partly by graphic illustration, the union and close connection between Painting, Sculpture and Architecture . . . another purpose is, the natural desire of leaving these works of Art subject as little as possible to the chance of their being removed from the positions relatively assigned to them; they having been arranged as studies for my own mind and being intended similarly to benefit the Artists of future generations.

In the earlier edition of this work (1830) Soane had outlined some of his rather extravagant sentiments on architecture:

What surprising geniuses! – what prodigies then, must those be who are born architects! How much above every other order of men must geniuses be who emerge at once as complete Architects!

His ambition was to see 'our houses with their plaster outsides . . . converted into grand hotels, with facades of solid stone, worthy of the metropolis of this mighty empire'.

This attitude is reflected in the Classical and Neo-Classical sculpture, fragments of columns and capitals that form the largest part of the collection. The most important piece of this kind is the Sarcophagus of Seti I, which Soane bought in 1824. Belzoni unearthed the sarcophagus in 1817 and offered it to the British Museum. After some deliberation they rejected it, and so Soane was able to buy it for the sum of £2000. It is an interesting purchase in that it demonstrates Soane's acumen as a collector. He could not have known its full significance at the time as the hieroglyphics were not deciphered until 1831, but presumably his appreciation of the line drawing of the figure of the Queen of Heaven led him to realise that it was of exceptional value and interest. Certainly he regarded its acquisition as a great triumph.

But perhaps the most interesting aspect of the collection is that it demonstrates the wide diversity of Soane's interests. He was a generous patron to contemporary

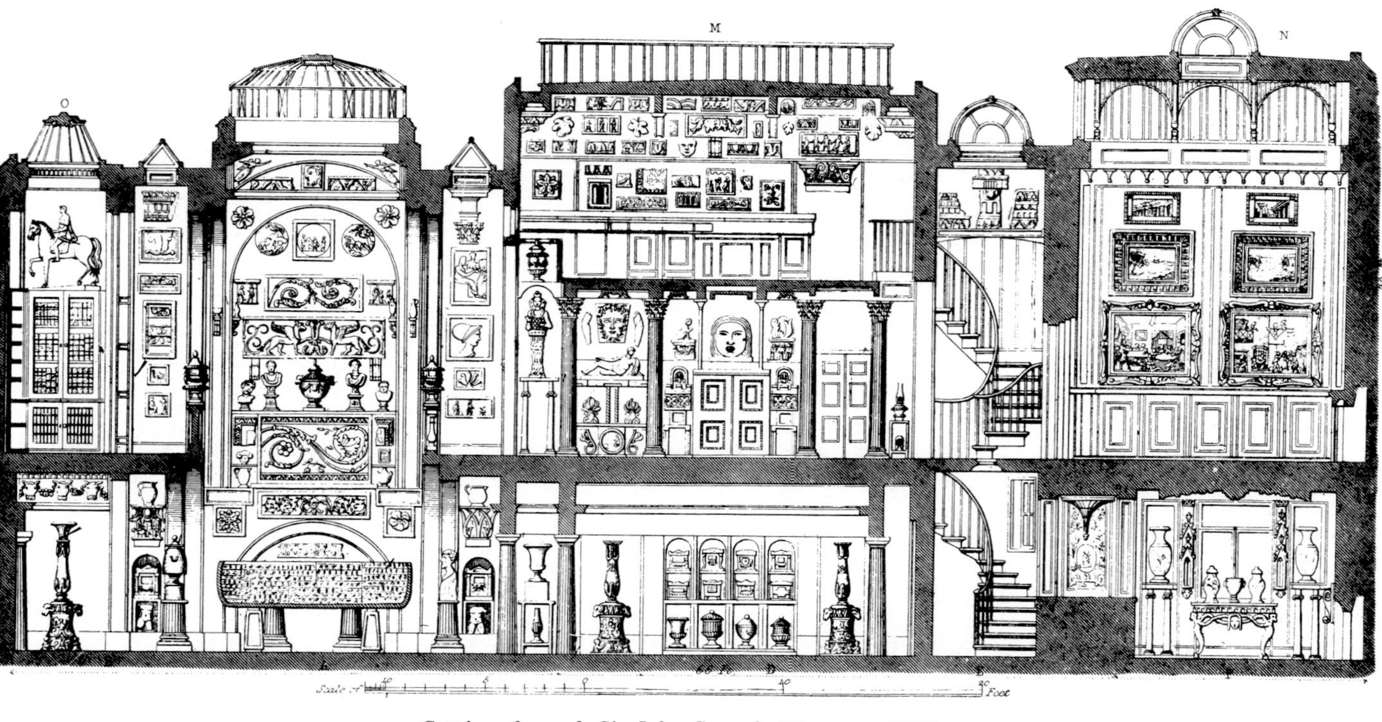

Section through Sir John Soane's Museum, 1827

artists, although by nature tight-fisted and even harsh towards those who were in his debt. Arthur Bolton* considers his patronage 'not always well directed; he had not apparently the same prophetic instinct in painting as in other forms of collecting. His courage in essaying the quicksands of contemporary art must however be applauded.' The following extracts from his correspondence give some idea of his taste in pictures.

To Thomas Stothard L.I.F. 8 May 1814

Dear Sir,

When you mentioned the circumstance of having sent the picture painted for me to the Exhibition, you added that if you had not considered it as mine under a promise, you should have expected two hundred for it instead of one hundred, the sum I was to pay–now certainly I do feel somewhat uneasy at having that for one hundred that you could get two hundred for; and as my request was to have a picture painted from any incident in Shakespeare's plays, allow me therefore to hope, that under these circumstances it may be agreeable to you to paint me at your leisure a subject from Shakespeare *instead* of that of Telemachus. I do not wish to press this request, but can only say your compliance will oblige,

Dear Sir, your very obedient and faithful servant,

J. Soane

L.I.F. 30 April 1820

Mr Soane presents his compliments to Mr Stothard, and [having?] waited more than *six years* for the picture (for which he paid Mr Stothard one hundred pounds) Mr Soane concludes that Mr Stothard is too much engaged to attend to his commission. Mr Soane therefore requests to have the principal returned to him, the use of the money Mr Stothard is welcome to.

It appears, however, that Stothard had executed the commission but that Soane had been dissatisfied with the result. Stothard eventually produced the picture, but it was evidently not accepted as there are only three small drawings by this artist in the museum. The Shakespeare scene was obviously intended for the 'Shrine to Shakespeare' that is contained in an alcove on the staircase. The centrepiece is a replica of the bust of Shakespeare at Stratford-on-Avon, and on the walls, among others, are two pictures by Henry Howard: *Lear and Cordelia* and *The Vision of Shakespeare.*

* *Arthur Bolton was Curator of the Sir John Soane Museum from 1917 to 1945, and the author of* The Portrait of Sir John Soane, R.A. (1753–1837) Set forth in Letters from his Friends (1775–1837) *(London, 1927). The material here quoted from this book is reproduced by kind permission of the Trustees of the Sir John Soane Museum.*

Tuesday Feb 5 1822. Called on Mr [James] Ward. Paid Mr Ward for the painting of Fanny [Mrs Soane's lap dog] which he req[d] to make from the drawing £42!!!!!

From George Jones, R.A., Soane commissioned a painting of the opening of the New London Bridge in 1831:

Now my walls will not bear an acre of canvas, therefore I have to request you to paint me a moderate-sized picture of the Procession on the Bridge–not that I mean to limit you in price as well as size: say 500 guineas and I shan't quarrel with you if you make it a thousand.

There is another picture by Jones in the Soane museum, *The Smoking Room, Chelsea Hospital* and also two original sketches of the coronation of William IV and Queen Adelaide, 8 September 1831.

Other contemporary artists whose work is represented in the museum are Flaxman, Chantrey (from whom Soane commissioned a bust of himself) and Henry Howard. The latter painted two ceiling panels in the library and dining room as well as the Shakespeare scenes, and found Soane 'the most liberal patron I have ever had the fortune to meet with'.

Although Soane concentrated mainly on English contemporary works as far as painting was concerned, he did acquire three pictures by Canaletto: *A View of the Grand Canal*, which was previously in the Colonna Collection and which he bought from Beckford in 1807, and two smaller ones from the collection of the Earl of Bute. In the same room are two heads by Raphael, details from the cartoons, one a copy by John Sanders. Seven of the twelve famous cartoons were brought to England in about 1720. We know that these details of heads were bought by Jonathan Richardson, the painter and collector, but it is not clear precisely where Soane acquired them.

In 1802 he bought a Watteau: *Les Noces* or *L'Accordée du Village* for £42, and in 1841 Turner's *Admiral van Tromp's Barge*, for which he paid 250 guineas. He also acquired the two famous series by William Hogarth: *The Rake's Progress* and *The Election*. The former was bought by Mrs Soane at Colonel Fullarton's sale at Christie's in February 1802, where she paid £570 for them. Sir John Soane bought *The Election*, which was formerly in the collection of the actor David Garrick, also at Christie's in the sale of Mrs Garrick's effects in 1823; he paid 360 guineas for the eight pictures. After he had bought the second series Soane received a letter from George Garrard, the sculptor, relating how the pictures had come to be in Garrick's possession. Apparently Hogarth, despairing of finding a single purchaser for his pictures, had put them up for sale in a raffle. He asked Garrick to subscribe–Garrick unwillingly did so, and then took pity on the artist and bought the whole series for £200.

A number of the objects in his collection were offered to Soane by friends or admirers. A facsimile of the Sketchbook of Inigo Jones, for example, was given to him in 1832 by the Duke of Devonshire, who had had it made at his own expense.

The sculptor Frederick Tatham, on hearing that Soane's collection was 'deservedly celebrated', offered to sell him some of William Blake's drawings, sketches and copper plates 'of a very extraordinary description'.

But Soane's renown as an architect and collector was not without its drawbacks. He suffered a great deal of ridicule and criticism: in 1824 there appeared in the first issue of *Knight's Quarterly Magazine* of that year a witty lampoon on his architectural style entitled 'The Sixth or Boeotian Order of Architecture':

The most robust of the pure Boeotian Columns had not less than 25 diameters. In this country the best public example is exhibited in the columns of the central portico of the pile of building in Regent Street, a part of which is distinguished as the Emporium of Messrs Robins and Co, Auctioneers and Land Agents. [The only building in Old Regent Street by Soane – 1820–21.]

The author continues with an exposition of the 'Doctrines of the Boeotian Style':

(1) That the *Utility* of every building (not merly ornamental) may be sacrificed in any degree to further the architect's views of making it a work of *Fine Art*.

This is exhibited by the Professor *in his own private dwelling*. Situated in the heart of London it might appear to ordinary minds (as it did to ours) essential to admit as much light and air into the interior as possible. But the Professor had to distinguish his house, and to give an instance of the Boeotian style, amidst the mass of unpretending buildings by which he was surrounded . . . [and so on].

One has a sneaking sympathy for this early critic: in the fiercely individualistic character of the collection one can sense the melancholic disposition of its owner. In fact, the last contemporary account we have of Sir John Soane is provided by George Wightwick, a young architect whom he employed as an amanuensis towards the end of his life. Wightwick had hesitated to apply to Soane for a job, because his 'reported eccentricity of mind and irritability of temper occasioned me to reserve him as the desperate ultimatum of forlorn hope'. Nor was Wightwick impressed by the house and its collection, finding a 'positive sense of suffocation in the plethoric compendiousness' and felt he had never before seen 'such a conglomerate of vast ideas in little'. He recorded his interview with Soane in great detail:

. . . his countenance presented, under differing circumstances, two distinct phases. In the one, a physiognomist might read a mild amiability, as cheerful and happy as [it was] 'kind and courteous'; yielding, and requiring gentle sympathy; a delicate sensibility spiced with humour; towards men, a politeness in which condescension and respect were mingled; and towards women, a suavity, enlivened with a show of gallantry, rather sly than shy. The other phase of his countenance indicated an acute sensitiveness, and a fearful irritability, dangerous to himself, if not to others; an embittered heart, prompting a cutting and sarcastic mind; uncompromising pride, neither respecting nor desiring respect; a contemptuous disregard for the feelings of his dependents; and yet, himself, the very victim of irrational impulse; with no pity for the trials of his neighbours, and nothing but frantic despair under his own.

Although the term of office did not last long, Wightwick evidently became very fond of the old man, in spite of his first impressions and although Soane was impossible to work for, he never failed in his kindness towards his former employee.

Soane's style of architecture and tastes in collecting were not always to the liking even of his contemporaries. If we find it difficult to assess his collection objectively today, there is no doubt that his extensive patronage provided some excellent examples of early nineteenth-century art in both painting and sculpture. But the most striking aspect of the collection is its expression of a strongly individual, slightly morbid, temperament which has survived intact in its original form.

CAMILLA TYLER

SIR ROBERT PEEL

EVERY student of English history knows of Sir Robert's political activities and achievements, but few know that he was one of the foremost collectors of his day. He was principally interested in the Dutch School of painting. One of the most detailed descriptions of his collection occurs in Mrs Jameson's *Companion to the Most Celebrated Private Galleries of Art in London*, which was published in 1844. She dedicated the book to Sir Robert and appears to have known him pretty well. Parts of her account are rather sugary: perhaps excessive respect for this collector made her style unusually cloying. There is a fascinating passage in her introduction to the whole work where she is obviously talking about Peel without, in fact, mentioning him by name.

' "I cannot express to you," a most distinguished statesman of the present day [said to me] as we stood in the midst of his beautiful pictures, "I cannot express to you the feeling of tranquillity, of restoration, with which in an interval of harrassing official business I look around me here." And while he spoke in the slow, quiet tone of a weary man he turned his eyes on a forest scene of Ruysdael,[1] and gazed on it for a minute or two in silence, a silence I was careful not to break.'

Sir Robert's pictures were divided between his official residence (as Prime Minister, at the time Mrs Jameson was writing) at 4 Whitehall Gardens, and his country residence at Drayton Manor. She lists 128 paintings, and of the 78 by

Drayton Manor

Dutch and Flemish Masters, only eight were *not* in London.[2] Sir Robert loved his collection very dearly, and liked to have his favourite paintings near at hand. He chose them with an infinity of care.

'It is as if the owner had intended to compromise within the smallest space the largest amount of excellence and beauty and invested wealth. With the exception of about twenty portraits of the English school, and two *chefs d'oeuvres* by Rubens all the pictures are of one school and one age – the Dutch school, properly so called, and by painters of the seventeenth century; all are cabinet pictures; each is a *chef d'oeuvre* of its class and style. Not only is there not one mediocre picture in the collection but there is not one which is not of celebrity and first rate.'

[1] The picture in question, *A Pool Surrounded by Trees and two Sportsmen coursing a hare*, is now in the National Gallery (No. 854). See Plate 66. It was one of three Ruisdaels in Sir Robert's collection.

[2] Of the 56 canvases by English painters, fourteen were portraits by Sir Thomas Lawrence, six by Sir Joshua Reynolds, one by Gainsborough (of William Pitt), and four were attributed to Sir Peter Lely.

Peel had bought most of his paintings through C. J. Nieuwenhuys,[1] John Smith,[2] and occasionally from Buchanan and Woodburn. In the majority of cases Mrs Jameson quotes the price he had paid to the previous owner. It is interesting that Peel was perfectly prepared to have this information publicised. He appears to have had a shrewd sense of values. In a letter dated 7 October 1826,[3] he instructed John Smith to bid for him at the Beckford Sale at Fonthill.[4] Smith obtained a Frans Mieris of a woman feeding a parrot (National Gallery No. 840) for him for 305 guineas. Peel had suggested 250 guineas, or slightly more. Smith also bought a Gerard Dou, *The Poulterer's Shop* (National Gallery No. 825) for 1270 guineas. Peel had suggested £1300.

However, not everybody shared Mrs Jameson's admiration of Peel as a knowledgeable connoisseur. He had become a trustee of the National Gallery in 1827 and it was he who had recommended the appointment of Eastlake as keeper,[5] in succession to William Seguier, in 1847. But it was Eastlake who noted 'that Sir Robert Peel rather opposed the purchase of works by the early Italian masters; his expression always was "I think we should not collect curiosities".'[6] On the strength of another letter from Peel to Smith (2 May 1827), Armstrong and a number of subsequent writers have dismissed Peel as lacking in knowledge and judgement of art. But the truth was that both as a private collector, as well as in his political career, Peel knew exactly what he wanted.

Among his paintings described by Mrs Jameson there were three by Cuyp; *the Poulterer's Shop* by Gerard Dou already mentioned; four by Hobbema including *The Avenue, Middleharnis* (National Gallery No. 830, see Plate 65) two by Pieter de Hoogh (National Gallery Nos. 834, 835), three by Karel du Jardin, two by Metsu; three by Netscher; one by Adriaen and two by Isack van Ostade; a Paulus Potter; three Rembrandts; the *Chapeau de Paille* and another by Rubens; three by Jacob van Ruisdael; a Jan Steen (National Gallery No. 856); three by David Teniers (the Younger) and his *Four Seasons*; a Terborch; two portraits by van Dyck; three by Adriaen and eight by Willem van de Velde; and six by Philip Wouwermans. It was truly 'the finest series of such things ever collected by an amateur'.[7]

In 1842 Mrs Jameson had lamented on the paucity of Dutch masters in the National Gallery. 'We are as yet most poor in the fine masters of the Dutch school.

[1] Author of *A Review of the Lives and Works of some of the most Eminent Painters, with Remarks on the Opinions and Statements of Former Writers*, 1834, and a remarkably successful dealer.

[2] Author of the immense *Catalogue Raisonné of the Works of the most eminent Dutch, Flemish and French Painters*. Nieuwenhuys and Smith had at one time been associates.

[3] Quoted by Sir Walter Armstrong, Director of the National Gallery of Ireland, in *The Peel Collection and the Dutch School of Painting*, 1904.

[4] '. . . and if you should succeed in purchasing them, I don't wish it to be known that they were bought for me.' The sale was made and recorded in the name of S. T. Howe.

[5] Eastlake resigned as such in 1847, and was appointed as first *director* in 1855. See also page 303.

[6] Quoted in *The Making of the National Gallery*, Sir Charles Holmes and C. H. Collins Baker, 1924.

[7] *The Making of the National Gallery*, page 46.

There is not a single specimen of Hobbema or Ruysdael. . . .' She did not live to know that the cream of Sir Robert's collection would one day go to the National Gallery. He died in 1850. In 1871 the National Gallery bought 77 paintings and eighteen drawings from his collection from his descendants for £75,000.[1]

FRANK HERRMANN

THE HOUSE OF SAMUEL ROGERS

SAMUEL Rogers was a banker, a man of letters and a poet as well as a connoisseur. He was born in 1763 and died in 1855, and his lifetime spanned–more than any other man's with a consuming interests in the arts–the period during which English collecting reached its zenith.

His charming house, just by Green Park, at 22 St James's Place, was filled with treasures that had been arranged with quite as much care as Walpole had bestowed on Strawberry Hill, and for many years Rogers entertained here the most distinguished figures in the political, literary and artistic world of the day at his celebrated breakfasts. The literature of the time abounds in enraptured comments on the house. Thus Macaulay wrote in a letter to one of his sisters in June 1831 'I breakfasted with Rogers yesterday. What a delightful house it is! The furniture has been selected with a delicacy of taste quite unique . . .', and Byron, who later quarrelled with Rogers, wrote in his diary 'If you enter his house–his drawing room–his library–you, of yourself, say, this is not the dwelling of a common mind. There is not a gem, a coin, a book, thrown aside on his chimney piece, his sofa, his table, that does not bespeak an almost fastidious elegance in the possessor.'

Rogers' entire collection of paintings, drawings and engravings; Egyptian, Greek and Roman antiquities; his sculptures, Greek vases, coins and furniture; and his enormous library was sold by Christie's in April and May 1856, during a sale lasting twenty days.[2] It realised £45,188. The National Gallery bought a number

[1] Many of the Drayton pictures were sold at Fisher and Robinson in 1901.

[2] Redford in his *Art Sales*–and a host of later writers who appear to have got their facts from him, including W. Roberts in his *Memorials of Christie's* (2 vols., 1897)–refer to the sale as lasting only 18 days. Two additional days were devoted to Rogers' plate, furniture and personal effects and were catalogued separately.

CATALOGUE

OF

THE VERY CELEBRATED COLLECTION

OF

WORKS OF ART,

THE PROPERTY OF

SAMUEL ROGERS, Esq., Deceased;

COMPRISING

ANCIENT AND MODERN PICTURES;

DRAWINGS AND ENGRAVINGS;

EGYPTIAN, GREEK, AND ROMAN ANTIQUITIES;

GREEK VASES;

MARBLES, BRONZES, AND TERRA-COTTAS, AND COINS;

ALSO,

THE EXTENSIVE LIBRARY;

COPIES OF ROGERS'S POEMS, ILLUSTRATED;

THE SMALL SERVICE OF PLATE AND WINE:

Which will be Sold by Auction, by

MESSRS. CHRISTIE AND MANSON,

AT THEIR GREAT ROOM,

8, KING STREET, ST. JAMES'S SQUARE,

On MONDAY, APRIL 28, 1856,

AND EIGHTEEN FOLLOWING DAYS,

AT ONE O'CLOCK PRECISELY.

——o——

May be publicly viewed on Thursday, the 24th, and two following Days, and Catalogues had, price One Shilling, at Messrs. CHRISTIE and MANSON's Offices, 8, *King Street, St. James's Square.*

G. BASSANO.

241.10 709 The good Samaritan, in a crimson dress, raising the wounded Jew, in order to place him on his mule, which stands by ; a silver bottle of wine and two dogs in the foreground ; the Levite seen in the open landscape distance. *This noble study of colouring, full of dignity and feeling, is from the Collection of Sir J. Reynolds, who kept it always hanging in his studio* Bentley — for Nat. Gall.

VELASQUEZ.

1270.10 710 Don Balthazar, son of Charles IV. of Spain, in a black and white dress, with crimson scarf, on a black charger, in the tennis court at Madrid ; a cavalier, attended by a page, and other figures around ; the royal mews are seen in the background. *This noble work was purchased in Spain, by Mr. Woodburn, for Mr. Rogers, at the recommendation of Sir David Wilkie* Nieuwenhuys

N. POUSSIN.

367 10 711 The Campagna of Rome ; a grand composition of broken rocky scenery : a convent in a ravine at the foot of the mountainous background ; a peasant and family resting on a bank beneath a fine group of trees ; a stream of water on the left. *This important work, highly commended by Mrs. Jameson and Waagen, for poetic composition and careful execution, is from the Collection of A. Champernowne, Esq.* Radcliffe

WILSON.

110 5 712 An Italian landscape, with a convent on a rocky height, two figures in conversation in the foreground, and distant view of a river. *From President West's Collection* Sharpe

GAINSBOROUGH.

204 15 713 A landscape, with a group of cattle and peasants on the bank of a river, in which vessels and boats are lying and landing fish. *Painted with wonderful transparency and brilliancy* Holloway

A typical page from an annotated copy of the catalogue.

of the paintings, and Rogers also bequeathed three major works to the Gallery, of which he had become the first untitled trustee in 1834.

Rogers' finest paintings were of the early Italian and the English schools. In fact, he was one of the first English collectors to show an interest in the Italian Primitives. In all his collecting activities he seems to have been guided by his own taste, rather than by the dictates of fashion, though we learn from Redford that Rogers' 'love of art never led him to pay extravagant prices for pictures or objects he admired; indeed, like most city men he seems to have had a dread of paying a large sum for any work of Art, and was never known to exceed £250. Fortunately for his estate, and not less so for the quality of his collection he began to buy . . . as far back as 1816.'

The piece which follows was presumably written after Rogers' death, but before his furniture and belongings were moved to Christie's for the sale. The footnote material with sale prices has been added by Redford.

FROM *The Athenaeum*, 29 December 1855 (also quoted by Redford in *Art Sales*, Vol. I, 1888).

THE poet's house consists merely of a front and back room on each floor, separated by the staircase, and is a narrow strip extending from St James's Place to the Green Park, where its contracted frontage is distinguished by a triple bow-window and curved gilt balcony. The street entrance conducts by a long narrow passage by the side of the staircase direct to the dining-room door. On entering this apartment the large window, shaded by evergreens, at once removes the confined feeling connected with a town house. In front of the window rises, dark and monumental, a handsome mahogany pedestal, surmounted by a beautiful vase; the latter is antique, the former work of Chantrey when a journeyman. Viewed from the window the pedestal has a stove-like appearance. To the right of the door on entering is a sideboard supporting ancient painted Greek vases, and Roubillac's terra-cotta model of the head of Pope. Above the glass is a portion of a fresco from the Carmine at Florence by Giotto.* In the corner to the left and towards the fireplace is the original terra-cotta model by Michelangelo for his well-known statue of the Duke Lorenzo dei Medici. Over the chimney-piece is the sketch by Velasquez of 'The Infant Don Balthazar'.† Between the fireplace and the window is the poet's writing-table, and immediately on a level with his eye were three small pictures. The right-hand one 'Christ on the Mount of Olives',‡ was painted by Raphael when about two-and-twenty. It is one of a series of pictures that ornamented the *predella* or step of the great altar-piece executed by Raphael

* *Bought for the National Gallery for* £78 15*s.*

† *It was sold for* 1210 *guineas to Sir Richard Wallace in the Rogers' Sale. Rogers had bought it through an agent in Spain in* 1827.

‡ *Purchased at the sale for the Baroness Burdett-Coutts for* 450 *guineas and in her Collection still. It was once in the Orleans Gallery, and afterwards in Lord Eldin's Collection, Edinburgh.*

for the nuns of St Antonio at Perugia. The large picture is in the Royal Palace at Naples:* the other compartments of the *predella* belong to Mr Miles of Leigh Court,† and Mrs Whyte of Barron Hill.‡ The remaining subjects over Mr Rogers' writing-table are a Virgin and Child worshipped by six saints, by Ludovico Carracci, and a lovely landscape ('The Mill') by Claude,§ No. II of the *Liber Veritatis*.

On this side of the room is the magnificent sketch by Tintoretto for his celebrated picture of the 'Miracle of the Slave'.|| It formerly belonged to Pilkington. Near, on the same wall hangs a fine original study by Titian of Charles V on horseback. Low down, next the window, is one of the most powerfully painted heads by Rembrandt–being his own portrait.** The touches and texture are truly marvellous. On the wall facing the fireplace is the large study by Paul Veronese†† for the celebrated picture in the Durazzo Palace, from which it differs in many respects. Mr Rogers purchased it from the Hope Collection in 1816 for £90. This is the picture which he actually crawled on his hands and knees to obtain. Near it are a superb sketch by Rubens for the picture 'The Horrors of War' in the Pitti Palace at Florence, and the head of our Saviour, by Guido‡‡–one of the three destined to grace our National Gallery.§§ Many of the largest pictures in this room are contrived by very simple machinery to advance from the wall and turn in almost every possible direction.

Immediately from the dining-room door to the left the staircase leads by a curved and unbroken flight of steps to the first floor, opening by a door upon a covered gallery connecting the drawing-room with the small square apartment in front, which is the poet's celebrated library. The gallery is lighted by a glazed window from the staircase, the walls of which are relieved by choice casts from the marbles of the Parthenon. Here, scarcely to be seen, is hung the sketch, by Titian for the famous 'Gloria'|||| at Madrid. Here, in semi-darkness, are some of the choicest painted Greek vases and Egyptian sculptures. Some of the rarest objects of *vertu* are laid out on a table, including an especially fine specimen of a Greek Rhyton. The library is lined with bookcases surmounted by Greek vases, each one remarkable for its exquisite beauty of form. Upon the gilt lattice-work of the bookcases are lightly hung in frames some of the finest original sketches by Raphael, Michelangelo, and Andrea del Sarto, and finished paintings by Angelico da Fiesole and Fouquet of Tours. Modern works also by Turner, Wilkie, and Mulready are there. The large painting by Reynolds of Cupid and Psyche is over the fireplace in the same apartment. Over the drawing-room fireplace, sculptured by Flaxman, is the study by Rubens*** from Andrea Mantegna's

* *Since sold to a Spanish nobleman for the ex-king.*

† *Sold in the Leigh Court Sale,* 1884, *for* 560 *guineas (Agnew for Lord Windsor).*

‡ *Bought by Mr Whyte at Sir Thomas Lawrence's Sale in* 1830.

§ *Bought by Baroness Burdett-Coutts for* £693.

|| *Bought by the Baroness Burdett-Coutts for* £430 10*s and in her Collection.*

** *Bought by Mr Rogers for* £69, *sold for* £325 10*s*.

†† *Bought by Baroness Burdett-Coutts for* £399.

‡‡ *Bequeathed in* 1855 *to National Gallery. Cost Mr Rogers* £26 15*s* 6*d*.

§§ *The Rubens was purchased by the National Gallery at the sale for* £210.

|||| *Bought by Lord H. Vane for* £283 10*s*.

*** *Purchased at the sale by the National Gallery for* £1102 10*s*.

triumphal procession of Julius Caesar, now at Hampton Court. Beneath this picture is a range of interesting miniatures and various relics, including orange-blossoms under glass. The chief picture towards the window is the beautiful 'Noli me Tangere' by Titian. It is fortunately destined to pass to the National Gallery.* Over the sofa hang pictures by Watteau, Le Nain, and Jan van Eyck, the latter a most exquisitely painted figure of Madonna and Child, surmounted by the richest ornamental architecture. Facing the window is a bold allegorical picture by Rembrandt, and a mellow moonlight scene by Rubens. Opposite the chimney-piece a cabinet of light wood is panelled with pictures by Stothard. The subjects are the characters of Shakespeare, the Canterbury Pilgrims, the characters of the Decameron, and the Sans Souci. In the centre of this side of the room is a fine picture of Annibal Carracci of 'The Coronation of the Virgin'; another repetition of this subject hangs to the right, but is very different in treatment. It is a small altar-piece by Lorenzo di Credi.† Near this again hangs the well-known Madonna and Child from the Orleans Gallery, attributed to Raphael, but certainly differing in feeling, form, and tone of colour from others of his known works at that period.‡ An extraordinary *riposo* by Correggio, § remarkable for power of handling and incorrect drawing, is possibly one of his early genuine works. The famous 'Puck', by Sir Joshua Reynolds,|| graces this room, and the collection possesses altogether seven excellent specimens of this English master.

THE COLLECTION OF SAMUEL ROGERS

THIS description of Rogers' collection was the final item in Mrs Jameson's *Companion to the Most Celebrated Private Galleries of Art in London*. It is not given in its entirety here. It was followed by a detailed catalogue of the paintings. Mrs Jameson also included a brief description of the separate collection of Rogers' sister, who at that time shared her brother's house. One gathers that she was an unassuming person, with a remarkably fine taste for early Italian and Flemish, and contemporary English paintings. Some of these she had inherited from another brother.

---

* *Bequeathed by Mr Rogers.*

† *Purchased by the late Lord Overstone for* £399, *and now in the Collection of Lord Wantage at Lockinge House, Berks.*

‡ *Mr Rogers is said to have given only* 60 *guineas for this beautiful little picture, which now brought* 480 *guineas.*

§ *Sold for* £252. *Cost Mr Rogers* £53 11*s.*

|| *Bought by Lord Fitzwilliam for* £1029. *Mr Rogers gave* £215 15*s. Reynolds sold it to Boydell for* £105.

ANNA JAMESON

EXTRACTED FROM Mrs Anna Jameson's *Companion to the Most Celebrated Private Galleries of Art in London*, 1844.

PICTURES are for use, for solace, for ornament, for parade; –as invested wealth, as an appendage of rank. Some people love pictures as they love friends; some, as they love music; some, as they love money. And the collectors of pictures take rank accordingly. There are those who collect them for instruction, as a student collects grammars, dictionaries, and commentaries: these are artists; such were the collections of Rubens, of Sir Peter Lely, of the President West, of Lawrence, of Sir Joshua Reynolds. There are those who collect pictures around them as a king assembles his court–as significant of state, as subservient to ornament or pride; such were Buckingham and Talleyrand. There are those who collect pictures as a man speculates in the funds–picture-fanciers, like bird-fanciers, or flower-fanciers–amateur picture-dealers, who buy, sell, exchange, bargain; with whom a glorious Cuyp represents £800 sterling, and a celebrated Claude is £3000 securely invested–safe as a bank; and his is not the right spirit, surely. Lastly, there are those who collect pictures for love, for companionship, for communion; to whom each picture, well-chosen at first, unfolds new beauties–becomes dearer every day; such a one was Sir George Beaumont–such a one is Mr Rogers.

To select a cabinet of pictures which, within a small space, shall include what is at once beautiful, valuable, and rare is a matter of time as well as of taste. It cannot be done easily–it cannot be done in a hurry. It requires a profound knowledge of the immutable principles on which high art is founded; and not merely the perception of truth and beauty, but a certainty of tact and judgement, which is perfectly independent of the variation of fashion, or the competition of vanity. To choose, not that which appears beautiful *now*, tempting to the fancy, new to the eye, coveted by others, but that which is crowned with perennial beauty, sanctified by ages of fame, beyond the power of fashion, or caprice, or change of time or place, to take anything from its intrinsic merit and value–that is the difficulty. And if few know how to select pictures, I know nothing that requires more taste, feeling, and experience, than their arrangement when selected. A public gallery should be arranged with a view to instruction; a certain system of classification and chronological progression should be aimed at. The Pinnakothek, at Munich, and the Museum at Berlin, for instance, are models of correct and instructive arrangement. In a private collection, which is usually a part of our *domesticité*, such a formal system would be chilling and pedantic. The pictures should be so hung as to produce a harmony in variety. Schools and artists of every style may be intermingled with good effect, provided that in colour they do not eclipse each other, nor produce a harsh contrast to the eye, nor in subject strike a discord in the mind or the fancy. They are dwellers with us under the same roof, and their presence should be felt often when not observed. One would not hang a group of drunken boors, by Ostade, though a *chef-d'oeuvre* in its way, under a Madonna of Raphael or Correggio; nor a Rubens where he would *kill* his next neighbour–beside the pale pathos of Guido, for instance. It is very seldom that you can hang a modern picture near an old one, and this, in many cases, more from the contrast in tone and feeling, than the positive difference in point of value

COMPANION

TO THE

MOST CELEBRATED

PRIVATE GALLERIES OF ART

IN LONDON.

CONTAINING

ACCURATE CATALOGUES, ARRANGED ALPHABETICALLY,
FOR IMMEDIATE REFERENCE,
EACH PRECEDED BY AN HISTORICAL & CRITICAL INTRODUCTION,
WITH A PREFATORY ESSAY ON ART, ARTISTS,
COLLECTORS, & CONNOISSEURS.

BY MRS. JAMESON.

THE GALLERY OF HER MAJESTY THE QUEEN.
THE BRIDGEWATER GALLERY.
THE SUTHERLAND GALLERY.
THE GROSVENOR GALLERY.
THE COLLECTION OF THE MARQUESS OF LANSDOWNE.
THE COLLECTION OF THE RT. HON. SIR ROBERT PEEL.
THE COLLECTION OF MR. ROGERS.

LONDON
SAUNDERS AND OTLEY, CONDUIT STREET.
1844.

3 The Good Samaritan.—Most admirable for character as well as colour, and far more dignified in feeling than is usual with Bassano.

In both these pictures the subjects are in harmony with the painter's particular turn of mind, and therefore excellent. 3 ft. 4 in. by 2 ft. 7 in.

4 The Nativity.—Treated in his usual homely, familiar style, as a group of peasants. The animals, and the colouring, excellent.

BAROCCIO (Federigo), b. 1528; d. 1612.

[A painter who is *sometimes* very sweet in colour and elegant in design; but generally he affected a rosy tint in his hues, and a flimsy prettiness in his compositions, ill adapted to the large sacred subjects he treated. Though he studied in the Roman school, he was strongly influenced by Correggio and Parmigiano.]

5 A Holy Family—called the "Madonna del Gatto." A repetition of the same subject now in the National Gallery. 3 ft. 8½ in. by 3 ft.

CARRACCI (Ludovico), b. 1555; d. 1619. See p. 84.

6 The Virgin and Child, with Six Saints.— A small and beautiful picture, a repetition of the same subject which is in the collection of the Marquess of Lansdowne, (No. 8,) and already described. It was brought by Mr. Rogers from Bologna.*

CARRACCI (Annibal), b. 1560; d. 1609.

7 The Coronation of the Virgin—by the Father and the Son. In the centre of the picture, the Holy Virgin, with the Father and the Son on each side, seated on a semicircular throne; a crowd of angels attending, some of whom perform a heavenly concert, in the foreground; while myriads of angelic spirits seem to float around, and melt into the dazzling abyss of light behind.

* I have heard that Lord Lansdowne gave 500*l.* for his picture. Mr. Rogers, who had long admired it, and at the sale had coveted it, found this little picture, also a genuine original, hanging in the house of a nobleman at Bologna, and purchased it for a sum not exceeding 30 guineas.

A typical page from Mrs Jameson's 'Companion'.

and merit. Mr Rogers has hung Sir Joshua Reynolds' Laughing Girl close to that splendid vivid sketch of Tintoretto, the Miracle of St Mark–and Sir Joshua stands it bravely, does not lose a tone or a tint; but anything else painted in the last fifty years would look like chalk and brickdust beside it. A private collection confined to works of one particular class –as the Queen's Gallery, or Sir Robert Peel's–is less exciting and agreeable than one in which the schools of art are mingled; but to mingle them with judgement is the difficulty. In short, it is the highest criterion of an exact, as well as an elevated taste in art, to select a small collection of pictures of various date, style, and feeling; to hang them in the same room; and so to hang them, that neither the eye shall be offended by inharmonious propinquity, nor the mind disturbed by unfit associations.

The small but most beautiful collection which we are now to consider, is a very perfect example of all that has been alluded to. It comprises about seventy pictures, which have been brought together at intervals during a period of nearly fifty years. In its gradual formation, we trace the same union of exquisite taste with good sense–the same symmetry of mind, in short, which has apparently governed the whole existence of the poet who formed it. He appears to have arranged his cabinet and his life on the same plan, and both are the true reflection of his genius: everywhere the graceful and elevated prevail–everywhere the feeling of harmonious beauty; simplicity polished into consummate elegance, pathos which stops short of pain. . . .

Had I undertaken to educate the eye and the mind of one not deficient in sensibility, but whose taste was yet to be formed, I should desire nothing more or better than occasional access to such a collection as this. An acquaintance with and a due appreciation of what is here, would fix the standard of excellence at such a height, even while it extended the sphere of sympathy and enjoyment, that the former could not be easily lowered, nor the latter easily narrowed, after such an initiation. . . .

What we call, in speaking of pictures, *colour–colouring*–may be most happily illustrated in this collection; the variety of perfection is brought within so small a compass, and the power of immediate comparison is so easy and delightful. An eye for colour is like an ear for music; where deficient, it cannot be imparted, but where it exists, it may be cultivated up to a keener and more discriminating sense of enjoyment. Pictures in which colour is a predominant charm, demand in the spectator a corresponding faculty of colour, to appreciate them wholly. There are certain pictures of Rubens, which, before we are near enough to discern form or subject, affect the senses like a bed of flowers with the sunshine playing over them. Others of old Bassano, which gleam with inward light, like a handful of rubies and emeralds, and others of Giorgione and Titian, which with their voluptuous richness of blended hues, intoxicate the sense, like mingled perfume and music. Here the various styles of colour, so called, may be distinguished from each other, and the significance of the epithets by which they are characterised, may be *felt*. The golden hue of Titian, the more fervid and fiery (*fiammeggiante*) glow of Giorgione, the gem-like radiance of Bassano, the vivid contrasts of Tintoretto, the rainbow-like magnificence of Rubens, and the more sober splendour of Paul Veronese; the luminous depth of Rembrandt, the pallid tenderness of Guido, the massive effects of Guercino, the roseate delicacy of Baroccio; and then comes our own Sir Joshua, and takes his place, unreproved, in the near neighbourhood of Rubens, Titian, and Tintoretto, gaining, rather than losing, by a propinquity, which would have annihilated any other. . . .

But though the colourists, so called, may be said to predominate in this collection, and to give it a particular and most attractive charm, it possesses as a school of study, a yet higher value. There are certain pictures here, which may be said to *epitomise* the characteristic merits of the greatest painters. For instance, Titian: not colour merely, every beauty for which the great Venetian is celebrated, is concentrated in the little picture of the 'Noli me tangere'–dignity, impassioned sentiment, luxuriant colour, and that peculiar richness of landscape, of which he and Giorgione gave the first examples. It adds to every other merit, that of perfect preservation, so that the very workmanship of the painter may be here illustrated in detail.

Another picture, most particularly characteristic, is the 'Coronation of the Virgin', by Annibal Carracci. It is not only a perfect example of all the best qualities of Annibal, but it illustrates a particular era in his career as an artist. Nearly the same may be said of the Tintoretto; all the unbridled fancy, the *furia*, the union of colour and chiaroscuro, the ready, felicitous execution, the happy adaptation of natural incident in a miraculous story–in short, all the characteristics of Tintoretto, are brought together in so striking a manner, that no one who has looked on this picture can fail to understand at once the man and the painter. So the sketch by Rubens is a combination, on a small scale, of every quality for which Rubens is remarkable, his sumptuous fancy, his turn for allegory, his potent luxuriance of colour, his ardent life and movement, his energy and facility of touch – all are here. There is not, perhaps, a more interesting picture in the world, than Rubens' version of Andrea Mantegna's 'Triumph of Julius Caesar'. It is so far from being a *copy*, that it is a kind of double original. It is the blended reflection of two master minds, the antipodes of each other, and here meeting midway. It is as wonderful as a psychological curiosity, as it is beautiful as a work of art.

Another picture, so characteristic as to be in itself an epitome of the mind and manner of the painter, is the head of Christ, by Guido; the same which has been so finely engraved by Sharp, with the inscription, 'Behold and see if there was ever sorrow like unto my sorrow.' It is a sketch, which Mr West declared must have been painted in one day. There is no retouching, no varnish; the impasto is so thin, that the canvas is merely covered. It is what Coleridge would call 'a single projection of mind', and the certainty of hand, the grace of the execution, as such, is quite inimitable. With regard to the mental part of the picture it has more of pathos and beauty than of character, and in this, also, it is most *characteristic* of the master.

The pictures most valuable, as illustrating the progress of art, are those of Giotto, Angelico, Lorenzo Credi, Van Eyck, and Hans Hemmelinck [Memlinc]; but these, like all the others, have been selected for their beauty and sentiment, not as mere curiosities.

Some other pictures add to their own intrinsic value all the charm and sanctity of memory – they have belonged to great men or personal friends, Sir Joshua Reynolds, West, Lawrence, Ottley, &c.

As the history of each picture is given in detail in the catalogue, I will not trust myself to enlarge further. The eye cannot fall on a single object around us, which is not suggestive of a thousand fancies: words in which to clothe them rush to the pen, but there is discretion in knowing where to stop – and I stop here.

ON THE HAZARDS OF SHOWING ONE'S COLLECTION

THE text of the book, *The Print Collector*, from which the following quotation is taken, has a charming affinity with books of sermons published at about the same period. Its anonymous author was, in fact, the Rev. J. Maberley. It abounds in such ingenuous observations as 'there is a strong and very general propensity in human nature to be perpetually acquiring and appropriating', or 'pity it is that the elegant pursuits of the intellect cannot be indulged without the necessity of being contaminated with the mercenary considerations of pounds, shillings and pence'. However, any collector will sympathise with the passage that follows.

THE PRINT COLLECTOR

EXTRACTED FROM *The Print Collector*, 1844.

THE collector must be warned to prepare himself for certain unpleasant inconveniences which will arise out of this very quality of the popularity of the objects of his pursuit. He will soon discover that though all may be amused, there are but few who judiciously admire; and he must not expect, while a whole company crowd round his portfolio, that his finest specimens will be in any degree appreciated, and, except on special occasions, when he may have reason to think that they will be so, he will grow reluctant to display them. Nevertheless, he should not be too jealous of the intrusion of the uninitiated, but endeavour to possess himself of sufficient magnanimity to suppress that contemptuous sort of feeling which his brethren are sometimes too apt to entertain with respect to all who have not a kindred taste; he should bear in mind that there are many who, though ignorant, are desirous to learn; many who have good natural taste, though untutored and indisciplined; and he will find pleasure in discerning indications of these qualities, and will, on such occasions, hazard a display of his divine things, even at the risk of hearing his gods blasphemed.

It must be confessed, indeed, that the temperament of an exhibitor is sometimes put severely to the test: remarks will now and then be made which are not at all germane to those feelings which the contemplation of the work displayed is calculated properly to excite. When a print, which has been previously proclaimed to be of importance, is produced before an assembly of uninitiated, the first secret feeling, is generally, disappointment, and the first observable effect a solemn pause of decorous silence; but presently an observation is hazarded, in a low tone, which awfully discloses the total insensibility of the

speaker to any one quality for which the work is admirable. 'What can it be?' said a young lady after contemplating a fine print of the Fall of Phaeton. 'Do look, mamma; what is it?' The old lady looked attentively. 'Really my dear, I do not know what it is; but it seems to be a sad accident.' Gentle reader, if when you have become a collector, and are exhibiting the large 'Descent from the Cross' by Rembrandt, and are expecting exclamations of admiration at the wonderful flood of light which is streaming in bright beams from heaven, blazing on the wood of the cross, and on the fur cap, back and arms of the man who is leaning over it, do not sink into the earth, if, instead of any such burst, you hear uttered in a whisper, 'Do look at the man on the ladder; what a great patch he has got on his trousers!' Endeavour, also to reconcile yourself to the very general, but sickening phrase, '*They* have made'; 'How large *they* have made the men in the boats'–as if a fine picture or print were like a piece of machinery, manufactured by such a one 'and Co.', which, by the way, with respect to prints of the present day, is an idea in some measure realised; of which more hereafter. Neither lose all patience, if, when you display your 'John Sylvius', your spectators, without noticing the portrait, immediately begin spelling, with great industry, the words around and underneath, puzzling out the Latin for the ladies; or if the only exclamation be, 'Bless me, how like Mr Dash!'

Even these disheartening shocks are less terrible than the smile of incredulity, so often ill concealed, when an antiquary produces to view something, which no-one chooses to believe to be what it professes to be, and is. Incredulity is often very undeserved. A friend of ours has a genuine curiosity, which we have frequently seen him exhibit, and then, for one that reverenced, there were ten that smiled. It is a small portion of the hair of Edward the Fourth, King of Scotland. Our friend, when a boy was present with Mr Emlyn, the architect, at the time of the discovery by the latter, in St George's Chapel, at Windsor, of the tomb of this king, in the year 1789, as described fully in the publications of the Antiquarian Society, 'Vetusta Monumenta', vol. iii, pl. 7 and 8. He then and there made this rape of the lock, and wrapped it in a piece of newspaper, which also he preserves, as it bears the stain of the liquid in which the king's body was found immersed. So difficult is it to obtain credit for the genuineness of an article of uncommon or unexpected occurrence; and the conclusion is, that the line of collecting is the best to take up, in which there is least vantage ground for scepticism to chill enthusiasm.

THE FOUNDING OF THE NATIONAL GALLERY

THE most important event in the whole of the history of English collecting was the foundation of the National Gallery in 1824. A multitude of enlightened collectors had striven for this during the previous forty years.[1] But the clamour began to become really vocal about 1805, and was concentrated largely in the Royal Academy and the British Institution. Sir Joshua Reynolds, James Barry, John Opie, Benjamin West and Sir Thomas Bernard were all fervent advocates of the cause. Travellers–and most connoisseurs were great travellers–brought back reports from the Continent of the opening of other fine public galleries: Vienna in 1781, Paris in 1793, Amsterdam in 1808, Madrid in 1809 and even Berlin had decided to go ahead in 1821 (though the musuem was not opened until 1830).

Conversely Mrs Jameson had written in 1842, 'it has been a subject of astonishment to intelligent foreigners that, in a country like England, possessed of such vast resources both in wealth and power, no National Gallery of art belonging, or at least accessible, to the public at large, should have existed till within the last twenty years.'

Curiously enough, to this day there is still no single, detailed and authoritative history of how the National Gallery came into being and of its early days.[2] Yet the piecemeal literature is immense. William Whitley's sober account of the correspondence that brought the National Gallery into being is an excellent summary of the final course of events, and it gives Sir George Beaumont the share of the credit that is his due. Mrs Jameson seems to think that Lord Liverpool, who had been Prime Minister since 1812 and who was certainly struggling with more than his fair share of problems over the collapse of trade, unemployment and civil unrest that were the natural sequels of a great and exhausting war, was made more hesitant about the proposal of buying the Angerstein Collection for the nation, than one might gather from the correspondence that follows: 'He and his other ministers were absolutely intimidated by the fierce attacks of the economists, and

[1] We have already seen the fierce obsession which Buchanan shared with many of his clients that the masterpieces they had been able to acquire from the Continent should eventually find a place in some major public gallery in England.

[2] The nearest thing to it is a 1s 6d pamphlet published in 1924 to mark the Gallery's first centenary. But as the authors (Sir Charles Holmes and C. H. Collins Baker) themselves state, it is 'the most hurried of summaries' and there is much evidence of the haste with which it was compiled. It is sad that the National Gallery, which probably has the best departmental catalogues of any major picture gallery in the world, should lack a reliable history of its formation, and a critical account of the periods of office of its many distinguished directors, but a major work on the subject is now in preparation.

scarcely dared propose such a measure themselves, dreading the apathy of some and the animosity of others.'

What Mrs Jameson did not appreciate was that Lord Liverpool's hand had been considerably strengthened by the unexpected return, at least in part, of two loans which had been made to Austria twenty-five years earlier in order to involve the Austrians in the war against the French. The sum concerned was approximately £6 million. After endless debates in Parliament and enquiries by special sub-committees, the Prime Minister decided against extending the facilities of the British Museum to include a national collection of pictures, and to set up a separate gallery for the purpose.

In a letter which Beaumont wrote to Lord Dover in 1823, after hearing that Lord Hertford was bidding for the Angerstein pictures, he said: 'I would rather see them in the hands of his Lordship than have them lost to the country; but I would rather see them in a Museum than in the possession of any individual, however responsible in rank or taste; because taste is not inherited, and there are few families in which it succeeds for three generations. My idea, therefore, is, that the few examples which remain perfect can never be so safe as under the guardianship of a body which never dies; and I see every year such proofs of the carelessness with which people suffer these inestimable relics to be rubbed, scraped, and polished, as if they were the family plate, that I verily believe, if they do not find safe asylum, in another half century little more will be left than the bare canvases.'

After Lord Liverpool had taken the plunge, and his offer for the collection had been accepted, Beaumont wrote in another letter to Dover: 'I think the public already begin to feel [that] works of art are not merely toys for connoisseurs, but solid objects of concern to the nation; and those who consider it in the narrowest point of view will perceive that works of high excellence pay ample interest for the money they cost.'

In 1826 Beaumont made good his earlier promise of supporting the new gallery in kind as soon as accommodation had been found for it, and made a formal gift of his pictures, then valued at £7500, to the nation. 'This,' says Mrs Jameson, 'was the first example given of private munificence.' She points out how much greater is the personal sacrifice to a collector of making a *gift* of this sort rather than a *bequest*. In fact, this action led to the famous story of how Sir George begged to have returned to him Claude's little *Hagar and the Angel*, until such time as he died, because he was so miserable without it.

In 1831 the Rev. William Holwell Carr's valuable collection of 35 paintings was bequeathed to the gallery as he too had promised many years earlier. It included Tintoretto's *St George and the Dragon* and Rembrandt's *Woman Bathing*. There was so little room left in the gallery at Pall Mall by this time that Seguier could only hang a few paintings from the new bequest. Constable much admired the Rembrandt when he saw it displayed, as well as Gaspar Poussin's *Storm: the Union of Dido and Aeneas*. This was in strange contrast to his much quoted letter written when the idea of a National Gallery was still being mooted in December 1822: 'Should there be a National Gallery (which is talked of), there will be an end of the art in poor old England, and she will become in all that relates to painting as much a nonentity as every other country that has one. The reason is plain; the manufacturers of pictures are then made the criterion of perfection, instead of nature.' But it was good to know that one of the few opponents to a national gallery (known to us now), should have been so fully converted in its favour.

When the painter Haydon visited the gallery soon after its opening, he wrote in his diary 'it was delightful to walk into the gallery just as you felt inclined, without trouble or inconvenience. I argue a great and rapid advance to the art of the country from the facility of comparison this will afford the public.'

The gallery at 100 Pall Mall was administered by a staff of seven and for many years the total cost of running it was less than £1000 per annum. Initially under Seguier, a Major Thwaites acted most conscientiously as Assistant Keeper and Secretary for some thirty years, always at his original salary of £150 a year! For the first three months Seguier and Thwaites were left undisputedly in charge, but in July 1824 a 'Committee of six gentlemen' was nominated by the Treasury 'to undertake the Superintendence of the National Gallery'. It consisted of Lords Liverpool, Ripon, Aberdeen, Farnborough, Sir George Beaumont and Sir Thomas Lawrence. In 1827 the number was increased to eight by the nomination of Lord Dover and Sir Robert Peel. Formerly no officially minuted meetings had been held, but the businesslike habits of Sir Robert Peel brought about the innovation of occasional formal meetings of the Trustees, as they were by then called.

The arrangement of the pictures in the gallery left much to be desired, and the use of the remaining wall space needed for additional gifts, bequests and purchases only made matters worse. The pictures were hung frame to frame, and reached from floor to ceiling.[1] Criticism of the lack of classification and of some of the purchases soon began to be heard. By 1831, the Trustees were beginning to devote a great deal of time to the plans and arrangement of a new building that was to be erected in the newly named Trafalgar Square (on the site of the old King's Mews). William Wilkins was to be the architect. He had defeated John Nash in a limited competition.

Building operations began in 1833; the young Queen inspected the new museum early in 1838 and it was opened to the public on 9 April that year. The premises were shared with the Royal Academy for many years.

Finally, two lots of statistics are of interest. During the year 1835 the number of visitors to the Pall Mall Gallery was 130,000. The number admitted to the

[1] On his first visit to England in 1835, Dr Waagen wrote: 'The house in which these treasures of art are for the present deposited is in Pall Mall, but [it is] by no means worthy of them. The four rooms have a dirty appearance; and, with great depth, so little light, that most of the pictures are but imperfectly seen. They are hung without any arrangement, as chance has decided.' *Works of Art and Artists in England*, Vol. I.

Trafalgar Square Gallery from October 1839 to October 1840 had risen to 768,244. The number of visitors to the (now vastly enlarged) National Gallery in 1966 was 1,520,621.[1]

Nearly a hundred years after its foundation, in 1922 the number of paintings owned by the National Gallery had reached a total of 2863. Of these only 701 had been purchased, at a total cost of £814,648 16s 7d; an average of £1162 per picture. In 1961 a single painting by Rembrandt was sold at Parke-Bernet for £821,000.[2] However much the value of money may have changed, the earlier figure is a remarkable tribute to the stewardship of the National Gallery's first eight Keepers and Directors,[3] as well as to the generosity of the English collectors and artists who gave or bequeathed their pictures to the nation.

EXTRACTED FROM William T. Whitley's
Art in England 1821–1837, 1930.

THE month of May, which saw the hanging of the new picture of Trafalgar by Turner, also witnessed the opening of the National Gallery. . . . The need of such an institution had been urged on the Government for many years by the press, and by private persons of influence. Of the latter none was more ardent or more unselfish than Sir George Beaumont. His friend Lord Dover,[4] when speaking of him after his death, said that the foundation of a National Gallery was the object that Sir George had most at heart. 'During the years 1821, 1822 and 1823', said Lord Dover, 'he was constantly talking to me on the subject, and urging the various reasons which rendered such an institution desirable in this country. He frequently begged me to speak to the Prime Minister, Lord Liverpool, about it, and always assured me he would give his own pictures to the nation, as soon as he saw a place allotted for their reception.'

Beaumont's desire was realised in 1824 owing to the death in 1823 of John Julius Angerstein, a wealthy London merchant of Russian extraction who owned one of the most famous collections of pictures in England.[5] Sir Thomas Lawrence, who had been

[1] The number of visitors on a single Sunday afternoon in November 1967 to the Metropolitan Museum in New York was over 54,000. This was not a record. The interested crowds in American museums, particularly on Saturdays and Sundays, seem quite astonishing to visitors from England.

[2] *Aristotle contemplating the Bust of Homer*, Alfred W. Erickson Sale, Parke-Bernet, New York, 15 November 1961.

[3] William Seguier, 1824–1843; Charles Eastlake, 1843–1847; Thomas Uwins, 1847–1855 – all as *Keepers*; Charles Eastlake, 1855–1866, as first *Director*; William Boxall, 1866–1874; Frederick Burton, 1874–1894; Edward Poynter, 1894–1904; Charles Holroyd, 1906 (the post had been vacant for eighteen months) – 1916; Charles Holmes, 1916–1928.

[4] Formerly the Hon. George Agar Ellis (see Plate 31).

[5] For two recent and informative biographical accounts of J. J. Angerstein, see 'The Angersteins of Woodlands' by Cyril Fox, reprinted from the *Transactions of the Greenwich and Lewisham Antiquarian Society*, 1966, and an article by Christopher Lloyd in *History Today*, June 1966.

Angerstein's intimate friend and had helped him to form the collection, was now asked by his son John to advise as to its disposal. The Prince of Orange was mentioned as a possible purchaser and Lawrence wrote instantly in reply:

Russell Square

Dear Angerstein,

I do most sincerely think that you should not ask less then £70,000 from the Prince of Orange; and as sincerely do I pray and implore that at that price he may not have them.

At least, before they are sold, as just patriotism and duty to our country, they should be offered for a less sum to the Government – to Lord Liverpool.

Ever most truly yours, but at this moment with great anxiety and dread!

Thomas Lawrence

Lawrence's advice was followed, but, to his great annoyance, he was not consulted during the negotiations with the Government after the pictures had been offered to Lord Liverpool, who, as his correspondent indicates, had already taken expert opinion as to their value. That he had made up his mind to secure them for the nation some time before the first approaches were made to him by Angerstein's heir and executors is shown by a letter written to Elizabeth, Duchess of Devonshire, in which he says:

'We are about to lay the foundation of a National Gallery in this country by the purchase of Mr Angerstein's pictures. You know that Sir George Beaumont has announced his intention of leaving his pictures to the public, and I am persuaded that when a gallery is once established there will be many bequests. The great object is large pictures of eminence.[1] Small pictures are as well dispersed in private collections but there are scarcely any houses in London capable of containing large pictures, and the consequence is that they are either not bought or are sent to great houses in the country where few can see them.'

This letter was written by Lord Liverpool on 19 September 1823, but it was not until two months later that his negotiations commenced with the owner of the pictures. They were preceded by some correspondence between Angerstein's son and Sir Charles Long,[2] who was one of the leading connoisseurs of the time and the virtual chief of the British Institution, and who enjoyed the confidence both of the King and of the Prime Minister. Long had enquired the price of the collection, and John Angerstein answered him in the following note which was accompanied by a communication from his father's executors, Sir George Martin and Mr A. H. Thomson:

[1] And large pictures is what the newly-created National Gallery soon had in excess. There was Sebastiano del Piombo's *Raising of Lazarus* (150″ × 113″), Rubens' *Peace and War* (78″ × 116″) presented by the Duke of Sutherland in 1828, Titian's *Bacchus and Ariadne* (69″ × 75″) bought from the Jeweller Hamlet in 1826, as well as a host of enormous, but also enormously impressive, Claudes and others.

[2] Later Lord Farnborough.

My Dear Sir,

I have the pleasure of enclosing my father's executors' price for the pictures, and I trust you will admit that we have been far from immoderate in our valuation.

Believe me, my Dear Sir,
faithfully yours,

John Angerstein

Pall Mall, *Monday*, 17 *Nov.* 1823

The following is the letter from the executors. The 'Mr Young's work' mentioned is a catalogue of the Angerstein pictures prepared by John Young the engraver,[1] and the Keeper of the British Institution:

London, 17 *Nov.* 1823

Sir,

In reference to the communications with which you have favoured Mr Angerstein on the subject of his late Father's Collection of Pictures in Pall Mall, which we, as his Executors, are instructed to dispose of, we have the honour to state to you, that well knowing the great satisfaction it would have given our late Friend, that the Collection should form part of a National Gallery, we shall feel much gratified by his Majesty's Government becoming the purchasers of the whole for such a purpose.

Understanding from Mr Angerstein that we should state the price we think ourselves authorized to take for the Collection under the above circumstances, we beg to name the sum of Sixty Thousand Pounds, as the price we are prepared to accept. We should state that the whole of the pictures described in Mr Young's Work are included in the above offer with the exception of Mrs Angerstein's Portrait by Joshua Reynolds, and the three Pictures by Mr Fuseli.

We have the honour to be, Sir,
Your most obedient humble Servants,

George Martin
A. H. Thomson

Sir Charles Long.

Long forwarded both the letters to the Prime Minister, whose answer was as follows:

Nov. 21 1823

My dear Long,

I have received your communication on the subject of Mr Angerstein's pictures.

I understand that he proposes that the Government shall purchase them for £60,000. You are well aware that I had taken measures to ascertain the value of them, and none of the valuations amount to that sum.

In a transaction of this nature it is impossible not to take into consideration the honour

[1] See note, page 236.

that will attach to Mr Angerstein's family from the circumstance of his collection forming the foundation of a National Gallery, and it appears that Mr Angerstein was himself so fully aware of this advantage that he expressed to you his belief that his father would have disposed of the collection for such an object upon more liberal terms than if they were sold in any other manner.

I must further observe that as this is a public transaction and as I have to justify it to Parliament I cannot consider myself as warranted in offering a price for the pictures beyond their fair valuation.

I should at the same time deem it unworthy of the Government to endeavour to strike a hard bargain in any transaction of this nature.

But I conscientiously believe that when I make the offer of £50,000 I am offering that which will be liberal on the part of the Public and, under all the circumstances of the case, advantageous to Mr Angerstein to accept.

Ever sincerely yours,
Liverpool

This brought forth a long and interesting statement from Mr Thomson addressed to John Angerstein but intended for Lord Liverpool, to whom it was sent. It contains information about the pictures and explains why the executors valued them at £60,000. The artist mentioned as the highest authority in the kingdom, was, of course, Lawrence; and the reference to Beckford and Sebastian del Piombo's *Raising of Lazarus* concerns an offer of which I shall speak later. Mr Thomson writes:

Austin Friars
24 *Nov.* 1823

My dear John,

Thank you for your communication of Sir C. Long's note, enclosing Lord Liverpool's letter of the 21st, in which he states that the sum of £60,000 named by Sir George Martin and myself for the Pictures in Pall Mall was more than he should feel justified in giving on the part of the Public, and proposes £50,000 as a sum that will be liberal on the part of the Public and advantageous to your family. As Sir C. Long may consider that we, as your father's executors, have endeavoured to obtain too high a price for the collection, I think it right, in justification of Sir George Martin and myself, to remind you of the grounds on which we thought ourselves authorised to expect the first-mentioned sum from the Government.

First, you will recollect your father's lowest valuation was £76,000–a sum which before we took the opinions of artists on the subject we had none of us thought overrated the merits of the works. Mr Woodburn gave us reason to suppose some collectors might give in order to keep the whole entire in the country, £60,000, and an artist whom we must consider the highest authority in the Kingdom had assured you that he had given his opinion publicly when a lower sum was named, that they ought not to be sold under £60,000 to which the valuation of Mr Seguier approached so nearly (being £57,000) and which we understood that gentleman would be prepared to justify in case any public enquiry should be instituted, that we could hardly, in justice to the property entrusted to our management fix upon a less sum, even without considering the large price offered at one time by Beckford, for the Sebastian with a few other minor pictures.

In reply to one of Lord Liverpool's expressions, alluding to what would have been your father's feelings on the advantage of the collection becoming the foundation of a National Gallery, I am not of opinion that he would have sold the pictures for less than their actual value, to the Public, tho' had it been a question of contribution he might have given a part or the whole for such a purpose.

For myself, I should not, as an executor, feel justified in accepting Lord Liverpool's offer, but I should not hesitate to abide by Mr Seguier's valuation, which must appear of high authority to Sir George Martin and myself, as it was obtained in consequence of Sir C. Long's own recommendation.

You are quite at liberty, if you think proper, to communicate my ideas to Sir Charles Long–my belief is that Sir George Martin, who is not in town, will agree with me in what I have stated.

I am always, Dear John,
Very truly yours,
A. H. Thomson

Lord Liverpool's next communication offered a basis for a settlement, which was approved by Mr Thomson, and by the end of the year 1823 the Angerstein collection was the property of the nation. The following are the letters from Lord Liverpool, and from Mr Thomson on behalf of himself and Sir George Martin, which led to the completion of h is most important business:

Fife House
25 Nov. 1823

My dear Long,

I have received your letter with the enclosures from Mr Angerstein and Mr Thomson, and in order to bring the matter to which they relate to a conclusion I am quite ready on the part of the public to purchase Mr Angerstein's collection of pictures for any sum between fifty and sixty thousand pounds which Mr Seguier and Mr Woodburn will state in writing to be their price upon *a fair and reasonable valuation.* I say *fair and reasonable valuation* because I am aware that upon these occasions there is sometimes an extreme valuation as distinguished from the former, and though this may occasionally be admitted in the case of a single picture, I cannot think it maintainable in respect to a collection in which every picture is valued separately.

I have no objection to your communicating this letter to Mr Angerstein.

Believe me to be,
My dear Long,
Ever sincerely yours,
Liverpool

Austin Friars,
19 *December* 1823

Sir,

I have the honour to acknowledge your note of this date, accompanying Lord Liverpool's letter, in which he consents on the part of the public to purchase Mr Angerstein's collection at the sum Mr Seguier named as their value, and I will take care to procure from that gentleman a more formal document than the short note Mr Angerstein sent to you, presuming that Mr. Seguier can have no objection to furnish one. In the meantime I will communicate to Sir George Martin, and to Mr Angerstein, Lord Liverpool's acquiescence to the terms proposed, which, of course, brings the matter to a conclusion–the purchase money for the thirty-eight pictures being £57,000.

I have the honour to be, Sir,
Your most faithful, humble servant,
A. H. Thomson

To Sir Charles Long

The 'more formal document', which was duly supplied by Seguier, was a detailed valuation of all the pictures in the collection. Some of its estimates are curious, for Wilkie's *Village Holiday* was regarded by Seguier as the most valuable of the English pictures and worth twice as much as Sir Joshua's splendid portrait of Lord Heathfield. Wilkie's picture is also rated in value above the famous *Portrait of Gevartius*, then so called but now known to represent Cornelius van der Geest.[1] The following is the document sent to Lord Liverpool.

Having very carefully examined the Collection of pictures of the late J. J. Angerstein, Esq., in Pall Mall, I am of opinion that the said Collection, containing the 38 pictures named in the accompanying list, is of the value of £57,000.

To this valuation I subscribe my name, the 26th day of December, 1823.

William Seguier

To the Executors of the late Mr J. J. Angerstein

Titian	Ganymede	£2000
Rubens	Rape of the Sabines	£2500
Vandyck	Emp. Theo expelled the Church by St Ambrose	£2500
Claude	Embarkation of the Queen of Sheba	£5000
Claude	Marriage of Rebecca	£3500
An. Carracci	St John in the Wilderness	£500
Lud. Carracci	Susannah and the Elders	£600
Velasquez	Philip IV of Spain and his Queen	£300
N. Poussin	Bacchanalian Triumph	£1500
Domenichino	Erminia with the Shepherds	£600

[1] See Plate 2.

Titian	Venus and Adonis	£3500
Claude	Landscape – Morning	£2500
Claude	An Italian Seaport	£1500
S. del Piombo	The Raising of Lazarus	£8000
Titian	A Concert	£500
Raphael	Pope Julius the Second	£600
Correggio	Christ on the Mount	£800
Vandyck	Portrait of Gevartius	£700
Rembrandt	The Nativity	£1200
Rembrandt	The Woman taken in Adultery	£4000
Wilkie	The Village Holiday	£800
Claude	The Embarkation of St Ursula	£4500
An. Carracci	Apollo and Silenus	£500
Hogarth	Six pictures of Marriage à la Mode	£2500
G. Poussin	A Land Storm	£1200
do.	Abraham and Isaac	£2500
Cuyp	Landscape with Cattle and figures	£900
Rubens	Holy family in a Landscape	£400
Vandyck	Portrait of Rubens	£400
Sir J. Reynolds	Portrait of Lord Heathfield	£400
Correggio	Study of Heads	£250
do.	do.	£250
Hogarth	His own portrait	£100

The following nine pictures in the above list are not now attributed to the artists to whom they were assigned by the advisers of Angerstein: *Ganymede; Philip IV of Spain and his Queen; Erminia with the Shepherds; A Concert; Pope Julius the Second; Christ on the Mount; Holy Family in a Landscape;* and the two Studies of Heads.

The pictures now purchased for the nation had been for many years under the care of William Nirling, an old servant of Angerstein's in whom he placed great trust, and were insured for £40,000 in the Sun and Phoenix Offices. On 10 January this was raised to £57,000 by Lord Liverpool, through William Seguier, who was looking after the pictures for the Government although he had as yet no official appointment. Lord Liverpool did not know where to exhibit the new acquisitions and Seguier recommended as suitable some rooms in Old Bond Street, of which Sir Charles Long approved when he saw them. This idea, however, was abandoned when it was discovered that Angerstein's executors were willing to sell the remainder of the lease of the house, No. 100 Pall Mall, in which the pictures were hanging. The lease was purchased and this at once removed any difficulties that stood in the way of exhibiting the collection until a proper gallery should be built.

Seguier was appointed Keeper of the National Gallery on 30 March, and in six weeks prepared the house for its new purpose. But until 10 May, when the pictures were on view, their acquisition had been mentioned by only one journal, the *Guardian,* which stated in

61 One of the greatest English collectors of all time was Edward Solly, a merchant who lived in Berlin from c. 1800 to 1821. The Prussian king bought his tremendous collection of 3000 paintings in 1821 as the nucleus of the Royal Berlin Gallery. This museum was built to a design by Schinkel to house it. Dr Waagen was its first director.

62 The side panels of van Eyck's polyptych, *The Adoration of the Lamb*, seen on the walls of the old Berlin Royal Gallery in the second half of the nineteenth century. Solly had bought the panels from the dealer Nieuwenhuys for 100,000 guilder in 1818. They came from the Cathedral of St Bavo in Ghent and were returned there under the terms of the Treaty of Versailles in July 1920.

63 Solly had a particular penchant for variations of the Madonna and Child theme, of which he owned several hundred, including examples by Taddeo Gaddi, Lippo Memmi, Verrocchio, Botticelli, Giovanni Bellini, Gentile Bellini, Mantegna, Jacopo da Valenzia, Cima and Raphael. He also owned this magnificent *Adoration in the Wood* by Fra Filippo Lippi and two other paintings by the same master.

64 Solly also had a wonderful eye for portraits. One of the best known in his collection was *The Merchant, Georg Gisze* by Hans Holbein, the Younger. Solly bought this in Switzerland for 60 guineas in about 1810.

65 Sir Robert Peel formed one of the most important collections of Dutch pictures in England, and it was acquired by the London National Gallery in 1871. Mrs Jameson tells us that he bought Hobbema's *The Avenue, Middelharnis* for £800 in 1829. He owned three other paintings by Hobbema.

66 Peel told Mrs Jameson how much reassurance and comfort he obtained from his pictures amid the harassment of political life. It seems that he was looking at this Forest Scene by Ruisdael as he was speaking to her.

67 Annibale Carracci's *Coronation of the Virgin* was the sort of picture much loved by English collectors in the nineteenth century. Mrs Jameson wrote of it in 1844: 'there is a sublime simplicity in the arrangement of the figures, a fertility of fancy, and richness of effect in the management of the accessories, a unity in the midst of variety, which renders this picture very remarkable.' It came from the Aldobrandini Collection in Rome; was inherited by the Pamfili and Borghese families; Alexander Day brought it to England about 1800; at the Samuel Rogers' sale in 1856 it fetched 400 guineas and was bought by the Duke of Newcastle, who showed it at the Manchester Art-Treasures exhibition in the following year. The present owner, Mr Denis Mahon, bought it for 48 guineas at a Christie's sale in June 1937 where it had been sent by the Earl of Lincoln.

68 One of two panels discovered by Sir Martin Conway in a French antique shop in 1903 and later attributed by him to Giorgione. For the full story of the discovery see page 366.

69 Many English artists were considerable collectors in their own right. Lely, Lawrence and Reynolds are outstanding examples. *The Agony in the Garden* by Giovanni Bellini was included in the sale of Sir Joshua Reynolds' extensive collection in 1795. It had been owned earlier by Consul Smith. Later it passed through the collections of, first, William Beckford and, second, the Rev. W. Davenport Bromley, where Waagen saw it and identified it as the work of Bellini and not Mantegna, to whom it had been attributed previously. It was shown in Manchester in 1857 and bought for the National Gallery in 1863.

70 Bertucci's *Incredulity of St Thomas* at one time belonged to Edward Solly. It was sold after his death in 1847 to Sir W. Domville, and later in 1850 to John Smith, the celebrated dealer. He sold it to Lord Northwick, who regarded it as one of his finest paintings and made a note to this effect on his copy of the catalogue of the Solly Sale. Waagen saw it at Thirlestane and selected it for the Manchester Exhibition. The attribution of authorship changed almost every time the picture was sold. For full details see page 322.

71 Raphael's *Madonna del Passeggio* once belonged to Queen Christina of Sweden and later became part of the Orleans Collection. When this was sold in London by Bryan in 1798 it was bought by the Duke of Bridgewater. It is still in the collection of his descendent, the present Duke of Sutherland.

72 *The Virgin and Child with SS John the Baptist and Catherine* by Andrea Previtali. This was one of the finest pictures belonging to the Duke of Buckingham and Chandos sold at the great Stowe Sale in 1848. It was bought by Sir Charles Eastlake (as *The Marriage of St Catherine* by Giovanni Bellini) for his personal collection for 36 guineas and subsequently by the National Gallery at Lady Eastlake's Sale in 1894 after her death.

74 *Portrait of a Man* by Dieric Bouts was at one time in the Aders Collection. Aders was a German merchant living in London and probably a friend of Solly's. Later the picture belonged to Samuel Rogers. It was exhibited at Leeds as 'Memblinc by himself', and went to the National Gallery in 1876 as part of the Wynn Ellis Bequest.

73 *Portrait of a Girl* painted in the Studio of Domenico Ghirlandaio was for a long time in the collection of James Whatman, the paper maker. In 1859 it was exhibited at the British Institution and in 1868 at the Leeds Art Exhibition, which was modelled on the Manchester Exhibition of 1857. It was sold in 1887 at the Whatman Sale at Christie's for 225 guineas and bought by the National Gallery.

75 *The Conversion of Saint Bavo* by Sir Peter Paul Rubens. Another of the great Rubens pictures which Irvine found for Buchanan. It came from the Carrega Palace in Genoa. It was bought by the Rev. W. Holwell Carr, who was an ardent collector and, for a time, also in partnership with Buchanan. It was shown at the British Institution in 1815 and left to the National Gallery by Holwell Carr in 1831.

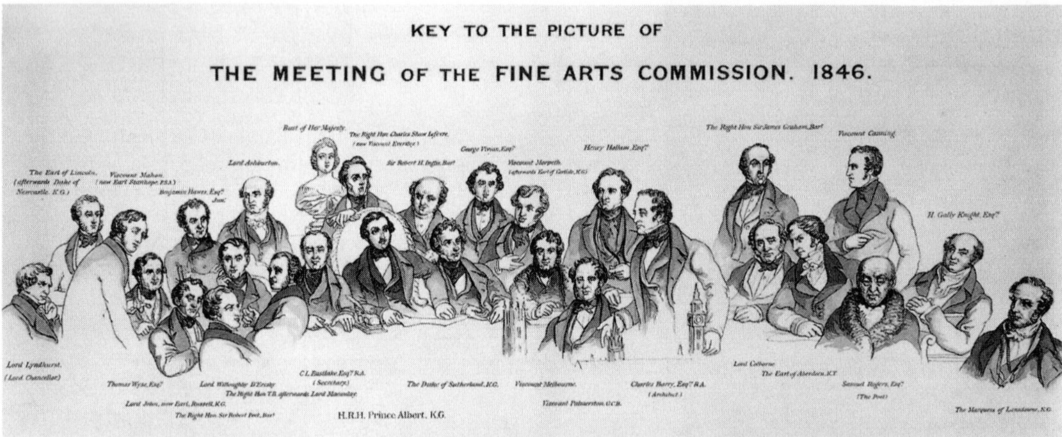

76, Prompted by the need for the internal decoration of the new Houses of Parliament designed by Barry, Sir
77 Robert Peel, the Prime Minister, appointed a Royal Commission in 1841 'to take into consideration the Promotion of the Fine Arts in this country'. As Chairman Peel selected Prince Albert, then aged only 22. His commissioners included Sir Charles Eastlake and a fair balance of collectors and connoisseurs on the one hand, and men concerned with the arts as educational and sociological factors, on the other. This painting by John Partridge is dated 1846.

78 H. J. Brooke's *Private View of the Old Masters Exhibition at the Royal Academy* in 1888. The tradition of an annual winter exhibition had started at the British Institution and was carried on by the Royal Academy after the expiry of the British Institution's lease in 1867. Many prominent collectors attended this private view.

January that they had been purchased 'by desire of his Majesty'. The King, according to Sir Charles Long, was the first to suggest the acquisition of the Angerstein pictures for the nation. Incredible as it may seem, the opening of the National Gallery on 10 May, so long desired, passed with little or no notice. The daily journals that, three or four weeks earlier, had described in long articles the inauguration of the new gallery of the Society of British Artists, almost ignored the opening of the first gallery of pictures owned by the State. *The Times*, on 11 May, announced the event as follows:

'Mr Angerstein's collection of pictures. Yesterday, for the first time the "national gallery" of pictures was opened to the public at 100 Pall Mall, formerly Mr Angerstein's town residence. At present the exhibition consists of these pictures only. It was visited by numbers of the Nobility and Gentry in the course of the day. It will continue open every day.'

THE STOWE SALE

One of the saddest events among the records of great sales in the middle of the nineteenth century was the dispersal of the property of Richard Plantagenet Temple Nugent Brydges Chandos Grenville, Second Duke of Buckingham and Chandos, in 1848 when he was fifty-one. Here was an accumulation of property and works of art by many generations of an illustrious family–and it was going for a song. It was literally the greatest bargain hunt of its era. Among a host of avid collectors, Ralph Bernal and Sir Robert Peel came to do their own bidding, and did remarkably well.

When Grenville inherited the title from his father in 1839, he succeeded to a rent roll of £100,000 a year. But the estates were very heavily encumbered, for his father had lived luxuriously and entertained lavishly on a scale which, wealthy though he was, even he could not sustain. The new Duke indulged extensively in buying land on borrowed money, where the interest was far greater than the resulting rent. The crash was finally precipitated by a visit to Stowe of Queen Victoria and Prince Albert in January 1845. The building and preparation for the visit cost vast sums and on 31 August 1847 the effects at Stowe and the Duke's other residences were taken possession of by bailiffs. A fortnight later the Duke left England with debts said to be upwards of £1,000,000. His estates in Buckinghamshire, Oxfordshire and Northamptonshire were sold in May 1848 for £262,990. The sale described here followed in August.[1] Others again came later.

EXTRACTED FROM George Redford's *Art Sales*, Vol. I, 1888.

THE vast accumulation of works of Art of almost every kind contained in the noble modern classic mansion of Stowe, near the town of Buckingham, from which the title of the Duke is taken, was sold by auction on the premises by Messrs Christie & Manson, the sale beginning 15 August and continuing for forty days. The sale created the greatest interest as will be gathered from the following article which appeared as 'a leader' in *The Times* the day before the sale:

The Times, 14 August 1848.

During the past week the British public has been admitted to a spectacle of painful

[1] There were two catalogues. The one issued before the sale by Christie's cost 15s and admitted four persons. A fully priced, annotated and illustrated catalogue edited by Henry Rumsey Forster was issued to subscribers by David Brogue of Fleet Street later in 1848.

interest and gravely historical import. One of the most splendid abodes ot our almost regal aristocracy has thrown open its portals to an endless succession of visitors, who from morning to night have flowed in an uninterrupted stream from room to room, and floor to floor–not to enjoy the hospitality of the lord or to congratulate him on his countless treasures of art, but to see an ancient family ruined, their palace marked for destruction, and its contents scattered to the four winds of Heaven. We are only saying what is notorious and what therefore it is neither a novelty or a cruelty to repeat, that the most noble and puissant prince, his Grace the Duke of Buckingham and Chandos, is at this moment an absolutely ruined and destitute man. Our advertising columns have introduced to the public the long list of estates, properties, and interests which are no longer his, and will not revert to his heirs. The last crash of this mighty ruin is that which now sounds. Stowe is no more. This morning the tumultuous invasion of sight-seers will once again be endured, and tomorrow the auctioneer will begin his work.

As every thoughtful spectator has spoken to the peculiar and most lamentable character of the scene, one may be permitted to dwell for a while upon circumstances of such rare occurrence and indelible recollection. Under the lofty arch which crowns the long avenue from Buckingham, and opens the first view of the magnificent Palladian facade, has lately passed a daily cavalcade which, except in its utter absence of style, might remind one of the road to Epsom on a Derby day. Barouches, flys, stage-coaches, 'busses' pressed from the metropolitan service, and every gradation of 'trap' down to the carrier's cart hastily emptied of groceries, dragged to Wolverton, and filled with unfortunate holders of return tickets to town, constituted a dreary antithesis to the *cortège* which so lately brought Royalty to Stowe. An elaborately circuitous road conducted the impatient visitors to the park front, before which in the vast amphitheatre formed by its side colonnades, so often the scene of rural festivities, the enemy encamped, one might imagine a great country picnic had suddenly gathered at Stowe; even stalls were there. From the branch of a noble beech hung a pair of huge scales on which venison was weighed. An advertisement posted on the front door particularised the very moderate prices at which a back, a half, or a quarter might be obtained. In the distance were fallen trees, timber waggons and extempore sawpits. The enormous edifice was a human hive, every window showed the crowd within passing to and fro. But once admitted–once standing under the Pantheon-like vault of the central saloon, and glancing right and left at endless vistas of gorgeous apartments, then one indeed realised the sacrilege that was going on. Every scholar must have thought of the scene related by Aeneas when the Greeks had burst open the gates of Priam's palace, and when the splendid interior, the spacious halls, and the sacred haunts of the ancient dynasty were presented to the eyes of the furious assailants.

The house was well set out for the distinguished visitors. Neither Louis the 18th, nor the Duke of Orleans, nor Queen Victoria, nor any of the great ones of the earth, whose visits are recorded with pillars and with trees planted by their own hands saw Stowe so nobly arrayed as the British public have seen it this week. The bride was dressed for the altar, the victim for the sacrifice. No thrifty coverings, no brown holland, no neat chintzes were there. King Mob had it all of the best, the richest Damask furniture and the newest state hangings; only as that personage rode literally rough shod through the palace and brought with him cartloads of gravel, there was just an attempt to save the carpets from excessive trituration. In the state dining room was set out 60,000 ozs of gold and silver plate; one was involuntarily reminded of the weight for the scales were at work there also, and men were weighing and noting down lot after lot.

On a table 20 yards long, and on a dozen sideboards stood forests of vases, candelabras, epergnes, groups, goblets, tankards, and every other form and variety of plate, from the elaborate designs of Italian artists to the simple elegance of the old English school, and the pretentious richness of the last generation. Among fifty other pieces of historic value, the gift of royal personages and distinguished men, stood a vase formed from snuff boxes presented by the cities and corporations in Ireland 1779, the mace of the old corporation of Buckingham purchased by the Buckingham conservatives and presented to the Duke as an everlasting possession, and the Chandos testimonial for which the gentry and yeomanry of the Country lately subscribed we believe £1,500. During the whole week this testimonial has been surrounded by a crowd of agriculturists, the very originals of the figures thereon represented, telling of the guineas they had contributed to the ill-fated fabric, but avowing with unvaried gratitude of a safer, if not better cause, that they would gladly give the money over again.

The galleries of family portraits and collections of family memorials seem to connect all the great men and all the great achievements of modern Europe with the name of Chandos, Temple, Cobham, and Grenville. But beyond the somewhat extensive circle of family affection, the original portraits of famous men and women here assembled are of the greatest interest and value. Here, too, is the victor's portion in the celebrated sieges, the memento of historical friendships, and the favourite gem of royalty or beauty. In the manuscript room is the most extensive and valuable collection of Irish documents anywhere to be found. For the pictures, marbles, bronzes, antique articles of virtu, curiosities, china, glass and wines, we leave them to the auctioneer and his catalogue of 5,000 items. It is not our purpose to speak of that which money had collected and may collect again. Such things are only scattered for a fresh reunion elsewhere under new and more favourable auspices. But the heirlooms of many great families, the records of many great events, and the memorials of many great persons, all spontaneously collected into one great whole, constitute a most singular and significant fact, the obliteration of which we can only compare to the overthrow of a nation or a throne.

And everything is to be sold. The fatal ticket is everywhere to be seen. The portrait of Charles Brandon, Duke of Suffolk,* the founder of the family, by Holbein, is Lot 51 in the 21st day's sale. That every other ancestor should go to the hammer, whether Vandyke or Lely, or Kneller or Gainsborough or Reynolds, follows of course. But there is one item of which no preparation can remove the shock. The Chandos family is descended from Frances Brandon, eldest daughter of the above Charles Brandon, by Mary, daughter of Henry VII, and Queen Dowager of France. Some time since savages or dilettanti at Bury exhumed that Mary Brandon from her grave, and took from her head a lock of silken hair, which thus constitutes a visible link between the present Duke of Buckingham and the throne of these realms, to which he has a reversionary claim. That lock of silken hair in its glass case is now to be sold to the highest bidder.†

IVOKY TANKARD

EXTRACTED FROM George Redford's *Art Sales* Vol. I, 1888.

As a collection, it was more remarkable for costly ornamental objects of display than for fine works of art, selected as such. The pictures could not be regarded as a representative collection, as there were few works of the great masters, and the portraits formed

* *This was purchased by the Duke of Sutherland for* £50.

† *This relic sold for* £7 10*s*, Owen, *just* 20*s more than was paid for it by the last Duke of Chandos, at the sale of the Duchess of Portland's museum in* 1786. *The lock was of a most brilliant gold colour, and rather more than* 12 *inches long.*

the chief part of the collection. Of these the most important was the portrait of Shakespeare, said to have been painted either by John Taylor, the player, to whom it belonged, or by Richard Burbage, and the history of which is well authenticated. This was purchased by Lord Ellesmere at the sale for £372 15s; and afterwards, in 1856, presented by him to the National Gallery. The copy of it, by Sir G. Kneller, which he did as a present to Dryden, is in the Collection of Lord Fitzwilliam, at Wentworth Wood House. A very good priced catalogue was published by Bogue, 1848, illustrated with woodcuts of the house and the various 'temples in the grounds',[1] and a mezzotint from the picture by Rembrandt of 'The Unmerciful Servant' which was bought by the Marquis of Hertford for £2300; besides most of the objects of ornamental art. The sale catalogue was charged 15s, admitting four persons to the private view, from August 3rd to the 15th, and many thousands of persons visited the sale. The pictures had come from time to time from Gosfield, the seat of Earl Nugent, in Essex; from Minchenden House, near Southgate the seat of Mr Nicoll, whose heiress married the Marquis of Caernarvon, afterwards third Duke of Chandos; from Avington, another seat of the Chandos family, in Hampshire. When the Duke of that day, 1848, succeeded to the title, he sent about 1000 pictures to be sold at Christie's and they only realised some £600. For weeks after the shops in Wardour Street were crammed with those pictures. The only modern commissions given by the Duke to artists were to John Martin for his 'Destruction of Herculaneum and Pompeii' – £800, and this was sold with others from Buckingham House, Pall Mall, at Christie's in 1848, for £105; Stanfield's 'Wreckers off Calais' was bought by the Duke in the sale of Mr Watson-Taylor's Collection, 1823, for £315, and now sold for £430 10s. The following were the important pictures by Old Masters: A. DURER (?) St Catherine – £157 10s, and St Barbara – £168. PRIMATICCIO, Diane de Poictiers at her toilette, with an attendant at a robe chest – £111 (*Ryman*). REMBRANDT, The enraged Prisoner – John, Duke of Cleves with two black boys, said to be a duplicate of the pictures in Berlin Museum and at Dresden – £85 (*Snare*); 'A Negro with bow and arrows' – £263 (*Marquis of Hertford*);[2] 'A Burgomaster', seated, his right hand raised, from the Orleans Collection, 52 × 43 in. – £850 (*Lord Ware*); 'The Unmerciful Servant', four figures nearly life-size 70 × 84 in. – £2300 (*Marquis of Hertford*). DOMENICHINO, 'Sybilla Persica' from the Orleans Gallery – £724 (*Marquis of Hertford*). CORREGGIO, An old copy of the 'Mercury and Venus teaching Cupid', brought to England by George Villiers, Duke of Buckingham, in the time of Charles I – £157 (*Ryman*). S. ROSA, 'The Finding of Moses', 48 × 79 in. – £1050 (*Farrer*). A. CUYP, 'Philip baptising the Eunuch', 66 × 45 in., from Count de Vismes' Collection – £1543 (*T. B. Brown*). The portraits sold for small prices generally, and some were bought in for the family. The ornamental objects brought nothing near the prices they would bring at the present time. The beautiful little majolica vase, painted with a battle, was bought by Mr Mark Philips, of Manchester for 50 guineas. The large majolica cistern – £67, to Mr Hope of Deepdene. Some of the choicest candelabra and other objects were purchased by Mr R. S. Holford; others by Mr Baring, Sir A. Rothschild, Mr Neaufoy,

[1] See illustrations on pages 274 and 275.

[2] See also the next article.

and Mr S. M. Peto. The bust of Prior, by Roubiliac, was bought by Sir Robert Peel for £136 10s. The fine bronzes of the Laocoon and the Mercury, by G. di Bologna, were bought the first by the Duke of Hamilton for £567; the Mercury by the Marquis of Londonderry for £112; and the beautiful antique marble of the Marine Venus, found in the baths of Agrippa, Rome, about 54 in. high, was purchased for the Queen.*

The amount of the chief day of the pictures was £10,821 16s 6d; another day was £5219. The plate &c., averaged from £5000 to £6000 a day, the total amounting to £75,562 4s 6d.

A SIDELIGHT ON STOWE

THE fascinating correspondence between one of the greatest collectors of the nineteenth century, Lord Hertford, and his agent, S. M. Mawson, is preserved in the archives of the Wallace Collection. Hertford rarely attended sales and these two letters are typical of his instructions to his faithful agent.

Mawson did, in fact, buy all the paintings mentioned and they can all be seen at the Wallace Collection. He paid £263 11s 0d for the Rembrandt. Since 1913 this has been catalogued as by Govert Flinck (P 238, *A Young Negro Archer*). Mawson obtained the Domenichino Sybilla (P 131, *The Persian Sybil*) for £690 and the Murillo (P 105, *The Assumption of the Virgin*) for £58 16s 0d. It is interesting to note that Redford knew that Lord Hertford had bought these paintings despite his strictures on secrecy.

Sepr. 10th 1848

My Dear Sir

I intended being at Stowe on the 15th Oct. but find that it is not certain whether I shall be able to attend the sale on that day. I think we must have the Unmerciful Servant by

* *There was a rather sharp contest for this at the sale, and it was bought by M. Grüner for £163 16s. It was announced, in the* Morning Post, *that the purchase was made for H.R.H. Prince Albert. The story goes that the Queen, when visiting Stowe in January 1845, admired the statue, and when the sale occurred, commissioned M. Grüner to buy it. The newspaper was handed by the Queen to the Prince Consort, congratulating him on so beautiful an acquisition to his collection; but the Prince expressed his surprise, as he knew nothing of it, when the Queen, with some* naïveté, *requested her Royal Consort to accept the statue as a birthday present, and it was at once placed at Osborne, the Marine Residence of the Queen.*

Rembrandt and hope the price will not be so unmerciful as the subject–but you know that I place all confidence in you and depend upon your kindness on this occasion.

I am also *very anxious* to have the Sybilla by Domenichino No. 432 as much for the frame as for the picture. So I hope you will purchase it for me. If the little Murillo No. 390, the Conception of the Virgin, was sold at a reasonable price I should like to have it but the Rembrandt and the Domenichino are my favourites and I depend upon you for doing the best.

Pray have the kindness not to mention to *anybody* that you buy on my account. I am very anxious my name should not appear.

In the event of my being in time for the sale you would see me there and then my *hat* would play the same part it has already acted in similar circumstances.

You will be so good as to have the picture *most* carefully packed and sent to your house. The great frame will require great care else it is sure to be broken. Pray have the goodness to answer this *by return of Post* as there is no time to be lost and if you cannot go to Stowe or are absent from London I must have recourse to other means which I shall much regret as you may suppose. You will be pleased to direct as below.

Believe me
Yours very truly
(Sgd.) HERTFORD

Hotel des Bains
Boulogne sur Mer
France

The Negro if cheap

Boulogne Sepr. 12/48

My Dear Sir

I have received your letter in answer to mine and thank you for your kind promise of doing my little affair at Stowe. It cannot I am convinced be in better and more honourable hands and I trust you entirely. I am very anxious to have the Domenichino Sybilla *with the frame* of course, so I hope you will secure her and it. I depend upon your not mentioning the name of your client. You will be asked by several persons and I dare say much pressed.

I think, as you do, that the Rembrandt ought to travel to your house without its frame, that may be left at Stowe for, if I remember right, it is clumsy and bad.

Yours very truly
(Sgd.) HERTFORD

Pray write to me when returned to town and direct Hotel des Bains, Boulogne sur Mer.

LORD HERTFORD AND HIS AGENT

PROBABLY the finest example of a collection that has come down to us, where succeeding members of the same family have taken on a really active role as collectors, can be seen in the Wallace Collection in Manchester Square. The Hertford family structure is highly complex, but explained in great detail in the current museum catalogues[1] so there is no need to recapitulate it in detail here. The two most interesting members of the family from our point of view were Richard, 4th Marquess of Hertford (1800–1870), and his son, Sir Richard Wallace (1818–1890). Both men lived a large part of their lives in France and the collection is dominated by their taste for French art and furniture. In fact, only part of their total treasures can be seen at Manchester Square: the story of the dispersal of another part of the collection is given in a later extract.[2]

Lord Hertford tended to shun public life and though Sir Robert Peel felt that his 'abilities might have carried him to the place of Prime Minister', he was so engrossed by his interest in art and the enlargment of his collection that he took little interest in anything else. He emerges in a particularly human light in his correspondence with S. M. Mawson, who was his chief agent in London and enjoyed Hertford's complete trust, as will be seen from the letters. Over and over again one reads in them such phrases as '. . . the unbounded confidence I have in your good taste and judgement, for I rely as much on you as I do on myself and besides your knowledge of pictures is of course much greater than mine'; or 'our Collection, which owes a great deal of its splendour to the interest you have always taken in it'.

Hertford frequently adjured Mawson to secrecy but Mawson was not always successful in concealing his master's interest. One is fascinated too that a man whose income in the 1850s was about £240,000 a year (and virtually untaxed) should be constantly worried about spending too much on individual paintings: 'I have bought a great deal this year and nothing but a bargain can tempt me. . . .'

Of the paintings mentioned in the ensuing correspondence Mawson only purchased the Lancret which Hertford so much desired (P 465) for £735 and the Velazquez (P 12) for £1680.

---

[1] See in particular the *General Guide to the Wallace Collection*, 1966; *Pictures and Drawings*, 1968; *Furniture*, 1956. The last two catalogues give an enormous amount of detail. In this respect the Wallace Collection has served the enquiring visitor better than any other museum in London. For interesting accounts of the Hertford family history see also *Old Q's Daughter* by Bernard Falk, second edition 1951 and *Pepita* by V. Sackville West, 1936 (Re-issued in 1970).

[2] 'The Wallace-Bagatelle Collection', page 354.

LORD HERTFORD

Paris Rue Laffitte 2
July 10th 1852

My dear Sir

The late Sir J. Murray's collection of pictures is to be sold at Messrs Christie & Manson on Thursday 17th. I am told there are some very good pictures. A very fine Van Dyck (the sleeping nymph) a good Hobbema and Rubens and several other pictures that might suit me. You most probably know this collection but if you do not as they are to be viewed three days preceding the sale you would have time by writing to me in time for the post on the 1st day of exhibition, to let me know details and your opinion of the pictures.

Pray have the kindness to do so without loss of time as I might run over if your account is favourable and you know my confidence in you that I am certain you will never betray.

I went to Brussels and attended the Ghent sale, but bought nothing of importance. The Mieris was pretty but rather dark–it was sold at a very high price. I suppose it is in England but I do not know for whom it was bought. The Ostade, the Hobbema and a Rubens fetched immense prices.

Yours very sincerely
(Sgd.) HERTFORD

Pray have the kindness to let this little communication rest *entirely* between you and I.
(Intd.) H

Write to me as soon as possible to give me time to cross the water. Si cela en vaut la peine.

Paris May 5th 1853

My dear Sir

Many thanks for your kind letter that I received yesterday. So there is no time to be lost in making up my mind. Unfortunately I do not remember the pictures you allude to but I think I should like No. 163 the Conception with the Angels &c. by Murillo: No. 150 Portrait of M.A. of Austria by Velasquez. Pray have the goodness to buy me these two pictures and I leave it entirely to your judgement and kindness to decide about the price. You know my confidence in you and I feel quite secure that what you will do will be well done.

Pray contrive that it should not be known for whom you make these purchases and if you really think them good acquisitions I hope you will secure them for me.

Believe me my dear Sir,
Yours very truly,
(Sgd.) HERTFORD

If 72 Murillo sold at a tolerable price you might buy it also.

Paris May 12th '53

My dear Sir

Many thanks for having had the kindness to give me some details concerning the sale. I begged you to buy me the pictures I mentioned in my last letter because you told me you thought them good and recommended them to me. I am very glad that upon further examination you discovered that they were not altogether right and I am obliged to you for having let them escape our notice. You know I rely upon your judgement and taste and depend also upon your kindness and attention to my little interests. With respect to the portrait by Murillo, I have no doubt it is fine, as you say so. But I confess I do not much like the portrait of an old man however fine it may be: it is not pleasing, so I should not like to give much for it and do not much mind if I have it not. If we had time to question and answer I should ask you if you thought it would fetch 500 gns. I dare say that if it is very magnificent it will sell for much more, tho' an unpleasant subject. I am now well aware that, with the exception of this picture, that I have, after all, no very *decided* fancy for, there is nothing else for me in *this* sale. Pray tell me *when* the Standing Vente begins. Do not give yourself the trouble of sending me a catg. as I have several; but the sale day may be changed. If there is anything worth mentioning, I am sure you will have the goodness to do so.

Without of course mentioning me, try and have a look at the Lancret and tell me what state it is in. I remember it but imperfectly.

I have been in my bed almost ever since you left Paris and if I go on in this deplorable state I shall certainly beg Monsieur V—— G—— to do me the honor to call upon me.

Yours my dear Sir,
Very Truly
(Sgd.) HERTFORD

Paris May 24th/53

My dear Sir

Many thanks for the fresh details you give me of the L.P. sale. I regret the fine portrait by Murillo as by your account of it, it is different from what I thought I remembered it–I had intended to run over to see all these pictures and for many other things too, but I am still too unwell to move. Between *you* and *I* (and to no other person but you should I make this *confidence*) I must have the Lancret, called Watteau in the Standish Collection. So I depend upon you for *getting it for me*. I need not beg you not to mention a word about this to *anybody* either *before* or *after* the sale. You will take the picture to your own house and I will send you, by return of post, a cheque to pay Messrs Christie & Manson.

I expect a letter from you tomorrow or the day after on the subject of this sale. There is not a moment to be lost and if you had anything very pressing to say you may have recourse to the telegraphic affair and I might answer you in the same way, but I have no doubt we understand each other.

Yours my dear Sir
Most Sincerely
(Sgd.) HERTFORD

Paris May 25/53

My dear Sir

I have just received your letter, many thanks for it.

I *depend* upon your getting the Lancret (Watteau in the Catg.) for me – I have no doubt it will sell for a good sum, most likely more than it is worth, but we *must* have it, as I suppose it will not *dépasse* 3 thousand Pds. I mention this to make you comfortable and you are the only person to whom I would say as much. I leave it to you, but I must have it, unless by some unheard of chance it were to go beyond 3000 Gns. Of course it will not, and on all that is honourable, don't mention one word of what I have just said. I will write to you tomorrow about the Velasquez.

In great hurry My dear Sir,
Yours very sincerely,
(Sgd.) HERTFORD

Paris May 26th/53

My dear Sir

I hope that by this time our Lancret is comfortably settled down in your house.

I do not at all remember the Velasquez you allude to. By your account of it, it must be very good and on the strength of your judgement you may purchase it for me if it does *not* go to an extravagant price and not much beyond what you think I might get for it in the improbable event of my not liking it. You know fancy has a great deal to do with pictures as well as with everything else. I hope I shall get some good news tomorrow as I should be extremely annoyed not to have the Lancret.

Yours most sincerely
(Sgd.) HERTFORD

I depend upon your not mentioning my name. You *may* have bought them for yourself and you will see what offers you get for them.

I dare say we shall have given as much as anybody would give.

Paris June 11/53

My dear Sir

Now that you have, I suppose, often looked at our new acquisitions, I hope you still like them. I am very glad indeed to have the Lancret for I think it very pretty and tho' it is well paid I would have given more (a *little* more) with pleasure. As for the Velasquez I do not remember it at all, ainsi je ne puis rien dire; what frightens me a little is that it appears never to have struck me at the Louvre as I do not remember it at all. You gave a *prodigious* price for it, but as I have unbounded confidence in your taste and judgement, as well as in everything else, I dare say I shall like it and I long to have a look at it which I hope soon to be able to do as the fine weather, that has at last made its appearance, has done me good and I trust that I am gradually recovering. So you see it was known the Velasquez was for me, it was mentioned in the Journal des Débats, my name en toutes lettres. How singular! for I am quite certain you never mentioned it–however it is not of much consequence.

Many thanks for the details you were good enough to give me respecting the picture by Landseer that was sold a few days ago. By your account of it I think it would not have suited me. I should like to have a picture by that Master but it must be *first rate* and a pleasing subject. Perhaps we may find one some day.

You might do me a *great service and oblige me very much*. You know there is at present an exhibition of works of art at Gore House. I should very much like to have drawings made of some of the principal and most beautiful articles of *furniture* NOT of the middle ages, but of the times of Louis XIV, XV and XVI, ESPECIALLY the *fine Cabinet* by *Gouthieres* sent by the *Queen*. I should like these drawings to be most *accurately made*, with *sides and backs*, with exact *dimensions* and *plans* of the *shapes*. The ornaments *very* carefully copied as well as all other details. For that purpose it would be necessary to employ a *first* rate artist accustomed to ornamental drawing etc. I have no doubt you could procure such a person and if you will do so, I shall be very *grateful*. Of course you will *not mention* that the drawings are for me. No time is to be lost as I believe the exhibition remains open only a short time.

You can make your own terms with the artist, provided the copies are *accurate* and *perfectly executed*, whatever you will do will be well done. I should like the scale to be generally large–say one half of the original. In short large and *distinct* enough to be easily used if I choose to have anything made from them–so the larger the better.

Yours My dear Sir
Very sincerely
(Sgd.) HERTFORD

Nothing copied of the time of the renaissance.

P.S. It might perhaps be as well, if you are good enough to undertake my little affair, to desire the Artist *not* to mention that he is employed by *you*, for everybody knows that we are friends and it would be immediately guessed that I am under the rose.

I have another favour to beg–I wish *very particularly* to know when the Duchess of Bedford's sale takes place. I believe it is at the end of this month. Pray have the goodness to find out and let me know, as soon as possible, *when* and *where* it will *come off* and if possible be so good as to send me a catalogue.

With amities
(Intd.) H

Paris July 6th 1853
CONFIDENTIAL

My dear Sir

Many thanks for your kindness in having sent me a Catalogue of the Duchess of Bedford's sale. As you intend paying a little visit to the Lodge you would very much oblige me if you would *carefully* examine the articles I call your attention to. I should like to know if they are *old* or whether they are imitations or made up, half new and half old, as is so often the case here and I dare say in London also. If you are not quite *sure*, you will most likely take an opportunity of consulting some *great* authority on the subject. As for the paintings I want no other opinion but yours. No. 774 (Landseer) sounds pretty well. These are the things I wish you to look at–287 Secretaire and book case–326 a magnificent old secretaire–914 Sevres vases. Then come in the Louis XIV drawing room the following articles that are described as being very beautiful and very likely are so and I hope you will find out whether they are *really* old or not–1017 An exquisite cabinet–1018 a most recherché secretaire–1019 a fine buffet–1020 a cabinet of great beauty–1021 a marqueterie table–1027 a work table in old marqueterie–1031 a magnificent folding screen. Now My dear Friend if you could let me have an answer by Friday's post you would much oblige me as I might like to run over and look at the things if you think them good. If, on Thursday after your visit, your impression is *good*, pray send me a *word* by the telegraph–*yes* if you approve and *no* if you do not, I shall know what those two words mean and by this means I may have a moment to prepare, in the event of my wishing to run over. Pardon all this trouble but I know how kindly disposed you always are towards me.

I am very glad our pictures were approved of by so distinguished a person as Sir Charles Eastlake. I am glad too that the drawings are going on favourably. I am sure, that under your inspection, they will be what I desire.

Yours My dear Sir
Most sincerely
(Sgd.) HERTFORD

Turn over

If you can write me a little description of what you have seen on *Thursday* and send it me by THAT DAY'S POST, it will be *perfection*. A word for each article will be quite sufficient.

(Intd.) H

THE TASTE FOR OBJETS D'ART

EXTRACTED FROM John Steegman's
Consort of Taste 1830–1870, 1950.

ALTHOUGH the collecting of pictures and Old Master drawings was a long-established tradition among English connoisseurs, the collecting of *objets d'art*, and especially of porcelain and bronzes, did not become a habit much before the middle of the [nineteenth] century; during the 1850s, however, it developed very rapidly. Ralph Bernal was one of the first English connoisseurs to collect such objects on a grand scale. Porcelain, glass, miniatures and silver were all represented so magnificently that his son Bernal Osborne used to say that the South Kensington Museum had its cradle in his father's house, 93 Eaton Square.* When Ralph Bernal died in 1854, an attempt was made to secure the collection for the nation.[1] This failed, and the result was one of the half-dozen outstanding sales of the nineteenth century. The 4300 lots, realising between £60,000 and £70,000, were dispersed, and severally formed the nucleus of most of the important collections of the next few decades. The collection as a whole had been offered to the nation for £50,000 and its acquisition had the support of the Prince Consort, Layard, Ford and many others. Gladstone, it appears, was interested, but, as Chancellor of the Exchequer, would only go as far as £20,000; to that extent Government did buy, but would not go a penny further. *Punch*† thought the Government was crazy even to go as far as that. Porcelain and glass formed, in 1855, a new departure in taste for *Punch* and its readers and, since Bernal was a very rich Jew, he and his 'crockery' were considered fair game. *Punch* gave a mock account of the 'Aarons Collection' to be sold by Messrs Aminadab Brothers of Whitechapel and consisting of cheap and common objects like teacups, tumblers and umbrellas, all with romantic and bogus historical associations attached to them. Not very funny, perhaps, nor very intelligent, but a good measure of the distance by which adventurous connoisseurs were (as they always are) ahead of the general public.

A story more fortunate in its outcome is that of the Soulanges[2] collection. A Monsieur Soulanges, of Toulouse, had a very fine collection, chiefly of majolica and bronzes, which,

* *P. H. Bagenal,* Life of Ralph Bernal Osborne, 1884.

[1] A much less well-known collector who deserves mention in this context is Felix Slade (1790–1868). A man of considerable wealth, who was attracted to the arts at an early age, he assembled a magnificent collection of glass representative of various ages and countries. He left this to the British Museum together with valuable collections of coins and medals, Japanese carvings in ivory and metal, engravings and etchings, manuscripts and bookbindings. His name has been perpetuated through his endowment of three professorships in fine arts at Oxford, Cambridge and London Universities, as well as a number of exhibitions and scholarships. Ultimately this led to the foundation of the Slade School of Fine Arts.

† Punch, *Vol. 28, 1855.*

[2] Steegman spells it thus throughout his book. The normally accepted spelling is 'Soulages'.

thanks to the great porcelain manufacturer Herbert Minton, was brought to the notice of South Kensington in 1856. Henry Cole* was sent down to Toulouse to inspect and ended up by buying the collection, through guarantors, for £11,000. This seems to have been a purely private undertaking and Government was in no way committed; which, at first, was unfortunate for the guarantors. When the collection was brought to England in October 1856 and shown (very badly) at Marlborough House, it was inspected by Palmerston. His feeling was wholly for classical art, and he had no sympathy whatever with medieval or Renaissance Italy. 'What is the use', he enquired, 'of such rubbish to our manufacturers?' So the Treasury refused to support the purchase and the Soulanges collection was sold to the Manchester Exhibition Committee of 1857. In the end, the Museum got round the Treasury and acquired the collection from the Manchester Committee piece by piece over a period of years.[1] 'Thus', said Sir Henry Cole, 'the nation acquired possession of a collection of medieval art of the greatest value to manufacturers, which has influenced pottery and furniture to a great and perceptible extent.' It is clear enough that Lord Palmerston and Sir Henry Cole were agreed upon one thing at least, and it is a point on which they will certainly have met with general consent. From whatever motives Mr Bernal or Monsieur Soulanges may have formed their great collections–porcelain, bronzes, majolica, Palissyware, silver miniatures, German glass, Renaissance furniture–these were to be regarded not as works of art, but as exemplars for modern manufacturers. Since long before the Great Exhibition, the guidance of public taste had been resigned into the hands of manufacturers, and they, encouraged thereto by the Schools of Design, were expected to find their inspiration in the Museums. The Museum and educational authorities tended to lose sight of the beauty that lay in the objects themselves, and to see the objects merely as sources of a second-hand beauty that was admirable only so far as it was derivative. The 1840s had regarded the exhibition of works of art as a means of moral improvement; the 1850s regarded it as a means of commercial advancement.

* *Sir Henry Cole:* Fifty Years of Public Life.

[1] For a full account of how his collection was acquired, see next piece.

OFFICIAL COLLECTING · THE SOULAGES COLLECTION PURCHASED

COLE was one of the outstanding public administrators of the nineteenth century, though he has so far been neglected by a modern biographer. It is largely to him that we owe the foundation of the third of the three great museums in this country after the British Museum and the National Gallery, namely the Victoria and Albert Museum in South Kensington. The difficulties of official collecting and, in particular, the financing of new purchases, are particularly well highlighted in the piece which follows.

According to the introduction of J. C. Robinson's 1857 edition of the Soulages Collection Catalogue, Jules Soulages undertook repeated tours through Italy between 1830 and 1840 'with the express purpose of acquiring specimens of Art . . . [according to] a definite scheme'. This was to collect 'a complete series of decorative objects of utility, and of those minor productions of great artists, which are not usually thought to deserve the designation of *high art*'. Robinson pointed out the 'novelty' of the Soulages plan, which meant that there was little competition for such objects and that they could be bought for very low prices. 'M. Soulages, being not only one of the earliest but most systematic of collectors, was thus able to acquire, in a few years, such a collection as could now scarcely be got together by any individual in the course of a lifetime. As a proof of the importance of his acquisitions, he has been more than once alluded to, in terms of regret, by Italian writers, as one of the most successful and untiring ravishers of the art treasures of their country.'

There were 749 numbered items in the catalogue, which included quantities of fifteenth- and sixteenth-century maiolica, Palissy ware, Venetian glass, ivories, Limoges enamels, bronzes, Italian sculpture, painted glass, medals and medallions, a few paintings, textiles and tapestries and decorative furniture.

EXTRACTED FROM Frank Davis' *Victorian Patrons of the Arts*, 1963.

THE fourth member of this influential quartet[1] was Henry Cole (died 1882), an astonishingly industrious individual, who, among other achievements, played a considerable part in establishing the Public Records Office, and was the Prince's right-hand

[1] Of enlightened individuals who could look beyond the taste of their time: the other three were the Prince Consort; Sir Charles Eastlake, Director of the National Gallery (see page 302);

man in promoting the Great Exhibition of 1851, from which sprang the Museum of South Kensington. He was Director of the South Kensington Museum and one of the founders of the National Training School, later reorganised as the Royal College of Music, and he was never so happy as when writing papers on such varied subjects as Army reform or the management of the Paris Exhibition of 1855. He was also the inspirer of the first Christmas card, designed for him by John Horsley in 1845, and so may perhaps be considered as the co-inventor with Charles Dickens of the English Christmas.

In his *Fifty Years of Public Work*, published in 1884, two years after his death, the first part written by himself, the second compiled by his son and daughter from his papers, Cole stands revealed as indefatigable and imperturbable, adroit in his dealings and–once he had reached what seemed to him a correct decision–hanging on with bull-terrier-like tenacity. He tells his story simply enough and in considerable detail, providing a vivid picture of the manoeuvres he sometimes found necessary to achieve the intended result.

A typical campaign was that undertaken to acquire the Soulages collection for the nation. When Cole was in Paris as Commissioner for the British Section of the Paris Exhibition of 1855, he was shown some photographs of maiolica, bronzes and other subjects which had been gathered together over many years by M. Soulages, an advocate of Toulouse. Cole went to Toulouse in October, spent two days examining the collection and came to the conclusion that 'it was my duty to effect the purchase if possible for the nation, and that it would be of great use to manufacturers'. On his return to England he met with all kinds of objections–even his colleague and assistant, Richard Redgrave, R.A., was against him. The Prince Consort, however, as on many other occasions, gave him his support in a very practical manner by guaranteeing £1000, and in due course Cole got promises of other guarantees up to £24,800.

Meanwhile the collection was valued, item by item, by John Webb, to a total of £11,782, and Webb negotiated the purchase with M. Soulages for £11,000–£3000 down and the balance by a bill payable in three years. Freight, insurance and various unavoidable expenses brought up the total cost to £13,500. The £3000 was advanced by Coutts and Co., and the vendor agreed to accept Cole's personal promissory note for £8000. Cole explains he had to arrange this as his two co-trustees were abroad and it was necessary to conclude the business in order to obtain possession of the collection.

The collection duly reached London in October 1865, and was catalogued and arranged at Marlborough House in December. Thanks to Palmerston's obtuseness, the Treasury refused to have anything to do with it. Cole must have been more than annoyed at the time, though his narrative gives the impression that he regarded this kind of set-back as all in the day's work. He immediately looked about him and remembered that by the trust deed the collection, if not bought by the state, was to be sold by the trustees.

and Sir Augustus Wollaston Franks, Keeper of the Department of British and Medieval Antiquities and Ethnography in the British Museum from 1866 to 1896. He refused the post of Principal Librarian, and thus the Directorship of the British Museum once, and the Directorship of the Victoria and Albert Museum twice. He left his immense private collection to the British Museum on his death.

It so happened that Manchester was just then organising that landmark in the history of exhibitions, the Manchester Art Treasures Exhibiton of 1857—the first of its kind to be held in England. The committee asked for the loan of the Soulages collection. Cole explained that he and his co-trustees had no power to lend, but only to sell; so he sold the collection to the Manchester executive under these conditions:

(1) If the Art Treasures Exhibition yielded a balance, the balance was to be used to found an art museum in Manchester with the Soulages collection as a beginning.

(2) If there was no balance, the collection was to be sold by auction, Cole and his co-trustees and the Manchester executive having joint and equal rights of purchase at the sale. This presumably meant that they would not bid against one another but would come to an amicable arrangement as to which items they wanted.

The committee promptly borrowed £13,500 from its bankers at four per cent interest, and paid up. M. Soulages was then asked if he would be so kind as to accept the whole amount due to him with interest, giving up Cole's promissory note for £8000; to which he replied, that 'he preferred to hold the promissory note of an Englishman to any other security'. However, it was at length explained to him that if Cole happened to die in the meantime there might be difficulty about payment, so he finally agreed to take the money. At this point Soulages disappears from the story, leaving behind him a pleasant old-world fragrance; one would like to know more about him.

No doubt at this stage a lesser man than Cole would have thrown in his hand. Instead he made another application to the Treasury asking them to buy the collection for the nation, and he received the accustomed dusty answer; a sale by auction in Manchester seemed inevitable. There now occurred a change in high places; Lord Derby took office with Lord Salisbury as Lord President of the Council. Cole applied to the Treasury for the third time and was again refused. Having failed in no fewer than three frontal attacks, he threw in his reserves upon an unguarded flank. On the authority of a Board of Trade minute of 1852, the Practical Art Department was in the habit from time to time of hiring objects and paying a rental for them. The Manchester Committee was accordingly asked to rent the collection to the Department and to give it the right to purchase individual objects annually as funds were available until the whole had been acquired. The Manchester Committee was amenable and Lord Salisbury, no less readily, sanctioned the agreement.

Purchases began immediately and, continues Cole, were made at the rate of about £2000 per annum. The Treasury reacted promptly, accusing the Department of not only acting without sanction, but also of incurring debt. In reply, Mr Lowe, Vice-President of the Committee of the Council on Education, drafted a letter pointing out that no debt had been incurred, that rent was not interest, and that the entire transaction was in accordance with normal practice. 'Thus', crows Henry Cole with justifiable pride, 'the nation acquired possession of a collection of medieval art of the greatest value to manufacturers, which, in the course of a quarter of a century, had influenced pottery and furniture to a great and perceptible extent. It has proved a most profitable investment and, if it were sold now, would realise much more than the money paid for it.'

SALE OF THE BERNAL COLLECTION

To Ralph Bernal, a highly intelligent man trained as a barrister and a Member of Parliament for thirty years, more than to any other single individual in the history of English collecting, we owe the shift of interest among collectors from the work of the artist to the product of the craftsman. Bernal's collection, almost in its entirety, was the stuff museums are made of.[1] Even if Bernal's taste was very much his own, the quality of the objects was such that we very rarely see their like in salerooms nowadays. With the gift of hindsight we can regret today that museum authorities bought objects of this sort so avidly as 'models for manufacturers' in the middle decades of the last century, but we can take comfort from the fact that so many have been so perfectly preserved in this country for this very reason.

Although a number of authors writing about him seemed to think that Bernal was a man of unlimited wealth, he was not in fact a rich man and he had a marvellous eye for a bargain. This is well illustrated by the following story told by Redford.

'Mr Bernal had such a reputation that whenever he was observed to admire anything it was quite enough to enhance its value in the eyes of the dealers, and thus it required no small diplomacy on his part to obtain the object he wanted at a reasonable price. A good story was told by the late Mr Carpenter, the keeper of the prints in the British Museum. Mr Bernal had called at Colnaghi's, the great print sellers in Pall Mall, as he often did, and found Dominic Colnaghi, who was the best expert in the line, looking over a heap of prints bought at a sale. Bernal glancing over his shoulder spied one of Hogarth's "Midnight Modern Conversation", and said carelessly, "I say, Dominic, you seem to have got there a pretty good impression; what do you want for it?" Colnaghi, busy with his searching for better things and without examining the print, said, "Oh, three guineas". "I'll take it," said Bernal. "Shall I send it home for you?" asked Colnaghi. "No, thank you, I'll take it now," answered Bernal rolling up the print, and walking out of the shop, chuckling over having thus got the rare early impression in which the word 'Modern' is spelt 'Moddern', as his quick eye had told him at a glance. When this print was sold in the Bernal sale of books and prints at Sotheby's, Feb. 1855, Mr Carpenter determined to have it for the Museum, but he had to pay £81 18s for it.'

---

[1] For full details see Christie's illustrated catalogue of March 1855. This was republished by Henry G. Bohn in 1862 as *A Guide to the Knowledge of Pottery, Porcelain and other Objects of Virtue*, because he had bought the wood engravings 'for a mere trifle'. The latter were the work of A. J. Mason from drawings by Henry Fitzcook. Bohn included the prices obtained at the sale and the buyers of the pieces.

SALE OF THE BERNAL COLLECTION

EXTRACTED FROM W. Roberts' *Memorials of Christie's*, A Record of Art Sales from 1766 to 1896, Vol. 1, 1897.

MR Ralph Bernal's sale in 1855 marks an epoch in the history of such events. The collection comprised 4294 lots, it occupied 32 days in selling, and realised the grand total of £62,690 18s, whilst the prints, books and furniture brought it up to £70,954 4s. In a note prefixed to the sale catalogue of Messrs Christie and Manson, J. R. Planché wrote: 'Distinguished amongst English antiquaries by the perfection of his taste, as well as the extent of his knowledge, the difficulty of imposing upon him was increased by the necessity of the fabrication being fine enough in form, colour or workmanship, to rival the masterpiece it simulated: to be, in fact, itself a gem of art which it would not *pay* to produce as a relic of antiquity. Mr Bernal could be tempted by nothing that was inferior. Even his pictures, though avowedly not selected for their value as paintings, but for their illustration of costume, have probably, taken as a whole, more merit in them than any similar collection in Europe.'

Ralph Bernal, who was of Hebrew descent, was born about 1783, and was educated at Christ's College, Cambridge, where he graduated B.A., 1806, and M.A., in 1809; he was called to the Bar at Lincoln's Inn, 5 February 1810. Not being a Jew by religion he was eligible for Parliament, which he entered as member for Lincoln in 1818, and, in 1820, for Rochester, which he represented in nine Parliaments; in 1841 he stood for Weymouth and was seated on petition: at the dissolution of 1852 he retired from Parliament. In 1830, Mr Bernal was appointed Chairman of Committees of the House of Commons, at a salary of £2000 a year, and this office he filled for twenty years. He died on 26 August 1854. 'He lived', writes Mr Humphrey Ward, 'at a time when no one either knew or cared about the choice things which nowadays ten thousand collectors seek for with frenzy. No one of his contemporaries in England–though Sauvagest and others were equally fine judges in France–knew so much as he about old armour or mediaeval goldsmiths' work, or the steel inlaying of the Milanese, or the makers and the decorators of the *pâte* tendre of Sèvres, or about majolica, or those infinitely delicate kinds of Chinese porcelain for which English and American connoisseurs are prepared to pay any price. What times those were for the collector! one is tempted to say as one looks through the priced Bernal catalogue with its pretty engravings by Mason after Fitzcook's drawings. The things sold for what we should consider literally nothing, though in almost every case they marked a considerable advance on the price Mr Bernal paid. As you walk through the South Kensington Museum, you can discover numbers of specimens of Limoges

PILGRIM-SHAPED GRÈS BOTTLE.

Dresden Porcelain Clock.

enamel, or of the "ruby-backed" oriental plates, or of a score of other curiosities with labels marking the price at which they were obtained in the Bernal sale: £3 for the plates, £50 or £60 for the pieces of Limoges, and so forth – in every instance about one-tenth or one-twentieth part of what would be paid now, so tremendous has been the effect of the spread of education, the diffusion of wealth and the desire to possess at least some of the choice works of the past. What was remarkable however, in the Bernal collection, was not the low prices at which things had been bought and were sold, but the faultless taste that had presided over their acquisition. Mr Woods, the present well-known and accomplished head of Christie's firm, is fond of quoting this Bernal sale as the supreme instance of a perfect collection; there was nothing, out of all the 4294 objects that was not good, genuine, and may it almost be said in intact condition.'*

The sale began on Monday, 5 March 1855, and concluded on 30 April. As a cheap edition, with illustrations, of the catalogue is published in Bohn's Illustrated Library, anything like an exhaustive analysis of the sale is unnecessary, and we must content ourselves with enumerating a few of the more interesting or important items. Dresden porcelain: a pair of small sceaux scalloped, each with eight small subjects of figures, £40 – these beautiful specimens were purchased by Mr Bernal for £5; an egg-shaped scalloped vase, with two subjects after Watteau, flowers on gold ground, 40 guineas; a clock in the form of a temple, with pilasters at the angles, and dome top, surmounted by two female figures, dated 1727, 18 in. high, £120 (Sir A. de Rothschild), see illustration; a pair of superb candelabra, each formed of a female draped figure bearing several branches for five lights, 24 in. high, 220 guineas (Marquis of Bath), see illustration; a pair of two-handled vases and ewers, painted with Chinese figures, and colours, £54 (Baron M. Rothschild). Old Chelsea: a pair of beautiful globular scalloped vases and covers, deep blue, painted with exotic limes, 105 guineas (S. Addington); and an écuelle, and cover and stand, with pink scalloped edges, 26 guineas (F. Baring). Grés de Flandres: a blue and white pilgrim-shaped bottle, with perforated ridges at

Dresden Candelabrum.

* Scribner's, *December 1890.*

FAENZA WARE—A PILGRIM'S BOTTLE.

the sides, inscriptions relating to the shield and arms of the Prince of Orange, and medallion of a helmeted head, date 1590, £18 (British Museum), see illustration on page 000.

Faenza and Raffaelle ware: a salt-cellar of Raffaelle ware, of triangular form, painted with rich ornaments of cupids and negroes' heads, date 1532, $2\frac{6}{8}$ in high by 6 in. long, £61 (British Museum): a Tazza-shaped dish, deep blue, with ten cupids supporting banners, date 1520, 10 in. diameter, £61 (A. Fountain); a flat-shaped pilgrim's bottle, with cover, snake handle, embellished with arabesque ornaments, camei, and subjects of Hercules and the Centaur, date about 1540, $12\frac{1}{2}$ in. high, 11 in. wide, 40 guineas (Baron A. de Rothschild),–see illustration; and a plate of the most rare and interesting character, in very strong colours; the subject believed to be Raffaelle himself and the Fornarina seated in the studio of an artist, who is occupied in painting a plate; $9\frac{1}{4}$ in. diameter, £120 (Marlborough House) [see Plate 82] this lot realised at the Stowe sale, 17 August 1848, only £4, and it was afterwards sold to Mr Bernal for £5. Palissy ware: a circular dish, on a foot, a lizard in the centre and with very rich border, $12\frac{1}{4}$ in. diameter, £162 (Baron G. de Rothschild)–a true specimen of the extremely rare Palissy ware, purchased in a broken state in Paris for 12 francs, and after being admirably restored, sold to Mr Bernal for £4.

Sèvres: an écuelle, cover and stand, gros-bleu, painted with six subjects of cupids by Chabry, 1771, £125 (Marlborough House); an elegant vase, with handles of goats' heads, gros-bleu, with frieze and gold, with an exquisite medallion of Fame recording the events of Time, 14 in. high, 121 guineas (S. Addington)–this article cost Mr Bernal 17 guineas; a gros-bleu vase and cover of beautiful form, with two handles, and festoons and leaves falling from the centre of the neck to the bottom of the handles painted with Venus, Adonis, and Cupid in front, and bouquet of flowers on reverse, $16\frac{1}{2}$ in. high, 213 guineas (S. Rucker); a magnificent cabaret of the finest gros-bleu, with wreaths of gold, consisting of plateau, teapot, sucrier and cover, milkpot, and two cups and saucers painted by Leguay, 1775–6, £465 (Marquis of Bath)–said to have cost Mr Bernal 65 guineas; a pair of fine vases and covers, green ground pencilled with gold, each with two bouquets with flowers in medallions by Dodet, 17 in., 305 guineas (C. Mills); a pair of oval jardinières, a very fine bleu de Vincennes ground, with children

SÈVRES VASE, ROSE DU BARRI.

after Boucher, 1754, £100 (Lord Falmouth); a pair of vases rose du Barri, each painted with two groups of cupids in medallions, the curved leaf-shaped lips forming handles, 14½ in., £1942 10s (Hertford)–see illustration; this magnificent pair of vases were formerly in the possession of Henry Baring, who sold them to Mr Bernal for about £200; a pair of vases of very elegant form, turquoise, with oval medallions of a shepherdess, and a girl bathing her feet, by Dodet and Drand, 18 in. £1417 10s (the same); a noble oviform vase and cover, green with gilt busts forming the handles, exquisite painting of a peasant family, in the manner of Greuze, 18 in. high, £388 10s (the same), see illustration; a pair of tall vases, and covers of rare form, gros bleu, delicately pencilled with gold stripes with medallion of a sacrifice to Venus and Bacchus, 14 in. high, £700 (S. H. Sutherland); a centre vase and cover, gros-bleu with upright handles, the centre with an exquisite painting of a peasant and two girls gathering cherries, donkey with panniers at their side, 18 in. high, £871 10s (Marquis of Hertford); a pair of vases and covers of equally high quality, gros-bleu, on the necks are two exquisite paintings by Gremont of a nymph at the bath, 15½ in. high £900 (Sir A. de Rothschild)–see illustration; and a pair of oviform vases and covers of equally high quality, gros-bleu, with flat handles, the front nearly covered with an exquisite painting of Bacchus seated, with a nymph presenting a wreath to Cupid in landscapes, 13 in. high, £590 (Marquis of Bath).

SÈVRES VASE.
(Bernal Sale.)

The antique jewellery, rings, crosses, brooches, and ormanents included an ancient Gaelic brooch, of silver, of circular form, scalloped and surrounded by small upright obelisks, each set with a pearl at top; in the centre is a round crystalline ball, considered a magical gem, 4¾ in. diameter, £71 (British Museum). This Scottish brooch is traditionally said to have been made by a tinker on the estate of Lochbury in Mull, from a silver one found there in or about the year 1500, and it was successively the property of Dr Lort, at the sale of whose effects 15 July 1791 it was purchased by Samuel Tysson; from them, at Tysson's sale, 18 May 1802, it was purchased by Mr Bindley, and at his sale by Mr Thomas, and again at Thomas's sale by Mr Bernal, for 10 guineas. The armour and arms comprised complete suits, cross-bows, daggers, gauntlets, guns, pistols, halberds, helmets, swords, shields, bucklers, and so forth. The Byzantine metal work, included King Lothaire's magic crystal, a highly interesting relic, engraved with the whole history of Susannah, in copper gilt, gothic frames set

OLD SÈVRES VASE AND COVER.

with imitations of precious stones, the crystal 4½ in. diameter £267, (British Museum)–this object was purchased in the Low Countries for 12 francs, and sold to Mr Bernal for £10. The more interesting examples of medieval work included Sir Thomas More's brass candlesticks, or rather flower vases, with flowers and leaves enamelled in blue and white, 221 guineas (Duke of Hamilton); the celebrated copper formed Reliquaire of the kings, copper gilt enamelled with blue and turquoise, presented by Pope Eugenius IV to Philip le Bon Duke of Burgundy, containing at the time the relics found in the Chatreux at Dijon in 1430, £66 (British Museum); and the St Thomas à Becket Reliquaire, a small coffer of copper gilt, richly enamelled with blue, on the front is represented the martyrdom of the saint, 4¾ inches long, nearly 2½ inches wide and 6½ inches high (see illustration) £28 17s 6d (Col. Sibthorp, M.P.)–this is said to have cost £12. Of the large number of Limoges enamel we can only mention an elegant ewer, with a fine subject of an equestrian combat around the body, and with busts in medallions of Henri II or Francis I, 10 inches by 4 inches, 130 guineas (S. Addington); and a beautiful casket in original silver gilt chased mounting, highly embellished with gems, camei, etc., and composed of five plaques of enamels in panels representing the sibyls in black and white, 4½ in. long by 5½ in. wide (see illustration), 240 guineas (Mr T. Smith, M.P.).

St. Thomas à Beckett Reliquaire.

Finally, the pictures included: Largillière, Pretender, in red dress wearing the Order of the Garter, and his sister in white satin at his side, 26 × 21, 111 guineas (Farrer); Mignard, Madame de Maintenon, in a yellow damask dress and blue robe lined with ermine, 52 × 40, 80 guineas (Duke of Hamilton); and Princess Henrietta, Duchess of Orleans, in a blue and white dress, ornamented with fleurs-de-lys, 40 × 33, 78 guineas (Vardon), 'this beautiful portrait is one of the last works of the master'; Drouais (not Greuze as catalogued), Madame de Pompadour in a white flowered dress, with a muff, oval, 185 guineas (S. Lyne Stephens); Mytens, Charles I, in a pink silk dress with slashed sleeves with lace collar, and the ribbon and badge of the Garter, 46 × 36, 80 guineas (Duke of Hamilton); Sir Peter Lely, Nell Gwynne, in a white dress and blue mantle, seated on a bank in a landscape, 49 × 40, 62 guineas (J. Neeld, M.P.); Cuyp, William II, Prince of Orange, in a white dress, edged with gold on a brown horse, 19 × 13, 100 guineas

A Casket of Limoges Enamel.

(Marquis of Londonderry); Primaticcio, the Cardinal of Chantillon, in a crimson damask dress and cloak, with a broad front of ermine, a small red cap on his head, half-length, 36 × 28, dated 1531, £163 (H.R.H. the Duc d'Aumale); S. Coello, Anna Maria of Austria, Queen of Philip II of Spain, in white silk dress, ornamented with broad gold bands of arabesque pattern, 'a noble *chef-d'oeuvre* of the great Spanish portrait painter', signed, 205 guineas (Sir H. H. Campbell); W. Mieris, Portrait of the artist in a yellow silk dress and crimson velvet cloak fastened by a jewel, oval 34 in. high, 62 guineas (Nieu wen huys); Palomino, Isabella de Valois, wife of Philip II in a black dress with pink sleeves, with necklace of pearls and jewels 75 × 43, 110 guineas (C. Mills); Janet, Elizabeth of Austria (not Isabel), Queen of Charles IX of France in white dress, beautifully ornamented with jewels, three-quarter length, 14 × 10, 147 guineas (Duc d'Aumale); Janet, or more probably Bernard Van Orley, Eleanor of Portugal, Queen of Francis I, in a black dress with slashed sleeves, three-quarter length, 15½ × 12, 212 guineas (the same); Holbein, Anne of Cleves in a black dress ornamented with broad stripes of gold damask, gold chain around her neck, a flat gold cap on her head, half-length, 15 in. × 14 in., 'an exquisite portrait on vellum', 175 guineas (Morant); Holbein, Lady Johanna Abergavenny, in a crimson dress with yellow sleeves, a gold head dress embroidered with initials, A.I., half-length, from Strawberry Hill, 16 × 12, 52 guineas (R. Neville); and the Portrait of Nicholas Lord Vaux, the poet and musician in a black dress and cap, seated at a table, an open book before him, he holds a viol de gambe in his left hand, green drapery behind, 17½ × 17, 'a most beautiful portrait of the highest interest', 100 guineas (Morant); and a Portrait by an unknown artist of Edward IV, in a gold dress and crimson cloak edged with fur, 150 guineas (Duke of Newcastle).

A GENEROUS DONATION

THERE have been many references to the generosity of English collectors in giving works of art to museums. The delightfully casual air which concealed such benefactions in the nineteenth century is particularly well demonstrated by the following correspondence now in the archives of the Department of Western Art in the Ashmolean Museum, Oxford.

The donor in this case was the Hon. W. T. H. Fox Strangways (1795–1865) who succeeded as 4th Earl of Ilchester in 1858.[1] He was a diplomat. In 1828 he had already given a collection of paintings to Christ Church, where he had been a

[1] For an earlier mention of the Ilchester family as collectors, see page 92.

student from 1813 to 1824[1]. He had collected these while he was secretary to the British Legation in Florence between 1825 and 1828. The remaining collections at Abbotsbury, the Ilchester family house,[2] were destroyed by fire early in the present century.

The letters were addressed to the Rev. Dr Henry Wellesley (1791–1866), natural son of Richard, Marquess of Wellesley. He became Vice-President of New Inn Hall, Oxford in 1842 and Principal in 1847. He was a curator of the University Galleries, and himself formed an important collection of Old Master drawings which deeply impressed Dr Waagen, even though his inspection of them was brief. Waagen described Wellesley as 'a man of the kindest and most refined manners, who unites the warmest love of art with the choicest taste. The strength of his collection consists in drawings by Titian and Claude, and I know no collection, either public or private, which possesses so rich a series of specimens by both masters.'[3]

There were thirty-nine paintings in the Fox Strangways' gift to the Ashmolean. They included work by Fra Filippo Lippi, Morone, Orcagna, Pintoricchio, Cosimo Rosselli, Sano di Pietro and Uccello, and include some of the most famous pictures in Oxford's museum.[4]

LETTER 1

31 Old Burlington St
11 Feby 1850

My dear Wellesley,

As I hear from various quarters that the picture gallery at Oxford is now finished [it was opened in 1845], and in a state to receive works of art to which it is destined, I should feel greatly obliged to you if you could let me know whether the Trustees would accept from me the present of a few works of the very old Masters, somewhat similar to those which I formerly gave to Christ Church?

They were bought at Rome some years later than the others and comprise works of rather a different style and school, but of the same age.

[1] For a full description, see J. Byam Shaw's Catalogue of *Paintings by Old Masters at Christ Church Oxford*, London, 1967.

[2] A detailed catalogue of the Earl of Ilchester's Collection was published in two volumes. The first (1883) listed pictures at Melbury, Redlynch, Abbotsbury and 42 Belgrave Square; the second (1904) listed those at Holland House.

[3] It was sold by Sotheby's after Wellesley's death in June 1866. The sale lasted fourteen days and realised just over £20,000, though Redford (*Art Sales*, Vol. I) tells us that some of the prices were ridiculously low even by the standards prevailing in 1888.

[4] This donation in some ways resembles the bequest by Charles Brinsley Marlay to the Fitzwilliam Museum in Cambridge in 1912. The quality here was not so high and 84 pictures only were retained out of a much higher total. The others were sold at Christie's in 1916 and 1924, and from the proceeds of the sales eight further pictures were purchased.

I had them slightly touched and put in order by Woodburn [the dealer] when they first came over, since when they have been lying in a case in Landsdowne House, and would have been offered to the Trustees last year, but that Woodburn intimated to me he was in treaty to sell a large collection of that sort of his own, to the Oxford Gallery–which I find on enquiry today, has not been brought to bear.

Let me know how the case can be addressed and sent so as to come safely to its destination, and sometime in the next month, if not before, I will take care it shall be forwarded to Oxford.

Often enquiring after you, and much wishing to see you
believe me yrs most truly

W. Fox Strangways

LETTER 2

Melbury
6 March 1850

My dear Wellesley,

I am very glad to hear that the pictures arrived safe and that you approve of them as far as you have been able to judge. I have not the List of them here but I will look for it as soon as I can and send it you. I believe most of them have a name or indication on their backs.

I have only one request to make respecting them which is that if you find any of them from injury or any other cause unworthy to be put up in the Gallery, you will not scruple to use your own judgement and put them aside at once without considering me. My object is to shew a respectable set of paintings without reference to number.

Some time after Easter I hope to be able to revisit Oxford, of which I will not fail to give you notice.

Yours most sincerely

W. Fox Strangways

LETTER 3

11 March 1850

My dear Wellesley,

I think our last letters must have crossed each other. However I will not delay answering yours and saying that I shall be much obliged to you if you will set apart the two heads after Guido which certainly do not belong to the old collection.

I will take possession of them when I come to Oxford–they were painted by Trajan Wallis, a very promising artist when I was at Florence but of whom I have heard nothing since.

Believe me yours sincerely

W. Fox Strangways

LETTER 4

31 Old Burlington St
25 Octr 1850

My dear Wellesley,

I did not tell you when I was at Oxford that there remained one case more of pictures I intended to complete the series I presented to the Institution. In fact I was so struck by the dimness and dustiness of some of those last sent, that I thought it better to have these, not cleaned professionally, but carefully dusted and washed, nothing more, before sending them. It was then vacation time and I considered it might be more convenient to wait till you were at Oxford again, and I in London, before expediting them.

If you please then I shall send this case down, addressed to you, or to Mr Fisher, Taylor Instn, Oxford in the course of next week. One painting in it, I think I may anticipate will particularly engage your attention.

Pray give my best compliments to Mr Smith and believe me sincerely

yr.

W. Fox Strangways

THE EASTLAKES ON TOUR

THERE have already been frequent references both to Sir Charles and to Lady Eastlake. In everything to do with the arts in England Charles Eastlake dominated the scene between 1840 and 1865. He was born in Plymouth in 1793. First he attended the grammar school at Plympton; then he went to Charterhouse, and while there he struck up a friendship with the painter Benjamin Haydon. He left early to set about the study of painting, both in England and on the Continent. In fact he travelled a great deal. During 1814–15 he was in Paris and saw the Louvre full of Napoleon's looted pictures. He went to Greece and Italy and settled for some time in Rome. He had acquired a considerable reputation as a painter by his middle thirties and, with his fabulously retentive memory, a knowledge of pictures that was probably rivalled in Europe only by Dr Waagen. Similar though the two men were, Eastlake was in every respect the greater man and possessed a more forceful and outstanding personality. The tidiness of mind, which probably restricted him from rising above the level of a painter of second rank, came into its own where administrative capacity was concerned.[1] The rare combination of artistic insight and administrative ability was soon much in demand for official posts. Eastlake filled many and refused more. Those that concern us most are his presidency of the Royal Academy, his secretaryship of the Royal Fine Arts Commission, and his ten years as Director of the National Gallery from 1855 to 1865.

Eastlake had a remarkable gift for getting on with people. A contemporary described 'his easy, yet courteous manners, his graceful way of conveying information, his highly cultivated mind and musical voice, together with his readiness to converse with the least as with the most important guests [which], left a strong impression on all. . . . I met Sir Charles Eastlake at many houses after 1843, but nowhere so frequently as with the Poet Rogers and his Sister, where he was always the most intimate friend and "much desired guest". Well do I remember the anxiety with which they awaited answers from their invitations to him! "If Eastlake can come we are sure of a pleasant party," Mr Rogers would say, and "what are we to do without Eastlake?" was often said by him, and by many others, and always found an echo.'[2]

Of his innumerable friendships three were to have the greatest effect upon Eastlake's life. The first was with Sir Robert Peel. 'Peel felt both affection and admiration for Eastlake: he also felt in some degree responsible for him.'[3] Most of the little we know of Eastlake's life is drawn from a *Memoir* of him compiled by his widow and published in 1870, five years after Sir Charles' death.[4] Here Lady Eastlake describes the relationship between the two men.

'Another very highly valued result of the position now occupied by Mr Eastlake was the friendship entertained for him by Sir Robert Peel. His visits to Drayton[5] – and on one occasion he was the only guest – opened scenes of domestic English life of peculiar attraction to him. He here saw the great statesman in all the variety of character that belonged to him – the country gentleman – the ardent farmer – the kind neighbour – the philanthropist – the man of letters – the patron of art – and the centre of happiness in his own family; while occasionally he touched on those larger and profounder topics to which his life was mainly devoted. The subjects of

[1] Waagen's rather starchy tribute to Sir Charles is of interest here: 'I had the pleasure of meeting here with Mr Eastlake, the painter, whom I had become acquainted with when he was on a visit to Berlin [in 1828]. Of all the present historical painters in England, he is distinguished by solid study, correctness, and refinement of taste, and by his colouring, which, though brilliant, is not offensively glaring, as is too often the case here, but kept within due bounds. He is at the same time one of those rare instances of artists who, like Schinkel, have acquired a general knowledge of art in all its branches, and commencing with enthusiastic devotion to their art, have gradually attained a very clear intuitive idea of the essential nature and the fundamental laws of the plastic arts.' *Works of Art and Artists in England*, Vol. I.

[2] *Sunny Memories, containing Personal Recollections of Some Celebrated Characters*, M.L. (Mrs M. Lloyd), 1880.

[3] John Steegman, *Consort of Taste*, 1950. Steegman was certainly the first authority in recent times to recognise the importance of Eastlake in his era.

[4] *Contribution to the Literature of the Fine Arts* (second series) by Sir Charles Eastlake, 1870.

[5] See page 247.

art and artists and the best mode of promoting and benefitting each took of course the lead in the *tête-à-tête* walks on the noble terrace, interspersed with plans for obtaining more space for the National Gallery, and for enlarging the sculpture-room at the Royal Academy. And while Mr Eastlake wondered how his distinguished host could give his mind to so many topics – and to all with thoroughness – it was with no little surprise that he discovered that Sir Robert had read and mastered the Handbook of Italian Painting, by Kugler, lately edited by himself.[1] At Drayton, too, he met the leading men of every class and country, who offered points of contact with Sir Robert Peel's extended interests and duties.'

As a direct consequence of this friendship, Peel decided to appoint Eastlake Keeper of the National Gallery in succession to Seguier. (The post of Keeper was up-graded to Director later. Eastlake resigned as Keeper in 1847 and was re-appointed as first Director in 1855, five years after Peel's death.) The correspondence is of interest.

Peel wrote to Eastlake on 15 November 1843: 'The death of Mr Seguier has occasioned a Vacancy in the Office of Keeper of the Pictures of the Royal National Gallery.

'Being convinced that there is no person better qualified than yourself for the discharge of the Duties of that Appointment, I have recommended to the Lords Commiss[rs] of the Treasury that an offer of it, which I trust will be acceptable, should be made to you.'

And Eastlake replied to Peel on 16 November 1843: 'Thus honoured by your choice, and deeply grateful for such notice, I do not for a moment hesitate to express my own willingness to undertake the office in the hope that, at least by integrity and attention to the duties connected with it, I may not be unworthy of the confidence which you have placed in me.'

And when the Duke of Newcastle wrote to Peel proposing two candidates of his own for the job, Peel explained that he could do nothing for them: the appointment was given to Eastlake, 'one of the Eminent Artists of the Country'.[2]

Eastlake had long been consulted by friends, colleagues and remote acquaintances who wanted to buy or sell paintings. Yet there was curiously little consultation when museum trustees were considering purchases. Lady Eastlake describes how her husband effectively changed this rather cavalier attitude.

[1] It had been published by Murray in 1842 as a volume in his celebrated 'Handbook for Travellers' series. Its influence and popularity was such that by 1874 Lady Eastlake was editing a fourth 'revised and re-modelled' and greatly enlarged edition. The third edition had appeared in 1855. As Lady Eastlake herself acknowledged, it was the monumental five-volume *History of Painting in Italy* by Crowe and Cavalcaselle (also published by Murray), the last two volumes of which had appeared a little earlier, that forced the large-scale revision of Kugler. In *Consort of Taste* Steegman gives an interesting account of the collaboration between Crowe and Cavalcaselle that resulted in this outstanding work.

[2] The three letters quoted are in the British Museum: Add. MSS 40, 536 ff 3, 22 and 24. The editor is most grateful to Professor David Robertson for drawing his attention to this correspondence. There has long been a need for a full biography of Eastlake. Professor Robertson's is nearing completion.

79–82 The collection formed by Ralph Bernal was one of the first, and also one of the most remarkable, ever assembled, of *objets d'art* rather than pictures or antiquities. It was hoped at one stage to purchase it for the nation, but when this failed it was sold by Christie's in 1855. Many of its treasures ultimately became the nucleus of various museum collections.

Shown here (top left) is a coloured Limoges enamel plaque of a head of Christ by J. Pénicaud, c. 1550; (bottom left) a fifteenth-century German or Flemish silver gilt chalice; (top right) an Italian maiolica plate of about 1450; and (bottom right) another maiolica plate showing a painter at work, of about 1515. It fetched £120 at the Bernal Sale. All four pieces are now in the Victoria and Albert Museum.

83 Ralph Bernal, one of the first and greatest collectors of *objets d'art.*

84 Alexander, 10th Duke of Hamilton, had married the younger daughter of William Beckford, and many of the Beckford treasures passed to the Duke, who was an ardent collector in his own right in the grandest of grand manners.

85 At the time of the Sale, Hamilton Palace was described by *The Times* as 'a stone edifice of vast size built in the debased classic style of the seventeenth century'. New wings had been added in 1838 to house the Beckford library on the West and the new state rooms on the East. The Palace contained 'probably the finest single collection ever to come on the market'. Christie's sold it in 2213 lots in seventeen days in 1882.

86, Two of the more fabulous items from the Hamilton Palace Sale, which altogether fetched a total of nearly
87 £400,000. They were described as: (above) 'Limoges enamel, quadrangular tablet, very exquisitely painted in grisaille on a black ground, from the Collection of M. Defournet, Paris 1820'; it was bought by G. Allenborough for £1328 5s. Below is 'a Louis XVI commode, of ebony, inlaid with shaped panels of lacquer, with birds and plants in gold on black ground, mounted with ormolu by Gouthiere, with friezes formed of wreaths of flowers and ribbons, and the monogram of Marie Antoinette'. It was bought by Wertheimer for £9450.

88 A picture sale at Christie's, 1888 (see page 344).

89 A book sale at Sotheby's (in their saleroom in Wellington Street, Strand) in 1892.

90 A photograph of a collection of some 200 bronzes (Egyptian, Minoan, Greek, Etruscan and Roman) on the vast desk which had once belonged to Warren Hastings in the study of Captain Spencer-Churchill at Northwick Park in 1965. He kept his favourite pieces on the mantelpiece (on the left).

91 The Northwick Park Collection was one of the largest single collections to come up for sale for many years (Christie's, 1964/5). The early English portraits shown here were among what Captain Spencer-Churchill called the 'Northwick Rescues'; for his particular delight was the rediscovery of works long lost or wrongly attributed or simply unrecognisable through layers of grime and varnish.

92 A sale of modern British sculpture held at Sotheby's in December 1966. The head of Sir Winston Churchill is by Sir William Reid Dick. Another Churchill head by Sir Jacob Epstein made £6000 in the same sale.

93 Peter Wilson, Chairman of Sotheby's from 1958-1979, auctioning Picasso's *Mother and Child* in April 1967. It reached a then record figure of £190,000 for a work by a living artist. The picture was put up for sale again at Christie's in December 1971, but failed to reach its reserve and was withdrawn at £287,000.

94 Arthur Grimwade, silver expert at Christie's for many years, has given English silver a new stature in the collecting world. Here he is examining items during the cataloguing of Lord Brownlow's collection. It was sold in May 1963 and fetched £141,000. In 1994 he published a charming autobiography entitled *Silver for Sale: Christie's in the Thirties.*

95 England still has a multitude of unrecorded treasures. This set of Lambeth Delftware drug jars in mint condition (four more not in the photograph were in use) were seen in a chemist's shop in the Midlands in 1968. They had been acquired for the original chemist's shop about 1740.

96 The artist as collector: all but two of these sketch-models of what probably constitutes his finest work were retained by Henry Moore for himself and his daughter.

'At that time, it must be remembered, there was an almost entire absence of connoisseurship in this country. Fine pictures by the old masters, of all schools, were purchased and highly valued by the English nobility and gentry, but these were usually so attested by their previous history that no niceties of knowledge were required respecting them. The purchasers and eliminators, for instance, of the Orleans Gallery, just referred to, suffered no qualms of doubt as to whether real Raphaels and Titians had fallen to their share. The contents of that gallery needed little guarantee beyond the fact that they were such. This very certainty may even in some measure be said to have retarded the progress of true connoisseurship, for works admitting of no question invited no analysis. Mr Rogers was a singular instance of a man who thought and felt for himself in matters of art, and though he had small pretensions to those subtleties of knowledge only obtainable by long experience–the acquirement of which, while it must be always rare, is indispensable now–yet his taste was so fine that he made few mistakes in his private selection, and, as a Trustee of the National Gallery his vote was always in harmony with the true interests of the public. The Trustees also, though endowed with unquestionable authority to purchase pictures, had but rare opportunities of exercising those powers, while such acquisitions as they did make–that, for example, of the two grand Correggios in 1834[1]–though of the highest value, needed no real discrimination on their parts. But the time was now approaching when only knowledge could decide as to the genuineness of a picture, and when no consciousness of ignorance had as yet suggested any diffidence in such matters. The following transaction reflects too much credit on the admirable sense of Sir Robert Peel, as well as on the knowledge of the history of art possessed by Mr Eastlake, to be omitted here.

'Mr Eastlake writes, 3 May 1841: "I mentioned that the Trustees of the National Gallery invited me to give an opinion of a soi-disant Raphael which they have some idea of purchasing. The proposition to consult artists before making these purchases was made at the last meeting of the Trustees *for the first time*, and it was made (so Sir Martin Shee tells me, who was present) by Sir Robert Peel. The President of the Royal Academy, Howard, Etty, Callcott, and myself were named. Today the Trustees meet, and having only seen the picture the day before yesterday, it was only yesterday that I sent in my report. I am afraid it will be rather humiliating to them (*entre nous*), but at least it will show that Sir Robert Peel was right. I have been able to give the whole history of the picture, for it is described in more than one work, and this kind of lore (with the help of the artistic library which I have by degrees collected) I have, as you know, at my fingers' ends. I have given them my own opinion, confirmed by a mass of evidence, dates, &c., which I think must show them that they need a little enlightening on these matters. On Saturday I so far let out my own opinon that I observed to ——— at the Academy dinner that the picture was certainly not by Raphael. 'Not by

[1] See page 208.

Raphael!' he exclaimed. 'Bless me, we never had any doubt about that! the only question was what it was worth, and we wished you to say whether it would be an acquisition as a specimen of the painter.' They had believed some spurious story about Raphael's having painted the picture at a certain time and place. I have given the clearest proof that all this is unfounded–in short, my only fear is that I have given them too strong a dose. I have, however, said, without pretending to judge of the price, that it would be an acquisition to the Gallery as the work of the painter to whom I attribute it (on grounds amounting to proof). When Sir Robert Peel made his proposition, ——— who piques himself on being a judge of Italian art, said he thought it would be imposing too much trouble on the members of the Academy to consult them. Sir Martin Shee, with his usual readiness, said the very object of the Academy was to promote the interests of the arts. There might be many cases of doubtful pictures on which I could not have pronounced; and, above all, in which I might not have had documentary evidence at command. It is particularly fortunate in support of Sir Robert Peel that I have been able to furnish the information I have sent. What the other painters have done I don't know, and of course I have not communicated with them, but I am very certain that none are in possession of the historical facts I have adduced. This letter is full of boasting, but it is true; and as I have sometimes been thought to have wasted time in acquiring this kind of knowledge and, I may add, spending a good deal of money gradually in collecting materials, it is a satisfaction to know that all this tells at last."

'An official letter from the Secretary (Col. Thwaites) acknowledged the information supplied, and the picture was not bought.*

'It was not long before this that he went to see "a Titian" which had been mentioned to him, and which was about to be raffled for at £6000. After a careful inspection he pronounced it to be "a fair copy, not even done by a Venetian painter". Mr Seguier afterwards confirmed his judgement. The instances in which he stood between spurious pictures and would-be purchasers were innumerable. These are only mentioned to show how rare was such knowledge out of the mere dealer class at that time.'

A second great friendship which was to have enormous consequences in Eastlake's life was with the Prince Consort. So anxious was Albert that Sir Charles (or Mr Eastlake as he was at the time) should become President of the Royal Academy following upon Sir Martin Archer Shee's death that the Queen was induced to write to Landseer to ensure Eastlake's appointment. Eastlake had been the Academy's librarian for a time and regularly attended General Assembly meetings. He was popular with the membership and was duly elected. In the first year of his presidency the Great Exhibition of 1851 took place. He had been working on it for two years or more as one of the twenty-six official Commissioners. Albert, who had first met Eastlake on the Royal Fine Arts Commission, took the unprecedented

* *The work in question was an unfinished Holy Family by Fra Bartolommeo–purchased several years later by Mr Thomas Baring, and now in his gallery.* [It is now in the Courtauld Gallery. Ed.]

step of attending the Academy Dinner and singing the new President's praises. Eastlake, who was at heart a man of great humility, was deeply touched.

The third important friendship began at a dinner party given by their mutual publisher, John Murray, for Elizabeth Rigby, the celebrated Edinburgh writer and art critic, and Sir Charles in May 1846. Other guests included Turner, Landseer, Kinglake (the author of *Eothen*) and the redoubtable Mrs Jameson (another Murray author). Eastlake took Miss Rigby in to dinner. The friendship blossomed. Three years later, in 1849, they were married. It was a remarkable partnership. Socially it drew the intelligentsia not only of London, but of the Continent too, to their house in Fitzroy Square.[1] In his work, Lady Eastlake was a stimulating and knowledgeable catalyst.[2] There can be little doubt that it was she who made possible the annual search for new paintings on the Continent after 1855, when 'in addition to his other occupations, Sir Charles accepted the office of Director to the National Gallery. In this position, the most interesting and delightful at that time which the painter, the connoisseur, and the man of taste could hold, though one of no exemption from toil, he found employment of a peculiarly congenial nature, and reaped the choicer fruits of his life of labour.'[3] Lady Eastlake continues: 'The fortunate necessity of travelling in quest of pictures was the best restorative for mind and body, after the fatigues of a London official life. Year after year the happy tour was made, always to Italy, once to Spain, and frequently on fruitful errands besides to France, Belgium, Holland, and Germany. And all the charms of travel were enhanced by a purpose, honourable and responsible, which kept up those habits of thought and industry, without which pleasure would have been none to him. No fatigues or discomforts deterred him from visiting the remotest parts of Italy: wherever the prospect was held out of securing (and in most cases it was rescuing) a work of interest, he patiently made his way; and before every picture, whether in church, convent, or private house, worthy of his investigation, accurate notes were taken, and every evening carefully transcribed.*'

For much of her life Lady Eastlake kept a journal. A selection from this, and from her voluminous correspondence, was edited by Sir Charles' favourite nephew, Charles Eastlake Smith, and published in two volumes in 1895. It is from the journal that the extract which follows is taken. At about this time Lady Eastlake wrote to her mother: 'We see a good deal of a certain class of man, namely picture-dealers–not educated, but sharp and cute! Poor devils! They are the only class

[1] One of Lady Eastlake's most delightfully recounted memories was the meeting between Waagen and Passavant in her house in 1850. The two elderly continental gentlemen caused great embarrassment by embracing each other upon first meeting there for a dinner party.

[2] Though we gather from Sir Charles' note-books, which are still extant in the library of the National Gallery (see footnote* on this page), that she did not often participate in her husband's day-to-day labours at home or in the actual search for pictures abroad.

[3] The *Memoir*, page 190.

* *A large collection of notes remains in my possession, which have been copied and catalogued alphabetically, and put at the service of the present Director of the National Gallery.*

who know anything of art, and they have a native drollery which sends us into fits. Some are fine-hearted creatures, honest, and would be generous if they could; but the majority are sly and intriguing and require such a cautious character as my husband to be their match.'

During Eastlake's directorship 139 pictures were bought for the National Gallery and they are among the cream of its possessions. Regrettably, the picture by Ghirlandaio that was the object of so much vexation in the passage which follows, finally eluded Eastlake's grasp. It represented *The Virgin enthroned with the Child and a band of angels, on her right the Archangel Michael and S. Justus, on her left the Archangel Raphael and S. Zenobius.* It had been executed for the Ingesuati of San Giusto near Florence. In 1529 it was moved to the cloister of I Disciplinati di San Giovanni Battista; and after the suppression of that confraternity, purchased with the cloister by the Congregazione dei Sacerdoti di Gesù Salvatore.[1]

Lord Normanby, who kept his principals in London thoroughly informed, described it thus in a letter: 'It is in a small room off a deserted dormitory . . . reduced by years of continual neglect to a condition so nearly hopeless that it requires more confidence in the endless resource of art than in my inexperience I possess to believe in the possibility of restoration.'

Eastlake's enthusiasm for the picture was matched by the generosity of his offer for it, considering its condition; namely £1200. The Tuscan government ultimately refused Eastlake permission to take the picture back to England and bought it for roughly a third of what Eastlake had offered for it. It went to the Uffizi in 1857.

Lady Eastlake's reference to the usefulness of Murray's *Guides* was echoed by many other English travellers of that period. The *Handbook for Travellers to Central Italy*, for example, had reached its third edition by 1853 (the first appeared in 1840). J. C. Robinson, Superintendent of the Art Galleries at the South Kensington Museum while Eastlake was at the National Gallery, frequently went to Italy to make purchases of sculptures and to arrange for the making of casts for the museum, and he also depended heavily on Murray's *Guides*.[2]

Sir Charles died on another such journey, after a lingering illness, in Pisa on Christmas Eve in 1865. Lady Eastlake survived him until 1893. As well as the 139 pictures he bought, 29 were bequeathed and presented during the time of his directorship.[3] Upon his death, and also upon Lady Eastlake's, a number of pictures

[1] One of the predella panels is now in the National Gallery (No. 2902).

[2] Some of these, with his annotations and sketches, are in the Victoria and Albert Museum library.

[3] It appears, in fact, that these figures are an underestimate. Professor Robertson assesses that Sir Charles purchased 175 pictures and that rather more than 70 were given or bequeathed during his directorship.

from their personal collection went to the National Gallery. His remarkable judgement and distinction as Director were demonstrated particularly well in 1965, on the centenary of his death, when the National Gallery placed a golden rosette beside each picture acquired during his time. Eastlake had raised its status from that of a provincial collection to one of international pre-eminence.[1]

EXTRACTED FROM *Journals and Correspondence of Lady Eastlake*, edited by Charles Eastlake Smith, 1895.

Coire, 20 *Oct.* 1854. On Monday we took the rail to Treviglio–thence the diligence to Bergamo, where we devoted ourselves to seeing the city. After driving up to the high town, which stands magnificently upon long lines of old fortifications, we explored churches and what not, seeing pictures and exquisite architecture. Our object is always to break into private houses, which are sure to retain pictures by native painters; and thus we effected an entrance into a Count Moroni's–some descendant of the great Bergamasque painter, Moroni–and saw some fine family portraits.

Certainly the appetite for seeing pictures *vient en voyant*, and the knowledge too. The different schools of painters, which clustered in the North of Italy–Milanese, Bergamese, Brescian, Paduan, and Venetian–are now getting disentangled in my mind, and I begin to know their differences and affinities. My husband is a fountainhead of knowledge, and seldom quits a collection of any kind without having cleared up some doubtful masters for the owners. I find his worth is unfailingly recognised: those who are pompously eager to teach him when we enter, are humbly asking his opinion before we leave. The way in which he smashes a false name is sometimes very amusing.

The next morning we were off early to Crocetta, the country house of a Count Lochis, of whose collection we had been informed. We were so early that the 'Signore' was not 'in toiletta', but a manservant showed us into two little rooms, where there were chiefly Flemish pictures–seldom genuine in Italy. We were beginning to think it a failure when he opened 'la rotonda', a large circular room where one glance showed us that we were in one of the richest temples of *cinquecento* art. The light was bad, but nothing could obscure the beauties, and we proceeded to feast. In half an hour the Count came in, all smiles and bows, and took us into other rooms surpassing the rotunda in value of contents.

Milan, 19 *Sept.* 1855. My dear husband is (between ourselves) in full treaty for some *prizes*, and has more prospect of getting what is really grand and fine than we could have expected. But this requires much patience, and prudence, and caution. Last year he made acquaintances which now serve his purpose, and we are taken to one palace after another–

[1] This opinion was first expressed by a French critic (Charles Clément in the *Journal des Débats*, 8 February 1866) and echoed in a number of obituaries after Sir Charles' death. One of the most informative was by F. T. Palgrave in the *Fine Arts Quarterly Review*, Vol. 1, July–October 1866, page 52.

such enormous structures, splendid and comfortless. Most of the owners are needy and in debt; and now these late Paris fêtes are likely to play into our hands for Dukes, &c. &c. are returning with more than empty pockets, and glad to have good prices for things, which, in their opinion any modern daub would replace. . . .

We got back by five o'clock, and then went to dine with the Castelbarcos. We were shown up wide, rough stone stairs, and went through commonish rooms–all 'en suite'–till we came to a large gallery, where the old Count met us. He is a kind-looking old gentleman, but, like most Italians, affected great negligence of toilette, and perfectly succeeded–having on most unmitigated old clothes, and not a particularly clean shirt. He has an immense number of pictures, very few of which are genuine except in his own estimation, and in that of another old gentleman, as kind-looking as, and rather shabbier than, himself, whom we took at first for his brother, but who turned out to be his head servant. From the gallery, full of soi-disant Raphaels, Leonardos, and Michael Angelos, we went through room after room–all full of pictures, and all increasing in beauty and richness of furniture and objects of *vertu*. The rooms appeared numberless, and, instead of ending, they debouched into another gallery–far larger and more magnificent than the first, with everything truly *en prince*. Then we went downstairs, and again through a suite of beautiful rooms to a large salon, where the Countess, a little old lady–eagle-eyed, and -nosed too–received us with true courtesy. Then through further rooms to dinner, which was in excellent style. Everything was exquisitely cooked, and we were obliged to eat more than we wanted, as some things had to be eaten because they were Italian, and others because our host hoped they were English.

Florence, 11 *Oct.* 1855. Here we are still, from reason of business of a rather vexatious nature. The laws here, as in Russia, are meant to be evaded; but Englishmen, and especially one like my husband, naturally begin by acting according to them, and are punished for their upright dealing by every kind of annoyance. Our business concerns a very important picture, and my husband wished that every formality should be complied with. They are so shamefully indifferent here about the preservation of their works of art, that the most glorious things are allowed to perish from sheer contempt and ill-treatment. It would wring the commonest artistic heart to see the most precious specimens of their best time dying a lingering death in their filthy churches–all defiled and bespattered, stuck through with hundred of nails and even of pins, with the dust and drought of centuries upon them. Such a long-suffering picture by Ghirlandajo, one of the giants of the olden time, Sir Charles has been in treaty for more than a twelvemonth–before we came out last year–and on arriving here the purchase was duly completed. It is a picture in a church belonging to the priests and congregation. The offer made by my husband was most liberal, and the treaty was carried on between him and the Venerable 'Signor Canonico Penitenziere'–a magnificent old man–in the most courteous way. The offer was accepted, and the Canonico obtained the consent of the 'Congregazione', and of the Archbishop, the more readily because the money was to be devoted to found a charitable institution. The consent of the Pope to sell the picture for that purpose had been obtained beforehand. Then the consent of the Academy was got, and then that of the Government; but by that time the Academy had found out that it was destined for the English National Gallery, and vowed that such a treasure–a picture of the highest importance–could not be allowed to leave the country. In short, all permission was withdrawn, and the Canonico and the Congregazione thrown into despair. It so happened, that we were just going to dine with Lord and Lady Normanby (he the English Minister) when this news reached us; and as my husband has a letter from Lord Clarendon to all ministers and consuls to assist him in any difficulty, he took it at once, and has set his Lordship to work to overrule, if possible, the intrigues of the Academy. But all this takes time, and though we have waited three days, we seem no nearer the end. However, priests and congregation, and Archbishop, and Pope all make common cause with us, and with Lord Normanby besides–so there is little doubt of the final result. The priests promise to sell it to no one else, and least of all to the Government, which only offers half the amount. At first I went to good old Count Buonarotti, who is one of the ministers; but it is not his department, and though he kindly said he would do his best, he warned me to 'expect nothing from Italians', and to rely on Lord Normanby entirely. The Countess has been most honest between her English and Italian sympathies, but she knows the nature of the laws, and only laments that Sir Charles ever paid them the compliment of complying with them. Certainly my husband will never try that plan again, but will do as all private purchasers do, and smuggle what they are not allowed to pass honestly. The picture is in such a wretched state, that it will require much time and expense to put it in order. The zeal for its retention, which they now show out of jealousy, had not prevented them from letting the picture perish by inches–all the *predella* pictures stolen and vanished, frame gone, and itself sure to disappear in time. It is worse than the dog in a manger, for the object in question is never to be replaced, and they won't even take care of it. Plenty of glorious things are ruined too far to be ever repaired.

Florence, 13 *Oct*. 1855. My husband has heard from Lord Normanby that his first appeal to the chief minister had met with a negative, on the score of the Government attaching too much importance to this poor, defaced Ghirlandajo to be able to give it up to oblige him. He had, therefore, made a second and far stronger appeal, which he hardly thought they could resist. Also he begged my husband to send the old 'Canonico' straight to him, so that he might know every particular. We hope, therefore, for the best. This transaction has given us but a poor opinion of the honesty of the Tuscan Government. The reason for the whole lies in the spite and ignorance of the Director of the Academy, a man we hear, without the slightest knowledge of art, under whose *régime* everything is neglected. He is jealous of anyone who knows more than himself. Sir Charles's choice of the picture has proved to him that it is one of value; and though, had the choice not been made, he would have let it perish with perfect indifference, yet he now affects a zeal for the preservation of it for the Florence gallery, and, as he is a trumpery marquis, all the ministers think themselves bound to support him. He has gone the length of making all believe, as they are as ignorant as he is himself, that this is the only specimen of the master left in Tuscany. In answer to this, Sir Charles has supplied Lord Normanby with a list of other examples, scattered through Florence, Lucca, &c., neglected by and unknown to the Government though Murray's 'Handbook' and many other English sources proclaim them to us. Also the 'Canonico' expects to prove that the picture is the church's entire property, independent of the Government, in which case they need not even give their ungracious consent.

Venice, 18 *Oct.* 1855. We reached Ferrara about noon on the 14th, and our eyes were soon opened to the real present character of this renowned spot. It is a deserted place, with everything going fast to ruin, including buildings of the highest interest. The grass grows thick in the streets, and on the church and house walls, on window sills, and thresholds, and upon the people too, for they seemed as stagnant as their town. The buildings are splendid –the Cathedral an unfinished mass of stone tracery–no end of palaces with the most sumptuous architectural decorations, either in stone or the far more beautiful terra-cotta–all crumbling and crumbled away. And in the centre, in a totally different style and character, the stern, strong castle, with turrets and towers, and a moat still full of water round it, looking like the most despotic tyrant and quite ruining the little faith I was ever disposed to place in the elegance and civilisation of its Alfonsos and Leonaras. No wonder Tasso went mad in Ferrara, even in its best days. The deserted wretchedness of the city, standing in a flat marsh which the Po, with any of its *scherzi*, can convert into a lake, so struck us that we had but one wish–to get away from it. The school of painters is original, but far less interesting than we had expected. In fact, the pictures that remained had, like the rest of Ferrara, been allowed to drop to pieces; and, though they have been furbished up to deck a public gallery, which is twenty times too big for them–such an old granary of a palace–yet they had been too far ruined ever to recover. House-rent in Ferrara I should think is nothing. The only tempting things in the palace were the gardens attached to every old ruin, which, as an old picture-dealer told us, are as big as a country seat. Next day we turned our backs most gladly on the city of Ariosto and Tasso, coming by Padua to our beloved Venice.

THE GREAT MANCHESTER EXHIBITION –AND THE NEW CONNOISSEURSHIP

THE first opportunity for the public at large to inspect and to study the pictures, sculpture and ornamental art which private collectors had been amassing in the previous fifty years occurred in Manchester in 1857. Manchester, not to be outdone by London, had sought the Prince Consort's advice about an occasion to rival the Great Exhibition of 1851, and Albert had suggested that the theme on this occasion should be art rather than industry. Waagen, with his unrivalled knowledge of what was available in private collections, was charged with a considerable part of the organisation. Apparently he did not in the end approve of everything that was exhibited: 'in so large a collection there is necessarily much of inferior interest, and many erroneous titles occur, by which the visitor may be misled.'[1]

But one gathers from another rival of the official catalogue[2] that even though the outside of the 'Transept Gallery' was forbidding, 'the scene within, when the visitor has fairly cleared the turnstile, is a wondrous contrast to the building's exterior [see Plate 51]. One long central gallery or nave, with its deep coloured walls, its bronzed columns, its Greek and Vetruvian ornamentation; its cold blue panelled roof; the long line of sky, tapering like a fairy wand of silver to the distant organ at the further end; the passage, formed by groups of milk-white sculpture; the restless, chattering crowd; the glittering cases of gold and silver work, and sparkling jewels; the martial armour, mounted imposingly on modelled steeds; and, looking down upon all, the living faces of the great, and brave, and good of England, make up an effect on which we have better reason to pride ourselves–aye–than upon the industrial wonders of the world the year 1851 saw in Hyde Park; for we have here not only marvellous pictures and perfect sculpture, but also the history of art and industry told in its choicest works . . . the show is a glorious one, in truth.'

The 'show' consisted of 1079 'paintings by Ancient Masters' plus an additional saloon of 44 paintings specially lent by the Marquess of Hertford; of 689 'paintings by Modern Masters' (which included names as diverse as Hogarth, Augustus Egg, William Etty, Raeburn, Rosa Bonheur, Romney, Landseer, Constable, Turner, Lawrence, Michael Dahl and John Wootton); then there was the British Portrait Gallery of 386 items (which incensed Waagen because of the number of unlikely attributions!); the enormous conglomeration known collectively as the Museum of Ornamental Art, to which was added the whole of the Soulages Collection and 'the Government Contribution from the British Museum and Marlborough House'; and nearly a thousand water-colours and fifty-nine miniatures.

Wealthy landowners sent their employees into Manchester on special outings so that they could see the Art Treasures Exhibition. Even eight weeks after the opening the daily attendance figure still averaged nine thousand a day despite the depressing news of the Indian Mutiny, which occurred at just this time. According to contemporary reports the Italian pictures, particularly the earliest ones, made the deepest impression upon the visitors. There can be no doubt that this first great art exhibition in England, which had been made possible through the magnaminity of the greatest English collectors of its day, was an enormous success and had an effect on national artistic taste and trends that even the Prince Consort had never envisaged.

In the long piece that follows, John Steegman uses the Manchester Exhibition

[1] *A Walk Through the Art-Treasures Exhibition at Manchester*, under the Guidance of Dr Waagen; a companion to the official catalogue, 1857.

[2] W. Blanchard Jerrold, *How to See the Art-Treasures Exhibition*, 1857.

as a starting point and discourses skilfully on the connoisseurship of the fifties of the last century. Of particular interest is the discussion of Sir Austin Henry Layard,[1] who while on terms of great friendship with the Eastlakes still held views on many aspects of art, and Italian painting in particular, which diverged widely from theirs.

In 1957 the Manchester Art Gallery held an exhibition of European Old Masters to commemorate the passing of a century since the first great exhibition. A proportion of the paintings included had been exhibited in 1857, but the exhibition demonstrated very clearly the extent to which pictures in the intervening century had crossed the Atlantic and had passed from private to public ownership both in England and the United States. Of most interest in the catalogue was the echo of those few distinguished, ancestral names which still featured as lenders of paintings.

EXTRACTED FROM John Steegman's
Consort of Taste 1830–1870, 1950.

COLLECTORS' fancy in the fifties followed and developed the tendencies which had begun to appear during the late thirties and the forties, which marked the final breaking away from the correct taste prevailing at the beginning of the century, still being followed by some of the older generation who clung to Reynolds' *Discourses* as their guide. . . .

In 1803 the vogue was still for the Eclectic Masters:[2] for the Carracci, Guido, Albano, Guercino and Domenichino. Half a century later, a number of collectors were already beginning to compete for works bearing the names of Giotto or Orcagna, of any Sienese or Florentine fifteenth-century Master and even, occasionally, of their Flemish contemporaries. The Manchester Exhibition was to show how strongly the tide, which had already begun to turn, was now flowing in the direction of the early Schools.

This epoch-making exhibition sprang from the same root as did the Crystal Palace Exhibition of six years earlier: zeal for educational usefulness. For the first the Prince was solely, for the second he was largely, responsible. Unlike most educationalists before or since, he did not confuse education with instruction. Education of the people was for him an object of which instruction was but a part, and, while he believed firmly in the intrinsic importance of factual knowledge, he also believed that such knowledge could only be fully fruitful if fertilised by the imagination.

The preliminary stages leading to the Manchester Exhibition make that clear enough.

[1] 1817–1894, a great traveller, writer, archaeologist, diplomat and eventually politician. He was, incidentally, related to Lady Charlotte Schreiber (see page 329).

[2] The author is referring to the exhibition held in Paris of the pictures assembled from all over Europe by Napoleon's Commissioners. For a full account of their activities, see Cecil Gould's *Trophy of Conquest*, the Musée Napoleon and the Creation of the Louvre, 1965.

They also make clear the extraordinary position of authority which the Prince came to enjoy after, and as a result of, 1851. The Manchester project was originally, it seems, for a general exhibition on the lines already becoming familiar. In the end, thanks to the Prince's advice, it grew into something of much more lasting importance; the first large exhibition for the public of works of art from private collections in England, including the inherited collection of the Queen and the personal collection of the Prince. The organisation was largely entrusted to Waagen, who probably had a greater factual knowledge of the private collections of this country than any other one man, however limited his critical gifts may have been. His *Treasures of Art in Great Britain* had been published in 1854, and possibly helped in inspiring the idea of this exhibition.

In the summer of 1856 a deputation from Manchester waited upon the Prince to explain their objects and to ask his advice. Although Manchester men, they were prepared to take advice from Prince Albert, if from no one else outside Lancashire. The Prince's views were set out after the meeting in a letter from him to Lord Ellesmere.* After describing the discussions with the deputation, H.R.H. went on to state the principles which he thought should govern the organisers. As he pointed out, Manchester would be at a disadvantage if it contemplated a general exhibition, since it had already been preceded by the Great Exhibition of 1851 and by those at Dublin and Paris in 1853 and 1855. They should therefore avoid a mere repetition, and produce something distinctive by having only an Art Treasures Exhibition.† The Prince's characteristic line of thought is expressed very clearly. 'In my opinion', he wrote to Lord Ellesmere, 'the solution will be found in the *usefulness* of the undertaking . . . in the *educational direction* which may be given to the whole scheme.' It was not enough to provide intellectual entertainment for the connoisseurs. The Exhibition must serve to instruct the uneducated in art-history. The Prince was was not far wrong when he told Lord Ellesmere that no country invested a larger amount of capital in works of art than England or did less for art education. It was quite clearly the Prince's belief that what he called art education (that is, both instruction in art-history and also the opportunity of experiencing works of art) was an important factor in general education; and it was also his belief that such instruction and such experience would ultimately produce a more critical taste in the general public, and thus would raise the standard of design in manufacture. That is probably why he identified himself so closely with such an exhibition in such a centre as Manchester. The Prince's beliefs were not shared by many other people either in his lifetime or for many years after. . . .

The Manchester Exhibition gave a new impetus to the science, in the Eastlake sense, of connoisseurship; and it also pointed a new direction in which persons of taste might profitably move. It revealed on an important scale for the first time the possibilities of the

* *Published in the* Manchester Guardian, 8 *July* 1856.

† *The Manchester Exhibition, as finally arranged at Old Trafford, included sections for Paintings by Ancient Masters, Modern Pictures by Foreign Masters, Engravings and Etchings, Ornamental Art, Oriental Art and, as a section to itself, the Contribution of the Marquess of Hertford (from what is now the Wallace Collection). The three-volume Catalogue and a Guide were compiled by Waagen, and a series of articles on each section, originally printed in the* Manchester Guardian, *were reprinted as Handbooks.*

early Italian and Northern Masters–thanks principally to the loans from the Prince's collection. As one of the critical notices in the *Manchester Guardian* pointed out,* the taste for early Italian art was not a recent development in this country only; it was a novelty even in Italy. At the beginning of the century Italian connoisseurs still regarded Perugino as the ultimate point to which investigation might be carried. A first important step had been taken early in the century by Lasinio, the *conservatore* of the Campo Santo at Pisa, in saving the Giotto frescoes from wanton destruction. Subsequent steps had been taken by Lasinio's English disciple William Young Ottley, who made careful drawings of frescoes at Pisa, Florence and Assisi, and, towards diffusing the new taste, by Seroux d'Agincourt in Paris and William Roscoe in Liverpool. But the new taste was slow in spreading, for there was almost no knowledge by which it could be supported. Before 1850 there was no English translation of Vasari,† although he had for many years been translated into most other European languages. When Waagen in the early fifties compiled his survey of English private collections, he found them still rich in works of the 'Grand Style'. Indeed, no private collector, even so late as that, would have considered himself correct without them. Yet their day in England was over. Lady Eastlake, trained to critical observation, yet capable of enthusiasm, could write from Florence in 1855 that the Carracci and all their tribe no longer interested the English of the present day, and that for her part she was fairly bitten with all the true Pre-Raphaelites;‡ there were, she added, already a chosen few in England who adored them. The fashion had begun very slowly to change even before the Manchester Exhibition, and, as that Exhibition showed, a taste for the Pre-Renaissance masters was far from rare among collectors at the end of the fifties. As many as one-third of the catalogue attributions were to names between Cimabue and Raphael, while two-thirds were to names later than Michael Angelo, the masters of the Academic conventions.

A few contemporary observers, like Layard, attributed this change of fashion to a revival of feeling for 'the pure, simple and devotional character of the early Italian masters'; some modern observers have said much the same, supporting themselves on the supposed influence of the Pre-Raphaelite Brotherhood. The argument, however, is not based on a true premise. The taste for the Early Masters was the sophisticated predilection of a few connoisseurs, like the Rev. W. Holwell Carr, William Young Ottley, Davenport Bromley, the Prince, Thomas Gambier Parry and Samuel Rogers.§ The taste for the late eclectics, on the other hand, had been in the previous generation the average educated taste of the day, filtered down from the sophisticates of the late eighteenth century. Nevertheless Raphael continued, and was to continue for many years to come, to be the ultimate authority by which excellence was judged. Subject to the agreed supremacy of Raphael the notable development of connoisseurs' taste in the fifties was in the direction of the

* *Reprinted in* A Handbook to the Paintings by Ancient Masters in the Art Treasures Exhibition, *published by Bradbury and Evans, 1857.*

† *Mrs Foster's version was published in Bohn's edition, 1857.*

‡ *Meaning painters earlier than Raphael.*

§ *The taste appears in America in the fifties with the notable collection formed by J. J. Jarves, bought from him in* 1871 *by Yale University.*

fifteenth century, of the Quattrocentists, and especially of the later ones, like Mantegna, Cima, the Bellinis and a hitherto unknown master whose planet now began to move into the ascendant: Botticelli. Layard in 1857* wrote of 'Sandro Botticelli, who holds so important a position in the transition period of the fifteenth century', and said that he was beginning to be very popular amongst collectors in this country. Three years earlier, Lady Eastlake had written that 'Sandro Botticelli is worthy to stand in the Florentine genealogy between Giotto and Michaelangelo'. That a critic of Elizabeth Eastlake's experience could say that, with no reference to Masaccio, suggests the enthusiasm natural to a new discovery, but it was not a bad estimate, all the same. Botticelli was a newly-realised Master, and the critics were still uncertain where to place him. The art-critic of the *Manchester Guardian* at the time of the exhibition made a more perceptive estimate when he compared Botticelli with the equally unfamiliar Lucas Cranach. It was a brilliant comparison of two still unexplored personalities; the Gothic German and the Renaissance Florentine linked by their nude and pagan Venus. When Layard discussed† the fifteenth-century Florentine and Umbrian masters he placed Piero della Francesca first in order of genius and omitted all reference to Botticelli, though even Filippino Lippi was given a place.

The promotion of Botticelli, after centuries of neglect, to an immense popularity towards the end of the nineteenth century would have confirmed Layard in his realistic view of Taste. In some quarters it was being advocated that the National Gallery should be primarily a collection of the most admired Masters; Layard urged that it should rather be fully representative of all Schools. 'Who are the best Masters?' he enquired in 1859. 'What School is most deserving of study and imitation? What works should be selected to improve or form the public taste? Within the last 25 years how great has been the change in the estimation of pictures!' Twenty-five years earlier taste had flowed strongly, still following the precepts of Reynolds sixty years before that, in the direction of the Bolognese and the Eclectic Masters, and collections formed during the two or three decades after Waterloo still abounded in pictures hopefully attributed to Guercino, Domenichino, the Carracci and Guido Reni.‡ 'But', exclaimed Layard, 'a violent reaction has now [since 1850] taken place, leading taste and artists to an opposite extreme, equally vicious and hurtful. German archaism, English Pre-Raphaelitism and the extravagant price now paid for the vilest daubs of what is called early or Gothic art, are symptoms of it.'

Layard's taste in pictures, as expressed in his *Quarterly* articles, was influential. It was evident that he much disliked the early Northern Masters, but that he was prepared to put up with the quite early Italians: Giotto, Ambrogio Lorenzetti, Simone Memmi and, particularly, Orcagna. His handsome tributes to Piero della Francesca and Benozzo Gozzoli savoured rather of obligation than of personal feeling; but his dislike of sixteenth- and seventeenth-century Academism was obviously genuine. 'Theatrical groups of muscular apostles and anatomic saints', he snorted. Perhaps what Layard really liked best were the

* *A. H. Layard:* Quarterly Review, *Vol.* 102, 1857.

† *A. H. Layard:* ibid., *Vol.* 104, 1858.

‡ *The dates of acquisition of nearly all the examples of these Masters in the National Gallery confirm this. See Catalogue of the National Gallery,* passim.

Venetians, though his choice of descriptive adjectives might not be our choice today. In an article of 1859, discussing National Gallery masterpieces, he described the Sebastiano del Piombo 'Raising of Lazarus' as 'probably the most precious in money value we possess';* Titian's 'Bacchus and Ariadne', on the other hand, was given no stronger adjective than 'excellent'.

It is on the subject of contemporary connoisseurship, however, that Layard is most revealing and most entertaining. Very evidently, he did not belong to the Charles Eastlake school of thought, for which he had some contempt, but then he did not have to bear the responsibility of being Director of the National Gallery. He was a romantic rather than a scholar in his approach to pictures, and had an intense repugnance for the German type of scholarship of which Waagen was an example and with which, unfairly and wrongly, he identified Eastlake. To Layard, that modern type of criticism seemed merely captious, throwing a cold damp upon all sentiment and imagination, disputing the authenticity of every great picture, however much hallowed by tradition, and leaving 'scarce one fragment of art in Italy unassailed'. There was undoubtedly a Waagen side to Eastlake the scholar, but it was balanced by the romantic side of Eastlake the painter. It was that balance between the two which made Eastlake so much more intelligent a man and so much more sensitive a connoisseur than Waagen could ever have hoped to become, or than Ruskin ever was.

A fair interpretation of connoisseurship as Eastlake understood it is provided by his wife.† Though the phrasing is hers, the message is his. They were concerned, it must be remembered, to establish for their generation a standard of serious criticism in a field where none existed. Connoisseurship, Lady Eastlake insisted, being clearly influenced by the views that her husband had expressed twenty years earlier, is neither just a knack nor an instinct with which some individuals are born; it requires 'unwearied diligence, sound sense and true humility'. It also, she maintained, required essentially the same education as that of the student in the exact sciences. Here and in her next contention she went beyond the limits of the Eastlake personal creed, but did so with the deliberate overstatement of a case that is common to all who have tried to instil a new spirit into the criticism of any subject at any time throughout the history of thought. 'Works of Art', Lady Eastlake rather unhappily said, 'must be treated as organic remains, subservient to some prevailing law, which it is the critic's task to find out and classify by a life of observation and comparison.' 'But', she added as an essential condition, 'there must be enthusiasm, pure and engrossing.' Connoisseurship, as the Eastlakes saw it, was of no avail without a deep love of art; together, those two qualities might become the most valuable corrective to materialism. The Eastlakes were among the thinkers who could see the danger of their age, and who aimed perhaps beyond their reach in trying to avert it.

The career of Layard, on the other hand, especially as an archaeologist, at a time when

* *This picture is No.* 1 *in the National Gallery Catalogue. From the Orleans and Angerstein Collections. Bought with Angerstein's other pictures on the foundation of the National Gallery,* 1824.

† *Lady Eastlake reviewing Waagen's* Treasures of Art in Great Britain; Quarterly Review, *Vol.* 94, 1854.

precisely scientific excavation was seldom undertaken, illustrates his reliance on imagination and flair. As a writer on art he showed much the same qualities. Moreover, not only did he despise scientific connoisseurship, but he greatly mistrusted it, believing that no Germans and very few English were above being taken in and fooled by forgeries. He was probably quite right there. There was an immense demand for pictures of certain schools, and the demand was met by an assiduous and steady supply. *Expertise* was exceedingly rare, and the great majority of collectors at home and on their travels trusted to their own judgement. The result was, in Layard's words, 'very mischievous'.* As he said, since Raphaels have always been in request, so Raphaels have always been made for sale. In the forties, when the Eclectic School was still in the fashion, Carraccis flooded the market. Nor was that by any means a new phenomenon. Forgery had begun before many of those forged were dead.† With the change in taste towards earlier masters, the practice received a fresh stimulus. 'Picture-dealers', said Layard, 'of Rome, Florence and other cities frequented by wealthy travellers send their agents through the length and breadth of the land to buy up every work of art whatever its merits.' These were then ingeniously converted wholesale into productions by Bellini, Mantegna, Leonardo, Luini, Perugino and other favourite and highly prized masters. That was written in 1857, and gives an interesting incidental glimpse of the newly developing taste for the late *quattrocento*. Those Masters could not possibly have been described in 1840 as favourite and highly prized. Still less could Fra Angelico, Taddeo Gaddi or Ghirlandajo have been so described, yet by 1857 there was evidently a big profit to be made out of faking them; there was even a market in Giotto by then.

If the wealthy traveller showed any inclination to doubt the dealer's honesty, his suspicions would be lulled and his self-esteem flattered when he was taken into the dealer's confidence and shown several pictures stacked in a corner with their faces to the wall. These, if he were English, would be described as merely 'roba Americana', rubbish for the American market; if he were American, they would be 'roba di milordo', rubbish for an English lord. Then he would be shown an Andrea del Sarto, proper for a person of his discrimination who so evidently was not one of those *ignoranti*. Layard tells a little story about a young American traveller, to whom an Englishman said, 'You have often spoken to me of your father's gallery at New York. What Masters, may I ask, has he got?' 'My father's gallery', was the reply, 'consists almost entirely of Raphaels and Leonardos, but he also has a few Correggios.' Anyone at all familiar with what remains today of the country-houses of Britain will agree that such ambitious attributions were not confined to America.[1] Incidentally, Layard, when discussing the Manchester Exhibition of 1857 in the *Quarterly*, assured his readers that even there, in Manchester, ancient paintings were being manufactured to a vast extent for the American market. . . .

* * *

* *A. H. Layard:* Quarterly Review, *Vol.* 102, 1857.

† *Thus, in England, Richard Wilson was being forged within five years of his death, so early as* 1785, *by his Welsh pupil Thomas Jones, who at that time, on his own confession, was forging the still-living Zuccarelli.*

[1] See also pages 199 and 201.

It was the Italian schools which captured the attention of the more perceptive scholars and collectors. Each in his different way, the Prince, Lord Lindsay, Ruskin and Eastlake had drawn attention to certain aspects of Italian art, and the Manchester Exhibition of 1857 served both to concentrate and to widen the interest; to concentrate it on Schools and Masters previously neglected, and to widen it by giving some hundreds of thousands of people the opportunity of seeing a form of art which they could not at that time find in the National Gallery.

THE NORTHWICK COLLECTION

NORTHWICK is one of the hallowed names among English collectors. The original great collection was begun by John Rushout, 2nd Lord Northwick, who was born in 1769. He inherited the title in 1800, after spending eight successive years in Rome in the study of painting, sculpture and architecture. He was, as Tancred Borenius wrote,[1] 'a collector of very high intelligence and discrimination. Living as he did at a time when the value of works of art in the market was one of taste and appreciation rather than of mere commerce, he was able to avail himself of an ample fortune to buy the finest specimens of the Fine Arts which came into the market'. Although in 1832 he added an extensive picture gallery to his home, Northwick Park, he soon owned such a multitude of pictures that he was forced to buy a second enormous mansion called Thirlestane House, just outside Cheltenham, which during his long lifetime he also gradually filled with pictures and antiquities of every sort. The collection was particularly rich in early Italian, Flemish and German paintings, but the Dutch and English schools were well represented too.

Lord Northwick never married and died intestate in 1859. This fact inevitably meant a forced sale of all his property including the collection, and caused a great stir in its day. A leader on the subject in the *Morning Post* is included in the quotation that follows. A small, but important portion of the vast collection was bought by the 3rd Lord Northwick, a nephew of the second Baron, who succeeded to the title, and some continuity in the family collection was thus established. What is more interesting from our point of view is that in 1912 Captain George Spencer-Churchill inherited this rump collection from his grandmother, widow of the 3rd

[1] In his preface to the *Catalogue of the Collection of Pictures at Northwick Park*, 1921.

CATALOGUE

OF THE LATE

LORD NORTHWICK'S

Extensive and Magnificent Collection

OF

ANCIENT AND MODERN

PICTURES,

CABINET OF MINIATURES AND ENAMELS,

And other Choice Works of Art,

AND THE

FURNITURE, PLATE, WINES, AND EFFECTS,

AT

THIRLESTANE HOUSE,

CHELTENHAM.

Which will be Sold by Auction by

MR. PHILLIPS

AT THE MANSION,

On TUESDAY, the 26th of JULY, 1859,

AND TWENTY-ONE SUBSEQUENT DAYS,

Commencing at One o'Clock precisely each Day,

BY DIRECTION OF THE ADMINISTRATOR.

May be Viewed on and after Friday, the 15th of July, by Catalogues only, at Five Shillings each, to admit Three Persons, to be obtained at the Lodge of the Mansion; of Messrs. AGNEW and SONS, Manchester; Mr. ISAACS, Liverpool; Mr. KERSLAKE, Bookseller, Bristol; Mr. HOLMES, Birmingham; Mr. BENTLEY, Worcester; Mr. DAVIES, Cheltenham; Mr. GREENWOOD, York; and at Mr. PHILLIPS' Auction Offices, 73, New Bond Street, London.

J. DAVY & SONS, Printers, 137, Long Acre, London.

Lord Northwick, and during the half century that followed built it up once more into one of the finest collections to be in private hands during this century.

Captain Spencer-Churchill also inherited Northwick Park, where the 3rd Lord Northwick had removed all the paintings he had bought at his uncle's sale, as well as his uncle's library and those effects which had come to him as a third share of the old man's property. Among them was a collection of sale catalogues which the 2nd Lord Northwick had collected and studied assiduously throughout his life. These were one of the most complete records of works of art dispersed by auction between the 1750s and 1850s.[1] Many of them were annotated by the great collector and we can learn from one of them in particular how extensive was his knowledge of pictures in England and how methodically he pursued those paintings that had eluded him when first they came up for sale.

The catalogue in question was that of 42 Italian pictures which had belonged to Edward Solly[2] and which were sold after Solly's death by Christie's on 8 May 1847. Lot 21 was catalogued as by Pietro Vanucci Detto il Perugino (see Plate 70). At the Solly sale it was bought by Sir W. Domville for 415 guineas. It came up for sale again in 1850 (lot 31) where it was bought by the famous dealer John Smith, still as a Perugino. Later that year Lord Northwick bought it from Smith: we know this from an entry on page 120 for 17 July 1850 in Smith's Day Book (1848–67) which is preserved in the Victoria and Albert Museum. But we also know it because Northwick annotated his copy of the Solly sale catalogue as follows: 'This picture now at Thirlestane House is I think undoubtedly painted by Raphael. Purchased 1850 off Messrs Smith. It is one of my most valued pictures. N.'[3] Waagen saw the painting at Thirlestane House during his visit in 1852 and subsequently selected it for display at the Manchester Art Treasures Exhibition in 1857. There it was catalogued as by Raphael (No. 211). In his book[4] Waagen had attributed the painting to Girolamo Mocetto. His comment is interesting: it is 'here, without the slightest foundation, called a Perugino. It is in feeling, colouring, and execution, an estimable work'. In fact, although Waagen held Lord Northwick (to whom he had, as it happens, been introduced on his first visit to England in 1835 by Edward Solly) in high esteem, he was not uncritical of the collection, which on this occasion he saw in the absence of its owner. He wrote somewhat smugly: 'the reputation of this collection, and the impression it produces on the mind, are injured by two circumstances – the first is, that the majority of the pictures bearing high-sounding, but too often erroneous, names, are either badly restored, or in themselves insignificant works; and the second, that, with

[1] See Christie's *Catalogue of Printed Books from the Northwick Park Collection*, 24 November 1965, lots 199–208, etc.

[2] See page 202.

[3] It is now in the National Gallery where it is catalogued as *The Incredulity of St Thomas* (No. 1051) by Giovanni Battista of Faenza, known as Bertucci. It was bought by Colnaghi for one of Edward Solly's descendants, a Miss Solly, in the Northwick Sale in 1859 and bequeathed to the National Gallery by Sarah Solly in 1879.

[4] *Treasures of Art in Great Britain*, 1854, Vol. III, page 201.

the exception of a few rooms, pictures of the most various times and schools are mingled together in the most arbitrary way. The number of those friends of art who have either time or patience to work their way through the whole collection and discover what is really valuable, is very small, and a superficial view can only lead to an unfavourable opinion. But whoever, like myself, spared neither trouble nor time in the inspection would find himself richly rewarded. I noted down no less than 200 pictures,[1] some remarkable, and some very beautiful, of all schools and periods . . . there are few collections in England which contain so many estimable pictures of the Italian school of the fifteenth century.'

Captain Spencer-Churchill's first love in the realm of collecting was for Egyptian antiquities. He had been sent to Egypt at the age of 13 for reasons of health. His interest soon spread to objects from Greece and Rome, and the Far East, particularly China. To the 400-odd paintings he inherited in 1912 he had added another 200 by the time he died in 1964. Many of these he used to refer to as the 'Northwick Rescues'. For he acquired not only remarkable expertise but also an uncanny flair for spotting what on many occasions turned out to be major and minor masterpieces concealed behind layers of grime and blackened varnish. In his will he stipulated that his collection should be sold in its entirety, as indeed it was, in a long series of memorable sales held by Christie's in 1965 which realised well over £2,000,000. Many of the items sold, among both the paintings and the immense mass of antiquities, ceramics and bronzes of diverse nationalities, already seem by today's standards to have been considerable bargains for their new owners.

QUOTED FROM George Redford's *Art Sales*, Vol. I, 1888.

THE sale commenced Tuesday, 26 July 1859, and continued for 21 days, Mr Phillips, of Bond Street, being the auctioneer, on the premises of Thirlestane House, Cheltenham. As a collection it was decidedly of importance, both as regards the interest of the pictures, and as one of the largest ever formed in England. It has also some special interest from being the work of a nobleman amateur, at a time when comparatively few students were engaged upon old masters, though Lord Northwick did not pretend to be more than a *dilettante*. It is evident, however, that he knew the masters historically, if not practically, for we find many names given to pictures, which at his date must have been quite unknown generally. Probably very few of these are truly assigned, but the pictures represent the art of the period, and I have purposely named them as a record of such examples, and the value attached to them in the sale. We must conclude that most of these were good, as they were bought often by such eminent connoisseurs as Lord Lindsay, the Duke of Newcastle, Lord Elcho, Duc d'Aumale, the Duke of Hamilton, Duke of Buccleuch, Mr Drax, the

[1] Out of 800.

Marquis of Lansdowne, Mr Davenport Bromley, Lord Taunton, and several expert dealers who attended the sale from abroad and all parts at home. The Director of the National Gallery, Sir C. L. Eastlake, P.R.A., selected four pictures at a cost of £2078 3s, viz., Masaccio–portrait of himself; Moretto of Brescia–St Bernardino and other saints; Giulio Romano–'The Infancy of Jupiter'; Girolamo da Treviso–'Madonna and Child'. There were no less than 1430 pictures, besides 83 miniatures, many antique engraved gems, with many bronzes. The total realised by the pictures and works of art, was £94,722 18s, in 18 days' sale, one of which amounted to £16,482 7s 6d, another to £10,770 7s 6d.

The bedrooms and upper chambers were hung with pictures, and the various galleries were named–The Parthenon Gallery, The Platform Gallery, Vestibule, The Principal Gallery, The Giotto Room, Venetian Room. Some were bought for Northwick Park; the Lord Northwick, the successor in the title, purchasing pictures and other works of art, to the amount of £7984 10s 6d. And Sir Thomas Phillips to about £1000, many of which remained in the galleries of Thirlestane House for some years, during which he occupied the mansion at Cheltenham.

A testimonial was presented to Lord Northwick, signed by upwards of 700 noblemen and gentlemen of the town and neighbourhood of Cheltenham, in replying to which Lord Northwick said, 'I had myself the good fortune to commence my travels through foreign lands at an early period of my life, and it was in the year 1792 that I first saw Rome, where I sojourned during the greater part of eight successive years, and was impressed with a profound veneration–which during the course of a long life has never since been effaced from my memory–for the stupendous monuments of falling greatness, with which it is on all sides surrounded–an unbounded admiration for the works of the most refined art in painting, sculpture, and architecture, with which it then abounded, and to which I had the advantage of a most free and unlimited access. These were the seductive amusements of my youth: they have clung to me through a long life, and they are now the solace of my old age.' Lord Northwick's family name was Rushout–John Rushout Baron Northwick.

Thirlestane House, where Lord Northwick had his pictures, and where he lived at Cheltenham, is a spacious mansion built of Bath stone, in the classical style, with a handsome portico of four Ionic columns and a façade on each side with two storeys [see Plate 21]. The gallery was a long one, with a transept at the end a little raised, the whole being lighted from skylights. He himself was a most pleasant and cheerful gentleman, extremely simple and unpretending in his manner, with a slight, rather short figure, and a face round, smiling and fresh in complexion. I remember him well as an *habitué* of Christie's, more than forty-two years ago, and in summer he generally wore a suit of Nankeen, a kind of cool dress which has long since disappeared. I visited Thirlestane House when forming the collection of pictures for the Leeds National Exhibition, in 1867, and was received by the late Sir Thomas Phillips, whom I found almost buried in his piles of books, his head just visible, peering over them at me, his strange visitor, as he was taking his luncheon from a tray on a heap of large quartos as high as his chin nearly. He waved his hand, directing me how to find my way through the lanes of books stacked up all over the floor of a large room, till at last I came upon the small open space where the great bookworm was standing in the midst of his treasures. In a few kindly words he welcomed me, and assured me that any pictures that seemed to me desirable for exhibition he should be most happy to lend, and bid me go round the gallery. This I soon did, but found nothing of any special interest, though there were many pictures which had belonged to the Northwick collection, mostly rather poor school pictures, with the exception, however, of some four or five good examples of Glover's landscapes–largish works in oil. I did not ask for any picture.

The following notice of Lord Northwick's Collection appeared in the *Morning Post*, 30 August 1859.

THE DUTY OF MAKING A WILL–The disposal of Lord Northwick's pictures, collected during a life extending for nearly a quarter of a century beyond the average term allotted to man, occupied 18 successive days, attracted buyers or buyers' agents from all parts of the kingdom, and realised a sum amounting in round numbers to nearly £100,000. So extensive a collection has not been sold for many years. The residents and visitors of Cheltenham knew its value, and will long lament its unfortunate dispersion. The galleries at Thirlestane House were the pride of Cheltenham. They were to that thriving town what the National Gallery is to the metropolis. They were open all the year round, without fee or charge of any kind, and their liberal owner had no greater pleasure than that of knowing that his pictures drew visitors by the hundred. In like manner, at Northwick Park, near Campden, his Lordship had built a spacious gallery, which was never closed at any hour of the day to the public, and, being the only gallery for many miles round, was greatly valued by all the neighbourhood. Until within the last year or two Lord Northwick spent much of his time every day among his pictures, and took great delight in pointing out their beauties to any intelligent visitor who might ask permission to see the collection. He had a kind way of getting into conversation with young people, and would explain the difference between one school of painting and another, and show how to discern the great points in a picture, where to look for merits, and how to distinguish between good and bad. It was a pride and pleasure to him to know that either at Cheltenham or Northwick Park his treasures were appreciated by the public. Few men of his rank and retired habits had more public spirit. Not his pictures only, but his whole house and park were at the service of the public. Those who have frequented that lovely spot for picnics or parties of pleasure know well the hospitality with which its noble owner would send out choice fruit or other refreshment by way of welcome to his often unknown visitors. As for Thirlestane House, it was for all practical purposes a public institution, of which Cheltenham and its visitors reaped the benefit.

These splendid collections are now scattered to the winds. They were brought together in the course of a very long life, they cost immense sums of money, and repaid their owner by the gratification they afforded to his own refined taste and the pleasure they afforded to others. But they are scattered, and it may be a whole generation before another collection at all approaching to it in number, value and public usefulness shall be formed. And it is this thought that suggests these remarks. We contemplate the dispersion of these pictures with two painful reflections, which, by way of caution or suggestion to other collectors, we wish to impress upon the public. The first is the comparative uselessness of collecting works of art without some provision for their preservation. Here was a most accomplished nobleman devoted to art, especially pictures. He spent enormous sums of money in the collection of choice specimens, and was a liberal patron of young artists of ability and promise. In the course of years he had galleries of which any peer or millionaire might be proud. Now where are they? He has gone, and his pictures are scattered all over the country and the continent. They are no longer a school of art. The galleries of Thirlestane and Northwick no longer form a school for the student or a refreshment to the amateur. The purpose of a life is dissipated, and a new illustration is given to the preacher's moral '*Vanitas vanitatis et omnia vanitas.*'

It was the belief in Cheltenham, we know not on what authority, that the pictures at Thirlestane would be left for the benefit of the town, or, at least, that some provision would be made by which they would be preserved there for the use of the public. This turns out to be a mistake. Those works of art have gone to the highest bidder, and their sale is regarded as a great calamity. Undoubtedly, he who collects treasures of art in the way Lord Northwick did, and gives the public the benefit of them during his life, does a great service in his day and generation; but it is impossible not to remember how much greater a service he renders who not only forms a collection, but provides for its perpetuity. To collect pictures at great cost and then sell them by auction is to throw to the winds a large amount of money. The difference between purchase and sale is the price of the owner's enjoyment during his lifetime, and a costly price it often is; whereas a comparatively small addition to this expense would save the labour and thought of years from the auctioneer's hammer, and, what is worse, from uselessness and oblivion. In the next place, see the duty of making a will. These collections are dispersed because they form a portion of the personality of the deceased, and there being no instructions as to their disposal, there is no choice but to sell them, and appropriate their proceeds among the heirs-at-law. Next to the mischief of making an unfair will is that of making none at all. Had Lord Northwick ordered by will the sale of his pictures, however disappointed the world might have been, it would have felt that he had a right to do as he liked. But dying intestate, the sale follows as a matter of course, and the results of a long life and large fortune devoted to works of art are just nowhere. Many of our readers are men of fortune and collectors of art treasures; we think the fate of Lord Northwick's pictures is a lesson to them. A gallery of pictures left to a family or to the public is an offering at the shrine of art; but, sold by auction and dispersed among innumerable private purchasers is sheer vanity and labour lost.

AN EARLY TURNER COLLECTOR

In the second quarter of the nineteenth century, when the great flow of art treasures from the Continent was reduced to a mere trickle, a number of men made wealthy by their enterprise in the Industrial Revolution turned to the patronage of living artists instead of the more risky investment in the works of masters long dead. Vernon (see Plate 33), Bicknell and Sheepshanks were among them; so was the pen-maker, Gillott. It was the enthusiasm of these self-made connoisseurs that drove up the prices of works by living artists and enabled painters like William Collins, Müller, Landseer and Linnell to make substantial incomes out of their creative work. Gillott's collection was sold by Christie's in 1872 and consisted of 525 paintings and water colours. There were only sixty foreign Old Masters among them. The six-day sale fetched a grand total of £164,530.

A particularly interesting explanation of the difference in subject matter and presentation between English and Continental nineteenth-century artists is given in the introduction by Richard Redgrave to the Inventory of the Sheepshanks Collection.[1] This was compiled after the collection had been given to the nation. In fact it is now preserved in the Victoria and Albert Museum. 'Art here has flourished from the demands of those who love it as a home delight', and 'the subjects chosen by British painters have been disparagingly classed with those of the Dutch School, but they are of a far higher character, and appeal to more educated and intellectual minds. . . . The works of Teniers, Terberg [sic], Ostade, Jan Steen, de Hooge, Dow, Mieris . . . seem to be productions of men who never read.' Redgrave goes on to disparage documentary art and to laud subjects culled from literature. (Also interesting in this connection is William Carey's *Observations on the Probable Decline or Extinction of British Historical Painting*, 1825.)

Probably the most distinguished Turner collector of his time was John Ruskin, who wrote in *Praeterita* 'the pleasure of one's own first painting everyone can understand. The pleasure of a new Turner to me nobody ever will and it is no use talking of it.'[2]

---

[1] *Inventory of the Pictures, Drawings and Etchings etc. in the British Fine Art Collections deposited in the New Gallery at Cromwell Gardens, South Kensington. Being for the most part the gift of John Sheepshanks Esq.*, HMSO, 1857.

[2] For a very full account of Ruskin's passion, see Luke Herrmann's *Ruskin and Turner: A Study of Ruskin as a collector of Turner based on his gifts to the University of Oxford incorporating a catalogue raisonné of the Turner drawings in the Ashmolean Museum*, London, 1968.

AN EARLY TURNER COLLECTOR

Extracted from George Redford's *Art Sales*, Vol. I, 1888.

Mr Gillott, a Yorkshireman, born at Sheffield, was evidently far before his time among the men of his class, and certainly gifted naturally with fine feeling for pictures. . . .

After he had become so successful as a maker of steel pens, and when only about thirty years of age he became acquainted with Mr Dawes and Mr Birch, both like himself engaged in trade at Birmingham, and both great lovers of pictures. They possessed fine works of David Cox, who was also a native of Birmingham, and of Turner. He was ambitious of rivalling them, and soon went in for pictures with the same enterprise that has carried him so successfully in his trade. He found that it was not easy then to get pictures by Turner, for the painter was proud and chary of selling, especially as one of his finest works, 'The Building of Carthage', which he afterwards bequeathed to the Nation, had passed on the walls of the Academy Exhibition of 1815, unnoticed; or rather laughed at by the art-critics of the day, and no one bought it at the price fixed by the painter– £200. In fact, Turner lived in dudgeon in his house in Queen Anne Street with this and a great many other pictures, some hung on the walls, others piled against the wall on the floor; and one or two, it is said, were actually used to stop the wind and rain in a broken window. Few persons who wanted to buy of Turner could get into his house at that time, and he had a sort of female Cerberus in the shape of his old housekeeper, who kept stealthy watch at the door.

Mr Gillott, however, was an original in his way, and liked a joke as much as anybody, and he planned an attack upon Turner's stronghold which is amusing, and most characteristic of the two men. He used to tell the story of his first interview with Turner with the greatest glee, and with no small pride at the success he achieved. The story was repeated to me at the time of the sale by a friend who had often heard it from Gillott, and I made note of it on the fly leaf of my catalogue. When Gillott knocked at the door the old housekeeper opened it only just enough to see who it was, and gave the usual answer 'Mr Turner's particularly engaged; he won't see anybody.' Gillott, however, contrived by parleying with her to get a footing on the door-mat and soothing her with the charm of a piece of silver in the palm persuaded her to go and tell Mr Turner that a man from Birmingham wanted to speak to him. While Gillott was standing in the passage, presently Turner came out looking very surly, and eyeing the stranger as he came close up to him, when Gillott addressed him with, 'My name's Gillott–I come from Birmingham to see your pictures.' 'What the pen-maker?' exclaimed Turner. 'What do you know about pictures?' 'Oh, I know enough to like yours.' 'Ah, but you can't buy of me,' said Turner gruffly. 'No, I know that, but I want to swop with you.' 'Swop. What with?' 'Oh some pictures.' 'Pictures? what pictures?' 'Well, I've got my pictures in my pocket,' says the Birmingham wag, as he pulled out a handful of £1000 notes, and waved them before the eyes of the grim painter, whose face broke into a smile at the sight and the humour of his new visitor, while he said, 'You're a rum chap; come in and have a glass o' sherry.' With this Turner led him into his room and Gillott soon began to point to this and that picture he should like, at which Turner generally replied with 'Ah, don't you wish you may get it.' One of these was the 'The Building of Carthage' which attracted Gillott's eye especially. Gillott said 'I should like that and that,' pointing to 'Sun rising in Mist',* and held out his bunch of banknotes as he said 'Come, Mr Turner; I'll swop these with you for those two.' 'No, thank ye, I'll never sell them. They might have been had in the Academy for a couple o' hundred a piece, but the press made fun of 'em, and wrote 'em down, and now nobody shall have 'em.' As may be supposed however the visit was not a fruitless one, for Turner was not insensible to the touch of crisp banknotes; and a bargain was struck for several pictures, Turner stipulating for the price in guineas, at which Gillott was ready enough to say, 'Of course, I expect to pay in guineas.' 'Well', said Turner, 'you're the only man that ever came prepared to pay in guineas and for the frames.' The pictures were taken away in a cab.

This account has been told in a much less extended shape in the biography of Gillott which says, 'When he had got into Turner's room he looked round at the walls, and startled the painter by saying, "Well, what will you take for the lot?" Turner half joking, and thinking to frighten Gillott, named a very large sum, many thousands, when Gillott opened his pocket book, and, to Turner's amazement, paid down the money in crisp Bank of England notes.' Now, I rather think that two occurrences are here confused. What my imformant† told me was – that some years afterwards Mr Gillott offerred to pay £35,000 for the pictures in the house in Queen Anne Street, and to take charge of the old housekeeper while Turner went abroad, as he was complaining of being much knocked up and wanting a change. Turner took a week to consider the offer but declined it; and fortunately so for our National Collection to which he preferred to bequeath all his magnificent works.

LADY CHARLOTTE SCHREIBER

THE three women who dominated the nineteenth-century collecting scene because of their remarkable intellectual capacity, their scholarship and their fantastic energy were Lady Eastlake, Mrs Jameson and Lady Charlotte Schreiber (see Plate 35). While Mrs Jameson will be remembered by her writings and Lady Eastlake by her influence on her husband (as much as by her largely anonymous authorship), Lady Charlotte will remain known as one of the earliest, most active

* *This was the picture he bought back in Lord de Tabley's Sale at Christie's in* 1827, *for* £514 10*s* *and bequeathed to the National Gallery.*

† *Mr Cox.*

and successful English collectors of ceramics, and of many other *objets d'art* including particularly lace, fans and playing cards. One gathers that she was a lonely child and kept a journal from a very early age. Her son, Montague Guest, assisted by Egan Mew, published a selection from this journal of the years between 1869 and 1885. There are more than a thousand pages of these 'Notes Ceramic' and they give a most revealing insight into Lady Charlotte's zealous collecting career.

The piece that follows is a typical excerpt. It occurs very near the beginning of the first published volume. Lady Schreiber's expertise was already considerable. Her evident familiarity with every variant of fake and forged mark must have been almost unique a century ago. The excerpt also shows, incidentally, a facet of collecting now often overlooked in the face of constantly rising values: that the collector only bought if he or she thought the price was right; that is, if the desire to possess the object exactly matched what the dealer wanted for it; or even better, if the collector thought he or she was getting a bargain and was getting the better of the dealer! A passage from Mr Guest's introduction to his mother's journal is of particular relevance here. It should be remembered that this was probably written about 1909 when he was seventy.

'When Lady Charlotte began to collect china, which may be put down roughly at between forty and fifty years ago, it was an easier matter than it is today; I myself began about the year 1860, and I know from experience that, amongst the ordinary dealers, ignorance was the prevailing characteristic of the period. The names of Chelsea, Bow, Worcester, Bristol, Plymouth and Derby were but barely known, and if some of the marks of these factories were understood it was about all one expected to find, unless indeed they happened to have a Marryat,[1] or a Chaffers[2] (then a new publication) at hand to refer to, which was not often the case, while if a specimen was unmarked it was totally unrecognised. Any person with a very small amount of knowledge could go round the old shops and pick up the untold treasures of today for the most trivial sums; there was an enormous supply, and very little demand, in consequence, the "fake" hardly existed. Then, in regard to English furniture many people were turning out their fine old examples, which were not appreciated, or in many cases not thought worth repairing, for a more modern kind, and the old brokers' shops were teeming with the most glorious and beautiful specimens of the earlier periods, which could be obtained for almost nothing. The name of Chippendale was hardly known, while those of Sheraton, Hepplewhite, Adam, etc., which today are upon everybody's tongue, were then absolutely unknown. As a proof of the estimation in which they were held, I may say that, in 1860, I bought a fine copy of Hepplewhite's book for 2s 6d. I believe it now realises somewhere about £16. . . . It was very much the same with the English School of

[1] Marryat, J., *Collections towards a History of Pottery and Porcelain in the 15th, 16th, 17th and 18th Centuries*, London, 1850; enlarged and reprinted in later editions as a *History of Pottery and Porcelain.*

[2] Chaffers, W., *Marks and Monograms in Pottery and Porcelain*, London, 1863.

painting, and miniature painting, while in regard to old silver, my brother was buying rat-tail spoons and three-pronged forks, and I think I may say Old English Silver generally, of the best periods, for an average sum of about 5s an ounce. Nobody wanted Old Sheffield Plate, Pinchbeck, old English jewellery, needlework pictures, old English glass, pewter, Staffordshire ware, excluding Wedgwood, old steel, brass, etc., all those things in fact about which every man, woman, and child seems to have gone mad in the present day.

Such, then, being the state of the antique trade, it may easily be conceived that my mother was able to pick up the finest specimens of china and other such articles for quite a moderate outlay. I have in my possession her priced catalogue of the collection in the Victoria and Albert Museum, at South Kensington; the amounts she paid are astounding to the present-day ideas and notions of the value of such things.'

Lady Charlotte was born in 1812, the only daughter (there were two sons) of Albemarle Bertie, 9th Earl of Lindsey, a general in the Guards, who had married a second time at the age of 65 in 1809. At 21, after a mild flirtation with Disraeli – who was clearly attracted not only by her intellect but also by her delightful personality – she married Sir John Guest, a man more than twice her age, owner of a very large Welsh Ironworks, a Fellow of the Royal Society and M.P. for Merthyr Tydvil for many years. Their marriage was extremely happy. She not only bore Sir John ten children, but also assisted him materially in the running of his business. She undertook negotiations on his behalf, kept the accounts and had a room next to his office in the city for her own use.

She was a voracious reader and as a child she had learned and made herself proficient in French, German and Italian and, with the help of her brother's tutor, had studied Greek, Latin, Hebrew and Persian. After her marriage she taught herself the Welsh language and as a result translated and published *Mabinogion* or the Tales of King Arthur's Round Table. It was the reading of this which inspired Tennyson's 'Idylls of the King', and later in his life he went out of his way to meet Lady Charlotte.[1]

In 1852, after twenty years of marriage, the ageing Sir John died suddenly and unexpectedly. For some years Lady Charlotte continued single-handed to run the Dowlais Ironworks. At one stage during this time she was faced with the most daunting decisions to end a difficult strike among the workers in the entire Welsh mining area.

Naturally she was most occupied with the education of her children. Soon after her husband's death she appointed a tutor, a Fellow of Trinity College, Cambridge, for her eldest son, Ivor (who later became the first Lord Wimborne). This was

[1] For many years too Lady Charlotte and her sons ran a private press, the Canford Press. There are frequent references to its productions in her journals. These included some unpublished poems by Tennyson.

Charles Schreiber, son of Lieutenant Colonel James Schreiber of Melton, in Suffolk, who had fought as a cavalry officer in the battle of Waterloo. Charles Schreiber came to Dowlais as tutor at a salary of £400 a year. Three years later he and Lady Charlotte were married. This union caused great distress among her family and it was years before some of her children forgave her. It was nevertheless remarkably happy.

Lady Charlotte gradually withdrew from the management of the family business, and, perhaps inspired by the example of her two sons, she began to take an interest in the collecting of antiques, particularly ceramics. She was over fifty when she was bitten in earnest by the bug she always referred to as her 'China Mania'. It soon became the all-absorbing interest in her life and she and her husband travelled across Europe in an unending search for items for their collection. Lady Charlotte soon discovered that what was known about many forms of porcelain and pottery amounted rather to lore than to hard fact, and she was one of the first to take a scholarly interest in the manufacture of wares, going through old catalogues and account books in well-known manufacturies and even helping in the excavation of kiln sites.[1] There can be little doubt that her connoisseurship, particularly where English porcelain was concerned, was greater than that of most of her contemporaries.

In fact, she herself prepared the first catalogue of the English part of her collection which she gave to the Victoria and Albert Museum after the death of Charles Schreiber in 1884.[2] There were just over 1800 items including porcelain, earthenware, glass and a fine collection of enamels. In January 1915 there appeared the first volume of an extensively revised catalogue of the porcelain section only, by Bernard Rackham. He linked descriptions of the pieces with references to their purchase in the *Journals*. In 1928 a revised edition of this first volume, on which W. B. Honey had assisted Rackham, appeared. The second volume on earthenware, on which Honey and Herbert Read had done the lion's share of the work under Rackham, came out in 1930.[3] Volume III, on the enamels and glass, had already

[1] See her introduction to the 1885 catalogue of the Schreiber Collection. It is here that she modestly describes some of her more outstanding discoveries during the course of her researches as 'interesting incidents'.

[2] She received a good deal of help from Sir Wollaston Franks of the British Museum (he had gone there in 1851 and was Keeper of the Department of British and Medieval Antiquities and Ethnography, which included ceramics). Franks had got together privately a superb collection of English earthenware and then offered it to the museum. To supplement this magnificent gift he had recommended the purchase of the collection of Henry Willett of Brighton, who had already made many gifts to the musuem in the seventies and eighties.

[3] Rackham and Read had been working together on earthenware for a long time. In 1924 they had published their monumental *English Pottery: its development from early times to the end of the 18th century*. It assuredly set the seal on the respectability of collecting earthenware rather than porcelain. As Rackham and Read say in their introduction: previously 'such collecting has not always been marked by discrimination. To possess characteristic pieces from all the leading potteries had been the first aim; to add to a collection of representative specimens productions of little-known factories or examples of unrecorded marks had been counted a stroke of good fortune. In short, the collector of English

appeared in 1924. Again Rackham had been assisted by Herbert Read in its preparation.

It will be evident from the passage from her journals which follows that Lady Charlotte was an enthusiastic collector of lace, which was widely collected in the second half of the nineteenth century. During the last four years of her life she supervised the production of two immense series of catalogues of her extensive collections, firstly of fans and fan-leaves and, secondly, of playing cards. The two volumes on fans were published by Murray in 1888 and 1890 and form the basis of the British Museum catalogue of 1893. The three volumes on playing cards were published by Murray in 1892, 1893 and 1895 and again the British Museum catalogue of 1901 is largely based on them. For Lady Schreiber had bequeathed both her collections to the British Museum after her death in 1895.

She had known for a long time that the deterioration of her eyesight might result in blindness and the preparation of these catalogues – with help from both the British Museum and the Victoria and Albert Museum – had virtually been a race against the time that the dreaded moment of complete loss of sight would arrive. Her mind remained sufficiently flexible at the age of 75 to take advantage of two modern developments during her approaching blindness. She learned photography in order to accelerate the illustration of the catalogues (but found the work 'fidgety'); and she was an early patient to undergo electric treatment for her glaucoma. She persevered with this treatment for some time, though in fact she felt that it had not been very efficacious.

However, she retained some sight until 1890, and a touching moment is recorded in her journal when the packers from the Victoria and Albert Museum arrived to remove what was now known as the Schreiber Collection of English ceramics[1] to the museum. Lady Charlotte at once set about the reorganisation of her even larger collection of continental wares and its redistribution among her several houses and to various members of her family (by this time she had forty grandchildren!). After her death five years later she still left an immense residue of ceramics, pictures, furniture and other *objets d'art* to several of her children.

For those interested, two volumes of Lady Charlotte's journals scanning a much longer part of her life (1833–1852, 1853–1891) were edited by her grandson, the Earl of Bessborough, and published in 1950 and 1952. The first volume is particularly interesting because it is confined to the years of her marriage with Sir John Guest. Her diaries, quite apart from their specific interest to collectors, are an outstanding sociological document on the attitude to life of a great Victorian. If at

Pottery had been led on by the same ambitions as a stamp collector or numismatist. Rarity had been the chief recommendation; the test by standards of good craftsmanship has been too seldom applied.'

[1] This collection can still be seen in its entirety in Gallery 139 on the upper floor of the Victoria and Albert Museum. It is interesting that Lady Charlotte strongly disliked the ceramic portraits of her husband and herself displayed there. These had been made at Murano at the instigation of Henry Layard (see page 314) who was both her cousin and her son-in-law; he had married her daughter Enid in 1869. Layard figures prominently in the journals.

times Lady Charlotte's views may seem a little condescending to twentieth-century ears, this is more than compensated for by her breadth of vision, by her interest in all sections of the community,[1] by her intense stoicism and by a general goodness of heart that is hard to imagine today. But most of all her dynamic spirit is reflected in her travels. Travelling, even in the second half of the nineteenth century, could be highly uncomfortable and uncertain, and there were constant political (and belligerent) upheavals. Lady Charlotte seems to have been quite undaunted by all this. As a final glimpse of her, Montague Guest's celebrated story is revealing: 'She hunted high and low, through England and abroad; France, Holland, Germany, Spain, Italy, Turkey, all were ransacked; she left no stone unturned, no difficulty, discomfort, fatigue or hardship of travel daunted her, or turned her from her purpose, and she would come back, after weeks on the Continent, to Langham House, Portland Place, where she lived, rich with the fruits of her expeditions. Mr Duveen (who was afterwards knighted[2]) told me a curious little story about her in connection with himself. He happened to be over in Holland searching for "objets d'art" when he heard of some wonderful pieces of china in a little village a long way from any town or railway; to get to this out-of-the-way place entailed a long and tedious journey by carriage. He started off on his expedition, but as he was nearing his destination he observed a fly driving out of the village towards him; he looked into it as he passed, and he saw the face of my mother; he felt at once that he had been forestalled, and he continued his journey, only to find that she had snatched the prize, which she was carrying off with her.'

EXTRACTED FROM Lady Charlotte Schreiber's *Journals*, Vol. I, 1911.

Turin

21 *May* [1869]. Visited 8 or 9 curiosity shops. Very little to be seen in any of them and that little extravagantly dear. Samson, Via San Filippo, has a very fine pair of Battersea enamel candlesticks, large size, of unusual form, and in good order, but he asks £20 for them which is absurd! Gherardo, Via San Teresa, had two fine (unmarked) Wedgwood tureens, ornamented with shells. Queen's ware uncoloured. He asked about £2, and they were worth it, but were too cumbrous to transport. Gherardo was very civil, took us to other shops, and sent us to see the private collection of General della Chiesa, No. 13 Piano 3°30 Via Providenza, with which we were much interested. The General received us very courteously and showed us his things which fill two or three rooms, and are very well

[1] She was constantly engaged in work for public and private charities. In fact, her obituary in *The Times* was largely concerned with her work on behalf of London cabbies (for whom she built a shelter and, after she became blind, knitted red comforters at the rate of one a day) and her labours on behalf of the disturbed Turkish community after the war of 1878.

[2] This was Sir Joseph Joel Duveen (1843–1908), father of Joseph, 1st Lord Duveen (1869–1939).

arranged. He has especially collected specimens of Turin china (Vinovo) of which he appears to have resuscitated the recollection, and he has some very good pieces, especially the figures. This Vinovo fabric seems the great ambition of the Turin antiquaries, and in the shops they all strive to show some of it, just as in Switzerland they aspire mainly to 'Nyon'. Neither fabric is very rich or original, but rather pretty and neat, and in imitation of Sèvres. In Turin they do not scruple to put on marks in a very superficial manner. Alloatti (a sort of private dealer, who seems the chief man; Via Ficenza) offered us a Vinovo pedestal with the correct mark in blue, but beneath it the good old D.V. of Mennecy stamped in the paste, which had doubtless escaped the observation of the modern who had put on the mark of Turin! At Doctor Michele's the Venice anchor had been unscrupulously painted at the bottom of some of his goods. We saw two or three very bad and imperfect specimens of enamel in one or two shops, at ridiculous prices. No purchases. Went to the Museum (Via Gaudenzio Ferrari) to see the small collection of Turin china kept there. Some of the pieces I should doubt, especially as Alloatti told us he had furnished most of the specimens arranged there. After our ceramic chasse, visited the Gallery of pictures and drove about.

22 *May*. Left Turin at 7, and reached Genoa soon after 12. Only 7 or 8 shops for antiquities and they are very, very bad. Isaac Tedesche (a furniture shop in the Via Orefice) had two pretty specimens of Battersea enamel, one a green étui, the other a snuff box. They are upwards of £3 3s apiece. Too dear. In another small shop we saw one or two Viennese dishes. No purchases. The thing in our line which has interested me most here is a magnificent display of old blue and white vases, for drugs, of the old Genoa Ware, which decorate a chemist's shop and which we went in and examined. The address is 'Farmacia De Negri, Genova in Seziglia'. The owner told us these things had been transmitted to him through several generations,[1] having originally belonged to a chemist of the family of Papagrande, the tracery on some of them is beautiful and the whole effect extremely good. As in Turin 'Vinovo', and in Switzerland 'Nyon', so in Genoa the prevailing would seem to be 'Savona'. At a dilettante shoemaker's in the Via Carlo Felici, Paladini by name, we were shown some Queen's ware cups very coarsely painted in red landscapes. On two of these the name of Jacques Boselly had been supplied, and we were assured they were specimens of 'Savona' although two others of the set had the name 'Wedgwood' impressed in the glaze. I confess the English name was rather faint so that the ingenious foreigner might be excused from expecting that it would escape ordinary inspection, but the mark was quite strong enough to be quite clear to any one initiated.

24 *May*. Visited Palazzi Balbi, Reale, Durazzo, Brignole, Pisa. Two shops at Pisa, but nothing in them.

27 *May*. Florence. Corpus Domini; no shops or museums open. Looked at Mr Spence's collection at Palazzo Georgini, then went to his Villa at Fiesole, where we dined and spent

[1] Happily this sort of experience is still possible. The editor walked into a chemist's shop on a market square in the Midlands in 1968, and was astonished to see a set of 24 perfectly preserved Lambeth Delft drug jars. They had belonged to the same establishment since 1742 and had been passed from owner to owner. (See Plate 95.)

the evening. [In the autobiography of Sir Henry Layard this gentleman is mentioned as being the son of Dr Spence, the author, in conjunction with Kirby, of a well-known work on Entomology.][1]

28 *May*. Went out with Mr Spence. Visited a great many curiosity shops. Found very little in them to our taste. A great quantity of earthenware (qy. if to be trusted), modern Capo di Monte, and pictures. Our only purchases were, enamel box with subject printed and coloured, 16s; small printed plaque, good, 4s; two small enamel buttons painted with a vase, 4s; Elers ware teapot with effigies of King and Queen, in relief and letters G.R. (qy. George I, or II) 8s. The only other English goods we saw were some indifferent pieces of Wedgwood, chiefly modern, and a white and gold dessert basket, Worcester (matching the pair we bought of Wharton for £2 10s) considered by Gagliardi to be Capo di Monte, and priced by him at £5. Also at Ribli's shop an unimportant little Derby group. At the shop of Capello (San Spirito) saw a magnificent work of Luca della Robbia, being a life size representation of Adam and Eve and the tempter, forming the back of a bed or sideboard. It resembles the sculpture in marble in the North transept at Pisa, a grand work. They say Colnaghi bought it for a £1000, but the Government prevented it being sent out of the country.

29 *May*. More shops today, without result. Mr Spence took us to see the Art collection at the Bargello, where there are some pieces of furniture of his, on loan, and fine Majolica, etc. Found Mr Sloane at his Palace, and joined him in the evening at his Villa Careggio, formerly belonging to the Medici. Two charming hours. [Mr Sloane was at one time tutor to the family of Count Bourtolin. Later in life he became a rich man. He died at the Medicean Villa about 1875.]

30 *May*. Not out till evening. To Mr Spence's Villa. Gordigiani (painter), Prati (poet), Holman Hunt and others there.

31 *May*. Accompanied Mr Spence Junr. to several shops, and to the Uffizi.

1 *June*. Went with Mr Spence and his son to see the Demidoff Villa.[2] Very fine Sèvres vases, and turquoise dessert set which had belonged to the Prince de Rohan.

2 *June*. At the banker's. To the Uffizi and the Pitti. To Palazzo Gingini to meet Mrs Spence. Agreed to buy five pictures which Mr Spence had had left with him for sale, viz. small portrait of a little girl by Allessandri di Verona, £14 8s. Portrait of Cosimo the 3rd of Tuscany, as a boy, by Sustermans, he wears the cross of the order of St Stephen, instituted by Cosimo I, £10 16s. Portrait of a man by Rubens, painted at Genoa, of which also the engraving, £27. St Bruno, by Domenichino (from the collection of Cav. Fineschi, a famous collector, connoisseur, and restorer of pictures, who died about 30 years ago) £63. Total, £142 4s viz. £158 less 10 per cent. To this is to be added £7 16s for which sum Mr Spence undertakes carriage and insurance to England. Full total, £150. Drove with Mrs Spence. Afterwards we called on Mrs Layard's friend, Mlle Caroline Sorelli, at the Bourtolin Palace. [Mrs H. P. J. Layard, née Austin, was the mother of Sir Henry

[1] The comments within square brackets are by Lady Schreiber's son.

[2] The contents of the Villa Demidoff were sold by Sotheby's in April 1969 for a total exceeding £300,000. The villa belonged to Prince Paul of Yugoslavia.

Layard, the well-known diplomat and connoisseur, and discoverer of Nineveh, who married Lady Charlotte Schreiber's third daughter, Enid.]

3 *June*. Went to the Belle Arti Collection of Medieval pictures with Mr Spence and his son. Afterwards, with the latter to Santa Croce. Left Florence at 4. During our short stay we ransacked all the shops we could find for English china, with no success, with the small exceptions above mentioned. We bought one teapot of old Ginori with figures, well painted in lilac, for 4s. We tried to find a pretty present for Blanche (Guest) but failed. The national jewellery, of which Marchesini, on the Ponte Vecchio, had much, is of an unsubstantial flimsy character, and they ask large prices for it. Young Spence took us to see one or two private collections of pictures and porcelain, for sale. Of these the best was that of Dr Guasdella, Piazza della Independenza, who has some good specimens of Italian china and earthenware. Signor Corsi, Via Valfondo, has chiefly pictures. Dr Foresi, who discovered the Florentine (Duomo) china, was unfortunately from home. We called twice in hopes of seeing him. His wife showed us a piece of the china, without the Duomo mark, but with the word PROVA underneath. She gave me his pamphlet on the subject. Mr Spence had a notion that a member of the Guacciardini family once possessed a fan-shaped toilet box made of Chelsea china, with smaller boxes inside; we failed to trace its existence; but from what I can make out I think it must be one which for the last two years I have admired in Joseph's shop in Bond Street. English china seems unknown at Florence. Yet I am aware that five fine figures (of Apollo and the Muses) with pedestals of most exquisite Chelsea came from Florence not long ago. We missed them last year at Solomon's, in Baker Street, whence they went to Nixon and Rhodes, who asked high prices for them. So much for our ceramic experience.

4 *June*. Bologna. Hunted the few curiosity shops here, and found nothing. Visited Minghetti's shop or Galerie, as they call it, where we saw his imitations of Majolica and all the ancient Faiences, a very useful lesson. Went to the Palazzo Hercolani, which is to be sold. There was nothing English, some fine Oriental vases, and some Dresden, probably not very old. The way the sale is managed is as follows–A catalogue is made and each article numbered. On a certain day (the first of July in this case) prices are affixed to the articles, you are invited, while the collection is on view, to bespeak the refusal of any of the articles, which you thus secure at the price assigned to them on the day of sale, with power of rejection if you consider the price too high. We signed for a pair of very fine Oriental vases, 3 feet high (No. 182), a set of Buen Retiro white (moulded) china, all marked, viz. 3 jugs and covers with finely twisted handles (one cracked), 2 Moutardiers and covers with stands, 1 plain pot and cover, with flowers embossed; this lot of 6 objects (No. 84). Dresden écuelle, cover and stand, with enamelled embossed flowers (No. 79). Figure of a man in white porcelain, 'Wood carrier', badly broken, marked Buen Retiro (No. 86). The porter, Bettramini Pietro, took the number of the lots, and is, on the 1st of July, to let us know at what figure they are priced in the list of sale, awaiting our reply. There was a fine set of 5 Oriental vases, enamelled highly with fine red borders. But we thought they would go beyond our limits, besides they were not of such high quality as those for which we signed, Lot 182.

5 *June*. Up at 4. By 6 in the train for Ravenna. We took letters to curator of the Mosaics and public buildings there, who is a Mosaicist himself. Found him copying the mosaic of the Good Shepherd from the Mausoleum of Galla Placidia, for the South Kensington Museum. He took us to all the chief objects of interest, viz. S. Appollinare Nuovo, S. Maria in Cosmedin, San Vitale, the Duomo and its Baptistery, the tomb of Galla Placidia. Thence, passing by the house formerly resided in by Lord Byron, and the Church where Dante is buried, to the Mausoleum of Theodoric outside the walls, a wonderful spot, with a beautiful grass avenue leading to it. Water standing in the lower part of the building. After luncheon at the Hôtel San Marco, M. Ribel went with us to S. Apollinare, and thence to the delicious Pineta. Theodoric's Sarcophagus was removed from his tomb and is now built into the wall of the building which goes by the name of Theodoric's Palace, near the Apollinare Nuovo. Nothing in the way of china, at Ravenna, no 'antiquaire' shops.

6 *June*. Strolled about, visited again the Academy. In the evening went to the Campo Santo, and there made the tour of the town outside the gates. While at Bologna, bought for Blanche an old silver cross and ornament, of Coltello, Via del Ospedale, £5.

7 *June*. Up at 3 o'clock, off to Ferrara at 6, arriving about half-past 7. Spent there above 4 hours. Visited the Castle and its dungeons; Dosso Dossi's ceiling in the Sala de Giganti might, with many modifications, give ideas for decorating the ceiling of the Canford drawing-room; Tasso's prison, Ariosto's house, the Cathedral, one curiosity shop, 'Mello' in the Ghetto, but containing nothing of our sort. We heard there was china in the Palazzo Costabile, and went there, but after waiting some time, failed to get into the Gallery, as the old steward could not manage to get the doors open. It was from this Palace that Ivor procured some of his finest pictures. [This is, of course, the first Baron Wimborne, the eldest son of Sir John Guest and Lady Charlotte.] Left Ferrara about 12; reached Venice after 4. Put up at the Pension Suisse.

17 *June*. Have been in Venice ever since and hope to stay another 10 days. Spent most of our time on the water and in hunting the curiosity shops. Most of these are filled with fine objects (qy. original) but out of our line. We have made on the whole a good many purchases, however; Guggenheim's is the largest shop. With him we only found a small enamel snuff box with a transfer printing of a girl, in black, milking, on the inside, £1 4s. Richetti is the next largest repository. He has a delightful service of Milanese ware, decorated with representations of Harlequin and Columbine; for the whole service of 80 or 90 pieces he asks £60. We bought 5 dishes of the service (2 of them marked) for £5 5s. Oval enamel, with Saviour on the Cross, printed in black, 8s. Pink enamel double inkstand, £1. A small Persian mug, £1 12s and a pair of fine Venetian soup tureens and covers, ornamented with flowers in bold relief as a handle, £7. Of all this lot amounting to £17, only the 2 objects in enamel are English. Next in order of importance comes the shop of Favenza, in course of moving to the banks of the Grand Canal. We found some fine old glass with him, and a few specimens of fine Venetian china, but nothing English, except 3 enamels and here again we have been tempted out of our line to the following extent. A large plaque of Smalto glass, with landscape in brown, £8, this is quite equal in size and decoration to the framed pieces in the Correr Collection. It has the extra merit

of being perfect, whereas two out of the Correr pieces are sadly broken, but it falls short of them, in that the Correr pieces are decorated with views in Venice, and ours has only a fancy landscape, but very good. A pair of Smalto glass vases, painted with amorini in pink, £4. Also resembling a vase in the Correr, though of a different subject. A circular plaque in Smalto glass with representation of San Rocco, done in red, £1 12s. A pair of Trembleuses and Stands, ruby glass, with white Smalto inside, decorated with red and gold ornaments, £7. A pair of Venetian cups and saucers finely painted in landscapes and figures, £2 8s. Two similar cups without saucers, £1. Four Venetian cups, rude painting, four of them marked, £4 10s. Eleven plates and 12 soup plates Venetian, marked, with wreathes and insects in centre, £3 14s 9d. Two pictures on glass, one done in gold, the other in silver, signed E.F. one has the arms of Cardinal Barberigo upon it, £7. A small unimportant enamel snuff box, £1 4s. A snuff box in the form of a bird, £1 10s. A small female head, enamel, black transfer-printing, 1s 3d. An Oriental teapot, gold ground, £1 (matching some egg-shell cups I have at home). This completes a sum of £43. All, I believe, well spent. As to the glass, we got Signor Montecchi, the Director of the Salviati Works, to come and give us his opinion of it. He considered the large plaque very fine indeed, as also the Trembleuses, which are of a colour very difficult to execute and still more difficult to get to stand. He pronounced these pieces undoubtedly old. About the Amorini vases he seemed rather more doubtful. It ended by our rejecting Favenza's 2 glass vases with Amorini, for on washing them we found the colouring defective. We added, however, an old metal frame and brought the lot, in settling with him, down to £40. We also made a change in our dealings with Ricchetti, exchanging the two marked Milan dishes, and two cups and saucers for a pair of Sucriers and stands (the latter both marked) to which we added a Venetian basket, bringing up the total paid him to £19. Another dealer, Rietti, principally sells figures of old Faience and Majolica, and Luca della Robbia. He has secured the whole make of the Nove works, who turn out very pretty terraglia, which he sells as old Nove pottery, and he has a quantity of Minghetti's copies of the antique. One piece of very fine Nove china he showed us, viz: an Ecuelle, cover and stand, beautifully painted with subjects in panels. He wanted 400 francs for it. I think we have traced that it must have come direct from the proprietors of the Nove works; it is marked N.O. in the glaze. At Rietti's we found a number of old knives and forks. Twisted handles of turquoise enamel, and silver, very beautiful; but of the lot only 7 were in good order. These 7 we bought for £2 2s as also 12 buttons of enamel with hunting subjects, in black transfer-printing, for £1 2s. This was arranged after a great deal of bargaining, more than double the price having been originally asked for them. At a little shop on the Piazza Sta. Maria dei Frari, we found a small enamel head, 1s 6d, and a piece of Buen Retiro exactly matching the pot and cover for which we 'signed' at Bologna, and making a pair with it. At a Librarian's named Colbachini, near the Belle Arti, we got a pair of very good Oriental cups, painted with cocks for 10s, and a much broken but very interesting enamel order of Frederick the Great, for 2s. There is an officious, meddling, tiresome old man named della Rovere, who keeps a shop with very little in it in the Palazzo Berchtold, from him we got 4 printed Wedgwood cups and saucers like the Milan set, only done in black transfer instead of red, 16s and also 4 small enamels of seasons, 12s, and 2 coloured enamel pegs, 4s. This man took us over the part of the Palace in which Mme Berchtold herself is living. She is a natural daughter of old Lord Hertford's by Lady Strachan. It is a tawdrily furnished uninteresting house, but has one fine hall in it hung with good tapestry, for which she wants some £2000. Everything in the house is for sale, but the prices asked are exorbitant. He also sent us to the Palace of a Count Albrizzi where also what little remains is to be sold. We looked at the things but liked nothing. What was then our surprise when the Count's servant brought all his china to us at our Hotel in the evening inviting us to make an offer? Of course we declined. There was a metal cast of Briot's, of a large dish. This we rather admired, but knowing nothing of this branch of the arts, we doubted of its value. To our digust della Rovere forthwith wrote off to Cortelazzo at Vicenza telling him we wanted to consult him about it, and Cortelazzo actually came to Venice to see us on the 16th accordingly. The pertinacity of this Count Albrizzi, who would hardly take a refusal from us, was very amusing, but we did not buy anything from him. The only good della Rovere did us was in introducing us to an industrious little dealer called Ruggieri, living near the Ponte della Piavola. We paid him many visits and got a few things from him on good terms for us, and doubtless for him also. There was a small Nove milk jug, well painted with buildings, but imperfect, 8s. A Nove écuelle, cover and stand, with a rose decorated with black spots, and signed with the star in gold, £2. A small Venetian vase, purple border, and bouquet of flowers, £1 4s. A pair of Nove cups and saucers (red star) with grotesque figures, 14s. One of the oldest established (I should think) and most respectable shops in Venice is kept by an old man, with a fine venerable countenance, named Len. He is giving up business and had not many things left. It is said he had not been prosperous, owing to his having refused to fee the Laquais de Place, but this is hardly credible. From him we bought a dish, matching the plates we got from Favenza, 8s, and a pair of Battersea enamel candlesticks, exactly like those we saw at Samson's at Turin. They are a good bit injured in the sunk part near the base (where, however, they can be well repaired by a band of filigree work) and the price we gave for them was only £2. Rather a different amount from that asked by Samson! but his were perfect. An amusing incident occurred the evening before we left Venice. Ruggieri had brought us some broken vases matching the one we bought of him, and a very good 'Frederic the Great' enamel snuff box and modern enamel bracelet, which he said belonged to a lady in distress who wanted to dispose of them. The price he wanted for the snuff box was £6. We did not purchase, but in hunting about the Spaderia, on the evening of the 28th, we found all these things at the shop of a little jeweller, 'Morchio', Calle Larga S. Marco 659, and bought the Frederic the Great box for £2 16s. On the same occasion we found a small teapot, Venetian, imitating Oriental, in a rubbish shop in the Spaderia, for which we paid 3s 6d. This exhausts the list of our Venice purchases. We went over to Murano one day with Signor Montecchi to see the glass works which interested us much and took the opportunity of going over the Museum and temporary Exhibition; the former of which contains some fine specimens of early manufacture. We also went into the Duomo, now undergoing repair, and there met the Cav. Abbate Zanetti, who is the Director of the Murano

Museum, and with whom we made an appointment to visit the Museum again on the following Monday, the 21st; on that occasion Zanetti had the case opened for us, and we examined carefully the pieces of old glass. Next morning a little dealer, into whose shop we had strolled at Murano, came over to Venice with some of the goods we had looked at. They were of little value, but more from charity than anything else we bought of him 4 old Nove ware trays, 3s; a smaller one, 1s 6d, and an earthenware plate with blue tracery, 2s 6d. On a later day he came over again bringing 2 glass bottles with the arms of Murano and those of Miotto done in gold, about a century old. These we bought for £1 4s. In order to verify this 'Stemma di Miotti' he showed us a circular 'seal' of Smalto glass, having on it in relief the Miotto insignia, an ape holding an apple and inscribed 'Pusopo Miotto, Murano'. This, he said, was the trade mark put by the Miotti on their cases of manufactured articles when shipped. He was very unwilling to part with it, and for a long time refused to do so, saying that it belonged to his brother who had only lent it to him to show us, giving authority for the decoration of the bottles. But at last we persuaded him to do so, mainly by telling him we would not buy the bottles without it, and so we ultimately secured it for £1. On a subsequent visit to Murano (25th) we showed this seal to Zanetti, who was quite excited at our having obtained it, considering it a most valuable and curious specimen. There is a similar one in the Murano Museum of the Barberis who were manufacturers in 1793 at the Sign of 'Alle Nave'. This seal or stamp is impressed, 'F.B. ALLA NAVE BETTINA' (and a ship with 2 masts and flag at the stern). The date of our Miotto was supposed by Zanetti to be about 1723–4. I have now enumerated every purchase. As I said above, our object was rather to enjoy and benefit by the air of Venice than to devote ourselves to sight-seeing. Let us hope to become better acquainted with its wondrous treasures of art on a future occasion. Of course we made frequent visits to S. Mark's (where I think I got some ideas for the Canford Hall) and to the Belle Arti, where we specially delighted in the Older Masters, Bonifaccio, Carpaccio, Gentile Bellini. Amusing ourselves by the study of the room containing the pictures of the two latter, C.S. is inclined to hope that the pictures we bought of Band on the 11th of May may turn out to be one or the other of them. We went over the Ducal Palace, saw Sta. Maria della Salute, Sta. Maria dei Frari, Santi Giovanni & Paolo. Some delicious pictures of the legend of St George by Carpaccio. We went over the Pesaro and Giovanelli Palaces, the latter done up in gorgeous modern taste, and paid two long visits to the Correr Museum, being on the second occasion (Wednesday, 25 June) accompanied by one of the Director's Sigr. Urbani, who gave us much information, and caused all the cases to be opened for our more complete examination of their contents. At Venice we became acquainted with Sir Robert and Lady Arbuthnot, who lent us Ruskin's books, and took us to see some glass (a service, not very old, decorated in gold) belonging to two old bachelor brothers, the Messrs Malcolm, who have been in trade many years. [Sir Robert was the 2nd Baronet, born in 1801. He married the younger daughter of Field Marshal Sir John Forster Fitzgerald.] We also made acquaintance with Mr Rawdon Brown, who is a resident of some 30 years and has made deep researches into matters relating to the Art and Literature of Venice.

[He worked for the English Rolls Office in the Venetian Archives and was the editor of the Venetian State papers in many volumes.] He mainly supplied the materials for Mr Drake's books on Venetian China. [This was a well-known collector and member of a firm of solicitors. He was knighted as Sir William Drake.] Having admired our little Nove cups and saucers (bought of Ruggieri) we secured a similar pair to give to him, and in return he gave us a pretty pair of Venetian cup and saucers, blue fish scale, Oriental figures in panels, probably of the Cozzi date. On Friday, 25th, we went over to Torcello, taking Murano on our way and again visiting Zanetti and the Museum, a delightful excursion. On our return went through Burano. Enquired there about lace, and found one old woman making a little, but it was very coarse bad stuff. Our enquiries were first made in a respectable, but humble dwelling (glittering, however, with brazen utensils) which we found to belong to the village tailor. His wife, a pretty young woman, who was tending twins in two cradles, not only received and directed us courteously, but insisted on our returning (after seeing the Church) to partake of coffee. The Burano people exhibit a taste I have not seen elsewhere, arranging their gaily coloured earthenware plates and dishes against the walls of their houses on racks which are constructed in pyramidical form. All the Islands seem very poor, but this is the best of them. Amongst the interesting sights of Venice I must not forget the Scoule of San Rocco, San Giovanni, and San Marco, the public Gardens (where the lime flowers were just going out of bloom) and the Lido. Also numberless excursions around the City, the Giudecca, etc. The name of our Gondolier, Luigi Moloso, No. 129. Hotel, Pension Suisse. On the morning of Saturday the 26th, we got up early and went for the day to Padua, remaining there till evening, a most charming expedition. We spent a very long time in the Giotto Chapel, and visited the Churches of S. Antonio (well remembered for the Marble Boys supporting the Candelabra, in 1838) and of Sta. Giustina. We fell in with a little antiquaire, Celin. He had nothing himself, but he took us to others. At another little shop we bought a pair of striped cups and saucers, Venetian, 4s, and a Persian pot and cover, 12s. I had been enquiring for lace at Venice and found it awfully dear. La Pompeia has the best selection. Some of it is very fine, but extravagant. For a flounce like one bought last year by Ivor she wanted £200. Of course this was out of the question. Happening to mention lace to Celin, he took us to a draper's shop, the master of which Barzillai, brought out a series of bundles to show us. Among them was a flounce of near 20 yards, 14 inches deep (very nearly resembling Ivor's, for which he had given £125). To our astonishment we were only asked £32 for it. The flounce was not to be resisted, even in the light of an investment, at that price, so we bought it. After this we went to the house of 'Giuseppe Bassani, San Cassiano'. He had some very fine things which we promised to visit again; from him we got a Venetian fruit basket and stand, 16s. From Barzillai 4 Venetian cups and saucers, Japanese pattern, 8s. Small pedestal of the same pattern as ours of Bow china, 4s. Four glass heads, unimportant, 8s. A moulded cream ware tray (qy. Treviso), £1. When we had completed our purchases, the jovial Barzillai asked us to stay and dine with him, which diverted us vastly. The following Monday, Lady Arbuthnot came to see our lace with Mme Usedom and Mr Trevelyan (the latter a great judge) and they pronounced it wonderful, both as to quality and price. This (Monday 28th) was our last day at Venice. We took a sorrowful farewell, devoutly hoping ere long to return to it.

29 *June*. Up at 3. Left Venice at 6. . . .

A PICTURE SALE AT CHRISTIE'S (1887)

THE English would never have become the enlightened collectors they did if it had not been for London's art auction houses. One might argue the case the other way round were it not for the fact that the first, venerable, James Christie started life as an auctioneer of property of every sort and gradually became more interested in pictures and books. He was by no means the first auctioneer to achieve success in London, but he was certainly the first *great* auctioneer, who, by dint of personality, intelligence and charm, rose to become a nationally popular figure.

This is not the place to enlarge upon the unquenchable excitement involved in any auction of great works of art, but two factors in collecting which are often overlooked do deserve mention. In the eighteenth and early nineteenth centuries it was largely in the auction room that the budding connoisseur had an opportunity to see a steady flow of works of art. Public museums hardly existed; private collections in the great houses were not open to everyman;[1] photography of paintings only became a reliable reality after the middle of the nineteenth century; engravings, common though they were, could never give a really life-like representation of a great picture. So in England it was only on the walls of the saleroom that a man could really study whatever school of painting appealed to him.[2]

Although the earlier English collectors could depend to some extent on the advice of their favourite dealers, by and large the majority did their own choosing and bidding. But it is all too easy to overlook the difficulty of selection, of personal choice. This is really where connoisseurship comes into its own. A walk round Sotheby's or Christie's today before a picture sale will readily demonstrate how difficult it is to choose a picture that is genuinely good. Admittedly in the nineteenth century the quantity displayed was probably not so great as it is now and pictures of genuine quality came up for sale more frequently. But copyists were just as active then and there was the additional hazard of bad condition. Methods of picture cleaning were primitive in the extreme. Following upon the disastrous

[1] An obvious exception was the Duke of Bridgewater's Gallery (see pages 125 and 140).

[2] Unless examples happened to appear in an exhibition at the British Institution (see page 226).

habit of 'picture scrubbing' in the late eighteenth and early nineteenth centuries, a preference for the 'golden glow of gallery varnish' became widely established. As often as not this concealed repairs and restorations.[1] One must also remember that the intellectual and scholarly equipment which we take for granted today when the purchase of works of art can be tantamount to investment pure and simple, did not begin to exist until well into the nineteenth century. So that when it came to bidding to win in the auction room, a collector depended largely upon taste and flair and an elastic purse.

While it may have been the private collector who stole the limelight on great occasions, it is clear from the records that then, as now, it was the professional dealer who dominated the saleroom. It appears to have been the better dealers who began to exercise more care over skilful restoration (particularly for their American customers) and it is easy to understand why after the middle of the nineteenth century the wealthier collectors preferred to buy from dealers whom they knew and could trust. Often this initially commercial relationship developed into genuine friendship and became the keystone of important collections. After a while a dealer learned exactly what would appeal to his client and thus became, as it were, a collector at second remove.

The description of the Christie sale which follows was written by George Redford, who was *The Times* Art Sale correspondent for many years. He was one of the first men to take an interest in the history of art auctions and is the author of the monumental, two-volume history of *Art Sales,* which was published in 1888.

The history of Christie's is particularly well documented. The firm has almost complete records since 1766. For further histories see *Memorials of Christie's,* a Record of Art Sales from 1766 to 1896 by W. Roberts in two volumes, 1897; *Christie's* 1766–1925 by H. C. Marillier, 1926; *Christie's Seasons* 1928, 1929, 1930 edited by A. C. R. Carter; and *Christie's since the War*, 1945–1958, which contains a particularly interesting essay on 'Taste, Patronage and Collecting' by Denys Sutton.

QUOTED FROM George Redford writing in *The Graphic,* 10 September 1887.

THE illustration [on Plate 88] represents a scene which may be witnessed any Saturday afternoon at the famous Rooms in King Street, St James's Square, during

[1] The cleaning and restoration of pictures is inextricably linked with collecting, and references to this topic occur throughout this book. The whole contentious subject is admirably discussed from a historical, technical and ethical point of view in Helmut Ruhemann's *The Cleaning of Paintings*, 1968, which also contains an immense bibliography of the relevant literature by Joyce Plesters.

the London season, when some great collection of pictures is being sold; it may be of works of Old Masters, for a century and more the treasures of some old family mansion, brought from abroad by some travelled lord of Horace Walpole's day, or more probably it is the collection of modern pictures upon which some merchant prince in his prosperous days lavished his too ready wealth. The picture upon the easel is the only one allowed to be seen, for all the others, which have been exhibited for several days before, are either covered up, like the large one, or taken down to be ranged in proper order behind the green baize screen at the side, so as to follow the catalogue quickly.

Mr Woods will be recognised in the rostrum, which tradition says is the very same old polished mahogany from which Mr Christie, the founder of the house more than a century ago in the Rooms in Pall Mall, vacated by the Royal Academy in its youth, pronounced the ultimatum of the hammer. The anxious moment of the last bid has come, as we see by the eager faces of the young ladies, and Mr Agnew, sitting close by the side of the rostrum is about to take the telegram handed to him, which may tell him to buy the picture at any price. Whether he will have to bid two or three thousand guineas, however, depends somewhat upon his rival, Mr Vokins, who turns with a smiling face towards his client. Amongst the audience watching the contest we may recognize several well-known *habitués* of Christie's. There is Mr Knowles, the Editor of the *Nineteenth Century*, and next to him Lord Normanton, who is one of the most constant observers at Christie's, and a most intelligent one, too, as a buyer especially. Then there is Lord Rosebery and a gentleman who, though his face is turned away, is surely Mr Butler, who buys pictures by the early Italian and Flemish masters, and has a fine collection. In the group standing behind the rostrum – a rather favourite place for the *cognoscenti* to compare notes – our artist seems to have seen Sir W. Gregory (Trustee of the National Gallery), with Lord Powerscourt and his friend Mr Doyle (the Director of the National Gallery of Ireland), who never misses a chance of adding a good picture to his Gallery. Other heads here seem to call to mind old Mr Quilter, who sold such a fine collection of water-colour drawings here some years ago at an enormous profit, Sir Charles Tennant, the Glasgow Croesus in the picture line, and Mr John Pender, of Oriental Telegraphian renown, who has some fine pictures, but is rarely a buyer now. If we could see the crowd of those who stand upon raised steps at the angles of the room – which is a long octagon in shape – and fill up the space just within and without the doorway, we should be pretty sure to find there Sir F. Burton (the Director of the National Gallery), the Duke of St Albans, Mr Salting, Dr Hamilton, Mr Disraeli (brother of the late Earl of Beaconsfield), Dr Percy, Sir Frederick Leighton occasionally, Mr Woolner the sculptor, but seldom other of the Academicians, who seem to be rather shy of picture auctions, which sometimes show a falling market even for good names.

So densely packed is this part of the room on the occasion of a great sale like that of the Bicknell Collection in 1863, or the Gillott sale in 1872, and the later sales of Mr Mendel's, Baron Albert Grant's, and the Duke of Hamilton's above all, that bidders who come late are obliged to stand on chairs out in the ante-room, and use their catalogues as semaphores on the chance of catching the eye of the auctioneer. This, however, has been obviated since the building of the handsome new Gallery in 1885, which at the same time gave access to the saleroom by a back staircase, admittance to which was given by tickets before the front door was opened. The sale of any celebrated picture, such as Turner's 'Venice', Müller's 'Chess-Players', or beyond all of a first-rate portrait by Sir Joshua or Gainsborough, is an exciting affair. The moment the picture comes upon the easel, it is received with loud clapping of hands, repeated as often as the bidders outvie one another in their advances of perhaps a thousand guineas, and when the hammer falls at last to a lumping sum there is a perfect uproar, just as the crowd roars its delight when the Derby is run, for the Christie audience revels in high prices simply for money's sake, though of course some of the applause is meant for the picture. But the sensational price seems to have lost its effect, since such extravagant sums have become common. For example, when the beautiful Gainsborough picture of 'The Sisters' was sold this season in the Graham sale for £9975 there was not half the applause it met with when in 1873 Mr Agnew bid £6615, and bought it for the late Mr Graham of Glasgow. But the greatest sensation of high price was over the Gainsborough Duchess of Devonshire portrait, the notorious stolen picture, at the Wynn Ellis sale in 1876, when, almost as the picture came upon the easel, Messrs Christie got a wire from Lord Dudley in Paris, telling them to go to 10,000 guineas for it. His bidding was done; but, while the audience shouted their applause or held their breath in amazement, Mr Agnew sent them into wild ecstasy by a further advance to 10,100 guineas, and so gave the final *coup* to this extraordinary sale of a picture which all the critics refused to accept as the work of Gainsborough, at the highest price ever paid at auction.

These sale audiences, however, only represent those who mean business – the dealers and their clients, who sit by them trembling with nervous hope and fear; with a sprinkling of the curious in these matters, who rush off to the Club and the dinner-table with the prices of the fine pictures which all the world of rank and fashion has been admiring and discussing while they were exhibited during the week. And it goes without saying, that the exhibitions before the sale day are the most interesting and the most instructive of any in London, or anywhere else in the world, for they have brought before us from time to time many masterpieces of ancient and modern Art – pictures by the Old Masters, which have been treasured away beyond the reach of most people in ducal palaces like those of Hamilton and Blenheim, or those magnificent displays of which English painters may well be proud, when the Bicknell, Gillott, Monro, and Mendel collections were to be seen upon the walls of Christie's Gallery. Nothing that the Academy can collect at Burlington House in any one year can be compared for variety and excellence with these exhibitions of Christie's, whether the works be those of Old Masters or modern painters, English and foreign. Then as the Gallery is the best lighted, and best adapted in form for exhibiting pictures, they always look their very best, and it is not too much to say that people enjoy a visit to Christie's more than anything else in the way of picture-seeing.

Here, in the early hours of the forenoon, come City men, lawyers, judges, Cabinet Ministers, editors, and art critics on their way to their labours. The Prince of Wales himself generally looks in when any great collection is 'on view', and other royal and distinguished personages, with many ladies of the highest rank and beauty. After luncheon time the rooms get more crowded on these great occasions, and continue so till late. That some thousands of persons pass before the pictures is told not so accurately as by a turnstile, but by the quantity of silk fluff upon the floor, swept off from the dresses of the ladies; and more substantially by the number of catalogues sold for the benefit of the artists' benevolent societies, to whose funds considerable sums are presented by Messrs Christie. In the old days of Christie's in Pall Mall, and at other auction rooms, catalogues were only to be had for half a-crown, and to keep out improper persons there was no admission without one. But these important sales were at rare intervals then, not, as we know them [now], going on almost every day, and always on Saturday, which being a non-Parliament day, is reserved for the chief sales of the season.

For considerably more than a century Christie's has been the centre of attraction for all works of Art, whose owners wish to turn them into money at once, as in the division of family properties. Of late, through the change in the law of entail, the number of sales has been vastly increased, as we have seen in several most important instances. The records afforded by the catalogues preserved so carefully, would give, had we space to enter upon it, a most curious history of the vicissitudes of Fine Art properties, and their owners. There is scarcely a name from King George IV, the Royal Dukes, and Queen Charlotte, all through the peerage, which is not to be found at some time in the list of sales: even the collection of Pope Paul IV, which contained many old drawings, came to Christie's in 1770. The wreck of the famous Orleans Collection, after the Duke of Bridgewater, Lord Carlisle, and Lord Stafford had taken their pick, went to another auctioneer in Spring Gardens, and so did the great collection of M. de Calonne, the French Ambassador, in 1795, the same year that Christie sold Sir Joshua Reynolds' collection after his death in 1792, for the executors, Edmund Burke, Malone, and Metcalf. But Christie was to have sold the Desenfans Collection in 1785, only the sale was postponed on account of the great excitement over Lunardi's going up in a balloon from the Artillery Ground; and in the end Desenfans never sold his pictures, but left them to his friend Sir F. Bourgeois, and we may see them now at the Dulwich Gallery. So many fine pictures were sent or brought to London during the troubles and dangers of the French Revolution that sales were constantly going on, and we find several 'the property of emigrant noblemen' about this time, and the important collections of Mr Trumbull and Mr Udney, with others, were sold by Christie in 1797 and in 1802–4. Then in 1811 came the notable sales of the Ottley and the Henry Hope Collections. In 1814 or 1815 the Prince Regent sent some of his pictures to Christie's, and soon afterwards there came to the hammer the collection of West, the President of the Academy, in which a Titian, 'The Death of Actæon', sold for £1785, a high price for those days. In the following year, 1821, came the famous Lady Thomond collection of the works of Sir Joshua, which he bequeathed to her, his favourite niece. Next came the sale of Mr G. Watson Taylor's pictures in 1823, in which was that most celebrated of Sir Joshua's portraits, the 'Mrs Siddons as the Tragic Muse', which the Earl Grosvenor was so fortunate as to get for the trifling sum of £1837, a price that now, were the present Duke to part with his inestimable treasure, would assuredly run into many thousands. So we might go on recounting the long roll of famous collections dispersed, down to those which in our own time have created such constant interest, and have been of such unspeakable value in developing our National Gallery. Thus it will be acknowledged that Christie's is not a mere picture mart; it has wide relations with Art, and well deserves to be named amongst the Art institutions of this country, though it be only with that unwritten charter of repute which the nation grants to private enterprise employed for the public benefit, and conducted with that integrity which is the pride of Englishmen.

THE HAMILTON PALACE COLLECTION

ALEXANDER, 10th Duke of Hamilton, married the younger daughter of William Beckford and many of the Beckford treasures passed to the Duke, who was an ardent collector in his own right in the grandest of grand manners. When his vast accumulation of treasures came to be sold at Christie's in 1882 it was, as Reitlinger says, 'probably the finest single collection ever to have come under the hammer'. It took seventeen days to sell 2213 lots and they fetched a record auction total of £397,562.

The preliminary account of the collection was written by George Redford. Redford, and the art world of 1882 in general, were delighted that for once the National Gallery had sufficient funds at its disposal to acquire most of the paintings which the Director, William Burton, wanted to purchase.

Two complete catalogues of the sale exist. One, illustrated with collotype reproductions, was the official Christie catalogue. The other, with a series of engravings, was published by Remington in conjunction with a French art journal (*Librairie de l'Art*) after the sale and contains the names of the purchasers and the prices paid. It was published because of the immense interest in the sale. Both versions can still be found fairly frequently.

QUOTED FROM George Redford writing in *The Times*, 6 February 1882.

THE Duke of Hamilton has determined that the noble collection of pictures, statues and splendid decorative furniture of this ancient ducal mansion, with the exception of the family portraits and articles possessing a purely family interest, shall be disposed of about the same time with the Library.* . . . It is intended we understand that the sale, which will form one more of the many important dispersions of Art Treasures which have made the galleries of Messrs Christie famous in the annals of Art Sales for more than a century, shall take place during the coming summer. Hamilton Palace dates back to times as early as the old kings of Scotland, having got its name of Palace long before the Lords of Hamilton of olden times became possessed of it as the appanage of their possessions at Hamilton, now grown into a busy town of trade and manufacture. Enclosed within the domain is the Moat Hill, an ancient seat of justice, with a Runic cross near it and an old gateway. Cadzow Castle and Chatelherault are other interesting relics of the ancient Dukes of Chatelherault created by Henri II of France in the Hamilton family. The present mansion, however retains nothing of the ancient palace, and is a stone edifice of vast size built in the debased classic style of the seventeenth century, with parts added at the wings forming the Beckford Library at one side, and the new state rooms built in 1838 on the other, presenting a front by no means imposing but rather heavy and gloomy in appearance, with indifferent approaches. Having a *souterrain* of vast mineral wealth it has suffered like many other great residences in the North from the encroaching spread of coal and iron works, and numerous mills and factories, the tall chimneys pouring forth their perpetual fumes of smoke and noxious vapours in every direction, and rendering it every year more and more unsuitable as a residence for a great nobleman.

It may be described as quadrangular in plan with a central block about 264 ft. long, flanked by wings enclosing a courtyard open to the south with the entrance door in the middle of the central façade, under a fine portico of columns 25 ft. high, each of a single block from the Dalserk quarries, and on the model of those of the Temple of Jupiter Stator at Rome. The main front of the building faces the garden, and looks north, the Beckford Library standing out on the west wing, the new state apartments on the east. A remarkable feature in the massive structure is the entrance hall which is a hall of columns placed in five rows and supporting a groined stone ceiling, lit by windows on the garden front, and ornamented with busts on pedestals among which are prominently placed those of Peter the Great and the Empress Catherine which remind the visitor that Duke Alexander was ambassador to Russia. It is to this Duke that is due the merit of having formed the extraordinary assemblage of works of Art as well as the Library distinguished by his name from the Beckford Library. He appears indeed to have been a virtuoso of heroic mould for he not only surrounded himself with all this magnificence of Art while he lived but built for himself a sepulcharal monument or mausoleum, and here he rests in the ancient Egyptian sarcophagus enclosed within it. This structure is like an ancient Egyptian tomb in its extraordinary massiveness; it stands in the Park, and is seen from afar, being no less than 120 ft. high, with grand flights of steps, fine bronze doors copied from those of Ghiberti, and a basement of vaulted tombs, intended to be occupied by the future Dukes of Hamilton.

The pictures and statues are arranged in the grand suite of apartments forming the

* *The splendid library was sold by Messrs Sotheby, Wilkinson and Hodge; the Beckford section in* 1882 *and* 1883; *the Hamilton in* 1884.

principal part of the Palace, extending over the hall of columns and to the wings at each side. This grand tier is reached by a staircase entirely made of black marble entered by a doorway at the right-hand corner of the hall. On the staircase is the large altarpiece by Girolamo dei Libri of the Virgin and Child, with Saint Augustine and another saint under a tree with landscape background, the largest and one of the finest of the works of this florid painter of the Veronese school. Here also is a very fine antique statue in Parian marble of the Venus of the Capitol, and busts in red Egyptian porphyry of Augustus and Tiberius and of Vespasian in black basalt, with draperies in jasper. The marble hall, entered from the stairs, is a very imposing apartment, as here are the heroic bronze statues of the Diana of the Louvre (Diane à la Biche), the Fighting Gladiator, the Apollo Belvedere, the Antinous of the Vatican and the group of Hercules and Telephus. These are important bronzes and of great historic interest, for they were cast in Rome for Francis I and once adorned his 'Chateau de Ville Roy'. Some rare specimens of Rouen ware are other noticeable objects in this hall; four busts of heroic figures representing the Seasons painted *au naturel* with pedestals of the same *fabrique*. The large altar-piece by Botticelli, the Assumption of the Virgin with the zones of Heaven in which are ranged the patriarchs, prophets, apostles, evangelists, martyrs, &c., which will be remembered in the Burlington House Exhibition of Old Masters in 1873, is a remarkable picture, painted as Vasari relates, for Matteo Palmieri, a learned Florentine, who gave the scheme to the painter, and had the mortification of being charged with heresy and seeing his picture interdicted and covered up from the public view.* This picture hangs above a most beautiful Renaissance mantelpiece of Florentine work of the fifteenth century in black limestone, in front of which is a superb specimen of Florentine mosaic in a table of large size.

The long gallery, which may be entered from this marble hall, is principally filled with portraits, among which is the fine Vandyck of the Earl of Denbigh in an eastern hunting dress with his gun and a boy in Persian dress, with a landscape background. But the great feature in this gallery is the large picture by Rubens of Daniel in the Lion's Den, of which the great painter spoke in his letter to Sir Dudley Carleton, published in Mr Carpenter's pictorial notices, as having been entirely painted by his own hand. There are nine lions and lionesses full life-size, painted with all the amazing power and spirit of the master such as we see displayed in the wonderful lion now exhibited at Burlington House, belonging to Lord Normanton. This is a picture of unique interest, being one of Charles I Collection, and known to have been presented to him by Lord Dorchester. It was engraved by Bloteling, and more recently by James Ward in mezzotint.[1] Another work by Rubens of great beauty is the landscape with the figures of Centaurs, known as 'The Loves of the Centaurs'.

* *This most interesting work of the master was purchased at the sale, for the National Gallery for* £4777 10*s*.

[1] However, by 1963 few people except Rubens experts remembered the painting. It came up for sale at Bonham's, attributed to Jordaens and de Voss, and was bought prior to auction for £500 by an American dealer. At that figure it escaped the net of the Reviewing Committee on the Export of Works of Art, and after Knoedlers had re-established its well-known pedigree it was sold to the National Gallery in Washington D.C. for £178,500. The dealer is said to have commented that he made 'a comfortable profit'!

The state dining salon which is between the Hamilton and the Beckford Libraries, and adjoins the Tribune at the end of the Long Gallery, contains some extremely fine full-length portraits, among which is that of Philip IV by Velasquez,* wearing the Order of the Golden Fleece, which according to Stirling was a spoil of the Peninsular War taken from the palace at Madrid by General Dessôlée. The equestrian portrait of Charles the First by Vandyck in this room is a fine replica of the famous Windsor Castle picture, but with variations. Here are also the portrait of Henrietta Maria; a whole length of Charles the First in a crimson slashed dress with the Order of the Garter; the Duchess of Richmond full length in a white dress, with her son as Cupid, in a landscape with buildings: a picture of striking elegance and beauty in brilliant tone of colour. The portrait of Henrietta Princess of Phalsburg, is a full length mentioned in the catalogue of Charles I Collection, and engraved by Vois. A remarkable portrait in this stately dining room is the full-length life-size one of Napoleon the Great by David; whom the Emperor especially favoured although he had been one of the most frantic revolutionists of '92, and who painted the well-known picture of Napoleon crossing the Alps. This full-length portrait was painted expressly for the Duke of Hamilton, and is a very fine work by this eminent painter of the French school. The large bronze of the Laocoon, which was in the Stowe Collection, stands at the top of the room, and other fine pieces of statuary are a bust of Venus which Waagen considered to be the work of a Greek chisel, and comparable in style with the Venus of Milo, and earlier than Venus de' Medici; a bust in red porphyry of the Dying Alexander, taken from the Florence marble, and wonderfully executed in this hard stone, and a magnificent tripod in giallo antico of the most costly and beautiful work. The rooms on the east side of the marble hall, consisting of drawing rooms, music rooms, boudoirs and private apartments, and the new state rooms, have the walls hung with fine tapestry; that in the new state rooms being Gobelins work by Nouzou bearing the date 1735.

It would be impossible however by any account which our limits permit, to describe the extraordinary collection of the most costly and rare works of Art which form the *ameublement* of this grand ducal palace. There are cabinets of odd Florentine mosaic and pietra-dura work, one of which is said to have been designed by Michel Angelo; another of the finest Milanese work of the sixteenth century in iron elaborately chiselled and damascened with arabesques in gold, which excited so much admiration in the Loan Collection at South Kensington in 1862; with a chess-table of similar Milanese work from the famous Soltikoff and De Bruges Dumesnil collections. The old French furniture is considered to be quite unique of its kind, especially the suite of marquetrie designed and made by Riesener in 1790 for Marie Antoinette, consisting of a secrétaire, and étagère, and cabinet, beautifully inlaid with wreaths of natural flowers, festoons and trophies with ormolu medallions and mounts by the greatest *ciseleur* of the time, Gouthière. These were described by Mr J. C. Robinson in the South Kensington catalogue as 'probably the most beautiful work of its kind produced in the age of Louis XVI'. We have besides these the Duke of Choiseul's writing-table and Cantonnière with clock with other fine specimens of the style of Louis XIV, and a set of four large candelabra by Gouthière of unusual excel-

* *Purchased at the sale for the National Gallery for* £6300.

lence. The specimens of Buhl work include a pair of splendid armoires once in the Louvre;* the D'Artois cabinet, and various other pieces among which is a large sarcophagus by Buhl in his finest style. There are state bedsteads, sofas and fauteuils, which once belonged to the Palace of Versailles, covered with Beauvais tapestry.

Besides those pictures which have been already named as holding a prominent place on the walls of the different rooms, there are many others of the highest interest to which attention must be drawn in taking a general survey of the collection. Among the Italian pictures are some works of importance. By Andrea Mantegna, there are six examples, the two fine half-length portraits of the Duke of Gonzaga and the Duchess of Mantua, his great patrons, mentioned by Vasari, and the engravings of which will be found in the portfolios of the collection, though Dr Waagen while praising the fine colour and animated expression, thought them not refined enough for this great master. Next two small panels with full-length figures of St Sebastian and St George exquisitely painted in colours and which probably once formed the wings of a triptych. Two similar panels in monochrome with two figures of vestals are equally remarkable for high finish and the perfect preservation of the pictures.† By Botticelli there is an 'Adoration of the Magi'‡, a picture painted like a miniature with many small figures admirably drawn and grouped, in a landscape, which Dr Waagen pronounced to be a 'gem by Fillipo Lippi erroneously called a Botticelli'. By the rare master Antonello da Messina, the Italian pupil of Van Eyck in learning his invention of oil painting, there is a portrait§ dated 1474 inscribed *Antonellus Messaneus me fecit*; by Leonardo, the 'Boy with a horn-book', a picture often spoken of as having been in the famous Arundel collection and bequeathed by Lady Betty Germaine to Sir W. Hamilton.|| There are many other pictures of various schools besides those we have pointed out as remarkable examples, which make the collection as varied and complete in the illustration of pictorial art as it is distinguished especially by works in statuary of bronze and marble, by mosaic and pietra-dura work of the highest excellence, and by decorative objects of every kind upon a scale of great magnificence and extraordinary beauty. In these respects the sale will certainly surpass in interest the celebrated sales of Stowe, Strawberry Hill, and the Bernal Collection, as it will the San Donato, and other great continental collections dispersed in recent times.

* *These sold for the enormous price of* £12,075 *in the sale.*

† *Purchased at the sale for the National Gallery for* £1785.

‡ *Also bought for the National Gallery for* £1627 10*s.*

§ *Purchased at the sale, for the Louvre, for* £514 10*s.*

|| *Purchased at the sale for* £2205, *by Mr Winckworth.*

ON THE USE OF PHOTOGRAPHY IN THE STUDY OF PAINTING

It is easy to overlook the importance of the invention of photography in the history of collecting. Engravings often introduced a subjective element into an objective reproduction. Bernard Berenson, whose influence in English collecting circles was certainly as great as among American, here makes this point in his own notebook.

Taken from Bernard Berenson's Notebook for 14 October 1893.[1]

. . . Printing itself scarcely could have had a greater effect on the study of the classics than photography is beginning to have on the study of the Old Masters. If most people are still incredulous about the possibility of giving a rational, systematic basis to the criticism of art, it is largely due to the fact that until very recently any accurate comparison of pictures was out of the question. The basis of connoisseurship is the assumption that an artist in his work develops steadily and gradually, and does not change his hand more capriciously or rapidly in painting than in writing. Unsigned works, therefore, are ascribed to this or that master, as are fragments of the classics when they come to light, by fancied or actual resemblances to signed or otherwise perfectly authenticated works. But the hitch in connoisseurship has always been in comparison. In the days of slow travel, when there were no photographs of old pictures to be had, the connoisseur was obliged to depend largely upon prints. But a moment's comparison of even the best print with its original will show how utterly untrustworthy and even misleading such an aid to memory must be. No engraver, however well intentioned, can help putting a great deal of himself into his reproduction. His print has no other value than that of a copy. The connoisseurs and art historians, therefore, who had to depend on prints, no matter how good a general notion of a painter's various compositions they might have drawn from this source, could have next to no acquaintance with those subtlest elements in his style which distinguished him from the mere copyist or clever imitator.

Is it surprising then, that really accurate connoisseurship is so new a science that it has as yet scarcely found its way into general recognition? Few people are aware how completely it has changed since the days before railways and photographs, when it was more or less of a quack science, in which every practitioner, often in spite of himself, was more or

[1] This entry was written in Venice and is quoted from *The Bernard Berenson Treasury*, selected and edited by Hanna Kiel, London, 1964.

less of a quack. Quackery in the criticism of art is unfortunately not less common now than it was then, but the difference is that the quack no longer has the least excuse for himself. Of the writer on art today we all expect not only that intimate acquaintance with his subject which modern means of conveyance have made possible, but also that patient comparison of a given work with all the other works by the same master which photography has rendered easy. It is not at all difficult to see at any rate nine-tenths of a great master's works (Titian's or Tintoretto's, for instance) in such rapid succession that the memory of them will be fresh enough to enable the critic to determine the place and the value of any picture. And when this continuous study of originals is supplemented by isochromatic photographs such comparison attains almost the accuracy of the physical science.

THE WALLACE-BAGATELLE COLLECTION

After the death of his father, the 4th Marquess of Hertford found himself the owner in London of Hertford House, Old Dorchester House, two houses in Piccadilly and one in Berkeley Square, besides various country seats. In Paris he owned the small house of Bagatelle in the Bois de Boulogne; another at 2 rue Laffitte and a third (occupied by his brother, Lord Henry Seymour) at 1 rue Tailbout. All these passed to his son, Sir Richard Wallace, in 1870. The son's collecting activities were less emphatically Francophile and ranged widely between the Renaissance and the eighteenth century. He had already sold an entire collection before starting again, often in collaboration with his father, in 1857. After the latter's death and the harrowing circumstances of the Franco-Prussian war and the *Commune*, Wallace began to remove many of the finest pieces to London. However, he also enlarged the buildings at Bagatelle.

The piece which follows is taken from Germain Seligman's *Merchants of Art: 1880–1960, Eighty Years of Professional Collecting*. Much of the book is devoted to the career of his father, Jacques, who bought the entire contents of the Chateau de Bagatelle 'blind' just before the first world war.

GERMAIN SELIGMAN

Extracted from Germain Seligman's *Merchants of Art*, 1961.

When it was announced, shortly after our return from the United States in the early spring of 1914, that Jacques Seligmann had purchased a marble bust by Jean-Antoine Houdon, representing the eighteenth-century tragedienne, Sophie Arnould, from the Paris collection of the late Sir Richard Wallace, it created something of a sensation in the art world. Rumours about the fate of the collection had been rife for more than two years; here at last was something definite. An American art journal reported that Mr Seligmann had confirmed his purchase of the Houdon, but denied that he was taking any steps toward the acquisition of the rest of the collection. Yes, the interview quoted him, it was true that the Wallace Collection was valued at around two million dollars; no, he knew nothing of the rumour that it was to go to Widener. My father must have had a lot of fun with that interview. It was strictly true that he was taking no steps toward the purchase of the rest of the Wallace Collection from the Chateau of Bagatelle. He already owned it.

The transaction, which he closed before we left for the United States, remains unique in the history of art dealing.[1] It is the only instance I know of a dealer taking the tremendous gamble of paying nearly two million dollars, in cash, for a collection which he had never seen and for which there existed no catalogue, no expertise, nor even an adequate inventory!

Considered in the light of the history of the Wallace-Bagatelle Collection and its founders, this spectacular gamble seems a fitting final episode to a story of strange legend and stranger fact. Involved in it are great names of England and of France, names which made headlines for daily papers and gossip for contemporary tongues. An aura of mystery and strangeness seemed to enshroud the actions of almost everyone connected with the Wallace Collection. The men who made it and the persons who inherited it were pronounced individuals with driving personalities. Jacques Seligmann himself was by no means the least of these, and the circumstances under which the sale was made were strictly within the tradition.

The Chateau de Bagatelle had its origins in the eighteenth century. It was charmingly situated near the banks of the Seine in the Bois de Boulogne, once the property of Madame la Maréchale d'Estrées, a *grande dame* of the court of the Regent, who built a house there in 1720. Just across the river there already existed another small pavilion belonging to the Duc d'Orleans which was called Brimborion, a trifle, and thus it seemed quite natural to call the new house a bagatelle. Located as it was on the road to Versailles and not far from the Chateau de La Muette where Louis XV was to find considerable charm, Bagatelle became a convenient halt in the restless movement of the court and one reads of the brilliant receptions the Maréchale gave there for the Regent and later for the young and dashing Louis XV.

[1] Though perhaps it was rivalled in more recent times (1945) by the purchase for £100,000 of Sir Thomas Phillipps' incredible collection of manuscripts and books, in uncatalogued and crated form, by the brothers Lionel and Philip Robinson.

In 1756 the property passed to the Marquise de Monconseil, and from 1770 to 1775 was owned by the Prince and Princesse de Chimay. All of them entertained lavishly for kings and court with plays, luncheons, and supper parties. One such occasion was a fête honouring the father-in-law of Louis XV, King Stanislas of Poland.

In 1775 the estate took the fancy of the younger brother of Louis XVI, the Comte d'Artois, later to reign briefly as Charles X. He was a profligate young man with no consideration for popular feelings or public funds, and in true princely fashion, decided to do away with the now somewhat shabby old house, and build another more in keeping with his exalted position. François-Joseph Belanger was designated architect, and Thomas Blaikie was called from England especially to landscape the grounds in the new vogue of the so-called English garden, a change involving major rearrangements of natural contours to accommodate the intricate paths, grottos, miniature rivers, and waterfalls. Such small, intimate houses, exquisite in every detail, served as weekend hideaways or hunting lodges for Paris society and were commonly called by the often-not-inappropriate name of *folie*. Bagatelle quickly became known as the Folie d'Artois. Even in the Comte's time, however, the original name was not forgotten.

Teased by his sister-in-law, Marie Antoinette, about the slow progress which his new *folie* was making, d'Artois is said to have made a wager with her that the new house would be ready to receive her *en fête* when the court returned to Versailles from its annual trek to Fontainebleau, just sixty-four days hence. And this master stroke was achieved in a grandiose manner. Contemporary accounts tell us that nine hundred workmen were employed night and day, and that scarce materials were commandeered on the roads without regard for their true destinations.

The wager between the Queen and the Comte, we are told, was for a stake of 100,000 francs, but the first accounting of the cost of the *folie* showed an expense of 600,000 francs, before interior decorations, furniture, and works of art. It is difficult to express eighteenth-century values in modern terms, but there can be little doubt that this represented more than a million dollars. When d'Artois received the congratulations of the Queen, and presumably the hundred thousand francs, he is supposed to have replied, 'Ce n'est rien qu'une bagatelle.'

In 1789, at the outset of the Revolution, d'Artois was one of the first to emigrate, and twenty-five years were to pass before he again saw Bagatelle. The Revolution of 1830 once more upset the ownership, and it is with the advent of the Orleans branch that we approach the final royal relinquishment of the chateau. Louis-Philippe, a constitutional king who had to keep his private expenses separate from the nation's budget, and was thus less profligate, decided to sell the *folie*. In September 1835, it was purchased by an Englishman, Richard Seymour, Lord Yarmouth, later to be the Fourth Marquess of Hertford. Lord Yarmouth, like his father, the Third Marquess of Hertford, was a great collector, a lover of works of art, and an extremely wealthy man. He was also, with other members of his famous family, a Francophile who spent most of his time in Paris, where he already owned a town house in the rue Laffitte, then a particularly brilliant residential section.

Yarmouth immediately began to restore Bagatelle to its original beauty and to furnish it in keeping with its style and his own predilection for the French eighteenth century. Once finished, and its name restored, Bagatelle again became the scene of royal entertainment, for Yarmouth numbered among his close friends the Emperor Napoleon III and his wife, the Empress Eugénie. It was in the *parc* of Bagatelle that the Prince Imperial received his first riding lessons, in a ring especially built for his use.

In 1842, Lord Yarmouth succeeded to the title and fortune of his father. That same year, a young man known to all familiars of the household as 'Monsieur Richard', legally changed his name from Richard Jackson to Richard Wallace. Exactly who he was remains uncertain. Some claimed him to be the son of the 3rd Marchioness, whom he always called 'Tante Mie Mie', and thus the half-brother of the new Lord Hertford. Others believed them to be father and son, though Lord Hertford referred to Wallace only as 'a dear friend'. Later historians say that Wallace was actually the son of the 4th Marquess and one Agnes Jackson whose family name was Wallace. Whatever the relationship, the two men were strongly alike in taste, manner, and political tendencies, as well as in their love for France and for works of art. Exquisite taste and refinement were exhibited by Richard Wallace in the purchases he made with and for Lord Hertford as they added further sumptuous works of art to the collection. The few existing documents lead one to wonder whether Richard Wallace may not have become a greater collector than his benefactor. It is quite conceivable that the later acquisitions of the Wallace Collection, as it is today at Hertford House in London and as it was at Bagatelle and rue Laffitte, were actually made by Richard Wallace rather than by Lord Hertford, as has been generally believed–perhaps a rather academic question, but puzzling to art historians.

By the end of the 1860s the political fortunes of France were rapidly deteriorating. The weak and sick Emperor, lost in dreams dominated by the memory of his majestic uncle, Napoleon I, ill-advised by court flatterers, and misled by his military chiefs, fell headlong into the trap of Bismarck, the Franco-Prussian War. Lord Hertford, old, ailing, and disheartened by this blow to his beloved France, passed away in August of 1870.

Richard Wallace was revealed as his heir.

Devoted to France as had been his benefactor, Wallace remained there throughout the war, helping with every means in his power to alleviate the sufferings which followed in its wake–the siege of Paris and the bloody Commune during which so many great monuments, spared by the Revolution of 1789, became a prey to fire and looting. He organised and financed three ambulance corps, founded and endowed the Hertford British Hospital, and spent vast sums to aid the besieged. Later he installed the hundred drinking fountains 'for man and beast' still known as 'Wallaces' to Parisians.

In recognition of his many benefactions, Richard Wallace was made a Commander of the Legion of Honour in France and knighted by Queen Victoria. Lady Wallace, however, was never received at Her Majesty's court; Sir Richard did not marry her until after the death of Lord Hertford, though she had already borne him a son. She lived quietly at Hertford House, while Sir Richard divided his time between London and Paris.

The situation in France had driven Richard Wallace to ship a large portion of his French collection to England, where many of its objects were included in the great Bethnal Green exhibiton of 1872, while the London home, Hertford House, was being readied for it. As might be expected with so celebrated a collection there was much speculation as to the intentions of Sir Richard regarding its final disposition. His English friends believed tha- he would leave it to England, while his French intimates asserted that he had often expressed his intention of giving it to the city of Paris. He did neither. When Sir Richard died in 1890, his entire estate, with the exception of a few specific legacies, was left to his widow. When Lady Wallace herself died in 1897, it was her will which left the art contents of Hertford House to the British nation. The will also brought another stranger into the Wallace story: John Murray Scott, to whom she bequeathed, except for minor bequests, the entire residue of this incredible estate, including the Chateau de Bagatelle.

If a link of consanguinity existed between Hertford and Wallace there was no such tie to explain the fabulously generous gesture to Scott. John Murray Scott was the son of a Scottish doctor living in Boulogne who had attended Lord Hertford. The charming manners and brilliant qualities of the young man had apparently attracted Hertford and Wallace, who employed him as their secretary. He gradually rose from this post to one of confidence and high trust, becoming finally the indispensable friend and man of affairs. It is said that Lady Wallace, after Sir Richard's death, relied upon Scott for everything and that it was on his insistence that the London portion of the Wallace Collection went to the nation, rather than to Scott himself, as she had wished. The evidence seems to indicate that in this she was also carrying out the wishes of Sir Richard. . . .

Scott's death added one more curious chapter to the saga of Bagatelle and created a stir which my generation has not forgotten. Lady Sackville, wife of the 3rd Baron Sackville of Knole, was willed the sum of £150,000 and the entire contents of the house on rue Laffitte. Although Sir John[1] left the bulk of his estate, amounting to well over a million pounds, to his brother and his two sisters, they nevertheless contested the bequest to Lady Sackville, on the grounds of 'undue influence', and the ensuing trial became a *cause célèbre*. In 1913, after memorable days spent in court fighting the case, Lady Sackville emerged victorious, the sole owner of the Paris portion of the Wallace Collection.

It is impossible to give in a few words a description of this beautiful and high-spirited lady, whose own life was so colourful and romantic, and I leave this to her daughter, Miss Vita Sackville-West, whose book [about her] *Pepita* is vivid and charming. I would give a great deal, however, to have been present at the various interviews which took place between Lady Sackville and my father, for it is now that Jacques Seligmann steps into the story. The meetings of two such determined individuals, of pronounced personality, must certainly have had their own special flavour.

Actually, they had met a few years earlier when my father had arranged the sale of the twenty-nine Knole House tapestries to J. Pierpont Morgan. Just when Jacques Seligmann first approached her, or, perhaps, she approached him, about the sale of her French holdings, I am not sure. I do know that it was well before the settlement of the lawsuit. Lady Sackville was not averse to selling. She was extravagant by nature and perhaps the heavy

[1] He had been knighted by Queen Victoria.

expenses of an earlier legal battle over the succession of her husband to the Sackville title, the death duties, and the upkeep of Knole House, made the prospect of a large sum of ready money a welcome one. Obviously, however, she could take no definite steps until the suit was settled. Furthermore, the house on the rue Laffitte was under legal seal, and the objects it contained could not even be seen. Nevertheless, Jacques Seligmann entered into a legal covenant with Lady Sackville whereby, should she win the suit, he would become the sole and absolute owner of the entire French collection of Sir Richard Wallace at an agreed price. Because of the loss of the firm's Paris records during the recent war, I cannot state the exact amount involved, but my recollection is of a figure slightly under two million dollars. I should like to emphasise that in accordance with my father's invariable practice, this sum was paid in cash, from his own funds, without recourse to loans or to mortgages. Miss Sackville-West states in *Pepita* that her mother received £270,000, which accords well enough if one takes into consideration deductions necessarily made for attorney's fees, inventory costs and other expenses. The *New York Times* front-page story of the purchase used the figure of $1,400,000.

At this point one must marvel at the courage and instinct of Jacques Seligmann, for *he had never seen the collection.* With its history and all that has been written of the Wallace-Bagatelle Collection, it would be natural to assume that all the world was familiar with the contents of Bagatelle and of the rue Laffitte house, but such an assumption would be erroneous. These were private houses, open only to friends of the families who lived in them. Thus as a basis for making his offer, colossal even for a man used to deals of magnitude, Jacques Seligmann had only three indications.

The first was knowledge of a few objects which Wallace had lent during his lifetime to certain important public exhibitions in Paris, and he may have read two articles on the contents of Scott's rue Laffitte house which had appeared in the English magazine *Connoisseur* in 1910 and 1911. The second was a manuscript list on which there was no description whatsoever, simply the barest indication, often insufficient to identify the items even after we had seen them, and useful only to check them by number and to help in a process of elimination. My father, perusing the list, tried to identify the items he knew, but ran into such laconic lines as 'a marble statuette', which he surmised might be the Cupid of Bouchardon, or 'marble figure of a woman', which might mean the Lemoyne portrait of Madame de Pompadour, or 'portrait of a young woman with head-dress', possibly referring to the Houdon. The third indication available to him, and the most valuable, was what he knew of the quality of the Wallace Collection at Hertford House in London. He reasoned that if items of such exceptional quality and importance as those he could identify were on the manuscript list with such insignificant captions, it was likely that others would prove of equal consequence. . . .

Long after the event, I continue to believe that no man but Jacques Seligmann would have had the courage to take such a huge gamble. If the enormity of what he did left my father openly unperturbed, it was still with relief that we viewed the profusion of riches when we were at last allowed to inspect the house at 2 rue Laffitte. I knew, of course, that millions of gold francs had been paid for these accumulated works of art, and I had perused the non-commital list, but I had not seen even the few objects which my father already knew. To me it was like entering Ali Baba's cave. His simple but daring reasoning had been correct. Almost every item was of the quality of Hertford House–but in what confusion!

All over the floors, piled up in corners, some carefully covered with slips, others wrapped in papers or, more often, with only a heavy coating of dust to protect them from sight, were some of the greatest sculptures of the eighteenth century and luxurious pieces of furniture made for the royal family. There, rolled in a corner, was the famous set of tapestries after cartoons by Boucher, now in the Philadelphia Museum. Standing on a table was the small figure by Lemoyne. Over there, its companion in size and quality, was the first version of the *Cupid Bending His Bow* of Bouchardon. Yonder was the superb Houdon bust of Sophie Arnould, now in the Louvre as a bequest of Edgar Stern.

Most belonged to the so-called decorative arts of the French eighteenth century, but objects which exhibit such perfection in proportion, repect for the essence of wood and the chiselling of gilded bronze are beyond the realm of the purely utilitarian. One feels that a table such as the Riesener, now in the Frick Collection, or a delicately conceived bit of bronze and enamel such as the Veil-Picard chandelier, now in the Louvre, deserve special cases, like bibelots, to preserve what they reveal of a civilisation which attained for a few years a pinnacle of refinement.

All the great cabinet-makers were represented: Riesener, Oeben, Weisweiler, Saunier, and Martin Carlin in pieces of furniture so perfect architecturally that they remind one of the glorious buildings of a Gabriel or a Mansard, yet so delicate in texture that the hand longs to stroke them. Here, too, were the *bureaux du roi*, which my father later gave to the Metropolitan Museum; sets of furniture upholstered in tapestries designed by Casanova and Le Prince; busts by Houdon; drawings and gouaches and paintings by Nattier, Lancret, Boucher, Prud'hon; all sorts of documentary drawings, including those ordered by Louis-Philippe as models for the engraver who recorded the historical paintings which the King had gathered for the Chateau of Versailles. Among the most impressive of the sculptures were the Coysevox busts of the Grand Dauphin and the Duc d'Orleans, which must certainly have adorned Versailles. They are now a part of the Samuel H. Kress Foundation in the National Gallery at Washington. . . .

The first private collector to see this collection while it was still at rue Laffitte was Henry C. Frick, who came straight from the golf course, dressed in plus-fours and a plaid cap. With him came Elsie de Wolfe, who was advising him in purchases for his new home. A selection was made on the spot, neither of them being at all disconcerted by the untidiness, the junkshop atmosphere of the cluttered rooms. Miss de Wolfe's recollection of this episode in her book, *After All*, is faulty on several points. She states that it was Lady Sackville who approached Jacques Seligmann, which may be true, and that the arrangement was for the selling rights to the collection in return for financing her lawsuit, which is not true.

The deal was an outright purchase. Nor could Miss de Wolfe, as she relates, have gone with my father to the rue Laffitte house while it was still under seal. The seals had been placed by the courts for the protection of all parties concerned and were not lifted until the ownership of the collection had been definitely decided by the court. I stress this because the extraordinary feature of this huge transaction was the fact that my father was willing to pay a remarkably large sum for a collection he had never seen.

A few days after Frick's visit, the entire collection was moved to Sagan.[1] There it was installed in the new building on the far side of the garden. The exhibition was the sensation of the season, with collectors coming from North and South America, and from all over Europe, to admire and to buy.

Sadly, it was one of the last international gatherings in Paris for many years to come, for the year was 1914 and the month was June. On 2 August, France mobilised, and for four years, Europe abandoned the enjoyment of art for grimmer pursuits.

THE ROTHSCHILDS OF WADDESDON MANOR

A UNIQUE dynasty in the annals of European collecting were the descendants of Mayer Rothschild, some of whom had already settled in England in the first half of the nineteenth century. Quality was the keynote of the many collections the Rothschilds formed. One can see this in the splendidly formal setting at Waddesdon Manor which James A. Rothschild left to the National Trust in 1957; in the Waddesdon Bequest of jewels, plate, enamel and carvings left by Baron Ferdinand to the British Museum; or in the Christie catalogue of the sumptuous contents of 148 Piccadilly (Victor's house) sold up in 1937. And yet, one gathers, the collections were built up with humility and humanity, with scholarship as well as with a particularly sophisticated taste unremarkable in the *most* affluent among the very affluent.

As someone who must have seen more magnificent collections than most of us, Lord [Kenneth] Clark is fascinating in his comments upon the Rothschilds:

'Up to the last war the style of Sir Richard Wallace was still to be seen in private hands in the house of the Rothschild family. Indeed, if all their collections could

[1] The magnificent showrooms into which Jacques Seligmann had moved his business in 1909.

have been united they would, I believe, have put the Wallace Collection in the shade. A visit to a Rothschild Collection was always a memorable experience. Hushed, inviolate, almost indistinguishable from one another, they were impressive not only by their size and splendour, but by a sense of the solemnity of wealth which hung about them. In a Rothschild Collection I always found myself whispering, as if I were in church.'[1]

Though it should be said that the house and collection at Ascott, also in Buckinghamshire, which was left to the National Trust in 1945 by Anthony de Rothschild is in marked contrast to this.

The piece that follows is accompanied–in a single (English language) issue of Georges Wildenstein's celebrated *Gazette des Beaux Arts* devoted to Waddesdon–by a description of the French eighteenth-century furniture, also by Francis Watson; the porcelain by Arthur Lane; the English pictures by Ellis Waterhouse; the French and Italian pictures by Michael Levey; the Dutch and Flemish paintings by Christopher White; the sculpture by Denys Sutton and the library by Anthony Hobson.

TAKEN FROM F. J. B. Watson's article on 'The James de Rothschild Collection' in *Waddesdon: the Manor, the Collections*, Edition de la Gazette des Beaux Arts, 1959.

BARON Ferdinand de Rothschild (1839–1898), the creator of Waddesdon Manor and the founder of its collections, was a member of the Austrian branch of the famous banking family. He took no part in the business, however, and after being educated at Paris (where he had been born) and in Vienna, he settled in England in 1860 and six years later married his cousin, Evelina, the daughter of the head of the English branch of the bank, Lionel Nathan Rothschild. After her death a little over a year later, he decided to dedicate his life to forming a cabinet of works of art of the highest quality. It was to house this collection that, in 1874, he purchased a tract of land at Waddesdon near Aylesbury, some forty miles from London, from the Duke of Marlborough and engaged the well-known French architect, Gabriel-Hippolyte Destailleur, to build a house there. Waddesdon Manor is in the French Renaissance style, a style which Baron Ferdinand himself tells us in a brief note on the house, which he printed for circulation amongst his friends and relations, had captured his fancy during a holiday in Touraine.

Baron Ferdinand's interest in the arts was far from being the mere hobby of a wealthy man. It was essentially serious.[2] He was at great pains to include in the collection only works of the finest quality of their kind. In his own words 'their pedigrees are of un-

[1] *Great Private Collections*, London, 1963, page 15.

[2] Though, sad to relate, he destroyed his receipts for anything he bought, because he was afraid that his descendants would regard the prices he paid as excessive!

impeachable authenticity . . . I have only acquired works of art the genuineness of which had been well established.' From the moment of his appointment as a Trustee of the British Museum until his death, he took an active interest in its work, an interest which led him to bequeath one whole section of his collection to that institution at his death. This is the famous 'Waddesdon Bequest' consisting chiefly of Medieval and Renaissance goldsmiths' work (particularly jewels and enamel), sculpture and armour which occupies a unique position even in that great treasure-house, for it alone, amongst the bequests received by the museum, is kept together as a tribute to its outstanding quality.

In some degree Baron Ferdinand was fortunate in the age in which he began to collect, for the agricultural crisis of the eighteen-seventies and eighties brought about the partial break-up of a number of old English family collections. It was this which enabled him to assemble the quite remarkable group of English eighteenth-century portraits now at Waddesdon. This is of such importance as to compensate for the losses in this particular field suffered during the 1920s when, under the encouragement of Lord Duveen, American collectors made such extensive purchases from the great English collections of family portraits.

Baron Ferdinand, possibly because he was born in Paris, had a particular interest in French history and art. Many of the medieval objects he left to the British Museum were French, especially the enamels and armour. During his lifetime he published a book, *Personal Characteristics from French History* (1896), based on a wide reading of French memoirs and chronicles. As with the English eighteenth-century portraits it was from English collections that much of the French eighteenth-century furniture and Sèvres porcelain was acquired. In particular he made considerable purchases at the Hamilton Palace sale of 1882, perhaps the most important single dispersal of French eighteenth-century furniture to have taken place since the period of the French Revolution. He bought likewise at the San Donato and other outstanding auction-sales of the last third of the nineteenth century, as well as acquiring many works of art privately. His aim was to acquire only what was the best, and he devoted much thought to eliminating from his collection as opportunity offered anything which he had come to regard as second-class in any respect. Thus it is not unknown to find works of art, particularly English eighteenth-century portraits of very high quality, which were at one time at Waddesdon but which did not come up to the exacting standards he set himself as a collector. When he died *The Times* wrote in his obituary notice: 'many Rothschilds are and have been collectors of works of art, but Baron Ferdinand surpassed almost all of them in the variety and scope of his collections.' Only those who have enjoyed the rare privilege of visiting the houses of various members of this family so renowned in the history of collecting, will realise not only the truth of what *The Times* wrote in 1898, but the extraordinarily high standards that the comparison implies.

The Waddesdon Bequest to the British Museum comprised the contents of a single room only at the Manor. The rest of the collections consisting of English, French and Italian paintings of the eighteenth century, Dutch seventeenth-century paintings, French eighteenth-century furniture, carpets, Sèvres porcelain and objects of art, mostly of the same period, were left by Ferdinand de Rothschild to his sister Alice who lived there until her death in 1922. Her main interests were in the country life, and the gardens at Waddesdon meant more to her than the art collections. Nevertheless she added a few things to the collection she had inherited, notably Boucher's portraits of the duc d'Orleans (Philippe Egalité) as a child, two important pieces of Renaissance armour from a suit made for the Emperor Charles V together with a considerable group of snuff-boxes and miniatures. When she died, she left the house and its contents to her great-nephew, Mr James de Rothschild.

Although of French birth, Mr James de Rothschild had long resided in England and associated himself with English life. Shortly after the 1914–1918 war, throughout which he served with great distinction in the ranks of the British Army, he became a naturalised English citizen and took an active part in the public life of his adopted country, becoming Member of Parliament for Ely from 1929 to 1945, just as Baron Ferdinand had been for Aylesbury from 1885 until his death.

Although he made a few additions to the collection, especially in the 1930s, they were not such as to change its general character or increase its scope in any appreciable degree. In 1934, however, at the death of his father, Baron Edmond de Rothschild of the French branch of the family, his elder son James inherited a considerable part of his collections. These consisted chiefly of French furniture, sculpture (including Lemoyne's bust of Mme de Pompadour from the Salon of 1761), porcelain and objects of art of the eighteenth century as well as a certain number of paintings, notable amongst which are three Watteaus and a Rubens of great importance, the *Jardin d'Amour*. In this way the very remarkable collection already at Waddesdon Manor was materially strengthened in those fields in which it was already rich.

When he died, in May 1957, Mr de Rothschild bequeathed Waddesdon Manor, its contents and its extensive gardens to the National Trust. At the same time he created a fund of £750,000 to be administered by Trustees for the maintenance of these properties. By his munificent gift he joins that small but exceedingly distinguished band which includes Lady Wallace, the duc d'Aumale, Madame Jacquemart-Andre and Mr Henry Frick who have presented their fellow-countrymen with private art collections of truly international significance.

The collection at Waddesdon Manor inevitably provokes comparison with the Wallace Collection. Their scope is somewhat similar and although the Wallace Collection is far larger, its paintings in particular being more numerous, more catholic in their choice and of higher quality, the two groups of French eighteenth-century furniture and Sèvres porcelain resemble one another both in quality and size, and in certain fields the collection of Waddesdon Manor supplements the great national treasure-house in Manchester Square. Thus the extraordinary assemblage of royal French Savonnerie carpets at Waddesdon, as well as the *boiseries* taken from eighteenth-century Paris houses, show aspects of the French decorative arts of the period which are not be to found at Hertford House. Equally the group of eight terra-cottas by Clodion illustrate a side of French eighteenth-century sculpture hardly represented in the Wallace Collection or, indeed, in any public museum. Taken together the two museums show French furniture and porcelain on a scale and of a quality not perhaps to be seen anywhere else in the world. By a curious paradox which contains matter for reflection, both collections came to the English public as gifts from donors who were themselves of French birth, the Wallace Collection being bequeathed in 1897 by Lady Wallace, *née* Julie-Amelie-Charlotte Castelnau, and the collection at Waddesdon by a leading member of the Paris branch of the Rothschild family.

THE SPORT OF COLLECTING

MARTIN Conway (1856–1937), one of the last old-style *amateurs*, was a man of many talents and a forceful personality. His two principal interests in life were mountaineering and the arts. However, Miss Joan Evans has shown with withering clarity in her recent portrait of him[1] that ultimately he never attained the goals he might have reached. He tried a good many things but lacked a sense of purpose, or it may well have been that his determination was often sapped by an over-generous, American millionaire father-in-law. However, he did become Slade Professor of Art in Cambridge from 1901 to 1904 and he was a passionate and devoted collector. He gave an account of his pursuits in this field in *The Sport of Collecting*, from which the three pieces which follow have been extracted. Conway published a spirited defence of his attribution of the two paintings in 'The Dream Come True' to Giorgione in the *Burlington Magazine* of September 1925.

THE DREAM COME TRUE

In the summer of 1903 we made an extensive motoring tour throughout the length and breadth of France, and wherever we went we searched the antiquity shops with patient thoroughness. It was not till we reached Biarritz that we began to strike a fertile field; but there and thereabouts many good things were on sale which had drifted over out of Spain. We made a certain number of acquisitions, under quite ordinary circumstances, which it would be tedious to linger over; but one adventure is worth describing at length.

In those days motor-cars were not the safe and sound means of locomotion they are now supposed to be. Ours, at any rate, perhaps through our own fault, was always providing us with surprises, especially after it had collided with a cow somewhere in the

[1] *The Conways:* A History of Three Generations, London, 1966.

neighbourhood of Bayonne. The cow did not mind, but our car did, and its internal mechanism was never quite the same again. This delayed us at Biarritz. I had a passionate desire to go to St Jean de Luz, but next day something occurred to prevent our start, and took us to the garage instead. At last, after lunch the third day, we succeeded in starting, and gaily ran about five miles. Then bang!–a tyre burst, and we had to halt and put on another. That punctured, and so did a third. I was for turning back. I said, 'We are not intended to get to St Jean de Luz. It's just as well to bow to the decrees of Fate first as last'. But my wife said, 'No. You've had a queer and apparently insensate desire to go to this place, and go we must. There's something for us there, and we've just got to go and get it.' So we travelled slowly on, with only some perilously old tubes on our wheels, expecting every moment that our last tyre would burst and we should be left stranded. That did not happen.

We presently reached St Jean de Luz and proceeded to investigate the dealers' shops. There were one or two in the main street, and they contained nothing worth looking at. I said, 'Let us have tea and go back to the hotel.' My wife said, 'No; there must be another shop. I am certain there is something for us in this place.' So we turned down a side street and came out on a flat expanse leading off to the sea. 'What nonsense it is,' I said, 'to be looking for anticas here! You might as well dig for them in the sand.' An old fisherwoman, or someone of that class appeared, and I was bidden to ask her whether there was not an antica-shop hereabouts. The notion of asking her seemed to me absurd. What could an old fisherwoman know of such things, and who on earth would dream of keeping an antica shop in such a neighbourhood–off the track of visitors and in the midst of a fishing population? However, I am nothing if not docile, so I pursued the old woman and asked my question. 'Yes!', she replied. 'Just round that corner there is a house where they sell all sorts of old things; you will have no difficulty in finding it.' Round the corner we went, and there was a house with the door open. Through it we could see the glitter of brass, the chaos of old furniture, and pictures on the walls. I entered amidst the usual rubbish, and was about to go out again and say there was nothing, when I saw an open door at the end of the room, and through it I could look into a room beyond. My attention was instantly arrested by two pictures hanging high up on a wall at the farthest end of that. I did not move or speak, but kept the corner of my eye on those pictures while occupied with objects close at hand. The pictures were quite far away, and the light was poor, but there was no doubt we were now close to something very good. I went out to my wife and said, 'In the far corner of the second room are two Venetian pictures which just might be Carpaccios. Don't seem to look at them, but come in and let's look at everything else.'

When we came near them I felt my heart thumping within me like a piston. I whispered that they were early Giorgiones, and that we must certainly buy them at any price. Finally, we had them taken down and placed in our hands, one after the other, the last things we looked at. It is hard under such circumstances to hide one's emotions, but we succeeded. A price was quoted–thank goodness, moderate. The purchase was made then and there. In a few minutes we were back in our car and away for Biarritz as hard as we could go. Somehow it seemed as though punctures were no longer to be expected. None occurred, at any rate, and we were able to travel fast; but the hour that intervened before we could reach our rooms and examine the new treasures at leisure and with minute attention seemed like a long afternoon. It was past midnight before we had rejoiced enough to be able to think of sleep.

The two panels were not in the best state of preservation. One was cracked right across, and the paint had begun to 'bubble off' both; but all the figures were intact, and the damage was confined to relatively unimportant parts of the painting.

I forget whether it was Mr Herbert Cook or Mr Robert Ross who first told me the meaning of the subjects, the 'Finding of Paris' and 'Paris being put out to Nurse'. In the first [see Plate 68] the child lies on a white cloth on the ground at the foot of some rocks near a stream; a man is pointing him out to two others, and two more are following them over a foot-bridge. In the middle distance is a village and a castle-crowned hill, and across the background are blue hills beneath a blue sky. The figures are all in brightly tinted costumes, and the whole is a delightful pattern of brilliant colours. By what is perhaps merely a curious coincidence, the child is almost identical, though in reverse (as if seen in a mirror), with a child drawn in outline by Dürer on a page of sketches made by him in Venice in 1495–probably the very year in which Giorgione painted this picture likewise in Venice. Certainly Dürer 'dürerised' his drawing, as he did in every case when he sketched an Italian original; but I find it difficult to believe that there is no connection between the two.

In the second picture a woman receives the child from one of a group of three men. Further back, two others are seated talking, near a herd of kine. There is again a village in the middle distance and blue hills behind. I have never wavered in the assurance that these pictures were painted by the youthful Giorgione and no other. Some of the figures are actually the same models as those employed by him in works universally accepted as his, but the palette is his likewise, and so are a quantity of little tricks of design and of technique, as well as certain weaknesses too tedious to set down in long-winded detail. The dealer from whom I bought the pictures stated that they had been in the Duke of Ossuna's collection, and this statement is verified by the seal on the back of each. They likewise had written labels bearing the name of Carpaccio, and the seal of the Venetian Academy, doubtless impressed when permission was given to export them. Their last Italian owner was revealed as follows.

By a strange coincidence, just when I was finding these pictures at St Jean de Luz, Mons. Ugo Monneret de Villard was enquiring for them in Italy. In the process of preparing his book on Giorgione* he had examined in the Communal Library at Verona a manuscript catalogue† of the Albarelli collection, entitled 'Gabinetto di quadri o raccolta di pezzi originali esistenti in Verona presso il sig. Gio. Albarelli, disegnati da Romolo Caliari, con illustrazioni. Verona, 1815.' In this volume he noticed two carefully made outline drawings of pictures which had been attributed to Carpaccio, but which he had no difficulty in recognising as compositions by Giorgione in his early period. After his book was already

* '*Giorgione da Castelfranco.' Studio critico. Bergamo*, 1904.

† *MS*, 1847, *Cl. Arti*, *Ubic.* 82. 6, *Busta* 5.

printed, but before it was issued, Mons. de Villard saw the photographs of the pictures themselves, which were published in the *Burlington Magazine*, and thus was enabled to insert in time an extra page, with copies of the reproductions facing the reproductions of the drawings.

It happened also, that at this very time Mr Herbert Cook was bringing out a revised edition of his Giorgione (London, 1904), and its pages were already printed off. Knowing his interest in the great Venetian master, I made haste to show him the panels as soon as they arrived in London, and he not only at once published them in the *Burlington Magazine* (November 1904, p. 156), but felt obliged to insert an extra leaf into his book, with the following note:

'As the second edition of this book goes to press comes the announcement of the discovery and acquisition by Sir Martin Conway of two pictures which appear to be by none other than Giorgione himself. Not only so, but, from the nature of the subjects represented and the style of painting, these panels would seem to have formed the last two of a series of which "The Birth of Paris" was the first portion. "The Discovery by the Shepherds of the Young Paris" and "The Handing Him over to Nurse" naturally complete the story, of which the first scene is given to the engraving, whilst the statement of the Anonimo that the "Birth of Paris" was one of Giorgione's early works is amply confirmed by the style of the newly found paintings, which must have been produced by a very youthful hand. Indeed, there is every reason to hold that they ante-date the little pictures in the Uffizi, and thus rank as the earliest known works of the young Giorgione.'

The pictures under discussion received what I may call 'first aid' at the hands of Mr Roger Fry; but the mischief was progressive, and had to be radically taken in hand and stopped once and for all. When they were last exhibited at the winter exhibition of the Burlington Fine Arts Club in 1911–12, all the best authorities urged me to have the work of restoration put in hand without delay, and the two panels were accordingly shipped off to Cavenaghi's without further delay. Several months later we followed them to Milan. It was a joyous moment when we found ourselves once more in our kind friend's presence and saw one of our pictures on the easel before him.

It was not the same studio to which we had been taken just twenty-five years before by Morelli, but it was the same kind welcome that greeted us, the same hand that clasped ours in friendly greeting, and the same common interest that continued to unite us. Even a quarter of a century ago Cavenaghi was the best restorer of Italian pictures in the world – so Morelli was never tired of proclaiming, and as all men agreed. If he was unrivalled in 1887, it is easy to understand at what height of pre-eminence he now stands, with the added knowledge that comes from an unexampled experience in dealing with the most precious Italian paintings in the world. I was naturally more than a little anxious to know what a restorer, through whose hands several works by Giorgione had already passed, might have to say about our pictures, for nothing can afford so good an opportunity of learning the hand of a master as the necessity of dealing so intimately with his work as a pre-eminent restorer like Cavenaghi is called upon to do.

By an admirable stroke of good fortune there was another Giorgione under treatment by him at this very time. It was the 'Orpheus and Eurydice' belonging to the Lochis collection in the Bergamo Gallery. This panel, out of its frame, was standing on an easel and faced us as we entered. Of course, one of the first questions I asked was whether Cavenaghi was satisfied that our pictures were by Giorgione. He replied, 'Undoubtedly', and, taking up one of them and the Bergamo picture, he placed them close together upon a single easel, remarking, 'You see, either of those might be a piece cut out of the other,' so absolutely did they agree in colour scheme, in forms, in construction, and all the elements that unite to make a picture. It would not be possible for anyone in presence of the two, thus displayed together before him, side by side, without frames, and under the same illumination, to doubt for one instant that both had been painted about the same time by the same artist using the same colours, similarly mixed and employed.

It occurred to me at that moment that I had before me a concrete example of what the labours of a connoisseur are directed to providing. A connoisseur is a person who, by long years of training and observation, has educated himself to retain in his mind, stored up and able to be produced at will to his internal vision, the aspect of any one of a multitude of works of art, and that not merely in a general sense, but in every detail of colour, texture, form, and chiaroscuro. What a thoroughly equipped and competent connoisseur of painting can do is to call up a mental image of any one of a great number of pictures with such vividness as to see its details and its totality almost as clearly as if the picture itself were before him. When he comes into the presence of a picture new to him he must be able to place beside it, before his mind's eye as it were, on the same easel, any other picture he has elsewhere seen with which to compare it; in fact, to be able mentally to produce just such a comparison as we had actually and visibly before us at that moment.[1]

LUXOR

The next collecting adventure I can remember was a wonderful night at Luxor, a village that in those days was a perfect hive of illicit antiquity dealers. No doubt most of the things they sold called for no secrecy, but it suited their notions of how best to impose on travellers to represent every object in their shops as a priceless treasure which the whole power of the local government was eager to seize for the glory of the Cairo Museum. They had plenty of forgeries, some almost perfectly made. Best were the scarabs. There must have been a genius at work producing them. I am told that he was as proud of his craft as Bastianini himself, and was indignant if anyone suggested that his scarabs were really old; but the dealers who bought from him had no such compunction.

I had spent two or three evenings in the dark native houses of Luxor, finding nothing

[1] The two paintings were shown in the 1955 Giorgione Exhibition in Venice (Nos. 1 and 2) when they belonged to Conte Paolo Gerli of Milan. The attribution is not considered certain in the catalogue. Catena is suggested by two authorities, and it is thought possible that Giorgione painted the landscapes and someone else the figures. The paintings had previously been sold at Sotheby's on 31 January 1951 as *Giorgione* (*Attributed to*).

but the ordinary poor rubbish that came to the surface everywhere in Egypt. At last I was taken, with what seemed no more than the usual precautions, into an inner room within the courtyard of a specially secluded house, and there, to my astonishment, they showed me a few quite extraordinary treasures. I knew enough to recognise them at once as work of the eighteenth dynasty, the most attractive period of ancient Egyptian art. We were in a low-roofed room with a little ramshackle furniture. The mud walls were naked. The floor was of hard mud. The place was very dirty. It was otherwise empty when we entered. Women, veiling their faces, brought things in from the background, one by one. First there was the head of a limestone statue of a woman, very finely wrought and with remains of paint on the voluminous wig. The long face, the drooping chin, the broken fragment of what must have been a long neck, were unmistakable. It was the head of some member of the family of the heretic King Amenhotep IV. A friend who was with me promptly acquired it. Then came a number of small objects, some of very fine quality, but they were all late, and prices were high. It was no use trying to bargain. Then there was a delay. The whole affair was excellently stage-managed. Faint sounds in the back quarter indicated that a heavy object was coming. Two persons brought it into the room and set it on the table. The cloth that covered it was removed, and I beheld a seated limestone figure about two feet high and in faultless preservation, the portrait statue of a princess of the family of the same Amenhotep. I have never seen a more perfect work of ancient Egyptian sculpture. It was admirable in design, delicate in finish, entirely portrait-like, and yet as completely incorporating the ancient Egyptian ideal of repose as it if had been solely imagined to that end. The limestone bust of Amenhotep IV in the Louvre, which I did not know then, may have been a work by the same sculptor, but that is damaged, while this had not a scratch. It must have been recently removed from the tomb in which it had remained untouched and even unbeheld for upwards of three millennia. I ought at once to have recognised that these people had found access to royal tombs of the family of that Pharaoh who moved the capital of Egypt to Tel-el-Amarna. But I did not put two and two together till later. For half an hour I lingered regretfully over this beautiful object, whose price was far beyond my reach. In its presence all other objects seemed relatively little desirable. A Russian nobleman bought it next day, I believe, and I have never since heard tell of it.

THE FAILURE OF AN AMATEUR 'SCOUT'

I spent a week walking up hills in the neighbourhood of the Italian Lakes, and it was while seated on the summit of one of them that a sudden and irresistible desire came upon me to turn my back on the snow-laden Alps, and take up again in the cities of North Italy the old hunt which had been so successful in 1887.[1]

I had observed that the great dealers in London, Paris, and elsewhere obtained much

[1] When Morelli had encouraged Sir Martin and his wife to look for works by Vincenso Foppa among the dealers' shops in and around Milan. Ultimately, after many disappointments, Conway found several works by Foppa and other painters of the Milanese School, principally in Brescia, and elsewhere in Northern Italy.

of their stock from smaller but still important dealers who were themselves, respectively, the most important in such cities as Milan, Venice, Florence, and the like. These dealers in turn gathered what they had for sale by going the rounds of the yet smaller men beneath whom again were the scouts who visited the villages and attended the country sales. As at each step up this scale prices were at least doubled, it was evident that whoso would buy cheap must go as near the fountain-head as possible. My former campaign had been amongst the smaller dealers, but it occurred to me that if I pursued my search into the villages themselves I might be yet more fortunate. It was a pretty plan, but there were a good many villages and country villas in Italy, and it had not occurred to me that to ransack them would be work for several lifetimes, rather than for a few autumnal weeks, which were all I had to spare.

There was, however, a district famed for its beauty which I had long wished to visit. It was actually at my feet on the hill where I was at the moment sitting when my determination was formed. It was the Brianza – that region of chaotic little hills and lakes, with villas and villages patched about, which lies between Como and Lecco, and stretches out somewhat southward, having been shaped and fashioned out of the terminal moraines of the vast Alpine glaciers of the Ice Age, reaching out at their furthest toward the great Lombard Plain. I decided to traverse this region on foot, combining the enjoyment of its beautiful landscapes with a hunt for works of art in its villages, farmhouses and villas. I started early one morning a few days later from Bellaggio, with Burton's story of his journey to Mecca in one pocket, and some light provisions in another. How well I still remember the the beauty of the way as I mounted along the backbone of the ridge dividing the two arms of Como Lake, with a fine disregard of roads and even footpaths, and no kind of idea whither I was going or what I was going to do.

Presently I passed over a col, and began the descent of Val Assina. I lunched by the roadside near a village, and instituted casual enquiries as to whether anyone about had any old things to sell. It soon became apparent that everything not new was alike 'antica' in these parts. Before long I thought I was hot on the scent of something really precious; exactly what it was I could not learn. It was to be very beautiful, very old, I gathered, and I should find it in that farm away off up a long hillside on which the sun was shining hotly. I toiled exceedingly in the ascent, and arrived gasping at the door. My enquiries elicited an immediate response. I was taken into a room, and the thing proved to be a much damaged spinet of London make! It was not exactly what I had expected, and I went on my way rather crestfallen. I need not describe the other like adventures and disappointments in detail. One day was as little fruitful as another. I pursued false scents and found nothing; or what I found was absurdly different from what I wanted. The hunt, however, was very amusing. There was talk with all sorts and conditions of men and women – farmers, priests, road-menders, labourers, carriers, and what not. I slept in curious places; the scenery everywhere was lovely. Most beautiful of all was an evening spent at Erba, where I dined on a terrace commanding a most glorious view over all the Brianza, flooded with the blue shadows that drown it at sunset, when the hilltops are golden and all the sky aflame.

At last, however, I met with a very intelligent person, who seemed to understand exactly what I was after. 'Would you like to find an old sculptured figure?' he asked, 'because I think I can tell you where to look for one which is really very precious and beautiful. It belongs to some people at the village of Barni, who you will easily find if you care to walk there.' I had been at Barni and found nothing, but then, no doubt, I had missed these people. I did not want to go back on a wild-goose chase; so I made very careful enquiries. 'What kind of figure was it?' I enquired .'Male or female? And how big?' 'Oh, it was the figure of a man about one metre high and finely made. It was very old, very, very old; as old as the figures you can see all over the Cathedral at Milan, and as fine as any of them.' 'Was it a marble figure,' I asked, 'or one of commoner stone, or, perhaps, terracotta?' 'It was surely marble, very beautiful marble, and there was some colour on it, but not much. Perhaps it was once coloured all over, but now there is only colour on some parts–the hair, I think, and, perhaps, the clothes, but that I don't rightly remember.' 'How did the owners of it get it? Did it come from a church or did it belong to their house?' 'I don't know how they got it. I only know that they and their forefathers have owned it as long as anyone remembers. People have wanted to buy it, but they would not part with it. But now the old man is dead, and the children sell it so as to divide the price between them.'

Accordingly I set off and walked back to the village of Barni, and the people sought were soon found. Yes! They had a beautiful figure for sale, very old, and sculptured in stone, a thing of great value. Sad were they to have to part with it, but there was no help for it. People had offered good prices for it, but not what it was worth, and I might have it if I paid what they were asking. Could I see the figure? Alas, no! It was no longer in their house. Up till yesterday it had been, but then they had sent it away to their relative at Bellaggio. He was a man of influence and position, sacristan and bell-ringer at the parish church there. He would have no difficulty in getting a good price for it from the foreign visitors there. Perhaps he had already sold it.

This talk took place beside a fountain where the water gushed out from a pipe protruding from a roughly carved sandstone head intended to represent Victor Emmanuel–a type of fountain-head common in these parts. The evening was coming on, and the shadows were creeping down the hills; the water splashed musically into the great stone trough where the village girls had been washing their linen, which was now spread to dry. By this time I was fairly determined to run the elusive sculpture to earth, so I decided, without hesitation, to go back to Bellaggio, and hunt up the 'man of influence and position'.

It was the following day before I reached Bellaggio Church and enquired for the sacristan. He was not forthcoming. He had gone away for the day on business of importance. My heart sank within me. What other business could he have but to dispose of the statue? Did they know whether he had a statute to sell, or whether he had taken it away with him? Oh, yes, he had a statue to sell, a fine old statue! It was brought to him from the country only the day before. But he had not taken it away with him. He had caused it to be carried up into a chamber in the church tower, and there he had locked it in. When he went away he took the key with him, and till he returned no-one could enter. But he would be back tomorrow and then I could see it. Till tomorrow I should have to wait. I asked what the statue was like, but no one could describe it. All they knew was that it was very old, very beautiful, and very precious, worth perhaps hundreds of francs. If I chose to wait I should see it, and could judge for myself.

Next day I was early on hand in a regular fever of impatience, which I did my best to hide. The sacristan was forthcoming, and the key. We entered the tower and mounted what seemed interminable steps. The old fellow was very garrulous, and full of praise of his treasure, but I paid little attention to him, as in a moment I should be able to see for myself. We came to the door of the bell-chamber, and the lock would not open. The key was tried one way and another. Much kicking and banging followed. They were just going to send for a locksmith when the door gave way, and we entered a pitch-dark place. I could dimly discern something standing upright in the far corner. As I was making my way toward it, the shutters opened and a burst of sunlight illumined the vast moustache of another figure of Victor Emmanuel, if anything worse than the fountain-head of Barni! 'Is this your wonderful statue?' I cried. 'Certainly, that is it. Is it not beautiful? It is very, very old!' That was the end of my attempts to go behind the little dealers and discover Old Masters for myself in North Italian villages.

THE GREAT EXODUS

PASSAVANT had commented on the flow of fine pictures out of the British Isles late in the eighteenth century. The pattern repeated itself a century later. Not only had great wealth been accumulated by individuals on the Continent and in America, but the official collectors from some of the principal museums of the world found for the first time that money was forthcoming to fill obvious gaps in their collections. Prince of the official collectors was undoubtedly Wilhelm Bode, the director of the picture gallery of the Kaiser Friedrich Museum in Berlin. He was one of the first to mobilise private wealth for public purposes. He did this through the Kaiser Friedrich Museum Verein, a body of wealthy and knowledgeable art lovers to whom he could turn as soon as any work of stature came onto the market. Bode was a frequent visitor to London and one can study the shrewdness of his purchases either through Christie's or Sotheby's catalogues of that era or in the annual reports of the Kaiser Friedrich Museum Verein (see in particular the years 1896–1914).[1] If Solly[2] provided the nucleus of the Berlin Museum's picture gallery, the

[1] See also page 388. [2] See page 202.

London art market certainly provided many of its finest acquisitions before the first world war.[1]

Another great surge in the export of works of art was initiated by intelligent dealers, who had detected a vast new potential for their trade in America. From France it was Seligmann[2] and Gimpel[3] who were constantly crossing the Atlantic; from England it was Joseph Duveen (1869–1939), dynamic son of an already unusually enterprising father (Joseph Joel Duveen, 1843–1908) who led the way. So much is known about Lord Duveen that there is little need to enlarge upon his activities here.[4]

Sir Robert Witt devoted a long life towards encouraging a greater appreciation of the arts in this country. He was a distinguished collector of British drawings and brought together a unique photographic record of every sort of painting, which is now one of the mainstays of the Courtauld Institute. In 1950 he gave a short lecture on 'The Art of Collecting'[5] in which he stressed the importance of the critical faculty in collecting, and hence the importance of knowledge of his subject in a collector. He said very truly '. . . it is happier to be a collector, than to be the owner of a collection. It is the chase, not the quarry, that counts; the pursuit of the unobtainable, the discovery of the unexpected, with all its vicissitudes of success and failure.'

The extract that follows is taken from one of his earliest books *The Nation and its Art Treasures* (1911) which was unusually and delightfully outspoken. 'Hitherto the attitude of the State had been to do the minimum that public opinion required, to follow not to lead, indeed to follow at a safe distance of some fifty years.' And again 'in America there is a vast empty continent to be filled, and with the steadfast conviction that what time has done for Europe, money can do for America, and that, moreover, it is well worth the doing, the Americans have come crowding into our auction rooms, after first prudently removing their own twenty per cent import duty which stood in their way'. And finally, 'an anthology longer than the present volume[6] could be compiled to demonstrate the continuous inertia of succeeding governments where the reasonable acquisition of works of art is

[1] See, for example *Die Gemäldegalerie des Kaiser Friedrich Museums*, Vol. I: die Romanischen Länder, Dr Hans Posse, Berlin, 1909; particularly pages 103, 174, 178, 183, 226–7, 229, 234–7. See also Vol. II: Die Germanischen Länder–pages 99, 101, 106, 150, 151, 178, 180, 186 in particular, 200, 203, 212, 273, 300, 337 and 345 in particular. (The pages referred to usually show illustrations of the paintings concerned. This list is by no means exhaustive.)

[2] See *Merchants of Art: 1880–1960*. Eighty Years of Professional Collecting, by Germain Seligman, New York, 1961.

[3] See *Diary of an Art Dealer*, René Gimpel, London, 1966.

[4] See *Duveen*, S. N. Behrman, London, 1952, which originally appeared as a series of articles in the *New Yorker*. The book has been frequently reprinted; also *The Rise of the House of Duveen*, J. H. Duveen, London, 1957; *Collections and Recollections*, J. H. Duveen, 1935; *Secrets of an Art Dealer*, J. H. Duveen, New York, 1938–a most curious book, seemingly written in total unawareness of the laws of libel!

[5] *The Art of Collecting*, a lecture by Sir Robert Witt, C.B.E., D.Litt., F.S.A., published by the National Art Collections Fund in July 1950.

[6] Sir Robert was referring to his own book, not *The English as Collectors*: however, the remark could still apply!

concerned'. The relevance and cogency of his remarks nearly sixty years after they were written–particularly where taxation and death duties are concerned–is thoroughly discomforting.

Even Sir Robert's book did not bring about the establishment of an official committee to review and permit (or reject) the export of works of art from this country, and though it did much to stir the official conscience action was not finally taken in this matter until just before the second world war. The system was revised in 1952, but even today the approach to the problem is still ham-handed. One of the most cogent critical articles on it in recent times was by Sir Philip Hendy in the National Gallery's Report for 1965–1966. He pleaded, at the end of his tenure of office as Director of the National Gallery, for two things: firstly, the establishment of a national art purchasing fund, which should be automatically or periodically replenished; and, secondly, for an adjustment in the British laws governing death duties which would go some way to counteract the United States (and now the Dutch and West German) death duty structure under which over 80 per cent of art donations to public galleries are virtually free–and permanently free–of tax.

EXTRACTED FROM Robert C. Witt's *The Nation and its Art Treasures*, 1911.

IN England the museums and galleries are lacking in the prestige that should be theirs. Services to the State are recognised by the Government in almost every department of activity save that of Art. In consequence it is impossible for our directors to compete on equal terms with their foreign colleagues, apart altogether from the private collector, whether American millionaire or not. We are falling behind, and must continue to fall if steps are not taken without delay.

Instances abound of the losses which the country has already suffered, and are too well-known to need more than a passing reference. In the years 1909 and 1910 the value of the works of art exported from this country was stated in Parliament to be £581,304 and £595,829 respectively. To refer only to pictures upon which, owing to the publicity their exodus has received, attention has been chiefly directed, some few familiar instances may be cited out of a much larger number. Among those that have actually passed from our private collections to foreign galleries, the Kaiser Friedrich Museum at Berlin has secured Fra Angelico's Last Judgement from the Dudley Collection, Botticelli's series of drawings illustrating Dante's Divine Comedy, Signorelli's Pan, refused by the then Director of the National Gallery, the Butler Masaccios, also offered and declined by the Director (though the master is entirely unrepresented in the National Gallery), the Sebastiano del Piombo Portrait from Blenheim, the Heytesbury and Nieuwenhuys Van Eycks, the Marquis of Exeter's Petrus Cristus, the Marquis of Lothian's Virgin and Child [by Rubens], and the Hamilton Palace and Cholmondeley portraits by Dürer (an artist who is also unrepresented except by a somewhat doubtful though attractive panel), a fine example of Schongauer (of whom again we have no example), the two Blenheim Rubenses, the pair of Genoese Van Dyck portraits from the Peel Collection, the great Ashburnham Rembrandt, the Joseph and Potiphar's Wife by the same master, and the Portrait of a Man by Giorgione, a painter also unrepresented in the National Gallery, this picture having been offered to the Trustees for a relatively small sum and declined. The Metropolitan Museum has acquired the superb Adoration of the Shepherds by El Greco, offered to the National Gallery for only £1600, the Van Dyck Portrait of the Duke of Richmond from Lord Methuen's Collection, and the Carpaccio Pieta from the Abdy Collection. Again the Louvre secured Perugino's Apollo and Marsyas, formerly ascribed to Raphael, and offered by the late Morris Moore to the Trustees for £100, for £8000, while Raphael's Three Graces, from the Dudley Collection, passed to the Musée Condé at Chantilly. The late Mr Rudolph Kann captured Ghirlandajo's portrait of Giovanna Tornabuoni from the Willett Collection, though it had been for many years on loan to the National Gallery, which contains no unquestioned picture by the master, as also the Rembrandt Philosopher with Bust, both of which have since passed to America. Indeed, when we come to American collectors the list is far longer, and only a few of the most famous need be referred to. The National Gallery possesses no work by Roger van der Weyden, yet one of his largest and most important pictures from the Ashburnham Collection passed into the Kann Collection, and subsequently into private hands in America. It can boast no authentic example of Giotto, yet Mr Willett's Presentation in the Temple is now in the Gardner Collection at Boston, as are Titian's Rape of Europa from Cobham (offered to the National Gallery for £12,000 and refused), and Velazquez's Don Balthazar Carlos and Dwarf from Castle Howard. Mr Frick has secured the Ilchester Rembrandt and Mr Widener Lord Landsdowne's mill [also by Rembrandt]. Lastly, the marvellous Gainsborough portrait of Miss Linley and her brother from Knole has lately passed into American hands.*

It is not of course suggested that it was either possible or necessary for the State to retain all of these masterpieces, however supreme their importance in the field of art. But their alienation is irrestible evidence, if such be needed, of the drain that is going on and may be expected to continue.

The reason for this drain is clear. It has been aptly described as the combined pressure of taxation and temptation. To a considerable extent the increasing art sales from the country are a by-product of the recent Budgets. Fiscal taxation operating during life as well as upon death is reducing both income and capital. Meanwhile the demands of society involve increased expenditure, and the pleasant provisions of the Settled Land Act enable owners to sell even what has been strictly settled. And while at the same time many great owners are willing or unwilling sellers, there are in this country today few if any buyers, especially of works of first-rate importance.

Such is the position with which the wealthiest nation in the world is faced at the opening of the twentieth century.

* *The above are for the most part selected from the lengthy but even so, unfortunately, not exhaustive list published by Mr Robert Ross in 1909.*

PROBLEMS OF CONNOISSEURSHIP

MAX Friedländer succeeded Bode as director of the picture gallery at the Kaiser Friedrich Museum in 1929. His was one of the greatest intellects in the field of critical art history during this century. His *magnum opus* was *Die Altniederländische Malerei,* which appeared in fourteen volumes between 1924 and 1937. Friedländer's influence was wide in both Europe and America. Regrettably he was much given to the continental habit of issuing certificates of authentification for individual paintings. Though his attributions are much quoted, they are not by any means invariably accepted. *Art and Connoisseurship,* from which the piece which follows was extracted, was the fruit of much thought and deliberation during Friedländer's exile in Holland between 1933 and 1941.

Tancred Borenius, who translated *Art and Connoisseurship* from the German manuscript, explains in an introductory note to the book the difficulties of rendering into English the author's tersely idiosyncratic style without editorial amendment. One gathers that Herbert Read assisted in some of the knottier problems of translation.

EXTRACTED FROM Max J. Friedländer's *Art and Connoisseurship,* 1942.

DEALERS and collectors are not served by suppositions; they demand a positive decision. The expert not infrequently gets into a difficult position, since more is expected of him than he can honestly give. Let us say that he has recognised a picture as a work by Rembrandt. Out of confidence in him somebody acquires it at a high price. Later he arrives at the conviction that he has made a mistake. Even if his love of truth now overcomes his vanity, he is yet reluctant to harm someone who has believed in him. An expert of determined character did once, in such a situation, take over the doubtful picture at his own expense, but declared another time coldly and resolutely that the financial risk had to be borne by the person who had consulted him. Most people have less character; they do not confess their mistake or they try to confuse the hard facts, more particularly as they know from experience that their clients never forget a financial loss, whereas grateful memory is developed on a singularly slight scale.

Every work of art has a financial value, which largely depends on the view taken of its authorship. This value also depends on its artistic value, which is difficult to assess, and in any case can be sent considerably up or down through the verdict of the expert. The expert comes up against financial interests and gets regrettably caught up in them.

At the same time, let us be lenient towards human weaknesses. Satisfaction of his vanity, the exalting consciousness of authority and the power that goes with it, must compensate the expert for much that is disagreeable in his questionable profession. Honest recognition of positive performance hardly ever comes his way, least of all from his professional colleagues, who quote him only when they contradict him. Anything true that today he has been the first to find, is common property tomorrow and at everybody's disposal. Mistakes survive, on the other hand, under his name and call up memories of him. Dubious things, which he was unable to attribute, are over and over again submitted to him with a silent reproach; while the works to which he, without being contradicted, has assigned such and such a name, disappear without further ado, and without earning for him any gratitude.

The quality of the works of art which drift about in the market is declining. The number of the dealers and agents who want to live by the sales in the art market grows continuously. The difference in value between a picture by Rembrandt and one by Ferdinand Bol is increasing. The hunt for valuable things becomes ever madder and more relentless. Connoisseurship becomes more and more specialised, takes on the character of a mystery, so that even a highly regarded and experienced dealer can no longer say to his customers: 'I regard the picture as a work by Titian and assume the guarantee; there is no need for an expert opinion.' All these are circumstances which contribute to an increase in the power of the expert, and to the danger of misusing this power.

'Expertising' is felt to be mischievous, but as things are it is bound to be ineradicable and a necessary evil. The need to establish whether a picture really is the work of Rembrandt by consulting an authority, a disinterested and conscientious writer of expert opinions, appears urgent. The difficulty lies in the regrettable uncertainty as to who is a well-informed and honest writer of expert opinions. All suggestions made, and measures taken, in order to combat the degeneration of 'expertising' have done more harm than good. Museum officials have thus in many places been forbidden to give written opinions, which means that a number of the best experts have been excluded, and the field has been thrown open to unofficial, professional writers of expert opinions. As a result the average standard of truth of the expert opinions has declined. The official may pronounce himself only verbally. The verbal opinion is naturally formulated with less sense of responsibility than the written opinion; and, moreover, it is usually distorted when subsequently handed on. The French institution of the *experts* as government officials has certainly proved its worth in the administration of justice, since a financial guarantee is linked with an attribution put forward; but it has not succeeded in asserting itself against free, unattached, specialised connoisseurship; it has been unable to replace it or eliminate the latter.

There is no choice but optimistically to rely upon the fact that ignorance and unscrupulousness will gradually be discovered in the circles of the collectors, and that the dealers as a result will be induced to exercise circumspection in the choice of the writers of expert opinions.

The complaints regarding frivolous and untruthful expert opinions are all too justified. They have caused a reaction, so that timorous minds nowadays go to extremes in judging negatively or with reserve. The people concerned say 'no' in order not, at all events, to be confused with the 'yes-men'. Now prudence is not only the mother of wisdom but also the daughter of ignorance. What must be done is to steer the right course between the rocks of a conciliatory complaisance on the one hand and a negative attitude, on principle, on the other.

THE TATTON TURNERS

A. C. R. Carter was immensely knowledgeable about the history of collecting in England. He wrote for many years on the subject in the *Daily Telegraph* and edited *The Year's Art*. Unfortunately he tended to concern himself largely with the anecdotal elements of collecting.

Extracted from A. C. R. Carter's *Christie's, 1929 Season.*

When Mr Lance Hannen mounted the rostrum on 14 December [1928] he saw before him one of the most crowded audiences of his career and, as the first half-hour had to be devoted to the Turner drawings, he must have thought of many celebrated sales in which Turner had won posthumous triumphs.* The continuous championing of Turner's pictures and drawings at auctions by the Agnew family forms a very proud chapter of achievement. As their first Turner purchase at Christie's was in 1859 (eight years after the death of the great painter), the period of the Turner-Agnew association has now reached seventy years, and it is doubtful whether it can be matched by any analogous record in the chronicles of art sales. Many instances of the Agnew ardour could be cited. Suffice it to mention an outstanding example. In the Bullock sale, 1870, the late Sir (then Mr) William Agnew gave 2560 guineas for that celestial vision of Venetian sunshine, the picture of *The Dogana and Salute*. In the Sir John Fowler Sale, 1899, he raised the price to 8200 guineas. In 1927, one of his grandsons, Mr Colin Agnew, paid the Turner

* *That Turner foresaw his future triumphs at auction is proved by the fact that, as far back as 1827, he attended the Lord de Tabley sale and bought his own* Sun Rising in a Mist *for as much as 490 guineas. This is one of the famous pair which he bequeathed to the nation on condition that they should be hung between two paintings by Claude.*

maximum, 29,000 guineas, for this superb work in the sale of the collection of James Ross of Montreal, once an engine-driver in Aberdeen. Therefore, as Mr Hannen looked on Mr Gerald Agnew sitting to his right, he would remember his grandfather, Sir William Agnew, his father Morland, his uncle George, and his cousin Lockett, who used to occupy that chair and bid up manfully for Turner's masterpieces. He would also remember that, despite the great sums given at Christie's for Turner drawings by these Agnews of a bygone day, it was Mr Gerald Agnew who beat every family record by giving 6200 guineas in the Drummond sale, 1919, for the beautiful *Zürich* bought by his grandfather for 1200 guineas in the Novar Sale, 1878. This was one of the now renowned drawings for which Turner tried hard to obtain 1000 guineas from Griffith of Norwood in 1842, but in the end had to be content with 800 guineas, that is, 80 guineas apiece. As the magnificent Tatton Turner drawing of *The Rigi at Sunset* or *The Red Rigi* was another of the famous ten, and had captivated every Turner lover on the view-days, Mr Hannen soon divined that Mr Gerald Agnew had come to fight for it *contra mundum* in the old style. It was evident, too, that his chief opponent would be a well-known shipowner sitting close by, as this gentleman showed his mettle in winning at 2400 guineas a *Lausanne* drawing which had been preserved in the old portfolio from W. G. Rawlinson's collection. The *Rigi* was the thirty-sixth and last Turner in the catalogue, and, as soon as it was placed on the easel, the bidding began at 1000 guineas, and almost in the time it takes to write this sentence, Mr Gerald Agnew had beaten the shipowner at the maximum Turner drawing price of 7900 guineas.

I remember this selfsame drawing falling to the bid of Lockett Agnew at 2000 guineas in the Taylor sale, 1912, and I remember, too, an old curmudgeon stigmatising the price as 'mad'. Let us hope that he is now having many a pleasant chat in the Elysian Fields with Turner–and with Lockett Agnew. He should, too, meet that eminent business man and statesman, the Right Hon. W. H. Smith, truly a real worshipper of Turner for, many years ago, seeking a sure distraction from affairs, he asked 'Old Woods' of Christie's to pick for him half a dozen Turner drawings. He always kept the soothing six in a portfolio and it was his wont to contemplate them in quietude. At his death they were found in his house–still in the portfolio–and Lockett Agnew (who told me the story) bought them, eventually letting old Sir Joseph Beecham have them. At the Beecham sale, 1917, the precious six brought the 'mad' total of 14,850 guineas. About the time that Mr Smith bought these six Turners, he also gave 4200 guineas for that Rosa Bonheur picture which realised only 46 guineas last season.

This Tatton collection, which caused this furore on 7 December, was formed in the last century by the owner's forebear, Robert Townley Parker and, when the 36 drawings and 27 pictures constituting it had been sold, the total for this alone came to £112,927–an average of nearly £1800 a lot. The average for the twenty-seven pictures was as much as £3300, and as the highest bid was 12,500 guineas given on two occasions, first for the Reynolds portrait of *Anne, Viscountess Townsend*, and second, for a small Vandyck portrait of a *Genoese Officer*, it will be gathered that the all round bidding was unusually high.

A very interesting theory concerning this Reynolds picture has been propounded. Up to its appearance at Christie's it was always held that, although the "original" portrait could never be discovered, this Townley Parker version was only a replica. But at the time of sale documentary evidence was produced which established this portrait to be really the lost original. It is certain that it was acquired about fifty years ago from a descendant of the Lady Townshend portrayed in somewhat secretive circumstances. As for the Vandyck bringing also 12,500 guineas, this had been acquired in 1823 from a collection in Madrid at a frugal sum. The portrait was now bought by Messrs Vicars, acting for the owner of many telling Vandycks.

Notwithstanding these, the company found the chief attraction to lie in the superb set of Canalettos, proved by accompanying documents to have been painted in 1725–6 for Signor Conti of Lucca for 90 sequins (about £45). As the quartet realised 24,500 guineas, the highest price being 6400 guineas given by Messrs Colnaghi for *The Rialto*, and the second 6300 guineas, paid by the Savile Gallery for the *Church of SS. Giovanni e Paolo*, every previous Canaletto auction figure was surpassed. In days to come I am convinced that many art lovers will talk proudly of having had the privilege of seeing these magnificent masterpieces, about which there could be no possible doubt whatever as being by the master in his young strength and vision.

One of the surprises was the courageous bid by Mr Frank Sabin of 7200 guineas for Titian's portrait of *Daniello Barbaro*, which, in less appreciative times, had brought only 38 guineas in the Tarral sale, 1847, and 60 guineas in the Beauclerk dispersal, 1877. I mention this as illustrating the Sibylline process now governing picture valuations. Year by year the number of works of the first rank becomes more depleted owing to their absorption by national and public institutions, so that the market keenly awaits every available opportunity. In addition to the Tatton Turner drawings, there was an early work in oils, *Bonneville Savoy*, with a view of Mont Blanc in the distance. This had been bought as recently as 1919 in the Camperdown sale at 3600 guineas, but the price advanced to 5800 guineas. When Ruskin saw the sketch for this he declared that mountains had never been drawn before at all, and would never be drawn so well again.

THE COLLECTION OF SAMUEL COURTAULD

PROBABLY the best known among English collectors active in the present century was Samuel Courtauld (1876–1947). With amazing generosity he not only left the bulk of his pictures by the French Impressionists to the nation, but with remarkable vision he also made available the money for the foundation of an institute for the study of the arts and gave the trustees his own house for the purpose.

The full catalogue of the Courtauld Collection appeared in 1954. It begins with a perceptive memoir of 'Samuel Courtauld as Collector and Benefactor' by Sir Anthony Blunt, from which the extract which follows is taken. The actual catalogue is preceded by a long introduction by Douglas Cooper. The last chapter of this is a masterly account of 'Modern French Painting and English Collectors' which is essential reading for anyone interested in the history of collecting in recent times. This was the first place in which Alex Reid, the Glasgow art dealer and one-time friend of Vincent van Gogh, received credit for his share in the sale–for a long time utterly unsuccessful–of French Impressionist pictures to British collectors.

Courtauld's mother, Sarah Sharpe, was descended from a family with a traditional interest in the arts. Her great grandfather had been Samuel Rogers' brother-in-law. Courtauld's enthusiasm for painting seems to have been kindled by a visit to Rome and Florence with his wife in 1901. After the spectacle of Italian paintings of the Renaissance in the great galleries of Florence he wrote: 'The Old Masters have come alive to me and British academic art died.[1] In the former I now perceived a wonderful mastery allied with strong emotion and with life itself; I felt strong and exciting currents still flowing beneath the surface of the paint. In the latter I felt nothing but artificiality and convention, and could detect no progress in technique.'

Not long afterwards he took an increasing interest in *modern* painting. At first it was in Monet, Manet and Degas. Then he saw the Hugh Lane Collection exhibited at the Tate Gallery in 1917. He himself described this as an 'eye-opener' to painters such as Renoir, Cézanne and later Seurat. The most active period of collecting came between 1924 and 1929 when Mr and Mrs Courtauld bought no fewer than forty oil paintings and a large group of drawings and prints. These included works not only by the painters already mentioned but also by Gauguin, Rousseau, van Gogh, Vuillard, Pissarro, Sisley and Toulouse-Lautrec.

Most of them can now be seen in the Courtauld Institute Galleries. This is one

[1] He had previously been very interested in this.

of the nicest museums in London but since it now includes the collections of Lord Lee of Fareham,[1] of Roger Fry, of Sir Robert Witt's drawings, the very much earlier Gambier-Perry Collection,[2] and the William Spooner bequest of English drawings and water-colours, the early sense of spaciousness and informality–something akin to a drawing-room atmosphere–has sadly disappeared.

EXTRACTED FROM *The Courtauld Collection: a Catalogue,* 1954.

ONCE Courtauld's enthusiasm for French painting was fully aroused, he became intensely aware of the indifference and even hostility with which it was generally viewed in this country. And he very soon formulated definite plans, first to build up a collection of Impressionist and Post-Impressionist painting and secondly to gain recognition for this school among the English public.

The first part of the scheme was relatively easy to carry out. Although many of the finest works of nineteenth-century French painting had already been bought by enlightened German and American collectors, it was still possible to acquire masterpieces at reasonable prices, and there would have been plenty of dealers and experts ready to advise a new and wealthy collector in the choice of his pictures. This method, however, would not have suited Courtauld in any way, though from one dealer, the late P. M. Turner, he certainly obtained much help over a long period. He was not remotely interested in knowing what he ought to buy, and the concept of what was fashionable, or what was admired by the best authorities, was of no significance to him. Certain kinds of paintings aroused in him strong feelings, and those were the pictures which he wanted to buy. He was deeply concerned to analyse these feelings to clarify and understand them; but above all he attached importance to the enlargement of spiritual experience which they gave him. Once he had satisfied himself that the emotions aroused by a work of art were valuable he did not care whether those who set up as experts agreed with him. He was only concerned about the attitude of others in so far as he wanted his friends to share in whatever he though important and worth while, and to experience the same widening of the spiritual horizon.

Those who knew him best while he was forming his collection all agree in asserting that from first to last the process of deciding whether or not to buy a picture was a matter to be worked out in his own mind and heart. He would himself search the stocks of dealers in London and Paris, receiving and personally investigating reports of works which might be available, never buying on reputation and always–unless circumstances absolutely prevented it–taking the picture to his own home to live with it for a time before coming to

[1] See page 394.

[2] There are separate catalogues available for each collection. For a detailed account of the Gambier-Perry Collection see the *Burlington Magazine* for March 1967.

a decision about its purchase. It is for this reason that his collection had in so high a degree the stamp of his own personality and lacked the ready-made character so often to be found in the accumulations of rich men in the present century – a fact which was perhaps first fully appreciated when it was shown in its entirety at the Tate Gallery after his death.

To further his plan for spreading public appreciation of French nineteenth-century painting Courtauld's most decisive action was his gift to the Tate in 1923. The fund which he created was to be administered by a committee consisting of himself, Lord Henry Bentinck, Sir Charles Holmes, Sir Michael Sadler and Mr Aitken, then Director of the Tate. The terms of the trust gave the trustees unusual freedom, allowing for instance, the exchange of paintings already bought when other and better works appeared on the market. During the next few years the Tate in this way acquired twenty-three works by Manet, Renoir, Van Gogh, Monet, Cézanne, Degas, Pissarro, Seurat, Sisley, Utrillo, Bonnard and Toulouse-Lautrec. Most of them still belong to the gallery, but some have been exchanged or sold, including Sisley's *Pont de Moret* and a Renoir *Baigneuse*. The most spectacular acquisition was the purchase in 1924 of Seurat's *Baignade*, but the *Self-Portrait* and the *Paysage Rocheux* by Cézanne, the Manet *Servante de Bocks*, the *Première Sortie* by Renoir, and the *Tournesols* and the *Chaise* by Van Gogh were hardly less important.

ANTHONY BLUNT

COLLECTING COSTUME

WILLETT Cunnington was a natural collector, with an almost obsessive interest in the past. His highly methodical mind and scientific training brought to all his collecting activities a constant questing for fact. When was it made? Why was it made like this? Who made it? What was it used for? These were the sort of questions that came to him as soon as he saw anything for the first time, whether it was antique furniture, silver, ceramic ware or costume. And for many years he provided the answers – anonymously – to readers' queries in an antiques journal. Aesthetics, as will be apparent from the piece that follows, interested him much less.

Together with his wife, Phillis, who was also a doctor, he began – as a collector – to take an interest in dress when he was over fifty, and it was their joint objective and scientific study of the origin and dating of English costume that brought them fame. Almost the first published result of their researches was the delightful and definitive *English Women's Clothing in the Nineteenth Century* (1937). After the war there followed a series of costume *Handbooks* that are among the most authoritative works on the subject.

But probably the greatest ultimate benefit of the Cunningtons' researches on costume was not so much the establishment of mere fact, but the social and psychological deductions on fashion which they established. Their collection eventually grew to such a size that they could no longer look after it themselves. Some 1100 complete dresses and 2000 dress accessories were acquired for the Costume Museum at Platt's Hall, Manchester, in 1947. The Cunnington Collection thus became a striking example of a collecting interest that made a major contribution to our knowledge of one facet of social history.

EXTRACTED FROM C. Willett Cunnington's
Looking over my Shoulder, 1961.

It was near the end of 1930 that I happened to see, in a little antique shop in Hampstead, a gorgeous-looking old silk dress for sale. Thinking that perhaps an evening cloak for Phillis could be made out of its ample material I bought it for a trifle. However, we hesitated to have it cut up until we knew its age; so we took it to the Victoria and Albert Museum to find out. Someone there very obligingly examined it and declared it to be undoubtedly 'Victorian'–perhaps about the 1870s, but we could get nothing more definite than that.

It was usual, at that time, for English museums to be content to label period costumes very vaguely in terms such as 'late Georgian', 'early Victorian' and the like. Apparently our specimen was not old enough to be a rarity and therefore a museum could not be expected to know much about it.

We decided that we should have to solve our problem-piece by our own efforts and this meant collecting fashion journals of the nineteenth century and searching in them for more precise evidence.

To us as doctors, it represented an agreeable change from ordinary medical diagnosis. Here was a case displaying queer-looking features presumably symptomatic, but of what? The dress had evidently broken out in a rash of colours; its shape was remarkably unlike that of the human body; it must have given the wearer much physical discomfort. In short, here was a capital example of the malady which is popularly known as 'fashion'.

Our medical instinct was agog to trace this particular epidemic to its origins.

Soon after, we bought from a patient half a dozen dresses which were said to be of the 'Empire period'. They proved to be a hundred years later.

We began to scour 'junk shops' in the outskirts of London and in the various places we visited on our holidays, and the number of specimens rapidly increased, for at that time collectors of 'antiques' paid little attention to items of the Victorian period and dealers knew nothing about period costume. Sometimes our enquiries seemed to suggest that we were seeking comic clothes for a music hall turn and we would be offered garments suitable 'for comedians like yourselves'. In that guise we got them quite cheap. Sometimes in a pile of old clothes dumped on a shop floor you might see a promising bit of material sticking out; in this way I rescued a beautiful white muslin dress of the Regency period at the cost of a shilling.

We were fortunate in having a patient who was an excellent washerwoman and she loved to clean and iron specimens in our collection that required it.

I discovered an institution that collected gifts of old clothes and sold them, the money going to a charity. I arranged that we should have 'first pick' and by this means a good number of specimens were obtained.

We sometimes paid visits to that notable hunting ground, the Caledonian Market in Islington. There, once a week, you would find every conceivable form of 'antique', genuine and otherwise, from Gothic chests to bits of bicycles laid out on stalls or in heaps on the cobbles with persuasive dealers bidding you 'to sort 'em out, they're lovely!' A customer pitted his knowledge against a salesman's whose shabby looks often concealed an expert; it was a form of gambling; if you knew more than he, you might get 'something for nothing'; more often the customer got 'nothing for something'.

However Victorian dresses had not, at that time, attracted collectors and we managed to pick up some desirable bargains.

It should be understood that while artists and others had often collected a certain number of period costumes, it had always been specimens chosen for their intrinsic beauty. We, however, approached the subject from the historic and scientific rather than the artistic viewpoint. We were trying to discover what Englishwomen liked to wear at a given period. We learnt from their contemporary fashion journals (of which we were collecting a substantial library) that 'fashion' was not governed by aesthetics; that often enough a 'beautiful' style would be discarded for an ugly one. We soon realised that such terms as 'beautiful' and 'ugly' applied to costume begged the question; for every fashion has been called beautiful by those who wore it and generally condemned as 'ugly' by those who presently discarded it.

Our researches were aimed at discovering why such changes of popular taste should have occurred, and our collection of specimens we regarded as psychological evidence revealing the tastes and prejudices of past generations, and inasmuch as human beings usually prefer beauty to ugliness there must have been some overwhelming influence causing ugliness to be the more favoured in certain epochs.

Ugly fashions will, to a scientist, therefore, have a peculiar interest of their own.

Visitors inspecting our collection would often express surprise that we should have some specimens that were 'so dreadfully ugly'. I tried, usually in vain, to explain why these were so interesting, pointing out that one doesn't collect prehistoric flint implements because they are 'pretty'.

We were not seeking dresses that had belonged to notable persons, but those of ordinary folk, for we were concerned with mass psychology not with the psychology of the individual.

By the end of 1932 the collection had expanded to include some two hundred dresses together with a mass of other garments, headgear and accessories. To house all this, we had converted the space immediately under the roof into a closed-in loft to which access was obtained by a sliding step-ladder. Here they were closely packed and it was becoming a task extracting specimens to bring downstairs.

We were shortly to be faced by a question which many collectors are bound to meet sooner or later. The need for more space demanded an answer – should we go on collecting more and more? If so it was evident that we should have to erect a building and this at a considerable cost. Could we afford this? Or should we exercise prudence and call a halt at the point already reached?

We had certainly learned a good deal both from the dresses and the library of fashion periodicals which I had by now accumulated; but we felt that there was much more to learn about Englishwomen's clothing in the nineteenth century. The collection was large but there were still many gaps. It was not yet the comprehensive collection that I had in mind.

Fortunately we chose the bold course and had a large hut some fifty feet long, built in our garden. It was constructed to be damp-proof and protected against moth. A year or two later this was followed by a second hut similarly constructed and ultimately the two proved to be only just sufficient for our purpose.

THE TWENTIETH CENTURY

DURING the seventy years of the present century the interest in collecting works of art and examples of the decorative arts has spread to such an enormous extent that only a very sophisticated econometric model could give a clear idea of the scale of its growth. It is therefore an unenviable task to try to summarise this development, and yet the present book would be curiously deficient if the attempt was not made. It would be simplest, of course, to devote a whole volume to the period.

In some ways the story is simplified both by the economic circumstances prevailing in England during the last seventy years and by the strong dominance of fashion of what was deemed collectable by a clearly defined majority. As usual, history was made largely by those collectors who sailed against the wind. Generally this was because such pioneers considered whatever it was they collected – be it Impressionist paintings or Japanese pottery or seventeenth-century Dutch seascapes or examples of the Italian Mannerist school or English Delftware—aesthetically attractive and desirable for some considerable time before a sizeable corpus of collectors followed their example.

Contrary to sentimental recollections of the 'good old days', the opening of the new century was not conducive to large expenditure on works of art. By the seventies and early eighties of the nineteenth century two harsh economic factors were already forcing English dealers to seek customers across the Channel and the Atlantic. One was the decline in land values, and thus in rentals, following upon the agricultural depression; the other was the burgeoning competition from Europe in the realms of industrial production. The gradual shift of emphasis in economic strength from agriculture to industry started much later on the Continent, but manufacturing processes and techniques were consequently often more technologically advanced and competitive. This meant that English industrialists had to compete for export markets with much reduced profit margins against foreign rivals, and thus there was no surplus for pastimes such as collecting.

Certainly it was such factors that brought about the greatly increased number of historic collections at famous sales and the 'Exodus' described earlier (see page 373) by Robert Witt. It also brought to this country perspicacious buyers like Wilhelm Bode, Director of the Kaiser Friedrich Museum in Berlin. Thus he stated quite openly in a publication to commemorate his active association with that musuem for half a century[1] that the England of about 1880 and after was a paradise for the really knowledgeable connoisseur of painting who wanted to build up an official collection. He wrote: 'Since 1873 I had made repeated journeys to England and had observed after my many visits to sales and the London dealers that there was a strong prejudice against certain sorts of subject, as well as whole periods of art; that there was an appalling lack of knowledge about the work of numerous painters; and that sales were poorly attended if some big collecting name was not attached to them. All this, as well as the wholly uncritical description of items in sales catalogues, was evidence that there were wonderful opportunities here for new acquisitions for our museums.'

It is certainly worth recording that like Waagen (his predecessor in the same post fifty years earlier) Bode thereupon applied for a prolonged leave of absence in order to buy pictures in England. His application was turned down because higher officialdom considered that there were insufficient funds available to make purchases openly on this scale in the London art market. Nothing daunted, Bode replied that he would use his leave for study purposes and go at his own expense. The first thing he did was to familiarise himself in every detail with Waagen's *Treasures of Art* and used this as a foundation for studying English private collections. He also visited exhibitions, particularly those at Burlington House. He bought many pictures while in London (largely with funds subscribed by the 'Friends of the Kaiser Friedrich Museum') and made notes of those he wanted to

[1] *Fünfzig Jahre Museumsarbeit*, Bielefeld and Leipzig, 1922.

acquire later. He then employed a knowledgeable Paris dealer to contact the unsuspecting owners who were usually delighted to accept quite unexpected offers for their pictures at a time when money was generally in short supply. By these shrewd, but perfectly legitimate methods, Bode acquired very reasonably great works by Rubens, Tiepolo, Rembrandt, Dürer and many others.

But Bode was by no means the only man to recognise the opportunities prevailing at the close of the nineteenth century in England. Joseph Duveen made his reputation and his fortune by his acute awareness of the buying climate. If it was the landowning and industrial upper middle class who had been the backbone among English collectors and who had now lost interest in collecting, there were new tycoons and young men with taste and perspicacity to take their place.

Despite Bode's contempt for English expertise in some areas, scholarship and the dissemination of factual knowledge about pictures and every form of decorative art had greatly expanded and continued to do so. A new generation with a different outlook began to take an interest in collecting objects that in the nineteenth century had been acquired almost accidentally. The first issue of *The Connoisseur* appeared in September 1901. Each month this magazine described collections that had been visited. At first it was pictures: Sir Charles Tennant's rather traditional assembly of canvases by Gainsborough, Reynolds, Hogarth, Turner and other painters of the English school. Next came a description of Arthur Sanderson's collection of 'Old Wedgwood'. The article stressed the curious fact that it was largely the French who had collected Wedgwood in the past. Though, of course, there were precedents in England too: hadn't Joseph Mayer bought the entire showroom stock of Wedgwood's Liverpool warehouse? And there had been the earlier collections of Barlow, de la Rue, Dr Sibson, William Bartlett, Shadford Walker, Streatfield, Felix Joseph, Sir Richard Tangye, Cox, Hulme and Holt. Most of these had been dispersed. At least four of them went entire to provincial museums after their owners' death.

A little later *The Connoisseur* began to take an interest in more out-of-the-way and specialist collections: Lord Cheylesmore's mezzotints; the famous collection of early English pottery got together by Mr Solon, who wrote his own two-part account of it; Lady Dorothy Nevill's very personal collection of porcelain: she considered them almost as knick-knacks – today hers would be regarded as a major collection;[1] Michael Tomlinson's enormous collection of Japanese lacquerwork,

[1] One passage from her article is particularly fascinating:

'. . . Often do I regret not having devoted my attention to collecting old English furniture at a time when it was almost a custom to consign even the finest pieces to the garret or to the servants' hall, their place being taken by the shapeless monstrosities which did duty as furniture in the early Victorian era. The generation of today [1901], which attaches such importance to period and style, cannot realise the artistic crimes which were perpetrated at that time, which, indeed, may be called the dark age of decoration. . . . Now, of course, almost everyone has, or pretends to have, some knowledge of or appreciation for books, pictures, engravings, china, or furniture; but at the time of which I speak such a thing was confined to the very few, and the taste of even the most

ivory, porcelain, metalwork, textiles, painting and engraving (*The Connoisseur* showed a superb photograph of the *tout ensemble* in 'the Japanese Gallery at Franche Hall' in Worcestershire).

Next *The Connoisseur* visited and marvelled at the superb quality of everything in Mr Alfred de Rothschild's collection, then in Seamore Place. Here were masterpieces of English, French and Dutch painting, and porcelain, bronzes, clocks and enamels hardly to be matched elsewhere. In contrast, during the following month, there was a description of an outstanding collection of book plates (Julian Marshall); and there were repeated articles to show what was happening across the Atlantic–thus the fate of the fantastic Garland Collection of china and porcelain was settled when Pierpont Morgan bought it, and it did not, as had been forecast, come to England.

In October (and December) of 1902 Louise Richter described the magnificent collection of Italian art assembled by Dr Ludwig Mond (much of it now in the National Gallery); this was followed by an account of the Dyson Perrins collection of early Worcester; and a little later there followed another visit to Europe: this time Bernard Berenson's two-part account of the collection of Italian pictures at Bergamo formed by the celebrated art historian, Morelli, part of which had been left to the museum in that town. In January 1903 a review of John Eliot Hodgkin's three-volume *Rariori: being Notes of some of the Printed Works, Manuscripts, Historical Documents, Medals, Pottery, Engravings etc. collected between 1858 and 1900* describes the widely catholic tastes of the 'Ideal Collector'.

Julia Frankau's Notes on the Harland-Peck Collection begins: 'Is Mr Harland-Peck a collector in the finest sense of the word, or is he only a connoisseur, an art lover, a *dilettante* to whom beauty has an irrestible appeal? Seeing that he can turn from prints to pictures, from marble to miniatures, from Louis Seize bibelots to sixteenth-century lustre with equal zest; seeing that he buys, understands, appreciates, *but fails to specialise*, I think that the answer must be that he is all this, and expert besides; and the proof of it is to be found at 9 Belgrave Square . . . for it is a "house beautiful" from the moment one leaves the hall . . . everywhere, on the walls, in china cabinets, on console tables, this eclecticism of taste, this multiplicity of interest strikes one afresh.' An even more diverse collection described later was that of Randolph Bevan at Princes Gardens, where the illustrations show perfect groups of Japanese bronzes, Austrian pewter, Tanagra figures, old English china cups with animals' masks (largely foxes), Turkish and Greek embroidery, and old English oak furniture.

In May 1903 *The Connoisseur* visited that bastion of the 'old' establishment, the Bridgewater and Ellesmere Collections at Bridgewater House; and tradition was continued at Belvoir Castle, where Lady Victoria Manners described the magni-

skilled of these would, I fear, compare none too favourably with that of the expert of today, when everything has become so specialised, with, I think, good results.' From *The Connoisseur*, March 1902.

ficent paintings in two articles. In August of that year there was an article on the superb collection of Bow, Chelsea and Derby figures belonging to Francis Howse.

By the beginning of 1904 an anonymous contributor proclaimed definitively the change that had taken place in collecting. It was an old cry in fresh phrases, but for us it makes a good epitaph on what had gone before, and marks the real start of the way in which collecting was to develop.

> The broad distinction between the old and new collector in all departments may be said to lie in the prevalence of emulation over enthusiasm. Formerly, while those who were led by some more or less casual circumstance to engage in the accumulation of what were vaguely denominated curiosities, and which it may be fitter to describe as miscellaneous objects of antiquity, the competition was languid, and a man, who was not very wealthy and not very fastidious, had no difficulty in making himself master of a very respectable assemblage of items belonging to the various branches of archaeology. He might not aspire to the highest prizes; but he lived before it was the cue of amateurs to struggle for the possession, not of articles which pleased them, *but of those which pleased other people.*

The Victorian predilections were fading fast; Edwardian taste was becoming established. There was far more curiosity about what was happening in Europe. More and more often *The Connoisseur* visited public and private collections in Holland, France, Spain, Italy and Germany. The revolutionary outlook of the Impressionist school in France was beginning to be regarded with some seriousness, even though this had happened twenty years earlier in Germany, Russia and the U.S.A.[1] The Scottish dealer, Alex Reid (1854–1928), after living in France for some years, imported the works of Corot, Daumier, Degas, Monticelli, Courbet, Puvis de Chavannes, Monet, Pissarro, Sisley and two canvases by his close friend, Vincent van Gogh. Though his gallery was in Glasgow, he held an exhibition of such works in London as early as 1891. In 1919 he held the first Vuillard exhibition in Scotland and a year later he held a large exhibition of French pictures at the McLellan Galleries in Glasgow, where twenty-nine artists were represented by 171 works,[2] and made a considerable impact on collectors.

Meanwhile in England that forceful, highly-strung Irish eccentric connoisseur-dealer, Hugh Lane,[3] had been pushing the cause of the Impressionists and the Post-Impressionists. Certainly this met with some success among private collectors, though it made no impact on the official collectors in London, an exact repetition of earlier attempts to gain representation for their work in the Louvre.[4]

[1] For more detail see page 402.

[2] See Ronald Pickvance's Introduction to the catalogue of an exhibition entitled 'A Man of Influence – Alex Reid' held by the Scottish Arts Council in 1967.

[3] See *Hugh Lane's Life and Achievement, with some Account of the Dublin Galleries* by Lady Gregory, London, 1921, and *Hugh Lane and his Pictures* by Thomas Bodkin, 1932 (reprinted 1956).

[4] For a full account of the Louvre's official attitude towards the work of the Impressionists, see Germain Bazin's introduction to his *Impressionist Paintings in the Louvre*, London, 1963 (fourth, revised, edition). Thus in 1923 the Council of Trustees of the Louvre only accepted the gift of Renoir's *The Bathers* by six votes to five.

The principal English disciple of the Post-Impressionists was Roger Fry, who staged his first exhibition of their work at the Grafton Galleries in 1910.[1] But there was strong public reaction: *The Times* complaining most vociferously of all. The pictures of Cézanne, Gauguin, van Gogh, Picasso, Signac, Derain and Finesz were universally ridiculed. Only Sir Charles Holmes, later Director both of the National Portrait Gallery and the National Gallery, had anything to say in their favour. In October 1912 Fry tried again. This time he showed the work of the rising generation of English painters like Duncan Grant, Eric Gill, Vanessa Bell, Wyndham Lewis and Stanley Spencer beside those of the 'Old Masters' from France. Again there was antagonism, but it was less vicious, and there can be no doubt that the two exhibitions made an immense impression upon the discerning public and many potential collectors.

Thus Professor Michael Sadler bought pictures by Kandinsky in 1911; Clive Bell bought works by Vlaminck, Finesz, Marchand, Juan Gris and Picasso between 1912 and 1913; Roger Fry himself frequently purchased examples of the artists whose works he had exhibited; Frank Stoop bought a large Degas from the great dealer Vollard before 1914 and a Picasso in 1920; Montague Shearman, an enlightened Foreign Office official, bought two female portraits by Matisse during the first world war, and went on to buy works by Bonnard, Vuillard and Utrillo, while Stoop later acquired pictures by Matisse, Picasso and the Douanier Rousseau. A few years later the trend was rolling along and collections of such works were becoming more common. The greatest of them, of course, was Samuel Courtauld's (see page 382). Others, whose collections became well documented, were Lord Keynes, Dr W. T. Cargill (his collection was dispersed in the U.S. in the second world war), William McInnes (an early customer of Alex Reid's), Mrs A. E. Pleydell-Bouverie and the Misses Davies who, advised by Hugh Blaker, formed the superb collection now in the National Museum of Wales in Cardiff.

The tradition of collecting the works of Old Masters declined somewhat as the most representative works disappeared into museums and prices increased. But one must remember what volume of them was available when one considers that Christie's have probably held *at least* two Old Masters sales a *month* during the present century and that Sotheby's have done so for about half of these seventy years; that few sales contain less than 150 pictures; and that a host of less well-known salerooms have been auctioning old canvases with absolute regularity. So it would be no exaggeration to say that a minimum of a million pictures by masters long dead will have changed hands in the past seventy years. Any collectors' names one selects from the great mass of possibles, therefore, are only those which have been much discussed in the periodical press because of the particular

[1] For a detailed account, see Virginia Woolf's *Roger Fry: a Biography*, 1940 (reprinted 1969), pages 153 *et seq.*

quality of their collections; or those whose collections have been given to the national museums, or whose catalogues are so authoritative as to be used as source books. (A good deal of information on the latter will be found in Parts 2 and 3 of the select, annotated bibliography on page 418.)

One or two such collections, begun in the nineteenth century, were still being added to in the twentieth and made a considerable impact on their generation. Probably the most outstanding was that of Sir Francis Cook (died 1901), who left a superb assembly of maiolica, bronzes, jewellery, ivories, enamels and miniatures to his son, Wyndham Francis Cook, who died only four years later (and the collection was dispersed on his widow's death in 1925). To his other son, Sir Frederick Cook, Sir Francis left the greater part of his vast collection of paintings at Doughty House, Richmond, Surrey. When Sir Frederick himself died in 1920 the collection was bequeathed to his son, Sir Herbert Cook, who added important works by Velazquez, Giorgione, Rembrandt and others. By 1932 there were 545 pictures in the galleries and private rooms of Doughty House: 201 Italian; 22 early Netherlandish; 197 later Flemish and Dutch; 46 Spanish; 32 French; 11 German and 32 English. The Cooks were always generous in the loan of their pictures to public exhibitions and every time a portion of their collection has come up for sale, prices have broken world records.

The roots of the Iveagh Bequest, the collection of the first Lord Iveagh, now at Kenwood, also stemmed from the 80s and 90s of the previous century. Kenwood was specifically bought so that it could be saved for the nation as it stood and Lord Iveagh spent the last four years of his life vigorously adding to his collection in anticipation of its opening as a public museum in 1927. A considerable number of paintings remained within the family.

Most intriguing of all, but relatively sparsely documented, was the immense and heterogeneous collection of George Salting. He was born in Australia in 1836, where his father made a fortune from sugar estates and farming. In middle life Salting settled in this country and associated almost immediately with a body of active English collectors. As a collector he followed his own methods but took care – while seeking the best advice available – to form his own judgement on every item. He was superbly endowed with natural taste and a flair for fine things. He was also – it was said – exceedingly mean and haggled endlessly about prices, though he combined great persistence with this and usually obtained any piece he really desired. Anecdotes about him abounded: most persistent was the story that his income was so enormous that he lived from the income of the original income re-invested. Yet his standards were of the highest and he was always eliminating objects he later considered second-rate. He lived in chambers in St James's Street. These were far too small to house his enormous and diverse collections – even in the cramped and overcrowded conditions in which he was prepared to exist – so that he used the Victoria and Albert Museum as a depository – on loan – of most of his treasures. Ultimately he left them the best of what came within the scope of that institution. The National Gallery also benefited extensively from his bequests, and he gave his finest prints and drawings to the British Museum. Finally he left a great deal of the remainder to his niece, Lady Binning, a vigorous collector in her own right. He died in 1909.

If Salting was remarkable for the wide range of his collecting activities, Robert and Evelyn Benson were specialists. For thirty years they sought after examples of the Sienese, Florentine, Umbrian, Ferrara-Bologna, Milanese and Venetian schools of painting in London, Paris and all over Italy. Evelyn was the daughter of Sir George Holford, so collecting was in her blood. (In fact, her husband Robert edited the great two-volume catalogue of the Holford Collection at Dorchester House of 1927.) The Bensons were also intimately acquainted with William Graham, Charles Butler and George Salting, that distinguished trio of late nineteenth-century collectors. They learned from them, imitated them and bought extensively from their collections when these were dispersed. They produced a memorable catalogue in 1914, listing 114 paintings but, alas, it is unillustrated.[1] Later the Bensons also collected English pictures, but no catalogue was published. Their collection has never stood out greatly because it was very personal and was not widely recorded. It was dispersed after Duveen bought it for a vast sum in 1927. He in turn sold a considerable number of the pictures *en bloc* to the American banker, Jules S. Bache, who left his collection to the Metropolitan Museum in New York in 1949.

Another born collector who parted with his first great collection and then formed another was Viscount Lee of Fareham (1868–1947). A tremendously active man, he devoted most of his life to public service. He was Minister of Agriculture, personal secretary to Lloyd George, First Lord of the Admiralty and chairman of several royal commissions. He had bought Chequers, for four centuries the family residence of the Hawtrey family, with all its contents in 1909, and added to it for many years. In 1921 he gave the house and all it contained to the nation, to serve as a country residence for the Prime Minister in office.[2]

Although this gesture considerably depleted his personal fortune, Lee soon started collecting again. At first it was pictures of the fourteenth and fifteenth centuries. On the whole he disregarded expert advice and used his own flair and taste. Later he also formed a collection of metalwork which he presented to Hart House in Toronto, and some fine illuminated manuscripts which he bequeathed to Cambridge.

[1] A small, 'extra-illustrated' edition was published later, but it is rarely found.

[2] 'Chequers is in no sense a museum, equipped with collections acquired and arranged for the enjoyment of students or the public. Such a conception of the house would be the very negation of the main objects of the donors, which was to provide an undisturbed sanctuary and place of recreation for overworked Prime Ministers. This catalogue, therefore, is more in the nature of a descriptive inventory of the principal contents of an official residence, in which an attempt has been made to show that art is not incompatible with domestic comfort and that beauty and utilitarianism can go hand in hand.' From Viscount Lee's Introduction to *A Catalogue of the Principal Works of Art at Chequers*, H.M.S.O., 1923.

But it had become clear to him quite early in his collecting career that England lacked an institute for training scholars in art appreciation and history to match those on the Continent. In the late twenties he became acquainted with Samuel Courtauld. The two men became firm friends and between them provided the drive and funds to found and to endow the Institute now known to all of us as London University's Courtauld Institute. Each man also bequeathed his own collection to the Institute.

Another assiduous collector who took a great interest in the Courtauld Institute was Sir Robert Witt. At the time of his death he left his magnificent library, which included some 600,000 reproductions of paintings and some 3500 drawings, to the Institute. The latter was a deliberately documentary collection, brought together to show representative works of artists, 'who while interesting or charming, were slightly below the highest rank, or temporarily out of fashion'. About a third of the drawings are by British masters. Sir Robert collected vigorously for over forty years and achieved a considerable reputation for his encouragement of other collectors.

A fourth outstanding collector who became another major benefactor to London University was Sir Percival David, a retiring man who had spent many years of his business career in China. He became immensely interested in Chinese culture and ceramics and formed a collection particularly rich in examples of objects of the Sung, Yüan, Ming and Ch'ing Dynasties. David acquired a considerable number of fine and inscribed specimens from the former Chinese Imperial Collection in Peking. It is said that these had been deposited with a bank as a surety against a loan with a valuation put upon them by Sir Percival. When the works became the property of the bank, David was able to acquire them. No fewer than fourteen hundred items from the complete collection can now be seen in the Percival David Foundation of Chinese Art at 53 Gordon Square, London.

In fact, Percival David was only one of a host of men of his generation who became fervent collectors of Oriental ceramics during the first half of the present century. Probably David's most distinguished rival was George Eumorfopoulos (1863–1939). He was born in Liverpool of Greek parentage and became a successful merchant banker as Vice-President of Ralli Brothers. In the introduction to the first volume of the magnificent catalogue of his collection (see page 428) he wrote: 'It was in 1891 that I first became interested in ceramics as a collector, but then I made what I now regard as a false start. I began by collecting English and Continental porcelain. To those a few pieces of Oriental came to be added, and as these grew in number it soon became clear that the European had to go.' He mentions how little was known about early Chinese ware, about T'ang in particular and, like Sir Percival David, he became as much a scholar as a collector. Bernard Rackham wrote of him after his death, 'Eumorfopoulos was so modest and unassuming, so entirely free from self-importance, that strangers meeting him for the first time were hardly able to estimate his full worth; they perhaps little suspected they were in the presence of a man whose learning, if he had chosen to display it in writing, might have won for him academic distinction (as was indeed recognised by his election to a Fellowship of the Society of Antiquaries).'

But Eumorfopoulos also had a marvellous eye for beauty and quality. Again he wrote, '. . . to enter my collection it was indispensable that [an object] should appeal to me aesthetically in some way or another.' In addition to ceramics, his collection included bronzes, gold ornaments, lacquer, jade, glass and other works of art that hailed not only from China but also from Korea, Japan and Persia. A substantial portion of them was sold to various museums, principally the British Museum, in 1934, and some five hundred items were sold in a four-day sale at Sotheby's in May 1940 for a total of £26,000. Not surprisingly, in view of the international situation at the time, most of the prices obtained seem unbelievably low by today's standards.

Probably the high water mark of interest in the collecting of Chinese works of art, but particularly of ceramics, was the International Exhibition of Chinese Art held at the Royal Academy during the winter of 1935–1936. It was organised by Sir Percival David, who also lent a vast number of pieces. The names of the other collectors whose possessions were exhibited reads almost like a roll call of prominent members of the Oriental Ceramic Society founded a few years earlier, though a great many pieces came over from China and from many other major museums in the rest of the world.

It seems that collecting Chinese ceramics between 1900 and 1930 had a twofold appeal. On the one hand, there was the undeniable beauty of the pieces, the strong aesthetic element, the appeal to the senses; and, on the other, there was a need for discriminating scholarship and connoisseurship in the then relatively uncharted history of Chinese pottery production, the appeal to the intellect and a crossword puzzle mentality. Furthermore, the two could be combined within a range of prices that was not wildly extravagant.

Many of the great collectors of Chinese ceramics of the period were bankers, merchant bankers and merchant princes. A number of them had, in fact, spent long periods in the Orient. They were fascinated not only by ceramics – mostly of the earlier periods – but also by bronzes, ivories and jade.

But Chinese painting, and even more so calligraphy, they left severely alone. These required a depth of immersion in an alien culture that was rarely achieved. Thus in 1935 Oliver Brown of the Leicester Galleries exhibited an unusually fine collection of early Chinese paintings assembled over many years by the French poet, Charles Vignier. But sales were poor, because collectors preferred ceramics.[1] Though one must also remember that ceramics were much easier to house and to display.

William Honey, who had a great respect for Vignier, explains the English preference for the work of the Oriental potter with great cogency: '. . . enjoyment

[1] See *Exhibition, the Memoirs of Oliver Brown*, London, 1968, page 121.

of works of art is surer and more lasting when it comes as the incidental half-conscious accompaniment of some other interest. Just as the potter himself was seldom concerned with the pure art of creating form, but rather with some practical problem of utility or technical excellence, so also should the connoisseur concern himself with some other problem or task, even one which may be in the strict sense irrelevant, such as classification and dating, but one which allows his enjoyment to come incidentally. The general argument rests on the necessity that taste should be informed taste. To appreciate the merits of a piece of pottery it is necessary at the outset to have a certain gift of eye, sensitive to what is original and creative in shape and colouring; and it is doubtful whether this faculty will ever be acquired by one not naturally possessing it. But even the gift must be cultivated. Without taste in this sense a man may fail to perceive beauty, or may find merit in an object clumsy or empty or merely clever. But without an informed taste he will tend to like one sort of thing only; he will lack the flexibility needed to adjust his standard to the varying ideals of potters in different periods.'[1]

Perhaps this underlines what a peculiarly *personal* fashion the collecting of Oriental ceramics is. Almost all of the outstanding collections formed in the first thirty-five years of the present century have been dispersed at auction after the deaths of their owners or have been absorbed into museum collections. Thus if one seeks out the names that figured most frequently among owners of fine pieces who loaned the best of what they had to exhibitions, one discovers W. C. Alexander (sold at Sotheby's in 1931); Sir Alan Barlow (now bequeathed to Sussex University) (see also page 23); G. H. Benson; R. C. Bruce (sold at Sotheby's); Chester Beatty (sold at Sotheby's); Sir John Buchanan-Jardine; Alfred Clark (partially sold at Sotheby's in 1953); Anthony de Rothschild (National Trust); the Hon. Mountstuart Elphinstone (171 monochrome pieces were given to the Percival David Foundation in 1952); Leonard Gow (sold to the United States);[2] Sir Neill Malcolm (retained, exceptionally, by his descendants); H. J. Oppenheim (all left to the British Museum); Oscar Raphael (divided between the British Museum and the Fitzwilliam Museum, Cambridge); Charles E. Russell (sold at Sotheby's in June and February 1936); Charles Rutherston (some sold at Sotheby's, but also at Bluett's); Ferdinand Schiller (left his very fine collection to his brother Max, who bequeathed it to the Bristol Museum in 1948); Dr Lindsey Scott (sold at Sotheby's); Professor C. G. Seligmann (left a large part

[1] William Bowyer Honey, *The Ceramic Art of China*, etc., London, 1945, page 2.

[2] In 1931 R. L. Hobson compiled a sumptuous catalogue of Gow's collection, which consisted in the main of eighteenth-century pieces. Gow was a wealthy shipowner, and after his death the collection was disposed of *en bloc* to two museums in the USA through the agency of Alfred de Pinna, who was considered one of the great judges of eighteenth-century Chinese porcelain. Although he was a dealer in his own right, he was consulted by many other firms of dealers (at a fee) as well as by a host of collectors. There was a final sale of pieces from the Gow Collection at Sotheby's in May 1943. The quality of these remaining pieces was still exceptional, though prices were depressed by wartime conditions.

to the Arts Council as a circulating exhibition and some sold); Captain A. T. Warre; Stephen Winkworth (sold at Sotheby's in April 1933 and April 1938); Mackinnon Wood (sold at Sotheby's in 1927).

Another collection formed during the same period but sold much later, which consequently fetched prices that were incomparably greater, was that of the dealer H. R. N. Norton. This was dispersed in three extensive sales in 1963, and really marked the end of the era we have been describing.[1] Norton had a small shop in Museum Street, Bloomsbury. The beauty of the pieces displayed in his window was a constant joy to those who passed by regularly. (Almost opposite was the remarkable emporium of Mosheh Oved, Cameo Corner, where – it might be said – the appreciation of Victorian jewellery was born.) The two shops were a delightful prelude of what was to come for the visitor approaching the British Museum.

English table glass began to be collected at the beginning of the century and four major collections have enriched museums. That formed by Sir Richard Garton, largely between 1927 and 1934, went to the London Museum. The collection belonging to Mr and Mrs Rees-Price of about 500 pieces and largely eighteenth century, was given to the Victoria and Albert Museum in 1925, where it became an important nucleus within the relevant department. The Donald H. Beves Collection went to the Fitzwilliam Museum in Cambridge and that formed by William Somerville Marshall to the Ashmolean Museum in Oxford. In addition in the late twenties and early thirties a number of really fine collections were dispersed and these were to form the backbone of the collections of the next generation. The outstanding primary collections that came up for sale included those of Wilfred Buckley (who was unusual in specialising in Continental glass), Alfred Trapnell, Frank Lloyd, the Wrigley Collection, Henry Peech, Lewis Evans, David Davis, Rev. H. A. Bull, C. Kirkby Mason, H. C. Levis, Hamilton Clements and Alexander Young.

Glass collecting has become particularly popular in England in recent years (there is much less interest in it on the Continent). But decorative and portrait glasses of the seventeenth century, and eighteenth-century drinking glasses with multi-spiral air-twist stems, have gone up enormously in price. Thus an example of the latter sold at auction in 1966 for £70, went for £160 in 1968 and £230 in 1969; a 1715 wine glass sold for £60 in 1956, went for £620 in 1968; and a 1550 goblet sold at Sotheby's in 1947 for £14, fetched £1,650 in 1969. It is an understandable concomitant that as prices went up dealers specialised increasingly in antique glass.

The story of the collecting of English tinglazed earthenware, known popularly as delftware, is very similar to that of glass and, incidentally, at their best, both

[1] However, it would be quite wrong to give the impression that the interest in the collecting of oriental ceramics has abated, as the fact that the membership of the Oriental Ceramic Society is currently (1971) in excess of 500 clearly shows.

table glass and delftware are particularly fine forms of English craftsmanship, which accounts for their appeal to collectors. It was the early enthusiasts who wrote books on the ware and these in their turn started off many other collectors. Thus Hugh Owen's *Two Centuries of Ceramic Art in Bristol*, published in 1873[1] was followed by W. J. Pountney's *Old Bristol Potteries* in 1920. Pountney was descended from a family of Bristol potters and his work was exceptional in that it was largely based on kiln excavations and research among the old pottery company's records. 1919 had seen the publication of Father E. A. Downman's rather more specialist *Blue Dash Chargers* (particularly useful because it lists all collectors who had fine examples of this form of pottery) and R. G. Mundy's more general *English Delft Pottery* appeared in 1927. The profuse illustrations were taken largely from examples in the author's own collection and those of his friends: in particular from the fine collection of Major-General Sir Gilbert Mellor which was sold at Christie's in 1966. The subject remained of continuing interest to scholar collectors. Thus Bernard Rackham and Herbert Read's *English Pottery* (1924)[2] and F. H. Garner's rather later *English Delftware* (1948) set completely new standards in the scientific detachment of their scholarship and each book gave the collecting of delftware new impetus.

More recently (1968) Anthony Ray's *English Delftware Pottery*, which is in fact a catalogue of the Robert Hall Warren Collection now in the Ashmolean Museum, made some advance on Garner's work. Mr and Mrs Warren, who lived in Bristol, formed the bulk of their collection between 1920 and 1939. Its inception was largely a matter of chance. A grandson of William Pountney, while still a young boy at school, came to tea at the Warren's house. He noticed a fine delft plate and said that he thought his grandfather would be interested to see the piece. Old Pountney subsequently came along, held forth ardently about the charm of delftware in all its forms and thus started the Warrens on getting together a particularly fine collection.

Delftware was one variety of ceramic antique where knowledgeable dealers helped to arouse interest in the subject. In the twenties and thirties Louis Gautier, R. P. Way, the redoubtable Fred Elsom of Christmas Steps in Bristol, the Mannheim family, Frank Tilley and A. F. Allbrook specialised in it. Collectors abounded everywhere, not simply in the West Country. Among the most renowned were Dr Glaisher of Trinity College, Cambridge, whose collection is now in the Fitzwilliam Museum, Dr Beaumont, Mr and Mrs J. E. Hodgkin (largely tiles), Professor F. H. Garner, Sir Francis Oppenheimer, Celia Hemming, Agnes Lothian, who collected all delftware associated with apothecaries on behalf of the Pharmaceutical Society, and more recently, Louis Lipsky who has specialised in dated pieces.

[1] This was published four years before Llewellyn F. Jewitt's finely illustrated *The Ceramic Art of Great Britain* and ten years before L.M. Solon's *The Art of the Old English Potter*.

[2] See page 332, note 2.

A very different genre of collecting which has gained enormously in popularity in the last half century is the collecting of drawings, and this has moved from strength to strength since the last war. The number of collectors in this field is legion, but a few names stand out. Near the beginning of the century Harry Oppenheimer bought aggressively. In 1912 he acquired most of the famous collection of drawings by Old Masters of J. P. Heseltine. The Oppenheimer Collection, which was particularly rich in its aggregation of drawings by Italian masters, was sold at Christie's in July 1936. The catalogue (see Bibliography) was introduced by C. J. Holmes and compiled by Sir Karl Parker. A much smaller, though fine, collection was assembled by Alfred de Pass, which he left to the Truro Museum in 1936. Among particularly distinguished collectors of drawings (and water-colours) by British artists we must name Sir Bruce Ingram, Sir Robert Witt, Gilbert Davies, Paul Oppé and D. C. T. Baskett. Tom Baskett was a dealer (a partner in Colnaghi's) who encouraged a multitude of collectors and is remembered by them with affection. It should also be stressed that it was the enthusiasm and scholarship of experts like A. E. Popham, Johannes Wilde and Sir Karl Parker[1] that made it possible for less knowledgeable collectors to buy with courage and discretion in an area where complete certainty is rare.

A number of particularly fine exhibitions organised by the Arts Council soon after the last war did much to foster a wider interest in the collecting of drawings. Prices rose enormously, and this in its turn encouraged more dealers to specialise in the subject. Water-colours are a natural pendant to the collector of drawings, and the great wealth of material by eighteenth- and nineteenth-century artists, both professional and amateur, makes collecting relatively easy.

I have stressed repeatedly the importance in the study of collecting of the enlightened dealer, who will not only seek out and provide what is in fashion and demand, but will also use his own judgement in making available the work of artists that have not already captured public interest.

A remarkable example of such a firm was the Leicester Galleries run by the Phillips brothers. Soon after the arrival there in 1903 of Oliver Brown the three partners pioneered not only the sale of what are probably the most interesting English artists of the present century, but also one-man exhibitions of the great Impressionists and Neo-Impressionists. As already mentioned, it is true that the latter had become accepted much earlier in Germany, France and the United States, and that in Britain a taste for the Barbizon School, and for Highland cattle and men-of-war remained deeply entrenched, particularly in the north country and in Scotland; while in London and the south of England the taste of the wealthy collectors continued to favour eighteenth-century portraits of pretty women and children by Romney, Hoppner, Gainsborough and Reynolds. As Oliver Brown wrote,[2] 'English taste, otherwise, favoured illustrative and literary subject

[1] See page 49, note 1. [2] Much of the information which follows, and all the quoted excerpts, are taken from his seminal, but largely forgotten, *Exhibition, the Memoirs of Oliver Brown*, of 1968.

matter', and Brown recounts that when he walked home through Kensington at the end of his working day he 'used to see through the windows of the tall houses pictures hung in three or four rows almost to the ceiling'.

The first stirrings for something different were fostered by the famous Durand-Ruel Exhibition of Post-Impressionists at the Grafton Gallery in 1905. The favourite painters among visitors appeared to be Monet and Sisley, while the Leicester Galleries themselves made some impact with an exhibition of the work of Eugène Boudin in 1906, followed by a second Boudin exhibition in 1909, though this also included the work of Stanislas Lépine. Boudin, Brown says understandably, was regarded 'as the link between the men of Barbizon and the Impressionists', though the pictures Boudin painted around 1870 were not easy to sell in 1906 'because of what were then considered the ridiculous and hideous old costumes'.

At the time of which Brown is writing most galleries were interested simply in dealing and not in the staging of public exhibitions of the works of a single painter, at which some examples of his work could be bought. In fact, one-man shows were exceptional, and the Leicester Galleries had little competition in this area, as museums did not mount such shows (and there was no Arts Council: only the Winter Exhibitions at the Royal Academy).

Brown used the auction rooms as one of his alternative sources of supply of paintings. He makes the interesting and highly valid point that before the last war these were regarded by dealers as places for finding bargains. The point is underlined by his comment that after the death of collectors – particularly of more modern pictures – relatives and executors were often dismayed by the poor results obtained by sending such pictures to public auctions. Famous Old Masters might make higher prices, 'but the moderns and living English artists brought such small totals that they were little help to poor relatives, and none at all to estates that were threatened with high death duties'.

A good example of the sort of collection that might sometimes come the way of a dealer was that of James Staats Forbes, who had occasionally visited the Leicester Galleries in his quest for pictures. When he died he left some four thousand of them. They were stored at Victoria Station, for Forbes was Chairman of the London, Chatham and Dover Railway. The Galleries were allowed by the executors to pick out pictures as and when they felt that they could sell them. In fact, a number of special exhibitions and sales were arranged, including one of a hundred fine Jean François Millet drawings, another of water-colours by Henri Harpignies, a combined assembly of works by Corot, Daubigny, Rousseau, Diaz and Jacques, and another of Crome, Stark, Bonington, Cotman and the Norwich School. Many of the pictures went to museums, including both the British Museum and the National Gallery in Dublin.

Another interesting point Oliver Brown makes was how uncommercially minded most of his early clients were. Edwardian collectors, in contrast to the impression Galsworthy gave of Soames Forsyte, 'seemed to be uninfluenced by the commercial aspect of the picture market and did not think of their collections as a property or investment. Indeed it was a delicate matter to ask our clients to sell a picture and they were sometimes offended. If they favoured only "costly" pictures it was for "snobbish" reasons and not as an investment. In these present times picture collectors are sometimes the shrewdest picture dealers of all.'

It was after the first world war that Brown began to get into his stride with the showing of the work of French painters. He sought the advice of Michael Sadleir, author, publisher and diligent collector (and son of another). Sadleir advised staging a one-man show of a *living* artist, and their choice fell upon Henri Matisse, even though the latter's work had been criticised particularly vituperatively when it was on show at the Grafton Gallery in 1910 and 1912. The exhibition was held in 1919. Most of the paintings came from Paris. The artist himself lent some of the pictures and came over to London. Pictures to the tune of more than £5000 were sold: a considerable sum at the time. No one was more surprised than Matisse himself. Brown commented: 'his surprise was tinged with amusement: "Ils sont foux–les Anglais!" he cried when he saw us putting red spots on the frames'. Collectors who bought examples of Matisse's work were Brandon Davis, a South African, Sir Michael Sadler (the adviser's father, who was Master of University College, Oxford), Maynard Keynes, George Eumorfopoulos and Walter Taylor, a rich artist friend of Sickert's (whose own work the Leicester Galleries often showed, but only rarely with success). A smaller exhibition of terracotta sculptures by Aristide Maillol was put on show together with the Matisse paintings.

An exhibition of works by Picasso in 1921 was a bold step but not a great financial success. Both the public and the critics were puzzled. But another in 1922 of paintings, drawings and pastels by Degas did rather better, though Brown muses somewhat sadly how low most of the prices were. The whole of Degas' little-known sculpture was shown in the following year.

Another show in 1922 was of the work of Lucien Pissarro, son of Camille. The results of this were encouraging. But the biggest coup was yet to come. Oliver Brown heard through a visitor to the Galleries that a great number of paintings by Vincent van Gogh were in the possession of the widow of Vincent's brother, Theo. He asked her why she had never shown a selection in England. 'Nobody', she replied, 'has ever asked me.' A little later Brown visited Amsterdam. Mme van Gogh Bonger was ill, so Vincent's nephew, V. W. van Gogh, received him. After lunch in the city, Brown writes, 'he took me to his little house in a suburb of the town. The walls in every room were crowded with his famous uncle's pictures. I was astonished to find so many together. Nearly all of them were for sale, save for a few to be retained if possible for Holland. Even in the bathroom upstairs I noticed several canvases propped between the bath and the wall. It looked as if two exhibitions would be possible and I found it difficult to make a choice for the first, but I finally selected about forty pictures and drawings. They included what are now world-famous masterpieces. Among the paintings were: 'A pair of boots',

Paris, 1887; 'Park at Asnières', 1887 (at Asnières van Gogh met Seurat and this picture shows a slight influence); 'The Postman', Arles, 1888 (the postman was Roulin who became van Gogh's affectionate friend at Arles and whose wife nursed van Gogh when he became seriously ill); 'Orchard in Arles', 1888; '*Berceuse*', 1888–89; 'Vincent's bedroom in Arles', 1888; 'The Sunflower', Arles 1888 (probably the best of his seven 'Sunflowers'); 'The Yellow Chair', Arles, 1888; 'The Bridge of Arles', 1888; 'The Zouave', Arles, 1888; 'The Olive Orchard', Saint Remy, 1889; and 'The Cornfield with Rooks', Auvers, 1889.'

The exhibition was a great success, though in the end more of the paintings were bought by foreign dealers than by English collectors.

By July 1924 the Leicester Galleries had assembled between seventy and eighty works by Paul Gauguin, and though this artist was virtually unknown in England, the exhibition caused a great public stir. It contained a number of Gauguin's paintings of Tahiti, and the extent and patience of Brown's search for this artist's work in every medium demonstrated just how creative the perceptive scholarship of the gifted dealer can be.

A year later he staged an extensive Cézanne exhibition (the artist had died in 1906). Cézanne had never had a great following in England. D. S. MacColl scorned his work. Roger Fry championed it. Only Samuel Courtauld bought it. Even in France the work of Cézanne had not been widely appreciated until Vollard organised an exhibition of some 150 works in 1895. But in London, Cézanne was widely discussed in the press at the time of the exhibition and praise began to be lavished on his work. It was another tribute to the efforts of the Leicester Galleries.

The works of French painters, both living and recently dead, of a lesser stature than the greatest masters also figured in exhibitions. Thus in 1926, paintings by Marie Laurencin and Odilon Redon were shown and in the summer of 1927 Brown first exhibited the work of Armand Guillaumin and then a collective exhibition, which had the blessing of the French authorities, of works by Dérain, Marquet, Friesz, Vlaminck, Dufy, Matisse, Vuillard, Forain, Bonnard and Despiau.

Another great milestone in 1926 was a Renoir exhibition. Brown felt that his Galleries had never looked so beautiful as when the walls were covered with Renoir canvases, but he 'was forced to conclude at that time that there was some quality in Renoir's painting that did not appeal to English taste', and there were relatively few sales. A second and third van Gogh exhibition also took place about this time, but although in the final exhibition the pictures were no less powerful than on the earlier occasions, they were not for sale and this appeared to act as a deterrent upon public interest.

Brown's love for sculpture resulted in an endless series of exhibitions of it, which were by no means common at the time. The list of artists was again highly distinguished. It included Rodin, Epstein, Maillol, Bourdelle, Zadkine and a little later Henry Moore, but collectors, though enthusiastic, often had difficulty in knowing where to put the sculptures they had acquired.

The early thirties saw 'a serious change of the taste in a section of the public. There was a revived interest in the not very remote past. In spite of the wave of excitement caused by modern painting and sculpture, the hitherto despised Victorian age began to fascinate a number of people.' What appeared to interest the public was not the Pre-Raphaelites but the paintings that showed actual life in the nineteenth century. This emerged particularly well in the work of painters like James Tissot, and an exhibition of his work was shown in 1933. A French equivalent was Constantin Guys, the long-lived painter and illustrator (1802–1892), who had produced such charming studies of horses.

One of the last exhibitions in this great tradition of showing the work of trend-setters was that of the work of Marc Chagall in 1934, but financially the results were modest once again.

We have dwelt rather on the exhibitions of continental painters, but the Leicester Galleries were equally perceptive in the work being shown of living English artists, many of whom reached great eminence later. In the earlier days they included Max Beerbohm, Sickert, Wilson Steer, Robert Bevan and Wyndham Lewis, and later on such well-known names as Mark Gertler, Barbara Hepworth, Ivon Hitchens, Paul and John Nash, Stanley Spencer, Augustus John, Matthew Smith, Graham Sutherland, John Piper and Ben Nicolson.

Thus the importance of the Leicester Galleries as a formative influence on English taste for and during the period described was very great, and the pleasure given to collectors was enormous. Like other great social institutions of our time such as the Webbs, Sir Thomas Beecham, Lord Reith and *Picture Post*, it was simply taken for granted during its heyday *because it was there*. Without its endeavours some of the major collections of the last forty years would never have been formed, and without their subsequent dispersal our museums would now be a great deal poorer in examples of French art of the nineteenth and twentieth centuries, and of English art of the last fifty years. Probably the value of Oliver Brown's slightly shapeless recollections will only be appreciated when some 'researcher' has produced a detailed and indigestible analysis of the contents of all the Leicester Galleries' exhibitions.

Since the last war the degree of specialisation among collectors has become even more marked. Glass, silver, porcelain, furniture–for each there is a multitude of enthusiasts. Overlapping, 'polymorph' collections have become exceptional, though what does stand out in the occasional exhibitions all over the country of newly-formed collections is how often a husband and wife team up to collect *together*, complementing each other's taste or developing a shared discernment. One of the most interesting examples of this is the small but very fine collection of Old Masters brought together by Sir John and Lady Heathcote Amory.[1] A rather

[1] Shown publicly for the first time in King's Lynn in 1965. The collection was formed with the help of the dealer Geoffrey Agnew. In his Foreword to the catalogue he recounts the following delightful exchange: 'Sir John Amory said "I've always wanted to know more about pictures. Will

earlier example was the Daisy Linda Ward collection of Dutch still lives, which was lodged with the Ashmolean Museum as early as 1940, and finally bequeathed to the museum by Mr T. W. H. Ward in memory of his wife in 1948.

When such collections become known beyond the circle of friends and acquaintances of the collectors, it has usually been due to enthusiastic directors of provincial museums, who have shown selections from such collections in their museums for a limited time. Two museums where this practice has been particularly rewarding are the Bristol Museum[1] and the Manchester City Art Gallery.[2]

Perhaps the last word should go to Sir Karl Parker, who said: 'The twentieth century ought to be looked at in quite a different light, because standards of taste and availability changed so completely and there are many collections formed in the last thirty years, the importance of which has yet to be assessed.' Any survey which embraces the activities of such diverse collectors as Queen Mary and Mrs Nellie Ionides, Sir Edward Marsh and Sir Roland Penrose, Somerset Maugham and William Cargill, Douglas Cooper and Paul Mellon can be at best only sketchy. Money alone is never enough. 'Going for a song', one of the most popular television programmes of recent years, involves the accurate identification of antiques of every kind both by amateur collectors and by experts. This programme has shown an enormously wide public that almost anything old and certainly anything beautiful has a market valuation. Yet, though it has greatly increased the general appreciation of antiques, it has also highlighted the uncertainty that confronts collectors when they 'find' something and has shown that collecting is not merely a question of expectable expenditure. Despite the huge increase in values and prices that daunts the man who collected before the war and still does today, connoisseurship, recognition of quality, a constancy of vision and the seeing eye are as important as ever to the true collector.

FRANK HERRMANN

you show us something really great, really out of the ordinary, just to mark the difference?" As it happened, I had recently bought the Metsu from the Cook Collection and had half promised it to a collector in Holland. I produced it and there was a long silence. "What's that worth?" said Sir John eventually. I told him and there was another silence. Then, meditatively, came the answer, "Well, I could always sell a farm." We all protested, explained that such a picture would not hang with what he had already bought, suggested waiting, thinking it over, seeing other pictures on another occasion. But the answer was firm – "I couldn't live without it now that I've seen it."

[1] An example is the collection of pictures, furniture, silver and pottery collected by Mr and Mrs. R. C. Pritchard, which was shown in 1968.

[2] Thus the delightful collection of modern paintings of Dr H. Rowland was shown here in 1962. Dr Rowland commented: 'I am not tired, as so many are nowadays, of the subject picture, nor afraid of sentiment. I am fond of the poetic element in pictures and of colour that sings. I also enjoy the type of abstract art which draws its inspiration from the visual world and retains an evocative quality. And I expect a positive attitude to man and life.' It is not often that a collector expresses his outlook so concisely.

SIR KARL PARKER · SURVEY OF A RECENT STEWARDSHIP[1]

By now it will have become increasingly clear to the reader that the last word in collecting today very often rests with the official collector, the museum curator. Although in this country he is constantly hampered by a lack of funds, when the really exceptional work of art appears on the market the odds are usually in his favour. In the United States, this is even more strongly the case. But the discerning official collector had really remarkable opportunities to exercise his skill ahead of vogue and fashion during the period from 1931[2] to 1954. In the fantastic scramble for outstanding works of art and antiques today it is all too easy to overlook those fifteen lean years for the art trade. Few official collectors spent the limited funds at their disposal more wisely than Sir Karl Parker on behalf of the Ashmolean Museum in Oxford. As the piece which follows also shows, the generosity of collectors towards a museum which they hold in high esteem has continued unabated in more recent times.

From 'Sir Karl Parker and the Ashmolean' by J. Byam Shaw and Ian Robertson, *Burlington Magazine*, October, 1962.

On 1 October Sir Karl Parker retires from Oxford after twenty-eight years' service, first as Keeper of the Department of Fine Art (now Department of Western Art) in the Ashmolean Museum, and from 1945 as Keeper of the Museum as a whole. An exhibition arranged by his staff in the department, during Sir Karl's absence on special leave, has drawn attention in the museum to the quality, variety, and extent of the acquisitions made during his Keepership; but it will not be superfluous to review, for a wider public, what may be called without exaggeration one of the great achievements of modern museum history. In doing so, the writers hope to avoid the flavour of an obituary notice; for friends and admirers are still expecting the fruits of Sir Karl Parker's great range of artistic and historical interest.

[1] Or, 'Making a little go a long way!'

[2] In the history of *Agnew's* (printed privately, 1967) Geoffrey Agnew writes: '. . . the autumn of 1931 . . . was a grim juncture at which to become a picture dealer, even for someone who had never wanted to be anything else. For three months, except for a sprinkling of visitors to a modern exhibition, some personal friends and an occasional "runner" with a picture under his arm (but even he soon became discouraged) hardly a visitor came in, certainly none with the intention of buying. . . . For the second time in its existence the firm was on the point of foundering. . . . Debts had accumulated, sales were non-existent, to buy was out of the question.'

When he took over the department in 1934, the new Keeper's name was chiefly associated with the study of the drawings of the old masters. His early publications on German and Swiss drawings had quickly drawn the attention of continental scholars (and also of one great English scholar, Campbell Dodgson, at the British Museum), and he had already published the first serious work on the drawings of Antoine Watteau. Above all, the quarterly publication, *Old Master Drawings*, was begun under his editorship in 1926, when he was at the British Museum, and by 1934 had a high reputation. It was, therefore, to be expected that on finding himself in a position to make the acquisitions of his choice, in a museum which was already a treasure-house of drawings by Michelangelo and Raphael, and contained the Douce and Chambers Hall Collections, he should make the most of his special connoisseurship and buy drawings. The final result of this could not be more than indicated, for lack of space, in the recent exhibition at Oxford. But the two volumes already published of the Ashmolean catalogue of drawings (Continental schools other than Italian in 1938, and Italian in 1956) tell the tale plainly enough: including the English schools–where no less important acquisitions have been made but not yet catalogued in print–well over 3000 drawings have been added to the collection during Parker's term of office.

These include examples of early masters who have always been famous and relatively expensive to buy–Rogier van der Weyden, Lucas van Leyden, Dürer, Holbein, Giovanni Bellini, Filippino Lippi, even Raphael; and of some later draughtsmen–Rembrandt and Watteau for example–whose works have generally commanded high prices. Somehow these were acquired, mostly by purchase, occasionally by gift, by seizing an opportunity when it occurred. But no less remarkable was Parker's success in building up the background of the picture, by the purchase of drawings by masters not previously represented, by concentrating on groups of drawings by one distinguished hand, and by anticipating–or perhaps setting–a fashion for a particular draughtsman. Splendid examples of Parmigianino were gathered in, long before that master began to attract four-figure prices in the saleroom; Guercino, Bernini, and the Tiepolos before the rest of us were quite awake to their importance; Samuel Palmer, before he became a bone of contention among the richest collectors; and David Wilkie, when he could still be got for small money. No school was neglected, from the early Germans to the French Impressionists, so far as the money would go.

The years from 1934 to 1945 or so were lean years for the art trade, and those collectors who were devoted enough to search for things, and buy them, had their reward. There has been nothing secretive about Parker's method of collecting–although this was ungenerously suggested by the writer of an otherwise valuable review of the second volume of the Ashmolean catalogue, who complained that no information was given as to the immediate provenance of many recent acquisitions. In fact, he simply cast his net wide, and was assiduous in his visits to the most likely fishing-grounds. Other museum officials might have done the same in this respect. But one advantage, apart from his own perceptive judgement, Parker certainly enjoyed over the majority of his colleagues: he was given a free hand, within the limits of his resources, by the Visitors of the Ashmolean, to take what he wanted on the spot. It was not necessary for him to refer individual purchases for approval to any superior authority; he had simply to justify his policy in the Visitors' Annual Report. This Report, for the years 1934 to 1962, is a striking testimonial to the success of the Oxford system.

In 1934, 236 drawings were acquired by purchase; 210 in 1950; in several years more than 100, and in no year less than fifty; not counting various albums and sketch-books, such as that of Palma Giovane acquired in 1954. Out of a purchasing grant of less than £2000, plus somewhat less than that in certain funds specifically bequeathed for the benefit of the Fine Art Department, one might suppose that not much would be left for buying pictures. But in that field, where prices are proportionately higher, the tale is equally astonishing. The Tallard *Madonna*, bought in 1949, and attributed by many authorities to Giorgione himself, heads the list of a very distinguished group of Italian paintings, which includes the important *Christ disputing with the Doctors* of Jacopo Bassano (1935), a Paolo Veronese (1952), and a rare Bernini (1950); a beautiful Barocci sketch, in oil on paper (1942); and, among later masters, Solimena, Pellegrini, and Pittoni, all at their best. Of other schools, there are an exquisite *Madonna* by Morales (1954), the Terbrugghen *Bagpiper* (1944), and a small landscape by Samuel Palmer (1947).

These are a few of many which might have been expected, even at the dates when they were acquired, to be beyond the means of a university museum. And to these must be added some important paintings (Montagna, Poussin) presented by the National Art-Collections Fund at the Keeper's suggestion; and still more, both paintings and drawings, acquired by bequest or private gift: from Mrs Weldon, Mr G. O. Farrer, Mr Ward, Mr Hindley Smith, Mr Campbell Dodgson, Sir Bernard Eckstein, Lord Donoughmore, and others; and particularly, in more recent years, from Dr Grete Ring, from the family of Camille Pissarro, and from Mr F. F. Madan. Not least among practical benefactors, in his unobtrusive way, has been Sir Karl Parker himself. Many drawings of interest, and some of high importance and value, have been presented by him to the department in the course of his Keepership: among them fine examples of Francesco Guardi and Domenico Tiepolo, a Guercino, a John Raphael Smith, and a splendid Urs Graf, a great rarity in England, bequeathed to him personally by Henry Oppenheimer, whose collection he knew so well. The last two were generous gifts indeed from one to whom the Ashmolean Museum and the University of Oxford were to owe so much in so many other respects. Such gifts and bequests, apart from the Keeper's own contributions, were no doubt often due to the courtesy and advice which he invariably offered to visitors; and they extended to other fields besides paintings and drawings. The collection of musical instruments bequeathed by Mr Alfred and Mr Arthur Hill in 1939, and the ivories, enamels, watches, and other *objets d'art* left to the museum by Mr Francis Mallett or given by his daughter, Miss Elizabeth Mallett, have added treasures which very few other museums in this country can boast; while as a result of the Farrer, Carter and Conway bequests and gift, the Ashmolean collection of English plate has within fifteen years become one of the best in the country. To attract benefactions, without importunate begging, is not the least of services which a keeper or director can render to his museum; and those we have referred to specifically here represent only a part of all that has accrued in this way during the last twenty-eight years. But even in these wider fields, Sir Karl has not been content to rely on benefactions, and has taken opportunities of buying sculpture and bronzes not unworthy of the standard set at the Ashmolean by the Fortnum Collection.

FILLING THE GAPS

We saw earlier that one of the first exponents of systematic purchasing to fill gaps in a museum collection was Dr Waagen. Museums in this country too had soon learned this but were usually hampered by the lack of available funds. Sir John Rothenstein, until recently Director of the Tate Gallery, here describes the particularly exhilarating–and probably unique–results of an official shopping spree on the Continent soon after the end of the second world war.

Extracted from John Rothenstein's
Brave Day, Hideous Night, 1966.

During the war and its immediate aftermath another of the Tate's three constituent collections–that of Modern Foreign painting–also suffered relative neglect. Since communication between Britain and the Continent was severed no foreign paintings were imported. Nevertheless, thanks to bequests, gifts and the careful expenditure of our tiny resources,[1] the Modern Foreign collection did not stand still. Between the beginning of the war and the end of 1948 we had acquired examples, in certain instances outstanding examples, of the work of Utrillo, Ernst, Munch, Matisse, Lautrec, Vuillard, Modigliani, Cézanne, Chagall, Bonnard, Kokoschka, Rouault, Gris, Morandi, and four Klees, one a gift and a group of three purchased for £290. But in 1949 it was decided to concentrate upon some of the most urgent requirements of the Foreign collection.

Not long after the reopening of the entire Gallery in the February of that year I went to Paris for the purpose of assembling for the consideration of the Board a group of works

[1] It should be pointed out that although the Tate Gallery was opened in 1887, it had no official purchase grant until 1946! The initial sum given then was only £2000.

by artists in whom they had expressed a special interest. I visited Léger, Giacometti, Laurens, Mme Lipschitz and other artists and their representatives. On several visits I went with Douglas Cooper, whose knowledge of Paris and Parisian painters and sculptors, which greatly exceeded my own, was most useful. I recall one incident that illustrates the minuteness of his knowledge. Looking through Léger's paintings I was much impressed by 'Feuilles et Coquillages' and I asked Léger if he had a photograph of it. 'I'm afraid not,' replied Léger. Douglas Cooper, who was looking through some drawings on the far side of the studio, observed, without turning his head, 'Right hand pile of photographs under the table by the window; the fourth from the top.' There indeed it was. It was an enjoyable visit; Léger and Douglas Cooper were in friendly accord and Léger was continually pleased and amused by the detailed knowledge of his work displayed by 'Dooglass'.

At a special meeting held in August I submitted this set of paintings and sculptures to the Trustees.[1] I shall not easily forget the looks of delighted dazzlement on the faces of the Trustees as they came in and looked at the paintings that covered the walls of the Board Room and the sculpture standing about. They comprised some thirty extremely fine works by Picasso, Gris, Dufy, Matisse, Rouault, Braque, Léger, Vlaminck, Giacometti, Brancusi, Lipschitz, Bourdelle, Despiau, Renoir. It was decided to buy 'Femme nue assise' by Picasso, 'Notre-Dame' by Matisse, 'L'Italienne' by Rouault, 'Feuilles et Coquillages' by Léger, 'Interior' and 'Man Seated' by Giacometti (the two together, if my memory serves, cost little over £100) and 'La Guitare Jaune' by Gris. (It subsequently appeared that the price of this last was £3000 and not £2500 as had been supposed, and the Board decided not to buy it.) The two Giacomettis, the artist later told me, he believed to be the first examples of his painting to enter a public collection.

Among Trustees of highly individual character and strong convictions unanimity, let alone unanimity of enthusiasm, must be an uncommon occurrence. I long looked back to the pervasive enthusiasm and good will which on that August afternoon was given such unanimous and unreserved expression–more especially in times, not so very far ahead, when enthusiasm had been forgotten and replaced by other and very different emotions. At the same meeting the Board also welcomed a further bequest of eight splendid Blakes as a gift of the Trustees of Graham Robertson.[2] About the same time they acquired

[1] Rothenstein's comments on the traditional character of museum Trustees in this country is interesting: 'The years of my directorship saw several changes, some of them regrettable, in the qualities deemed relevant to the making of a good Trustee. In the past Trustees had, as often as not, been members of the aristocracy, who still embodied an uneroded tradition of public service: they gave their services as a duty of their station; by education, training and class ethos they were highly disinterested; in the way of social advancement or personal aggrandisement they had nothing, of course, to gain from being Trustees of the Tate. They tended also to be men of mature years.' He might also have added that many Trustees were collectors in their own right.

[2] Graham Robertson was one of the most remarkable artist/collectors of recent times. In 1939 he had written to Rothenstein as follows: 'I am looking round to find a place of safety for my London pictures and it has occurred to me that, as some of them are dedicated to the Tate Gallery in my will, you might care to take charge of them. For instance, the set of 9 large colour-printed designs by William Blake which you admired much at my house–'Elohim creating Adam', 'Hecate', 'Newton', 'The Good and Evil Angels', 'Nebuchadnezzar', 'The Court of Death', 'Lamech', 'Pity', and 'Elijah in the Chariot of Fire'–Blake's most important pictures and the very

Picasso's 'Buste de Femme', Chagall's 'Bouquet of Flying Lovers' and two bronzes by Degas. Negotiations were begun and completed the following year for the purchase –for about £3500–of Renoir's two most ambitious bronzes 'Venus Victrix' and 'La Laveuse', which I had first seen and coveted on my visit to Paris shortly after the Liberation.

In 1949 and for some time later the most conspicuous additions were those made to the Modern Foreign collection. Although we were aware of the increase in the prices of works of art, in particular those of nineteenth- and twentieth-century continental masters, I do not believe that we foresaw quite how spectacular this was to become. However that may be, we did in fact avail ourselves of the last chance afforded to a Gallery of such severely limited resources as the Tate to buy a group of paintings and sculpture which, only a very few years later, would have been infinitely beyond our reach.

The two cubist Picassos, the Matisse Landscape, the Rouault, the Léger, and the two Giacomettis bought at the August meeting cost the Gallery, I think, less than £9000. In fact a considerably smaller sum was paid not only for this group of paintings, but for all the other purchases of foreign works made between 1938 and 1952 than would, only a few years later, have sufficed to buy Picasso's 'Femme nue assise', bought on that afternoon for £3250.

THE NEED FOR MORE

Such splendid accretions as the one described in the last extract were all too rare. A few years later, the introduction to an annual Tate Gallery report–presumably the author was again Sir John Rothenstein–bemoaned the enormous increase in prices of pictures, while purchase funds had remained virtually unchanged. The whole piece demonstrates rather well another facet of the viewpoint so commonly expressed, that all good things are disappearing from the private sector of the art

flower of his work. I am rising 74 and pretty shaky, and the return of peace is not likely to find me here so–if you cared to find a harbour of refuge for these pictures–I could present them to the Tate at once. I have also willed to your gallery Rossetti's 'Proserpine' (the best of his studies from Mrs Morris), Whistler's 'Valparaiso', my portrait by Sargent, Melville's 'Venetian Night' and my grandmother's portrait by Andrew Geddes. I don't know if you could manage to protect these also, or if there are any among them which you would not care to include in the collection. Perhaps you could let me have a line to tell me your wishes so that I may–if necessary–make other arrangements.

3 Sept. 1939'

The pictures were evacuated to safety with the rest of the Tate Collection during the war.

market. But here the *official* collector is seeing his chances slipping because of the greater wealth of many more recently established museums, particularly, of course, those in the United States.

EXTRACTED FROM *The Tate Gallery: Report of the Trustees,* 1961–2.

A CONSTANT theme of these reports has been that the sadly thin representation of modern foreign art in British collections, both public and private, is serious enough to be treated as a national artistic emergency. The twentieth century has been a period of exceptional inventiveness and daring and will certainly be regarded as one of the turning points in the history of visual arts. Yet, in all the other public galleries in Great Britain there is not a single early Cubist picture; only three or four examples of Surrealism; and no paintings at all by such famous twentieth-century artists as Gris, Miro, Chagall, Soutine, Kandinsky, Mondrian and Delaunay, to name only a few. These Galleries are, of course, much stronger in their collections of modern British painting, but it has to be admitted that British painters have so far played only a minor role in this visual revolution of the twentieth century. The number of twentieth-century foreign works in British private collections which might be given or bequeathed to the nation is also very small by comparison with those in other countries; in fact there are probably more major twentieth century French paintings in private collections in, for example, the city of St Louis, Missouri, than in all the private collections in Great Britain put together.

This general poverty throughout the country in works of a most important period makes it doubly necessary that the Tate should make a special effort to acquire such works to fill the gaps in the central national collection of twentieth-century painting. For example the Tate still has no works by such well-known artists as Mondrian, Marquet, Vlaminck, Villon, Feininger, Nolde, Kirchner, Franz Marc, Beckmann, Dali, Boccioni, Severini, Barlach and Gonzalez. In the last ten years there has been such a striking increase in public interest in modern art in this country that the Trustees believe it to be more than ever in the public interest that this state of affairs within the national collection of modern art should be specifically dealt with and made good.

A high proportion of the masterpieces of the first half of this century are already in museums abroad or are promised to one or other of them; the demand for those which remain in private hands therefore increases. This is especially true of works marking some of the most epoch-making phases, which may only have lasted for a few years and of which the number of examples is accordingly limited. Foremost amongst these is analytical Cubism, which culminated in the years 1909–12; a phase of crucial importance in the history of modern art, the significance of which was widely recognised in other countries with the result that most of the finest examples are already enshrined in their museums.

Though at the start of this year the Gallery's collection contained two analytical Cubist paintings by Picasso of 1909–10, there was no early work by the co-founder of Cubism, Georges Braque, who was represented in the Gallery only by three pictures dating from 1925–27. When therefore an opportunity arose during the year of buying a fine analytical Cubist Braque of 1909–11, 'Still Life with Fish', the Trustees decided that every effort should be made to secure it. About the same time a large recent Braque of 1952, 'The Bench', came up for sale, a work which would have filled another serious chronological gap in the collection. The Treasury was therefore asked for a special grant towards the purchase of these two works, one early and one late; but unfortunately, because of the economic crisis the Trustees were told that no special grant could be made. When the Trustees repeated how particularly important to the collection they considered the 'Still Life with Fish' to be, and urged the Treasury to reconsider its decision, the Chancellor felt himself unable to do more towards meeting the price of this picture than to advance £19,000 from the following year's purchase grant. It was accordingly bought by the Gallery, the rest of the price coming out of the current year's grant.

The Trustees naturally regretted having to dip so deeply in advance into the purchase grant for 1962–63, but they considered that the importance of the picture to the Gallery was such as to warrant this exceptional measure, even while they regarded it as a precedent to be deplored. It is of interest that the cost of this painting was well over three-quarters of the total sum which the Gallery now receives as an annual purchase grant. A purchase so disproportionate, financed entirely out of the 'normal' funds, has of course obliged the Trustees to neglect other excellent possible additions to the collection which will meanwhile themselves become more expensive.

SIR WILLIAM BURRELL'S PURCHASE BOOKS (1911-1957)

OUR final excerpt describes the means by which one of the last great collectors[1] in the grand manner kept records of his purchases. Even though they only begin in 1911–many years after Sir William started collecting–such records kept personally by a collector are rare indeed. Sir William Burrell died in 1958 at the age of 96. The source of his wealth was shipping and he was known to have sold a fleet of some thirty vessels after the first world war. He lived, from 1927, at

[1] For the purists it should be stated that though Sir William was born and spent his life in Scotland, his family was of Northumberland descent.

Hutton Castle, outside Berwick-on-Tweed, and this housed as furnishings much of his enormous accumulation of early stained and painted glass; sculpture; woodwork and furniture; a superb collection of Gothic tapestries and over seven hundred and fifty paintings and drawings. These include a few early Italian, German and Flemish paintings, some seventeenth- and eighteenth-century pictures (chiefly Dutch and British) and an outstanding assembly of nineteenth-century French pictures. There were also quantities of Egyptian and other antiquities, much European silver and glass and a collection of over one hundred pre-T'ang examples of Chinese pottery and a much larger number of T'ang, Sung and Ch'ing pieces of stoneware and porcelain. Sir William gave this enormous collection of *objets d'art* to the City of Glasgow in 1944. He also gave £450,000 towards the building of a special gallery to house his collection. It has proved difficult to meet the stipulations for the siting of this museum, but it now seems likely that plans for it will mature in the middle seventies. The author of the piece that follows is the first Keeper of the Burrell Collection.

TAKEN FROM an article of the same title by William Wells in *The Scottish Art Review*, Vol. IX, No. 2, 1963.

THE discovery at Hutton Castle last summer of the twenty-eight note books in which Sir William recorded additions to his Collection between 1911 and 1957 has made an invaluable addition to the meagre information contained in the inventories.

The aim of the latter was to list the collection under thirty-one different categories (paintings, tapestries, stained glass, etc.) with a number, title, size and insurance value. Clearly there was no point in repeating in the inventories all the additional facts and theories about each object which he had already copied into the notebooks at the time of purchase–at least there would have been no point if the two records had been cross-referenced.

Unfortunately, this is not the case, and before the notebooks can be made use of fully it is necessary to scrutinise each entry and if possible provide it with the correct inventory number, a task that has hitherto only been completed for the books covering the years from 1934 onward and which becomes progressively more difficult for the earlier books. Clearly, Sir William became more and more aware of the value of documentation as the years went by and of the difficulty of distinguishing one object from others of a similar kind if the descriptions in the purchase books omitted, as they tend to do in the earliest of them, the basic facts such as size.

Apart, however, from the information they provide about specific acquisitions, the purchase books reveal as nothing else could Sir William's methods of collecting, and the breathtaking scale of his expenditure on works of art which probably exceeded on average £20,000 a year during the half-century or so he kept records, or at any rate, records that have survived.

Perhaps one day purchase books covering the period prior to 1911 will come to light, for obviously he did not begin collecting in that year. He was in fact in possession of quite a considerable collection by 1901, the year of Glasgow's International Exhibition, when he lent over one hundred and sixty works of art including pictures by Géricault, Daumier, and Manet, as well as tapestries, stained glass, Persian carpets, furniture, metalwork, and carvings in wood and ivory to the big loan exhibition held in the newly opened Art Gallery and Museum at Kelvingrove. A number of these loans can be recognised in old photographs of the interior of his house at No. 8 Great Western Terrace where the walls of the dining room were lined with six fifteenth- and early sixteenth-century Franco-Flemish tapestries, all of which still form part of the Burrell Collection.

There is then no certain indication whether the earliest entries in the purchase books continue the rhythm of collecting established in previous years or represent a lull in Sir William's collecting ardour. If they are the first records of the kind he kept it may be assumed they indicate a new seriousness of purpose, a change perhaps from collecting for pleasure to collecting with some distant end in view. However this may be, his purchases during the first years were quite modest and chiefly confined to Chinese pottery and bronzes. The first recorded picture purchases occur in 1915 when he bought the Master of the Brunswick Diptych *Annunciation*, Le Nain's *Peasant Children*, the School of Lorraine *Ecce Homo*, together with twenty-three Chinese ceramics and bronzes and two paintings by Eckhout and La Croce for a total expenditure of £1172.

During the following ten years or so the highest sums Sir William spent each year were almost always for pictures and it was during this period that he acquired most of his paintings by French masters of the nineteenth century. In 1926, for example, he purchased Daumier's *Le Meunier, sons fils et l'âne*, Degas' *La Répétition* and Manet's *Au Café*.

From 1927 and onward for about an equal period of time pictures were ousted by tapestries and for many of these he was prepared to pay larger sums. In 1927, for example, he bought the large fifteenth-century Franco-Flemish tapestry called *The Vintagers* and on two other occasions he spent five-figure sums on tapestries. In 1937 he spent more on the fifteenth-century tapestry called *The Betrothal and Marriage* than on either Degas' *Jockeys sous la Pluie* or Cézanne's *Maison de Zola*, bought the same year.

During the following ten years Sir William's major purchases become unpredictable: 1939, set of three early seventeenth-century silver gilt steeple cups; 1940, the Dietrichstein Persian carpet; 1941, the Richard de Bury chest; 1942, Joseph Crawhall's *The Flower Shop*; 1943, a Chinese famille noire vase; 1944, a Chinese stone seated Lohan; 1945, early sixteenth-century Franco-Flemish tapestry of open-air banquet; 1946, Rembrandt's Self Portrait of 1632; 1947, fifteenth-century Franco-Flemish tapestry from Alexander set; 1948, Frans Hals' *Portrait of a Man*. The last mentioned, a three-quarter length portrait by Hals from Nonsuch Park where it had been discovered in the proverbial attic and shown in the Hals exhibition at Haarlem in 1957, was, incidentally, the most expensive purchase that Sir William ever made.

From 1947 onward Sir William, who was then in his eighty-sixth year, began to explore what was for him an almost totally new field and most of his purchases during these last ten years of his life were of Egyptian, Greek, Mesopotamian and Persian antiquities. His last major purchase was made in April 1957 when he bought an Urartian bronze head of a bull from Toprak Kale. By this time he was unable to make his own entries in the purchase books and from March of that year additions were recorded by a scribe.

Using the major acquisitions as a criterion, it is clear that Sir William's purchasing during the period covered by the purchase books was dominated by successive master interests, but in actual fact, with the exception of the final period when he was chiefly buying early civilisation antiquities, he was adding to all parts of the collection almost continuously. There was, for example, hardly a year in which he did not add to the collection of Chinese pottery and porcelain rising to a peak in the 1940s when, during four successive years, he acquired annually well over a hundred pieces. The Chinese bronzes were acquired more intermittently during the same long period; the acquisition of Chinese jades, on the other hand, was almost entirely concentrated within a few years (1946–51). The Persian carpets were mostly acquired prior to 1941; the Persian pottery almost entirely after 1945. The collections of English needlework, furniture, silver and glassware were spread out over many years and this also applies to the collections of European medieval wood, metal and stonework. The purchase books account for only a limited portion of the stained glass, the majority of which was presumably acquired prior to 1911.

In so far as expenditure is a guide, Sir William's annus mirabilis was clearly 1936 when he made over one hundred and fifty additions to the Collection which he bought at intervals throughout the year from twenty-six different firms and dealers. These included thirty-five fifteenth- and sixteenth-century tapestries of which the most expensive was a large so-called Credo tapestry, and several more almost equally costly – a set of six Sibyls from Rothamsted, a hunting scene with falconers, a large Adoration of the Virgin, a Trojan War episode and a fragment of the Seven Sacraments tapestry. The eleven pictures he bought this year included Memlinc's *Rest on the Flight*, Giovanni Bellini's *Madonna and Child*, Domenico Veneziano's *Judgement of Paris*, Manet's *Le Jambon*, Daumier's *La Baignade*, James Maris's *Souvenir of Dordrecht* and Gauguin's drawing of a Breton Girl. Apart from these major purchases he bought fourteen Chinese ceramics and bronzes, five Persian carpets, six pieces of needlework and lace, twenty-eight glass drinking vessels, eleven pieces of furniture, twenty-seven of metalwork and fourteen carvings in wood, stone, alabaster and ivory.

During his second peak year, 1948, Sir William spent rather less for a much larger and more widely spread number of objects (over 700) which he acquired from fifty-two different firms, dealers and agents, only eight of whom incidentally were the same as those he had traded with in 1936. Apart from the previously mentioned Hals portrait and Memlinc's *Virgin of the Annunciation*, a cut-down panel painting thought to be from the same altar-piece as the Flight into Egypt bought in 1936, Sir William made no spectacular purchases in so far as individual works of art were concerned, but spent larger and smaller sums constantly throughout the year on consignments of various antiquities, sometimes ten, sometimes twenty or thirty at a time from the same dealer. On 29 January, for example, he bought fourteen Chinese neolithic pots from the N. S. Browne Collection;

on 2 February an assortment of twenty Assyrian, Egyptian, Etruscan, Chinese and Persian antiquities; on 2 March twenty-seven Sumerian, Egyptian, Greek and Roman antiquities and this tempo continued with the result that at the end of the year the collection of Egyptian antiquities was augmented by 124 pieces, that of Chinese pottery and porcelain by 130 pieces and that of Persian pottery by 82 pieces. He also added considerably to the medieval and renaissance collections. On 7 October, for example, he acquired six Hispano-Moresque dishes at the Beit sale; on 18 October, thirty-two English earthenware pots of the fourteenth, fifteenth and sixteenth centuries; on 28 October, twenty-five panels of English, Flemish and French stained glass of the thirteenth, fourteenth and fifteenth centuries (including a masterpiece of the Norwich School from St Peter Mancroft). Nor was the remainder of the collection neglected.

The books in which Sir William recorded these purchases are ordinary exercise books of the type used by school children and students, mostly with hard bindings, but sometimes with soft. Two or more lean years may fill or partly fill the same book; a fat year may occupy two or more books. Each entry runs across the two open pages and is neatly arranged under eight headings ('Date paid', 'From whom bought', 'Description', 'Price paid', 'Received' (date and place), 'Insured' (date and amount), 'Photographed', 'All in Order') which, but for slight modifications from time to time to meet the altered circumstances, remained unchanged from beginning to end. Except for brief periods of indisposition or absence, Sir William wrote all the entries himself and his handwriting also remained uniformly constant in character and legibility until, about eighteen months before the end at the age of 96, his pen began to stagger across the pages leaving a trail of blots and scratches. With the exception of the last, all the copy-books are thumbed but magnificently unblotted. Sir William collected well; he also recorded well.

SELECT, ANNOTATED BIBLIOGRAPHY

PART I: GENERAL WORKS

AGNEW, GEOFFREY. *Agnew's, 1817—1967*. London, published privately, 1967.

A fascinating and highly readable history of the firm. One only regrets it is not six times as long and much more detailed.

ALEXANDER, BOYD (Editor). *Life at Fonthill, 1807–1822* with Interludes in Paris and London; from the Correspondence of William Beckford. London, 1957.

For many years Beckford wrote almost daily letters to his great friend and companion, Chevalier Gregorio Fellipe Franchi. Although the correspondence was entirely in Italian, Beckford's son-in-law, the Duke of Hamilton, felt compelled to buy it back for reasons of prudence. The letters throw a great deal of light on Beckford as a collector.

AMES, WINSLOW. *Prince Albert and Victorian Taste*. London, 1967.

ANONYMOUS. *An Account of all the Pictures exhibited in the Rooms of the British Institution from 1813 to 1823*, belonging to the Nobility and Gentry of England: with Remarks, Critical and Explanatory. London, 1824.

A very useful source of information, though the tables take a little getting used to. (Better still are the individual catalogues issued by the Institution for each exhibition.) There is a lively introduction in which the editor takes some pains to conceal his identity, signing himself only with a Gothic capital D.

ARMSTRONG, SIR WALTER. *The Peel Collection and the Dutch School of Painting*. London, 1904.

A curiously vapid work containing one interesting chapter on how Sir Robert Peel formed his remarkable collection. The book can still be found readily today.

BARLOW, SIR ALAN. *The Collector and the Expert*.

A paper first published in the Transactions of the Oriental Ceramic Society 1936–37, and republished in 1963 in honour of the author's retirement as President of the Society.

A charmingly modest and sanguine examination of the collector's place in society and his relationship with experts in other fields related to collecting. The author's principal concern is, of course, with oriental ceramics.

BARRY, JAMES. *An Inquiry into the real and imaginary Obstructions to the Acquisition of the Arts in England*. London, 1775.

Barry is not a good writer and one questions whether many of his criticisms were valid.

[BECKFORD, WILLIAM]. *Italy; with Sketches of Spain and Portugal*, by the Author of 'Vathek'. 2 vols. London, 1834.

Beckford's youthful travels were first recorded in 1783 in *Dreams, Waking Thoughts and Incidents*, which was suppressed by his family. But at least a part of this found its way into *Italy; with Sketches of Spain and Portugal*. This in turn was followed in 1835 by the publication of his *Recollections of an Excursion to the Monasteries of Alcobaca and Batalha*.

BEHRMAN, S. N. *Duveen*. London, 1952.

A delightful and deservedly popular account of the great dealer. Unfortunately the author reveals none of his sources.

BLUNT, ANTHONY (Editor). *Bibliography of the History of British Art*, Volume VI, 1946–1948. 2 volumes. Cambridge, 1956. Part I: Nos. 1–2109 General, Architecture, Sculpture; Part II: Nos. 2110–3974 Painting, Drawing, Engraving, Applied Art, Index to Vol. VI.

The last issue of an admirable enterprise carried out under the auspices of the Courtauld Institute that had started in 1936. Volumes I to IV cover the years 1934, 1935, 1936 and 1937 respectively, and Volume V (in two parts) the years 1938–1945.

BLUNT, ANTHONY, and WHINNEY, MARGARET. *The Nation's Pictures*, a Guide to the Chief National and Municipal Picture Galleries of England, Scotland and Wales. London, 1950.

The information on each gallery is useful and in some cases not readily found elsewhere. Unfortunately the many contributors appear to have interpreted the editors' brief rather individualistically and the introductions are therefore of uneven quality.

BODE, WILHELM VON. *Mein Leben*. 2 vols. Berlin, 1930.

The autobiography of one of the greatest 'official' collectors of all time. His links with this country were numerous. He also bought many of his finest acquisitions on the London art market.

BOLTON, ARTHUR T. *The Portrait of Sir John Soane, R.A.* (1753–1837); set forth in Letters from his Friends (1775–1837). London, 1927.

Very full – rather dry – documentation on the great eccentric.

BUCHANAN, WILLIAM. *Memoirs of Painting*, with a chronological History of the Importation of Pictures by the Great Masters into England since the French Revolution, 2 vols. London, 1824.

A key work. Buchanan was a dealer who realised the importance of documentary evidence. In these two volumes he set out to record the outstanding sales and transactions that had taken place during his initial career in the art world. (He had retired from it to write the book, but started dealing again a few years later.)

BYNG HALL, MAJOR H. *The Bric-à-Brac Hunter*, or Chapters on Chinamania. London, 1875.

An anecdotal period piece on the search for ceramic bargains throughout Europe. One sometimes wonders whether the author intended the reader to take it all seriously even in 1875!

CABANNE, PIERRE. *The Great Collectors*. London, 1963.

Translated from the French. Interesting material, but unfortunately the author does not reveal any of his sources.

COKE, DESMOND. *Confessions of an incurable Collector*. London, 1928.

Deserves inclusion despite its breathlessly anecdotal style. Yet this is probably the very sort of book that stopped other great collectors of the same era from publishing their own experiences.

CONSTABLE, W. G. *Art Collecting in the United States of America;* an Outline of a History. London, 1964.

A very lively summary of the events on the other side of the Atlantic during the last 120 years.

CONWAY, SIR MARTIN. *The Sport of Collecting*. London, 1914.

Highly readable reminiscences of a man now almost forgotten, who was a curious blend of scholar, collector, dealer, politician, mountaineer, explorer and entrepreneur.

COOPER, DOUGLAS. *The Courtauld Collection*: a Catalogue and Introduction. With a Memoir of Samuel Courtauld by Anthony Blunt. London, 1954.

Contains a brilliant assessment of the impact of Impressionism on English taste. The section called 'Modern French Painting and English Collectors' is a remarkable piece of scholarship and should be regarded as essential reading for anyone interested in the history of collecting.

—— (Editor). *Great Family Collections*. London, 1965.

—— (Editor). *Great Private Collections*. London, 1963.

Both these very fully illustrated volumes are international in scope (they are 'co-editions' *par excellence*), though English collections are well represented. The first is introduced by the editor and contains excellent pieces on Chatsworth (by Michael Jaffé), Althorp (by Kenneth Garlick) and Houghton (by Francis Watson). The second contains penetrating introductions by both Douglas Cooper and Lord [Kenneth] Clark. It will be interesting to see, in the course of time, how many great private collections become great family collections. The odds, in an age where death is the most viciously taxed undertaking of all, are heavily against.

DENUCÉ, J. *Art Export in the 17th Century in Antwerp: The firm Forchoudt*. Antwerp, 1931.

——. *The Antwerp Art Galleries: Inventories of the Art-Collections in Antwerp in 16th & and 17th Centuries*. Antwerp, 1932.

——. *Antwerp Art-Tapestry and Trade*. Antwerp, 1936.

These three studies of Antwerp as the centre of the art world in the seventeenth century contain fascinating detail. Unfortunately only the introductions are in English. The plates in the second book show a unique selection of pictures of contemporary art galleries (see also Plates 1 and 2, facing page 16).

DIBDIN, T. F. *Aedes Althorpianae*: an Account of the Mansion, Books and Pictures at Althorp, the Residence of George John Earl Spencer, K.G. 2 vols. Shakespeare Press, London, 1822.

DONATH, ADOLPH. *Psychologie des Kunstsammelns*. Berlin, 1911.

In fact, the psychological element plays a minor part in this book. It is more a brief historical appreciation of collecting that takes in the English scene. Its own bibliography is of some interest.

DUVEEN, J. H. *The Rise of the House of Duveen*. London, 1957.

EASTLAKE, SIR CHARLES LOCK. *Contributions to the Literature of the Fine Arts*. 2 vols. London, 1870.

The second volume contains an interesting biographical account of her husband's life by Lady Eastlake.

ECCLES, LORD. *On Collecting*. London, 1968.

A distinguished contemporary collector muses in print on his own experiences and the wider aspects of collecting. Recommended as a charming contrast to the same genre of 30 years earlier.

EDWARDS, EDWARD. *Anecdotes of Painters* who have resided or been born in England; with critical Remarks on their Productions. London, 1808.

Edwards – deliberately – began where Walpole left off. The title page actually states: 'Intended as a continuation to the Anecdotes of Painting by the late Horace Earl of Orford'. Full of useful facts on the English eighteenth-century scene.

ELLIS, SIR HENRY. *The Elgin and Phigaleian Marbles of the Classical Ages in the British Museum*. 2 vols. London, 1846.

The first chapter contains a very objective account of how Lord Elgin obtained the marbles and brought them to England.

ERSKINE, MISS STEWART (Editor). *Anna Jameson, Letters and Friendships* (1812–1860). London, 1915.

EVANS, JOAN. *A History of the Society of Antiquaries*. London, 1956.

Antiquaries were students of the past and not necessarily collectors, but many distinguished antiquaries were also outstanding collectors.

FARINGTON, JOSEPH. *The Farington Diary* (1793–1821) edited by James B. Greig. 8 vols. London, 1922–28.

A glorious rag-bag of trivia and yet an invaluable documentary source book of its time. A new, complete and scholarly edition is said to be in preparation. (The full manuscript is in the Royal Library at Windsor.)

FOTHERGILL, BRIAN. *Sir William Hamilton*, Envoy Extraordinary. London, 1969.

A detailed and lively biography that deals at some length with Sir William's collecting activities.

GIMPEL, RENÉ. *Diary of an Art Dealer*. With an Introduction by Sir Herbert Read. London, 1966.

Covers the era between 1918 and 1939, with fascinating information on great painters, dealers and collectors.

GRAVES, ALGERNON. *Art Sales from early in the eighteenth Century to early in the twentieth Century*. 3 vols. London, 1918–21.

The author's aim was to correct 'the many errors and omissions' of Redford's *Art Sales*. The list of pictures sold is vastly expanded, but there is no descriptive text.

GREENWOOD, THOMAS. *Museums and Art Galleries*. London, 1888.

Concerns itself largely with local and municipal museums.

[HAMILTON, W. R.]. *Memorandum on the Subject of The Earl of Elgin's Pursuits in Greece*. Second edition, London, 1815.

Hamilton had been Elgin's Secretary. The exceedingly rare first edition of this pamplet came out in 1811. One usually finds it bound up with one or more of the innumerable pamphlets that appeared around the time of the great Elgin *éclat*.

HASKELL, FRANCIS. *Patrons and Painters*, A Study in the Relations between Italian Art and Society in the Age of the Baroque. London, 1963.

HERVEY, MARY F. S. *The Life, Correspondence and Collections of Thomas Howard, Earl of Arundel*. Cambridge, 1921. [Reprinted New York, 1969].

A painstaking piece of scholarship that brings the great seventeenth-century collector wonderfully to life.

——. 'A Lumley Inventory of 1609', published in the sixth volume of *The Walpole Society*, 1918.

Miss Hervey's article was preceded by a general account of the Lumley Inventories by Lionel Cust. These had first been discussed in the *Records of* the Lumleys of Lumley Castle by Edith Milner and Edith Benham, published in 1904. The inventories of 1590 and 1609 list sculpture, unusual furniture, tapestries, carpets, pictures (mainly portraits) and are among the earliest English inventories of their kind. The first includes 19 pages of drawings representing marble furniture, which may have been at Nonsuch Palace, one of Lord Lumley's residences.

HILLES, F. W. (Editor). *Letters of Sir Joshua Reynolds*. Cambridge, 1929.

HOBBES, JAMES R. *The Picture Collector's Manual,* adapted to the Professional Man, and the Amateur, being a Dictionary of Painters. . . . 2 vols. London, 1849.

HOLMES, C. J. *Self and Partners (Mostly Self), being the Reminiscences of C. J. Holmes*. London, 1936.

A former Director of the National Portrait Gallery and, subsequently, of the National Gallery, looks back revealingly. Yet being essentially a modest man, he does not hit back at those who terminated his career before its time.

HOLMES, SIR CHARLES and C. H. COLLINS BAKER. *The Making of the National Gallery, 1824–1924*. London, 1924.

This 80-page pamphlet, hastily prepared to celebrate the first centenary of the National Gallery, is still the fullest historical account of its foundation and early growth.

HOLST, NIELS VON. *Creators, Collectors and Connoisseurs;* the Anatomy of artistic Taste from Antiquity to the present day. With an Introduction by Sir Herbert Read. London, 1967.

The author spent forty years gathering facts for this vast history of collecting. The English edition is presented with far more skill and erudition than the German, but somehow remains a little indigestible. The book contains a most useful bibliography.

HUTCHINSON, SIDNEY C. *The History of the Royal Academy, 1768–1968*. London, 1968.

IRWIN, DAVID. *English Neo-Classical Art:* Studies in Inspiration and Taste. London, 1966.

Contains a good deal about collecting.

JAMESON, MRS ANNA. *A Handbook to the Public Galleries of Art in and near London,* with Catalogues of the pictures, accompanied by critical, historical and biographical Notices and copious Indexes to facilitate reference. 2 vols. London, 1842.

——. *Companion to the Most Celebrated Private Galleries of Art in London,* containing accurate Catalogues, arranged alphabetically, for immediate Reference, each preceded by an historical and critical Introduction, with a prefatory Essay on Art, Artists, Collectors and Connoisseurs. London, 1844.

Mrs Jameson was unusually diligent in seeking out facts and wrote them up with verve and what amounted to remarkable critical honesty for her time. *Private Galleries,* in particular, is a key work in the history of collecting.

KEEN, GERALDINE. *The Sale of Works of Art*: A Study based on the Times/Sotheby Indexes. London, 1971.

The book is a symptom of our times in that it is probably the first general study to appear in England which discusses the art market largely in terms of investment. In the USA Richard H. Rush's *Art as an Investment* appeared in 1961 and has been reprinted several times since then. Mr Rush was one of the first to plot the increasing values of paintings in the form of graphs.

KENNEDY, JAMES. *A Description of the Antiquities and Curiosities in Wilton-House*. Salisbury 1769.

Contains one of the earliest accounts of the *principles* on which an outstanding collection was formed.

KETTON-CREMER, R. W. *Horace Walpole, a Biography*. First edition, London, 1940; second, revised edition 1946; third edition, 1964.

A fascinating and delightful study of Walpole's life and work. The book has changed publisher three times (see page 116n.), presumably because it deserves a wider audience than it has reached so far.

LANSDOWN, CHARLOTTE (Editor). *Recollections of the late William Beckford of Fonthill, Wilts. and Lansdown,* Bath. Bath, 1893. Re-issued Bath, 1970.

Contains a number of letters from her father to Miss Lansdown. They are long and detailed descriptions of meetings with Beckford towards the end of his life. The first is dated 21 August 1838 and begins: 'I have this day seen such an astonishing assemblage of works of art, so numerous and of so surprisingly rare a description that I am literally what Lord Byron calls "Dazzled and drunk with beauty" . . .'

LEES-MILNE, JAMES. *Earls of Creation.* Five great Patrons of Eighteenth-Century Art. London, 1962.

LESLIE, ROBERT CHARLES and TAYLOR, TOM. *Life and Times of Sir Joshua Reynolds,* with Notices of some of his Contemporaries. 2 vols. London, 1865.

A splendid quarry of information.

LEWIS, WILMARTH. *Collector's Progress.* London, 1952.

The author has devoted many years in search of anything and everything that had once been Horace Walpole's, and has created a new Strawberry Hill in Farmington, Connecticut. Anyone interested in the history of collecting is really indebted to his labours. The opening of the book is a delightful account of a young collector in the making.

LUGT, FRITS. *Les Marques de Collections.* Amsterdam, 1921.

——. *Répertoire des catalogues de ventes publiques.* Vol. I: the Hague, 1938.

Volume I contains 11,065 items and spans the years 1600–1825; Volume II, which appeared in 1953, covers the years 1826–1860 and items 11,066–25,909; Volume III appeared on Lugt's 80th birthday in 1964 and covers the years 1861–1900 and items 25,910–58,704. A fourth volume (1901–1925) was nearing completion at the time of the compiler's death in July 1970, and may take the number of sale catalogues analysed up to 110,000. Lugt is really the collecting devotee's bible.

MARILLIER, H. C. *Christie's, 1766 to 1925.* London/Boston, 1926.

A conscious continuation of Roberts' book, though less chronological and more general in its treatment. Contains a particularly useful set of illustrations.

[MARTYN, THOMAS]. *The English Connoisseur:* containing an Account of whatever is curious in Painting and Sculpture etc., in the Palaces and Seats of the Nobility and Principal Gentry of England, both in Town and Country. 2 vols. London, 1766.

The first general review in book form of collections of pictures in England. The work was published anonymously. For full details, see page 99.

[MATY, M.]. *Authentic Memoirs of the Life of Richard Mead, M.D.* London, 1755.

Dr Mead was an exceedingly successful physician (he is said to have earned £7000 in a single year), yet he was also generous and gave much to charity. He was a man of great learning, and an enthusiastic patron and one of the earliest English collectors of prominence. This study appeared a year after his death. It is a document of considerable sociological interest and was combined with a catalogue of Mead's possessions. Though there is a multitude of copies –with variations– in the British Museum, it is very rarely found in the antiquarian book trade.

MICHAELIS, ADOLF. *Ancient Marbles in Great Britain.* Translated from the German by C. A. M. Fennell. Cambridge, 1882.

Michaelis' is the most complete survey of Greek and Roman antiquities in private and public collections. The book was written between 1861 and 1878: the translation, printing and revision took another ten years. In exactly a hundred numbered paragraphs the author gives an excellent history of the collecting of antiquities in England. His style is readable (the translation is masterly); his scholarship immense, and the footnotes alone are a delight to anyone interested in the subject. The book is undoubtedly one of the landmarks in the documentation of English collecting. Michaelis himself wrote: 'Favourable circumstances having enabled me to become acquainted with those galleries to a greater extent than perhaps any other living archaeologist, I thought it my duty, putting aside for some years other tasks of a more inviting nature, to undertake the irksome, mosaic-like work of drawing up a descriptive catalogue of the marbles they contain.'

MILLAR, OLIVER. *Zoffany and his Tribuna.* London, 1966.

A detailed identification of every work of art and the multitude of English travellers whom Zoffany posed in the Uffizi in this remarkable documentary picture. (See Plate 12.)

[MCCLEARY, BRENDA]. *Colnaghi's, 1760–1960.* London, published privately, 1960.

A brief history of the firm. The illustrations show some of the finest works of art that have passed through its hands.

MACPHERSON, GERARDINE. *Memoirs of the Life of Anna Jameson.* London, 1878.

NIEUWENHUYS, C. J. *A Review of the Lives and Work of some of the most eminent Painters:* with some Remarks on the Opinions and Statements of former Writers. London, 1834.

The author was a member of the famous Dutch art dealing family who settled in England. The book is a curious mixture. It contains the first account in English of Rembrandt's own picture collection. In among the descriptions of the other paintings mentioned is a good deal of information about contemporary collections.

PASSAVANT, J. D. *Tour of a German Artist in England*, with Notices of Private Galleries and Remarks on the state of art. 2 vols. London, 1836.

Passavant toured English collections only a few years before Waagen. His principal purpose was to see all the works attributed to Raphael while he was engaged on his monumental study of that master. The 'Tour' contains interesting detail but is decidedly bitty.

[PATMORE, P. G.]. *British Galleries of Art.* London, 1824.

Distinctly vapid work made up of a series of twelve pieces first published (anonymously) in periodical form; but useful because it includes a very few rare, first-hand accounts of private collections.

PYE, JOHN. *Patronage of British Art*, an historical Sketch comprising an Account of the Rise and Progress of Art and Artists in London. . . . London, 1845.

Full of fascinating detail on collecting at the beginning of the nineteenth century. Clearly the emphasis is on patronage. Probably the first art-historical work in English in which the footnotes *in toto* are a good deal longer than the principal text!

REDFORD, GEORGE. *Art Sales:* A History of Sales of Pictures and other Works of Art, with Notices of the Collections sold, Names of Owners, Titles of Pictures, Prices and Purchasers. 2 vols. Published privately, London, 1888.

These two volumes are the fruit of a lifetime's work. Redford was *The Times'* Sales Correspondent for forty years and as such he was in a unique position to survey the subject. He has been more extensively quoted without acknowledgement than any other author on collecting since Buchanan. (See also Algernon Graves, *Art Sales.*)

REITLINGER, GERALD. *The Economics of Taste.*

Volume I: The Rise and Fall of Picture Prices, 1760–1960. London, 1961.

Volume II: The Rise and Fall of Objets d'art prices since 1750. London, 1963.

Volume III: The Art Market in the 1960s. London, 1970.

One marvels at the fantastic amount of work that has gone into the compilation of these three volumes, but they are not easy to read or devoid of error. However, their usefulness is assured because of the wealth of information they contain.

REVELEY, HENRY. *Notices illustrative of the Drawings and Sketches of some of the most distinguished Masters in all the principal Schools of Design.* London, 1820.

A very subjective account of the style of drawing of 300 well-known artists of all schools. Unusual in that it mentioned the private collections in which outstanding examples could be found. Thus 'perhaps the finest collection of Guercino's drawings in England is in the possession of Mr Hervey, of Welbeck Street. They are contained in about twelve volumes; and were inherited from his uncle Mr Bouverie, who purchased them of Francesco Forini at Bologna, into whose possession they had come from a great grandson of Guercino; being the same which are noticed by Carlo Malvazio, in his Lives of the Bolognese Painters.' William Carey published a list of *Addenda* to the book shortly after its publication, giving more detail and a list of prices.

RICHARDSON, JONATHAN. Two Discourses: I *An Essay on the whole Art of Criticism*, as it relates to Painting. Showing how to judge I. Of the Goodness of a Picture; II. Of the Hand of the Master; and III. Whether 'tis an Original, or a Copy. II An Argument in behalf of *the Science of a Connoisseur*; wherein is shown the Dignity, Certainty, Pleasure and Advantage of it. London, 1719. [Second edition, 1725.]

RICHARDSON, JONATHAN Senior and Junior. *An Account of Some of the Statues, Bas-Reliefs, Drawings and Pictures in Italy etc., with Remarks.* London, 1722.

The 'Discourses' are really the first books in English on collecting and connoisseurship; and their diffuseness and curious organisation must be judged in the light of this.

The Italian volume was a bold attempt (by father and son) to list the art treasures to be found in Rome (principally, though also in other Italian cities). One suspects that the volume was used as a plunderer's source book when the unfortunate owners or their descendants were forced into selling their possessions at the end of the eighteenth century.

RIGBY, DOUGLAS and ELIZABETH. *Lock, Stock and Barrel;* the Story of Collecting. Philadelphia, 1944.

A little-known book containing sane and sensible remarks on collectors and collecting–including the English scene–but it tries to tackle too much.

ROBERTS, W. *Memorials of Christie's: a Record of Art Sales from 1766 to 1896.* 2 vols. London, 1897.

This first effort to compress into continuous prose 'the essence of many thousands of catalogues' is a very useful historical account of Christie's. However, one regrets the many omissions and the fact that the author restricts himself to a purely chronological treatment.

ROBINSON, FREDERICK S. *The Connoisseur,* Essays on the Romantic and Picturesque Association of Art and Artists. London, 1897.

The author was a son of J. C. Robinson (below). The book is an early example of the anecdotal treatment of art in general and collecting in particular. The author's sources can be readily identified as Redford, Buchanan, Mrs Jameson, etc.

ROBINSON, J. C. *A Critical Account of the Drawings of Michel Angelo and Raffaello in the University Galleries, Oxford.* Oxford, 1870.

The author, who was Eastlake's opposite number at the Victoria and Albert Museum, includes considerable detail on the collection of Sir Thomas Lawrence.

ROTHENSTEIN, SIR JOHN. *Brave Day, Hideous Night:* Autobiography 1939–1965. London, 1966.

Contains fascinating information on the remarkably successful acquisitions policy of a recent Director of the Tate Gallery.

ST CLAIR, WILLIAM. *Lord Elgin and the Marbles.* London, 1967.

An excellent, lively and authoritative résumé of the whole Elgin saga.

SCHARF, GEORGE and others. *Catalogue of the Art Treasures of the United Kingdom* collected at Manchester in 1857. Manchester, 1857.

This was the *official* catalogue of the most momentous art exhibition held in England during the nineteenth century (see page 313). It showed for the first time the accumulated wealth of private collections formed in the previous hundred years, and its influence on contemporary taste was enormous. One usually finds the catalogue bound up with *A Walk through the Art-Treasures Exhibition at Manchester under the Guidance of Dr Waagen* (one of the principal organisers); *Jerrold's Guide to the Exhibition*; *What to see, and where to see it! or the Operatives Guide to the Art Treasures Exhibition,* and various similar publications.

SCHREIBER, LADY CHARLOTTE. *Journals;* Confidences of a Collector of Ceramics and Antiques throughout Britain, France, Holland, Belgium, Spain, Portugal, Turkey, Austria and Germany from the year 1869 to 1885. Edited by her son, Montague J. Guest. With annotations by Egan Mew. 2 vols. London, 1911.

Probably the earliest and most interesting account of the formation of a great ceramic collection that we have.

——. *Extracts from her Journal,* 1853–1891. Edited by the Earl of Bessborough, P.C., G.C.M.G. London, 1952.

—— [Lady Charlotte Guest]. *Extracts from her Journal,* 1833–1852. Edited by the Earl of Bessborough, P.C., G.C.M.G. London, 1948.

SELIGMAN, GERMAIN. *Merchants of Art: 1880–1960.* Eighty years of Professional Collecting. New York, 1961.

The biography of one of the leading French art dealers and of his father.

SKINNER, BASIL. *Scots in Italy in the Eighteenth Century.* Edinburgh, 1966.

Marvellously erudite; tantalisingly brief; wholly lacking in acknowledgement of sources. Perhaps the author will one day expand this slim volume whose *raison d'être* was an exhibition of the same title.

SMITH, A. H. *Lord Elgin and his Collection.* Reprinted (in book form) from the *Journal of Hellenic Studies,* Vol. XXXVI, London, 1916.

SMITH, CHARLES EASTLAKE (Editor). *Journals and Correspondence of Lady Eastlake.* 2 vols. London, 1895.

A discreet, albeit highly readable, insight into the private lives of Sir Charles and Lady Eastlake; and, in its way, a minor classic of a Victorian intellectual success story. Rarely found in the antiquarian book trade.

SMITH, JOHN. *A Catalogue Raisonné of the Works of the Most Eminent Dutch, Flemish, and French Painters*; in which is included a short biographical Notice of the Artists, with a copious Description of their Principal Pictures; a statement of the Prices at which such Pictures have been sold at Public Sales on the Continent and in England; a Reference to the Galleries and Private Collections, in which a large Proportion are at present; and the Names of the Artists by whom they have been engraved; to which is added a brief Notice of the Scholars and Imitators of the Great Masters of the above Schools. 8 vols. London, 1829–1837. Supplement: 1842.

This was another great labour of love, for Smith complained in the introduction to each volume as it appeared that he had bitten off far more than he could chew! But he finished the work *and* added the extensive supplement to it. It really needed another Graves to compile a complete index to it, but instead Hofstede de Groot used it as the basis of his own magnificent opus (see page 30).

SMITH, JOHN THOMAS. *Nollekens and his Time:* comprehending a Life of that celebrated Sculptor; and Memoirs of Several Contemporary Artists from the Time of Roubiliac, Hogarth and Reynolds to that of Fuseli, Flaxman and Blake. 2 vols. London, 1828.

Delightful contemporary gossip, yet full of useful information.

STEEGMAN, JOHN. *The Rule of Taste,* from George I to George IV. London, 1936.

A simple and perceptive account of the views on art in eighteenth-century England. The unqualified and straightforward character of Steegman's generalisations leave one gasping with admiration.

——. *Consort of Taste,* 1830–1870. London, 1950.

A very readable assessment of Victorian taste and a pioneer work when it first came out. Steegman was one of the first to realise the importance of the influence of the Eastlakes, Mrs Jameson, etc. on their own generation. (Re-published in 1970 as *Victorian Taste*, with an introduction by Sir Nikolaus Pevsner.)

SUMMERSON, SIR JOHN. *What is a Professor of Fine Art?* An Inaugural Lecture as Ferens Professor delivered in the University of Hull on 17 November 1960. Hull, 1961.

A masterly and beautifully written disquisition on the death of connoisseurship and its replacement by the verifiable facts of art history; the author makes an interesting comparison between the status of Ruskin and Roger Fry in England and Burckhardt and Wölfflin in Germany, and the shift from inspired amateurism to academic professionalism.

SUTTON, DENYS. *Christie's since the War, 1945–1958: an Essay on Taste, Patronage and Collecting*. London, 1959.

The 'Essay' is particularly interesting, and, had it been more extensive, there would have been no need for the present work.

TAYLOR, FRANCIS HENRY. *The Taste of Angels,* A History of Art Collecting from Rameses to Napoleon. Boston/London, 1948.

Invaluable as the first attempt of recent times to produce a historical survey of collecting. The effect is slightly marred by what one suspects was an attempt to introduce a popular element into an essentially scholarly work. It is our misfortune that the author, who was Director of the Metropolitan Museum in New York, never completed the second volume, from 1855 to the present time, but the book contained the most complete bibliography of the subject at the time of its publication.

TIETZE, HANS. *Treasures of the Great National Galleries:* An Introduction to the Paintings in the Famous Museums of the Western World. London, 1955.

Brief accounts of the establishment and history of the major European Galleries followed by a massive number of illustrations of their outstanding pictures.

VOLLARD, AMBROISE. *Recollections of a Picture Dealer*. London, 1936.

Ingenuous reminiscences of the most perceptive dealer of the twentieth century.

WAAGEN, G. F. *Works of Art and Artists in England.* 3 vols. London, 1838.

——. *Treasures of Art in Great Britain:* being an Account of the chief Collections of Paintings, Drawings, Sculptures, Illuminated MSS, etc. 3 vols. London, 1854.

——. *Galleries and Cabinets of Art in Great Britain:* being an Account of more than forty Collections of Paintings, Drawings, Sculptures, MSS, etc. visited in 1854 and 1856, and now for the first time described. London, 1857. [Published specifically as a Supplement to his three volumes of 1854.]

Though its accuracy on detail has always been questioned, Dr Waagen's encyclopaedic survey of art in England is the most important single work available to us in the history of collecting. *Works of Art in England* was written as thirty long letters in 1835 and was first published in German. It was translated by H. E. Lloyd. The 1854 edition, which was revised so extensively as to be virtually a new book, never appeared in German, and was edited and translated by Lady Eastlake. So was the 1857 supplement. Algernon Graves compiled a *Summary of the Index to Waagen* (both editions) which appeared in a limited edition in 1912.

WAETZOLD, WILHELM. *Deutsche Kunsthistoriker.* Berlin, 1965.

This is an uncorrected, single-volume reprint of the first two-volume edition of 1924. For those who read German the book is a mine of information (see page 219). It includes detailed accounts of the lives of Waagen and Passavant.

WALPOLE, HORACE. *Aedes Walpolianae:* or, a Description of the Collection of Pictures at Houghton Hall in Norfolk, the seat of the Right Honourable Sir Robert Walpole, Earl of Orford. London, 1747. Second edition with additions, London, 1752.

Horace's catalogue of his father's great collection. One of the earliest examples of this genre and a classic of its kind. For full details, see page 80.

——. *Anecdotes of Painting in England* with some Account of the principal Artists and incidental Notes on other Arts; collected by the late Mr George Vertue; digested and published from the original MSS by the Hon. Horace Walpole with considerable Additions by the Rev. James Dallaway. 5 vols. London, 1826.

This finely printed edition is probably the one most frequently found of the many that appeared of this most important source book on the history of art in England. For full details, see page 57.

——. *Journals of Visits to Country Seats*, edited by Paget Toynbee. Sixteenth Volume of the Walpole Society, 1927–1928. Oxford, 1928.

These *Journals* are contained in two handwritten notebooks, covering a period from July 1751 to September 1784, that came to light in 1913 and were transcribed and edited by Paget Toynbee. Some forty-five journeys are described, and often more than one house was visited. The *Journals* should be considered in conjunction with a list Walpole compiled entitled 'Collections Now in England', full details of which are given by F. H. Taylor in his *Taste of Angels*, pages 451–453.

WARING, J. B. and others. *National Exhibition of Works of Art at Leeds, 1868: official catalogue.* Leeds, 1869.

A successor to the Manchester Art-Treasures Exhibition of 1857. More highly organised, less exciting, but still important.

WATKIN, DAVID. *Thomas Hope, 1769–1831, and the Neo-Classical Idea.* London, 1968.

A detailed and remarkably perceptive biography of the man who set out to change the taste of Regency society and who was an important figure in the contemporary collecting scene.

WAY, R. P. *Antique Dealer.* London, 1956.

A charming and deservedly popular book, which is surprisingly memorable. (See, for example, the description of the sale in Ross-on-Wye on page 58.)

WESTMACOTT, C. M. *British Galleries of Painting and Sculpture*, comprising a general historical and critical Catalogue, with separate Notices of every Work of Fine Art in the Principal Collections. London, 1824.

Westmacott's style is appalling, but the book contains some interesting information about important collections and a few unique illustrations of galleries.

WHITLEY, WILLIAM T. *Artists and their Friends in England, 1700–1799.* 2 vols. London/Boston, 1928.

Immensely useful account of every aspect of the art world of the eighteenth century culled from a very wide range of primary sources.

——. *Art in England, 1800–1820.* Cambridge, 1928.

——. *Art in England, 1821–1837.* Cambridge, 1930.

Certainly these two volumes, which cover the period year by year, are the most informative source books on the era covered. Unfortunately their usefulness is limited by a complete absence of documentation. However, Whitley's original papers are readily available in the Department of Prints and Drawings in the British Museum, in conjunction with an excellent index compiled by Ruth Simon.

[WINSTANLEY, THOMAS]. *Observations on the Arts*, with Tables of the Principal Painters . . . their Scholars and Imitators. Liverpool, 1828.

Winstanley, who published this very successful little volume anonymously, was a Liverpool dealer and auctioneer specialising in Old

Masters. The book was a warning against the excessive credulity of young collectors in the second quarter of the nineteenth century.

WITT, ROBERT C. *The Nation and its Art Treasures*. London, 1911.

The book was a plea to put some sort of official brake on the number of great works of art that were being sold to America and Germany. It was also an appeal to the state to take more interest in the arts.

——. *The Art of Collecting*, a lecture delivered by Sir Robert Witt, C.B.E., D.Litt., F.S.A. Published by the National Art-Collections Fund, London, 1950.

A survey of the pleasures that collecting can give; Sir Robert is particularly eloquent on the collecting of drawings.

WOOLF, VIRGINIA. *Roger Fry, A Biography*. London, 1940.

A relatively little-known work which throws a great deal of light on the status of the art historian, the expert and the collector (both here and in the U.S.) during the first thirty years of the present century.

PART 2: SELECTED PRIVATE CATALOGUES

The English have never lapsed so lightly into producing lasting monuments to their collecting activities as have the Germans and the French. On the Continent, catalogue compilation became a minor industry for art historians towards the end of the nineteenth and the beginning of the twentieth centuries: not only for pictures, but also for collections of bronzes, glass and porcelain. Though certainly the labours of Tancred Borenius, Maurice Brockwell and the Chiswick Press between them, produced a continuing stream of English equivalents for many years.

It is probably flippant to suggest that the interest and value to us of private catalogues, particularly those produced in England just before and soon after the turn of the last century, often varies in inverse proportion to their size. But there can be little doubt that *some* of the elephantine, twin- or multi-volume works of that era contain little information that is of use to the student of collecting (either about the owners or the provenance of their pictures) though such works continue to fetch high prices at auction.

It is for this reason that the examples here selected are generally among the shorter, more useful and more readily available catalogues and handlists.

ANGERSTEIN COLLECTION. A Catalogue of the Celebrated Collection of Pictures of the late John Julius Angerstein, Esq. Containing a finished Etching of every Picture and accompanied with historical and biographical Notices by John Young. London, 1823.

ASSHETON BENNETT COLLECTION. Catalogue of the Paintings and Drawings from the Assheton Bennett Collection by Dr F. G. Grossman. Manchester, 1965.

Strictly this catalogue has no place here because it is issued by the City of Manchester Art Gallery. But it covers the 96 pictures unexpectedly received by Manchester from Edgar Assheton Bennett and his wife a few years ago. The paintings are predominantly of the Dutch School and exude the delightfully intimate atmosphere that so often reflects the eye of the selective but enthusiastic collector (and appeals far less to the art historian). It is now housed in a delightful, special gallery together with the superb collection of English silver which the same donors gave to Manchester in 1957.

BENSON COLLECTION. Catalogue of Italian Pictures at 16 South Street, Park Lane, London and Buckhurst in Sussex collected by Robert and Evelyn Benson. London, published privately, 1914.

Contains an informative preface of particular interest about several late nineteenth-century English collectors of Italian pictures, including William Graham, Sir George Holford, Charles Butler and George Salting. The Benson Collection was eventually bought by Duveen for £620,000. (See also page 394.)

BLENHEIM PALACE COLLECTION. Catalogue Raisonné of a list of the Pictures in Blenheim Palace with occasional Remarks and Illustrated Notes by George Scharf, F.S.A. By Authority of His Grace the Duke of Marlborough. London, 1862.

The first part deals with the contents of the Public Rooms; the second with those of the Private Apartments.

BURGHLEY HOUSE. A Guide to Burghley House, Northamptonshire, the Seat of the Marquis of Exeter; containing a Catalogue of all the

Paintings, Antiquities, etc. with biographical Notices of the Artists by J. Blore. Stamford, 1815.

There had been an earlier guide by J. Horn in 1797. There was a later one by W. H. Charlton in 1847.

Callaly Castle Collection. Catalogue of the Works of Antiquity and Art collected by the late William Henry Forman, Esq., Pippbrook House, Dorking, Surrey and removed in 1890 to Callaly Castle, Northumberland, by Major A. H. Browne, by W. Chaffers, F.S.A. Printed for private circulation, 1892.

Major Browne was a nephew of Henry Forman. The Forman Collection of antiquities ran to over 4000 items as listed by Chaffers, and was particularly strong in Greek vases. Mr Forman was also a great admirer of William Hogarth. He owned fifteen paintings by the latter, various associated items that had formerly belonged to David Garrick and Horace Walpole, many drawings and virtually all Hogarth's engravings.

Christ Church Collection. Paintings by Old Masters at Christ Church, Oxford, Catalogue by J. Byam Shaw. London, 1967.

The first catalogue of what was then known as the 'Library Collection' was prepared by Tancred Borenius in 1916. In order to mark the opening of the newly built Gallery in 1967 it was decided to sponsor this new catalogue of the gifts from General John Guise, the Hon. W. T. H. Fox-Strangways (see also page 299), W. S. Landor and Sir Richard Nosworthy to their former college.

Cook Collection. Abridged Catalogue of the Pictures at Doughty House, Richmond, Surrey in the Collection of Sir Herbert Cook, Bart. London, 1932.

A useful handlist of 550 pictures which were collected in the first instance by Sir Francis Cook between 1830 and 1860, and added to later, by Sir Frederick, and subsequently by Sir Herbert Cook. This catalogue is based on the large 3-volume work. (It may be helpful here to differentiate between the Cook Collection at Doughty House and that of Ernest Edward Cook, a grandson of Thomas Cook, the founder of the famous travel agency. When E. E. Cook, an exceedingly generous but retiring man who had shunned publicity all his life, died in 1955 he left a remarkable bequest of fine pictures to the National Art-Collections Fund. He had also given a number of properties to the National Trust, including Montacute and the Bath Assembly Rooms, and he ensured indirectly that a number of other estates would eventually go to the Trust.)

Corsham House. An Historical Account of Corsham House in Wiltshire; the Seat of Paul Cobb Methuen, Esq., with a Catalogue of his celebrated Collection of Pictures . . . by John Britton. London, 1806.

(See also page 100.)

Percival David Collection. A Catalogue of Chinese Pottery and Porcelain in the Collection of Sir Percival David, Bt, F.S.A. By R. L. Hobson. London, 1934.

This amazingly rich collection is now the property of the University of London and forms a museum in its own right at 53 Gordon Square, London W.C.1. (See also page 395.)

The Davies Collection. The Davies Collection of French Art by John Ingamalls. Cardiff, 1967.

For further details, see page 392.

Elton Hall. A Catalogue of the Pictures at Elton Hall in Huntingdonshire in the Collection of Colonel Douglas James Proby by Tancred Borenius and the Rev. J. V. Hodgson. London, 1924.

A supplement by Granville Proby appeared in 1939.

Eumorfopoulos Collection. The George Eumorfopoulos Collection: Catalogue of the Chinese, Corean and Persian Pottery and Porcelain by R. L. Hobson. 6 vols. London, 1925 ff.

Ultimately six magnificent folio volumes enshrined the details of this most outstanding of all the great Oriental ceramic collections formed in the first thirty years of this century in England.

Goodwood. Goodwood: its House, Park and Grounds with a Catalogue Raisonné of the Pictures in the Gallery of his Grace the Duke of Richmond, K.G. By William Hayley Mason. London, 1839.

Earl Grosvenor's Gallery. A Catalogue of the Pictures at Grosvenor House, London . . . by John Young. London, 1821.

The collection was begun by the then earl's father who had bought paintings from such celebrated primary collections as those of Sir Luke Schaub and Lord Waldegrave. Dalton, the King's Librarian and Royal Keeper of pictures, had foraged in Italy on the earl's behalf. The second earl bought the famous collection of Welbore Ellis Agar *in toto* and the greater part of the Marquess of Lansdowne's collection. He had also added assiduously from important continental collections. This catalogue lists 143 pictures.

HENDERSYDE PARK COLLECTION. A Catalogue of Pictures, Statues, Busts, Antique Columns, Bronzes, Fragments of Antique Buildings, Tables of Florentine and Roman Mosaic, Scagliola and inlaid Wood; Indian, Neapolitan and other China, etc. Printed for private circulation, 1859.

A charming, very personal catalogue of the possessions of John Waldie of Hendersyde Park, near Kelso in Roxburghshire. He appears to have travelled a great deal, particularly in Italy, and many of the paintings were acquired on his journeys abroad. There was an earlier catalogue in 1835.

HOLFORD COLLECTION. The Holford Collection, Dorchester House [edited by Robert Benson]. 2 vols. Oxford, 1928.

There had been an earlier volume in 1924 of the pictures, also belonging to Sir George Lindsay Holford, which were kept at Westonbirt in Gloucestershire. These two magnificent volumes showed the results of collecting by several generations of Holfords, but principally of Robert Holford (1808–1892) who had bought many of his finest pictures from or through the agency of William Buchanan. (See also 'Sales Catalogues'.)

ILCHESTER COLLECTION. 1. Catalogue of the Pictures belonging to the Earl of Ilchester. Published privately, 1883. (This included the collections at Melbury, Redlynch, Abbotsbury and at 42 Belgrave Square.) 2. Catalogue of Pictures belonging to the Earl of Ilchester at Holland House. Published privately, 1904.

LEE PRIORY. List of Pictures at the Seat of T. B. Brydges Barrett, Esq., at Lee Priory in the County of Kent, 1817.

Only sixty copies of this catalogue were printed, at the Lee Priory Press at Ickham, near Canterbury, by Sir Egerton Brydges. The design of the catalogue is unusual in listing the paintings on one page and including biographical material about the painters on the facing page. It was obviously an ingenious typographical exercise for the compositor of a private press. The collection itself consisted of Italian, Dutch and English pictures.

MAYOR COLLECTION. A Brief Chronological Description of Original Drawings and Sketches of the Old Masters of the different Schools of Europe from the Revival of Art in Italy in the XIIIth Century to the XIXth Century; formed by the late Mr William Mayor of Bayswater Hill, London. The Result of upwards of fifty years' Experience and Research. London, 1875.

Mayor had studied art in Haydon's studio and became friendly with such fellow students as William Bewick and the Landseers. After a prolonged tour of the Continent, where he bought a good many drawings, he got to know Sir Thomas Lawrence, who introduced him to his own collection. Thereafter Mayor collected drawings assiduously–and appears to have done little else–for almost fifty years. He became something of an authority and frequently disposed of items which he considered not good enough for his collection. This catalogue was, in fact, a sale catalogue prepared after his death by the dealer, J. Hogarth.

MELCHETT COLLECTION. Catalogue of the Greek and Roman Antiquities in the Possession of the Right Honourable Lord Melchett, P.C., D.Sc., F.R.S. at Melchet Court and 35 Lowndes Square, by Eugenia Strong, C.B.E., M.A., Ll.D., F.S.A., etc. Oxford, 1928.

Lord Melchett (1868–1930), the begetter of I.C.I., was the son of Dr Ludwig Mond (1839–1909) q.v., the brilliant chemical engineer, who left his splendid collection of Italian pictures to the National Gallery. Mond bought much on the advice of J. P. Richter at a time when there was a marked lack of interest in Italian pictures among English collectors; Lord Melchett was assisted in *his* collecting by the celebrated Miss Henriette Hertz of Rome, who formed an outstanding collection of antiquities in her own right. (Lord Melchett's older brother, Sir Robert Ludwig Mond (1867–1938), was also an enthusiastic archaeologist and keenly interested in antiquities.)

MERTON COLLECTION. A Catalogue of Pictures and Drawings from the Collection of Sir Thomas Merton, F.R.S., at Stubbings House, Maidenhead by Alfred Scharf. London, published privately, 1950.

A small, very personal, relatively little-known, but fine collection of Italian, German and Flemish works painted between 1450 and 1520.

Miles Collection. A Catalogue of the Pictures at Leigh Court, near Bristol; the Seat of Philip John Miles, Esq., M.P. . . . by John Young. London, 1822.

In its day this was one of the most celebrated collections in the West of England. It contained works attributed to Rubens, Claude Poussin, Titian, Velazquez, Murillo, Raphael, Leonardo da Vinci, Giovanni Bellini, Andrea del Sarto, van Dyck, Rembrandt, Holbein and a host of lesser Italian and Dutch masters. Many of the pictures had originally been in the collections of Richard Hart Davis and of Henry Hope. The Miles Collection was sold at Christie's in 1884 and many paintings from it eventually found their way into national galleries all over Europe.

Mond Collection. An Appreciation by J. P. Richter. 2 volumes. London, 1910.

Richter acted as adviser to Dr Ludwig Mond for twenty-five years in the formation of this magnificent collection of sixteenth- and seventeenth-century Italian paintings, predominantly of the Venetian School. The catalogue was published just after the collector's death and to some extent it is an expression of Richter's *credo.* There is a useful introduction about collecting in general, and Richter's adherence to the principles advocated by Morelli in particular, though at times Richter's style is a little ponderous: 'the art-collection proper is not a mere assemblage of heterogeneous rarities, but an organism of which the parts mutually supplement and comment each other'; or: 'there is nothing in a work of art which should be indifferent to a harmoniously developed man; even its soul . . .'. Many of the paintings were included in the Mond Bequest to the National Gallery in 1924.

Napier Collection. Catalogue of the Works of Art forming the Collection of Robert Napier of West Shandon, Dunbartonshire. Mainly composed by J. C. Robinson, F.S.A. London, published privately, 1865.

A splendid collection of 'Pictures, Carvings in Wood and Ivory, Bronzes, Decorative Furniture, Clocks and Watches, Arms and Armour, Locks and Keys, Silver, Pottery and Porcelain printed for the owner as a souvenir of his art gatherings'.

Northbrook Collection. A descriptive Catalogue of the Collection of Pictures belonging to the Northbrooks. London, 1929.

A fine collection of Old Masters, particularly strong in the Dutch and Flemish schools, largely sold up by private treaty between the wars.

Northwick Collection. Catalogue of the Collection of Pictures at Northwick Park. [Compiled by Tancred Borenius and Lionel Cust]. Published privately, 1921.

This handlist appeared nine years after Captain Spencer-Churchill had inherited the collection. For full details, see page 320.

Norton Hall. Catalogue of Pictures at Norton Hall by Beriah Botfield. London, 1863.

Botfield was a well-known bibliographer and published this catalogue, mainly of seventeenth-century Dutch and Italian pictures, in the year of his death. In an earlier work (*Stenemata Boteilvliana*) he says: 'the pleasing collection of second-rate pictures is distributed throughout the several rooms [of Norton Hall], care being taken that the Ancient and Modern pictures, and the Italian and Flemish painters, do not occupy the same apartment'.

Nostell Priory Collection. Catalogue of the Pictures and other Works of Art in the Collection of Lord St Oswald at Nostell Priory, by Maurice W. Brockwell. London, 1915.

A fine old family collection containing distinguished pictures, and furnishings that provide a noble setting for them. Paine and Adam did much of the interior decoration of the house. Chippendale made the greater part of the furniture (for which a number of the original invoices remain extant). The house has belonged to the National Trust since 1953.

Parnham House. Ancient Furniture and other Works of Art illustrative of a Collection formed by Vincent J. Robinson, C.I.E., Knight of the Legion of Honour, Fellow of the Society of Antiquaries, of Parnham House, Dorset. London, 1902.

A private catalogue *atypical* of the English as collectors; compiled by an interested amateur without professional assistance, whose taste went against the swim with his enthusiasm for furniture of the fifteenth and sixteenth centuries. The text is occasionally arresting for the perversity of its judgements.

Petworth Collection. Catalogue of the Petworth Collection of Pictures in the Possession of Lord Leconfield, by C. H. Collins Baker. London, 1920.

One of the oldest family collections of pictures

still extant. It was certainly well established by 1650 and a valuation of 1671 included the majority of van Dycks and Lelys still at Petworth today. The house became the property of the National Trust in 1947.

RADNOR COLLECTION. Catalogue of the Earl of Radnor's Collection of Pictures by Helen Matilda, Countess of Radnor. Third edition, edited and revised by William Barclay Squire, F.S.A. To be obtained from the Housekeeper, Longford Castle, 1910.

An extract from the preface will be found on page 123. The first edition of this smaller catalogue appeared in 1890. The third edition was, to some extent, based on the much bigger two-volume catalogue by W. B. Squire (see next entry). But it was, in fact, the Countess of Radnor herself who had found the inventories in the castle muniment room, which showed where and at what cost most of the pictures had been bought.

RADNOR COLLECTION. Catalogue of the Pictures in the Collection of the Earl of Radnor, by Helen Matilda, Countess of Radnor, and William Barclay Squire. With a Preface by Jacob, sixth Earl of Radnor. 2 volumes. London, 1909.

A magnificent catalogue, printed by the Chiswick Press, in a limited edition of 200 copies. The information given about each painting is extensive and useful. The second volume is devoted to the family portraits.

ROYAL COLLECTION. I. The Tudor, Stuart and early Georgian Pictures in the Collection of Her Majesty the Queen, by Oliver Millar. 2 vols. London, 1963. II. The Later Italian Pictures in the Collection of Her Majesty the Queen, by Michael Levey. London, 1964. III. The Later Georgian Pictures in the Collection of Her Majesty the Queen, by Oliver Millar. 2 vols. London, 1969.

These admirable volumes are the first three published of a complete, new catalogue of the entire Royal Collection. They replace the great multitude of earlier publications which would form a substantial library in their own right. The Phaidon Press has also published fourteen volumes by distinguished authors on the Drawings in the Royal Collection. These have become much sought after now that they are no longer in print!

A large literature also exists on the original collection of Charles I. The first catalogue generally available was the one copied by George Vertue from an MS in the old Ashmolean Museum (now in the Bodleian Library). This was published by W. Bathoe as *A Catalogue and Description of King Charles the First's Capital Collection of Pictures, Limnings, Statues, Bronzes, Medals and other Curiosities*... London, 1757. In fact, the MS he used was one of the four copies of an inventory compiled by Abraham van der Doort in the 1630s as Surveyor of the Royal Pictures. The most accurate transcription of this will be found in Oliver Millar's carefully collated and annotated text in the 37th Volume of the Walpole Society (1958–1960).

SCHREIBER COLLECTION. Catalogue of English Porcelain, Earthenware enamels, etc., collected by Charles Schreiber, Esq., M.P., and the Lady Elizabeth Charlotte Schreiber and presented to the South Kensington Museum in 1884. London, 1885.

Strictly speaking this is a museum catalogue and not a private one, but Lady Charlotte herself had compiled the catalogue of that part of her collection which she gave to the nation in memory of her husband. (See also page 332.)

SEILERN COLLECTION. [The catalogue is in three parts and six volumes: in each case one volume for the text and one for the illustrations.] I. Flemish Paintings and Drawings at 56 Princes Gate, London S.W.7. London, 1955. II. Italian Paintings and Drawings at 56 Princes Gate, London S.W.7. London, 1959. III. Paintings and Drawings of Continental Schools other than Flemish and Italian at 56 Princes Gate, London S.W.7. London, 1961.

This must be one of the most remarkable collections formed in recent years. The catalogues do not state that the collector is Dr Count Antoine Seilern. He repeatedly expresses his indebtedness to Johannes Wild in the formation of the collection and to Michael Kitson for the compilation of the catalogue.

SOULAGES COLLECTION. Catalogue of the Soulages Collection, being a descriptive Inventory of a Collection of Works of Decorative Art, formerly in the possession of M. Jules Soulages of Toulouse, now, by permission of the Committee of Privy Council for Trade, exhibited to the Public at the Museum of Ornamental Art, Marlborough House. By J. C. Robinson, F.S.A. London, 1856.

Again, strictly speaking this was an *exhibition* catalogue of a non-English collection published under the auspices of a museum. But the acquisition of the Soulages Collection for the nation was of such importance (see page 290) that it must be included here. A slightly different, Manchester Art-Treasures Exhibition edition, appeared in 1857.

STAFFORD GALLERY. Engravings of the most noble Marquis of Stafford's Collection of Pictures in London, arranged according to Schools and in Chronological order with Remarks on each Picture. By William Young Ottley, Esq., F.S.A.; the executive part under the Management of Peltro William Tomkins, Esq., Historical Engraver to her Majesty. London, 1818.

This catalogue, in four monumental quarto volumes, was probably the most luxurious to have appeared in England by 1818. The first volume contains charming plans which show how the paintings were hung on the walls of each room and also how some of the furniture in them was arranged. The collection was not only one of the most important of its day but one of the few open to the public, and frequent references to it will be found (see, in particular, page 125).

An earlier *Catalogue Raisonné of the pictures belonging to the most Honourable the Marquis of Stafford in the Gallery of Cleveland House* by John Britton had appeared in 1808. Cleveland House was built in 1626, and a first picture gallery was added to it by the Duke of Bridgewater in 1797. He left the house and his collection to his nephew, who became Marquis of Stafford in 1803. It was *he* who added a second picture gallery in 1805–6, after designs by C. H. Tatham, which became known as the *Stafford Gallery*.

TENNANT GALLERY. Catalogue of Pictures in the Tennant Gallery, 34 Queen Anne's Gate, S.W. London, no date.

This dreary little catalogue, which is still frequently found, does little credit to what was a fine collection of English and French pictures got together by Sir Charles Tennant (1823–1905), a hard-working, generous and intelligent businessman, whom Redford described as 'the Glasgow Croesus in the picture line'. (See page 345.) It was open to the public–free–two afternoons a week.

WANTAGE COLLECTION. A Catalogue of Pictures from the Collection of Lord and Lady Wantage at 2 Carlton Gardens, London and Lockinge House, Berkshire and Overstone Park and Ardington House. London, 1905.

The catalogue was compiled by A. G. Temple, Director of the Guildhall Art Gallery, with the assistance of Robert Benson. There had been an earlier catalogue compiled for Lord Overstone by George Redford in 1875. Lord Overstone, who was a highly successful banker and economist, started collecting in 1831 (when he was plain Mr S. J. Jones Lloyd). With Thomas Baring and Humphrey Mildmay he bought the celebrated Dutch collection belonging to Baron Verstolk van Soelen. One picture was bought from them by the King of Holland. The remaining 99 were divided at a private auction among the three partners and a Mr Chaplain, the dealer who organised the sale. Jones Lloyd acquired ten pictures in this way. Thomas Baring acquired forty-two, which later passed to the Earl of Northbrook.

WELBECK ABBEY COLLECTION. Catalogue of the Pictures belonging to his Grace the Duke of Portland, K.G., at Welbeck Abbey, 17 Hill Street, London, and Langwell House. Compiled by Richard W. Goulding and revised by C. K. Adams. Cambridge, 1936.

The collection, which is remarkably well documented, probably includes the largest accumulation of family portraits in England. This was because many other old-established collections (those of the Vere, Wriothesley, Cavendish, Holles and Harley families) became incorporated with the Bentinck family by marriage.

WILTON HOUSE. A Catalogue of the Paintings and Drawings in the Collection at Wilton House, Salisbury, Wiltshire compiled by Sidney, 16th Earl of Pembroke. London/New York, 1968.

There are many catalogues of the treasures at Wilton (see page 96). This latest one – unusual in being compiled by the present earl – is a highly professional and useful addition to the literature on the history of collecting.

PART 3: SELECTED SALE CATALOGUES OF PARTICULAR INTEREST

ALTON TOWERS. Christie's, July 1857.

The catalogue was 'of the Magnificent Contents of Alton Towers, the princely Seat of the Earls of Shrewsbury . . .', and the sale lasted 29 days. It was perhaps remarkable in only fetching £42,198 16s. Many of the pictures, Redford tells us, were bought in Rome in 1829 in one lot from Madame Bonaparte, mother of Napoleon, by the Shrewsbury family. The Earl Charles also bought pictures on the advice of Bryan, but, writes Redford, 'being a strict Roman Catholic the subjects were all in accordance with that feeling'. The 708 paintings fetched £12,940.

BARKER, ALEXANDER. Christie's, June 1874 and June 1879.

A marvellous collection, particularly of Italian Old Masters, formed by the son of a West End bootmaker.

BECKETT-DENISON, CHRISTOPHER. Christie's, June 1885.

Pictures and *objets d'art*. An outstanding collection rapidly assembled. Much came from Hamilton Palace.

BERNAL, RALPH. Christie's, March 1855.

4294 items. Probably the greatest collection of ceramics and *objets d'art* of its time (see page 293).

BLENHEIM PALACE (Duke of Marlborough). Christie's, August 1886.

Historical collection of Old Masters and porcelain.

BRETT, JOHN WATKINS. Christie's, April 1864.

2059 items. Pictures, antiquities, coins and medals.

ELDIN, LORD JOHN. Winstanley, 1833.

Approximately 700 items: pictures, drawings and antiquities. A fine collection, but the sale has become particularly celebrated because the floor of the Edinburgh building in which it was held collapsed during the proceedings. There is an addendum (usually found bound together with the catalogue) entitled *A Concise and Accurate Account of the Accident that occurred at the Sale of the late Lord Eldin's Pictures*.

FLETCHER, RALPH. Christie's, June 1838.

A very respectable collection of English, Dutch and French pictures (72 in all).

FONTHILL ABBEY (William Beckford). Phillips, September 1823.

This is the expanded catalogue based on the earlier Christie version. One of the most famous sales of the nineteenth century. For full details–particularly of pagination and collation–see page 214.

FOUNTAINE, SIR ANDREW. Christie's, June 1884.

Sir Andrew (1672–1753) of Narford Hall, Norfolk, Master of the Mint under Queen Anne and George I, was one of the very earliest of English collectors. When his magnificent collection of maiolica, Henry II ware, sixteenth-century faience, Limoges enamels and early Flemish drawings came onto the market 132 years after his death, there was immense competition for individual pieces and they fetched prices that have not often been exceeded even since that time. The collection was sold by a direct descendant who had added a considerable number of pieces of equal quality.

GARNER, PROFESSOR F. H. Sotheby's, October 1964, March and June 1965.

An interesting example of a recent, specialist collection. Professor Garner spent many years studying and collecting English Delftware and wrote the standard book on the subject (*English Delftware*, London, 1948). He also bequeathed some fine examples to the Victoria and Albert Museum. Prices at the three sales were high and brought about a new valuation of Delftware generally. This sort of economic pattern has become common in recent years and was repeated, for example, at the Walter Smith Sales of English glass at Sotheby's in 1967–68.

GRAHAM, WILLIAM. Christie's April, 1886.

Graham loved Italian Old Masters of the *trecento* and *quattrocento*, and pictures by Pre-Raphaelites such as Burne-Jones, Sir John Millais and Rossetti (to whom he acted as patron). His collection was sold in two parts, the Pre-Raphaelites fetching infinitely more. His early Italian pictures tended to be over-restored but were selected with scholarly care. Graham's Italian collection was probably one of the finest ever assembled in England.

HAMILTON PALACE (the Duke of Hamilton). Christie's, June 1882.

2213 items. Pictures, ceramics, French furniture. One of the most magnificent sales ever to be held in England: it lasted fifteen days and totalled nearly £400,000. The Duke was

Beckford's son-in-law and many of his pieces came from Fonthill. For a full description, see page 348. An illustrated, priced catalogue was published by Remington and Co. late in 1882.

HOLFORD, SIR GEORGE LINDSEY. Christie's, July 1927, May 1928.

There were two sales: the first of pictures by Italian Masters; the second contained those by Dutch, Flemish, French, Spanish and British artists. The Dutch part of the collection, which included four fine Rembrandt portraits, had remained almost as it had been formed by Robert Stayner Holford, a saleroom rival of Sir Robert Peel. The prices obtained were outstandingly high. (See also Bibliography of Private Catalogues.)

HOPE, ADRIAN. Christie's, June 1894.

This was a very fine collection of 75 Old Masters, mostly Dutch. Hope had excellent judgement and had bought them for less than £10,000 before 1860. They were now sold for about £50,000. Most of the pictures came from the dispersal of other famous collections and many were listed by Smith in his *Catalogue Raisonné*.

HOPE HEIRLOOMS. Christie's, July 1917.

The magnificent and highly personal collection of the great Neo-Classical protagonist, Thomas Hope (1796–1831), was preserved at Deepdene until 1917, when his descendant, Lord Francis Pelham Clinton Hope, was forced to sell it. The highlight of the sale were the two days devoted to the dispersal of the Greek, Roman and Egyptian antiquities, which fetched £67,709. Some of these had come direct from the collection of William Hamilton. The three most exceptional items were the statues of *Hygeia*, the Goddess of Health, in Pentelic marble found among the ruins of Ostia (£4200, Spink); an *Antinous*, of Parian marble, found in the ruins of Hadrian's villa at Tivoli (£5880, F. Partridge); and the 'Hope' Athena, a Pheidian statue of Carrara marble, 'also found at Ostia, 30 feet below the surface' (£7140, Agnew). Sadly one must report that this same *Athena* was bought in at Lady Cowdray's sale at £200, and that the same statue of *Hygeia* only fetched £589 10s at the Lady Melchett Sale in 1936. This was typical of the new valuation of antiquities after the great slump. It was due firstly to a declining interest by collectors and, secondly, to increased archaeological expertise which led to much closer scrutiny of the pieces concerned and a re-assessment of their authenticity. (See also Lansdowne Marbles.)

LANSDOWNE, THE MARQUESS OF ('The Lansdowne Marbles'). Christie's, March 1930.

One of the most famous collections of antiquities and sculpture (formed largely in the second half of the eighteenth century) ever to come on the market. The catalogue, which is immensely scholarly and a model of its kind, was based on A. H. Smith's *Catalogue of the Ancient Marbles at Lansdowne House*, 1899, which in its turn was based largely on Michaelis' *Ancient Marbles in Great Britain* (see pages 44 and 422).

LAWRENCE, SIR THOMAS. Christie's, May 1830.

This was the sale of Lawrence's collection of 127 paintings, which included several fine works by Italian and Dutch Masters, but principally consisted of examples of his actual and near contemporaries. For the full story of the dispersal of Lawrence's unique and enormous collection of *drawings*, see page 190.

MAGNIAC, HOLLINGWORTH (Colworth Collection). Christie's, July 1892.

Frequently described by contemporary observers as 'extraordinary', the sale of the collection included 1550 items. There were fine historical portraits, including many by Cranach and Holbein; Old Masters; metalwork; bronzes; enamels; goldsmiths' work; old furniture; glass; maiolica; faience; porcelain and examples of every variety of *objets d'art* purchased by selective collectors of the nineteenth century. A detailed catalogue of the collection had been compiled thirty years earlier (1862) by Sir Charles Robinson.

MICHELHAM, LORD. Hampton's, November 1926.

The collection was distinguished for a fine selection of eighteenth-century English pictures and portraits, and of eighteenth-century French pictures, tapestries, furniture and *objets d'art*.

NORTHWICK, LORD. Phillips, July 1859.

The twenty-day sale was another very famous one in its day. Full details are given on page 320. Sotheby's sold the coins, medals, etc, in separate sales in March 1860.

OPPENHEIMER, HENRY. Christie's, July 1936.

A fine catalogue of a magnificent collection of drawings; compiled by K. T. Parker and introduced by C. J. Holmes. Oppenheimer was born in Washington, but settled in England soon after 1900. His highly successful banking career came to an end in 1914 and with it his spending ability, for afterwards he only bought the occasional drawing. Nevertheless the 460 items sold included some of the finest early Italian, French, German and Netherlandish drawings to come on the market in the present century. They had apparently cost him about £45,000 and realised £92,000. The catalogue itself is increasingly sought after.

ROGERS, SAMUEL. Christie's, April and May 1856.

The editor's favourite collection of 'works of art' of every kind! For a full description see page 249.

ROTHSCHILD, VICTOR. Sotheby's, April 1937.

One of the greatest pre-war Sotheby sales, this was billed as *Catalogue of the Magnificent Contents of 148 Piccadilly, W.1*. As the preface states, 'the treasures of pictures, French furniture, carvings and tapestries . . . were mainly collected by the Baron Lionel Nathan de Rothschild who built the house to his own plans in 1865. His collections were mainly formed during the thirty years or so preceding that date and are mentioned by Waagen.' The catalogue contains some fascinating illustrations of the rooms as they were furnished before the dispersal. If only more catalogues of great collections did so.

SOLLY, EDWARD. Christie's, May 1847.

A catalogue of the finest of Solly's Italian pictures remaining at his death. Although there were only 42, the sale caused a great deal of interest. Almost more interesting–because he frequently stated that he did not like Dutch paintings–is the sale catalogue (Fosters, May 1837) of Solly's 91 *Dutch* pictures, because it is clear evidence that this Goliath among collectors (see page 202) had turned dealer after he settled in England upon his return from Germany. The latter catalogue is found exceedingly rarely.

SPENCER-CHURCHILL, CAPTAIN E. G. Christie's, October 1965.

One of the outstanding post-war sales. Captain Spencer-Churchill built magnificently upon the inherited foundations of the great Northwick Park Collection. The most important sales were those of pictures by Old Masters (1400–1600; 1600–1800) and antiquities. For more detail, see page 323.

STOWE HOUSE. Christie's, August 1848.

A tragic sale this, following upon the bankruptcy of the Duke of Buckingham and Chandos. It lasted thirty-five days and the prices were often incredibly low. This was probably because such a vast accumulation of treasure by many generations of a single family was just more than the trade, collectors and local gentry between them could absorb at one go, but in any case, saleroom history between 1830 and 1848 reflects a state of depression, of which Stowe was the last major example. (For full details, see page 274.) The original catalogue, which is surprisingly rarely found, is illustrated with delightful topographical lithographs.

Presumably because the sale aroused such enormous national publicity it was later considered worth publishing a fully priced and annotated catalogue. The work was undertaken by Henry Rumsey Forster and he contributed an interesting preface on the sale, and separate accounts of the family and the house. The catalogue is exceptional in printing both a list of subscribers *and* one of the purchasers. It contains a few illustrations.

STRAWBERRY HILL. George Robins, April 1842.

The engraved title page reads: *A Catalogue of the Classic Contents of Strawberry Hill collected by Horace Walpole*. Robins employed more promotional rhetoric than any contemporary auctioneer. His 'Prefatory Remarks' in this catalogue are an example of his fulsome style. The sale lasted 24 days, but aroused relatively little public interest and was poorly attended. It must be remembered that Walpole had started collecting almost a century earlier, and that his highly individual taste would have been regarded as merely curious in 1848 by almost everyone except William Beckford. Yet even he described Strawberry Hill as 'a miserable child's box; a species of Gothic mouse-trap; a reflection of Walpole's littleness, . . . some things I might have wished to possess: a good deal I would not have taken as a gift'. Yet he bought a lot of Walpole's drawings and books. In fact, the prints and drawings were not sold *in situ*, but in London during the following year.

SYDNEY COLLECTION. Knight, Frank and Rutley, June 1915.

Another first world war casualty on a magnificent scale was Frognal in Chislehurst, Kent, the seat of the Townsend family. It was Thomas Townsend, created Viscount Sydney in

1709, who had taken a prominent part in arranging the terms of the peace after the American Revolution, precipitated by his cousin Charles' Stamp Act. Thomas later had control of the Colonies and the newly-discovered harbour of Sydney in Australia was named after him. The family thus had a lot of possessions with important historical associations, including portraits, Americana, early views of Australia, two superb Books of Hours, English and French eighteenth-century furniture and very respectable pictures.

TAYLOR, JOHN EDWARD. Christie's, July 1912.
Taylor was one of the proprietors of the *Manchester Guardian*, and the sale of his magnificent collection of every form of antique and pictures was one of the greatest before the beginning of the first world war. It raised a grand total of £385,500. A great deal of interest centred in Taylor's Turner drawings when, during a single day, Lockett Agnew bought 49 out of 61 items.

WELLESLEY, FRANCIS. Sotheby's, June 1920.
This collection of drawings was fine by any standard, but particularly renowned for its plumbago drawings. Sotheby's were so delighted by the opportunity of such a sale that, exceptionally, they contributed a four-page introduction.

WERTHEIMER, CHARLES. Christie's, May 1912.
A relatively specialist collection of French snuff boxes and bijouterie that fetched enormous prices.

WILTON HOUSE. Sotheby's, July 1917.
In July 1914 Sotheby's sold the Wilton Library of early printed books which realised just short of £40,000 and, three years later, the Earl of Pembroke sent further treasures to the auction room. They consisted of a large collection of engravings; a particularly fine collection of drawings (including eight by Dürer); two famous suits of armour which had come into the possession of the 1st Earl after the battle of St Quentin in 1557; and two outstanding paintings: Mantegna's *Judith and Holofornes* and Rembrandt's *Portrait of his Mother*. The last fetched £11,500; the Mantegna was withdrawn and sold to Widener in the States; the suits of armour fetched £25,000 between them (but the more expensive was withdrawn at £14,500 because it did not reach its reserve); and the prices of the drawings must have been regarded as disappointing, even in the midst of the first world war, though a Veronese sketch went for £1650 and one by Correggio for £750. In 1929 the Wilton Diptych was sold to the National Gallery for the then enormous sum of £90,000. In 1951 and 1960 some 90 lesser paintings from Wilton were sold, and so was a limited number of Roman marbles in 1964.

PART 4: MUSEUM CATALOGUES

It would be invidious to list selected Museum Catalogues, but it should be said that many of the specialist catalogues produced by the Victoria and Albert Museum between 1870 and 1930 often covered individual collections bequeathed to the museum *in toto*, which are of great interest. (See, for example, the Schreiber, Allen, Jones, Salting, Ionides Catalogues. Some went through several editions.) Reference to the catalogues of the National Gallery is made on page 51 and to those of the Wallace Collection on page 282.

INDEX

[Book titles are in *italic* type; works of art are in quotation marks; plate references are given as final items, e.g. Pl. 29. Variants of accepted spellings of proper names which occur in the extracts are included in the index.]

INDEX

INDEX

INDEX

INDEX

INDEX

INDEX

INDEX

INDEX

INDEX

INDEX

INDEX

INDEX

INDEX

INDEX